ETYMOLOGICAL DICTIONARY OF

SCOTTISH-GAELIC

ETYMOLOGICAL DICTIONARY OF

SCOTTISH-GAELIC

ALEXANDER MACBAIN

HIPPOCRENE BOOKS
New York

For information, address:
HIPPOCRENE BOOKS, Inc.
171 Madison Avenue
New York, NY 10016

Cataloging-in-Publication data available from the Library of Congress.

ISBN 0-7818-0632-1

Printed in the United States of America.

Dedicated

TO THE

MEMORY

OF

REV ALEXANDER CAMERON, LL.D.

BIOGRAPHICAL NOTES

Alexander MacBain, the author of this book, was born in Glenfeshie of Badenoch, in Inverness-shire, in the year 1855. He spent his boyhood in his native district, and began his career there as a pupil teacher. Later on he was for a short time with the Ordnance Survey in Wales. In his nineteenth year he went to Old Aberdeen Grammar School; two years later, to King's College; graduated in 1880; and, in the same year, received the appointment of rector of Raining's School, Inverness. This post he held until 1894, when the school was transferred to the administration of the local Board. From that time until the close of his life he held a position in the High School of Inverness. In 1901 he was made an LL.D. by the University of Aberdeen.

The range of his studies in the Celtic field covered mythology, philology, history, manners and customs, and place and personal names. His literary output, extending over only 24 years, though not voluminous, involved much preparatory work, and is of great value for the acumen and originality exercised in the study and elucidation of the subjects which he took in hand.

A large number of his papers appeared in the Transactions of the Gaelic Society of Inverness, and also in pamphlet form. These comprise, besides others, articles on "Celtic Burial," "Who were the Picts?" "The Chieftainship of Clan Chattan," "Badenoch History, Clans, and Place Names," "Ptolemy's Geography," "The Norse Element in Highland Place Names," "Personal Names," and "The Book of Deer." In collaboration with the Rev. John Kennedy he brought out the two volumes of "Reliquiæ Celticæ," containing much matter for the student of Gaelic. He edited "Skene's Highlanders," to which he added a short but valuable excursus. Along with Mr John Whyte, Inverness, he prepared two useful Gaelic school-books and an edition of MacEachan's Gaelic Dictionary.

His most important work, however, is "The Etymological Dictionary of the Gaelic Language," issued in 1896, of which the present volume is the second edition. Unfortunately, he was prevented from personally superintending its publication by his sudden demise in April, 1907, when in the town of Stirling making arrangements with the publisher.

EDITORIAL NOTE

THE present edition of Dr MacBain's Etymological Dictionary consists of the text of the original edition, with interposed additions, amendments, and corrections drawn from the author's "Further Gaelic Words and Etymologies," from the "Addenda et Corrigenda" at the end of the first edition, and from written jottings on interleaved copies of these books.

Nothing has been added to Dr MacBain's work except the Supplement to The Outlines of Gaelic Etymology, the words and letters in square brackets, and a few slight changes from the original text, which are the work of the Rev. Dr George Henderson, Lecturer in Celtic Languages and Literature in the University of Glasgow, who found it necessary to abandon his intention of seeing the Gaelic Etymological Dictionary through the press, after reaching the sixteenth page of the "Outlines"; and a few suggestions in brackets followed by "Ed."

Nothing has been left out which could be deciphered, or applied with any measure of confidence. Even queried suggestions have been given, in the belief that mere flashes of thought by an expert may often point the way towards correct findings.

CALUM MAC PHARLAIN.

CORRIGENDUM ET ADDENDUM

At the foot of page 97 restore dropped *m*'s.

To **goireag** on page 391 add (= cock of hay; also in parts of Suth. *gòrag* = large coil of hay. See *coileag* in Dicty. Ed.)

PREFACE TO THE FIRST EDITION

THIS is the first Etymological Dictionary that has appeared of any modern Celtic language, and the immediate cause of its appearance is the desire to implement the promise made at the publication of Dr Cameron's *Reliquiæ Celticæ*, that an etymological dictionary should be published as a third or companion volume to that work. Some learned friends have suggested that it is too early yet to publish such a work, and that the great Irish Dictionary, which is being prepared just now by a German savant, should be waited for; but what I hope is that a second edition of this present book will be called for when the German work has appeared. Celtic scholars, if they find nothing else in the present Dictionary, will, at least, find a nearly pure vocabulary of Scottish Gaelic, purged of the mass of Irish words that appear in our larger dictionaries; and, as for my countrymen in the Highlands, who are so very fond of etymologising, the work appears none too soon, if it will direct them in the proper philologic path to tread. With this latter view I have prefaced the work with a brief account of the principles of Gaelic philology.

The words discussed in this Dictionary number 6900: derivative words are not given, but otherwise the vocabulary here presented is the completest of any that has yet appeared. Of this large vocabulary, about two-thirds are native Gaelic and Celtic words, over twenty per cent. are borrowed, and thirteen per cent. are of doubtful origin, no etymology being presented for them, though doubtless most of them are native.

The work is founded on the Highland Society's Gaelic Dictionary, supplemented by M'Alpine, M'Eachan, and other sources. I guarded especially against admitting Irish words, with which dictionaries like those of Shaw and Armstrong swarm. Shaw, in 1780, plundered unscrupulously from Lhuyd (1707) and O'Brien (1758), and subsequent dictionary-makers accepted too many of Shaw's Irish words. Another trouble has been the getting of genuine Irish words, for O'Reilly (1823) simply incorporated Shaw's Dictionary and M'Farlane's Scotch Gaelic Vocabulary (1815) into his own. For genuine modern Irish words I have had to trust to Lhuyd, O'Brien, Coneys, and Foley. For early Irish, I have relied mainly on Windisch, Ascoli, and Atkinson, supplementing them by the numerous vocabularies added by modern editors to the Irish texts published by them.

For the etymologies, I am especially indebted to Dr Whitley Stokes' various works, and more particularly to his lately published *Urkeltischer Sprachschatz*. I have, however, searched far and wide, and I trust I have not missed anything in the way of Celtic etymology that has been done for the last twenty or thirty years here or on the Continent. In form the book follows the example of Mr Wharton's excellent works on Latin and Greek philology, the *Etyma Latina* and the *Etyma Græca*, and, more especially, the fuller method of Prellwitz' *Etymolgisches Wörterbuch der Griechischen Sprache*.

The vocabulary of names and surnames does not profess to be complete. That errors have crept into the work is doubtless too true. I am sorry that I was unable, being so far always from the University centres, to get learned friends to look over my proofs and make suggestions as the work proceeded; and I hope the reader will, therefore, be all the more indulgent towards such mistakes as he may meet with.

ALEXANDER MACBAIN.

INVERNESS, 13th January, 1896.

PREFACE TO FURTHER GAELIC WORDS AND ETYMOLOGIES

SINCE the publication of my *Etymological Dictionary of the Gaelic Language* in January, 1896, I have had the benefit of criticisms of that work both publicly and privately, and the result of these, along with what I have gleaned from my own reading and thinking, I here give to the Gaelic Society and the public, so as to form a sort of *addenda et corrigenda* to my dictionary. I have to thank the critics of that work for their almost unanimous praise of it; its reception was very flattering indeed. The criticisms of most weight were from foreign scholars, the best in the way of addition and suggestion being that of Prof. Kuno Meyer in the *Zeitschrift fur Celtische Philologie*. In Scotland the *Inverness Courier* gave the weightiest judgment on the general philology of the work; and other papers and periodicals as well added their quota of fruitful criticism. Nor did the work fail to meet with critics who acted on Goldsmith's golden rule in the "Citizen of the World"—to ask of any comedy why it was not a tragedy, and of any tragedy why it was not a comedy. I was asked how I had not given derivative words—though for that matter most of the seven thousand words in the Dictionary are derivatives; such a question overlooked the character of the work. Manifest derivatives belong to ordinary dictionaries, not to an etymological one. This was clearly indicated in the preface; the work, too, followed the best models on the subject—Prellwitz, Wharton, and Skeat. Another criticism was unscientific in the extreme: I was found fault with for excluding Irish words! Why, it was the best service I could render to Celtic philology to present a pure vocabulary of the

Scottish dialect of Gadelic; the talk of the impossibility of "redding the marches" between Irish and Gaelic may be Celtic patriotism, but it is not science. As against this criticism, I was especially congratulated by Prof. Windisch for attempting to redd these same marches. A funny criticism was passed on the style of printing adopted for the leading words; no capitals are used at the beginning of each article. The critic had not seen a dictionary before without such capitals, and it offended his eye to see my work so "headless" as it is! Here again acquaintance with like philological works would have removed the "offence" and shown the utility of the style. In fact in Gaelic, with its accented vowels, capital initials are troublesome and unsightly, and the philological method is at once more scientific and more easy to work.

The following vocabulary contains (1) etymologies for words not etymologised in my dictionary; (2) new or corrected etymologies for words already otherwise traced; and (3) words omitted. These new words have come from the public and private criticisms and suggestions already referred to, and from another overhauling of such dictionaries as M'Alpine and M'Eachan.

ABBREVIATIONS.

1. LANGUAGE TITLES.

Ag. S. . —Anglo-Saxon
Arm. . —Armenian
Br. . . . —Breton
Bulg.. . —Bulgarian — O. Bulg. = Ch. Sl.
Ch. Sl. . —Church Slavonic
Cor. and Corn. —Cornish
Dan. . . —Danish
Dial. . . —Dialectic, belonging to a Dialect
Du. . . —Dutch
E. . . . —Early, as E. Eng.=Early English
Eng. . . —English
Fr. . . . —French
G. . . . —Gaelic
Gaul. . —Gaulish
Ger. . . —German
Got. . . —Gothic
Gr.. . . —Greek
H. . . . —High, as H.G. = High German
Heb. . . —Dialects of the Hebrides
Hes. . . —Hesychius
I. E. . . —Indo-European
Ir. . . . —Irish
Ital. . . —Italian
L. . . . —Late, as L. Lat. = Late Latin;
Lat. . . —Latin
Lett.. . —Lettic
Lit. . . —Lithuanian
M. . . . —Middle, as M. Ir.=Midd Irish
Mod.. . —Modern
N. . . . —Norse
N. . . —New, as N. Slav.=New Slavonic
N.H. . . —Dialects of the North Highlands
N. Sc. . —Northern Scottish
O. . . . —Old, as O. Ir.=Old Irish
O. H. G. —Old High German
Per. . . —Persian
Pruss. . —Prussian
Sc. . . . —Scottish
Shet.. . —Shetland
Skr. . . —Sanskrit
Sl. and Slav. —Slavonic
Slov.. . —Slovenic
Span. . —Spanish
Sw. . . —Swedish
W.. . . —Welsh
Zd.. . . —Zend or Old Bactrian

2. BOOKS AND AUTHORITIES.

A. M'D. . . . . . —Alexander Macdonald's *Gaelic Songs*, with vocabulary.
Atk. . . . . . . —Atkinson's Dictionary to the *Passions and Homilies from the Leabhar Breac*, 1887.
Arm., Arms. . . —Armstrong's *Gaelic Dictionary*, 1825.
B. of Deer . . . —Book of Deer, edited by Stokes in *Goidelica*, 1872.
Bez. Beit. . . . —Bezzenberger's *Beiträge zur Kunde der Idg. Sprachen*, a German periodical still proceeding.
C.S. . . . . . . —Common Speech, not yet recorded in literature.
Carm. . . . . . —Dr Alexander Carmichael ; see "Authors quoted."
Celt. Mag. . . . —The *Celtic Magazine*, 13 vols., stopped in 1888.
Con. . . . . . . —Coneys' *Irish-English Dictionary*, 1849.

Corm. . . . . —Cormac's Glossary, published in 1862 and 1868, edited by Dr Whitely Stokes.
D. of L. . . . . —*The Dean of Lismore's Book*, edited in 1862, 1892.
Four Mast. . . . —Annals of the Four Masters, published in 1848, 1851.
Fol. . . . . . —Foley's *English-Irish Dictionary*, 1855.
Hend. . . . . —Dr George Henderson, Lecturer in Celtic Languages and Literature in the University of Glasgow.
H. S. D. . . . . —The Highland Society's *Dictionary of the Gaelic Language*, 1828.
Inv. Gael. Soc. Tr. —Transactions of the Gaelic Society of Inverness, still proceeding.
L. na H. . . . —*Lebor na h-uidre*, or the Book of the Dun Cow, an Irish MS. of 1100.
Lh. . . . . . . —Lhuyd's *Archœologia Brittanica*, 1707.
Lib. Leinster . . —Book of Leinster, an Irish MS. of 1150.
M'A. . . . . . —Macalpine's *Gaelic Dictionary*, 1832.
M'D. . . . . . —Alexander Macdonald's *Gaelick and English Vocabulary*, 1741.
M'E. . . . . . —M'Eachan's *Faclair*, 1862.
M'F. . . . . . —M'Farlane's *Focalair* or Gaelic Vocabulary, 1815.
M'L. . . . . . —M'Leod and Dewar's *Dictionary of the Gaelic Language*, 1831.
Nich. . . . . . —Sheriff Nicholson's Gaelic Proverbs.
O'Br. . . . . —O'Brien's *Irish-English Dictionary*, 1768 and 1832.
O'Cl. . . . . . —O'Clery's Glossary, republished in *Revue Celtique*, Vols. IV. V., date 1643.
O'R. . . . . . —O'Reilly's *Irish-English Dictionary*, 1823.
Rev. Celt. . . . —*Revue Celtique*, a periodical published at Paris, now in its 17th vol.
R. D. . . . . — Rob Donn, the Reay Bard ; sometimes given as (Suth.).
Rob. . . . . —Rev. Chas M. Robertson, author of pamphlets on certain dialects of the Scottish Highlands.
S. C. R. . . . . —The *Scottish Celtic Review*, 1 vol., edited by Dr Cameron 1885.
S. D. . . . . . —*Sean Dana*, Ossianic Poems by the Rev Donald Smith.
Sh. . . . . . —Shaw's *Gaelic and English Dictionary*, 1780.
St. . . . . . —Dr Whitley Stokes ; see "Authors quoted"
Stew. . . . . —Vocabulary at the end of Stewart's Gaelic Collection.
Wh . . . . . . —John Whyte, Inverness : sometimes entered as (Arg.).
Zeit. . . . . . —Kuhn's *Zeitschrift f. vergl. Sprachforschung*, a German periodical still proceeding.

An asterisk (*) denotes always a hypothetical word ; the sign (†) denotes that the word is obselete. The numeral above the line denotes the number of the edition or the number of the volume.

AUTHORS QUOTED.

ADAMNAN, abbot of Iona, who died in 704, wrote a life of St Columba, edited by Reeves 1857, re-issued by Skene in 1874.

ASCOLI is publishing in connection with his editions of the MSS. of Milan and St Gall a "Glossary of Ancient Irish," of which the vowels and some consonants are already issued.

BEZZENBERGER edits the *Bez. Beit.* noted above, has contributed to it Celtic articles, and has furnished comments or suggested etymologies in Dr Stokes' *Urkeltischer Sprachschatz.*

BRADLEY'S *Stratmann's Middle English Dictionary.*

BRUGMANN is the author of the "Comparative Grammar of the Indo-Germanic Languages," a large work, where Celtic is fully treated.

CAMERON : The late Dr Cameron edited the *Scottish Celtic Review*, where he published valuable Gaelic etymologies, and left the MS. material which forms the basis of the two volumes of his *Reliquiæ Celticæ.*

CAMERON : Mr John Cameron of the *Gaelic Names of Plants*, 1883.

CARMICHAEL'S *Agrestic Customs of the Hebrides*, in the Napier Commission Report.

EDMONSTON is the author of an *Etymological Glossary of the Orkney Dialect.*

ERNAULT, author of an Etymological Dictionary of Middle Breton, and contributor to the *Rev. Celt.* of many articles on Breton.

FICK, compiler of the Comparative Dictionary of the Indo-Germanic Languages (not translated yet), completed in 1876. The fourth edition was begun in 1890 with Dr Whitley Stokes and Dr Bezzenberger as collaborateurs: the second volume of this edition is Dr Stokes' *Urkeltischer Sprachshatz*—Early Celtic Word-Treasure, 1894.

JAMIESON, author of the *Etymological Dictionary of the Scottish Language*, 2 vols., 1808, Paisley edition, 5 vols., 1879-1887.

DE JUBAINVILLE, editor of the *Rev. Celt.*, has written much on Celtic philology in that periodical and otherwise.

GUTERBOCK, author of a brochure on Latin Loan-words in Irish, 1882.

HENNESSEY, who offered some etymologies in his Criticism of Macpherson's Ossian in the *Academy*, August 1871.

KLUGE, compiler of the latest and best *Etymological Dictionary of the German Language*, 5th edition here used mostly.

LOTH, author of *inter alia* the *Vocabulaire Vieux-Breton*, 1884, the work usually referred to under his name

MACKINNON : Prof. Mackinnon in *Inv. Gael. Soc. Tr.*, in *Celt. Mag.* and in the *Scotsman.*

M'LEAN : Hector Maclean wrote many articles on Gaelic philology in newspapers and periodicals ; here quoted as an authority on the language.

K. MEYER, editor of *Cath Finntrága*, 1884, *Vision of MacConglinne*, 1892, &c., all with vocabularies.

MURRAY, editor of the Philological Society's *New English Dictionary* in process of publication.

OSTHOFF: especially in *Indogermanischen Forschungen*,[4] 264-294.

PRELLWITZ, compiler of an Etymological Dictionary of Greek, 1892.

RHYS: Prof. Rhys is author of *Lectures on Welsh Philology*, 1879, *Celtic Britain*, 1884, *Hibbert Lectures*, 1886, and a colophon to the *Manx Prayer Book*, 2 vols., on the Phonetics of the Manx Language.

SKEAT, author of the *Etymological Dictionary of the English Language*.

STOKES: Dr Whitley Stokes, author of books and articles too numerous to detail here. His *Urkeltischer Sprachschatz* was used throughout the work; it is to this work his name nearly always refers.

STRACHAN: Prof. Strachan's paper on *Compensatory Lengthening of Vowels in Irish* is the usual reference in this case.

THURNEYSEN, author of *Kelto-romanisches*, 1884, the work usually referred to here, though use has been made of his articles in *Zeit.* and *Rev. Celtique*.

WHARTON, author of *Etyma Græca*, 1882, and *Etyma Latina*, 1890.

WINDISCH, editor of *Irische Texte mit Wörterbuch*, used throughout this work, author of a *Concise Irish Grammar*, of *Keltische Sprachen* in the *Allgemeine Encyklopædie*, of the Celtic additions to Curtius' *Greek Etymology*, etc.

ZEUSS, *Grammatica Celtica*, second edition by Ebel.

ZIMMER, editor of *Glossæ Hibernicæ*, 1881, author of *Keltische Studien*, 1881, 1884, pursued in *Zeit.*, of *Keltische Beiträge*, in which he discusses the Norse influence on Irish, and many other articles.

OUTLINES OF GAELIC ETYMOLOGY.

INTRODUCTION.

GAELIC belongs to the Celtic group of languages, and the Celtic is itself a branch of the Indo-European or Aryan family of speech; for it has been found that the languages of Europe (with the exception of Turkish, Hungarian, Basque, and Ugro-Finnish), and those of Asia from the Caucasus to Ceylon,[1] resemble each other in grammar and vocabulary to such an extent that they must all be considered as descended from one parent or original tongue. This parent tongue is variously called the Aryan, Indo-European, Indo-Germanic, and even the Indo-Celtic language. It was spoken, it is believed, some three thousand years B.C. in ancient Sarmatia or South Russia; and from this as centre[2] the speakers of the Aryan tongue, which even then showed dialectal differences, radiated east, west, north and south to the various countries now occupied by the descendant languages. The civilization of the primitive Aryans appears to have been an earlier and more nomadic form of that presented to us by the Celtic tribe of the Helvetii in Cæsar's time. Here a number of village communities, weary of the work of agriculture, or led by the desire of better soil, cut their crops, pulled down their lightly built houses and huts, packed child and chattel on the waggons with their teams of oxen, and sought their fortune in a distant land. In this way the Celts and the Italians parted from the old Aryan home to move up the Danube, the former settling on the Rhine and the latter on the Gulf of Venice. The other races went their several ways—the Indians and Iranians eastward across the steppes, the Teutons went to the north-west, and the Hellenes to the south.

The Aryan or Indo-European languages fall into six leading groups (leaving Albanian and Armenian out of account), thus:—

I. INDO-IRANIAN or ARIAN, divisible into two branches:

(a) Indian branch, including Sanskrit, now dead, but dating in its literature to at least 1000 B.C., and the descendant modern (dialects or) languages, such as Hindustani, Bengali, and Mahratti.

[1] [2] See *Supplement to Outlines of Gaelic Etymology.*

(*b*) Iranian branch, which comprises Zend or Old Bactrian (circ. 1000 B.C.), Old Persian and Modern Persian.

II. GREEK or HELLENIC, inclusive of ancient and modern Greek (from Homer in 800 B.C. onwards). Ancient Greek was divided traditionally into three dialects—Ionic (with Attic or literary Greek), Doric, and Æolic.

III. ITALIC, divided in early times into two main groups—the Latin and the Umbro-Oscan. From Latin are descended Italian, French, Spanish, Portuguese, Rhoeto-romanic and Roumanian, called generally the Romance languages.

IV. CELTIC, of which anon.

V. TEUTONIC, which includes three groups—(*a*) East Teutonic or Gothic (fourth cent. A.D.); (*b*) North Teutonic or Scandinavian, inclusive of Old Norse and the modern languages called Icelandic, Norwegian, Swedish, and Danish; and (*c*) West Teutonic, which divides again into High German (whence modern German), the Old High German being a language contemporary with Old Irish, and Low German, which includes Old Saxon, Anglo-Saxon, English, Dutch, and Frisian.

VI. BALTO-SLAVONIC or LETTO-SLAVONIC, which includes Lithuanian, dating from the seventeenth century, yet showing remarkable traces of antiquity, Lettic, Old Prussian of the fifteenth and sixteenth centuries, now extinct, Old Bulgarian or Church Slavonic, into which the Bible was translated in the ninth century, and the Slavonic modern languages of Russia, etc.

These six groups cannot, save probably in the case of Latin[3] and Celtic, be drawn closer together in a genealogical way. Radiating as they did from a common centre, the adjacent groups are more like one another than those further off. The European languages, inclusive of Armenian, present the three primitive vowels *a*, *e*, *o* intact, while the Indo-Iranian group coalesces them all into the sound *a*. Again the Asiatic languages join with the Balto-Slavonic in changing Aryan palatal *k* into a sibilant sound. Similarly two or three other groups may be found with common peculiarities (*e.g.*, Greek, Latin, and Celtic with *oi* or *i* in the nom. pl. masc. of the *o*- declension). Latin and Celtic, further, show intimate relations in having in common an *î* in the gen. sing. of the *o*- declension (originally a locative), *-tion-* verbal nouns, a future in *b*, and the passive in *-r*.

[3] See *Supplement to Outlines of Gaelic Etymology.*

The Celtic group now comprises five living languages; in the 18th century there were six, when Cornish still lived. These six Celtic languages are grouped again into two branches, which may be named the Brittonic and the Gadelic. The former includes the Welsh, Cornish, and Breton; the Gadelic comprises Irish, Manx, and (Scottish) Gaelic. The main difference between these two branches of the Celtic group consists in this: the velar guttural of the Aryan parent tongue, which we represent here by the symbol *q*, when labialised, that is when the sound *w* or *u* attaches itself to it, becomes in Brittonic a simple *p* and in Gadelic a *c* (*k*, Ogam *qu*). Thus the Welsh for "five" is *pump*, Cornish *pymp*, and Breton *pemp*, Gaulish *pempe*. whereas the Gaelic is *cóig*, Manx *queig*, and Irish *cúig*: the corresponding Latin form is *quinque*. Professor Rhys has hence called the two branches of the Celtic the P group and the Q group (from Ogmic *qu* = Gaelic *c*). The distinction into P and Q groups existed before the Christian era, for the Gauls of Cæsar's time belonged mainly, if not altogether, to the P group: such distinctive forms as Gaulish *petor*, four (Welsh *pedwar*, Gaelic *ceithir*), *epo-s*, horse (Welsh *ebol*, Gaelic *each*), and *pempe*, five, already noted, with some others, prove this amply. At the beginning of the Christian era the Celtic languages were distributed much as follows: Gaulish, spoken in France and Spain, but fast dying before the provincial Latin (and disappearing finally in the fifth century of our era); Gallo-British or Brittonic, spoken in Britain by the conquering Gaulish tribes; Pictish, belonging to the Gallo-Brittonic or P group, and spoken in Scotland and, possibly, in northern England; and Gadelic, spoken in Ireland and perhaps on the West Coast of Scotland and in the Isles. The etymology of the national names will be seen in Appendix A. Our results may be summed in a tabular form thus:—

Celtic	Q Group	Gâdelic		Irish Manx Gaelic
		Dialects in Spain and Gaul (?)[4]		
	P Group	Gallo-Brittonic	Brittonic . .	Breton Cornish Welsh
		Gaulish—various Pictish[5]		

There are no literary remains of the Gaulish language existent; but a vast mass of personal and place names have been handed

[4] [5] See *Supplement to Outlines of Gaelic Etymology.*

down, and also a few words of the ordinary speech have been recorded by the Classical writers.[6] The language of Brittany came from Britain in the fifth and sixth centuries, and it may have found remains in Brittany of the kindred Gaulish tongue. The Brittonic languages—Welsh, Cornish, and Breton—appear first in glosses as early as the eighth century. These glosses are marginal or super-linear translations into Celtic of words or phrases in the Latin texts contained in the MSS. so "glossed." The period of the glosses is known as the "Old" stage of the languages—Old Breton, Old Cornish, Old Welsh. Real literary works do not occur till the "Middle" period of these tongues, commencing with the twelfth century and ending with the sixteenth. Thereafter we have Modern or New Breton[7] and Welsh as the case may be. In this work, New Breton and New Welsh are denoted simply by Breton and Welsh without any qualifying word.

The Gaelic languages—Irish, Manx, and Scottish Gaelic—have a much closer connection with one another than the Brittonic languages. Till the Reformation and, indeed, for a century or more thereafter, the Irish and Scottish Gaelic had a common literary language, though the spoken tongues had diverged considerably, a divergence which can be traced even in the oldest of our Gaelic documents—the Book of Deer. In the eighteenth century Scottish Gaelic broke completely with the Irish and began a literary career of its own with a literary dialect that could be understood easily all over the Highlands and Isles. Manx is closely allied to Scottish Gaelic as it is to the Irish; it is, so far, a remnant of the Gaelic of the Kingdom of the Isles.

The oldest monuments of Gadelic literature are the Ogam inscriptions, which were cut on the stones marking the graves of men of the Gaelic race. They are found in South Ireland, Wales and Eastern Pictland as far as the Shetland Isles, and belong mostly to the fifth, sixth, seventh, and eighth centuries. The alphabet, which is formed on a proto-telegraphic system by so many strokes for each letter above, through, or below a stem line, is as follows[8]:—

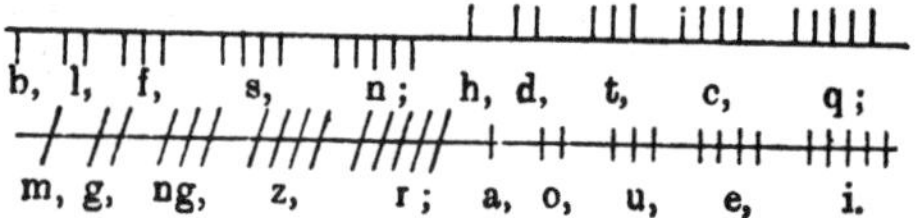

[6] [7] [8] See *Supplement to Outlines of Gaelic Etymology.*

Examples of Ogam inscriptions are :—

Sagramni maqi Cunotami
"(The stone) of Sagramnos son of Cunotamus."

Maqi Deceddas avi Toranias
"Of the son of Deces O' Toranis."

Cunanettas m[aqi] mucoi Nettasegamonas
"Of Cunanes son of the son of Nettasegamon."

Tria maqa Mailagni
"Of the three sons of Maolan."

These examples show that the state of declensional inflection was as high as that of contemporary Latin. The genitives in *i* belong to the *o* declension; the *i*, as in Old Irish, is not taken yet into the preceding syllable (*maqi* has not become *maic*). The genitives *os* and *as* belong to the consonantal declension, and the hesitation between *a* and *o* is interesting, for the later language presents the same phenomenon—the *o* in unaccented syllables being dulled to *a*. The Ogam language seems to have been a preserved literary language; its inflections were antique compared to the spoken language, and Old Irish, so near it in time as almost to be contemporary, is vastly changed and decayed compared to it.

Irish is divided into the following four leading periods :—

I. Old Irish: from about 800 to 1000 A.D. This is the period of the glosses and marginal comments on MSS. Besides some scraps of poetry and prose entered on MS. margins, there is the Book of Armagh (tenth century), which contains continuous Old Irish narrative.[9]

II. Early Irish, or Early Middle Irish: from 1000 to 1200 A.D. —practically the period of Irish independence after the supersession of the Danes at Clontarf and before the English conquest. The two great MSS. of *Lebor na h-uidre*, the Book of the Dun Cow, and the Book of Leinster mark this period. Many documents, such as Cormac's *Glossary*, claimed for the earlier period, are, on account of their appearance in later MSS., considered in this work to belong to this period.

III. Middle Irish: from 1200 to 1550 (and in the case of the Four Masters and O'Clery even to the seventeenth century in many instances). The chief MSS. here are the Yellow Book of Lecan, the Book of Ballimote, the *Leabar Breac* or Speckled Book, and the Book of Lismore.

IV. Modern, or New Irish, here called Irish: from 1550 to the present time.

[9] See *Supplement to Outlines of Gaelic Etymology*.

As already said, the literary language of Ireland and Scotland remained the same till about 1700, with, however, here and there an outburst of independence. The oldest document of Scottish Gaelic is the Book of Deer, a MS. which contains half a dozen entries in Gaelic of grants of land made to the monastery of Deer. The entries belong to the eleventh and twelfth centuries, the most important being the first—the Legend of Deer, extending to 19 lines of continuous prose. These entries form what we call OLD GAELIC, but the language is Early Irish of an advanced or phonetically decayed kind. The next document is the Book of the Dean of Lismore, written about 1512 in phonetic Gaelic, so that we may take it as representing the Scottish vernacular of the time in inflexion and pronunciation. It differs considerably from the contemporary late Middle Irish; it is more phonetically decayed. We call it here MIDDLE GAELIC, a term which also includes the MSS. of the M'Vurich *seanchaidhean*. The Fernaig MSS.,[10] written about 1688, is also phonetic in its spelling, and forms a valuable link in the chain of Scottish Gaelic phonetics from the Book of Deer till now. The term GAELIC means Modern Gaelic.

Scottish Gaelic is written on the orthographic lines of Modern Irish, which in its turn represents the orthography of Old Irish. The greatest departure from ancient methods consists in the insistence now upon the rule of "Broad to broad and small to small." That is to say, a consonant must be flanked by vowels of the same quality, the "broad" being *a*, *o*, *u*, and the "small" *e* and *i*. Gaelic itself has fallen much away from the inflexional fulness of Old Irish. Practically there are only two cases—nom. and gen.: the dative is confined to the singular of feminine nouns (*a*-declension) and to the plural of a few words as laid down in the grammars but not practised in speech. The rich verbal inflexion of the old language is extremely poorly represented by the impersonal and unchanging forms of the two tenses—only two—that remain in the indicative mood. Aspiration, which affects all consonants now, (though unmarked for *l*, *n*, *r*), has come to play the part of inflection largely; this is especially the case with the article, noun, and adjective. Eclipsis by *n* is practically unknown; but phonetic decay is evidenced everywhere in the loss of inflection and the uniformising of declension and conjugation.

There are two main Dialects of Gaelic, and these again have many sub-dialects. The two leading Dialects are known as the Northern and Southern Dialects. The boundary between them is described as passing up the Firth of Lorn to Loch Leven, and then across from Ballachulish to the Grampians, and thence along

[10] See *Supplement to Outlines of Gaelic Etymology.*

that range. The Southern Dialect is more Irish than the Northern, and it has also adhered to the inflections better (*e.g.*, the dual case still exists in feminine *a* nouns).[11] The crucial distinction consists in the different way in which the Dialects deal with *é* derived from compensatory lengthening ;[12] in the South it is *eu*, in the North *ia* (*e.g.*, *feur* against *fiar*, *breug* against *briag*, &c.) The sound of *ao* differs materially in the two Dialects, the Southern having the sound opener than the Northern Dialect.[13] The Southern Dialect is practically the literary language.

Modern Gaelic has far more borrowed words than Irish at any stage of its existence. The languages borrowed from have been mainly English (Scottish) and Norse. Nearly all the loan-words taken directly from Latin belong to the Middle or Old period of Gaelic and Irish ; and they belong to the domain of the Church and the learned and other secular work in which the monks and the rest of the clergy engaged. Many Latin words, too, have been borrowed from the English, which, in its turn, borrowed them often from French, (such as *prìs*, *cunntas*, *cùirt*, *spòrs*, &c.). Latin words borrowed directly into English and passed into Gaelic are few, such as *post*, *plasd*, *peur*, &c. From native English and from Lowland Scots a great vocabulary has been borrowed. In regard to Scots, many words of French origin have come into Gaelic through it. At times it is difficult to decide whether the Teutonic word was borrowed from Scottish (English) or from Norse. The contributions from the Norse mostly belong to the sea ; in fact, most of the Gaelic shipping terms are Norse.

I. PHONETICS.

Under the heading of Phonetics we deal with the sounds of the language—the vowels, semi-vowels, and consonants, separately and in their inter-action upon one another.

§ 1. Alphabet.

The Gaelic alphabet consists of eighteen letters, viz., *a*, *b*, *c*, *d*, *e*, *f*, *g*, *h*, *i*, *l*, *m*, *n*, *o*, *p*, *r*, *s*, *t*, and *u*. Irish, Old and New, have the same letters as the Gaelic. As this number of letters in no way adequately represents the sounds, signs and combinations are necessary.

Firstly, the long vowels are denoted by a grave accent: *à*, *ì*, *ù*, *è*, *ò*, the latter two having also the forms *é*, *ó*, to denote sounds analogous to those in English *vein*, *boar*. Whereas *à*, *ì*, *ù*, which have only one sound, represent corresponding Indo-European sounds (*ā*, *ī*, *ū*), none of the long sounds of *e* or *o* represent a simple corresponding I.E. sound.

[11] [12] [13] See *Supplement to Outlines of Gaelic Etymology.*

The Gaelic vowels are divided into two classes—broad and small. The broad vowels are *a, o, u;* the small, *e, i*. The Gaelic diphthongs[14] represent (1) simple sounds, (2) real diphthong sounds, or (3) modification of the consonants and carrying out of the law of "broad to broad and small to small." They are as follows:—

*ai, ao, [au]**	*ài*
ea, ei, eo, eu, eò	*éi, èi*
ia, io, iu, iù	*ìo*
*oi, [ou]**	*òi*
ua, ui	*ùi*

Here *ea, ei, eu* represent O. Ir. *e, é,* and are practically simple sounds, as certainly is *ao*. The forms *ia, ua* are genuine diphthongs, as are usually the long vowel combinations. The rest may be diphthongs, or may be a trick of spelling, as in the word *fios* (O. Ir. *fis*), where the *o* shows that the *s* has its normal sound, and not that of E. *sh*, as *fis* would imply.

Triphthongs occur in the course of inflection, and in the case of *ao* otherwise. These are—*aoi, eoi, iai, iui, uai, eòi, iùi.*

The consonants are classified in accordance with the position of the organs of speech concerned in their utterance:—

I. Liquids.—The liquids are *l* and *r*, with the nasals *n* and *m*. In writing, *m* only is "aspirated," becoming to the eye *mh*, to the ear a *v* with nasal influence on the contiguous vowels. The other liquids, *l*, *n*, and *r*, are really aspirated in positions requiring aspiration, though no *h* is attached to show it.[15] There is, however, only a slight change of sound made in these letters by the aspiration—a more[16] voiced sound being given them in the aspirating position.

II. Mutes and Explosives.—These all suffer aspiration when intervocalic. They are classified as follows:—

	Tenues.	Mediæ.	Aspirates.
Labials..................	*p*	*b*	*ph, bh*
Dentals..................	*t*	*d*	*th, dh*
Gutturals..............	*c*	*g*	*ch, gh*

The dentals *d* and *t* become spirants[17] when in contact with, or flanked by, the "small" vowels *e* and *i*. The other mutes are not affected by such contact.[18] The aspirate sounds are—*ph* = *f*, *bh* = *v*, *th* = *h*, *dh* and *gh* before *e*, *i* = *y*, *ch* = German and Scotch *ch*.

* Dialectal, before *ll, nn, mh, bh,* though not in the script.

14 15 16 17 18 See *Supplement to Outlines of Gaelic Etymology*.

III. THE SPIRANTS.—These, outside the above spirant-made mutes, are *f* and *s*. The sound [resembling E.] *sh* is represented by *s* flanked with "small" vowels. The aspirate forms of these are—*fh* (=the Greek open breathing or nothing practically), G. *sh* (=*h*).

Celtic Alphabet.

The Celtic alphabet, as deduced from the Neo-Celtic dialects, checked by Gaulish, possessed the following sounds :—

I. VOWELS :—
Short—*i, u, e, o, a*
Long—*ī* (=*ī, ē*), *ū*, *ē* (=*ei*), *ō* (=*au*), *ā* (=*ō, ā*)
Diphthongs—*ei, oi, ai, eu, ou, au*

II. LIQUIDS—*r, l, m, n*

III. SPIRANTS—(*h*), *s, j, v*

IV. EXPLOSIVES :—

	Tenues.	Mediæ.
Labials.	—	*b*
Dentals.........	*t*	*d*
Gutturals......	*k, kv,* (*p*)	*g, gv* (*b*)

It has to be noted that Indo-European *p* initial and intervocalic is lost in Celtic.[19] Before another consonant, it manifests its former presence by certain results which still remain. Thus I. E. *septn̥* is G. *seachd*, *supno-s* becomes *suan*.

Indo-European Alphabet.

By a comparison of the six Indo-European or Aryan language groups, the sounds possessed by the parent tongue may be inferred. The following is the form of the I. E. alphabet which is used in the present work :—

I. VOWELS : Short—*i, u, e, o, a, ə*
Long—*ī, ū, ē, ō, ā*
Diphthongs—*ei, oi, ai, eu, ou, au*
ēi, ōi, āi, ēu, ōu, āu

II. SEMI-VOWELS : *i̯, u̯*, represented in this work always by *j, v*. See the spirants.

III. CONSONANT-VOWELS : *r̥, l̥, m̥, n̥, r̥̄, l̥̄, m̥̄, n̥̄*

IV. LIQUIDS AND NASALS : *r, l, m, n*

V. SPIRANTS : *j, v, s, z*

[19] See *Supplement to Outlines of Gaelic Etymology.*

VI. EXPLOSIVES[20] :—

	Tenues.	Mediæ.	Aspirates.
Labial........	*p*	*b*	*ph, bh*
Dental	*t*	*d*	*th, dh*
Palatal.......	*k*	*g*	*kh, gh*
Velar.........	*q*	*g*	*qh, gh*

§ 2. VOWEL MODIFICATION.

In Gaelic the vowel or vowel combination of a syllable may undergo "mutation" (German *umlaut*) in the course of inflection or word-building. This mutation is caused by the influence exerted backward by the vowel of the next syllable now or previously existent. There are three classes of mutation in Gaelic caused either by a following (1) *e* or *i*, (2) *a* or *o*, or (3) *u*.

Mutation by "e" or "i."

a becomes (1) *ai* : *cat*, gen. *cait*, *damh*, g. *daimh*.
(2) *oi* (with double liquids usually): *dall*, pl. *doill*, *clann*, g. *cloinne*.
(3) *ui* (with liquids) : *ball*, pl. *buill*, *allt*, g. *uillt*. Also where Irish shows *o* : *balg*, O. Ir. *bolc*, pl. *builg ;* so *clag*, *falt*, *gal*, *fuil*, *car*.
(4) *i* : *mac*, g. *mic*. Dialectally *ai* becomes *ei*, especially with liquids, and in ordinary G. *eile* represents O. Ir. *aile ;* so *seileach*, too.

o becomes (1) *oi* : *sgoltadh*, *sgoilte*.
(2) *ui* : *bonn*, g. *buinn*, *post*, g. *puist*.

u becomes *ui* : *dubh*, comp. *duibhe*.

e becomes *ei* : *beir* for **bere*, catch thou.

à, *ò*, *ù* become *ài*, *òi*, *ùi* : *làimhe*, *òige*, *dùin*.

eo, *iu*, *ua* become triphthongs ; [the digraph *ao*+*i* forms a diphthong.]

ea becomes (1) *ei* : *each*, g. *eich*.
(2) *i* : *ceann*, g. *cinn ;* the usual mutation.

eu, with liquids, becomes *eòi* : *beul*, g. *beòil*. It sometimes becomes *ao* : *eudann*, *aodann*.

ia is restored to *éi* : *fiadh*, g. *féidh ;* irregularly—*fiar*, crooked, comp. *fiaire*, *biadh*, g. *bìdh*, [Dial. *béidh*, *beidh*, *bi-idh*.]

io becomes *i* : *fionn*, g. *finn*.

Mutation by "o" or "a."

o becomes *a*, a mutation of principal syllables rare in Irish : *cas*, Ir. *cos*, original **coxa* ; *cadal* for *codal*.

u becomes *o* : *sruth*, g. *srotha* ; *nuadh*, *nodha*.

e becomes *ea* : *cearc* from **cerca*.

[20] See *Supplement to Outlines of Gaelic Etymology*.

i becomes *ea* : *fear* from **viro-s*.
éi becomes *ia* : the stem *féidh* becomes *fiadh* in the nom. (**veido-s*).
ì becomes *ìo* : *fìor* from **vîro-s*.

Mutation by "u."

A succeeding *u* affects only *i* or *e*; it is a mutation which does not now operate. Thus *fiodh* comes from **vidu-* (O. Ir. *fid*); *bior* from **beru* (O. Ir. *bir*); *sliochd* from *slektu-*; *cionn* from the dat. **cennū*, from **cennō*.

§ 3. Indo-European and Gaelic Vowels.

The representation in Gaelic of the I. E. vowels is very complicated owing to the principles of mutation discussed above.

I. E. *i*.

(1) Gaelic *i*, O. Ir. *i*, W. *y*.
bith, world, O. Ir. *bith*, W. *byd*, Br. *bed* : **bitu-s*, root *gi*. So *ith*, *fidir*, *nigh*, *fir* (gen. and pl. of *fear*), as also *nid* from *nead*, etc.).

(2) G. *ea*, O. Ir. *e*.
beatha, life, O. Ir. *bethu* : **bitûs*, stem **bitât-*, root *gi*. So *eadh*, it, *fear*, *geamhradh*, *meanbh*, *nead*, *seas*, *seasg*, *sleamhuinn*, *sneachd*.

(3) G. *io*, O. Ir. *i*.
G. *fiodh*, wood, O. Ir. *fid*, W. *gwydd*, Br. *gwez* : **vidu-*. So *fios*, *iodh-*. The *io* of *fionn*, O. Ir *find* is due to the liquid and medial mute, which together always preserve the *i* and even develop it from an original *ṇ* or *en* (*ṇb*, *ṇd*, *ṇg*).

(4) G., O. Ir. *iu*.
This is a mutation by *u* : *fliuch*, wet, from **vliqu-*; *tiugh*, **tigu-s*.

I. E. *u*.

(1) G., O. Ir. *u*, W. *w* (*o*).
G., O. Ir. *sruth*, stream, W. *frwd* : **srutu-s*. So *bun*, *dubh*, *guth*, *muc*, *musach*, *slug*, *smug*, *tulach*.
Here add G. *ui* : *cluinn*, *luibh*, *uisge*.

(2) G., O. Ir. *o*.
bonn, bottom, O. Ir. *bond*, W. *bon*, **bundo-s*. So *bothan*, *con*, dogs', *do-*, *so-*, *domhan*, *dorus*, *tom*, *os*, *trod*.

I. E. *e*.

(1) G., O. Ir. *e*, W. *e*.
Simple *e* is rare in G. : *leth*, side, O. Ir. *leth*, W. *lled*, **letos*. So *teth*, hot.

(2) G. *ea*, O. Ir. *e*.
G. *each*, horse, O. Ir. *ech*, W. *ebol*, Lat. *equus*. So numerous words—*eadh*, space, *bean*, *beart*, *cearc*, *ceart*, *dearc*, *dearg*, *deas*, *fearg*, *geal*, *geas*, *meadhon*, *meanmna*, *meas*, *neart*, *reachd*, *seach*, *seachd*, *sean*, *searg*, *teach*, *teas*, *treabh*.

(3) G. *ei*, O. Ir. *e*.
G. *beir*, take, O. Ir. *berim*, W. *adfer*, Lat. *fero*. So *beil* (*meil*), *ceil*, *ceirtle*, *ceithir*, *creid*, *deich*, *deis*, [Dial.] ready, *meirbh*, *seinn*, *teich*, *teine*.

(4) G., O. Ir. *i*.
G., O. Ir. *fine*, tribe, root *ven*, O. H. G. *wini*, Ag. S. *wine*, friend. So *cineal*, *gin*, *ite*, *mil*, *misg*, *sinnsear*, *tigh*, *tighearna*.

(5) G. *io*, O. Ir. *i*.
G. *bior*, spit, O. Ir. *bir*, W. *ber*, Lat. *veru*. So *iol-*, *sliochd*, *smior*, *biolaire*, *ciomach*, *tioram*.

(6) G. *ui* in *ruith*, *ruinn* = *rinn* (bis), *ruighinn* and *righinn* : (Cf. *roinn*, [Dial.] did, for *rinn* ; *ruigheachd*). So *trusdair*, *stuthaig*.

(7) Compensatory long vowels in G. and O. Ir. These arise from loss of one consonant before another, one of which must be a liquid.

a. *ent* becomes G. *eud*, O. Ir. *ét*. G. *ceud*, first, O. Ir. *cét*, W. *cynt*. So *seud*, journey. Similarly **enk* ; G. *eug*, death, O. Ir. *éc* ; **brenkâ*, G. *breug*, lie, O. Ir. *bréc*, ; **enkt*, G. *euchd*, E. Ir. *écht* (Cf. *creuchd*, **crempt- ?*) ; **centsô* ; G. *ceus*, crucify. Parallel to these forms in *ent*, *enk* are those in *n̥t*, *n̥k*, such as *ceud*, one hundred, O. Ir. *cét*, W. *cant*, Lat. *centum* (so *deud*, *eug*, *geug*).

b. *ebl* : in G. *neul*, cloud, O. Ir. *nél*, W. *niwl*.
egr : in G. *feur*, grass, O. Ir. *fér*, W. *gwair*.
egn : in G. *feun*, O. Ir. *fén* : **vegno-s*.
etl : in G. *sgeul*, O. Ir. *scél*, W. *chwedl*.
etn : in G. *eun*, O. Ir. *én*, W. *edn*.

c. G. *eadar* and *thig* show short vowels for original **enter* and *enk*. This is due to sentence accent in the case of *eadar* and to the word accent in the case of *thig* or to both.

For *ceum*, *leum*, etc., see under *n̥*.

I. E. *o*.

(1) G., Ir. *o*.
G. *co-*, *comh-*, with, O. Ir. *co-*, *com-*, W. *cy-*, *cyf-*, **kom-* ; so *ro-* (= Lat. *pro*), *fo* (= Gr. ὑπό), *nochd*, naked, night, *ochd*, *mol*, *bodhar*, *gon*, *gort*, *roth*.

(2) G., O. Ir. *u*, *ui*.

G., O. Ir. *muir*, sea, W. *môr*, Br. *mor*, from **mori*. So *druim* (**dros-men*), *guidhe*, *guil*, *guin*, *sguir*, *suidhe*, *uidhe*, *uileann*, *uircean*, *gu*, to, *cu-*, *fu-*, *fur-* (*for* = **vor*).

(3) G. *a*, O. Ir. *o*.

G. *cas*, foot, O. Ir. *cos*, W. *coes*, **coxâ*. So *amh*, *balg*, *call*, *falt*, *gart*, *gar*, *calltuinn*. So, too, compounds. With *con* as in *cagainn*, *cadal*, *cagar*, *caisg*, as against *coguis* (O. Ir. *concubus*), with its *u* sound terminal.

(4) Compensatory long vowels.

G. *dual*, lock of hair, **doglo-*, Got. *tagl*, Eng. *tail*. So *òl* (**potlo-*), *buain*, (**bog-ni-* or **bongni-*), *cluain*, *cuan*, *bruan*, *sròn*, *còmh-*.

I. E. *a*.

(1) G. *a*, *ai*, O. Ir. *a*, W. *a*.

G., O. Ir. *can*, sing, W. *cana*, Lat. *cano*. So many words, such as *abhainn*, *ad-*, *agh*, *air*, *altrum*, *anail*, *anam*, *cac*, *damh*, *gad*, *mac*, *maide*, *marc*, *nathair*, *salann*, &c.

(2) G. *à* before *rd*, *rn*, *m*.

See *àrd*, *bàrd*, *bàrr*, *càrn*, *sgàird*, *càm*, *àm*, *màm*.

(3) G. *i*.

In two cases only : *mac*, g. *mic* ; *sile* [Dial. for *seile*], saliva, O. Ir. *saile*.

(4) G. *u*, *ui*.

This happens in contact with liquids. The prep. *air* becomes *ur-*, *uir-*, *urchar*, *uireasbhuidh*. So *muigh* from **magesi*. Common in oblique cases : *allt*, g. *uillt*, *ball*, *buill*, &c.

(5) G. *ea*, *ei* for *e*.

G. *seileach*, willow, E. Ir. *sail*, W. *helyg*, Lat. *salix*. So *ealtuinn*, *eile*, *eir-* for *air-*, *eilean*, [Dial.] training, *deigh*, ice.

(6) G. *oi*.

This change of I. E. *a* into Gaelic *oi* is due mostly to a liquid followed by a "small" vowel.

G. *oil*, rear, E. Ir. *ailim*, Lat. *alo*. So *oir* for *air-*, *coileach*, *goir*, *troigh*, *coire*, *loinn*, &c., and *goid*, *cide*.

(7) Compensatory lengthenings in G.

a. As *à*, *ài* :

G. *dàil*, meeting, O. Ir. *dál*, W. *dadl*, where *-atlo-* is the original combination. *-agr-* appears in *nàire*, *sàr*, *àr*.

b. As *eu*, *ao*, *ia* :

It has been seen that *ceud*, hundred, corresponds to W. *cant*, Lat. *centum*. The Celtic, in these cases, is regarded as having been *n̥t*, *n̥k*, (**kn̥to-n*). See under *n̥*.

An undoubted case of *a* landing by compensation into *eu* (=*é*) is *deur*, tear, O. Ir. *dér*, O. W. *dacr*, I. E. *dakru*. Prof. Strachan has extended this analogy to words like *meur*, *breun*, *léine*, *sgeun*, *mèanan*. The case of *deur* seems rather to be an anomaly.[21]

I E. ə.

This is the I. E. "indefinite" vowel, appearing in Celtic as *a*, in the Asiatic groups as *i*, and generally as *a* in Europe (Greek showing also ε). Henry denotes it by *ä*, a more convenient form than Brugmann's ə. Some philologists refuse to recognise it.

G. *athair*, father, O. Ir. *athir*, I. E. *pəter-*, Gr. πατήρ, Skr. *pitar*.

It is common in unaccented syllables, as G. *anail*, breath, W. *anadl*, **anə-tla*, Gr. ἄνεμος. In the case of syllables with liquids it is difficult to decide whether we have to deal with *a*, ə, or a liquid vowel ; as in G. *ball*, member, **bhal-no-*, root *bhəl*, whence Gr. φαλλός, Eng. *bole*.

I. E. *Long Vowels*.

I. E. ī and ū are so intimately bound with *ei* and *eu* (*ou*) that it is difficult to say often whether we have to deal with the simple vowel or the diphthong as the original. For ī see *lì*, *sìn*, *sgìth*, *brìgh* ; for ū, see *cùl*, *dùil*, element, *dùn*, *cliù*, *mùch*, *mùin*, *rùn*, *ùr*. The W. in both cases (ī, ū) show simple *i*.

I. E. ē appears in Celtic as ī, G. ì : as in G. *fìor* (*fìr*), true, O. Ir. *fír*, W. and Br. *gwir*, Lat. *vêrus*. So *lìon*, *mìal* (*mìol*), *mìos* *rìgh*, *sìth*, *sìol*, *sìor*, *tìr*, *snìomh*.

I. E. ō and ā appear both as ā in the Celtic languages—Gadelic *á*, W. *aw*, Br. *eu*. For ō, see *blàth*, *gnàth*, *làr*, *dàn*, *snàth*. For ā, see *bàn*, *bràthair*, *cnàimh*, *càr*, *clàr*, *dàimh*, *fàidh*, *gàir*. *màthair*, *sàth*, *tàmh*. But *ròin*, *ròn*, *nòs*, *mòin*, all from *â ? ò* in finals, etc., may equal *u* : **svesor* = O. Ir. *siur*, *fiur*, Med. Ir. *siúr*.

I. E. *Diphthongs*.

I. E. *ei* (*èj* ?) appears in G. in two forms—as *éi* and *ia*. Thus—

a. G. *éi*, O. Ir. *éi*, W. *wy*, Br. *oe*, *oa*. See *féith*, *géill*, *méith*, *réidh*, *séid*, *sméid*.[22]

[21] [22] See *Supplement to Outlines of Gaelic Etymology*.

b. G. *ia*, O. Ir. *ia*. This is due to the influence of a succeeding broad vowel. See *cia*, *ciall*, *cliathach*, *criathar*, *fiadh*, *fianuis*, *giall*, *iarunn*, *liagh*, *riadh*, *riar*, *sgiath*, *sliabh*. Consider these—*feuch*, *lèan*, *glé*, and, possibly, *gèadh*.

I. E. *oi* (*ōj?*). This consistently appears in G. as *ao* long, O. Ir. *ái*, *ói*, later *oe*, *ae*, (*óe*, *áe*), W., Br. *u*. See *caomh*, *claon*, *fraoch*, *gaoth*, *gaol*, *laogh*, *maoin*, *maoth*, *taobh*.

I. E. *ai* can with difficulty be differentiated from *oi*; certainly not on Celtic ground, nor, indeed, outside Greek and Latin. The following are real cases: G. *aois*, *caoch*, *saothair*, *taois*.

I. E. *eu* and *ou* are also confused together in the modern Celtic languages. They both appear as either G. *ua* or *ò*.

a. G. *ua*, O. Ir. *úa*, W., Br. *u*.
G. *buaidh*, victory, O. Ir. *buaid*, W. *bud*, Gallo-British *Boudicca*, "Victoria." See also *buachaill*, *cluas*, *luath* *ruadh*, *ruathar*, *truagh*, *tuath*, *uasal*.

b. G. *ò*; as *bòidheach* from *buaidh*, *tròcair* from *truagh*, *lòchran*, *còs* for *cuas*.

I. E. *au*[23] appears in G. as *ò* or *ua*, much as do *eu*, *ou*. Thus—G. *gò*, a lie, O. Ir. *gó*, *gáu*, W. *gau*, Br. *gaou*. Also *òigh*, virgin, from *augi-*, *fuachd*, *uaigneach*.

§ 4. I. E. Semi-Vowels and Consonant Vowels.

The semi-vowels are denoted by Brugmann as *i* and *u*, by Henry as *y* and *w*; and these forms are used by them not merely for intervocalic semi-vowels but also for the diphthongs which we have printed as *ei*, *oi*, *ai*, *eu*, *ou*, *au*, which Henry, for instance, prints as *ey*, *ew*, etc. In this work Fick is followed in the forms of the diphthongs, and also, where necessary, in his signs for the semi-vowels, viz., *y* and *v*, with *j* and *v* as signs for the spirants.

I. E. *y*, *j*, *v*.[24]

I. E. *y* and *j* disappear in Gadelic, but are preserved in the Brittonic as *i*. Thus *ìoc*, heal, O. Ir. *íccaim*, W. *jach*, I. E. *yakos*, Gr. ἄκος, Skr. *yáças*; see *deigh* and *òg*. For I. E. *j*, compare G. *eòrna*, for *eò-rna*, **jevo-*, Gr. ζειά, spelt, Skr. *yáva*; also *eud*, jealousy, **jantu-*, Gr. ζῆλος, zeal, Skr. *yatná*.

I. E. *v* is thus dealt with :—

(1) Initial *v*: G., O. Ir. *f*, W. *gw*, as in G. *falt*, hair, Ir. *folt*, W. *gwalt*; also *fàidh*, Lat. *vātes*, *feachd*, *fear*, Lat. *vir*, *fiadh*, *fichead*, *fine*, *fiodh*, with succeeding consonant in *flath* (**vlati-*), *fliuch*, *fraoch*, *fras*, *freumh*, etc.

[23] [24] See *Supplement to Outlines of Gaelic Etymology*.

(2) Intervocalic *v*. This disappears in G. leaving the vowels to coalesce with varying results, thus :—

a. *-ivo-* produces *eò*, as in *beò*, **givo-s*, Lat. *vivus*, or *ia* in *biadh* (**bīvoto-n*, cf. *dia*), *dian*.

b. *-evo-* produces *eò*, as in *ceò*, **skevo-*, Eng. *shower*; *deò*, W. *dywy*, **devo-*, Lat. *fûmus*, *eòrna*. Stokes gives *cliù* as **klevos*, Thurneysen as *kloves-*.

c. *-ovi-* gives *nuadh*, **novios*, *-ovo-* in *crò* (**krovos*), *-ovṇ-* in *òg*.

d. *-avi-* in *ogha* (**pavios*) ; *dàth* (**daviô*) ; *-avo-* in *clò*.

e. *-eivi-* in *glé*, *-eivo-* in *dia*.

(3) Post-consonantal *v*.

a. After liquids it becomes *bh*. See *garbh*, *marbh*, *searbh*, *tarbh*, *dealbh*, *sealbh*, *meanbh*, *banbh*.

b. After explosives it disappears save after *d*, (*gv*) : *feadhbh*, widow, O. Ir. *fedb*, *taobh*, *baobh*. For *gv*, see *g* below.

c. After *s*, it sometimes disappears, sometimes not. Thus *piuthar* is for **svesôr*, O. Ir. *siur*, whereas in *searbh* (**svervo-s*), *solus* (but *follas*), *seinn*, etc., it disappears.

The Consonant Vowels.

These are *ṛ*, *ḷ*, *ṇ*, *ṃ* ; *ṝ*, *ḹ*, *ṇ̄*, *ṃ̄*. The regular representation of *ṛ*, *ḷ* in G. is *ri*, *li* (mutated forms being *rea*, *rei*, *lea*, *lei*). See the following regular forms : *bris*, *britheamh*, *fri*, *lit*; also the modified forms—*bleath*, *bleoghainn*, *breith*, *cleith*, *dreach*, *leamhann*, *leathan* (?), *sreath*.

The numerous Gaelic *a* forms of I. E. *e* roots containing liquids fall to be noticed here. Some of them Brugmann explains as glides before sonants, somewhat thus : G. *mair*, remain, O. Ir. *maraim*, would be from *mṛra-*, root *mer*, Lat. *mora* ; so *sgar* from *sker* ; *garbh*, *marbh*.

Add the following :—*alt*, *carbad* (Lat. *corbis*), *bàrr*, *bàrd*, *cairt*, *garg*, *mall*, *dall*, *sgàird* (Lat. *muscerda*), *tart*, *tar* ; *fras*, *flath*, *fraigh*, *graigh*, *braich*. With modified vowels in—*coille* (**caldet-*), *doire*, *foil*, *goile*, *goirid*, *sgoilt*.

The long vowels *ṝ* and *ḹ* appear regularly as *rā* (?) *lā*. See *làn* (**pḹ-no-*, Skr. *pūrnas*), *slàn*, *tlàth*, *blàth*. Long *ṝ* seems to appear as *ār* in *dàir*, *màireach*, *fàireag* (?).[25]

Vocalic *n* and *m* may be looked for in G. *samhail*, which Brugmann explains as *sṃmḷli-s*, in *tana*, thin ; reversed in *magh* and *nasg*.

Compensatory *ṇ* plays a great part in G., appearing usually as *eu* (*ao*). We have *ceud*, hundred, W. *cant*, *deud*, W. *dant*, *teud*,

[25] See *Supplement to Outlines of Gaelic Etymology.*

eud, eug, eudann, éiginn, geug. The negative *ṇ* appears before vowels as *an,* before *c, t,* and *s,* as *eu, éi*: *eutrom, éislean,* &c. The most curious result arises from *-ṇgm-*, which ends in G. as *eum-*; see *ceum,* W. *cam, leum,* W. *lam,* and add *teum,* W. *tam,* from **tṇd-men.*

Before the medials *b, d, g,* both *ṇ* and *ṃ* become *in* (*ion*), *im* (*iom*), and original *in* retains its *i* (cf. *fionn*). Thus we have *im-*, *iom-* from *ṃbi,* Lat. *ambi,* also *ìm, ionga, imleag, ciomach.*

I. E. "*r*" and "*l*" Liquids.

Gaelic *r* and *l* represent the I. E. liquids *r* and *l.* Initially we may select *ràmh, reachd, ruadh, rùn, loch, laigh, labhair, leth;* after *p* lost—*ro, ràth, làmh, làn, làr.* Medially *r* and *l* are "aspirated," but the sounds have no separate signs—*dorus, tulach, geal, meil, eile, seileach,* etc. Post-consonantal *r* and *l* appear in *sruth, srath,* etc., *cluinn, fliuch, slug,* etc. In *-br, -tr, -dr,* the combinations become *-bhar, -thar, -dhar,* while in *-cr, -gr, -bl, -tl, -dl, -cl, -gl* the respective explosives disappear with lengthening of the preceding vowel. For *-sl,* see below (*-ll*).

Ante-consonantal *r* and *l* preserve the explosives after them—*àrd, bàrd, ceart, neart, dearg, dearc, allt, calltuinn, gilb, balg, cealg, olc,* etc.

Gaelic *-rr* arises from *-rs*; see *bàrr, èarr, carraig*; from the meeting of *r* with *r,* as in *atharrach*; from *rth,* as in *orra* from *ortha,* Lat. *orationem.* Again *-ll* comes from *-sl,* as in *uaill, coll, ciall,* etc.; especially from *-ln-*, as in *follas, ball, feall,* etc.; from *-ld-*, as in *call, coille,* and many others.

Gaelic *-rr* arises from *-rp*; *corran, searrach* (St.); Ir. *carr,* spear, *cirrim,* I cut, *forrach,* pole. KZ. 35.

I. E. "*n*" and "*m*" Nasals.

I. E. *n* and *m* appear normally in G. as *n* and *m,* save that I. E. terminal *m* in neuter nouns, accusative cases, and genitives plural, became in Celtic *n.* (1) Initial *n* appears in *nead,* Eng. nest, *neart, neul, nochd,* naked, night, *nathair, nuadh, nasg, na,* not, etc. (2) After an initial mute, *n* appears in *cnàimh, cneadh, cnò, gnàth,* etc. After *s,* in *snàth, snìomh, snuadh, snigh, sneachd.* After *b* it changes the *b* into *m* (*mnatha* for **bnâs*). (3) Intervocalic *n* is preserved—*bean, làn, maoin, dàn, rùn, dùn, sean,* etc. (4). Pre-consonantal *n* is dealt with variously:

a. Before the liquids, *n* is assimilated to *m* and *l,* and disappears before *r.*

b. Before the labials, *n* becomes *m* in modern Gaelic. Before *t*, *c*, the *n* disappears with lengthening of the previous vowel, as in *ceud*, first, *breug*, *cóig*. Before *d* and *g*, it is preserved, as in *cumhang*, *fulaing*, *muing*, *seang*, but it assimilates *d*—*fionn* (**vindo-s*), *bonn*, *inn-*, *binn*. For *-ngm*, see under *ṇ* and *g*.

c. Before *s*, *n* disappears as before *t* and *c*. Compare *mìos*, *feusag*, *grìos*, *sìos*.

(5) Post-consonantal *n* disappears after *l*, leaving *ll* (see under *l*), but is preserved after *r*, as in *càrn*, *eòrna*, *tighearna*, etc.

a. After *s*, that is, *-sn* becomes *-nn*; as in *dronn* for **dros-no-*, *donn*, *uinnsean*, *cannach*, *bruinne*, etc.

b. The mutes, *t*, *d*, *c*, *g*, *p*, disappear with compensatory lengthening of the previous vowel: *-tn-*, as in *eun*, *buan*, *ùin*; *-dn-*, as in *bruan*, *smuain*; *-cn-* is doubtful—cf. *tòn*, also *sgeun*, *breun*, *leòn*; *-gn*, as in *feun*, *bròn*, *uan*, *sròn*; *-pn*, as in *suain*, *cluain*, *cuan*; *-pn? tepno* = *tĕn*; *apnio* = *ăne* (Lit. *aps*); *lipn* = *lĕn*, follow; but *supn* = *suan*; *copn* = *cuan* (Stokes); *cn*, *gn*, and *tn* initial become *r* in pronouncing; but the vowel is nasal—*gnàth* is *gràth* with nasal *à*; *bn* becomes *mn*, as in *mnaoi*, pronounced *mraoi*; even *snàth* becomes dialectally *sràth*, especially in oblique cases.

c. After *b*, that is, *bn* changes into *mh-n*, as in *domhan* (**dubno-*), *sleamhuinn*.

The G. combination *-nn* arises therefore from (1) *n* before *n*, (2) *n* before *d*, and (3) from *-sn*; or (4) it is a doubling of *n* in an unaccented syllable at the end of a word (*tighinn*, etc.), or, rarely, of a one-syllable word like *cinn*, *cluinn*, *linn*. In Islay, *-in* becomes *-inn*; *duinne* is for *duine*; *minne* gen. of *min*, etc. In general, *gloinne* is comp. of *glan*.

Initial *m* appears in *mìos*, *muir*, *mil*, *maide*, etc. Before the liquids *r* and *l*, the *m* becomes *b*, as in *braich*, *brath*, *brugh*, *blàth*, *bleith*, *bleoghainn*. Intervocalic *m* is always aspirated—*geimheal*, *amhuil*, like, *cruimh*, *amh*, *damh*, *cnàimh*, *làmh*, *caomh*. In combinations with other consonants, various results occur:—

(1) Pre-consonantal *m*.

a. Before liquids, *m* is preserved in an aspirated form (*geamh-radh*, etc.), but there are no certain ancient cases. Of course, *m* before *m* results in preserved *m* (cf. *amadan*, *comas*, *comain*).

b. Before *s*, *m* should disappear, but no certain Celtic cases seem to occur. In the historic language, *m* before *s* results in *mp* or *p* as usually pronounced, as in *rompa* for *rom* + *so*, that is, **rom-sho*; so *iompaidh*, *umpa*.

c. Before the explosives. Original *mb* is now *m*, as in the prefix *im-*, *iom-*, in *imleag*, *tom*. I. E. *m* before *t* and *k* (*q*) became *n* (as in *ceud*, *breug*), and disappeared with compensatory lengthening. Compare also *dìdean*, *eiridinn*. Prehistoric *mg*, *md* fail us; in the present language both appear aspirated (*mhgh*, *mhdh*).

(2) Post-consonantal *m*. After the liquids *r*, *l*, and *n*, the *m* is preserved. Whether an intermediate *s* is in some cases to be postulated is a matter of doubt (as in *gairm*, from **gar-s-men*? W. *garm*). See *cuirm* (W. *cwrw*), *gorm*, *seirm*, *deilm*, *calma*, *ainm*, *meanmna*, *anmoch*.

After *s*, *m* becomes in the older language *mm*, now *m*; *druim* comes from **dros-men*. But *s* is very usual as an intermediate letter between a previous consonant and *m*: many roots appear with an additional *s*, which may originally have belonged to an *-es* neuter stem. We actually see such a development in a word like *snaim*, which in E. Ir. appears as *snaidm* (d. *snaidmaimm*), from a Celtic **snades-men*. In any case, a word like *ruaim* postulates a Pre-Celtic **roud-s-men*. See also *gruaim*, *seaman*, *réim*, *lom*, *trom*.

After the explosives the *m* is aspirated and the explosive disappears, as in the case of *freumh* (*vṛdmâ*); but seemingly the accented prefix *ad-* preserves the *m*: cf. *amas*, *amail*, *aimsir*.

Preserved G. *m*, intervocalic or final, may arise from (1) *m* or *n* before *m*, (2) *s* before *m* (also *-bsm*, *-tsm*, *-dsm*, *-csm*, *-gsm*), (3) *-ngm*, or *-ṇgm*, as in *ceum*, *leum*, *beum*, *geum*, or *-ndm* as in *teum*, (4) *ng* becoming *mb* as in *ìm*, *tum*, *tom*, etc., or (5) *mb* (*-mbh*), as in *im-*, *iom-*.

§ 5. Vowel Gradation or Ablaut.

The most characteristic roots of the I. E. languages are at least triple-barrelled, so to speak: they show three grades of vowels. The root *pet*, for instance, in Greek appears as *pet*, *pot*, *pt* (πέτομαι, fly, ποτάομαι, flutter, πτερόν, wing). The first grade—*e*—may be called the "normal" grade, the second the "deflected" grade, and the last—*pt*—the "reduced" or "weak" grade. The reason for the reduced grade is evident; the chief accent is on another syllable. Why *e* interchanges with *o* is not clear. The leading I. E. series of vowel gradations are six in number, as follows:—

	Normal.	Deflected.	Weak.
1. *e*-series	*e*	*o*	*nil*
but	*ei*	*oi*	*i*
2. *ē*-series	*ē*	*ō*	ə
3. *ā*-series	*ā*	*ō*	ə
4. *ō*-series	*ō*	*ō*	ə
5. *a*-series	*a*	*ā*	(*a*)
6. *o*-series	*o*	*ō*	(*o*)

Corresponding to the *e*, *o*, *nil* series are the two "strong" vowel grades *ē*, *ō*, as in *sed*, sit, *sod*, *sēd*, *sōd*, *si-zd*, found in Latin *sedeo* (*sed*), G. *suidhe* (*sod*), G. *sìth* [properly *sìdh*], peace (*sēd*), Eng. *soot* (*sōd*), Lat. *sīdo* (*si-zd*).

The *e*-series in full is as follows:—

	Normal.	Deflected.	Weak.
e simple	*e*	*o*	*nil*
ei	*ei*	*oi*	*i*
eu	*eu*	*ou*	*u*
er (or *el*, *en*, *em*)......	*er*	*or*	*r̥*

To all these correspond "reduced" long forms—to *ei* belongs *ī*, to *eu* belongs *ū*, and to the consonant-vowels correspond the long *r̥̄*, *l̥̄*, *n̥̄*, *m̥̄*. We may also here add the triple *ve*, *vo*, *u* (*vet*, *vot*, *ut*, as in G. *feitheamh*, *ùine*, *uiridh*; *vel*, *vol*, *ul* as in *falt*, O. Ir., Mod. Ir. *folt*, *olann*).

Some Gaelic examples will now be given.

(1) The *e*-series. G. *eadh*, *uidhe* from **pedo*-, **podio*-; *tigh*, *tugha*, from **tegos*, **togio*-; *geas*, *guidhe* from *ged*, *god*; *cleachd*, *cleas*, *cluich*, etc. In *ei* we have the complete set *meit*, *moit*, *mit* in *mèith*, *maoth*, *meata* or *miosa*; further *cliathach*, *claon* from *klei*, *kloi*; *fianuis*, *fios* from *veid*, *vid*; *gaoth*, *geamhradh* from *ghoi*, *ghi*; and others. The diphthongs *eu*, *ou* cannot be differentiated, but the short form of the root occurs, as in *ruadh*, *roduidh* from *roud*, *rudd*; *buail*, *buille* from *bhoud*, *bhud*; *cluas*, *cluinn* from *kleu*, *klu*; *nuadh*, *nodha* (?) The liquids show the changes also: *beir*, *br̥eith* from *ber*, *br̥*, and in the sense of speech we have also *bràth*, judgment (*br̥̄tu*-). The root *pel* is especially rich in forms: *iol* (**pelu*-), *uile* (**polio*-), *lìon* (**plēno*-, Lat. *plēnus*, from *plē*), *làn* (either **plōno*, *plō*, Eng. *flood*, or **pl̥̄-no*-, from *pl̥̄*-), that is, root forms *pel*, *pol*, *pl̥*, *plē*, *plō*, *pl̥̄*, meaning "full." In *n* we have *teann*, *tana* (**tendo*- *tn̥navo*-, according to Brugmann), and *teud*; from *gen* we get the long forms *gnē* in *gnìomh* and *gnō* in *gnàth*. In *nem* we have *nèamh*, heaven, O. Ir. *nem*, and *nàmhaid*, foe, from *nōm* (Gr. νωμάω).

(2) The *ē* and other series. One of the best examples of the *ē* series is *snē*, *snō* (*snā*), spin, which gives *snìomh* (**snēmu-*) and *snàth*, thread (**snātio-*). From *sē* comes *sìol* (**sêlo-*) and, possibly, *sàth*, transfix (*sôto-*). The *ā-* series is not differentiated in G. nor is the *ō-* series; but from *a* short we get, among others, the root *ăg*, lead, in *aghaidh*, etc., and *āg* in *àgh*, success, *àghach*, warlike. The diphthong *ai* has as its "reduced" grade *i*. The name *Aodh* in Mackay represents O. Ir. *Aed*, *aed*, fire, Gr. *αἴθω*, I burn.

§ 6. The Spirants.

The I. E. spirants were *j*, *v*, *s*, and *z*. We have already discussed *j* and *v* under the heading of semi-vowels, from which it is difficult to differentiate the consonantal *j* and *v*. Here we deal with *s* and *z*, and first with *s*.

(1) Initial *s*. Before vowels and the liquids, I. E. *s* remains intact in Gadelic. In Brittonic *s* before vowels becomes *h*; before *l*, *n*, and *m*, it disappears, while before *r* it or its resultant effect is preserved (see *sruth*, *srath*, *sròn*).

a. I. E *sv* appears in Gadelic as *s* usually, more rarely as *f* and *p* or *t*; in W. the form is *chw*. See *searbh*, *seal*, *sè*, *sibh*, *séid*, etc. The G. *piuthar* appears in Ir. as *siur*, *fiur*, from **svesōr*, while *pill* (**svelni-*) gives *fill* and *till*; compare also *séisd* (*téis*).

b. I. E. *sp* (*sph*) is treated in Celtic much as *sv*. And *spr* appears as *sr*; cf. *sròn*, *straighlich*, *slis*, *sonn*, *sealg*, *sine*.

I. E. *st* appears in Gadelic as *t*, as in *tigh*, *tà*, *tighinn*, *taois*. But *str*, *stl*, become *sr*, *sl*, as in *srath*, *sreothart*, *sreang*, *slios*, *slat*, *sloinn*, *slaid*. Some hold that *st* may appear as simple *s*, which is the case in Welsh, but the instances adduced can be otherwise explained (cf. *seirc*, *sàil*, *searrach* (St.), *seall*).

I. E. *sq*, *sqh*, appear in Gaelic as *sg*, O. Ir. *sc*, as in *sgàth*, *sgath*, *sguir*, etc. The W. precedes the *sg* with a *y* as in *ysgwyd*, Ir. *sgiath*, G. *sgiath*, shield : I. E. *sqv* is in W. *chw*, as G. *sgeul*, W. *chwedl*, *sgeith*, W. *chwydu*.

I. E. *skn* appears in Gaelic as *sn*, as in *sneadh*.

(2) Intervocalic *s*. This becomes *h* and disappears; compare *tagh* (**to-gusô*), *do-*, *chì*, etc.

(3) Terminal *s* disappears altogether; but in closely connected combinations of words its former existence is known from the so-called euphonic *h*, as in the article genitive feminine and

nom. plural before vowels (*na h-òighean* = **sen·lâs augeis*), also *O' H-* of Irish; and it may be the origin in most cases of prothetic *s*.

(4) Pre-consonantal *s*. A prehistoric case of *-sr* is not forthcoming, but *éirich* comes from **ek-s-regô*. Before *l*, *m*, and *n* the *s* disappears, and the liquid is doubled (*m* of Gaelic being for older *mm*), as already shown under these letters. Medial *sv* appears as *f* in the older language (see *seinn*), and it is still seen in *t ıbhann* (**to-sven-*), *feabhas*.

Before the explosives, *s* is preserved before the tenues, which in the modern language become mediæ. The combination *sp* is not certain; but *-sc* becomes *-sg* (see *fasgadh*, *seasg*, *measg*, etc.), *st* becomes *s* (older *ss*) simply, as in *seas* (= **sisto-*), *fois*, *fàs*, *dos*, etc. Before the medials *s* becomes *z*, which see for results in Gaelic; **sg* becomes *g*; *sp* becomes *s*.

(5) Post-consonantal *s*. After the liquid *r* the *s* is assimilated to the *r*, and the result is *rr*, as in *bàrr*, *èarr*, etc. From *-ls-* seemingly *s* results, at least in the later language; *-ms*, *-ns* become *s* with compensatory lengthening for the previous vowel; *-ds* becomes *t*, as in *an t-each* (= **sindos eqos*); Thn. adds *fitir* (= **vid-sar*). For *m-sh* = *mp*, see under *m*.

The explosives combine with the *s* and disappear into O. Ir. *ss*, now *s*, as in *uasal* (= **oups-* or **ouks-*), *lus*, *leas* (**led-so-*), *lios*, *as*, out (– *eks*), and many others.

Gaelic preserved *s* intervocalic, therefore, arises from (1) *st*, as in *seas*; (2) from *-ms*, *-ns*, as in *mìos*; and (3) from *-ps*, *-ts*, *-cs*. Gaelic *-st* arises from this *s* by a sort of modern restoration of previous *st*, only, however, *x* may also become modern *st* (as in *aiste*, now *aisde*, out of her). Final *x* disappears, as in *caora*, *sè*.

I. E. *z*.

Even in I. E. this is assured only before the medial explosives. Thus G. *nead*, nest, is from I. E. *nizdo-s*: so *maide*, *brod*, *cead*, *gad*, *séid*. Again *-zg* seems to have developed in G. into *g*; compare *beag*, *biog*, *mèag*, *griogag*, *eagal* (= *ex-gal-*), *rag*.

§ 7. The Explosives or Mutes.

The I. E. explosives formed a possible sixteen in number between tenues, mediæ and the double set of aspirates (*ph*, *bh*, *th*, *dh*, *kh*, *gh*, *qh*, *gh*). The tenues aspirate were "rare and of no importance" in the resulting languages, save only in Sanskrit and Greek. The mediæ aspirates are the predecessors of aspirates of the modern languages. But in the Celtic languages these mediæ aspirates were merged into the mediæ themselves, so that *b* and *bh* appear in Celtic as *b*, *d* and *dh* as *d*, *g* and *gh* as *g*, and *g* and *gh* as *g*. The Balto-Slavonic, in this matter, shares the peculiarity of the Celtic.

All the explosives, when intervocalic, are "aspirated" in Gaelic —*p* to *ph*, *b* to *bh* (= *v*), *t* to *th* (= *h*), *d* to *dh* (= *y*), *c* to *ch*, *g* to *gh*, (= *y*); the corresponding Welsh changes are the tenues to mediæ, and the mediæ to *f*, *dd*, and *nil* in the case of *g*. Intervocalic preserved explosives in Gaelic arise from a doubling of the explosive, the cause of which in many cases is obscure. The following are the leading cases and causes of intervocalic G. mutes:

(1) Doubling of the explosive in the course of inflection or word-building.

a. Inflection. The participle passive in *-te* preserves the *t* or *d* of the root as *t*; thus [*caith* gives *caithte*,] *bàth* (for *bàdh*) gives *bàite*, *ràdh* gives *ràite*, etc.

b. Word-building. The prepositional prefixes which end or ended in a consonant preserve the succeeding explosive; even vowel-ending prepositions like *air* (**are*), *aith-* (**ati*) do the same, if the accent is on the preposition. Thus—*abair* is for *ad-ber*, *aitreabh* is for *ad-treb*, *aidich* is for *ad-dam*, *faic* for *ad-ces-*, *agair* for *ad-gar*. In the way of affixes, we have *ruiteach* from *rud-t* and *ruicean* from *rud-c*, *creid* from **cred-dhô*; compare the compounds *boicionn*, *laoicionn*, and *craicionn*.

(2) After sunk *n* or *m*. Thus *deud* comes from *dṇt*, and so with *ceud*, *teud*; *ceud*, first, from **cento-*, so *seud*; *eug* from *ṇko-*, etc.

(3) After sunk spirant *z*. This is assured for *zd*, as in *brod* (**broz-do-*, Norse *broddr*), *cead*, *gad*, *maide*, *nead*; but *zg* giving *g* is doubtful—*eagal* seems for **es-gal* or **ex-gal-*, *beag* for *gvezgo-s* (Lat. *vescus*), *mèag* for *mezgo-*.

(4) Cases corresponding to double explosives in other languages: *cat* and Lat. *catta* (borrowing?), *cac* and Gr. κάκκη. Compare also *slug*.

(5) Doubtful cases. Many of these cases can be satisfactorily explained as due to suffixes immediately affixed to consonant-ending roots. Thus *brat* may be for *brat-to-*, *trod* for *trud-do-*, *ìoc* for **yak-ko-*, *breac* for *mṛg-ko-*. Even suffixes in *-bho-* and *-go-* (Eng. *k* in *walk*) are not unknown, and they might account for *reub* (**reib-bo-*, **reib-bho-*, Eng. *reap*, *rip*), *slug* for *slug-go-*, etc. Dr Whitley Stokes has given a different theory founded on the analogy of a Teutonic phonetical law, stated

thus by Brugmann : "*bn, dn, gn* became *bb, dd, gg* before the principal accent in primitive Teutonic, thence *pp, tt, kk* (by Grimm's law), which were further treated just the same as *pp, tt, kk*, which had arisen from *pn, tn, qn*, and from I. E. *bhn, dhn, ghn, ghn*. . . . O. H. G. *sluccho, slukko*, glutton [**sluk-no-*], M. H. G. *sluchen*, gulp, have hiccup, allied to Gr. λύζω, λυγγανάομαι, I have hiccup." These last words are allied to G. *slug*, which Dr Stokes refers to a pre-Celtic **slug-nó-*, the accent being on the suffix *-no-*. The weakness of this hypothesis lies in the fact that uniform results are not found from it. Thus *breac*, from *mṛg-nó-*, should be *breag*, not *breac*, on the analogy of *slug*.

I. E. *p*.

Initial and intervocalic I. E. *p* disappears in Gaelic, as in *athair*, Lat. *pater*, *eun* for **pet-no-*, *eadh* for *pedo-*, *iasg* against Lat. *piscis*, *ibh* against *bibo* (for *pibo*), *làn* against Lat. *plenus*, *làr* and Eng. *floor*, etc. For intervocalic *p*, see *fo* (**upo*), *for*, *teth*, *caora*, (**kaperax*), *saor*, (**sapiros*), etc.

Lat. and G. agree in the initial of the numeral five—*quinque* and *cóig*, though the I. E. was *penqe*. In *feasgar* the G. gutturalises an original *vesperos* without Latin countenancing it. Initial *sp* appears as *s* ; see *sealg*, spleen, *sonn*, *sliseag*, *sine*, *sir*.

When *p* appears before the liquids and *t*, *c*, or *s*, it is not lost in G. ; it leaves its influence either in a new combination or in compensatory lengthening. Thus *suain* is for *supno-s*, and see *cluain*, *cuan*. G. *dias* seems from **steip-s-â*, W. *twys*, and *uasal* may have had an original form like ὑψηλός, Eng. *up*. (Cf. *teanga* and *dingua*). In *seachd*, Lat. *septem*, the *p* is gutturalised ; we may add here **neachd*, O. Ir. *necht*, Lat. *neptis*, Eng. *niece* ; *creuchd*, *drèachd*. Possibly *leac* may be for *lep-kâ*.

G. intervocalic *p* is, of course, due to some combination. In *leapa*, genitive of *leabaidh*, it arises from **leb-tha* ; and we must explain similarly *tap* (**tabaidh* arising from **tab-tha*) ; so *raip*, *streap*.

For *t* taking the place of *p* through an initial *h* compare the derivations offered for *torc*, *turlach*, *tuil*, *tlàm*, *tlùs* for *lùths*.

I. E. *b*, *bh*.

These two become *b* in Gaelic and the other Celtic languages, I. E. *b* is rare in any language ; in G. it appears in *ibhim* (**pibô*). *treabh*, *domhain* and *drùchd* (**dhreub-tu-*).

(1) Initial I. E. *bh*, G. *b*. See *beir*, *balg*, *ball*, *bàn*, *blàth*, bloom, *bragh*, *bruthainn*, *buaidh*.

(2) Intervocalic I. E. *bh*, G. *bh* (=*v*), O. Ir. *b*, W. *f*. See *abhainn cràbhach*, *dubh*, *gobhal*.

(3). Pre-consonantal *bh* or *b*.

a. Before *r* it remains—*abhra*, *gabhar*, *dobhar*, Gaul. *dubrum*.

b. Before *l* it disappears with compensatory lengthening—*neul* for *neblo-s*.

c. Before *n* it becomes *mh* now—*sleamhuinn* is for **slibno-s*, Eng. *slippery*; so *domhain*. These are I. E. *b*.

d. Before *t*, I. E. *b* becomes *ch* as in *drùchd*.

(4) Post-consonantal *b*, *bh*. It is preserved after the liquids *r* and *l*—*carbad*, *cearb*, *earb*, *gilb*, *sgolb*. After *m* it preserves the *m*, as in *im-*, *iom-* from *m̥bi*, *ambi*. After *s* it is preserved in *eabar*; after *d* in *abair*, *leòb*, *faob*, *aobrann*; perhaps after *g* in *leabaidh*, **leg-buti-* (?).

(5) Gaelic intervocalic *b*. In *reub* and *gob* we seem to have a suffix *-bo-*, **reib-bo-*, *gob-bo*; also *cliob* from *clib-bo-*, root *ql̥g*, Gr. κολοβός, stumpy (?). Oftenest *b* is produced from a previous *d*, especially of the prefixes—as *abair*, *abadh*, *faob*, etc. (see the paragraph above).

I. E. *t*.

Initially this is Celtic *t*; intervocalic, it is aspirated, and otherwise it is variously modified.

(1) Initial *t*, G., O. Ir., W. *t*. See, among many, *tiugh*, *tar*, *teth*, *teich*, *tais*, *tora*, *tlàth*, *tnùth*, *tri*, *treabh*.

(2) Intervocalic *t*, G. *th* (=*h*), O. Ir. *th* (*d*), W. *d*. See *athair*, *màthair*, *ith*, *roth*, *ceithir*, *leth*, etc. Sometimes in non-accented syllables it appears as *dh*, as in *biadh* from **bîvoto-s*, and this is always the case with the infinitives in *-atu-* (*glan-adh*). Irregularly *fàidh* for *fàith*.

(3) Pre-consonantal *t* not initial. Before *r* it is preserved, as in *criathar*, *briathar*, etc. Before *l* it disappears with compensatory lengthening—*sgeul*, W. *chwedl*, *òl*, *beul*, etc.; so before *n*, as in *eun*. Before *s* the *t* disappears and the *s* is preserved, as in *miosa*, *ris*, *sàs*. Words like *fios* are from *vid-s-tu-*, formerly explained as from *vid-tu-*. Before another *t*, *t* is preserved in the resultant *t* of G., as in *ite*, etc.; *-td-* seems to become *-dd-*; *-tc-* becomes O. Ir. *cc*, G. *c*, as in *freiceadan*; *-tg-* becomes *gg*, that is *g*, as in *freagair*.

(4) Post-consonantal *t*. After *r* and *l* it is preserved, as in *beart*, *ceart*, *ceirtle*, *alt*, *falt*; after *n* and *m* it sinks to *d*, as in *ceud*, etc. As seen, *-bt* becomes *-chd*, as in *drùchd*, while *-pt* is in *seachd*. After *c* or *g*, the *t* sinks in G. to *d*, preserving the

guttural as an aspirate: *ochd*, *nochd*, *bochd*, *reachd*. O. Ir. has *-cht* here and W. *th*.

(5) Gaelic intervocalic t. The *t* of a root is preserved when the suffix begins in *t*, as [in *caithte*, spent,] in *ite*, O Ir. *ette*, **pet-tiá*, *lit*, **pḷt-tion-*. The *d* of the affixes preserves it, as in *aitreabh*, *taitinn*, *ruiteach*, *réit*. The *t* of the following does not belong to the ultimate root: *ciotach*, **sqvi-tto-*, Eng. *skew*, *creit*, root *kur*, *lot*, root *lu*.

I. E. *d. dh.*

This is a uniform Celtic *d* initial; Gaelic *dh* between vowels and W. *dd*.

(1) Initial *d*, *dh*. See *deas*, *dearc*, *deich*, *druim*, *dùn*, *damh*, etc., for *d*; for *dh*, *dubh*, *domhan*, *dearg*, *dorus*, *dall*; also *dlighe*.

(2) Intervocalic *d*, *dh*. See *fiodh*, **vidu-*, *eadh*, *suidhe*, *fiadh*, *guidhe*, etc.

(3) Pre-consonantal *d*, *dh* non-initial. Before *r*, *l*, *n*, the *d* disappears with compensatory lengthening, as in *àireamh* (**ad-rím-*) *àros*, *àrạch*, *buail*, (**boud-lo-*), but *buille* is for **bud-s-lio-*; *smuain* for *smoud-no-*, Before *m* it sometimes disappears, as in *freumh*, **vṛd-mâ*, but with an accented prefix the *d* and *m* become *m*, as in *aimsir*, *amal*, *amas*. With *s* it coalesces into *s*, as in *musach*, or in *uisge* for **ud-s-qio-*, or *fios* for **vid-s-tu-*. Before the explosives, with *b* it coalesces to *bb*, now *b*, as in *abair*, etc. So with *t*, as in *aitreabh*; with *d*, as in *aidich*; with c, as in *faic*; with *g*, as in *agair*.

(4) Post-consonantal *d*, *dh*. The liquid *r* preserves a following *d*, as in *àrd*, *bàrd*, *sgàird*, *òrd*, etc. It assimilates with *l*, as in *coille*, *call*, *moll*, *mullach*; and with *n*, in *fionn*, O. Ir. *find*, *bonn*, O. Ir. *bond*, *binn*. For *zd*, see next paragraph. The explosives before *d* are unusual, save *t* and *d*, for which see next paragraph.

(5) Intervocalic G. *d*. There are three sources at least for this *d*:—

a. The *d* from *nt* in *ceud*, *teud*, *beud*, etc.

b. The *d* arising from the spirant *z* before *d*, as in *brod*, **brozdo-*, *cead*, *gad*, *maide*, *nead*, *druid*.

c. From *-dd-* as in *creid*, *goid*, *rodaidh*, *trod*, etc.; also *aidich*, **ad-dam-*.

I, E. "*k*" and "*q*."

These appear in G. uniformly as *c*; but in the Brittonic languages *q*, if labialised, becomes *p* as in Greek.

(1). Initial *k*. See *cluinn*, *cù*, *ceud*, hundred, *cac*, *cridhe*, *caomh*, *còrn*.

Initial *q* simple. See *caraid*, W. *câr*, *ceud*, first, W. *cynt*, *coille*, W. *celli*, *cas*, W. *coes*, *coileach*, W. *ceiliog*, etc.

Initial *q* labialised, that is, *qv* : *casd*, W. *pâs*, *ciall*, W. *pwyll*, *ceithir*, W. *pedwar*, *ceann*, W. *pen*, *coire*, W. *pair*, *co*, W. *pa*, *cruimh*, W. *pryf*.

It seems clear that G. *g* at times represents I. E. *k*, *q*, as W. has the latter. Compare G. *geug* with W. *cainc*, Skr. *çañku* ; but W. *ysgainc* shows the reason for the anomaly—an *s* initial has been dropped, and in dropping it the G. reduced *c* to *g*. Further compare *garmainn*, *giomach*. Cf. *dias*.

(2) Intervocalic *k*, *q*. The G. is *ch*, W. *g*, *b*. Compare *cruach*, W. *crûg*, *fichead*, *deich*, *loch* ; also *each*, W. *ebol*, *seach*, W. *heb*, etc.

(3) Pre-consonantal *k*, *q*. Before *r*, *l*, *n*, the *c* disappears with compensatory lengthening as in *deur*, Lat. *dacrima*, *meur*, *dual*, *muineal*, *tòn* ; and compare Prof. Strachan's derivations for *mèanan*, *breun*, *càin*, *lèana*. With *s*, the result in G. is *s*, O. Ir. *ss*, W. *ch*, as in *uasal*, W. *uchel*. Before explosives, *cb*, *cd*, *cg* do not appear ; *ct* becomes *chd*, for which see under *t* (4) ; for *c-c*, see paragraph (5) here.

(4) Post-consonantal *k*, *q*. After *r* and *l*, the guttural appears as *c*, as in *cearc*, *uircean*, *malc*, *olc*, *falc*, etc. After *n* (*m*), it sinks to *g*, with a preceding long vowel, as in *eug*, *breug*, already discussed. After *s*, the *c* is preserved, but in G. it is written as *g*, as in *measg*, *nasg*, *teasg*, etc. After explosives, the *t* and *d* of the prefix or root preserves the *c* following, for which see under *t* and *d* pre-consonantal. For *c* or *g* before *c*, see next paragraph.

(5) Intervocalic Gaelic *c*. It may arise from *-tk*, *-dk*, *-kk*, *-gk*. From *-tk* in *freiceadan* (**frith-com-ét-án*) ; *-dk* in *faic*, *acarach*, *ruicean*, *acuinn* ; *-kk* in *muc*, **mukkus*, *cac*, *craicionn*, *ìoc*, *leacainn* ; from *-gk* in *bac*, *boc*, *breac*, *cnoc*, *gleac*. The word *mac*, son, postulates a Gadelic *makko-s* as against the Ogmic *maqvi* (gen.) and W. *mab* ; it is difficult to account for the G. form.

I. E. *g*, *gh* ; *g*, *gh*.

These consonants all, save in one case, appear in G. as *g*, aspirated to *gh*, and W. shows *g* and *nil* in similar circumstances. The exception is in the case of *g*, which when labialised, becomes G. and W. *b*. But *gh*, whether labialised or not, becomes *g* in G.

(1) Initial I. E. *g* : in *guth*, *gin*, *gnàth*, *geimheal*, *gò*. I. E. *gh* is in *geamhradh*, *gabh*, *gàg*, *geal*, white. I. E. *g* simple appears in *geal*, leech, *goir*, *goile*, *gearan*, *guala*, *gràdh* ; I. E. *gh* in

gar, *grian*, *gaol*, *guidhe*, *geas*, *guin*. Labialised *g* appears in *bean*, Eng. *queen*, *bior*, *beò*, *bó*, *brà*, quern, *bràghad*.

(2) Intervocalic Celtic *g*. See *deigh*, *aghaidh*, *greigh*, *truagh*, *bleoghainn*, *tigh*, *bragh*, etc. In the termination of words it appears often as *ch*: *teach* (**tegos*), *mach*, (**magos*), *imlich*, *im[th]ich*, *éirich*, *fuirich*. Intervocalic *g* labialised does not seem to exist in modern G.

(3) Pre-consonantal Celtic *g*. Here *-gr*, *-gl*, *-gn*, become *-r*, *-l*, *-n* with vocalic lengthening, as *feur*, **vegro-*, *àr*, *nàir*, *fuar*, *àl*, *fual*, *feun*, **vegno-*, *sròn*, *uan*, *tàin*, *bròn*, etc. Before *m*, *g* is found in the combination *ng-m*, which results in *m* with a preceding long vowel, as in *ceum*, *leum*, *geum*. Before *s* it becomes *x* and modern *s*, W. *ch*, as in *uasal*, W. *uchel*, *as* for *ex*, *os*, deer, W. *ych*, *cas*, *las*, *uiseag*. Before explosives the *g* is variously preserved: *-gb*, *-gd* may be passed over; *-ct*, *-gt* appear as *chd*, as in *seachd*, *bliochd*, *smachd*, *nochd*, *sneachd*, etc.; *-gk* ends in *-kk*, now *c*, for which see post-consonantal *k*; *-gg* appears as *g*, as in *slug*, *bog*, *clag*, *lag*, *slige*, *smugaid*.

(4) Post-consonantal Celtic *g*. After *r* and *l* the *g* is preserved in G., but often in W. becomes *y*; see *dearg*, *fearg*, *searg*, *garg*, *lorg*, *balg*, *cealg*, *dealg*, *tulg*. After *n* ordinary *g* is preserved, as in *cumhang*, *long*, *muing*, *seang*, *fulaing*. But labialised *g* became *b*, and then coalesced with the *n* into *mm*, now *m* as in *ìm*, butter, Lat. *unguentum*, *tum*, *cam*, *tom*, *ciomach*, and in modern times *cum*, keep, from **congv* in *congbhail*. For *ng-m* see the foregoing paragraph. For *sg* see the next paragraph. After the explosives, the *g* is preserved in the combinations *-tg* (*freagair*), *-dg* (*agair*), and *-gg*, which see below.

(5) Intervocalic Gaelic *g*. It arises from *-sg* firstly, which in pre-Celtic times was *-zg*, as in *beag*, *mogul*, *griogag*, *mèag*, *eagal*, etc., which see under I. E. *z* above. From the explosive combinations we have *tg* in *freagair*, **frith-gar-*, *eagna*, *eagar*; *dg* in *agair*, *agus*. The *-gg* must arise from a suffix in *-go-*, which was operative in early Gadelic, if we discard Dr Stokes' view already set forth. Cf. Eng. *walk*, *hark*, *lurk*, *skulk*, *smirk*. For this *-gg* see paragraph third above.

Intervocalic *g* may arise from a lost *n* before *c*, as in *breug*, *geug*, *eug*, etc. The previous vowel is lengthened save in a few cases where the word—or sentence—accent has brought about a short syllable. Thus *thig* has short *i*, and in G. *leig* is short. This is regularly the case with the results from the prefix *con*, confused with *cos*, as in *cogais*, O. Ir. *concubus*, *cadal*, *cagar*, *cogadh*, etc.

§ 8. Accent.

In Gaelic, only the stress accent exists, and it is placed always on the first syllable. The accent of the Old Gaelic was likewise on the first syllable, save in the case of the verb. Here in the compounded verbs the stress accent rested on, as a rule, the second syllable; but the imperative placed the accent on the first syllable, and this also took place after the negative and interrogative particles and after the conjunctions *gu'n* and *na'n* (*da'n*). Thus *faic*, see thou, is for *f-aid-c*, with accent on the preposition *ad*, for it is imperative; the future *chì* stands for the old present *at-chí*, videt, where the accent is on the root *cí*. Again in *cha'n fhaca* the negative brings the accent on the prefix *ad*, that is, *f-ad-ca*. When the accent is on the prefix, its ending consonant and the initial consonant of the root coalesce and result in a preserved G. intervocalic consonant, but the root suffers truncation: when the accent is on the root, these consonants are aspirated, and the root is preserved. The ten irregular verbs in G. present sufficient illustrations of this rule. The preposition *con*, when accented, was always *con*, when unaccented it was *com* (*comh*). In the unaccented syllables, long vowels become short (*àireamh* from **ád-rîm*, *anail* for O. Ir. *anál*), and in many cases change completely their grade, as from small to broad (*e.g. còmhnadh*, O. Ir. *congnam*, from *gnìomh*, and the compounds in *-radh* and *-lach*).

II. WORD-BUILDING.

Word-building consists of two parts—composition and derivation. The first deals with the compounding of separate words; the second deals with the suffixes (and prefixes) that make up the stem of a word from its root.

(1) The compound may be two stems welded together: *righ-theach*, palace, **rîgo-tegos*, "king's house"; *righ-fhàidh*, royal prophet —"king who is a prophet"; *ceann-fhionn*, white-headed, *penno-vindo-s*; *ceithir-chasach*, four-footed; *dubh-ghlas*, dark-blue; *crannchur*, lot, "casting the lot." These are the six leading relationships brought out in compounds. In Celtic the first stem is nearly always in *o*-, as *Teuto-bōdiaci*, G. *seanmhathair* (but *Catu-slôgi*, *Mori-dûnum*, G. *Muirgheal*). Consider the following compounds: *iodhlann*, *mìolchu*, *òircheard*, *buarach*, *cèardach*, *clogad*, *bàthach*, *eilthire*, *gnàth-fhocal*, *moirear*, *leth-chas*, *leth-trom*, etc.

The following are common prefixes: *ath-*, re-, *ath-ghlac*, recapture; *ban-*, she, *ban-altrum*, *bantrach*; *bith-*, ever-, *bith-bheò*, *bith-bhuan*; *il-*, *iol-*, many; *ion-*, fit; *sìr-*, *sìor-*, ever-, *fìr-*, *fìor-*, very, *saobh-*, pseudo-.

The following suffixes belong to this branch of word-building :—

-lach, from **slougo-*, now *sluagh ;* seen in *teaghlach*, *dòrlach*, *òglach*, youth, etc.

-radh, from **rêda*, W. *rwyd* (see *réidh*) ; seen in *reabhradh*, *madraidh*, dogs, *òigridh*, youth, *macraidh*, sons, *rìghre*, kings, *gnìomharra*, deeds.

-mhor, *-or*, from *mór*, great ; it makes adjectives from nouns, etc. : *lìonmhor*, etc.

-ail, like ; from *samhail*, *amhail* : *rìoghail* for *rìogh-amhail*, king-like.

-an, diminutive masculine, O. Ir. *án*, Ogmic *-agnos*, for **apo-gno-s*, root *gen*, bear (Stokes) : as in *fearan*, *truaghan*, etc.

-ag, diminutive fem. in G., O. Ir. *-óc* (masc. and fem.), from *óc*, *óg*, young : seen in *caileag*, etc.

-seach. This feminine termination has been explained by Stokes as from O. Ir. *es*, a fem. form, with the adjectival addition **iqâ*, and this *es* he deduces from W. *es*, which comes from Lat. *issa*. Cf. *baiseach*, *cláirseach*, *bonnsach*, *céirseach* or *ciarseach* (Ir.).

(2) The compound may be one noun governing another in the genitive : *mac-leisg*, and all the personal names in *mac*, *gille*, *maol*.

(3) Uninflected prefixes :

a. Negative prefixes—I. E. *ṇ*, G. *an* before vowels, *aineol*, *ion-*, *in-* before *b*, *d*, *g* (*iongantas*), *eu-* (*ao-*) before *t*, *c*, *s* (*aotrom* for *é-trom*, **ṇ-trommo-s*).

To this negative add also *mi-*, *neo-*, *as-* (*eas-*), *di-* (*der-* = *di-air-*).

b. Prefixes of quality : *do* (*do-char*), and *so-* (*so-char*) ; and the intensive *ro-*.

(4) Old adverbial forms and all prepositions. These prepositions are often combined with one or two other prepositions.

ad-, Lat. *ad* : *faic* = *f-ad-ci ; àireamh* (= *ad-rîm-*).

aith-, *ad-*, **ati-*, re-, continually confused with the above prep. (*aith* gives accented *é* as in *épiur* ; *ad* gives *a* as in *aca*) : *abair* (**ad-ber-*), *agair*, *aithreachas* (**ati-réc-*), etc. Compounded with *to-* in *tagair*, *tapaidh*, *taitinn*, *taitheasg*, *taisg*, etc. ; with *fo-* in *fàg* (*fo-ad-gab*).

air, by, on : *air-leag*, *eir-idinn*, *òir-dheirc*, *oir-thir*, *urchair*, *ùrlar*. Compounded with *com* in *comhairle ;* with *to-* in *tairis*, *tairg*, *tèarainn ;* with *di-* in *dearmad ;* with *imm-* in *iomar-bhaigh*, *iomarchur*.

as, out, *es-* : *as-eirigh*, *as-creideamh*, *eas-bhuidh*, *éi-rich*. Compounded with *air* : *aireasbhuidh* ; with *to-*, *teasairg* ; with *to-for-* in *tuairisgeul* ; with *to-fo-ar* in *tuarasdal* ; with *to-fo-* in *tuasgail*.

eadar, between ; *eadar-sgaradh*.

iar, after ; in **iarfaighim*, now *feòraich* ; *iarogha*.

in, in ; with *to-* in *tional* and *comh-thional*. With a double *nn* in *ionnsuidh*.

inn-, *ionn-*, to, Gaul. *ande-* : in *fionnogha* ; with *to-* in *tionnsgainn*, *tionndadh* (Zeuss). Confused with *in*, *ind*, above.

im-, *iom-*, about : *iomair*, *iomradh*, *imich*, *iompaidh* (**imb-sh*). Compounded with *com* in *caochladh* ; with *to-* in *timchioll*, *tiomsach*, *tiomnadh*.

od-, *ud-*, out, Eng. *out* : *obann*, *obaidh*. Compounded with *aith-* in *ìobairt* ; with *di-* in *dùisg*.; with *fo* in *fògair* ; with *to-* in *tobar*, *tog*.

con-, *comh-*, co- : *coimhead*, *comaidh*, *caisg*, *cogadh*. Compounded with *im-* in *iomchorc* ; with *con* in *cogais* (O. Ir. *concubus*) ; with *to-aith-* in *teagasg*, *teagamh*.

di-, *de*, de : *dìmeas*, *dìoghail*, *dìomhain*, *dìreach* ; also *deach*, *dèan*.

do-, to : this is the unaccented form of *to-*.

fo, under : in *foghnadh*, *foghlum*, *falach*, *fulaing*. Compounded with *to-* in *tòrachd*, *tuisleadh* (*to-fo-ess-*) *tuarasdal* (*to-fo-ar-as-*), *tuasgail* (*to-fo-as-*).

for, *far*, super : in *forail*, *forradh*, *fàrdorus*, *farmad*, *furtachd*. Compounded with *to* in *tormach*, *tuairisgeul*.

fri-, *ri*, to, **vrt*, Lat. *versus* ; it appears as *frith*, *fris* : in *freagair*, *fritheil*, *freiceadan* (*frith-com-*).

ro-, before : in *robhas*, *rosg*, *rabhadh*, *radharc*. Compounded in *rug* (*ro-ud-*).

tar, across, *tairm-* : in *teirig*, *toirmisg*.

Stem Suffixes.

The following are the most important suffixes used in Gaelic for stem formation :—

1. *o-*, *â-*, as in *cùl* (**cûlo-*), *aitreabh*, *cas* (**coxâ*).
2. *tro-*, *tlo-*, *trâ-*, *tlâ-* : *criathar*, *krei-tro-*, *anail*, (**ana-tlâ*), *sgeul*, *cineal*.
3. *jo-*, *jâ-*, *ijo-*, *ijâ-* : *eile*, *suidhe*, (**sod-i-on*). See *no-*, *ro-*, *tjo-*, *sqio-*.
4. *vo-*, *vâ-*, *uvo-*, *uvâ-* : *tarbh* (**tar-vo-*), *each* (**ek-vo-*), *beò*, (*bi-vo-*).
5. *no-*, *nâ-*, *n̥no-*, *eno-*, *ono-* : *làn*, *slàn*, *duan*, *domhan*, *leathan* (*letano-s*). It is secondary in *iarunn* ; cf. *tighearna* (**teg-er-nio-*).

6. *mo-*, *mâ-* : *trom*, *lom*, *caomh*.
7. *ro-*, *râ*, *ṛro-*, etc. : *sìor*, *mór*, *làr*, *àr*, *bodhar*. Here comes the Gaelic numeral stem *-âro-n*, as *aonar*, one person, *cóignear*, five persons ; it is allied to Lat. *-ârius*, *-ârium*, Gaelic *-air*, *-eir*, denoting agents or doers—*clàrsair*, harper, etc.
8. *tero-*, *ero-* : in *sinnsear*, *uachdar*, *eadar*.
9. *lo-*, *lâ-*, *ḷlo-*, etc. : *coll* (**cos-lo-*), *sìol*, *neul*, *ciall*, *giall*.
10. *dhro-*, *dro-*, *dhlo-*, *dlo-* : *odhar*, *uallach*.
11. *bho-*, *bhâ-* : *earb*, *gob* (**gob-bo-*).
12. *to-*, *tâ-*. This is the participial termination in most I. E. languages. In G. it is used for the past passive. Also in the adjectives *nochd*, *bochd*, *gnàth*, etc. ; nouns *dligheadh*, *dearmad*, *gort*.
13. *tjo-*, *tjâ-* : Gr. ἀμβρόσιος. This forms the passive participle in G. : *briste*, *caithte*, etc.
14. *tâ-* of abstract nouns : *ìobart*, now *ìobairt*.
15. *to-* comparative. This appears in the ordinal numerals : *deicheamh*, O. Ir. *dechmad*, for **dekṃmeto-*.
16. *ko-*, *kâ-* : *òg*, young, *juvṇ-ko-*.
17. *qo-*, *qâ-*, *qio-*, *āqo-* ; *sùileach* for **sûli-qo-s* ; *cuimhneach*, *creidmheach*. Especially the adjectives and nouns in *ach*, as *marcach*, *buadhach*. Further, the form *iche* (*-iqio-s*) denoting agent ; *maraiche*, etc.
18. *sqo-*, *sqio-* : as in *measg*, *seasg*, *uisge*.
19. *go-*, *gâ* : see *muing*, Danish, *manke* ; cf. Eng. *walk*, *hark*, etc.
20. Stems in *i-* : *àird*, *muir*, *maith*, *deigh*. In *ni-*, *tàin*, *cluain*, *buain* ; in *mi-*, *cruimh*, *cnàimh* ; in *li-*, *samhail*, *dùil* ; in *ti-*, *fàith*, *féith*, *breith*, *bleith*, etc.—a form in which some infinitives appear.
21. *tâti-*, that is, Celtic *tât-*, *tûs* : *beatha*, life, **bitûs*, g. **bi-tât-os*.
22. Stems in *u-* : *tiugh*, *fliuch*, *dub*, *loch*. In *nu-*, *linn*, O. Ir. *lín*, *lênu-* ; in *tu-* there are many—*bith*, *iodh-*, *fios* (**vid-s-tu-*), *guth*, *cruth* ; especially *reachd* and its like in *chd*. Here come the infinitives in *adh* (*-ātu-*).

    In G. *-eas*, *as* of abstract nouns, the form arises from *tu-* being added to an *-es* stem : *aois*, **aiv-es-tu-* ; so *dorus*, *follus*.
23. Stems in *-n* : *cù*, *àra*, *ìm*, *ionga*. In *-ien*, there is *'Eire*, *'Eireann*. The stems in *tiô* are very common ; the oblique cases are in *-tin-* ; see *eiridinn*, *faotainn*, etc. : common in infinitives. Similarly common is *-men*, *-mon*, in *ainm*, *cuirm*, *druim*, *leum* ; and masculine in *britheamh*, *ollamh*, *talamh*.
24. Stems in *-r* ; only the family names *athair*, *màthair*, etc.
25. Stems in *-t*, *-nt* : *nochd*, night : *caraid*, friend—a participial form.

26. Stems in *k* or *q* : G. *nathair*, g. *nathrach*, so *làir*, *lasair*, *cathair*, etc.
27. Neuter stems in *-es* : *teach*, *leth*, *magh*, *gleann*.
28. Comparative stems in *-jes*, *-is-*, *jôs* : *mò*, greater **mâ-jôs*, *sine*, Skr. *san-yas-*.

Adair in *tughadair*, *dialladair*, *figheadair*, *breabadair*, *etc.* (?)

Two or three stems peculiar to Gaelic may be mentioned. Adjectives in *-idh*, O. Ir. *-de*, as *diadhaidh*, come from an original *-dio-*. Endings like *maireann*, *firionn* have been correlated with the Lat. gerund, itself a much disputed form. The preserved *d* in words like *flichead*, moisture, O. Ir. *fliuchaidatu*, has been variously referred to **-antu-* or *-ato-tût* ; possibly the latter is its origin.

III. SYNOPSIS OF GADELIC ACCIDENCE.

A. Declension.

1. *o-* stems. Masc. o-stem *ball*, member.

	Gaelic.	Old Irish.	Gadelic.
Sing. Nom.	ball	ball	ballos
Gen.	buill	baill	ballī
Dat.	ball	baull	ballū (ballōj. *Jub.*)
Acc.	ball	ball n-	ballon
Voc.	bhuill	baill	balle
Dual N., A.	dà bhall	dá ball	ballō
G.	dà bhuill (?)		
D.	dà bhall	dib mballaib	ballobin
Plur. Nom.	buill	baill	ballī (balloi)
G.	ball	ball n-	ballon
D.	ballaibh	ballaib	ballobis
A.	buill	baullu	ballōs (ballons)
V.	bhalla	baullu	ballōs

Neuter *io*-stem *cridhe*, heart.

S. N., A.	cridhe	cride n-	kridion
G.	cridhe	cridi	kridiī
D.	cridhe	cridiu	kridiū
V.	chridhe	cride n-	kridion
Pl. N., A.	cridheachan	cride	kridia
G.	cridheachan	cride n-	kridion
D.	cridheachan	cridib	kridiobis
V.	chridheachan	chride	kridia

2. *ā*-stems : all feminine. *cas*, a foot.

	Gaelic.	Old Irish.	Gadelic.
S. Nom.	cas	coss	coxā
G.	coise	coisse	coxies
D.	cois	coiss	coxī (coxai)
A.	cas	coiss n-	coxin
V.	chas	choss	coxa
Dual A.	dà chois	dí choiss	coxē
G.	dà chois	dá choss	coxō
D.	dà chois	dib cossaib	coxābin
Pl. N.	casan	cossa	coxās
G.	cas	coss n-	coxan
D.	casaibh	cossaib	coxābis
A.	casan	cossa	coxās
V.	chasa	chossa	coxās

3. *i*-stems. Feminine noun *sùil*, eye.

S. Nom.	sùil	súil	sūlis
G.	sùla	súla	sūlōs (sūlous)
D.	sùil	súil	sūlī
A.	sùil	súil n-	sūlin
V.	shùil	shúil	sūli
Dual N.	dà shùil	dí shúil	sūlī
G.	dà shùil	dá súla	sūlō
D.	dà shùil	dib sulib	sūlibin
Pl. N.	sùilean	súli	sūleis (sūlejes)
G.	sùil	súle n-	sūlion
D.	sùilibh	súlib	sūlibis
A.	sùilean	súli	sūleis
V.	shùilean	shúli	sūleis

4. *u*-stems. Masculine noun *bith*, world.

S. Nom.	bith	bith	bitus
G.	bith	betho	bitous
D.	bith	biuth	bitū
A.	bith	bith n-	bitun
V.	bhith	betho	bitou
Pl. N.	bithean	bithi	bitois, (bitoves)
G.	bith	bithe n-	bition, (bitovon)
D.	bithibh	bithaib	bitubis
A.	bithean	bithu	bitūs
V.	bhithean	bithu	bitūs

5. Consonantal Stems.

(*a*). Stem in *r*; *athair*, father.

	Gaelic.	Old Irish.	Gadelic.
S. Nom.	athair	athir	atīr
G.	athar	athar	atros
D.	athair	athir	atri
A.	athair	athir n-	atren
V.	athair	athir	ater
Dual N., A.	dà athair	dá athir	atere
G.	dà athair	dá athar	atrō
D.	dà athair	dib n-athrib	atrebin
Pl. N.	athraichean	athir	ateres
G.	athraichean	athre n-	atron
D.	athraichean	athrib	atrebis
A.	athraichean	athrea	aterās (*aterṇs*)
V.	athraichean	athrea	aterās

(*b*). Stem in *men*; neut. *ainm*, name.

S. N., A.	ainm	ainm n-	anmen
G.	anme	anma, anme	anmens
D.	ainm	anmaimm	*anmṇbi*
Pl. N., A.	ainmeannan	anmann	anmena
G.	ainmeannan	anmann n-	anmenon
D.	ainmeannan	anmannaib	anmenobis

(*c*). Stem in guttural *c*; fem. *nathair*, serpent.

S. Nom.	nathair	nathir	natrix
G.	nathrach	nathrach	natracos
D.	nathair	nathraig	natraci
A.	nathair	nathraig n-	natracen (*natṛcṇ*)
Dual N., A.	dà nathair	dí nathraig	natrace
G.	dà nathair	dá nathrach	natracō
D.	dà nathair	dib nathrachaib	natracobin
Pl. N.	nathraichean	nathraig	natraces
G.	nathraichean	nathrach n-	natracon
D.	nathraichean	nathrachaib	natracobis
A.	nathraichean	nathracha	natracās
V.	nathraichean	nathracha	natracās

(*d*). Neuter stem in *-es*; *tigh*, house.

S. N., A.	tigh	teg, tech	tegos
G.	tighe	tige	tegesos
D.	tigh	tig	tegesi
Dual N.	dà thigh	dá thech	tegese

		Gaelic.	Old Irish.	Gadelic.
	G.	dà thigh	dá thige	tegesō
	D.	dà thigh	dib tigib	tegesobin
Pl.	N.	tighean	tige	tegesa
	G.	tigh	tige n-	tegeson
	D.	tighibh	tigib	tegesobis

6. Adjectives.

Adjectives belonged (1) to the *o-* and the *a-* declensions, as *marvos, *marvâ, *marvon, now *marbh*, declined like the nouns of *o-* and *a-* declensions; (2) *i-* declension, as *maith*, *matis, *matis, *mati, the neuter nom. being the stem ; (3) *u-* declension, as *tigus, *tigus (?), *tigu, now *tiugh ;* and (4) consonantal adj., *tepens, *te*, *téit*, etc. Comparison was in two ways—(1) *caomh* : O. Ir. cóem, coemiu, coemem : *koimos, *koimjôs, *koimimos ; (2) *luath* : O. Ir. lúath, lúathither, lúathem : *loutos, *loutiteros, *loutimos.

The numerals may be seen in the Dictionary in their Celtic form : *oinos, *dvâ, *treis, etc.

The pronouns are so phonetically gone astray that they cannot be restored.

B. Conjugation.

Active Voice. Indicative—Present. Verb *beir*, bear.

S. 1.	beiridh mi	berimm	berommi*
2.	beiridh tu	beri	beresi
3.	beiridh e	berid	bereti
Rel.	beireas	beres	beret-se
P. 1.	beiridh sinn	bermme	berommesi
2.	beiridh sibh	berthe	berete
3.	beiridh iad	berit	berenti (beronti)
Rel.	beireas	berte	berent-eis

Dependent Present.

S. 1.	bheir mi	do-biur	berô
2.	bheir tu	do-bir	beres
3.	bheir e	do-beir	beret
P. 1.	bheir sinn	do-beram	beromos
2.	bheir sibh	do-berid	berete
3.	bheir iad	do-berat	beront

The first sing. is from theme-vowel-less verbs : **ber-mi*. Cf. *orm*, *tharam* even *agam*, *asam*.

Secondary Present or Subjunctive.

		Gaelic.	Old Irish.	Gadelic.
S.	1.	bheirinn	no berinn	berîn (?)
	2.	bheireadh	no bertha	berethâs
	3.	bheireadh e	no bered	bereto
P.	1.	bheireamaid	no bermmis	berimmiss (?)
	2.	bheireadh sibh	no berthe	berethi
	3.	bheireadh iad	no bertis	berintiss (?)

Aorist.

S.	1.	do ghabh	ro gabus	gabassu
	2.	ghabh	ro gabis	gabassi
	3.	ghabh	ro gab	gabas-t
P.	1.	ghabh	ro gabsam	gabassomos
	2.	ghabh	ro gabsid	gabassete
	3.	ghabh	ro gabsat	gabassont

Imperative.

S.	1.	beiream	—	—
	2.	beir	beir	bere
			berthe	berethēs
	3.	beireadh e	berad	beretō
P.	1.	beireamaid	beram	—
	2.	beiribh	berid	berete
	3.	beireadh iad	berat	berontō

Passive. Indicative—Present.

S.	3.	beirear e	berir	beretor
P.	3.	beirear iad	bertir	berentor

Secondary Present or Subjunctive.

S.	3.	bheirteadh e	no berthe	—
P.	3.	bheirteadh iad	no bertis	—

Past Tense.

S.	3.	chanadh e	ro chét	cantos, "cantus"
P.	3.	chanadh iad	ro chéta	cantâs (n.f.)

Imperative.

S.	3.	beirear e	berar	—
P.	3.	beirear iad	bertar	—

Participle.

		cainte	céte	cantjos

SUPPLEMENT TO OUTLINES.

1. cf. Grierson's *Linguistic Survey of India* as to how far the statement is to be limited as embracing India. Concerning Asia the statement is to be restricted to living Aryan languages.

2. v. J. Hoop's *Waldbäume und Kulturpflanzen* (Trübner, 1905), pp. 113-114, 382-384. The question is far from being settled.

3. cf. G. Dottin: *Les désinences verbules en r en sanskrit en italique et en celtique.* He regards the passive in *r* in Celtic and Italic as an independent creation, the common element *r* going back to the period of Indo-European unity. Even the future in *-bo* he regards as a possibly analogous formation and different in origin and development. Compare critique in Revue Celtique, 18, 343, where M. D'Arbois de Jubainville takes exception to some points. Irish, contrary to the Latin, has conserved the Indo-European perfect. Further, see G. J. Ascoli: *Osservazioni fonologiche concernenti il celtico e il neolatino* in *Actes du dixième congres international des Orientalistes* ii. ème partie, Leide Brill, 1895; cf. *Indogerm. Forschungen Anzieger* vii., i., 70. Also Windisch in *Grundriss der Rom. Philologie*, where most of the relative literature is summarized and discussed. The views of M. D'Arbois were made accessible some years ago in a paper in the *Celtic Magazine*, ed. by Dr MacBain. cf. Giles's *Manual* § 449.

4. cf. Rhys's *Celtae and Galli* in *Proceedings of the British Academy.* Dr MacBain's notices of it in the *Scottish Historical Review* and in the *Celtic Review* are of interest, as also Sir J. Rhys's references in his *Celtic Inscriptions of France and Italy*, reviewed by the writer in the *Scottish Historical Review*, July, 1908.

5 See Stokes on *Pictish and Other Names* in *Bezzenberger's Beiträge*, Band 18. In the second edition of Skene's *Highlanders of Scotland*, Dr MacBain clearly summarizes the whole of the Pictish problem. Dr Zimmer's views were made accessible in a paper treating of *Matriarchy Among the Picts* given in the writer's *Leabhar Nan Gleann* (Edin.: N. Macleod).

6. See *Old Celtic Inscriptions* by Stokes in *Bezzenberger's Beiträge*, B. xi., 112-141; Rhys's *Celtic Inscriptions of France and Italy*, and reviews by Thurneysen in *Zeitschrift für Celtische Philologie.*

7. cf. Rhys and Jones: *The Welsh People*; v. Henry's *Lexicon Etymol.*, p. xxiii., where he refers to the dialects of Modern Breton. On the periods of Old Breton see Loth's *Vocabulaire Vieux-Breton*, Paris, 1884, ch. i.

8. The presence of *z* (for vowel-flanked *s*) can only be explained by assuming that the Ogmic alphabet was invented or imported before the regular disappearance of *s* between vowels—v. *Bezzenberger's Beiträge*, xi., 144. Mr R. A. Stewart MacAlister, in his work on *The Ogam Inscriptions* (London: D. Nutt), suggests a different value in the case of *z*; in which case, if we have *f* for *z*, we require to read *v* for the *f* of this transcription of the Ogam alphabet.

9 Add K. Meyer's old Irish treatise on the Psalter (Oxford: Clarendon Press), his edition in the Revue Celtique of the Old Irish version of *Tochmarc Emere*; and *Félire Oengusso* (2nd ed. by Stokes in Publications of Henry Bradshaw Society).

10. About one half of the contents was transliterated by the writer in *Leabhar Nan Gleann*; cf. Stern's critique in *Zeitschrift für Celtische Philologie.* One of the chief poems has since been found in a good version in an Irish MS. from Ratisbon, of which an account has been given by the writer in the forthcoming volume of the *Transactions of the Gaelic Society of Inverness.*

11, 12, 13, 14, 15, 16, 17, 18. cf. the writer's treatment of *The Gaelic Dialects* in *Zeitschrift für Celtische Philologie*; also Rev C. Robertson on the same subject in the *Celtic Review*; M. Macfarlane's *The Phonetics of Scottish Gaelic*; and Professor Mackinnon on Scottish Gaelic Dialects in a paper in the *Transactions of the Gaelic Society of Inverness.*

19. "*h* in anlaut before a vowel seems to come from *p*. So apparently in Irish *haue* = πάις, and *Hēriu* cognate with πιερία. This change is regular in Armenian, see Brugmann's *Grundriss*, § 30"—Stokes in *Bezzenberger's Beiträge*, 23, 44. In last ed. of the *Félire* Stokes regards *íre* as the cognate of the Greek word cited. But this does not affect the cases in which an historic *h* seems to represent a vanished *p*; compare the *m* for *n* in the derivation of *amharus*; and see Dr Pedersen's *Vergleichende Grammatik der Keltischen Sprachen*, as well as the second edition of Brugmann's *Grundriss der Vergl. Grammatik.*

20. A great levelling, as compared with what one must infer from the historic development of Indo-European, has taken place in Gadelic. Dr MacBain's Indo-European Alphabet is therefore simplified in the gutturals, although perhaps it would have been more regular to have put in a labio-velar series apart. Osthoff recognises three k-rows, labio-velar, velar, palatal, in the mother-

speech; v. *Indogerm. Forschungen*, 4, 246; Wharton's *Etyma Latina* recognise the three rows *c*, *k*, *q*; cf. Zupitza's treatment of the gutturals. In Gadelic the velar and the palatal series have fallen together, but there is a distinct treatment of the labio-velar.

21. Contamination may have been at work here. But although the Cymric cognate is *daigr*, and Old Latin shows *dacruma*, O. H. German, *zahar*, O. Icelandic, *tár*, Germ., *zähre*, in view of the Gadelic forms, we may take the pre-historic form to have been **dn̥kru*, which developed on the Brythonic side into a proto-Celtic **dakru*. Compare Dr Walde's *Lateinisches Etymologisches Wörterbuch*, p. 319, also p. 5, where L. *acer* is given as cognate with Irish Gadelic *ér*, high.

22. *méith* should be *mèith*, as in the Dictionary, with long open *è*; this is diphthongized in the Northern dialect as *mīath*—a case of diphthongization of long open *è* where there has been no compensatory lengthening.

23. See *Zeitschrift für Celtische Philologie*, Band 3, 264, 275, 591.

24. See Zupitza on *i*, *j* in Celtic, in *Zeitschrift für Celtische Philologie*, 2, 189-192.

25. See Foy in *Indogerm. Forschungen*, 6, 337, on Celtic *ar*, *al* = Indogerm. *r̥̄*, *l̥̄*; and Zupitza on *r̥*, *l̥* in Celtic, in Kuhn's *Zeitschrift*, 35, 253.

D

CORRIGENDA.

Page xxxiii.—In the third line from the bottom of the page, for krid on, read kridion; in the eleventh line from the bottom of the page, for the word in braekets, read (ballons).

ETYMOLOGICAL DICTIONARY OF

SCOTTISH-GAELIC

ETYMOLOGICAL DICTIONARY OF

SCOTTISH-GAELIC

A

a, vocative particle, Ir. *a*, O. Ir. *á*, *a* ; W., Corn., Br. *a* ; Lat. *o* ; Gr. *ὦ*.

a, his, her, Ir., *a*, O. Ir. *á*, *ái* (accented), W. *ei*, Br. *e*, Celtic *esjo*, *esjâs* ; Skr. gen. *asyá*, *asyâs*. The gen. pl. is **an,** their, O. Ir. *a n-*, Celtic *esjon* (Stokes gives *esan* = Skr. fem. gen. pl. *âsâm*).

a, who, that (rel. pron.). In G. this is merely the verbal particle *do* of past time, used also to explain the aspiration of the future rel. sentence, which is really paratactic, as in the past rel. sentence. Oblique cases are done by *an*, *am* (for *san*, *sam*, O. Ir. *san*, *sam*), the neut. of art. used as rel. (cf. Eng. *that*). The rel. locative is sometimes done by the prep. *an*, *am* : "An coire am bi na caoraich" (1776 Collection, p. 112).

a, out of, ex : see **as.**

a, from, in the adverbs **a nall, a nìos, a nuas, a null** ; Ir., O. Ir. *an-*, as *anuas*, etc. ; Celtic *a(p)ona*, a derivative from I. E. *apo*, whence Lat. *ab*, Gr. *ἀπό* ; Ger. *von*, from, is the exact equivalent of the Celtic. The **a** before *sìos* and *suas* is due to analogy with *a nìos*, *a nuas*.

a, in, to, as in **a bhàn, a bhos, a nis, a stigh, a steach,** is the prep. **an,** in, into, q.v.

a, as in **a ris,** &c., and before verbs, is the prep. **do,** q.v.

a', the, at ; see *an*, the, and *ag*, at.

ab, or **ab ab,** fie ! The Ir. *ab ab*, M. Ir. *abb*, is an interjection of defiance, *obo*, of wonder ; cf. Lat. *babæ*, Gr. *βαβαί*. Hence, doubtless M'A.'s **abab,** dirt.

aba, abbot, Ir. *ab*, O. Ir. *abb*, W. *abad* ; from Lat. *abbas*, *abbatis*, whence also Eng. *abbot*. Hence **abaid,** abbey. M. Ir. *apdaine*, abbacy, in M. G. "abbey lands," whence place-names Appin, older Abbathania (1310), Abthein (1220), "abbey lands."

abadh, syllable, utterance; E. Ir. *apad*, proclamation: *ad-ba-*, Celtic *ba*, speak; Lat. *fatur*, *fama*, Eng. *fame*.

abaich, ripe, Ir. *abaidh*, M. Ir. *abaid*, E. Ir. *apaig*, **ad-bagi*, O. Ir. *apchugud*, autumnatio; **ad-bog-*, Celtic root *bug*, as in *bog*, q.v.; *ad-bach*, root of Eng. *bake*; Gr. *φώγω*. The W. *addfed* is from a root *met*.

abaideal, colic (M'A.):

abair, say, so Ir., O. Ir. *epiur*, Celtic *ád-berô*; Lat. *re-fero*; see root in *beir*.

abaisd, a brat, trifling, impudent person:

abalt, expert (M'A.); from Sc. *apert ?* See *aparr*.

†**abar,** confluence; only in Pictish place names: O. Gaelic (B. of Deer) *abbor*, W. *aber*, O. W. *aper*, Celtic *ad-bero-*, root *ber*; see *beir*. Modern Gaelic pronounces it **obair** (so in 17th cent.), which agrees with the O. W. *oper*; this suggests *od-bero-*, "out flow," as against the "to flow" of *ad-bero-*. The *od* is for *ud*, allied to Eng. *out*. Aporicum: **ati-boro-n* (Holden).

abarach, bold; see *abair* above.

abardair, dictionary (Shaw); from *abair*, q.v.

abartach, talkative, bold; from *abair*, q.v.

àbh, hand net; from Norse *háfr*, pock-net. Also **tàbh,** q.v. Spelt less correctly **àmh** and **àbhadh.**

abh, bark of dog; an onomatopoetic word.

abhainn, river, Ir. *abhann* (gen. *abhann*, now *aibhne*), O. Ir. *abann*, W. *afon*, Br. *auon*, Gallo-Brit. *Abona*; Lat. *amnis* (**ab-nis*). Root *abh*; Sk. *ambhas*, water; Gr. *ἀφρος* (*ὄμβρος*, imber) (Zim. Neu., 270).

àbhacas, sport, irony; see the following word.

àbhachd, humour, sport, Ir. *adhbhachd*:

abhag, terrier, Ir. *abhach*; from *abh*, q.v. Cf. E. Ir. *abacc*, dwarf; W. *afanc*.

abhagas, rumour, false suspicion:

àbhaist, custom, Manx *oaysh*, Ir. *abhest* (O'R.), *abaise* (O'B.), *ad+beus ?* M. Ir. *ábaisi* (pl.). See *beus*, custom. Ascoli compares the O. Ir. *-abais* of *duabais*, teter, and *suabais*, suavis. Meyer suggests from N. *avist*, abode: unlikely.

abhall, an orchard, apple-tree, M. Ir. *aball*, apple-tree. See *ubhal*.

abharr, silly jest (M'A.):

abharsair, Satan, Ir. *aidhbherseóir*, E. Ir. *adbirseoir*; from Lat. *adversarius* (Eng. *adversary*). Also **aibhistear.**

abhcaid, a jest; see *àbhachd*.

abhlan, wafer, so Ir., O. Ir. *obla*, g. *oblann*; from Lat. *oblationem*, an oblation.

abhra, eyelid; see *fabhra.*

abhras, spinning, produce of distaff, Ir., M. Ir. *abhras,* O. Ir. *abras,* gestus, E. Ir. *abras,* handiwork, spinning, *abairsech,* needlewoman. Corm. (B) *abras,* who derives it from L. Lat. *abra,* ancilla.

abhsadh, the slackening of a sail, hoisting sail (N. H.); from Norse *hálsa,* clew up sail, from *hâls,* neck, allied to Lat. *collum.* Eng. *hawser* is also hence. Also **allsadh.**

abhsporag, a cow's stomach, tripe (H.S.D.), **allsporag,** cow's throttle (M'A.); borrowed evidently from a Scandinavian compound of *háls,* neck. Cf. *abhsadh* above.

ablach, a mangled carcase, Ir. *ablach,* carcase: **ád-bal-ac-,* from root *bal, bel,* die, I. E. *gel,* whence Eng, *quell.* Irish has *abailt,* death, O. Ir. *epeltu, atbail,* perit, from the same root and prefix; the first of them appears in our Gaelic dictionaries through Shaw. From Gaelic comes Scotch *ablach.*

àbran, abran (M'A. and H.S.D.), an oar-patch on a boat's gunwale; see *aparan.*

Abraon, April, so Ir.; founded on Lat. *Aprilis* (Eng. *April*). The form is due to folk-etymology, which relates it to *braon.*

abstol, apostle, Ir. *absdal,* O. Ir. *apstal,* W. *apostol;* from Lat. *apostolus,* whence Eng. *apostle.*

acaid, a pain, stitch; **ád-conti-;* see *urchoid.*

acain, sigh, complaint, E. Ir. *accáine,* W. *achwyn; ád + caoin;* see *caoin,* weep.

acair, anchor, Ir. *ancairé,* O. Ir. *ingor,* W. *angor;* from N. *akkeri:* **acarsaid,** anchorage, from N. *akkarsaeti,* "anchor-seat." From. Lat. *ancora,* whence Eng. *anchor.*

acair, acre, Ir. *acra;* from Eng. *acre;* Lat. *ager.*

acarach, gentle; Ir. *acarach,* obliging, convenient, which shades off into *acartha,* profit; W. *achar,* affectionate; *ád-car-;* see *càr,* friendly. M'A. has **acarra,** moderate in price, indulgence, which belongs to **acartha.**

acaran, lumber:

acartha, profit, so Ir.; see *ocar,* interest.

acastair, axle-tree; borrowed word from Sc. *ax-tree* of like meaning—Eng. *axle,* &c.

ach, but, Ir. *achd,* O. G. (B. of Deer) *act,* O. Ir. *act, acht,* **ekstos,* possibly, from *eks = ex;* cf. Gr. ἐκτός, without. For the change of vowel, cf. *as,* from *eks.* The Welsh for "but" is *eithr,* from *ekster;* Lat. *exter-.*

ach, interjection of objection and impatience; founded on above with leaning upon *och,* q.v.

achadh, a field, so Ir., O. G. *achad,* O. Ir. *ached* (locative?) campu lus (Adamnan), **acoto-;* Lat. *acies, acnua,* field.

achain, prayer ; dialectic for *achuinge*, q.v.

acharradh, dwarf, sprite :

achd, statute, so Ir., M. Ir. *acht* ; from Lat. *actum*, Eng. *act.*

achd, manner, condition, Ir. *achd* ; same as above. There may be a native *aktu-* (**ag-tu-*, **pag-tu-* ?) underlying some meanings of the word, especially in Irish.

achdarr, achdartha, methodical, expert (H.S.D.) :

achlaid, chase, pursuit, so Ir., M. Ir. *acclaid*, fishing, E. Ir. *atclaid*, fishes, hunts, pursues : *ad-claidim* ; see *claoidh.*

achlais, arm-pit, Ir. *ascall*, M. Ir. *ochsal*, W. *cesail.* The divergence from regular philologic equivalence here proves borrowing—from the Lat. *axilla* ; Norse *öxl*, Ger. *achsel*, Sc. *oxter.*

achlan, lamentation (M'L.) ; for *och-lan ?* from *och.*

achmhasan, a rebuke, Ir. *achmhusán*, E. Ir. *athchomsán* ; cf. *aithis* for root.

achuinge, supplication ; also **athchuinge**, so Ir., E. Ir. *athchuingid* ; *ath + cuinge* ; O. Ir. *cuintgim*, peto, *con-tek-* ; Eng. *thig.* See *atach.*

acras, hunger, Ir. *ocrus*, E. Ir. *accorus*, *occorus* : **ad-co-restu-*, possibly the root *pres* of Lat. *premo* : **careo* (F[4]. 422).

acuinn, acfhuinn, apparatus, accoutrements, Ir. *acfuinn*, E. Ir. *accmaing*, means, apparatus : *ad-cumang*, O. Ir. *cumang*, potentia ; see further under *cumhachd.*

ad, hat, M. Ir. *at*, W. *het* ; from Eng. *hat*, N. *hattr.*

ad-, adh-, inseparable prefix, in force and origin the same as Lat. *ad.* It is to be separated, though with difficulty, from the *ad-* arising from *aith-* or *ath-*, q.v.

adag, shock of corn, Ir. *adag* ; cf. Sc. *hat*, *hot*, *hut*, "to put up grain in the field, a small stack built in the field ;" M.E. *hutte*, heap.

adag, a haddock ; from the English.

adamant, àdamant, so Ir. ; from the English.

adha, ae, liver, Ir. *aeghe*, g. *ae*, O. Ir. *óa*, *ae*, W. *afu*, Br. *avu*, root *av.* Cf. *adha* for *ae*, *cadha* for *cae.*

adhan, proverb (M'A.) ; rather **aghan**, root *agh*, Lat. *ajo*, *adagio*, adage ; Skr. *ah*, say.

adhal, flesh hook (Sh.), so Ir., O. Ir. *áel*, tridens : **pavelo-*, Lat. *pavire ?* But cf. Eng. *awl*, M. E. and Ag. S. *awel*, awl, flesh-hook.

adhaltrach, adulterous, Ir. *adhaltranach*, E. Ir. *adaltrach* ; from Lat. *adulter*, whence Eng. *adulterous.*

adharc, horn, so Ir., O. Ir. *adarc* : *ad-arc* ; root *arq*, defend, as in *teasairg*, q.v. ; Lat. *arceo*, &c.

adharcan, lapwing, "horned bird;" from *adharc*; Dial. **daoireagan.** Ir. *adaircín* (P. O'C.).

adhart, pillow, so Ir., E. Ir. *adart*: *ad-art*; *art*, stone? See *airtein*.

adhart, aghart, "progress" (Dict.). This is a ghost-word, made from the adverbial phrase **air adhart,** which in M. Ir. is *araird*, forward, bring forward; in O. Ir. *arairt*, prorsum. Hence it is *air*+*àrd*, q.v.

adhastar, halter, Manx *eistyr*, Ir. *aghastor*, M. Ir. *adastar*; cf. W. *eddestl*, steed.

adhbhal, vast, awful, so Ir., O. Ir. *adbul*: **ad-bol-*; I. E. root *bhel*, swell, as in Eng. *bloom*, etc. Zimmer compares it with Skr. *bala*, strength. Stokes and Osthoff give root *bel*, *bol*, strong, big, Skr. *balam*, strength, Gr. *βέλτερος*, better, Lat. *de-bilis*, weak, Ch. Sl. *boliјĭ*, greater; whence **bailceach** (Osthoff) and **bail, buil.**

adhlac, burial, Ir. *adhlacadh*, O. Ir. *adnacul*, sepulcrum: *ad-nank-otlo* (**ad-nagtlo-*, Zim.): root verb *nankô*, I bring; Lat. *nanciscor*; further I. E. *nenk*, *enk*, as in *thig*, q.v.

adhna, an advocate (Macd.): H.S.D. cfs. Heb. *adhon*, sustentator.

ag, at, with inf. only; see *aig*.

ag, agadh, refusal, doubt; E. Ir. *ac*, refusal, O. Ir, *acc.* no! W. *acom*, to deny. It is onomatopoetic? See next.

agadh, hesitancy in speech, Br. *hak*, *hakal*; cf. Skr. *ac*, speak indistinctly. See foregoing word.

agair, plead, so Ir., O. Ir. *acre* (n.), from *ad-gar-*; root *gar*, cry; see *goir*.

agallamh, conversation, Ir. *agallamh*, O. Ir. *acaldam*, for *ad-glád-*, O. Ir. *ad-gládur*, I converse: for root, see *glaodh*.

agh, a hind, Ir. *agh*, O. Ir. *ag*, W. *ewig* (**agîko-*), Celtic *agos-*; Skr. *ajás*, buck; Lit. *ożýs*, goat. Zend. *azi*, Arm. *ezn* (St.).

àgh, also **àdh,** happiness, luck, Manx *aigh*, Ir. *ágh*, M. Ir. *ada*, *buada*, late M. Ir. *ád*, luck, *ádh*=sonas (P. O'C.); root *āg-*, bring; see next.

àghach, warlike, so Ir., E. Ir. *ágach*, *ág*, war, **āgu-*; Skr. *ājís*, contest; Gr. *ἀγών*, Eng. *antagonist*.

aghaib, essay (M'A.); see *oidheirp*.

aghaidh, face, so Ir., O. Ir. *aged*, **agitâ*; I.E. root *ag*, lead. It is usually referred to the root *oq*, Lat. *oculus*, etc., but the phonetics are unsatisfactory.

aghann, pan, so Ir., O. Ir. *aigen*, Celtic *aginâ*; Skr. *aga*, water jar; Gr. *ἄγγος*, a vessel.

agus, and, so Ir., O. Ir. *acus*, *ocus*, B. of Deer *acus*, O. W. *ac*, Br. *hag*; allied is **fagus,** near, O. Ir. *ocus*, W. *agos*, Br. *hogoz*:

**aggostu-, ad-gos-*; root *ges, gos,* carry; Lat. *gero, aggestu-s,* mound (Zimmer). Stokes refers it to the root *angh,* choke, narrow; Celtic *aggúst-,* from pre-Celtic *aghnústu-* (Lat. *angustus*), with accent on syllable after the root—*gn* with the accent on the following vowel being supposed, as in Teutonic, to produce *gg.* The derivation from root *onk, enk,* as in *thig,* is not tenable in view of the Welsh.

ai, sheep, swan (Carm.):

aibheil, huge (M'E.). See *adhbhal.*

aibheis, sea, the deep; Ir. *aibheis,* sea, abyss; E. Ir. *aibéis,* sea. This Stokes refers to a Celtic *abensi-s, abhent-ti-s*; root *abh,* as in *abhainn.* But cf. O. Ir. *abis,* from Lat. *abyssus*: W. *affwys,* bottomless pit.

aibheis, boasting; **aibhsich,** exaggerate; Ir. *aibhseach,* boasting: from the foregoing? Another form of *aibhsich* is **aillsich.**

aibhist, an old ruin (Stew.):

aibhistear, the Devil; another form of *abharsair,* q.v.

aibhse, spectre, so Ir.: see *taibhse.*

aibidil, alphabet, Ir. *aibghitir,* O. Ir. *abbgitir,* from L. Lat. *abgetorium, abecedarium,* the *a, b, c, d,* or alphabet. A dialectic form, **aibirsidh,** comes from the old learning system, beginning "A per se," *a* by itself = *a,* Eng. *apersie.* Analogised to *caibideal* (Meyer).

aice, proximity, Ir. *aice*; see *taic.*

aice, a lobster's burrow, also **faiche.**

àicheadh, deny, Ir. *aithcheo,* contradicting, M. Ir. *aithceód*: **ati-coud-* (?), "go back on;" cf. O. Ir. *atchuaid,* exposui, which Stokes refers to the root of *chaidh,* went, q.v.

aicheamhail, reprisal; cf. Ir. *athghabháil*; *ath + gabhail.*

†aicme, race, Ir., O. Ir. *aicme,* W. *ach,* pedigree, **akk-,* from *ak,* edge; Lat. *acies*? Stokes cfs. Skr. *anka,* lap, but this would give G. *àc-* (ā) and a W. *anc.* Norse *átt,* family, Ger. *acht,* property.

aidheam, joyous carol:

aidich, confess, Ir. *admhuighim,* O. Ir. *addaimim,* W. *addef*: *ad-dam-*; root *dam*; Lat. *domo,* Eng *tame.*

aifrionn, mass, so Ir., E. Ir. *oifrend,* W. *offeren*; from Lat. *offerendum* (Eng. *offer*).

aig, at, Ir. *ag,* O. Ir. *oc*; for root, see *agus.*

àigeach, young or entire horse; also **òigeach** = *òg + each,* q.v. M. Ir. *óc-ech,* young steed (Eriu[2] 11).

aigeann, the deep, Ir. *áigeun,* E. Ir. *oician,* W. *eigion*: from Lat. *oceanus,* Eng. *ocean.* There is also a by-form **aigeal.**

aigeannach, spirited, E. Ir. *aignech*; see *aigneadh.* Ir. *aigeanta,* meditative.

aighear, mirth, Manx *aigher* ; **ati-gar-* ; see *gàirdeachas* for root. Yet Ir. *aiéreach*, merry, aerial, from *aiér*, air, from Lat. *aer*, makes the matter doubtful. Ir. *aerach* (Hyde), merry, airy. Evidently the G. is borrowed from the Lat.

aigilean, ear-ring, tassel; cf. Sc. *aiglet*, tagged point, jewel in one's cap; *eglie*, needlework, from Fr. *aiguille*, needle; Lat. *acus*.

aigne, the swift, anything quick (Carm.):

aigne, aigneadh, mind, so Ir., O. Ir. *aicned* : *ád-gn-eto-*, root *gnā*, know, Gr. γιγνώσκω, Eng. *know*. Stokes refers it to the root of *aicme*, as he gives it. Ascoli makes the root *cen*, as in *cineal*. The Gaelic *g* is against any root with *c*.

àil, will; better **àill,** q.v.

ail, aileadh, ailt, a mark, impression, Ir. *oil*, mark (O'R.), M. and E. Ir. *aile*, fence, boundary (Meyer). A *t* stem : *oiledaib*, **al-et*.

†**ail,** rock, Ir. and O. Ir. *ail*, **alek-*, allied to Ger. *fels* ; see further under *mac-talla*.

ailbheag, ring; see *failbhe*.

ailbhinn, flint, precipice; from *ail*, rock.

àile, air, scent, E. Ir. *aél*, *ahél* ; W. *avel*, C., Br., *awel*, wind; Gr. ἀέλλα (St. Lec.), storm; **avel-*, root *ave*, *ve*, wind; Lat. *au-ra*, Gr, ἀήρ, Eng. *air*.

aileag, hiccup, Ir. *fail* ; cf. Lat. *hālo*, breathe, Eng. in-*hale*.

àilean, a green : **ag-li-*? Cf. Lat. *ager*.

àilear, porch :

ailis, blemish, reproach, O. Ir. *ail*, disgrace, Got. *agls*?

ailis, mimicing (Wh.); bad *atharrais*, *aith-lis*, (M'A.) *aithris*.

àill, desire, so Ir., O. Ir. *áil*, W. *ewyll*, Br. *ioul*, Celtic *avillo-* ; root *av*, desire, Lat. *aveo*, Eng. *avidity*. *áil*, pleasant, **pagli*, Eng. *fair* (St. Bez.[20] 24).

àille, beauty, E. Ir. *álde*, for *álnde* ; see *álainn*.

àilleas, àilgheas, will, desire; Ir. *áilgheas*, E. Ir. *ailges*, *áilgidim*, I desire; from *àil* and *geas*, request, q.v.

ailleagan, root of the ear, hole of the ear; also *faillean*, q.v.

àilleagan, darling, so Ir.; from *àille*, q.v.

aillean, elecampane: cf. Gr. ἑλενίον, Lat. *inula*. M. Ir. *eillinn* (Rev. Celt.[9] 231). inula quam *alain* rustici vocant (Isidor).

ailleant, shy, delicate; M. Ir. *ail* (O'Cl.), shamefaced.

ailleort, high-rocked; from *aill*, rock; see *mac-talla*.

aillse, diminutive creature, fairy, Ir. *aillse* ;

aillse, cancer, Ir. *aillis*, O. Ir. *ailsin*, cancerem :

aillseag, caterpillar; from above.

ailm, the letter A, elm; Ir. *ailm*, palm (fir?) tree, letter A; borrowed from Lat. *ulmus*, Norse *álmr*, Eng. *elm*.

ailt, stately, high ; Ir. *ailt*, Lat. *altus*, *àilt* (H.S.D.).

aim-, aimh-, privative prefix ; see *am-*, *amh-*. See its use in **aimhleas** (=*am-leas*), hurt, **aimhrea, aimhreidh,** confusion (=*am-réidh*), **aimbeart,** distress, etc. (=*am-bert*). The vowel in the root is "small", and hence affects the *a* of *am*.

aimheal, grief, Ir. *aithmhéal*, repentance ; *aith*+*méala*, grief, E. Ir. *méla*, sorrow, reproach ; **meblo-*, a shorter form of O. Ir. *mebul*, dedecus ; Gr. *μέμφομαι*.

aimhfheoil, ainfheoil, proud flesh ; from *aimh-* and *feòil*, q.v.

aimlisg, confusion, mischief :

aimrid, barren, so Ir., M. Ir. *immrit*, barren, E. Ir. *amrit* ; *am-ber-ent-*, "non-producing ;" root *ber* of *beir* ?

aimsichte, bold (Arms.) ; *am-meas-ichte*, "un-mannerly ?" See *meas*.

aimsir, time, so Ir. ; O. Ir. *amser*, W. *amser*, Br. *amzer*, possibly a Celtic *ammesserâ* ; either a compound of *am*, time (*ammen-sîrâ*, from *sír*, long ?), or *amb-mensura*, root *mens*, measure, Lat. *mensus*, Eng. *measure*. Ascoli and Stokes give the Celtic as *ád-messera*, from *ad-mensura*.

aimsith, missing of aim, mischance : am-*mis*-ith, Gaelic root *mis* of *eirmis*, q.v.

àin, heat (Dict.), light (H. M'Lean), O. Ir. *áne*, fulgor, from *án*, splendidus, latter a Celtic *āno-s* ; Got. *fôn*, fire (from *pân*) ; Pruss. *panno*. Stokes suggests rather **agno-s*, allied to Lat. *ignis*, Skr. *agní*, fire.

ain-, privative prefix ; see *an-*.

ainbhtheach, stormy, M. Ir. *ainbthech*, **an-feth-ech*, Gaelic root *feth*, breeze, from *vet*, Eng. *weather*, Lat. *ventus*, etc. See *anfadh*.

ainbi, ainbith, odd, unusual : *an-bith*, "un-world-like." See *bith*.

aincheas, doubt, M. Ir. *ainches*, E. Ir. *ances*, dubium :

ainchis, a curse, rage, Ir. *aingeis*, E. Ir. *aingcess*, *ánces*, curse, anguish ; *an*+*geas*, q.v., or Lat. *angustia ?*

aineamh, flaw, so Ir., E. Ir. *anim*, W. *anaf*, blemish, O. Br. *anamon*, mendæ ; Gr. *ὄνομαι*, blame.

àinean, a liver, liver of fish (N.H.) ; see *adha*.

àineartaich, yawning (*aineartaich*, M'A.) ; see *àinich* below.

aineas, passion, fury ; *an-theas*, from *teas*, heat.

aingeal, angel, so Ir., O. Ir. *angel*, W. *angel*, Br. *ael ;* from Lat. *angelus*, whence also the Eng.

aingeal, light, fire, Manx *ainle*, Ir. *aingeal* (Lh., O'B.), M. Ir. *aingel*, sparkling : **pangelos*, Ger. *funke*, M. E. *funke* ; further *ong*, fire, hearth ; Lit. *anglis*, coal, Skr. *añgâra*, glowing coal ; I. E. *ongli*, *ongôl* ; allied is I. E. *ognis*, fire, Lat. *ignis*. See

Fick[4] 14. Skeat derives Sc. *ingle* from the Gaelic. Also **ainneal,** a common fire.

aingealachd, numbness: *ang-eal-ach-*, root *ang*, choke (Lat. *ango*)?

aingealtas, perversity, malignity; from the following.

aingidh, wicked, Ir. *aingidhe*, malicious, O. Ir. *andgid*, *angid*, nequam, wicked, *andach*, sin; **an-dg-id*, root *deg* of *deagh*, good, q.v.

àinich, panting, also **aonach**; root *ān-*, long form of *an*, breath (see *anail*); Skr. *ânana*, mouth ("breather").

ainid, vexing:

ainis, anise; from the English. M. Ir. *in ainis*, gloss on "anisum cyminum dulce."

ainm, name, Ir. and O. Ir. *ainm*, pl. *anmann*, B. of Deer *anim*, W. *enw*, Br. *hanv*, **anmen-*; Gr. *ὄνομα*; Pruss. *emmens*, Ch. Sl. *imę*; root *ono*, allied to *nō* in Lat. *nomen*, Eng. *name*.

ainmhide, a rash fool; see *òinid*.

ainmhidh, beast, brute, Ir. *ainmhidhe*, M. Ir. *ainmide*, **anem-itio-s*, **anem-*, life, soul; Lat. *animal*, etc. Ir. is also *ainmhinte*, "animans."

ainmig, rare; *an-minig*, q.v.

ainneamh, rare; see *annamh*.

ainneart, force; *ain-*, excess (see *an-*), and *neart*.

ainnighte, tame, from *ainneadh*, patience (Sh.); possibly from *an-dam*, root *dam*, tame.

ainnir, virgin, E. Ir. *ander*, W. *anner*, heifer, M. Br. *annoer* (do.), **anderâ*; cf. Gr. *ανθηρός*, blooming, *ἀθάριοι*, virgins (Hes.), **νθαρ-*.

ainnis, ainniseach, needy: *an+dìth*, want?

ainstil, fury, over-fizzing: *an+steall*.

air, on, upon. This prep. represents three Irish ones:

(*a*) **air** = O. Ir. *ar*, *air*, ante, propter, W. *ar*, *er*, Br. *er*, Gaul. *are-*, Celtic *ari*, *arei*, Gr. *παρά*, *παραί*, by, before; Lat. *prae*; Eng. *fore*, *for*. This prep. aspirates in Irish, and in Gaelic idioms it still does so, *e.g. air chionn*.

(*b*) **air** = O. Ir. *for*, "super," O. W. and O. Br. *guor*, Br. *voar*, *oar*, Gaul. *ver-*; Gr. *ὑπέρ*; Lat. *s-uper*; Eng. *over*. This prep. did not aspirate; it ended originally in *r* in Gaelic; as an inseparable prefix (*vero-*, *viro-* in Gaul.) it aspirated, as in the modern form of old names like *Fergus*, now *Fearghuis* or *Fear'uis* (gen. case).

(*c*) **air** = O. Ir. *iar n-*, after, pre-Celtic *eperon*; Skr. *aparám*, afterwards, *aparena*, after; Got. *afar*, after, Eng. *af-*ter. Further come Gr. *ὄπι-*, behind, *ἐπί-*, to, Lat. *ob-*, *op-*. See *iar*.

This is the prep. that is used with the inf. to represent a perfect or past participle in Gaelic—*Tha mi air bualadh*; "I have struck."

airbhinneach, honourable; *air+beann?*

airc, distress, so Ir., O. Ir. *aircur*, pressura; cf. Lat. *parcus*, sparing.

àirc, the Ark, Ir. *airc*; from Lat. *arca*.

airchios, pity, clemency (Hend.): see *oircheas*.

aircill, to watch, listen, Ir. *aircill*; see *faircill*.

aircleach, a cripple; **airc-lach*, from *airc*, q.v.

àird, point (of the compass), Ir. *áird*, E. Ir. *aird*, Gr. *ἄρδις*, a point. Hence Sc. *airt*.

àird, preparation, activity:

àirde, height, Ir. *áirde*, E. Ir. *arde*; see *àrd*.

àirdeil, ingenious:

aire, heed, Ir., O. Ir. *aire*, Old. Brit. *Areanos*, native watchers who gave intimation to the Romans (Ammianus), pre-Celtic *parjâ*, *par*, seek; Gr. *πεῖρα*; trial, Lat. *ex-perior*, Eng. *experiment*.

àireach, keeper of cattle. There is confusion in Gaelic between *àireach* and O. Ir. *aire(ch)*, lord; the *bó-aire*, cow-lord, was the free tenant of ancient Ireland. For O. Ir. *aire*, see *airidh*. G. *àireach* owes its long vowel to a confusion with *àraich*, rear. See *àiridh* for root.

àireamh, number, so Ir., O. Ir. *áram*, W. *eirif*, **ad-rîm-*, Celtic *rîmâ*, number; Ag. S. *rîm*, number, Eng. *rhyme*; Gr. *ἀριθμός*, number.

airean, ploughman, herdsman; Ir. *oireamh*, g. *oireamhan*, ploughman, the mythic *Eremon*, *Airem(on)*, **arjamon-*, Skr. *Arjaman*, further *Aryan* (?); root *ar*, plough.

†airfid, music, harmony: see *oirfid*.

airgiod, silver, so Ir., O. Ir. *arget*, W. *ariant*, Br. *arc'hant*, Gaul. *Argento-*, *Argento-coxus* (a Caledonian prince): Lat. *argentum*; Gr. *ἄργυρος*. Eng. *argent* is from the Lat.

àiridh, better **àirigh**, hill pasture, sheiling (**airghe**, in Lh. for Gaelic); cf. E. Ir. *airge*, *áirge*, place where cows are, dairy, herd of cattle; E. Ir. *airgech*, herdswoman (of Brigit); Ir. *airghe*, pl. *áirighe* (O'B.), a herd of cattle; *airgheach*, one who has many herds; **ar-egia*; Lat. *armentum?* But see *àraich*, rear. Norse or Danish *erg* from Gaelic equals Norse *setr* (Ork. Sag.). This Norse form proves the identity of Gaelic with E. Ir. *airge*; *airge=ar-agio*, **agio*, herd.

airidh, worthy, Ir. *airigh* (Ulster), *airigh*, nobleman (O'B.), O. Ir. *aire(ch)*, primas, lord; Skr. *árya*, good, a lord; *ârya*, Aryan, *âryaka*, honourable man. *parci?

airilleach, a sleepy person; from †*aireal*, bed, M. Ir. *airel* (O'C.):

airleag, lend, Ir. *airligim*, O. Ir. *airliciud*, lending; from *leig*, let, which is allied to Eng. *loan*, Got. *leihvan*, Ger. *leihen*. See *leig*.

airleas, pledge, earnest, arles; from Sc. *arles*, older *erles*, which, through O. French, comes from. Lat. **arrhula*, dim. of *arrha*, pledge. Eng. *earnest*, whence W. *ernes*, is probably from the same origin. See *eàrlas*.

airleig, a strait:

airmis, hit; see *eirmis*.

àirne, a sloe, so Ir., M. Ir. *arni*, sloes, W. *eirin*, plums, Br. *irinenn*, sloe, Celtic *arjanio-* (Stokes); Skr. *araṇi*, tinder-stick "premna spinosa," *araṅka* forest.

àirneach, murrain in cattle:

airneis, àirneis (M'L. & D.), furniture; Ir. *áirneis*, cattle, goods, etc., M. Ir. *airnis*, tools, furniture. The word can hardly be separated from the Romance *arnese*, accoutrements, armour, whence Eng. *harness*, armour for man or horse. The word is originally of Brittonic origin (Br. *harnez*, armour), from **eisarno-*, iron; see *iarunn*.

airtein, a pebble, so Ir., E. Ir. *arteini* (pl.), O. Ir. *art*; possibly Gaul. *arto-* (*Arto-briga*), *Artemia*, name of a rock.

airtneal, airsneal, weariness:

àis, milk (Carm.), M. Ir. *as* (O'Dav.).

àis, wisdom (Carm.), *ais* (O'Cl.) See *cnoc* (Carm).

ais, back, backwards; so Ir., E. Ir *aiss*, *daraaiss*, backwards; Gaelic **air ais.** The forms *ais*, *rithisd* (*rìs*), *thairis*, seem compounds from the root *sta*, *sto*, stand; cf. *fois*, *bhos*, *ros*; **ais** may be for *ati-sta-* or *ati-sti-*. Ascoli refers *ais* to an unaccented form of *éis*, track, which is used after *tar* and *di* (*di a éis*, post eum; see *déis*) for "after, *post*," but not for "back," as is *air ais*, with verbs of rest or motion.

aisead, delivery (obstetrical), E. Ir. *asait*, vb. *ad-saiter*, is delivered; **ad-sizd-*; Lat. *sīdo*, *assīdere*; a reduplication of the root *sed*, of *suidhe*, q.v. From *ad-sem-t*, root *sem* as in *taom* (Stokes).

aiseag, a ferry, Ir. *aiseog* (Fol.):

aiseal, axle; it seems borrowed from Eng. *axle*, Norse *öxull*, but the W. *echel*, Br. *ahel*, **aksila*, makes its native origin possible, despite the absence of the word in Irish.

aiseal, jollity (Sh., Arms.); see *aisteach*.

aisean, rib, Ir., E. Ir. *asna*, W. *eisen*, *asen*, Cor. *asen*; cf. Lat. *assula*, splinter, *asser*, beam (Stokes). Formerly it was referred to the same origin as Lat. *os*, *ossis*, bone, Gr. *ὀστέον*, but the root vowel and meaning are both unfavourable to this etymology.

aisearan, weanling (Argyle) ; from *ais*?

aisg, a request (Sh.), E. Ir. *ascid* ; **ad-skv-*, root *seq.*, as in *sgeul*, q.v.

aisgeir, a ridge of high mountains, Ir. *eiscir*, *aisgeir* (Lh. for latter) ; **ad-sker-* (?), as in Eng. *skerry*, G. *sgeir*, q.v. Cf. W. *esgair* (Meyer).

aisig, restore, so Ir., E. Ir. *assec* ; possibly = **as-ic*, "out-bring," *ic* = *enk* ; see *thig*, come.

aisir, aisridh, path ; see *astar*.

aisith, strife ; *as-sìth*, *as-*, privative, and *sìth*, q.v.

aisling, a vision, dream, so Ir., O. Ir. *aislinge* ; possibly **ex-ling-ia*, "a jump out of one-self, ec-stasy," the root being *leng* of *leum*, q.v. Nigra suggested the root *sil* or *sell* of *seall*, see, q.v. ; he divided the word as *as-sil-inge*, Stokes as *ad-sell-angia* (Beiträge, Vol. VIII.).

aisneis, rehearsing, tattle, E. Ir. same, O.Ir. *áisndís* ; *aisnédim*, I relate ; (*as-ind-fiad-im*, O. Ir. *in-fiadim*, I relate) ; *fiad* = *veid*, know ; see *innis* ; root *vet*, Lat. *veto* (Stokes), but this does not account for *í* of O. Ir. *aisndís*.

aisteach, a diverting fellow, Ir. *aisdeach*, witty :

ait, glad, Ir., E. Ir. *ait*, O. Ir. *ait*, euge ! adverbium optantis :

àite, a place, Ir., E. Ir. *áit*. Possibly Celtic *pōd-ti*, **panti*? root *pōd*, *ped*, Lat. *oppidum*, Gr. πέδον, ground, Skr. *padám*, place ; as in *eadh*, q.v. Stokes has referred *áit* to the root that appears in Ger. *ort*, place, Norse *oddr*, O. Eng. *ord*, point, Teutonic *uzd-*, I. E. *uzdh-* ; but this in Gaelic would give *ud* or *od*.

àiteag, a shy girl, see *faiteach*.

aiteal, breeze, ray, small portion. In the sense of "ray," cf. Gr. ἀκτίς, ray ; in the sense of "quantulum," it may be divided as *ad-tel*, O. Br. *attal*, an equivalent, root *tel*, weight, money ; see *tuarasdal*. *actualis* ?

aiteam, a people, a tribe (Arms.) :

aiteamh, a thaw ; **aith-tā-m*, W. *toddi*, melt ; Lat. *tabes* ; Gr. τήκω, melt ; Eng. *thaw*. The Ir. word is *tionadh* (O. Ir. *tinaid*, evanescit), Manx *tennue*, the root of which is *ten*, Lat. *tener*, Eng. *thin*.

aith-, "re-" ; see *ath-*.

aitheamh, fathom, O. W. *atem*, filum ; **(p)etemā* ; Eng. *fathom* ; I. E. *pet*, extend, Lat. *pateo*, etc.

aithinne, fire-brand, Ir., O. Ir. *aithinne* : **aith-tén-io-* ? Root of *teine* ? The root *and*, kindle, as in O. Ir. *andud*, accendere, *adandad*, lighting up, is also possible, **aith-and-io-* being the form in that case. *amhailte* (Glen-moriston).

aithis, a reproach, affront, so Ir., O. Ir. *athiss* ; **ati-vid-tu-* ; Got. *idveit*, Eng. *twit* ; root *vid*, wit, know.

aithlis, a disgrace ; cf. *leas* in *leas-mhac*.

aithne, knowledge, so Ir., O. Ir., *aithgne*, W. *adwaen* : *ati-gn-io-* for Ir. ; I. E. *gen*, *gnā*, *gnō*, to know ; Lat. *cognosco* ; Gr. γιγνώσκω ; Eng. *know*.

àithne, command, Ir., O. Ir. *aithne*, depositum, command ; *immánim*, delego, assign ; W. *adne*, custody ; the root seems to be *ān* or *an*, judging from the verbal forms, though these scarcely agree with the noun forms. See *tiomnadh* further.

aithreach, repentant, so Ir., O. Ir. *aithrech*, Corn. *edreck*, repentance, Br. *azrec* (do.), **ati-(p)reko-*, **ati-(p)rekiâ* ; root, *prek*, Lat. *precor*, Ger. *fragen*, ask, etc. Ascoli makes the root *reg*, come (see *rach*).

aithris, tell, so Ir., **ati-ris*, E. Ir. *ris*, a story, **r̥t-ti*, *rat*, *rēt*, Ger. *rede*, speech, Got. *rathjo*, speak, Lat. *ratio*. Cf. O. Ir. *airissim*, from *iss*.

àitidh, damp :

aitionn, juniper, Ir. *aiteann*, O. Ir., *aitenn*, W. *aith*, *eithin*, Cor. *eythinen*, O. Br. *ethin* (gl. rusco), **akto-*, I. E. root, *ak*, sharp, Lat. *acidus*, Eng. *acid*, *edge*, Gr. ἄκρος, extreme, etc. The nearest words are Lit. *ákstinas*, sting, Ch. Sl. *ostinu*. Also **aiteal.** **at-tenn-*, "sharp bush or tree" ; from root *at*, sharp, E. Ir. *aith*, sharp, **atti-*, *atto-*. For *-tenn*, see *caorunn*. Cf. Ir. *teine*, furze.

aitreabh, a building, Ir. *aitreibh*, E. Ir. *aittreb*, W. *adref*, homewards, Gaul, *Atrebates* ; **ad-treb-*, the Celtic root *treb* corresponding to Lat. *tribus*, Eng. *thorpe*.

àl, brood, Ir., *ál*, W. *ael*, *al* : **(p)aglo-* ; cf. Lat. *propâgo*, Eng. *propagate*. Hence **àlaire,** brood mare. Ger. *adel*, nobility.

àlach, a brood, set, bank of oars (M'E.) :

àlach, nails : **āl-lach*, *āl-*, from *(p)agl-*, Lat. *pālus*, stake ; root *pag*, *pāg*, fasten, whence Gr. πήγνυμι, Lat. *pango*, fix, Eng. *page*.

alachag, alachuin, see *ealachainn*.

àlainn, beautiful, Ir. *áluin*, O. Ir. *álaind* ; **ad-lainn* ; see *loinn*. Stokes prefers referring it to *áil*, pleasant, **pagli-*, Eng. fair, root *pag*. But *ro-laind*, pleasant, **ad-pland* (Holden).

all-, over ; see *thall*.

allaban, wandering :

allail, noble, M. Ir. *all*, *aill*, **al-no-s*, root *al*, as in Lat. *altus*.

alladh, fame (either good or bad), Ir. *alladh*, excellency, fame, E. Ir. *allud* ; see above.

allaidh, fierce, wild, Ir. *allta*, O. Ir. *allaid*; possibly from *all-*, over, the idea being "foreign, barbarous, fierce;" cf. W. *allaidd* of like meanings, from W. *all*, other. See next.

allmharach, a foreigner, foreign, fierce; Ir. *allmharach*, foreigner, transmarine; E. Ir. *allmarach*. From *all-*, beyond, and *muir*, sea, "transmarine" (K. Meyer).

allsadh, a jerk, suspending, leaning to one side; see *abhsadh*.

allsmuain, a float, great buoy:

allsporag, cow's throttle (M'A.); see *abhsporag*.

allt, a stream, Ir. *alt*, height, (topographically) glen-side or cliff, O. Ir. *alt*, shore, cliff, O. W. *allt*, cliff, Cor. *als*, Br. *aot*, shore; all allied to Lat. *altus*. The Gaelic form and meaning are possibly of Pictish origin.

all-tapadh, mishap, ill-luck (Wh.); mischance: from *all-* and *tapadh*.

alm, alum; from the English.

almsadh, charity (Hend.), M. Ir. *almsain*.

alp, also **ealp** (Wh.), ingraft, join closely together: *alp* in tinkers' Ir. a job of work, hill; ealp = Sc. *imper*, graft.

alt, joint, Ir., E. Ir. *alt*, **(p)alto-s*; root *pel*, whence Eng. *fold*, Norse, *faldr*, Ger. *falz*, groove; Gr. -πλάσιος, doubled, for πλάτιος. "air alt" = in order that (Wh.).

altach, a grace (at food), Ir. *altughadh*, O. Ir. *attlugud*, rendering thanks, *atluchur bude*, I give thanks: **ad-tlukôr*, root, *tluq*; Lit. *tulkas*, interpreter; Lat. *loquor* for *tloquor*.

altair, altar, Ir., O. Ir. *altóir*, W. *allor*, Cor. *altor*, Br. *auter*; from Lat. *altare*, altar, "high place."

altrum, fostering, Ir. *altrom*, O. Ir. *altram*, W. *alltraw*, sponsor; root *al*, nourish, whence Lat. *alo*, Got. *alan*, grow, Eng. *old*.

àm, time, Ir. *am*, pl. *amanna*, E. Ir. *am*, **ammen-*, from **at-s-men-*, root *at*, Got. *aþn*, year; possibly Lat. *annus* (*at-s-no-*).

am-, privative prefix; this is the labialised form of *an-*, q.v.; and being labialised, it is also aspirated into **amh-**. The forms before "small" vowels in the subsequent syllable are **aim-**, **aimh-**.

amach, vulture, so Ir.:

amadan, fool, Ir. *amadán*: *am+ment-*, "non-minded," Celtic root *ment* (*dearmad*, *farmad*, etc.), mind; Lat. *mens*, *menti-s*, Eng. *mind*, etc. The shorter root *men* is found in *meanmna*.

amail, mischief; E. Ir. *admillim*, I destroy: *ad+mill*, q.v.

amail, hindrance: *ad+mall*, q.v. But Norse *hamla*, hinder.

amal, swingle-tree; **ad-mol*; *mol*, a beam, especially "a mill shaft," E. Ir. *mol*. Cf. Norse *hamla*, oar-loop.

amar, channel, mill lead; E. Ir. *ammor*, *ammbur*, a trough, **amb-or-*; Gaul. *ambes*, rivos, rivers, *Ambris*, river name;

Lat. *imber*; Gr. ὄμβρος, rain; Skr. *ambu*, water. Zimmer considers the Ir. borrowed from Ag. S. *ámber*, amphora, Ger. *eimer*; but the Gaelic meaning is distinctly against his theory. A borrowing from Lat. *amphora* is liable to the same objection.

amarlaich, blustering (M'A.):

amarlaid, blustering female; not *amarlaich*.

amart, need (Hend.). Hend. now questions it, *aimbeairt*.

amhailte, large ember of wood (Glen-moriston).

amas, hitting, O. Ir. *ammus*, an aim: **ad-mes-*; see *eirmis*.

amasguidh, aimsgith, profane, impure: **ad-mesc-id-*, "mixed;" see *measg*.

amh, raw, Ir. *amh*, E. Ir. *om*, W. *of*; root *om*, *ōm*, whence Gr. ὠμός; Got. *amsa*; Skr. *amsas*.

amhach, neck: **om-âk-â*; Lat. *humerus*, shoulder (**om-es-os*); Gr. ὦμος; Got. *amsa*; Skr. *amsas*.

amhain, entanglement by the neck (M'A.); from above.

a mhàin, only, Ir. *amháin*, E. Ir. *amáin*; cf. O. Ir. *nammá* (W. *namyn*, but ?) = *na-n-má*, "ut non sit major" (?). The main root is *má* or *mó*, more, with the negative, but the exact explanation is not easy; "no more than" (?). *amhàin* = *a*-(*a*[*p*]*o*) + *màin*, **mani*; Gr. μάνος, spärlich, μονος (St. Z.).

amhainn, river; better *abhainn*, q.v.

amhaltach, vexing; see *aimheil*.

amhan, a marsh, or *lòn* (Glen-moriston).

amharc, looking, seeing; so Ir., M. Ir., *amarc*, *amharc* = *a*-(*apo*) + *marc*, Ger. *merken*, perhaps Lith. *mérkti*, wink, blink (St.). Roots *marc*, *marg*.

amhartan, luck, Ir. *amhantur*, *abhantur*; from Fr. *aventure*, Eng. *adventure*.

amharus, suspicion, so Ir., O. Ir. *amairess*, infidelitas, *am* + *iress*, the latter meaning "faith;" O. Ir. *iress* = *air-ess*, and **ess* is from **sistâ*, standing, root *stâ*, stand, reduplicated; cf. Lat. *sisto*, etc. The whole word, were it formed at once, would look like **am*-(*p*)*are-sistâ*, or **am-are-sistâ*.

amhas, amhusg, wild man, beast man; Ir. *amhas*, a wild man, madman; E. Ir. *amos*, *amsach*, a mercenary soldier, servant. Conchobar's *amsaig*, or mercenaries, in the E. Ir. saga of Deirdre, appear misunderstood as our *amhusgan*, monsters; there is probably a reminiscence of the Norse "bear-sarks." Borrowed from Gaul. Lat. *ambactus* (= *servus*, Festus), through **ambaxus*; Cæsar says of the Gaulish princes: "Circum se *ambactos* clientesque habent." The roots are *ambi-* (see *mu*) and *ag*, go, lead (see *aghaidh*). Hence many words, as Eng.

ambassador, Ger. *amt*, official position, etc. Ir. J., 154, 156, has *amhas* in G. force.

àmhghar, affliction, Ir. *amhgar*; *am-* (not) +*gar*; cf. O. Ir. *ingir*, tristitia, from *gáire*, risus. See *gàir*, laughter, for root. E. Ir. *so-gar*, *do-gar*, **χαρα* (St.).

amhladh, distress, dismay (Hend.). See *amhluadh*.

amhlair, fool, boor, silly talker or behaver (Arg.); Ir. *amhlóir*, O. Ir. *amlabar*, mute; from *am-* (not) and *labhair*, speak, q.v. Cf. *suilbhir*.

amhlaisg, bad beer, taplash:

amhluadh, confusion, distress:

amhra, wonderful; **am-porios* (St.), ἄπειρος.

amhran, song, Ir. *amhrán*, *abhrán*, M. Ir. *ambrán*, Manx, *arrane*; see *òran*. Cf. Ir. *amhra*, eulogy, especially in verse; *amhra*, famous (Lec. 69).

amhsan (ansan), Dial. **osan,** solan goose; from Lat. *anser?*

amhuil, like, as, Ir. *amhluidh*, O. Ir. *amail*, *amal*, O. W. *amal*, W. *mal*, Br. *evel*; from a Celtic *samali-*, which appears in *samhail*, q.v.

amhuilt, a trick, deceit (H.S.D., M'E. **àmhuilt**): Cf. *aith-méla*.

àmhuinn, oven, Ir. *óigheann*; borrowed from Eng. *oven*.

amlach, curled, **amlag,** a curl, M. Ir. *amlach*, from the prep. *ambi-*, as in *mu*, q.v.

amraidh, àmraidh (M'E.), cupboard, Ir. *amri* (O'B.), W. *almari*; all borrowed from Eng. (Gaelic from Sc. *aumrie?*) *ambry* and M. E. *almarie*, from O. Fr. *almarie*, from Lat. *armarium*, place of tools or arms, from *arma*.

an, a', the, Ir. *an*, O. Ir. *in* (mas. and fem.), *a n-* (neut.); a *t-* appears before vowels in the nom. masc. (*an t-athair*), and it is part of the article stem; a Celtic *sendo-s* (m.), *sendâ* (f.), *san* (n.). *Sendo-s* is composed of two pronominal roots, dividing into *sen-do-*; *sen*, judging by the neuter *san*, is a fixed neuter nom. or acc. from the Celtic root *se* (I. E. *sjo*, beside *so-*), allied to Ag. S. *se*, the, *seó*, now *she*. The *-do-* of *sendo-s* has been referred by Thurneysen and Brugmann to the pron. root *to-* (Eng. *tha-t*, Gr. τό); it is suggested that *to-* may have degenerated into *do-* before it was stuck to the fixed form *sen*. *Sen-to-* could not, on any principle otherwise, whether of accentuation or what not, produce the historical forms. It is best to revert to the older etymology, and refer *do-* to the pronominal root appearing in the Latin fixed cases (enclitic) *-dam*, *-dem*, (qui-*dam*, i-*dem*, etc.), the Gr. δέ, -δε (as in ὅ-δε, this), Ch. Sl. *da*, he. The difference, then, between Gr. ὅ-δε and Gaelic *sen-do-s* is this: the Gr inflects the first element (ὁ = *so*) and keeps the δε fixed, whereas Gaelic reverses the matter by fixing the *sen* and inflecting the *do-*; otherwise the roots are the same ultimately, and used for almost similar purposes.

an, in, Ir. *a n-* (eclipsing), O. Ir. *i*, *i n-*, W. *yn*, Br. *en*; Lat. *in*; Gr. ἐν; Eng. *in*, etc. Generally it appears in the longer form *ann*, or even as *ann an*; see *ann*.

an, interrogative particle, Ir. *an*, O. Ir. *in*; Lat. *an*; Got. *an*.

an-, negative prefix, Ir. *an-*, O. Ir., *an-*, *in-*; W., Cor., Br. *an-*; Celtic *an*, I. E. *n̥-*, Lat. *in-*, Gr. ἀ-, ἀν-, Eng. *un-*, Skr. *a-*, *an-*, etc. It appears before labials and liquids (save *n*) as **am-**, aspirated to **amh-**; with consequent "small" vowels, it becomes **ain-, aim-, aimh-.** Before *g*, it becomes *ion-*, as in *iongantas*. Before *c*, *t*, *s*, the *an-* becomes *eu-* and the *t* and *c* become medials (as in *beud*, *breug*, *feusag*). See also next word.

ana-, negative prefix, O. Ir. *an-*, sometimes aspirating; G. **ana-creidimh,** disbelief, O. Ir. *ancretem*, but *ainfhior*, untrue; M. Ir. *ainfhír*. This suggests a Celtic *anas-* for the first, and *ana-* for the second, extensions of the previous *an-*; cognate are Gr. ἄνις, ἄνευ, without; Ger. *ohne*, Got. *inu*, without.

ana-, an-, ain-, prefix of excess; Ir. *an-*, *ain-*, M. Ir. *an-*; Ir. aspirates where possible (not *t*, *d*, *g*), Gaelic does so rarely. Allied are Gr. ἀνά, up, Got. *ana*, Eng. *on*. Hence **ana-barr,** excess; **ain-neart,** violence; **ain-teas,** excessive heat, etc.

anabas, dregs, refuse, also green, unripe stuff cut; from *an-abaich*.

anabhiorach, centipede, whitlow:

anacail, defend, save; Ir. *anacail*, protection, E. Ir. *anacul* (do.). This Ascoli refers to the same origin as *adnacul*; see *adhlac*.

anacair, sickness, affliction, so Ir., *an-shocair*. Ir. Jl. 156. See *acarach*.

anadas, regret (M'D.):

anagna, irregularity, unusualness (Hend.), *ana* + *gnáth*.

anail, breath, Ir. and O. Ir. *anál*, W. *anadl*, *anal*, Cor. *anal*, Br. *alan*, Celtic *anatlâ*; root *an*, breathe, Got. *anan*, to breathe, Skr. *anila*, wind. See *anam* also.

anainn, eaves, top of house wall:

anam, soul, so Ir., O. Ir. *anim* (d. *anmin*), Cor. *enef*, M. Br. *eneff*, Br. *ene*, Celtic *animon-* (Stokes); Lat. *animus*, *anima*; Gr. ἄνεμος, wind.

anamaint, lust, perversity (Hend.), *ana* + *mèin*.

anart, linen, Ir., E. Ir. *anairt*, O. Ir. *annart* **an-arto-*; root *pan*, *pān*; Lat. *pannus*, cloth; Gr. πηνός, thread on the bobbin; Got. *fana*, cloth, Ag. S. *fana*, small flag, Eng. *vane*, *fane*.

àнart, pride :

anasta, stormy ; **an-fadh-asta* ; see *anfadh*, storm.

ancachd, adversity (Hend.) :

an dràsta, now ; for *an-tràth-sa*, "the time here," q.v.

†anfadh, storm ; proper G. is *onfhadh*, q.v.

anfhann, weak, Ir. *anbhfann*, M. Ir. *anbfann*, *anband* ; *an+fann*, "excessive faint." See *fann*.

anlamh, annlamh, misfortune ; *an-* (not)+*lamh* ; see *ullamh* for *lamh*.

ann, there, Ir., O. Ir. *and*, **anda* (Stokes) ; Cyprian Gr. *ἄνδα* (=*αὔτη*, this, she) ; Lit. *àndai*, newly, *àns*, *anà*, ille, illa ; Ch. Sl. *onŭ*, that ; Skr. *ana*, this (he).

ann, ann an, in, Ir. *ann*, E. Ir. *ind*, O. Ir. *ind-ium* (in me), Celtic *endo* (Stokes) ; Lat. *endo*, *indu*, into, in ; Gr. *ἔνδον*, within, *ἔνδοθεν* ; Eng. *into*. The roots are *en* (see *an*), in, and *do* (see *do*), to. In **ann an**, the two prepositions *ann* and *an* are used. The form **anns** is used before the article and relative ; the *-s* properly belongs to the article ; *anns an*, in the, is for *ann san*.

†annaid, annoid, a church, M. Ir. *annóit*, O. Ir. *andoóit*, mother-church. Stokes refers it to L. Lat. *antitas*, for *antiquitas*, "ancient church." In Scottish place-names it appears as *Annet*, *Clach na h-Annaid*, etc. Cf. *annone*, church (O'Dav.), from Hebrew.

annaladh, era, calendar, Ir. *analach*, chronicle ; from Lat. *annalia*.

annamh, rare, M. Ir. *annam*, E. Ir. *andam* ; **an-dam-*, "non-tame"; root *dam*, home, etc. ; Eng. *domestic*, *tame*. Hence **annas**, rarity.

annlamh, vexation, etc. ; see *anlamh*.

annlan, condiment, E. Ir. *annland*, W. *enllyn* ; possibly *an + leann*.

annrach, ànrach, wanderer, stranger ; either from **ann-reth-ach*, root *reth*, run (see *ruith*, *faondradh*), or from **an-rath-ach*, "unfortunate," root *rath*, luck, q.v.

annrath, distress, Ir. *anrath* ; *an+rath* ; see *rath*, luck. The E. Ir. *andró* appears to be of a different origin.

annsa, dearer, better liked, so Ir., M. Ir. *andsa*, preferable :

ao-, privative prefix ; for *eu-*, that is, for *an-* (not), before *c* and *t*. See *an-*.

aobhach, joyous ; see *aoibhinn*.

aobhar, cause, Ir. *adhbhar*, O. Ir. *adbar*, **ad-bero-n* ; root *ber*, I.E. *bher*, whence Lat. *fero*, Eng. *bear*, etc.

aobharrach, a young person or beast of good promise, hobble-dehoy ; from *aobhar*, material.

aobrann, ankle, O. Ir. *odbrann*, W. *uffarn* : **od-bronn*, **ud-brunn-*, "out-bulge ;" *ud-*=Eng. *out*, and *brunn-*, see *brù*, belly.

Stokes (*Academy*, June, 1892) makes *od-* to be for *pod*, foot, Gr. πούς, ποδ-ός, Eng. *foot*, etc.

aodach, clothes, Ir. *eudach*, O. Ir. *étach*, **ant-ac-os*; root *pan*, as in *anart* q.v. Cf. Lit. *pinti*, plait, twine, Ch. Sl. *pęti*, wind, Lat. *pannus*, etc. Strachan cfs. Alb. *ent*, *int*, weave, Gr. ἄττομαι, weave.

aodann, face, Ir. *éadan*, O. Ir. *étan*, Celtic *antano-* (Stokes); Lat. *ante*; Gr. ἀντί, against; Eng. *and*; Skr. *ánti*, opposite.

aodraman, bladder, Ir. *éadtromán*; see *aotrom*.

aog, death; see *eug*.

aogas, aogasg, face, appearance, M. Ir. *écosg* (O'Cl.), O. Ir *écosc*, habitus, expression, **in-cosc*; see *casg*, check. Cf. O. Ir. *in-cho-sig*, significat.

aoghaire, shepherd, so Ir., M. Ir. *aegaire*, O. Ir. *augaire*, **ovi-gar-*; for *ovi-*, sheep, see *óisg*. The *-gar-* is allied to Gr. ἀγείρω, ἀγορά, meeting place, market.

aoibh, civil look, cheerful face, Ir. *aoibh*, pleasant, humour, E. Ir. *áeb*, O. Ir. *óiph*, beauty, appearance, **aibâ* (Thurneysen), mien, look, Prov. Fr. *aib*, good manners. Ascoli refers it to the root of *éibheall* (q.v.), a live coal, the underlying idea being "shining, sheen." This would agree as to the original force with *taitinn*, please, *taitneach*, pleasant.

aoibhinn, pleasant, joyful, so Ir., E. Ir. *áibind*, *óibind*. See above word for root.

aoideag, hair-lace, fillet; from root of *aodach*.

aoigh, guest, Ir. *aoidhe*, pl. *aoidheadha*, O. Ir. *óegi*, pl. *óegid*, *(*v*)*oig-it*; cf. the Teutonic **faig-iþ-*, whence Norse *feigr*, doomed to die, Ag. S. *fáege*, doomed, Eng. *fey* (Schräder). Stokes gives the Celtic as (*p*)*oik-it*, *poik*, whence Eng. *foe* (cf. Lat. *hostis*, *hospes*); but the Gaelic *gh of aoigh* is against this otherwise satisfactory derivation. As against Schräder's etymology, might be put a reference to the form found in Gr. οἴχομαι, go, Lit. *eigà*, going, further root *ei*, go; the idea being "journey-taker." Commonly misspelt **aoidh**.

aoigh, pleasant countenance, Ir. *aoibh*.

aoine, fast, **Di-haoine**, Friday, Ir. *aoine*, Friday, O. Ir. *oine*, fast, Br. *iun*; from Lat. *jejunium*, a fast, fast-day, Eng. *jejune*. Stokes suggests Gr. πεινάω, hunger, as cognate, making it native: **poin-io-*. Unlikely.

aoineadh, a steep brae with rocks, Manx *eaynee*, steep place:

aoir, a satire, Ir. *aor*, E. Ir. *áer*, O. Ir. *áir*. **aigrâ*, αἶσχος, Got. *aiviski*: *aigh* (St.). Prellwitz gives Gr. and Got. and root. Ascoli refers this word and O. Ir. *tatháir*, reprehensio, to *tàir*, q.v.

aoir, sheet or bolt-rope of a sail:

aoirean, airean, ploughman, herdsman, Ir. *oireamh*, g. *oireamhan*, ploughman, the mythic *Eremon*, *Airem(on)*, **arjamon-*, Skr. *Arjaman*, further *Aryan* (?) ; root *ar*, plough.

aoirneagan. See *aonagail.*

aois, age, Ir. *aois*, O. Ir. *áes*, *áis*, *óis*, W. *oes*, **aivestu-* ; Lat. *ævum*, *ætas*, Eng. *age* ; Gr. αἰές, αἰεί, always ; Eng. *aye*. From **ait-tu*, Lat. *oitor*, *utor*, δί-αιτα (Th. St. Arch. 276).

aol, lime, Ir. *aol*, O. Ir. *áel* : **aidlo-*, from *aidh*, light, fire, Gr. αἴθω, gleam, (St.). See *Mackay.*

aolach, dung, Ir. *aoileach*, O. Ir. *ailedu*, stercora, W. *add-ail*, eluvies. Ascoli compares O. Ir. *áil*, probrum, but this word is probably cognate with Got. *agls*, *aglus*, difficult, shameful, and may not be allied to *aolach.*

aolais, indolence :

aolmann, ointment : founded on the Eng. *ointment.* Cf. *iarmailt*, *armailt.*

aom, incline. Ir. *aomadh*, inclining, attracting :

aon, one, Ir. *aon*, O. Ir. *óin*, *óen* ; W., Cor., Br. *un* ; Lat. *unus* (= *oinos*) ; Got. *ains*, Eng. *one.*

aonach, moor, market place, Ir. *aonach*, fair, assembly, O. Ir. *óinach*, *óenach*, fair, **oin-acos*, from *aon*, one, the idea being "uniting, re-union." Some have compared the Lat. *agonium*, fair, but it would scarcely suit the Gaelic phonetics.

aonach, panting ; see *àinich.*

aonadh, ascent :

aonagail, aonairt, aoineagan, wallowing (H.S.D.) ; see *uainneart* ; *uan* = foam.

aonais, want ; see *iùnais.*

aorabh, bodily or mental constitution :

aoradh, worship, Ir. *adhradh*, O. Ir. *adrad* ; from Lat. *adoratio*, Eng. *adoration.*

aotrom, light, Ir. *éadtrom*, O. Ir. *étromm* ; **an + trom*, "non-heavy." See *trom.*

ap, ape, Ir. *ap*, W. *ab* ; from Eng. *ape.*

aparan, apron, gunwale patch (N.H.) : from the Eng.

aparr, expert ; from Sc. *apert*, from O. Fr. *aparté*, military skill, from Lat. *aperio*, open, Eng. *aperient*, *expert*, *etc.*

aparsaig, knapsack ; from Eng. *haversack.*

ar, ar n-, our, so Ir. and O. Ir. **(s)aron* ; this form may have arisen from unaccented *n̥s-aron* (Jub.), like Got. *uns-ar* (*us* of Eng. and *ar*), Ger. *unser*, Eng. *our* (Thurneysen). Stokes refers it to a Celtic (*n*)*ostron*, allied to Lat. *nostrum.* See further at *bhur.*

ar, seems; **ar leam,** methinks, Ir., M. Ir. *dar*, E. Ir. *indar*, *atar*, with *la*, O. Ir. *inda*, *ata*, *da*; where *ta*, *tar* is the verb *tha* (*thathar*), is, with prep. or rel. *in* before it. *Tha leam-sa* (Mrs Grant). See *na*, than.

àr, plough, E. Ir. *ar*, W. *ar*, ploughed land; Lat. *aro*; Lit. *ariù*; Got. *arjan*, Eng. *ear*, plough.

àr, battle, slaughter, Ir. and O. Ir. *ár*, W. *aer*, **agro-*; root *ag*, drive; Gr. *ἄγρα*, chase; see *àgh*.

àra, kidney, Ir. *ára(nn)*, O. Ir. *áru*, g. *áran*, W. *aren*, **n̥fron-*; Lat. *nefrōnes*; Gr. *νεφρός*; Ger. *nieren*. Stokes refers *ára* to *ad-rên*, the *ren* being the same as Lat. *ren*.

arabhaig, strife; cf. O. Ir. *irbág*, *arbag*, **air-bāg-*, Norse *bágr*, strife.

àrach, rearing; see *àiridh*, shealing. It is possible to refer this word to **ad-reg-*, *reg* being the root which appears in *éirich*.

àrachas, insurance, so Ir., E. Ir. *árach*, bail, contract, **ad-rig-*, root *rig*, bind, which see in *cuibhreach*.

àradh, a ladder, Ir. *aradh*, E. Ir. *árad*:

araiceil, valiant, important, Ir. *árach*, strength, *árachdach*, puissant, **ad-reg-*, root *reg*, rule, direct.

àraidh, certain, some, Ir. *áirighe*, M. Ir. *áiridhe*, **ad-rei-*; cf. W. *rhai*, *rhyw*, some, certain, which Rhys compares to Got. *fraiv*, seed.

ar-amach, rebellion; for **eirigh-amach*, "out-rising."

aran, bread, Ir., M. Ir., *arán*; root *ar*, join, Gr. *αραρισκω*, *ἄρτος*. See next.

arbhar, corn, so Ir., E. Ir. *arbar*; O. Ir. *arbe*, frumentum; Lat. *arvum*, field. Also Gaul. *arinca*, "frumenti genus Gallicum" (Pliny), Gr. *ἄρακος*, vetch, Skr. *arakas*, a plant.

arbhartaich, dispossess; **ar-bert-*; *ar* for *ex-ró?*

arc, fungus on decayed wood, cork, **àrcan,** cork, a cork, stopple, Ir. *arcan*, cork (Lh.):

archuisg, experiment (Sh.):

arcuinn, cow's udder:

àrd, high, Ir., E. Ir. *árd*, Gaul. *Ardvenna*; Lat. *arduus*; Gr. *ὀρθός*.

àrd-dorus, lintel, Ir. *ardorus*, *fardorus*; *àrd-* here is a piece of folk etymology, the real word being *ar*, *air*, upon. See *air* and *dorus*.

arfuntaich, disinherit; **ar-fonn-*. See *arbhartaich*.

argarrach, a claimant; **air+gar*; see *goir*.

argumaid, argument, Ir. *argumeint*, O. Ir. *argumint*; from Lat. *argumentum*.

àrlas, chimney, E. Ir. *forlés*, roof light; *air + leus*, q.v.

arm, weapon, Ir., O. Ir. *arm*, W. *arf*; from Lat. *arma*, whence Eng. *arms*. Stokes says unlikely from Lat.

armadh, working wool in oil, the oil for working wool. Cf. *aolmann*.

àrmunn, a hero, Ir. *armann*, an officer, E. Ir. *armand*, from an oblique case of Norse *ármaðr* (g. *ármanns*), harmost, steward.

àroch, hamlet, dwelling:

àros, a dwelling, Ir. *árus*, M. Ir. *aros*, W. *araws*, *aros*; **ad-rostu-*; Eng. *rest* is allied to *rostu-*.

arpag, a harpy; from Lat. *harpyia*, Eng. *harpy*.

arraban, distress: **ar-reub-* ?

arrabhalach, treacherous fellow; see *farbhalach*.

arrachar, rowing, steering (Arm.): **ar-reg-*, root *reg*, direct.

arrachd, spectre, Ir., E. Ir. *arracht*; **ar-rig-*; see *riochd* for root. Ir. has also *arrach*, contour, spectre.

arrachogaidh, the first hound that gets wind of, or comes up to the deer (Sh.):

arraghaideach, careless (Sh.):

arraideach, erratic: from the Eng. ? *earraid*, hermit ?

arraidh, farraidh, suspicion (M'D.).

arraing, a stitch, convulsions, so Ir.; **ar-vreng-* ? Eng. *wrench*, etc.

arral, foolish pride:

arronta, bold; see *farranta*.

àrrusg, awkwardness, indecency, **arusg** (M'A.):

ars, arsa, quoth, Ir. *ar*, E. Ir. *ar*. The *s* of the Gaelic really belongs to the pronoun *sé* or *sì*, said he, said she, "ar sé, ar sì." Cf. M.G., "ar san tres ughdar glic"—said the third wise author (*san* being the full art.; now *ars an*). The E. Ir. forms *bar* and *for*, inquit, point to the root *sver*, say, Eng. *swear*, *answer*. Stokes refers it to the root *ver*, *verdh*, Eng. *word*, adducing E. Ir. *fordat*, *ordat*, *oldat*, inquiunt, for the *verdh* root. Thurneysen objects that *ol* or *for* is a preposition, the *-dat* being the verb *ta* on analogy with other forms *indás*, *oldáte*. The original is *al*, propter, "further" (see *thall*), like Lat. *tum* ("tum ille"—then he), later *or* or *for*, and later still *ar*—all prepositions, denoting "further."

àrsaidh, old, Ir. *ársaidh*, O. Ir. *arsid*: **ar-sta-*; *sta*, stand. It was not observed that Stokes had the word; but the same conclusion is reached. His stem is *(*p*)*arostât*, from *paros*, before, and *stât*, Skr. *purástât*, erst.

arsnaig, arsenic; from the Eng.

arspag, large species of sea-gull, larus major:

artan, a stone; see *airtein*.

artlaich, baffle; see *fairtlich*.

àruinn, a forest; **ag-ro-ni-*, root *ag*, Gr. ἄγρα, the chase.

as, a, out of, from, Ir. *as*, O. Ir. *ass*, *a*, W. *a*, *oc*, Br. *a*, *ag*, Gaul. *ex-*; Lat. *ex*; Gr. ἐξ, etc. **As-** is also used as a privative particle.

asaid, delivery; see *aisead*.

asair, also **fasair,** the herb "asara bacca;" borrowed from Latin name.

asair, harness, shoemaker, Ir. *asaire*, shoemaker, *assain*, greaves, etc., O. Ir. *assa*, soccus; Gr. παξ, sandal (Hes.), Lat. *baxea*; root *pāg*, fit, Gr. πήγνυμι (Stokes).

asal, an ass, so Ir., M. Ir. *assal*, W. *asyn*, Cor. *asen*. G. and Ir. are borrowed from Lat. *assellus*, the W. and Corn. from Lat. *asinus*.

asbhuain, stubble; **as-buain*, "out-reaping," q.v.

ascaoin, unkind, wrong side of cloth (*caoin is ascaoin*); *as-*, privative, and *caoin*, q.v.

ascart, tow, Ir. *asgartach*, M. Ir. *escart*, W. *carth*, Br. *skarz*, **ex-skarto-*, **skarto-*, dividing, root *sker*, separate; Gr. σκώρ, dung; Eng. *sharn*; etc.

asgaidh, present, boon, E. Ir. *ascad*, O. Ir. *ascid* (Meyer); for root, see *taisg*.

asgailt, a retreat, shelter; see *fasgadh*, *sgàil*: **ad-scath-*, *asgaid*.

asgall, bosom, armpit, so Ir., Br. *askle*, W. *asgre*, bosom. The same as *achlais* (q.v.) by metathesis of the *s*.

asgan, a grig, merry creature, dwarf (Arm.). See *aisteach*.

asgnadh, ascending, so Ir.; **ad-sqendô-*; Lat. *scando*, etc.

aslach, request, Ir., O. Ir. *aslach*, persuasio, *adslig*, persuades; for root, see *slighe*, way.

aslonnach, prone to tell (Arm.), E. Ir. *asluindim*, I request; **ad-sloinn*, q.v.

asp, an asp, W. *asp*, from the Eng.

àsran, a forlorn object, Ir. *asránnach*, *astrannach*, a stranger: from *astar*?

astail, a dwelling; see *fasdail*.

astail, a contemptible fellow (M'A.):

astar, a journey, Ir. *usdar*, *astar*, E. Ir. *astur*; **ad-sod-ro-n*, root *sod*, *sed*, go; Gr. ὁδός, way, Ch. Sl. *choditi*, go; Eng. *ex-odus*. Stokes (Bez. Beit.[21] 1134) now gives its Celtic form as **adsîtro-*, root *sai* of *saothair*, toil.

àsuing, àsuinn, àsuig, apparatus, weapon; see *asair* (?).

at, swell, Ir. *at*, O. Ir. *att*, *(*p*)*at-to-*, root *pat*, extend, as in *aitheamh*, q.v. Stokes gives Celtic as *azdo-* (Got. *asts*, twig, etc.); but this would be in Gaelic *ad*.

†**atach,** request, B. of Deer *attác*, E. Ir. *atach*, O. Ir. *ateoch*, I pray, **ad-tek-*; Eng. *thig*.

atach, cast-off clothes (Uist, etc.) = *ath-aodach.*

ataig, atuinn, a palisade, stake :

atamach, fondling, caressing (M'A.) :

ath, next, again ; see *ath-*.

ath, flinch ; from *ath-*, back. Hence **athach**, modest.

ath-, aith, re-, so Ir., O. Ir. *ath-*, *aith-*, *ad-*, **ati*, W. *ad-*, Br. *at-*, *az-* ; Gaul. *ate* : Lat. *at*, but, *at-* (*atavus*) ; Lit. *at-*, *ata-*, back, Slav. *otŭ* ; Skr. *ati*, over. Stokes divides Celtic *ati-* into two, meaning respectively "over" and "re- ;" but this seems unnecessary.

àth, a ford, Ir., O. Ir. *áth*, **jâtu-* ; Skr. *yâ*, to go ; Lit. *jóti*, ride (Stokes). **Beul-àth** :

àth, a kiln, Ir. *áith*, W. *odyn*. Stokes refers this to a pre-Celtic *apati-*, *apatino-*, parallel to Eng. *oven*, Got. *auhns*, Gr. ἰπνός. Bezzenberger suggests the Zend. *âtar*, fire, as related.

athach, a giant, Ir. *fathach*, *athach* ; root *pat*, extend ?

†**athach**, a breeze, Ir., O. Ir. *athach* ; Gr. ἀτμός, vapour, Eng. *atmosphere* ; Ger. *atem*, breath ; etc.

athainne, embers, so Ir. ; **ath-teine* (?). See *aithinne*.

athailt, a scar ; *ath-ail* ; see *ail*, mark.

athair, father, so Ir., O. Ir. *athir* ; Lat. *pater* ; Gr. πατήρ ; Skr. *pitár-* ; Eng. *father*.

athair-neimh, serpent, Br. *aer*, *azr* ; for *nathair-neimh*, q.v.

athair-thalmhainn, yarrow, milfoil, Ir. and M. Ir. *athair talman* ; "pater-telluris !" Also **earr-thalmhainn**, which suggests borrowing from Eng. *yarrow*.

athais, leisure ; *ath* + *fois* = delay, q.v.

athar, evil effect, consequence (M'A., Whyte), **at-ro-n* from *ath*, "re-." See *comharradh*. Sc. *aur* = *athailt*.

athar, sky, air, Ir. *aiéur*, air, sky, O. Ir. *aér*, *aier*, W. *awyr* ; from Lat. *aer*, whence Eng. *air*. See St. for *aér*, **aver-* ? Cf. *padhal*, *staidhir*, *adhal*.

atharla, heifer ; possibly *ath-ar-laogh*, "ex-calf." Cf. E. Ir. *aithirni*, calf.

atharnach, second crop, ground cropped and ready for ploughing (N. H.) *ath-eòrn-ach* ? **ath-ar-nach*, root *ar*, plough.

atharrach, alteration, Ir. *atharrach*, O. Ir. *aitherrech*, Br. *adarre*, afresh, *arre*, **ati-ar-reg-*, root *reg* of *èirich*. Stokes analyses it into *ati-ex-regô*, that is, *ath-éirich*.

atharrais, mocking, imitating (M'K.) ; (Dial. *ailis*) : *ath-aithris*, "re-say," Ir. *aithris*, tell, imitation. See *aithris*.

B

ba! part of a lullaby; onomatopoetic. Cf. Eng. *baby*, Ger. *bube*, etc.

bà, bàth, foolish, Fernaig MS. *bah*: "deadly," (talky?), root *bā-*, kill (speak?); see *bàs*. Cf. Lat. *fatuus*.

babag, tassle; see *pab*.

babhd, a surmise (M'A.), a quirk; from Fr. *faut*.

babhsganta, baosganta, cowardly; see *bodhbh*; *babhsgadh*, fright, shock (Hend.).

bàbhun, bulwark, enclosure for cattle, Ir. *bábhún*. whence Eng. *bawn*, M. Ir. *bódhún* (Annals of Loch Cé, 1199); from *bó* and *dùn*, q.v.

bac, hindrance, Ir. *bac*, M. Ir. *bacaim* (vb.). See next word.

bac, a crook, Ir. *bac*, O. Ir. *bacc*, W. *bach*, Br. *bac'h*, Celtic *bakko-s*; **bag-ko-*, Norse *bak*, Eng. *back*. Hence **bacach,** lame, E. Ir. *bacach*, W. *bachog*, crooked.

bacag, a fall, tripping; from *bac*, q.v.

bac-mòine, turf-pit or bank (N. H.); from Norse *bakki*, a bank, Eng. *bank*. Hence also place-name *Back*.

bacaid, ash holder, backet; from Sc. *backet*, from Fr. *baquet*.

bacastair, baker, **bacaladh,** oven, Ir. *bacail*, baker; all from the Eng. *bake*, *baxter*.

bacan, stake, hinge, Ir. and E. Ir. *bacán*. From *bac*.

bach, drunkenness, Ir. *bach*; from Lat. *Bacchus*.

bachall, shepherd's crook, crozier, Ir. *bachul*, O. Ir. *bachall*, W. *bagl*, crutch; from Lat. *baculum*, staff; Gr. *βακτηριά*, Eng. *bacteria*. *Bachull gille*, slovenly fellow (M'D.).

bachar, acorn, "Molucca bean," Ir. *bachar*; borrowed from or allied to Lat. *baccar*, Gr. *βάκκαρις*, nard.

bachlag, a shoot, a curl, Ir. *bachlóg*; from *bachall* (Thurneysen).

bachoid, the boss of a shield, Ir. *bocoide*, bosses of shields; from L. Lat. *buccatus*, Lat. *bucca*, cheek. See *bucaid*.

bad, a cluster, thicket; cf. Br. *bot*, *bod*, bunch of grapes, thicket; common in Breton and Scotch place names; probably a Pictish word. Cf. Eng. *bud*, earlier *bodde*. Cf. Lat. *fascis* (**fað-scis*), **bað-sk-*, Norse, Eng. *bast*?

badhal, a wandering, **bàdharan**; possibly from the root *ba*, go, as in *bothar*, q.v. H.S.D. suggests *bà* + *dol*.

bàdhan, a churchyard (Sutherland), *i.e.* "enclosure," same as *bàbhun*.

bàdhar (H.S.D.), **badhar** (Carm.), placenta of cow:

bag, a bag; from the Eng.

bagaid, a cluster, troop, W. *bagad*, Br. *bagod*; from Lat. *bacca* (Thurneysen, Ernault).

bagaire, a glutton; from *bag* in the sense of "belly."

bagair, threaten, so Ir., E. Ir. *bacur*, a threat. The W. *bygwl*, a threat, etc., is scarcely allied, for it comes from *bwg*, a spectre, bogie, whence possibly the English words *bogie*, *boggle*, etc. G. *bagair* may be allied with the root underlying *bac*; possibly *bag-gar-*, "cry-back."

bagaisde, baggage, lumber (of a person) (Wh.), from *baggage*.

bàgh, a bay, Ir. *bádh*; from Eng. *bay*, Romance *baja*.

baghan, a stomach (*baoghan*, with *ao* short). Dial. **maghan** (Sutherland); cf. Eng. *maw*, Ger. *magen*, Norse *magi*.

baibeil, lying, given to fables; from Eng. *babble*.

baideal, tower, battlement, ensign, **baidealach**, bannered; from M. Eng. *battle*, *battlement*, which is of the same origin as *battlement*.

bàidh, love, Ir. *báidhe*, M. Ir. *báid*, *báde*, **bâdi-s* (Stokes). Cf. Gr. φώτιον, friendly (Hes.), for φώθιον; root *bhā* : *bhō*, whence Gr. φώς, man.

baidreag, a ragged garment; see *paidreag*.

bàidse, musician's fee; from the Eng. *batch*?

baigeir, a beggar; from Eng.

baigileis, loose lumber or baggage (Argyle); from *baggage*.

bail, thrift, Ir. *bail*, success, careful collection, M. Ir. *bail*, goodness, E. Ir. *bulid* : φυλλα; I. E. root *bhel*, swell, increase. See *buil*, *bile*. Hence **baileach.** Cf. *adhbhal*, βέλτερος.

bailbheag, a corn poppy; also **beilbheag, mealbhag, meilbheag.**

bailc, a ridge, beam, W. *balc*, from Eng. *balk*.

bailc, seasonable rain, showers:

bailceach, strong, a strong man, E. Ir. *balc*, strong, W. *balch*, superbus, Br. *balc'h*; Lat. *fulcio*, support, Eng. *fulcrum* (Stokes). Likely a Celtic *bal-ko-*, root *bal*, as in *bail*. So Ost.; Skr. *balam*, strength (*adhbhal*), Gr. βέλτερος; Wh. St. *bolijĭ*, greater; Lat. *debilis*.

baile, town, township, Ir., E. Ir. *baile*, **balio-s*, a pre-Celtic *bhv-alio-*, root *bhu-*, be; Gr, φωλεός, a lair; Norse *ból*, a "bally," further Eng. *build*, *booth*.

baileach, excessive; see *bail*. Also **buileach.**

bàilisdeir, babbler, founded on Eng. Scandinavian *balderdash*.

bàillidh, a magistrate, bailie; from Sc. *bailzie* (Eng. *bailiff*), Fr. *bailli*.

baineasag, a ferret, Ir. *baineasóg*; *bán* + *neas*, "white weasel," q.v.

bàinidh, madness, fury, Ir. *báinidhe*; Ir. *mainigh* (O'Br.), from Lat. *mania*; see *bà*.

bainisg, a little old woman, female satirist (Carm.) = *ban-éisg*; from *ban*, *bean*, *q.v.*

bainne, milk, Ir., M. Ir. *bainne*; also **boinne**, milk (Sutherland shire), a drop, Ir., M. Ir. *bainne*, milk. O. Ir. *banne*, drop,

Cor., Br. *banne*, gutta ; root *bha* ; O. Slav. *banja*, bath ; Eng. *bath*, etc.

bàir, a game, goal, Ir. *báire*, hurling match, goal, M. Ir. *báire* : **bag-ro-*, root *bāg-*, strive ; see *arabhaig*. **bàireach,** a ball.

baircinn, side timbers of a house (Sh.) :

baireachd, quarrelling (Carm.) ; cf. *bàirseag*.

†**bairghin,** bread, cake, Ir. *bairghean*, E. Ir. *bargen*, W., Cor., and Br. *bara*, panis, **bargo-* ; Lat. *ferctum*, oblation cake ; Ag. S. *byrgan*, to taste, Norse *bergja*, taste.

bàirich, lowing ; root of *bó*, cow. Cf. *bùirich*.

bàirig, bestow ; from Eng. *ware*, as also *bathar*.

bàirleigeadh, bàirneigeadh, warning, summons ; from the Eng. *warning*.

bàirlinn, rolling wave, billow ; *bàir-linn*, from †**bàir,** wave, borrowed from Norse *bára*, wave, billow. For *linne*, see that word.

bàirneach, a limpet, Ir. *báirneach* (Fol.), W. *brenig*, Cor. *brennic* : from M. Eng. *bernekke*, now *barnacle*, from Med. Lat. *bernaca*. Stokes takes *bàirnech* from *barenn*, rock, as Gr. λεπάς, limpet, is allied to λέπας, rock.

bàirneachd, judgment (Sh.), Ir., W., Br. *barn*, root *ber* in *bràth*, q.v.

bàirseag, a scold (Sh.), Ir. *bairseach*, M. Ir. *bairsecha*, foolish talk, *bara*, wrath, W. *bâr*, wrath. Stokes refers *bara* to the same origin as Lat. *ferio*, I strike, Norse *berja*, smite, etc.

baisceall, a wild person (Sh.) ; M. Ir. *basgell* (i. *geltan*), *boiscell* ; root in *bà*, foolish ? + *ciall*.

baiseach, a heavy shower, Ir. *báisdeach*, rain, *bais*, water ; cf. O. Ir. *baithis*, baptism, which may be borrowed from Lat. *baptisma* (Windisch). The root here is *bad*, of *bàth*, drown. Ir. *baiseach*, raining (Clare), from *baisteadh*, Lat. *baptisma* (Zim.).

baist, baptise, Ir. *baisd*, O. Ir. *baitsim* ; from Lat. *baptizo*, which is from Gr. βαπτίζω, dip.

baiteal, a battle ; from Eng. *battle*.

balach, clown, lad, Ir. *balach*, clown, churl ; cf. Skr. *bālakas*, a little boy, from *bāla*, young. But cf. W. *bala*, budding, root *bhel*. Rathlin Ir. *bachlach*.

balaiste, ballast ; from the Eng.

balbh, dumb, so Ir., E. Ir. *balb* ; borrowed from Lat. *balbus*.

balc, ridge, etc. ; see *bailc*. Also "calf of leg" (Wh.).

balc, misdeed :

balcach, splay-footed (H.S.D.). Cf. Gr. φολκός, bandy-legged (?).

balg, belly, bag, Ir. *bolg*, O. Ir. *bolc*, W. *bol*, *boly*, belly, Cor. *bol*, Gaulish *bulga* (Festus) sacculus ; Got. *balgs*, wine-skin, Norse *belgr*, skin, bellows, Eng. *belly*.

balgair, a fox :

balgum, mouthful, M. G. *bolgama* (pl.), Ir. *blogam* ; from *balg*. Cf. O. Ir. *bolc uisce*, a bubble.

ball, a member, Ir., O. Ir. *ball* ; Gr. *φαλλός* ; Eng. *phallus* ; root *bhel*, swell.

ball, a spot, Ir., M. Ir. *ball*, white-spotted on forehead (of a horse), Br. *bal* (do.). The Gaelic suggests a stem *bal-no-*, Celtic root *bal*, white, Gr. *φαλός*, shining, *φάλαρος* (phalāros), white-spotted (of animals) ; I. E. *bhēl : bhale*, shine ; whence Eng. *bale*-fire. Stokes says the Irish *ball* seems allied to the Romance *balla*, a ball, Eng. *bale* and *ball* (?). Hence **ballach,** spotted. W. *bal*, spotted on forehead.

ball, a ball ; from Eng.

balla, wall, Ir. *balla* (Four Masters), *fala* (Munster) ; from M. Eng. *bailly*, an outer castle wall, now in Old Bailey, from Med. Lat. *ballium*.

ballaire, a cormorant ; from *ball*, spot.

ballan, a vessel, tub, Ir. *ballán*, E. Ir. *ballan*. Stokes cfs. Norse *bolli*, bowl, Eng. *bowl*, and says that the Gaelic is probably borrowed.

ballart, boasting, clamour ; probably from Norse *ballra*, strepere, *baldrast*, make a clatter (Eng. *balderdash*), Ger. *poltern*.

balt, a welt : see *bolt*.

bàn, white, Ir., O. Ir. *bán* ; I. E. root *bhā*, shine ; Gr. *φανός* (*a* long), bright ; Skr. *bhânù*, light ; further away is Eng. *bale* (*bale*-fire).

ban-, bana-, she-, female- ; see *bean*.

banabachadh, worse of wear (M'D.) :

banachag, dairymaid :

banachdach, vaccination :

banair, sheep fold ; see rather *mainnir*.

banais, a wedding, wedding feast, Ir. *bainfheis*, wedding feast, M. Ir. *banais*, g. *baindse* ; from *ban* + *féisd* ?

banarach, dairymaid ; from *ban-* and *àireach*.

†**banbh,** a pig, Ir. *banbh*, E. Ir. *banb*, W. *banw*, Br. *banv*, *banc*, **banvo-s*. The word appears as *Banba*, a name for Ireland, and, in Scotland, as Banff. M'L. and D. gives the further meaning of "land unploughed for a year."

banc, a bank ; from the Eng.

bànchuir, squeamishness at sea (H.S.D., which derives it from *bàn* and *cuir*).

bangadh, a binding, promise (Sh., H.S.D.), Ir. *bangadh*. H.S.D. suggests Lat. *pango*, whence it may have come.

bangaid, a banquet, christening feast ; from Eng. *banquet*.

bann, a belt, band; from Eng. *band*. It also means a "hinge." Dialectic **spann**.

bannag, a Christmas cake; from the Sc. *bannock*. See *bonnach*.

bannag, corn-fan; from Lat. *vannus*, Eng. *fan*.

bannal, a troop, gang, Ir. *banna*; from Eng. *band*. Cf. E. Ir. *ban-dál*, assembly of ladies. Also **pannail.**

bansgal (Dial. *banasgal*), a female, a hussy, Ir. *bansgal*, E. Ir. *banscál*, O. Ir. *banscala*, servae; root of *sgalag*.

bantrach, a widow, E. Ir. *bantrebthach*, landlady: *ban+trebthach*, farmer, from *treb* in *treabhadh*, *aitreabh*.

baobh, a wicked woman, witch, Ir. *badhbh*, hoodie crow, a fairy, a scold, E. Ir. *badb*, crow, demon, *Badba*, the Ir. war-goddess, W. *bod*, kite, Gaul. *Bodv-*, *Bodvo-gnatus*, W. *Bodnod*; Norse *böð*, g. *boðvar*, war, Ag. S. *beadu*, g. *beadwe*, **badwa-* (Rhys). In Stokes' Dict. the Skr. *bádhate*, oppress, Lit. *bádas*, famine, are alone given. Also **baogh.**

baodhaiste, ill usage from the weather:

baoghal, danger, so Ir., O. Ir. *baigul*, *baegul*; cf. Lit. *bai-mė*, fear, *bai-gus*, shy, Skr. *bhayate*, fear.

baoghan, , a calf, anything jolly; from *baoth*.

baogram, a flighty emotion (Dialectic); founded on **baogadh**, a dialectic form of *biog*, q.v.

baoileag, blaeberry; cf. Eng. *bil*berry, Dan. *bölle*bær.

baoireadh, foolish talk; founded on *baothaire*, fool, from *baoth*, q.v.

†**baois**, lust, so Ir., E. Ir. *baes*, **baisso-* (Stokes); compared by Bezzenberger to Gr. φαιδρός, shining, and by Strachan to the root *gheidh*, desire, Lit. *geidu*, desire, Ch. Sl. *žida*, expetere, Goth. *gaidw*, a want. Possibly allied to Lat. *foedus*, foul.

baois, madness, so Ir., E. Ir. *báis*; from *baoth* (Zim. Z[32] 229) = *báithas*. Cf. *sgìth*, *sgìos*.

baoisg, shine forth: see *boillsg*.

baoiteag, a small white maggot; see *boiteag*.

baol, nearness of doing anything (M'A.); *baoghal?* Cf. its use in Fern. MS.

baoth, foolish, so Ir., O. Ir. *báith*, *baeth*; root *bai*, fear, as in *baoghal*; Cor. *bad*, Br. *bad*, stupidity, are not allied, nor is Goth. *bauths*, dumb, as some suggest. Hence **baothair**, fool.

bara, a barrow, Ir. *bara*, E. Ir. *bara*; from M. Eng. *barowe*, Eng. *barrow*.

barail, opinion, Ir. *baramhuil*, M. Ir. *baramail*: *bar+samhail*; for *bar-*, see *bàirneachd*, *bràth*.

baraill, a barrel, Ir. *báirille*, E. Ir. *barille*, W. *baril*; from M. E. *barel*, from O. Fr. *baril*.

baraisd, **barraisd**, borage; Ir. *barraist*; from the Eng. *borage*.

baran, a baron; Ir. *barún*, W. *barwn*; from the Eng.

barant, surety, warrant, Ir., M. Ir. *baránta*, W. *gwarant*; from M. Eng. *warant*, now *warrant*. So St.

barbair, a barber, Ir. *bearrbóir* (Fol.), W. *barfwr*; from the Eng.

barbarra, barbarous, Ir. *barbartha*: from Lat. *barbarus*, Eng. *barbarous.*

bar-bhrigein, silver-weed (Arm.); also **brisgean** (from *brisg*):

barbrag, tangle tops, barberry; from Eng. *barberry.* In Lewis, the former is called **bragaire.**

bàrc, a bark, boat, Ir. *bárc*, E. Ir. *barc*, W. *barg*, Br. *barc.* These words are all ultimately from the Late Latin *barca*, whence through Fr., comes Eng. *bark.*

bàrc, rush (as water), Ir. *bárcaim*, break out; cf. M. Ir. *barc*, multitude; Lat. *farcio*, cram, *frequens*, numerous.

bàrd, a poet, Ir. *bárd*, E. Ir. *bard*, W. *bardd*, Br. *barz*, Gaul. *bardos*, **bardo-s*; Gr. φράζω (φραδ-), speak (Eng. *phrase*).

bàrd, dyke, inclosure, meadow, Ir. *bárd*, a guard, garrison; from Eng. *ward*, enclosed pasture land (Liddell 35).

bargan, a bargain, W. *bargen*; from the Eng. *bargain.*

bàrlag, a rag, tatter-demalion; cf. Ir. *barlín*, sheet, for *braith-lín*, q.v.

bàrluadh, a term in pipe music; from Eng. *bar*+G. *luath.*

bàrnaig, a summons; from the Eng. *warning.*

barpa, barrow, cairn (H.S.D., a Skye word). Cape Wrath is *Am Parph* in Gaelic (*An Carbh*, Lewis); from Norse *Hvarf*, a turning, rounding, Eng. *wharf.*

bàrr, top, Ir. *bárr*, O. Ir. *barr*, W., Cor. *bar*, Br. *barr*, **barso-*; Norse *barr*, pine needles, Ag. S. *byrst*, Eng. *bristle, burr*; Lat. *fastiguim* (for *farstigium*), top; Skr. *bhṛshti*, a point. Hence **barrachd,** overplus. **bàrrlach,** refuse, flotsam (Wh.).

barra, a spike, bar, Ir. *bárra*, W. *bar*, nail, etc.; all from the Eng. *bar.*

barra-gùg, potato bloom, bud. See *gucag.* Also *barr-guc.*

bàrraisg, boasting, brag, **bàrsaich,** vain, prating; see *bàirseag.*

barramhaise, a cornice (A. M'D.); *barr*+*maise.* Also **barr-maisich** (verb), ornament (M'A.).

barrlait, a check (Carm.):

bas, palm of the hand, Ir., O. Ir. *bas, bass, boss*, Br. *boz*, **bostâ*; Gr. ἀγοστός.

bàs, death, Ir., O. Ir. *bás*; Celtic root *bā*, *ba*, hit, slay, whence Gaul. Lat. *batuere* (Eng. *battle*, etc.); Ag. S. *beadu*, war.

basaidh, a basin; from Sc. *bassie*, Eng. *basin.*

bascaid, a basket, Ir. *basgaod*, W. *basged*; from the Eng. *basket.*

basdal, noise, gaiety; from Norse *bastl*, turmoil.

basdard, a bastard, so Ir. and M. Ir., W. *basdardd*; all from the Eng. *bastard.*

basgaire, mourning, Ir. *bascarrach*, lamentation, clapping with the hands, M. Ir. *basgaire*; *bas+gaire*, "palm-noise;" for *gaire*, see *goir*. Also **basraich**.

basganta, melodious:

basg-luath, vermilion; from the obsolete adj. *basg*, red, E. Ir. *basc*, and *luath*, ashes, q.v. Stokes cfs. *basc* to Lat. *bacca* (for *bat-ca*), berry.

bat, bata, a stick, Ir. *bata*; from M. Eng. *batte*, stick, now *bat*, which comes from O. Fr. *batte*, from Gaul. Lat. *battuere*, as under *bàs*, q.v. The Br. *baz* seems borrowed from the Fr., though it may be native.

bàta, a boat, Ir. *bád*, M. Ir. *bát*, W. *bâd*; all from Ag. S. *bât*, Eng. *boat*, Norse *bátr* (Stokes). K. Meyer takes Ir. and G. from the Norse.

batail, a fight; see *baiteal*.

bàth, drown, Ir. *báthaim*, O. Ir. *bádud* (inf.), W. *boddi*, Br. *beuzi*; I.E. *gādh*, sink, Gr. *βαθύς*, deep, -*βδύω*, sink, Skr. *gāhás*, the deep. Gl. *fodio* (Ern.).

bàth, vain, foolish (Hend.); see **bà**. Skye.

bàthaich, a byre, Ir. *bothigh*, W. *beudy*; *bó+tigh*, "cow house."

bathais, forehead, Ir. *baithis*, pate, E. Ir. *baithes*, crown of the forehead; **bat-esti-*, from *bat*, I.E. *bhā*, shine, Gr. *φάσις*, appearance, *phase*. See *bàn* further. Lat. *facies*, face, appearance, may be allied, though the latest authorities connect it with *facio*, make.

bathar, wares; from the Eng. *wares*.

†**beabhar**, beaver, Ir. *beabhar* (Lh.), Cor. *befer*, Br. *bieuzr*, Gaul. *Bibrax*; Lat. *fiber*; Eng. *beaver*, Ag. S. *béofor*. Gaelic and Ir. are doubtful.

beach, a bee, so Ir., O. Ir. *bech*, W. *begegyr*, drone, **biko-s*; a root *bi-* appears in Eng. *bee*, Ag. S. *beó* (=**bija*), Ger. *biene* (=**bi-nja*), Lit. *bitis*. Stokes makes the Celtic stem *beko-s*, but does not compare it with any other language.

beachd, opinion, notice, Ir. *beacht*, certain, E. Ir. *becht*, *bechtaim*, I certify; **bhig-to-*; Lat. *figo* (St. Z.C.P. 71).

beadaidh, impudent, fastidious, Ir. *béadaidh*, *beadaidh*, sweet-mouthed, scoffing; E. Ir. *bet*, talking, shameless girl (Corm.): **beddo-*, **bez-do-*, root *bet*, *get*, as in *beul*.

beadradh, fondling, caressing, **beadarrach**, pampered:

beag, little, Ir. *beag*, O. Ir. *becc*, W. *bach*, Cor. *bechan*, Br. *bic'han*, *bian*, **bezgo-*; Lat. *vescus* (=*gvesgus*)? Some have connected it with Gr. *μικρός*, Dor. Gr. *μικκός*, and Dr Cameron suggested Lat. *vix*, scarcely.

beairt, engine, loom: see *beart*.

beairtean, shrouds, rigging; see *beart*.

bealach, a pass, Ir. *bealach*, pass, road, E. Ir. *belach*; cf. Skr. *bíla*, gap, mouth; *bilako-n* (C.RR. 174). Cf. W. *bwlch*, pass, etc? See *bile*.

bealaidh, broom, Ir. *beallÿi* (Lh. *Comp. Voc.*); cf. Br. *balan*, M. Br. *balazn*, O. Fr. *balain*; also Fr. *balai*, older *balain*, a broom. This might be referred to the common root *bhel*, bloom (prolific as a root, like the corresponding root of *broom*, as in W. *balannu*, to bud), but the W. for "broom" is *banadl*, Cor. *banathel*, which M. Ernault has compared with Lat. *genista*, broom (root *gen*, beget?). Jub. gives Br. as *banadlon* (R.C.[18] 106). The Br. might be a metathesis of W. *banadl* (cf. Br. *alan v. anail*). It is possible that Gaelic is borrowed from the Pictish; the word does not appear in the Ir. Dictionaries, save in Lh.'s Celt. part, which perhaps proves nothing.

bealbhan-ruadh, a species of hawk (Sh., O'R.); for *bealbhan*, cf. †**bealbhach,** a bit, from *beul*, mouth?

bealltuinn, May-day, Ir. *béalteine*, E. Ir. *beltene*, *belltaine*, **belo-te(p)niâ* (Stokes), "bright-fire," where *belo-* is allied to Eng. *bale* ("bale-fire"), Ag. S. *bael*, Lit. *baltas*, white. The Gaul. god-names *Belenos* and *Belisama* are also hence, and Shakespeare's *Cym-beline*. Two needfires were lighted on Beltane among the Gael, between which they drove their cattle for purification and luck; hence the proverb: "Eadar dà theine Bhealltuinn"—Between two Beltane fires.

bean, wife, so Ir., O. Ir. *ben*, W. *bun*, *benyw*, Cor. *benen*, sponsa, Celtic *benâ*, g. *bnâs*, pl. n. *bnâs*; Gr. γυνή, Bœot. Gr. βανά; Got. *ginô*, Eng. *queen*, Sc. *queyn*; Skr. *gnâ*.

bean, touch, Ir. *beanaim*, beat, touch, appertain to, O. Ir. *benim*, pulso, ferio, Br. *bena*, to cut, M. Br. *benaff*, hit; **bina*, root *bin*, *bi* (O. Ir, *ro bi*, percussit, *bithe*, perculsus), from I.E. *bhi*, *bhei*, hit; Ch. Sl. *bija*, *biti*, strike; O. H. G. *bîhal*, axe; Gr. φιτρός, log. Further is root *bheid*, split, Eng. *bite*. Usually *bean* has been referred to I. E. *ghen*, *ghon*, hit, slay; Gr. φεν-, slay, επεφνον, slew, φόνος, slaughter, θείνω, strike; Skr. *han*, hit; but *gh* = G. *b* is doubtful.

beann, top, horn, peak, Ir. *beann*, O. Ir. *benn*, pinna, W. *ban*, height, peak, M. Br. *ban*, also *benny*, horn, pipe (music), Gaul. *canto-bennicus* mons, "white peak" mount; proto-Gaelic *bennâ*; root, *gen-*, *gn-*, as in Eng. *knoll*, Sc. *knowe*. In Scotch Gaelic, the oblique form **beinn** has usurped the place of *beann*, save in the gen. pl.

beannachd, blessing, so Ir., O. Ir. *bendacht*, W. *bendith*; from Lat. *benedictio*, whence Eng. *benediction*.

beannag, a skirt, corner, coif, Ir. *beannóg*; from *beann*.
beantag, a corn-fan; see **bannag**.
bearach, dog-fish (M'A.); O. Ir. *berach*, verutus, from *bior*; cf. Eng. "picked or horned dogfish"; "bone-dog."
bearachd, judgment (Sh., O'R.); root *bera*, *brâ*, as in *bràth*, q.v.
bearbhain, vervain; from Eng. *vervain*, Lat. *verbena*.
bearn, a breach, cleft, Ir. *bearna*, E. Ir. *berna*; I. E. *bher*, cut, bore; Lat. *forare*, bore; Gr. *φάρος*, a plough, *φαρω*, split; Arm. *beran*, mouth; Ch. Sl. *bar*, clip; Eng. *bore*. Also *bern*, fen in E. Ir.
beàrr, shear, Ir. *béarraim*, O. Ir. *berraim*, O. W. *byrr*, short, Cor. *ber*, Br. *berr*, short, **berso-*; Gr. *φάρσος*, any piece cut off; root *bhera*, as in *bearn*.
bearraideach, flighty, nimble; from *beàrr*?
beart, a deed, Ir. *beárt*, load, action, E. Ir. *bert*, bundle, birth; Gr. *φόρτος*, burden; root, *bher*, in *beir*, q.v. Also **beairt**, engine, loom. It is used in many compounds in the sense of "gear," as in **cais-bheart**, foot-gear, shoes; **ceann-bheart**, head-gear, helmet, &c.
beartach, rich; from *beart*; W. *berth*, rich, *berthedd*, riches.
beatha, life, so Ir. O. Ir. *bethu*, g. *bethad*, Celtic stem, *bitât-*, divided into *bi-tât*; see *bith* (i.e., *bi-tu-*) for root. It is usual for philologists to represent the stem of *beatha* as *bivotât*, that is, *bi-vo-tât-*, the *bi-vo-* part being the same as the stem *bivo* of *beò*. While the root *bi* is common to both *beatha* and *beò*, the former does not contain *-vo-*; it is the O. Ir. nom. *beothu* (**bi-tûs*) that has set philologists wrong. Hence G. and Ir. **beathach**, animal. Ir. *beathadhach*, dial. of *beathach*.
beic, a curtesy; from Sc. *beck*, curtesy, a dialectic use of Eng. *beck*, *beckon*. Hence **beiceis**, bobbing, etc. (M'A.).
beil, grind; a very common form of *meil*, q.v.
beil, is; see *bheil*.
beilbheag, corn-poppy; see *mealbhag*. Also **bailbheag**.
béileach, a muzzle, Ir. *beulmhach*, a bridle bit, *-mhach* for *bach* termination from *bongim*, beat; from *beul*.
béilleach, blubber-lipped, **béileach** (H.S.D.); from *beul*. The first form suggests a stem *bél-nac-*. Cf. **béilean**, a prating mouth. Also **méilleach**.
beilleag, outer coating of birch, rind; also **méilleag**, q.v.
beince, **being** (H.S.D.), a bench; from Sc. *bink*; Eng. *bench*. Cf. Ir. *beinse*, W. *mainc*, Br. *menk*.
beinn, hill, ben; oblique form of *beann* (f.n.), used as a fem. nom., for *beann* sounds masculine beside *ceann*, etc. See *beann*.

beinneal, binding of a sheaf of corn, bundle; from Sc. *bindle*, a cord of straw or other for binding, Eng. *bundle*; from *bind*.

beir, catch, bring forth, Ir. *beirim*, O. Ir. *berim*, W. *cymmeryd*, to take, accept, Br. *kemeret* (= *com-ber-*); I.E. *bher*, whence Lat. *fero*, Gr. φέρω, Eng. *bear*, Skr. *bharami*.

beirm, bairm (Hend.), barm, yeast; from Sc. *barm* (pronounced *berm*), Eng. *barm*; Lat. *fermentum*.

beisear, plate-rack on dresser (Rob.).

béist, a beast, Ir. *bíast*, *péist*, O. Ir. *béist*, W. *bwystfil*; from Lat. *bestia* (Eng. *beast*). Also **biast**.

beith, birch, so Ir., O. Ir. *bethe*, W. *bedw*, Br. *bezuenn*, Celtic *betvâ*, Lat. *betula*, Fr. *boule*.

beithir, a serpent, any wild beast, monster, a huge skate, Ir. *beithir*, wild beast, bear, E. Ir. *beithir*, g. *bethrach*. In the sense of "bear," the word is, doubtless, borrowed; but there seems a genuine Celtic word *betrix* behind the other meanings, and the *beithir* or *beithir béimneach* is famed in myth. Cf. Lat. *bēstia*, for *bet-tia?* Norse *bera*, bear (fem.), *beirfjall*, bearskin, Eng. *bear* (Zim. K.B.[1] 286).

beitir, neat, clean (M'F.):

beò, living, Ir., O. Ir. *beò*, W. *byw*, Br. *beu*, **bivo-s*; Lat. *vîvus*, living, *vîta*; Gr. βίοτος, a living; Eng. *quick*; Skr. *jîvá*, living, ; I. E. *gei-*, *gi-*, live. See also *beatha*, *bith*.

beòir, beer, Ir. *beór*; from Ag. S. *beór*, Norse *bjórr* (Eng. *beer*).

beòlach, ashes with hot embers (M'A.); from *beò* + *luathach*, "live-ashes." Another **beòlach**, lively youth, hero, stands for *beò-lach*; for *-lach*, see *òglach*.

beuban, anything mangled:

beuc, roar, Ir. *béic*, O. Ir. *béccim*, W. *beichio*, *baich*, **beikkiô*; Cor. *begy*, Br. *begiat*, squeal, *baeguel*, bleat, **baikiô* (Stokes). The difficulty of the vowels as between G. and W. (*é* should give *wy*) suggests comparison with *creuchd*, W. *craith*, **crempt-* (Strachan). Thus *beuc*, *baich* suggests *benk-ko-*, further *gn̥k-ko-*, root *gem*, Lat. *gemo*, etc. The same result can be derived from the root *geng-* of *geum*, q.v.

beud, mischief, hurt, Ir. *béad*, E. Ir. *bét*, **bento-n*; allied to Eng. *bane*

beul, mouth, so Ir., O. Ir. *bél*, **bet-lo-*, I. E. *get-*, whence Eng. *quoth*, Got. *qithan*. The idea is the "speaker." Some connect W. *gwefl* (= *vo-bel*), but this is probably **vo-byl*, *byl*, edge (Ernault).

beulaobh, front, E. Ir. *ar-bélaib*, O. Ir. *bélib*; dat. pl. of *beul*; also mixed with this is the O. Ir. acc. pl. *béulu*.

beum, a stroke, cut, taunt, Ir. and O. Ir. *béim*, nom. pl. *bémen*, blow, from the root *beng*, *bong*, which appears in *buain*; cf. *ceum* from *ceng-men*, *leum* from *leng-men*. This agrees with Cor. *bom*, blow. Some suggest *beid-men* or *beids-men*, root *bheid*, Eng. *bite*, which suits G. best as to meaning. The favourite derivation has been **ben-s-men*, root *ben* of *bean*.

beur, beurra, beurtha, sharp, pointed, clear; gibe, jeer (Hend.); cf. Ir. *béarrtha*, clipped, from *beàrr*; from *berr-tio-s*, with *i* regressive into *berr*, giving *beirr*.

beurla, English, language, Ir. *beurla*, speech, language, especially English; O. Ir. *bélre*; *bél+re*, *bél*, mouth, and the abstract termination *-re* (as in *luibhre*, *buidhre*, etc).

beus, conduct, habit, so Ir., O. Ir. *bés*, Br. *boaz*, **beissu-*, **beid-tu-*, root *beid*, I. E. *bheidh*, Gr. πειθω, persuade, Lat. *fides*, English *faith*. Others derive it from *bhend*, bind, giving *bhend-tu-* as the oldest stem. Windisch suggests connection with Got. *bansts*, barn, Skr. *bhâsa*, cowstall. The Breton *oa* seems against these derivations.

bha, bhà, was, Ir. *do bhámar*, we were (*bhá-*), *do bhí*, was, M. Ir. *ro bói*, was, O. Ir., *bói*, *bái*, *búi*, a perfect tense, **bove*(*t*), for *bebove*; Skr. *babhūva*; Gr. πέφυ-κε; I. E. root *bheu*, to be, as in Lat. *fui*, was (an aorist form), Eng. *be*.

bhàn, a bhàn, down; by eclipsis for *a*(*n*) *bh-fàn*, "into declivity," from *fàn*, a declivity, Ir., O. Ir., *fán*, proclive, W. *gwaen*, a plain, planities montana, **vag-no-*, root, *vag*, bow, etc., Lat. *vagor*, wander, Ger. *wackeln*, wobble. Ir. has also *fán*, a wandering, which comes near the Lat. sense. In Sutherlandshire, the adj. **fàn**, prone, is still used.

bheil, is, Ir. *fuil*, *bh-fuil*, O. Ir , *fail*, *fel*, *fil*, root *vel* (*val*), wish, prevail, Lat. *volo*, *valeo*, Eng. *will*.

bho, o, from Ir. *ó*, *ua*, O. Ir., *ó*, *úa*, **ava*; Lat. *au*-fero, "away"-take; Ch. Sl. *u-*; Skr. *ava*, from.

bhos, a bhos, on this side; from the eclipsed form *a*(*n*) *bh-fos*, "in station," in rest, Ir. *abhus*, O. Ir. *i foss*, here, O. Ir. *foss*, remaining, staying, rest. See *fois*, rest, for root.

bhur, bhur n-, your, Ir. *bhar n-*, O. Ir. *bar n-*, *far n-*, **svaron* (Stokes), **s-ves-ro-n*. For *sves-*, see *sibh*. Cf. for form Got. *izvara*, Lat. *nostrum* (nos-*tero-*, where *-tero-* is a fuller comparative form than Celtic -(*e*)*ro-*, *-ro-* of *sves-ro-n*, *svaron*).

bi, bì, be, Ir. *bí*, be thou, O. Ir. *bíu*, sum, *bí*, be thou, O. W. *bit*, sit, *bwyf*, sim, M. Br. *bezaff*. Proto-Celtic *bhv-ijô*, for O. Ir. *bíu*, I am; Lat. *fio*; Eng. *be*; I. E. root *bheu*, be. See *bha*. Stokes differs from other authorities in referring *bíu*, *bí*, to Celtic *beiô*, root *bei*, *bi*, live, as in *bith*, *beatha*, Lat. *vivo*, etc.

bi, bigh, doorpost, threshold (Hend.), E. Ir. *di bí* = two posts. M'A. has *bìgh*, post, pillar.

biadh, food, so Ir., O. Ir. *biad*, **bivoto-n*, whence W. *bywyd*, vita, Cor. *buit*, cibus, Br. *boed*, food. *Bivoto-n* is a derivative from *bivo-* of *beò*, living, q.v.

bian, a hide, Ir., E. Ir. *bían*, **beino-*; root *bhei-*, as in Eng. *bite*, Lat. *findo*. For force, cf. Gr. δέρμα, skin, from *der*, split, Eng. tear. Cf., for root, *bean*, hit.

biasgach, niggardly; from *biast*. In some parts *biast* is applied to a niggardly person. H.S.D. refers it to *biadh* + *sgathach*, catching at morsels.

biast, a beast, worthless person; see *béist*. The word **biast,** abuse, is a metaphoric use of *biast*.

biatach, a raven (Sh.); cf. *biatach*, *biadhtach*, a provider, farmer, from *biadh*.

biatas, betony, beet, Ir. *biatuis*, W. *betys*; from Lat. *bētis*, *bēta*, Eng. *beet*. Also **biotais.**

biathainne, earth-worm, hook-bait, **biathaidh** (Dialectic); from *biadh*. Cf. Lat. *esca*, bait, for *ed-sca*, *ed* = *eat*. The word **biathadh** in many places means "to entice."

biatsadh, provisions for a journey, *viaticum*; formed from *biadh*, with, possibly, a leaning on *viaticum*.

bicas, viscount (Arm.). Founded on the Eng., and badly spelt by Armstrong: either **biceas** or **biocas.**

bicein, a single grain (Arg.). From *bioc*, *pioc*? (Wh.)

biceir, a wooden dish; from Sc. *bicker*, Eng. *beaker*. Also **bigeir, bigein.**

bìd, a very small portion, a nip, a chirp. In the sense of "small portion," the word is from the Sc. *bite*, *bit*, Eng. *bite*, *bit*. In the sense of "chirp, a small sound," O'R. has an Ir. word *bíd*, "song of birds." See **bìog.** Hence **bìdein,** diminutive person or thing. Cf. W. *bidan*, of like force.

bìdeag, a bit, bittie; from Sc. *bittock*, dim. of Eng. *bit*.

bidean, a fence (Stew.), **bid** (Sh.), Ir. *bíd*, *bídeán* (O'R.), W. *bid*, quickset hedge, *bidan*, a twig; **bid-do-*, root, *bheid*, split?

bidhis, a vice, screw, so Ir.; from Eng. *vice*.

bidse, a bitch; from the English.

bìgh, bigh, pith of wood, gum. See **bìth.**

bil, bile, edge, lip, Ir. *bil*, mouth, E. Ir., *bil*, *bile*, W. *byl*, **bili-*, *bilio-*. Root *bhi*, *bhei*, split; cf. Skr. *bíla*, a hole, mouth of a vessel, etc.; *vil*, edge: W. also *myl*.

bileag, bile, a leaf, blade, Ir. *billeóg*, *bileóg*, **biliā*, I. E. root *bhela*, *bhale*, *bhlē*, *bhlō*, as in *blàth*; Lat. *folium*; Gr. φύλλον, a leaf; further, Eng. *blade*.

bilearach, bileanach, sea-grass, sweet-grass; from *bile.*
bileid, a billet; from the Eng.
bilistear, a mean, sorry fellow, a glutton, Ir., E. Ir. *bille,* mean, paltry. In the Heb. it means, "rancid butter" (H.S.D.).
binid, also **minid** (Arg.), cheese, rennet, bag that holds the rennet, stomach, Ir. *binid,* O. Ir. *binit,* rennet; **binenti-,* "biter" root of *bean?* Cf. *muinne,* stomach.
binn, melodious, so Ir., O. Ir. *bind,* **bendi,* **bydi-*; O. Br. *bann* (St.); Skr. *bhandate,* joyful, *bhand,* receive loud praise, *bhandána,* shouting (Stokes, who adds Lat. *fides,* lyre). The idea may, however, be "high," root of *beann,* peak, *binneach,* high-headed. See next also.
binn, sentence, verdict; **bendi-,* **benni-,*; cf. E. Ir. *atboind,* proclaims, **bonnô,* I ban. Cf. Skr. *bhan,* speak, Eng. *ban.* It is clear that Gaelic has an ablaut in *e* : *o* connected with the root *bha,* speak.
binndich, curdle; from *binid,* q.v.
binnein, pinnacle; from *beann,* q.v.
bìoball, pìoball, Bible, Ir. *biobla,* W. *bebil*; from Lat. *biblia,* Eng. *bible.*
biod, pointed top; root in *biodag, bidean.*
biodag, a dagger, Ir. *bideóg* (O'R.), *miodóg,* W. *bidog,* O. Br. *bitat,* resicaret, **biddo-, bid-do-,* Celtic root *bid, beid,* I. E. *bhid, bheid,* Lat. *findo,* Eng. *bite,* Skr. *bhid,* split. Hence Eng. *bodkin,* possibly.
biog, bìog, a start, Ir. *bíodhg,* E. Ir. *bedg,* O. Ir. *du-bidcet,* jaculantur, **bizgo-,* root *bis-, gis,* root *gi-* of *beò.* Consider **bìogail,** lively, *quick.*
bìog, biog, chirp; onomatopoetic; cf. Lat. *pipe,* chirp, Eng. *pipe*; also Eng. *cheep.* Also **bìd,** q.v.
bìogarra, churlish; "cheepish," from *bìog,* cheep.
biolagach, melodious (M'F.); from †**biol,** violin; from Eng. *viol,* Fr. *viole,* violin.
biolaire, water-cresses, Ir. *biolar,* E. Ir. *biror,* W. *berwr,* Cor., Br. *beler,* **beruro-,* Lat. *berula* (Marcellus), Fr. *berle,* Sp. *berro.* Possibly allied to the root of Celtic *bervô,* seethe, O. Ir. *tipra,* well, G. *tobar,* Eng. *burn.* Cf. Ger. *brunnen kresse,* water-cress, *i.e.,* "well" cress. The dictionaries and old glossaries (Cormac, etc.) give *bir, bior,* as water or well.
biolar, dainty, spruce (Sh.); for *bior-ar,* from *bior,* "sharp"?
biolasgach, prattling, so Ir. (Lh., O'B.); from *bil,* lip.
bionn, symmetrical (Carm.): Sc. *bien.*
bior, stake, spit, Ir. *bior,* O. Ir. *bir,* W. *bêr,* Cor., Br. *ber,* Celtic *beru-*; Lat. *veru*; Gr. *βαρύες,* trees (Hes.); Lit. *gìré,* forest. Hence **biorach,** sharp.

biorach, a heifer, colt, Ir. *biorach,* cow-calf:

bioras, water-lily; same origin as *biolar,* q.v.

biorg, gush, twitch, tingle; from the roots of *biolar* (*bior-*) and *bior.*

biorraid, a helmet, cap, Ir. *birread,* cap; from Eng. *biretta,* from Late Lat. *birretum.*

biorsadh, a keen impatience: "goading"; from *bior.*

biorsamaid, a balance; from Sc. *bismar,* Norse *bismari.*

bior-snaois, bowsprit of a sailing boat (N. Lochaber), forepart of vessel:

biota, a churn, vessel; from Norse *bytta,* a pail, tub, Ag. S. *bytt,* Latin *buttis,* Eng. *butt.*

biotailt, victuals, E. Ir. *bitáill,* W. *bitel,* M. Br. *bitaill*; from O. Fr. *vitaille,* from Lat. *victualia.* Eng. *victuals* is from the French.

birlinn, a galley, bark, M. Ir. *beirling*; formed from the Norse *byrðingr,* a ship of burthen, from *byrðr,* burden, vb. *bera,* Eng. *bear.* The Sc. *bierling, birlinn* is from the Gaelic. Cf. *feòirlig = fjórðungr.*

birtich, stir up; from *bior,* goad.

biseach, luck; see *piseach.*

bith, the world, existence, Ir., O. Ir. *bith,* W. *byd,* Br. *bed,* Gaul. *bitu-,* **bitu-s*; root *bi, bei,* live, I. E. *gei, gi,* whence Lat. *vivo,* Eng. *be,* etc. Hence *beatha, beò, biadh,* q.v.

bith, being (inf. of *bì,* be), Ir., E. Ir. *beith,* O. Ir. *buith.* The O. Ir. is from the root *bhu* (Eng. *be,* Lat. *fui*) = **buti-s,* Gr. *φύσις.* The forms *bith* and *beith,* if derived from *bhu,* have been influenced by *bith,* world, existence; but it is possible that they are of the same root *gi* as *bith.* Stokes, in his treatise on the *Neo-Celtic Verb Substantive,* takes *bith* and *beith* from the root *ga,* go, Gr. *βάσις* (Eng. *base*), a root to which he still refers the O. Ir. aorist *bá,* fui (see *bu*).

bìth, resin, gum, birdlime, Ir. *bigh,* O. Ir. *bí,* pix, adj. *bíde,* **geis-,* a longer form of *gis-,* the root of *giuthas,* fir (Schräder). Otherwise we must regard it as borrowed from Lat. *pix, picis,* whence W. *pyg,* Eng. *pitch,* against which *b* and *í* (*i* long) militate.

bìth, quiet (Arm.):

bith-, prefix denoting "ever-," Ir., O. Ir. *bith-,* W. *byth-*; from *bith,* world.

biùc, difficult utterance:

biùthaidh, foe, Ir. *bíodhbha,* E. Ir., O. Ir. *bidbe, bidbid* (gen.) culprit, enemy.

biùthas, fame, **biùthaidh,** hero; see *fiù, fiùbhaidh.*

blabaran, stammerer, Ir. *blabarán*; from the Eng. *blabber*, speak inarticulately. It is of onomatopoetic origin. Cf. Eng. *babble*.

bladair, a wide mouth, a flatterer, Ir. *bladaire*, flatterer; from the Eng. *blatterer*, bletherer, blusterer, *blatter*, prate; from Lat. *blaterare*, prate. Also **blad,** a wide mouth (M'F.).

bladh, fame, Ir. *bládh*, E. Ir. *blad*; root *blad-*, *blat-*, speak, as in Lat. *blatero*, babble, Norse *blaðr*, nonsense, Sc. *blether*. See *bladair*. Cf. *glaodh*, shout. Hence **bladhair,** expressive, a boaster.

bladhail, strong, from **bladh,** pith, W. *blawdd*, active; **blâd-*; root *blā-*, swell, bloom, as in *blàth*, q.v.

bladhm, a boast, etc.; see *blaomadh*.

blad-shronach, blad-spàgach, flat-nosed, flat-footed; *blad-* is from Eng. *flat*.

blaisbheum, blasphemy; from Lat. *blasphemia*, Eng. *blasphemy*.

blanndaidh, rotten, stale; from Norse *blanda*, whey "blend."

blanndar, flattery, dissimulation, so Ir.; from Lat. *blandiri*, Sc. *blander*, Eng. *blandish*.

†**blaodh,** a shout, noise, Ir. *blaodh*, M. Ir. *blaeded*, W. *bloedd*. Hence **blaodhag,** noisy girl, **blaoghan,** calf's cry, etc.

blaomadh, loud talking, Ir. *blaodhmanach*, noisy person; from **blaid-s-men*; see *blaodh*.

†**blaosg,** a shell, Ir. *blaosc*, M. Ir. *blaesc*, testa, W. *blisg*; see *plaosg*.

blàr, a field, battle, peat-moss; from *blàr*, spotted, the idea being a "spot." See next word.

blàr, having a white face, or white spot on the face (of an animal); **blā-ro-s*, root *blā-*, from I. E. *bhale*, shine, *bhā*; Gr. *φαλαρός* (second *α* long), having a white patch (on the head, as on a dog's head). Cf. Dutch *blaar*, a white spot on the forehead (whence Fr. *blaireau*, badger), M. Dutch, *blaer*, bald. See for roots *bealltuinn*, *bàn*. Welsh has *blawr*, grey, iron-grey, which seems allied. This word enters largely into Pictish topography. It is not so used in Argyle (M'K.) nor in Ireland.

blas, taste, Ir. *blas*, O. Ir. *mlas*, W. *blâs*, Br. *blas*, **mlasto-*; Czech *mlsati*, lick, be sweet-toothed, Russ. *molsatĭ*, suck (Bezzenberger). Ultimately the root seems to be *mel*, as in *meli-*, honey, G. *mil*, and even *meil*, grind. Hence Fr. *blasé*?

blas-bheumnaich, blaspheme (Hend.). See **blaisbheum.**

blàth, bloom, blossom, Ir., E. Ir. *bláth*, W. *blawd*, *blodau*, Cor. *blodon*, M. Br. *bleuzenn*, **blâto-n*; I. E. root *bhela*: *bhlo*, blossom forth; Lat. *flōs*, flower; Eng. *bloom*, etc.

blàth, warm, kind, Ir., E. Ir. *bláith*, soft, smooth, *mláith*, **mlâti-*; root *mela*, *mlâ*, to grind. The original idea is "ground soft." Cf. W. *blawd*, meal.

blàthach, buttermilk, Ir., M. Ir. *bláthach* ; *mlā-tac-*, root *mel*, *mlâ*, as in *blàth*. The idea is "pounded, soured." Cf. *braich*, from *mrac-*, "soured," and Eng. *malt*, "soured," from *melt*. Hence Sc. *bladach*.

bleachdair, a soothing, flattering fellow, Ir. *bleachdaire*, flatterer, cow-milker; a metaphoric use of the last word, "cow-milker," from *bliochd*, milk, q.v.

bleagh, milk (vb.), Ir. *blighim* ; see *bleoghainn*.

bleaghan, a dibble for digging up shell-fish, a worthless tool; possibly from Norse *blað*, Eng. *blade*.

bleid, impertinence, solicitation, Ir. *bleid*, cajolery, impertinence. This seems another word formed on the word *bladair*, *blad*, just like Eng. *blatant*, *blate* (talk, prate).

bleideir, coward; from Norse *bleyði*, cowardice, and Sc. *blate* (?).

bleith, grind, Ir. *bleithim*, E. Ir. *bleith*, inf. to O. Ir. *melim*, I grind, W. *malu*, Br. *malaff* ; root *mel*, grind, Lat. *molo*, Eng. *meal*, etc.

bleoghainn, milking, E. Ir. *blegon*, inf. to *bligim*, *mligim* ; Lat. *mulgeo* ; Gr. *ἀ-μέλγω* ; Eng. *milk* ; Lit. *mélžu*.

bliadhna, year, Ir. *bliadhain*, O. Ir. *bliadain*, W. *blydd*, *blwyddyn*, Br. *bloaz*, *blizen*, **bleidni-*, **bleido-* ; I. E. *ghleidh*, whence Eng. *glide* : "labuntur anni" (Stokes). It is doubtful if I. E. *gh* becomes Celtic *b*.

blialum, jargon; from the Sc. *blellum*.

blian, the flank, groin, Ir. *bléin*, E. Ir. *blén*, O. Ir. *melen*, for *mleen*, **mlakno-* ; Gr. *μαλακός*, soft (Strachan, Stokes). The meaning, if not the phonetics, is not quite satisfactory.

blian, lean, insipid, **blianach**, lean flesh; cf. W. *blin*, tired, O. Br. *blinion*, inertes. These may be referred to **gleghno-*, Lit. *gležnus*, tender, weak, Gr. *βληχρός*, languid. See, however, the derivation suggested for *blian*, above. For the Brittonic words, Stokes has suggested the stem *blêno-* ; Skr. *glána*, tired.

bligh, milk; see *bleagh*.

bliochan, yellow marsh, asphodel, Ir. *bliochan* ; from **blioch* = **melgos-*, milk. For phonetics, cf. *teach*, from *tegos-*.

bliochd, milk, Ir. *bleachd*, E. Ir. *blicht*, W. *blith*, **mḷctu-*, root *melg*, milk. See *bleoghainn*.

blìonadh, basking (Islands): "softening"? See *blian*.

bliosan, artichoke (Sh., O'B., O'R.), Ir. *bliosán* : **blig-s-ān-*, "milk curdler?" Its florets were used for curdling.

blob, blubber-lipped (Sh.); from Eng. *blub*, puffed, protruding, *blubber*, etc.

blocan, a little block, **blog,** block (Dialectic), Ir. *bloc*, *blocán*; from Eng. *block*.

bloigh, fragment, half, Ir. *blogh*, *blógh*, fragment, E. Ir. *blog*, pre-Celtic *bhlog*; Eng. *block*, further away Eng. *balk*, Gr. *φάλαγξ*. Stokes refers it to the root of Eng. *pluck*. (St. now Eng. *plough*, Ger. *pflug*).

bloin'gein, any plant with crisped leaves, Ir. *bloinigain* (O'R.); G. and Ir. **bloinigean gàrraidh** is "spinage." Cameron refers the word to *blonag*, fat,

blomas, ostentation (Sh.). Ir. *blomas*; see *bladhm*. Ir. *blamaire*, means "boaster."

blonag, fat, Ir. *blonóg*, *blainic*, *blunag*, M. Ir. *blonac*, W. *bloneg*, Br. *blonek*, **blon-*, **blen-*, root, *bhle*, *bhel*, swell; a very prolific root. Rhys says W. is borrowed. [R.C.[17] 102.]

† **blosg,** sound a horn, Ir. *blosgaidhim*, resound, sound a horn, M. Ir. *blosc*, voice; W. *bloedd*, a shout, from **blogðo-*, for *bloðgo-*; cf. *mèag*, W. *maidd*. [Zeit[34] 502.] Cf. Gr. *φλοῖσβος*, din (= *φλοσ-γος*), Lit. *blázgu*, roar.

bó, a cow, Ir., O. Ir. *bó*, W. *buw*, O. Br. *bou-*, **bov-s*; I. E. *gôus*, whence Lat. *bos*, Gr. *βοῦς*, Eng. *cow*, Skr. *go*.

boban, bobug, a term of affection for a boy; cf. M. Ir. *boban*, calf, *bóban*, from *bó*. Eng. *babe*, earlier, *baban*, of uncertain origin, may be compared.

boban, a bobbin; from the Eng. *bobbin*.

bobhstair, bolster; from Sc. *bowster*, Eng. *bolster*.

boc, a buck, Ir. *boc*, he-goat, O. Ir. *bocc*, W. *bwch*, Cor. *boch*, Br. *bouc'h* **bukko-s*; Skr. *bukka*, goat. These may be analysed into *bug-ko-*, root *bug*, Zend. *bûza*, buck, Arm. *buc*, lamb, Eng. *buck*, Ger. *bock*.

bòc, swell, Ir. *bócaim*; cf. W. *boch*, cheek, from Lat. *bucca*, puffed cheek (Eng. *debouch*, *rebuke*).

bòcan, hobgoblin, Ir. *bocán*, E. Ir. *boccánach*. With these are connected W. *bwg* (*bwci*, Cor. *bucca*, borrowed from M. E. ?), Eng. *bug*, *bugbear*, *bogie*; the relationship is not clear (Murray). For Gadelic a stem *bukko-*, from *bug-ko-*, would do, allied possibly to Norse *púki*, a Puck, Ag. S. *puca*, larbula. *boc-sithe*, apparition, ghost (Perth : Wh.).

bochail, proud, nimble; cf. the interjection †**boch,** Ir. *boch*, heyday! "O festum diem."

bochuin, swelling, the sea (Carm.), *boch-thonn* (H.S.D.):

bochd, poor, so Ir., O. Ir. *bocht*; **bog-to-*, a participle from the vb. (Irish) *bongaim*, break, reap, Celtic *bongô*, break; Skr. *bhanj*, break, Lit. *banga*, breaker (wave). See *buain*.

bocsa, a box, so Ir., pronounced in Ir. *bosca* also, W. *bocys*; from Eng. *box*. Hence **bocsaid,** a thump, Eng. *box*.

bodach, an old man, a carle, Ir. *bodach*, a rustic, carle; **bodd-aco-*, "pēnitus," from **bod,** mentula, M. G. *bod* (D. of Lismore passim), M. Ir. *bod, bot*, **boddo-*, **bozdo-*; Gr. *πόσθη*, mentula. Stokes suggests the alternative form *butto-s*, Gr. *βύττος*, vulva, but the G. *d* is against this. He also suggests that *bodach* is formed on the O. Fr. *botte*, a clod.

bodha, a rock over which waves break; from Norse *boði*, a breaker, over sunken rocks especially.

bòdhag, a sea-lark:

bodhaig, body, corpus; from the Sc. *bouk*, body, trunk, Norse *búkr*, trunk, Ger. *bauch*, belly. The G. word has been compared by Fick with Eng. *body*, Ag. S. *bodig*, and Murray says it is thence derived, but the *d* would scarcely disappear and leave the soft *g* ending now so hard.

bòdhan, ham, breech, breast: **boud-āno*, **boud*, *bhud-*; cf. Eng. *butt, buttock*.

bodhar, deaf, so Ir., O. Ir., *bodar*, W. *byddar*, Cor. *bodhar*, Br. *bouzar*; Skr. *badhirá*.

bodhbh, bobh, a fright (Perthshire), E. Ir. *bodba*, dangerous, **bodv-io-s*; from *bodvo-* in *baobh*, q.v.

bodht, swampy ground:

bog, soft, Ir. *bog*, O. Ir. *bocc*, Br. *bouk*, O. Br. *buc*, putris; **buggo-*, **bug-go-*; I. E. *bhug*, bend, Skr. *bhugna*, bent, Got. *biugan*, Eng. *bow*, from Ag. S. *boga*.

bogha, a bow, so Ir., M. Ir. *boga*; from Ag. S. *boga*, Eng. *bow*. For root, see under *bog*.

bògus, a timber moth, bug; from Eng. *bug*, Sc. *bōg*.

boicineach, small-pox; root in *bucaid*, q.v.

boicionn, a goat skin, skin; **boc-cionn*, "buck-skin"; the word **†cionn** is in O. Ir. *cenni*, scamae, W. *cen*, skin, Cor. *cennen*, Br. *kenn-*, pellis; Eng. *skinn*, Norse *skinn*. *-cionn*, skin, Norse *hinna*, film (Leiden) I.F. 5A 127.

bóid, vow, Ir. *móid*, M. Ir. *móit*, **monti-*, root *mon, men*, think. A borrowing from, or leaning on, Lat. *vōtum* seems possible in view of the Gaelic form. M. Ir. *in uóit*; from Lat. *vôtum*, as is also *móid* (Stokes).

bòidheach, pretty; for *buaidheach*, "having virtues," from *buaidh*, q.v.

bòidheam, flattery (H.S.D.):

bòigear, puffin, ducker; also *budhaigir*, q.v.

boil, boile, madness, Ir. *buile*, E. Ir. *baile* :

bòilich, tall talk, boasting ; cf. Eng. *bawl*, cry like cows (*bó*).

boillsg, gleam ; **bolg-s-cio-* ; Lat. *fulgeo*, shine, Eng. *effulgent*, Lit. *blizgù*, glance, shine, Eng. *blink*, I.E. *bhleg*, **fulgeo*.

boineid, a bonnet, Ir. *boineud* ; from Eng. *bonnet*.

boinne, a drop, Ir. *bain* (d. pl. *bainnibh*), O. Ir. *banne*, Cor., Br. *banne* ; Celt. *bannjâ* (Stokes). See *bainne*. Hence **boinneanta,** healthy, well-built.

boirche, a buffalo (Sh., Lh.), so Ir. ; perhaps allied to Lat. *ferus*, Eng. *bear*.

boireal, a small auger (M'F.) ; founded on Eng. *bore*.

boiriche, rising ground, bank (M'D.) ; same root as Ger. *berg*, mountain, Eng. ice-*berg*.

boirionn, female, feminine, Ir. *bainionn*, *boinionn* ; **bani-*, from the word *bean*, *ban*, q.v. Hence **biorionnach,** a female, which is masc. in gender, having been originally neuter. Cf. *doirionn* for *doinionn* (Arg.).

bois, the palm ; see *bas*.

boiseag, slap in the face, palmful, Ir., M. Ir. *boiseóg*, buffet.

boiseid, a belt, budget ; from the English.

boisg, gleam ; see *boillsg*.

boiteadh, boiled food for horses (H.S.D.), Eng. *bait* :

boiteag, a maggot ; see *botus*.

boitean, a bundle of hay or straw ; for *boiteal*, from Sc. *buttle*, Eng. *bottle*, bundle of hay, from O. Fr. *botte*.

boitidh, the call to a pig, **boit,** a taste for (Dialectic) :

bòl, a bowl ; from the English.

boladh, smell, so Ir., O. Ir. *bolad*, **bulato-* ; Lit. *bu'ls*, dusty air (Bezzenberger). Stokes has compared Lit. *bulis*, buttock, Skr. *buli*, vulva.

bolanta, excellent ; root *bol*, as in *adhbhal*, q.v.

bolla, a boll ; from Sc., Eng. *boll*. Hence also **bolla,** a buoy.

bolt, a welt, Ir. *balta*, welt, border ; from the Lat. *balteus*, girdle, Eng. *belt*. Cf. Eng. *welt*, W. *gwald*.

boma, a bomb ; from the English.

bonn, foundation, so Ir., O. Ir. *bond* ; Lat. *fundus* ; Skr. *budhná* ; Eng. *bottom*.

bonn, a coin, so Ir. ; possibly from Lat. *pondo*.

bonnach, cake, bannock, Ir. *boinneóg*, oaten cake. This word, like the Sc. *bannock*, appears to be founded on Lat. *pānicum*, *pānis*, bread.

bonnanach, a strapping fellow (Mrs M'Ph.), *bonnanaich*, active young men (Skye) :

borb, fierce, so Ir., O. Ir. *borp* ; allied to, or, more probably, borrowed from, Lat. *barbarus*.

borbhan, a purling sound; **borvo-*, a stem identical with *bervo-*, seethe, Fr. *Bourbon,* Lat. *ferveo,* etc. Hence **borbhanach,** base, deep.

bòrc, sprout, swell; see *bàrc.*

bòrc-lunn, swell-wave (Hend.):

bòrd, a table, Ir., M. Ir., *bord,* W. *bwrdd;* from Ag. S., Norse *bord.*

bòrlanachd, mòrlanachd, compulsory labour for the proprietor; from Eng. *bordland,* as under *bòrlum.* Hence M'Morland. The *cairiste,* done for proprietor (M'K. and Carm.).

bòrlum, a strip of arable land (Hebrides); a frequent place name; from M. Eng. *bordland,* mensal land, especially the royal castle lands in the Highlands.

bòrlum, a sudden flux or vomiting, a flux; for *bòrc-lum;* see *bòrc.*

†**borr,** knob, pride, greatness, great, Ir., E. Ir. *borr,* **borso-*, *bhorso-;* Lat. *fastus* (for *farstus*), pride; O. H. G. *parrunga,* superbia; allied to *bàrr,* q.v. Hence **borrach,** a haughty man, a protruding bank, a mountain grass.

bòsd, a boast, Ir. *bósd* (O'R.), W., Cor. *bost;* all from Eng. *boast,* itself of unknown origin.

bòsdan, a little box, Br. *bouist;* the G. is from early Sc. *boyst,* M. Eng. *boiste,* from O. Fr. *boiste,* Med. Lat. *buxida* (*bossida*), which is the Gr. *πύξιδα.* Heuce also Eng. *box,* G. *bosca.*

bosgaire, applause (Sh.); *bas+gaire,* q.v., "palm-noise."

bot, a mound, river bank; cf. *bught, botach,* a reedy bog.

bòt, a boot; from M. E. *bote,* Eng. *boot.* Also **bòtuinn,** from Sc. *booting,* Fr. *bottine,* half-boot.

botaidh, a wooden vessel (size, half anker); formed from M. E. *butte,* Eng. *butt,* Fr, *botte.*

both, perturbation, a plash; see *bodhbh.*

both, bothan, a hut, bothie, Ir., M. Ir. *bothán, both,* W. *bod,* residence, Cor. *bod, bos,* **buto-;* Lit. *bùtas,* house; Eng. *booth,* Norse *búð,* Ger. *bude;* root *bhu,* be. Hence Eng. *bothie.*

bothar, a lane, street (A. M'D.), Ir. *bothar* (Con.), *bóthar,* E. Ir. *bóthar,* **bâtro-*, **bâ-tro-*, root *bā,* go; Gr. *ἔ-βην,* went, *βαίνω,* go; Skr. *gâ,* go; Eng. *path.*

botrumaid, a slattern, (M'F.); see *butrais.*

botul, a bottle, Ir. *buideul,* W. *potel;* from Eng. *bottle.*

botunn (Lewis), deep water pool (in moors); Norse, *botn.*

botus, a belly-worm; from M. E. *bottes,* pl. of *bot, bott,* of like meaning; Sc. *batts.* Origin unknown (Murray).

brà, bràth, a quern, Ir. *bró,* g. *brón,* E. Ir. *bró,* g. *broon,* mill-stone, **brevɔn-*, **bravon-;* Skr. *grâvan-;* Lit. *gìrnos;* Eng. *quern.*

brabhd-chasach, bow-legged:

brabhdadh, bravado, idle talk, **brabhtalachd,** haughtiness (A. M'D); from Eng. *bravado*?

bràc, curve as of waves before breaking, a bellow, branch or deer-horn (Carm.), reindeer (Carm.):

bracach, grayish, **braclach,** brake: see words in *broc-ach, -lach.*

brachag, a pustule; from **brach,** rot (vb.); see *braich,* malt. Also **brachan,** putrefaction.

bràchd, putrescence, fat, rich:

bradach, thievish, **braid,** theft, Ir. *bradach,* thievish, roguish, E. Ir. *broit,* g. *braite*: **mraddo-,* allied to *brath,* betray? Scarcely from *bṛ-ont-,* root *bher,* carry, Lat. *fur,* etc.

bradan, salmon, Ir. *bradán,* E. Ir. *bratan.* Cf. Lit. *bradà,* water, Ch. Sl. *brożdą,* wade through.

bradan, a ridgy tumour on the surface of the body (H.S.D.); metaphorically from above word?

bradhadair, a blazing fire, kindling of a fire (Hebrides). Possibly *braghadair,* from *bragh,* q.v. Cf. **braghadaich,** crackling.

brag (Lewis), a sudden creeking noise, Norse *brak.*

bragaireachd, vain boasting, Ir. *bragáireachd,* from *bragaire,* boaster; from the Eng. *brag.*

bragh, an explosion, peal, O. Ir. *braigim,* pedo; Lat. *fragor,* crash, *fragrare,* Eng. *fragrant.* See *bram.*

bràghad, neck, throat, Ir. *bráighid,* O. Ir. *bráge,* g. *brágat,* W. *breuant,* O. Br. *brehant,* **brâgṇt-*; Eng. *craw,* Ger. *kragen,* collar, M. H. G. *krage,* neck; Gr. *βρόγχος,* windpipe, Eng. *bronchitis.* Bezzenberger (Stokes' Dict.), refers it to the root of Norse *barki,* weazand, Gr. *φάρυγξ,* Eng. *pharynx. Bràghad* is really the gen. of *bràighe.*

bragsaidh, braxy; from Sc., Eng. *braxy.*

braich, malt, so Ir., E. Ir. *mraich,* W., Cor. *brag,* Br. *bragezi,* germinate, Gaul. *brace* (Plin.), genus farris: **mraki*; Lit. *mèrkti,* macerate, *márka,* flax-hole for steeping; Lat. *marcere,* fade, *marcidus,* decayed, rotten. From W. *bragod,* comes Eng. *brugget.*

braid, theft; see *bradach.*

bràid, horse-collar; see *bràighdeach.*

bràighde, captives, pledges, Ir. *bráighe,* pl. *bráighde,* E. Ir. *braga,* g. *bragat,* hostage, prisoner, *braig,* a chain; Gr. *βρόχος,* noose; Eng. *crank,* Ger. *kringel*; I. E. *gregh,* possibly allied to I. E. *grēgh,* neck, as in *bràghad.* Hence **braighdeanas,** captivity, also dialectic **braigh,** hostage, pledge.

bràighdeach, horse-collar, M. Ir. *braigdech,* older *bráigtech*; from *bràghad.* Also **bràid.**

bràighe, upper part (of places): this is the nom. case of *bràghad,* which also appears in place names, as *Bra'id-Albainn,* Braidalbane.

braile, a heavy rain (Sh.):

braile, braighlich, a rattling noise (Perth). Sc. *bruilze,* Fr. *brouille.* See **braodhlach.**

brailis, wort of ale, Ir. *braithlis,* M. Ir. *braichlis,* from *braich.*

braim, bram, crepitus ventris, Ir. *broim,* O. Ir. *braigim,* pedo, W., Cor., Br. *bram,* **bragsmen*, root *brag,* I. E. *bhrag*; Lat. *fragor,* crash, *fragrare,* etc. Hence **bramaire,** a noisy fellow.

braisleach, full-formed, bulky man, M. Ir. *bras,* great, W. Cor., Br. *bras,* grossus, **brasso-*; Lat. *grossus,* Fr. *gros,* bulky.

bràist, a brooch; from the Eng.

braithlin, linen sheet, so Ir.: **brath+lìn*; but *brath*? M'E. suggests *plài-linn.*

braman, misadventure, the Devil; also dialectic **broman.** M. Ir. *bromán* means a "boor," *brománach,* impertinent. The root seems to be *breg, brog, brag* of *breun, braim.*

bramasag, a clott-burr, the prickly head of a thistle (H.S.D.):

† **bran,** a raven, Ir., O. Ir. *bran,* W. *brân,* crow, Br. *bran,* crow; **branâ,* for *gvranâ,* with which cf. O. Slav. *gavranŭ,* raven, but not *vrana* (do.), as is usually done. The further root is *gra, gera,* cry, whence Eng. *crane,* Gr. γέρανος, crane, W. and Cor. *garan.* Used much in personal and river names.

bran, bran, Ir., W. *bran,* Br. *brenn*; G., Ir., and W. are from Eng. *bran,* from O. Fr. *bren, bran,* whence Br.

brang, a slip of wood in the head-stall of a horse's halter, resting on the jaw; horse's collar; **brangas,** a pillory; from the Sc. *branks,* a head pillory (for tongue and mouth), a bridle with two wooden side pieces, *brank,* to bridle; allied to Ger. *pranger,* pillory, Du. *prang,* fetter.

branndaidh, brandy; from Eng. *brandy,* that is "brand or burnt wine."

branndair, a gridiron; from Sc. *brander,* from *brand, burn,* etc.

braodag, a huff (Hend), also (Perth):

braodhlach, brawling, **braoileadh,** loud noise, Ir. *braóilleadh,* rattling; a borrowed word, seemingly from Sc., Eng. *brawl,* confused with Sc. *brulye,* Eng. *broil.*

braoileag, a whortleberry, Ir. *broileóg, breileóg.* Sc. *brawlins, brylocks,* comes from the Gaelic.

braoisg, a grin, Ir. *braos*:

braolaid, raving, dreaming; from *breathal*?

braon, a drop, rain, so Ir., O. Ir. *broen*; cf. Eng. *brine.* The attempt to connect it with Gr. βρέχω, or with Lat. *rigare,*

Eng. *rain*, is unsatisfactory. Stokes derives it from root *ver* (see *fearthuinn*), **vroen*, but unlikely.

braonan, praonan, an earth-nut, bunium flexuosum. Perhaps from *braon*, a drop—"a bead, nut."

bras, brais, active, rash, Ir. *bras*, E. Ir. *bras*, W. *brys*, haste: **bṛsto-*, I.E. *gredh-*, as in *greas*, q.v.? See also *brisg*, active.

brasailt, a panegyric (M'A.); E. Ir. *bras-scélach*, panegyrical; from O. Ir. *bras*, great, W. and Br. *bras*; cf. Lat. *grossus*, Eng. *gross*. See *braisleach*.

brat, a mantle, Ir. *brat*, O. Ir. *bratt*, W. *brethyn*, woollen cloth, Br. *broz*, petticoat, **bratto-*, **brat-to-*. For root *brat*, *brant*, see *bréid*. Ag. S. *bratt*, pallium, is borrowed from the Celtic. Hence **bratach,** flag.

bratag, the furry or grass caterpillar, Ir. *bratóg*, "the mantled one," from *brat*. Cf. *caterpillar* = "downy cat," by derivation.

brath, information, betrayal, Ir. *brath*, E. Ir. *brath*, treason, and *mrath* also, W. *brad*, treachery, Cor. *bras*, Br. *barat*, O. Br. *brat*, **mrato-*; Gr. ἁμαρτάνω (-μαρτ-), sin, miss, ἤμβροτον (past tense). Cf. *mearachd*. M. Ir. *mairned*, treachery.

bràth, judgment, **gu bràth,** for ever (pron. *gu bràch*) "till Judgment," so Ir., O. Ir. *bráth*, judgment, W. *brawd*, M. Br. *breut*, Gaul. *bratu-*, **brâtu-*; **brâ*, **bera*, judge, decide, from I. E. *bher*, in the sense of "say," as in *abair*. The Ir. *barn*, judge, and W. *barn*, judgment, are hence, and may be compared to Gr. φρήν, φρένες, soul, *phrenology*. Hence also **breath**, or **breith** (**bṛt-*), q.v. The sense "conflagration" given in the Dict. is due to "Druidic" theorisings, and is imaginary.

bràthair, brother, Ir. *bráthair*, O. Ir. *bráthir*, W. *brawd*, pl. *brodyr*, Cor. *broder*, pl. *bredereth*, Br. *breur*, *breuzr*, pl. *breudeur*, **brâtêr*; Lat. *frâter*; Eng. *brother*; Skr. *bhrâta*; etc.

breab, a kick, Ir. *preab*, M. Ir. *prebach*, kicking; perhaps from the root form of the following word.

breaban, a patch of leather, Ir *preabán*, parcel, piece, patch; from, or allied to, O. Fr. *bribe*, a piece of bread, alms, Sp. *briba*, alms; also O. Fr. *bribeur*, mendicant, *briberesse*, female vagabondage and harloting; cf. Ir. *preabóg*, a wenching jade (O'B.). Eng. *bribe* is from the French.

breac, speckled, so Ir., E. Ir. *brecc*, W. *brych*, Br. *brec'h*, small-pox, **mṛkko-s*, **mṛg-ko-*, root *mṛg*; Lit. *márgas*, speckled, pied; Gr. ἀμαρύσσω, twinkle. There is an O. Ir. *mrecht*, W. *brith*, of like meaning and origin, viz, *mṛk-to*, from *mṛg-to-*. Hence **breac,** small-pox, W. *brech*, and **breac,** trout, W. *brithyll*.

breacan, plaid, Ir. *breacán*, W. *brecan*, rug; from *breac*. Rhys regards W. as borrowed from Irish.

breac-shianain, freckles:

breacag, a pancake, W. *brechdan*, slice of bread and butter, *bṛg-ko-*, *bṛg*, as in *bairghin*, bread? (Rev. Celt. [17]102). See *breachdan*.

breachd, seizing = *beireachd*.

breachdan, custard (Lh.), M. Ir. *brechtán*, a roll, W. *brithog*; from *mṛg-to-*, Ir. *brecht*, W. *brith*, motley, mixed. See under *breac*.

brèagh, fine, Ir. *breágh*, M. Ir. *breagha* (O'Cl.), **breigavo-s*, root *breig*, *brîg* as in *brìgh*, q.v.? Ir. *breagh* or *breaghda* = *Bregian*, Tir Breg. (Ir. J. No. 119).

† **breall,** knob, glens mentulæ, D. of Lismore *breyl*, Ir. *breall*, *bṛs-lo-*, root *bers*, *bors*, as in G. *borr*, *bàrr*, Eng. *bristle*. Hence *brilleanach*, lewd, q.v. *breall* = *bod* (Glenmoriston).

breaman, tail of sheep or goat, podex; cf. Ir. *breim*, by-form of *braim*, q.v.

breamas, mischief, mishap, the Devil; an *e* vowel form of *braman?*

breanan, dunghill (Sh.); from *breun*, q.v.

breath, row, layer: **bṛtâ*, a slice, root *bher* of *beàrn*.

breath, judgment, so Ir., O. Ir. *breth*, **bṛtâ*, W. *bryd*, Gaul. vergo-*bretus*, **bṛto-s*. For root, see *bràth*. Spelt also **breith.**

breathas, frenzy (M'A.); see *breisleach*.

bréid, a kerchief, so Ir., E. Ir. *bréit*, **brenti-*, roots *brent*, *brat*; Skr. *granth*, tie, knot, *grathnâti*; Ger. *kranz*, garland, Eng. *crants* (Rhys). The Skr. being allied to Gr. *γρόνθος*, fist, seems against this derivation (Stokes), not to mention the difficulty of Gr. *θ* and Skr. *th* corresponding to Celtic *t*. Possibly from root *bhera*, cut, Gr. *φᾶρος*, cloth (Windisch). Cf. W. *brwyd*, braid.

breisleach, confusion, delirium, nightmare, Ir. *breisleach* (O'R., Fol.), *breaghaslach* (Lh.) from *breith-*, **bret*, **bhre-t*; *bhre*, mind, as in Gr. *φρήν*, mind? Cf. E. Ir. *Breslech* Mór Murtheimme; *·brislech*, "overthrow."

breith, bearing, birth, so Ir. and E. Ir., **bṛtí-s*; Skr. *bhṛti-*; Eng. *birth*; etc.: root *bher*, bear; see *beir*.

breitheal, confusion of mind; from *breith-*, as in *breisleach*. Also **breathal** and **preathal.**

breitheanas, judgment, Ir. *breitheamhnus*, E. Ir. *brithemnas*; from *brithem*, a judge, stem *britheman*, to which is added the abstract termination *-as* (= *astu-*). From *britheamh*, q.v

breo, breoth, rot, putrefy:

breochaid, any tender or fragile thing (M'A.); from *breo*.

breòcladh, clumsy patching, **breòclaid,** sickly person: *breódh* + *clad* (= *cail* of buach*ail*). See *breóite*.

breòite, infirm, Ir. *breóite*, *breódhaim*, I enfeeble (Keat.), **brivod-*; cf. W. *briw*, break, **brîvo-*, possibly allied to Lat. *frivolus*.

breolaid, dotage, delirium; cf. *breitheal*, etc.

breug, briag, a lie, Ir. *breug*, *bréag*, O. Ir. *brée*, **brenkâ*; Skr. *bhramça*, loss, deviation.

breun, putrid, so Ir., E. Ir. *brén*, W. *braen*, Br. *brein*; **bregno-*, **bragno-*, foul, from root, *breg*, *brag* of *braim*. Strachan takes it from **mrak-no-*; Lat. *marcidus*, rancid, as in *braich*, q.v.

briagail, prattling:

briathar, a word, so Ir. and O. Ir., **brêtrâ* (O. Ir. is fem.; G. is mas., by analogy?), **brê*, ablaut to *brâ-* of *bràth*, q.v. Bezzenberger would refer it to O.H.G. *chweran*, sigh (see *gerain*) and even to O. H. G. *chrâjan*, Eng. *crow*.

brìb, a bribe, Ir. *bríb*; from the Eng.

bricein-, a prefix to certain animal names; from *brcac*.

†**brìdeach,** a dwarf (Arm., Sh.), Ir. *brideach* (Lh., O'B.). See *brìdeag*, little woman. Shaw also gives it the meaning of "bride," which is due to Eng. influences.

brìdeag, a little woman, Ir. *brídeag*, a figure of St. Bridget made on the Saint's eve by maidens for divination purposes. See *Brighid* in the list of Proper Names. Shaw gives **bridag,** part of the jaw, which H.S.D. reproduces as **brìdeag.**

brìdeun, a little bird, sea-piet (M'A. for latter meaning): seemingly formed on the analogy of the two foregoing words.

brìg, a heap (H.S.D , M'A.): "brìg mhòine," a pile of peats; cf. Norse *brík*, square tablet, piece, Eng. *brick*.

brìgh, pith, power, Ir. *brígh*, O. Ir. *bríg*, W. *bri*, dignity, rank, Cor. *bry*, Br. *bri*, respect, **brîgâ*, **brîgo-*; Gr. βρῖ = βριαρός, strong, mighty, βρίμη (ι long), strength, anger; Skr. *jri*, overpower, *jrayas*, extent; an I.E. *gri-*, *grī-*, *grei-*. Bezzenberger suggests Ger. *krieg*, war, striving: **greigh?* This may be from the root *brî* above.

brilleanach, lewd, **briollair, briollan,** from *breall*, q.v.

brìm, pickle (Arg.); from Eng. *brine*.

brimin bodaich, a shabby carle; for *breimein*, a side form of *braman*; root *breg*, *brag?* But cf. Norse *brimill*, phoca fetida mas.

brìobadh, bribing; see *bríb*, which also has the spelling **brìob.**

brìodal, lovers' language, caressing, flattery; also **brionndal,** caressing, **brionnal,** flattery; possibly from *brionn*, a lie, dream (Ir.), as in *brionglaid*, q.v. M. Ir. *brinneall* means a beautiful young maid or a matron. Cf. *briagadh*. Arran *brìd*, whisper.

briog, thrust, Ir. *priocam*; from the Eng. *prick*.

briogach, mean-spirited:

brìoghas, fervour of passion; cf. W. *brywus*, *bryw*, vigorous.

briogais, breeches, Ir. *brigis*; from the Eng. *breeks*, *breeches*.

briollag, an illusion (Sh.); Ir. *brionn*, dream, reverie. The G. seems for *brion-lag*. See next.

brionglaid, a confusion, dream, Ir. *brionnglóid*, a dream; from *brionn*, a dream, a lie. In the sense of "wrangling," *brionglaid* is purely a Scotch Gaelic word, from Sc., Eng. *brangle*, of like force.

brionnach, pretty (M'F.), fair (Sh.), glittering, Ir. *brinneall*, a beautiful young woman, a matron:

brionnach, brindled, striped; from the Eng. *brinded*, now *brindled*.

brìos, mockery (A. M'D.), half-intoxication (M'A.):

briosaid, a girdle (Arm.), from Eng. *brace?*

briosg, start, jerk, so Ir.; from *brisg*, active, q.v.

briosgaid, a biscuit, M. Ir. *brisca* (F.M.); founded on Eng. *biscuit*, but by folk-etymology made to agree with *brisg*, brittle (Gaidoz).

briosuirneach, ludicrous; cf. *brìos*, mockery, etc.

briot, briotal, chit-chat, Ir. †*briot*, chatter, *briotach*, a stammerer: **bṛt-to*, **bṛ-t*, root *bar*, *ber*, as in Lat. *barbarus*, Gr. βάρβαρος, βερβερίζω, I stammer. The reference of *briot* to the name *Breatnaich* or Britons as foreigners and stammerers is scarcely happy.

bris, break, so Ir., O. Ir. *brissim*, **brestô*, I break, root *bres*, *bhres*; O.H.G. *brestan*, break, Ag. S. *berstan*, Eng. *burst*, Fr. *briser*, break. Distantly allied to **berso-s*, short, G. *beàrr*. Brugmann has compared the Gaelic to Gr. πέρθω, destroy, from *bherdho-*, giving a Celtic stem *bṛd-to-*, and *bṛd-co-* for *brisg*.

brisg, brittle, Ir. *briosg*, E. Ir. *brisc*, Br. *bresq*: **bres-co-*; root *bres* of *bris* above.

brisg, lively, Ir. *brisc*, W. *brysg*; all from the Eng. *brisk*, of Scandinavian origin (Johansson, Zeit. xxx.).

brisgein, cartilage; from Norse *brjósk*, cartilage, *bris*, Sw. and Dan. *brusk*; Ger. *brausche*, a lump (from a bruise).

brisgein, brislein, white tansy; from *brisg*, brittle.

britheamh, a judge, Ir. *breitheamh*, O. Ir. *brithem*, g. *britheman*; root *bṛt-*, of *breath*, judgment, q.v.

broc, a badger, so Ir., E. Ir. *brocc*, W., Cor., *broch*, Br. *broc'h*, **brokko-s*: **bork-ko-*, "grey one"; root *bherk*, *bhork*, bright, Gr. φορκός, grey, Lit. *berszti*, Eng. *bright?* Thurneysen cfs. the Lat. *broccus*, having projecting teeth, whence Fr. *broche* (from Lat. **brocca*, a spike, etc.), a spit, Eng. *broach*, *brooch*; he thinks the badger was named *broccos* from his snout, and he instances the Fr. *brochet*, pike, as parallel by derivation and analogy. If Gr. βρύκω, bite, is allied to Lat. *broccus*, the underlying idea of *broc* may rather be the "biter," "gripper."

Bezzenberger suggests Russ. *barsúkŭ*, Turk. *porsuk*, Magyar *borz*; or **brokko-s*, from **bhrod-ko-s*, Skr. *bradhná*, dun.

brocach, greyish in the face, speckled, Ir. *brocach*, *broc*, W. *broc*, grizzled, roan; from *broc*.

brochan, gruel, porridge, Ir. *brochán*, O. Ir. *brothchán*; *broth-chán*, **broti-*, cookery; root *bru*, I. E. *bhru*, whence Eng. *broth*, Lat. *defrutum*, must. See *bruith*.

bròchlaid, trash, farrago; root *bhreu*, *bhru*, as in *brochan*; *bhreu* varies with *bhrou*, G. *brò*.

bròcladh, spoiling, mangling; see *breòclaid*.

brod, a lid; from Sc. *brod*, side form of Eng. *board*.

brod, a goad, prickle, Ir. *brod*, E. Ir. *brott*, W. *brath*, Cor. *broz*, Br. *brout*, **broddos*, from *broz-do-*; O. H. G. *brort*, edge, Norse *broddr*, sting, Eng. *brod*, *brad*, Ag. S. *brord*, sting.

brod, the choice of anything; from the above, in the sense of "excess." Cf. *corr*.

bròd, pride, **bròdail**, proud, Ir. *bród*, etc. Iu Arran (Sc.) we find **pròtail**, which is a step nearer the origin. From the Eng. *proud*.

†**brodan**, mastiff, E. Ir. *brotchu*, W. *brathgi*; from *brod*, "good."

bròd, a crowd, brood, **bròdach**, in crowds; from the Eng. *brood*?

bròg, a shoe, Ir. *bróg*, M. Ir. *brócc*, E. Ir. *bróc*, pl. *bróca*, used in compounds for various nether garments; from Norse *brókr*, Ag. S. *bróc*, pl. *bréc*, Eng. *breech*, *breeks* (Zimmer, Zeit. xxx.). See *briogais*.

brog, stimulate, an awl; from Sc. *brog*, *prog*. Cf. W. *procio*, thrust, poke, from M. E. *prokien*, stimulare. Thurneysen takes Sc. and G. from Fr. *broche*, Lat. **brocca* (see *broc*). Hence **brogail**, "active," "in good form."

brogach, a boy, young lad, from *brog*?

broidneireachd, embroidery, Ir. *broidineireachd*; from the Eng. *broider*, *embroidery*.

†**broigheal**, cormorant, Ir. *broighioll*:

broighleadh, bustle; from Sc. *brulye* (Eng. *broil*), Fr. *brouiller*, It. *broglio*. See *braodhlach*.

broighleag, whortleberry; see *braoileag*.

broigileineach, substantial; from *broigeil*, a by-form of *brogail*; see *brogach*.

broilein, king's hood; pig's snout (Badenoch): root *bhru*, brow?

broilleach, a breast, Ir., E. Ir. *brollach*: **bron-lach*; for **bron*, see *bruinne*.

broineag, a rag, ill-clad female, **bronag**, a crum (Dialectic); possibly from the root of *bronn*, distribute. Shaw spells it *broinnag*, M'F. as above.

broinn, belly (Dialectic); the dat. of *brù* used dialectically as nom.; see *brù*.

broit, the bosom; properly the breast covering (H.S.D., for latter meaning); cf. G. *brot*, O. Ir. *broiténe*, palliolum. The word appears to be from *brat*, mantle, with a leaning for meaning on *bruinne*, breast.

brolaich, incoherent talk (as in sleep), **brolasg**, garrulity, Ir. *brolasgach*, prattling; cf. W. *brawl*, *brol*, boasting, Eng. *brawl*, Du. *brallen*, boast.

brolamas, a mess (D. C. Mc. Ph.) (Glenmoriston); same root as *brollach*.

broluinn, brothluinn, boiling, "æstus," tide-boiling; from *broth*, boiling, as in *brollach*, etc.

brollach, a mess; cf. E. Ir. *brothlach*, the Fénian cooking pit, from *broth*, as in *brochan*, q.v.

bromach, a colt, Ir. *bromach*: **brusmo-*, **brud-*, **bru*, as in Eng. em-*bryo*?

bròn, grief, Ir.. O. Ir. *brón*, W. *brwyn*, smarting, sorrow, **brugno-s*; Gr. *βρύχω* (*υ* long), gnash the teeth; Lit. *gráużiu*, gnaw, Pol. *zgryzota*, sorrow.

† **bronn**, grant, distribute, M. G. *bronnagh* (1408 charter), Ir. *bronnaim*, E. Ir. *bronnaim*, *brondaim*, bestow, spend: **brundo-*, **bhrud-no-*, I. E. root *bhrud*; Ag. S. *bryttian*, deal out, Norse *bryti*, a steward (cf. Gr. *ταμίας*, steward, "cutter"), *brytja*, chop, Eng. *brittle*, Teut. *brut*, chop; perhaps, Lat. *frustum*, bit.

brosdaich, stir up, Ir. *brosduighim*, E. Ir. *brostugud*, inciting. The word is from the root *bros-* in *brosdo-* of *brod*, q.v., being here *bros-to-*, which becomes *brosso-*, and later reverts to *brost*, *brosd*, or remains as in **brosnaich.** Stokes says it is founded on Low Lat. *brosdus*, *brusdus*, broidery, "done by a needle," or *brosd*, which is of Teutonic origin and cognate with G. *brod*, already given as the root. Hence **brosgadh,** stimulation, etc. The Ir. *brosna*, O. Ir. *brosne*, faggot, may be hence; the root *bhrud*, discussed under *bronn*, has also been suggested.

brosgul, flattery, fawning (especially of a dog); possibly from the root form *brost*, in *brosdaich*, *brosgadh*.

brosnaich, incite; see *brosdaich*. This is the best G. form; *brosdaich* is rather literary and Irish.

brot, broth; from the Eng. *broth*.

brot, a veil, upper garment, O. Ir. *broiténe*, palliolum; G. is a by-form of *brat*.

broth, itch, Ir. *broth*, **bruto-*; see *bruthainn* for root. Also (rarely) **bruth.**

broth, lunar halo (Arg.), or **brogh**; cf. O. Ir. *bruth*, heat, under *bruthainn*. Sc. *broch*, Ulster Ir. *broth*.

brothag, the bosom, a fold of the breast clothes; **broso-*, root *brus* of *bruinne*, breast.

brothas, farrago, brose, Ir. *brothus*, from M. E. *brewis*, Sc. *brose*. See *bruthaist*, the best G. form.

brù, g. **bronn,** belly, so Ir., O. Ir. *brú*, *brond;* W. *bru*: **brûs* **brus-nos*, root *brus*, I. E. *bhrus*, *bhreus*; Teut. *breust-*, Norse *brjóst*, Eng. *breast*, Ger. *brust*. Stokes refers it to the root *bru*, to swell, Gr. *βρύω*, am full, *ἔμ-βρυον*, embryo (whence Eng. *embryo*), or to Skr. *bhrûṇá*, embryo. See *bruinne*.

bruach, a bank, brink, Ir., O. Ir. *bruach*: **brou-ko-*, I. E. *bhrû*, brow, Gr. *ὀφρύς*, eyebrow, Eng. *brow*, Lit. *bruvis*, O. Ir. *brúad*, (dual). Also E. Ir. *brú*, bank, border. Stokes suggests either the root of *brùth*, bruise, or Lit. *briau-nà*, edge.

bruachaire, a surly fellow, one that hovers about, Ir. *bruachaireachd*, hovering about; from *bruach*.

bruadar, bruadal, a dream, Ir. *bruadair*, W. *breuddwyd*: **braud* or **brav-*: *fraus*, *fraud?*

bruaillean, bruaidlean, trouble, grief; from *bruadal* above.

bruais, crush to pieces, gnash (Dialectic): **bhraud-so-*, Lat. *fraus*, Eng. *brittle*.

bruan, thrust, wound; from the root of *brùth*.

bruan, a fragment; **bhroud-no-*, from **bhroud*, break, Ag. S. *bréostan*, break, Eng. *brittle*, etc., as under *bronn*. Strachan also suggests **bhroucno-*, Lett. *brukt*, crumple, and Stokes the root of *brùth*.

brùc, seaweed cast ashore (Lewis); Norse *brúk*, dried heaps of seaweed.

brucach, spotted in the face, smutted, Ir. *brocach*: "badger-like"; see *broc*. The Sc. *broukit*, *brooked*, is of uncertain origin (Murray). Hence **brucachadh,** irregular digging, **brucanaich,** the peep of dawn (M'A.), etc.

brucag, bruchag, a chink, eylet (Sh.), dim candle light (H.S.D.). Sh. gives *bruchag*, H.S.D. *brucag*, which appears only to apply to the "dim candle light"; from *brucach*.

brùchd, belch, burst out, so Ir., E. Ir. *brúchtaim*, eructo, vomo, W. *brytheiro* (vb.), *brythar* (n.).

bruchlag, a hovel; from *brugh*, q.v.

bruchlas, the fluttering of birds going to rest (Sh.):

bruchorcan, stool bent, heath rush; said to be derived from †*brú*, a hind, and *corc-an*, oats, "deer's oats." Also **bruth-chorcan.**

brudhach, a brae; see *bruthach*.

brudhaist, brose; see *bruthaist*.

brugh, large house, a tumulus, so Ir., E. Ir. *brug*, *mrug*, land, holding, mark, W. *bro*, country, region, land, *Cym-mro*, a Welshman, pl. *Cymmry* (**com-mroges*), Br. *bro*, country, Gaul. *Brogi-* : **mrogi* (for Gadelic); Lat. *margo*; Got. *marka*, border-country, Ag. S. *mearc*, border, Eng. *mark*, *march*.

bruich, boil, cook; gutturalised form of *bruith* (cf. *bràth*, *bràch*). See *bruith*. The Ir. *bruighim* appears in O'R., and has been compared to Lat. *frîgo*, Gr. *φρύγω*, roast; but it is evidently a bad spelling of *bruith*.

bruid, captivity, Ir. *bruid*, M. Ir. **brat*, g. *braite*, E. Ir. acc. *broit*, **braddâ*. For root, see *bradach*.

bruid, bruidich, stab, goad, Ir. *bruidighim* : the verb from *brod*, a goad.

brùid, a brute, Ir. *brúid*; from Eng. *brute*.

bruidheann, bruidhinn, talk, conversation, Ir. *bruíghinn*, scolding speech, a brawl (also *bruitheann*), O. Ir. *fris-brudi*, renuit, W. *cyfrau*, song, O. Br. *co-brouol*, verbialia, **mru*, say; Skr. *brû*, *bravati*, says, Zend *mrû*, speak. O'Grady (S. Gad. xvi.) connects E. Ir. *brudin*, hospitium; says meaning really is "quarrel" He gives Ir. as *bruidhen*. Stokes E. Ir. *brudin*, **brodìna*, Eng. *board* (Z. 33).

bruidlich, stir up; see *bruid*, stab, goad.

brùill, bruise, thump; a derivative from *brùth*, q.v.

brùillig, a person of clumsy figure and gait (H.S.D., which refers the word to *brù*, belly); from *brù*?

bruim-fheur, switch grass, so Ir.: from *braim-fheur*, a term to denote its worthlessness.

Brùinidh, the Brownie; from Sc. *Brownie*, the benevolent farm-house goblin, from Eng. *brown*. Cf. the Norse *Svart-álfr* or dark elves.

bruinne, breast, O. Ir. *bruinne*, W. *bron*, Cor. and M. Br. *bronn*, **brus-no*, root *bhrus*, *bhreus*; Norse *brjóst*, Ger. *brust*, Eng. *breast*. Stokes gives the root as *brend*, from I. E. *grendh*, swell, be haughty, Gr. *βρένθύομαι*, strut, bear oneself loftily, Lat. *grandis*, Ch. Sl. *grądĭ*, breast. Usually correlated with Got. *brunjô*, breastplate, M. H. G. *brünne*, N. *brynja*, coat of mail, M. Eng. *brynie*, Sc. *byrnie* : a satisfactory enough derivation, and ultimately from the same root as the first one given above (I. E. *bhru*). Indeed Stokes says the Teut. is borrowed from the Celtic.

bruinneadh, the front (Dialectic), O. Ir. *bruinech*, prow, Cor. *brenniat*, prow, **bronjo-*, to which Bez. compares Ger. *grans*, prow (I. E. *gh* = G. *b*?). From root of *bruinne*.

bruis, a brush, Ir. *bruis* (vulg.); from the Eng. *brush*.

bruiteach, warm; from **bruth*, heat; see *bruthainn.*
bruith, boil, cook, so Ir., E. Ir. *bruith*, cooking, **broti-*, from the root *bru*, I. E. *bhru*; Eng. *broth* (Teut. *broþo-*, I. E. *bhruto-*), and *brew* (I. E. *bhreu*); Lat. *defrutum*, must; Thrac. Gr. *βρῦτον*, beer.
brunsgal, rumbling noise; *bronn+sgal?* From *brù*, in any case.
brusg, a crumb, particle of food, Ir. *bruscán*, *brusgar*, broken ware, useless fragments, *brus*, refuse of corn: from **brus*, short form of **brūs* in *brùth.*
brutach, digging, the act of digging (N. H. according to H.S.D.): **brutto-*, **bhrud-to-*, root *bhrud*, break? See *bronn.*
brùth, bruise, pound, Ir. *brúighim*, E. Ir. *brúim*, **brūs*, strike, graze, pound; Pre. Celt. *bhreus*; Ag. S. *brýsan*, bruise, Eng. *bruise* (influenced by Fr.); perhaps O. Slav. *brŭsnąti*, corrumpere, radere.
bruthach, a brae: **brut-acos*, root *bru*, from *bhru*, brow; see *bruach.* Sc. *brae* is of a similar origin, founded on Norse *brá*, eyelid, brow (Murray).
bruthainn, sultriness, heat, Ir., O. Ir. *bruth*, fervor, W. *brwd*, hot, Br. *brout*, hot (fire), O. Br. *brot*: **brutu-*. For further root see *bruith.* Wider are Lat. *ferveo*, *fervor*, Eng. *burn*, etc.
bruthaist, brose; from early Sc., Eng. *browes*, Sc. *brose*; from the Fr., but allied to Eng. *broth.*
bu, was, Ir. *budh*, O. Ir. *bu*: Proto-Gaelic **bu* for a Celtic *bu-t*; Gr. *ἔφυ* (*υ* long), aorist tense; Lat. *fuit*; Skr. *ábhūt*, was; I. E. *é-bhū-t.* The root is *bheu*, *bhu*; Eng. *be*, etc. Both G. and Ir. aspirate, which shows the *t* of the 3rd sing. disappeared early.
buabhall, unicorn, buffalo, M. Ir. *buabhall*, W. *bual*; from Lat. *bubalus*, buffalo, gazelle, whence (*būfalus*) Eng. *buffalo.*
buabhall, a trumpet, Ir. *bubhall*, *buadhbhall*, M. Ir. *buaball*, W. *bual*, bugle; cf. M. Ir. *buabhall*, horn, W. *bual*, buffalo horn, M. Ir. *corn buabhaill*; whence the further force of "trumpet."
buachaill, a herdsman, so Ir., O. Ir. *bóchaill*, *buachaill*, W. *bugail*, Cor., Br. *bugel*; Gr. *βουκόλος*, cowherd (Lat. *bucolicus*, Eng. *bucolic*), *βου-*, cow, and *-κολος*, attendant, Lat. *colo*, *cul*tivate.
buachar, cow-dung, Ir. *buacar*, *buachar* (Con.), Br. *beuzel*; for the stem before the suffix *-ar*, cf. W. *buwch* (**boukkā*), though *bou-cor-* or *bouk-cor-*, "cow-offcast," may properly be the derivation for the Gadelic. See *bó* and, possibly, *cuir.* Cf. *salchar.*
buadhghallan, buaghallan, ragwort, Ir. **buadhghallan,** M. Ir. *buathbhallan*, *buathfallan*: "virtue bearing wort?" More probably it is *buaf-bhallan*, "toad-wort," from *buaf*, toad,

reptile, from Lat. *bûfo.* The Welsh call it "serpent's weed," *llysiau'r nedir.* Ir. *baufanan* is "mugwort"; *buadharlann* (Hend.).

buaic, a wick, Ir. *buaic*; from Eng. *wick*, Ag. S. *weoca ?*

buaic, bleaching lees, Ir. *buac*; from M. E. *bouken*, steep in lye, Eng. *buck*, Ger. *bauchen*; Fr. *buer*, from a Lat. type **bûcare.* See *fùcadh.*

buaicneach, small-pox (Suth.); founded on a later form of Lat. *bucca*, as in *bucaid*, q.v.

buaidh, victory, virtue, so Ir., O. Ir. *buaid*, W. *budd*, O. Br. *bud*, Gaul. *boud-*, in many personal names, whether as the only root (cf. *Boudicca*, "Victrix") or in compounds, either initial or as second part: **boudi-*; Norse *býti*, exchange, Ger. *beute*, booty, Eng. *booty*, Fr. *butin* (do.).

buaidheam, fits of inconstancy; cf. *buathadh.*

buail, strike, so Ir., E. Ir. *bualaim*: **budlo-* or **boudlo-*, **boud*, Pre-Celt. *bhoud*, *bheud*; Ag. S. *béatan*, Eng. *beat*, *beetle*, Ger. *beutel*, beetle (Strachan). See *buille.* Stokes gives the form **buglaô*, root *bug*, *bhug*, as in Ger. *pochen*, Eng. *poke.*

buaile, a fold, pen, so Ir., E. Ir. *buale*; Lat. *bovile*; from **bov-*, cow.

buaill, place for resting and milking (Lewis). Cf. Norse *ból.*

buain, reap, Ir., O. Ir. *buain*, inf. of *bongaim*, reap, break: **bogni-* or **bongni- ?* For root, see *bochd.*

buair, tempt, vex, Ir. *buaidhirim*, E. Ir. *buadraim*, O. Ir. *buadartha*, turbulentus: **boud-ro-*; possibly from *bhoud*, strike, the idea coming from a form **boudro-*, a goad, goading? G. has **buaireadh, buair,** a rage.

bual-chòmhla, sluice (M'L.) (*an fhamh bhual*, water vole); M. Ir. *bual*, flowing sluice water, E. Ir. *roth-búali*, water-wheel, **bogla*, Eng. *beck*, Ger. *bach* (St.) (Zim.).

bualtrach, cow-dung, so Ir. *buartlach* (Dial. Ir.); from *buar*, cattle.

buamastair, a blockhead:

buan, lasting, Ir. *buan*, lasting, fixed, E. Ir. *buan*: "being, during," from **bu*, be, I. E. *bhu*, be; Lit. *butinas*, being, during, from *buti*, be; Norse *búa*, dwell, Got. *bauan*, etc. Stokes gives the G. stem as *buvano-s*, and cfs. Skr. *bhûvana*, existence. Hence **buanaich,** persevere.

buana, an idle person who lives on the best his neighbours can afford (Lewis) (M'A.):

†**buanna,** a mercenary, a billeted soldier, so Ir.:

buannachd, profit; from *buain*, reap, with irregularly doubled *n* (see *cinne*, *linn*, *seann*, *bann-* for *ban-*, *miann*)? Cf. Ir. *buannacht*, soldiers billeting from a tenant (Joyce).

buar, cattle, so Ir., E. Ir. *búar*, cattle of the cow kind; from *bó*, cow: **bovâro-*; cf. Lat. *boarius.*

buarach, cow-fetter, Ir., E. Ir., *buarach* : for *bó-árach*, "cow-fetter," *árach* being for *ad-rig-os*, root *rig* of *cuibhreach*, q.v.

buathadh, a rushing, a mad fit :

bùb, roar, Ir. *bub* : onomatopoetic. Cf. Lat. *baubor*, bay, Gr. *βαΰζω*, bark, Lit. *bubauti*, roar.

bùban, coxcomb, Ir. *bubán* ; cf. Eng. *booby*.

bucach, a boy (dial.) : "growing one ;" founded on Lat. *bucca* as in the following word.

bucaid, a pustule, Ir. *bocóid*, a spot, E. Ir. *boccóit* ; from Brittonic Lat. *buccâtus*, from *bucca*, puffed cheek (Eng. *debouch, rebuke*).

bucall, a buckle, Ir. *bucla*, W. *bwcl* ; from M. Eng. *bukyll*, Eng. *buckle*, from Fr. *boucle*, from Lat. *bucula*, cheek-strap, from *bucca*, cheek.

bùchd, size (Sh. *buc*) ; from Sc. *bouk*, i.e., *bulk*.

buchainn, melodious (A. M'D.) :

buchallach, nestling (adj.) : **buth-chal*, "house tending ?" *buchallach* (M'L. Teachd. Gaidh.) :

budach, poult (Suth.) : see *pùt*.

budagochd, snipe (M'L.), woodcock (H.S.D.). It seems a reminiscence of Eng. *woodcock*.

budhaigir, the puffin, **buigire**, (M'A , for St Kilda), Sc. *bowger*, the coulter-neb ; somehow from Norse *bugr*, curve, "bent-bill ?"

budhailt, a window-like recess in a wall ; from Sc. *bowall, boal, bole*. Origin unknown (Murray).

budhag, a bundle of straw : root *bud*, which underlies Fr. *botte*, bundle ? See *boitean*.

bugha, a green spot by a stream (Skye), *bogha* (Rob.).

buideal, a bottle, cask, Ir. *buideul*, W. *potel* ; from Eng. *bottle*. See *botul*.

buidealaich, a conflagration, Ir. *buite*, fire, *buitealach* (Lh.†, O'Cl., O'B.), *bott* (O'Cl.) : **bud-do-*, root *bhud* (Lat. *fustis, bhud-tis*, Eng. *beetle*), giving the idea of "faggot, firewood ?"

buidhe, yellow, so Ir., O. Ir. *buide* ; Lat. *badius*, Eng. *bay*.

buidhe, now **buidheachas**, thanks, Ir. *buidhe*, O. Ir. *buide* [W. *boddaw*, please, *bodd*, will ?], **budo-*, I. E. *bhudh, bheudh* ; Gr. *πεύθομαι*, learn by inquiry ; Ag. S. *béodan*, command, Eng. for-*bid*.

buidhe, glad to, had to, O. Ir. *buithi*, participle of necessity, from the verb *bí*, be : "Is amlid is buithi do chách"—Thus ought it to be with every one (9th Cent. glosses) ; G. "Is buidhe do gach neach."

buidheann, a company, Ir. *buidhean*, O. Ir. *buden*, W. *byddin*, O. Br. *bodin*, manus, **bodînâ* ; O. H. G. *chutti*, troop, band, O. Fries. *kedde*, Ger. *kette*, covey ; I.E. *gô : go*, drive ; cf. Lit. *gůtas*, herd.

buidhinn, gain, win, **buinnig**, act of gaining, gain ; from the Eng. *win*, *winning*.

buil, effect, use, Ir. *boil*, **bol*, **bel* : Pre-Celt. *bhel*, *bhol* ; Gr. ὄφελος, advantage, ὠφέλέω, help.

buileach, total, entirely ; another form of *baileach*. E. Ir. has *bulid*, blooming.

buileastair, a bullace or sloe (M'D., Sh.) ; from M. E. *bolaster* = *bullace-tree*, from *bolace*, now *bullace*.

builionn, a loaf, Ir. *builín* ; from O. Fr. **boulange*, ball-shaped loaf (?), which Diez suggests as the basis of Fr. *boulanger*, baker.

buille, a blow, so Ir., E. Ir. *bulle*, *buille* = *bollia* = *bus-liâ* = *bhud-s-liâ* ; root *bhud*, beat, as in *buail*, q.v. Stokes gives the stem as **boldja*, allied to Lit. *béldžiu*, *belsti*, give a blow, *baldas*, a beetle ; Ger. *poltern*.

buillsgean, centre, Ir. *boilsceán*, M. Ir. *bolscén*, middle, midriff = *bolgán*, from *balg*, *bolg*, belly.

buin, belong to, Ir. *beanaim*. The Ir. is from the verb *bean*, touch ; the G., which has the idea of relationship or origin (*Cha bhuin e dhomh* : he is not related to me), seems to confuse *bean* and *bun*, stock.

buinne, a cataract, tide, Ir. *buinne*, a spout, tap, E. Ir. *buinne*, wave, rush of water : G. **buinneach**, flux, diarrhœa, so Ir. ; see *boinne*. Also *puinne* (Suth.) (W. Ross).

buinneag, a twig, sprout, Ir. *buinneán*, E. Ir. *buinne* : **bus-niâ* ; root *bus*, as in Eng. *bush*, *bosky*, Ger. *busch*, etc.

buinnig, winning ; see *buidhinn*.

†**buinnire**, a footman, so Ir. ; from *bonn*, sole of the foot.

bùir, **bùirich**, roar, bellow (as a bull), Ir. *búireadh*, roaring ; E. Ir. *búraim* ; **bû-ro-*, I. E. root *gevo*, *gû*, cry ; Gr. βοάω, shout ; Lit. *gauju*, howl ; Skr. *gu*, cry. Strachan gives as G. stem *bucro-*, root *buq* as in Lat. *buccina*, horn, Gr. βύκτης, howling, Skr. *bukkāras*, lion's roar, Norwg. *bura*, to bellow, Shet. *boorik*, cow.

buirdeiseach, a free man, burgess, Ir. *buirgéiseach* ; from the Eng. *burgess*.

buirleadh, language of folly and ridicule ; from the Romance *burla*, to jest, etc. See *burraidh*.

bùirseach, a deluge of rain ; a rousing fire (Heb.) :

buiseal, a bushel, Ir. *buiseul* ; from Eng. *bushel*.

bùit, bashful (Badenoch) : "fugy," as a fowl ; see *pùt*.

bùiteach, a threat (Suth.) : a form of *bòidich* ?

buitseach, a witch, so Ir. ; from Eng. *witch* ; "buidseach agus raitseach."

bùlas, pot hook; from the Sc. *bools*, a pot hook in two parts or "bools," M. Eng. *bool*, a pail handle, round part of a key, Ger. *bügel*, arc: from Teut. *beugan*, bend, Eng. *bow*. Dialectic **pùlas.**

bumailear, a bungler; from Sc. *bummeler*, from *bummil*, bungle, Eng. *bumble*; of onomatopoetic origin (Murray). Cf. Ger. *bummler*, a lounger.

bun, root, stock, bottom, Ir., E. Ir. *bun*, W. *bon*, stem, trunk, O. W. *boned*; Armen. *bun*; N. Pers. *bun*, Zd. *buna-* (Bugge). Rhys has suggested a connection with Ger. *bühne*, a stage, boards. Ag. S. *bune*, "stalk, reed," may be allied. It cannot be connected with *bonn*, for the stem there is *bhudh-no-*, root *bhudh*. The ultimate root of *bun*, in any case, is simply *bhu*, *bhû*, grow, swell, Gr. *φύω*, *φῦλον*, a tribe, Eng. *boil* (n.), Ger. *beule*, a swelling, Skr. *bhumis*, earth; *bhû*, grow, is identical with *bhu*, be.

bunach, coarse tow, refuse of flax, so Ir.; from *bun*.

bunait, foundation, Ir. *bunáit*: *bun* + *áit.*, q.v.

bungaid, a hussy (Dial.); from Sc.*bungy*, pettish.

bunndaist, a bounty, grassum, Ir. *bunntaiste*; from Eng. *poundage*.

bunnlum, steadiness, **bunntam, bunntamas,** solidity, shrewdness; from *bun*, foundation. Cf. Ir. *buntomhas*, well founded opinion: *bun* + *tomhas*, q.v.

bunnsach, a twig, so Ir., E. Ir. *bunsach*; see *buinneag*.

bunnsach, a sudden rush; from *buinne*.

bunntam, solidity; see *bunnlum*.

buntàta, potato, Ir. *potáta*, *fataidhe*; from the English. It contains a piece of folk-etymologising in the syllable *bun-*, root.

buntuinn, belonging; see *buin*.

bùrach, turning up of the earth, digging; from the Sc. *bourie*, Eng. *burrow*. The Sc. *bourach*, enclosure, cluster, knoll, heap, etc., is the Eng. *bower*.

burgaid, a purge, **Burgadoir,** Purgatory; see *purgaid*, *Purgadoir*.

bùrlam, a flood, rush of water (Arg.); see *bòrlum*.

burmaid, wormwood; from the Eng. M. Ir. *in uormoint*.

bùrn, water; from Sc. *burn*, water, spring-water, Eng. *bourne*, *burn*, a stream, Teut. *brunnon-*, a spring, Norse *brunnr*, well, Ger. *brunnen*.

burrachdadh, raging:

burraidh, a blockhead, Ir. *búrraidh*; from Sc. *burrio* (1535), Fr. *bourrieau*, Lat. *burræ*, nonsense, Eng. *burlesque*, etc.

burral, a howl, lamentation, so Ir.; for the root, which is here short (**bur-ro-* ?), see *búir*. Cf. *bururus*, however.

burras, a caterpillar:

burr-, as in **burr'caid**, clumsy person, **burr'ghlas**, a torrent of rage, etc , seems from *borr*, great, excessive, q.v. **Burr'sgadh,** a burst of passion, may be from Eng. *borasco*, squall of wind.

bùrt, mockery ; from Sc. *bourd*, M. Eng. *bourd*, jest, Fr. *bourde*, a lie.

bururus, infant lisping, warbling, purling ; cf. Eng. *purr* and *purl* (Skeat). Evidently onomatopoetic.

bus, a mouth, kiss, Ir., M. Ir. *bus*, **bussu-* ; Pre-Celt. *guss-* ; Teut. *kuss*, Ger. *küssen*, kiss, Eng. *kiss* (Kluge). Bezzenberger cfs. Lit. *buczúti*, kiss ; others give *buc-sa*, allied to Lat. *bucca*, cheek.

busgadh, dressing ; from the Sc., Eng. *busk*.

busgaid, a bustle (M'D.) ; formed from Eng. *busy* ; cf. Ag. S. *bysgu*, business.

bustail, puffing, blowing (Heb.) ; from *bus*.

butadh, a push ; see *putadh*.

butag, oar pin ; see *putag*.

bùth, a shop ; from the Eng. *booth*, Norse *búð*, shop, root *bhu*, be. See *bothan*.

buthainnich, thump, thrash, bang ; from the root *bhud*, beat (Eng. *beat*) ? See next.

buthuinn, long straw for thatch ; cf. **sputhainn**, straw not threshed, but seedless (Arg.), which seems from *spoth*.

butrais, butarrais, a mess :

C

c', for *co*, *cia*, who, what, q.v.

cà, ca, where, Ir *cá*, how, where, who ; a by-form to *cia*, *cè*, q.v.

cab, a gap, indentation, mouth, Ir. *cab*, mouth, head, gap, *cabach*, babbling, indented. The word is borrowed from two English words—*gap* and *gab* (M. E. *gabben*, chatter); G. has also *gab*, directly from *gab* of the Sc. Hence **cabach**, gap-toothed.

càbag, a cheese ; Sc. *cabback*, *kebbock*. The latter form (*kebbock*) is probably from a G. *ceapag*, *cepac*, obsolete in G. in the sense of "a cheese," but still used for the thick wooden wheel of wheel-barrows ; it is from G. *ceap*. Sc. *cabback* is a side form of *kebbock*, and it seems to have been re-borrowed into G. as *càbag*. The real G. word for "a cheese" is now *mulachag*.

cabaist, cabbage, Ir. *gabáisde* ; from the Eng.

càball, a cable, Ir. *cabla* ; from Eng. *cable*, which, through Fr., comes from Lat. *capulum*.

cabar, a rafter, caber, deer's horn, Ir. *cabar*, W. *ceibr*, rafters, O. Br. *cepriou*, beams ; from a Med. Lat. **caprio*, a rafter, *capro*, *caprones* (which exists as a genuine 8th century word),

Fr. *chevron*, rafter. *Caprio* is from *caper*, goat; Lat. *capreoli*, goat-lets, was used for two beams meeting to support something, props, stays.

cabasdar, cabstar, a bit, curb, W. *cebystr*, Br. *kabestr*; from Lat. *capistrum*, halter, "head-holder," from *caput*.

cabhag, hurry:

cabhlach, a fleet, Ir. *cobhlach, cabhlach*, E. Ir. *coblach*; **cob-lach*; from **kub*, **qug*, curve, root of Lat. *cymba*, boat, Gr. *κύμβη*, boat, cup, especially Lat. *cybaea*, a transport (**κυβαία*).

cabhladh, ship's tackle, Ir. *cábhluighe*; cf. *cabhlach*, and Eng. *cable*.

càbhruich, sowens, flummery, Ir. *cáthbhruith*; from *cáth* and *bruith*, q.v.

cabhsair, causeway, Ir. *cabhsa*; from Eng. *causey, causeway*, from O. Fr. *caucie*, from Lat. *calciata* (via).

cabhsanta, dry, snug; from Sc. *cosie, colsie*, Eng. *cosy*, whose origin is unknown.

cabhtair, an issue, drain in the body (M'D., who, as *cautair*, explains it as "an issue or cauter"); from Eng. *cauter*.

cabhuil, a conical basket for catching fish; from M. Eng. *cawell*, a fish basket, still used in Cornwall, Ag. S. *cawl*. Cf. Br. *kavell*, bow-net, O. Br. *cauell*, basket, cradle; from Lat. *cauuella*, a vat, etc. (Loth, Ernault).

càblaid, turmoil, hindrance, trouble (Wh.): See càpraid.

cabon, capon (M'D.), Ir. *cabún*; from Eng. *capon*.

cac, excrement, so Ir., E. Ir. *cacc*, Cor. *caugh*, Br. *kac'h*, **kakko-*; Lat. *caco*; Gr. *κάκκη*; Skr. *çáka*, g. *çaknás*.

cách, the rest, others, Ir., O. Ir. *cách*, quivis, W. *pawb*, all, Br. *pep*, **qáqe*; root *qō, qo, qe* of *co* and *gach*, q.v.

cachdan, vexation, Ir. *cacht*, distress, prisoner, E. Ir. *cachtaim*, I capture, W. *caeth*, slave, confined: **kapto-*, caught; Lat. *capio, captus*; Got. *haban*, Eng. *have*.

cachliadh (Arm.), **cachaleith** (H.S.D.), a gate; *co+cliath*, "co-hurdle;" see *cliath, cleath*, hurdle, wattle. Also **cachliag,** (C.S.). It has also been explained as *cadha-chliath*, "hurdle-pass." Carmichael gives alternate *cliath-na-cadha*.

cadadh, tartan cloth, hose tartan, Manx *cadee*, cotton; Eng. *caddow* (16th cent.), an Irish quilt or cloak; doubtless from Eng. *caddis*, worsted, crewel work, etc., Fr. *cadis*, woollen serge. See also *catas*.

cadal, sleep, Ir. *codladh*, O. Ir. *cotlud*, vb. *contulim*: **con-tul-*, root *tol*; Ch. Sl. *toliti*, appease, placare, Lit. *tilas*, quiet (Persson). The root *tol, tel*, appears in *tlàth*, gentle, Lat. *tolerare*, Sc. *thole*.

cadan, cotton (Sh.); from Eng. *cotton.* Properly **codan,** which is the usual dialect form. See *cotan.* For Ir. *cadás,* cotton, see *catas.*

cadha, a pass, narrow pass, entry; cf. Ir. *caoi,* way, road, E. Ir. *cái,* which Stokes, however, refers to the root *ci* as in Lat. *cio,* move, Gr. *κίω,* go, a derivation which does not suit the G. phonetically. *Cae* (Meyer).

cadhag, jackdaw, Ir. *cabhóg,* M. Ir. *caog*; **ca-óg,* the *ca*-er or crier of *ca, caw*; of onomatopoetic origin. Cf. Eng. *caw*; also *chough,* from a West Teut. *kâwa-.*

cadhag, a wedge (M'A. for Skye):

cadhan, wild goose, barnacle goose, so Ir.; cf. Eng. *caw,* for possibly the name is onomatopoetic. Corm. (B) *cadan.*

cadh-luibh, the cud-weed (Sh. gives **cad-luibh,** and O'B.), Ir. *cadh-luibh*; from M. Eng. *code,* a cud. M'A. omits the word; it is clearly Irish. The G. is **cnàmh lus,** which is its Lat. name of *gnaphalium* in folk etymology.

cadhmus, a mould for casting bullets; from Sc. *cawmys, calmes* (16th century), *caums,* Eng. *calm, came.*

cagailt, a hearth, Ir. *cagailt,* raking of the fire (O'R.):

cagar, a whisper, Ir *cogar,* M. Ir. *coccur*; *cechras,* qui canet, *cairche,* sound; root *kar,* of Lat. *carmen,* Gr. *κῆρυξ,* herald (Stokes).

cagaran, darling: **con-car-*; root *car,* dear, as in *caraid.*

caglachan, something ground to pulp or dust (M'D.):

cagnadh, chewing, Ir. *cognadh,* M. Ir. *cocnum,* O. Ir. *cocnom*: **con-cnámh*; see *cnàmh.*

caibe, a spade, turf cutter, Ir. *coibe, cuibe* (O'R., Fol.), W. *caib,* O. Cor. *cep.*

caibeal, a chapel (M'D.); from Lat. *capella.* The G. really is *seipeal,* q.v.

caibheis, giggling, laughing:

caibideil, caibdeil, a chapter, Ir. *caibidil,* E. Ir. *caiptel,* W. *cabidwl*; from Lat. *capitulum,* whence O. Fr. *chapitre,* Eng. *chapter.*

caidir, cherish, so Ir. See the next word.

caidreabh, fellowship, affection, vicinity, so Ir., M. Ir. *caidrebh,* Celtiberian *Contrebia*: **con-treb-*; see *aitreabh, treabh.*

caig, conversation, claque (Arg.); teaze (Perth):

caigeann, a couple (of animals), coupling: **con-ceann*; from *ceann,* q.v.

caigeann, a winding pass through rocks and brushwood, a rough mountain pass (Dial. = *cadha-éiginn*).

caigeann, scrimmage (M'D.):

càil, condition, vigour, appetite, anything (*càileigin*), Ir. *cáil*, W. *cael*, to have, get, enjoy, **kapli-*, **kapelo-* : root *qap* ; Lat. *capio*, Eng. *have*.

cailbhe, a partition wall (of wattle or clay, etc.) ; from *calbh*, q.v.

cailc, chalk, Ir., E. Ir. *cailc*, W. *calch* ; from Lat. *calx*, *calcis*, whence also Eng. *chalk*.

caile, girl, wench, Ir. *caile*, hussy, E. Ir. *caile* ; cf. Br. *plac'h*, girl ; Gr. παλλακή, concubine, Lat. *pellex*. Usually **caileag**, girl.

càileach, husks, Ir. *cáithleach* : *cáith-lach* ; see *càth*. From *càth* comes also **càilean**, a husk.

caileadair, philosopher, star-gazer ; from the Eng. *calender*, a mendicant dervish, from Pers. *qalander*.

cailidear, snot, rheum (M'F., **cailidhir** in Sh.). O'R. improves this into *cailidéar*.

cailis, chalice, Ir. *cailís* ; from Lat. *calix*, cup, Eng. *chalice*.

cailise, kails, ninepins (M'D.) ; from Eng. *kails*, M. Eng. *cailis*, from *keyle*, a peg, Ger. *kegel*, a cane, ninepin.

cailleach, old wife, nun, so Ir., O. Ir. *caillech*, "veiled one ;" from *caille*, veil, which is from the Lat. *pallium*, cloak, Eng. *pall*.

caillteanach, eunuch, so Ir. ; from *caill*, lose. See *call*.

càimein, a mote, Ir. *cáim*, a stain, blemish ; from *càm*.

caimeineach, saving (Carm.) :

caimhleachadh, caingleachadh, restraining (Carm.).

caimir, a fold :

caimleid, camlet ; from the Eng.

càin, a tax, a tribute, Ir. *cáin*, E. Ir. *cáin*, statute, law : **kap-ni-*, root *qap*, as in *càil* ? Stokes refers it to the root *kâs*, order, Skr. *çâs* (do.), Lat. *castigare*, *castus*, Got. *hazjan*, praise. Hence Sc. *cain*.

càin, white : from Lat. *cānus*.

càin, scold, revile, Ir. *cáin*, M. Ir. *cáined*, scolding : **kag-niô* or *kakniô* (?) ; Gr. καχάζω, laugh, καγχάζω, Lat. *cachinnus* ; O. H. G. *huohôn*, mock ; Skr. *kakhati*, laugh.

cainb, hemp, Ir. *cnáib*, M. Br. *canap* ; from Lat. *cannabis*, allied to Eng. *hemp*.

caineal, cinnamon ; from Sc. and obsolete Eng. *cannel*, *canel*, cinnamon, from O. Fr. *canelle*, from Lat. *canella*, dim. of *canna*, cane.

caingeann, a fine (Heb.), Ir. *caingean*, a rule, case, compact, etc. :

Caingis, Pentecost, Ir. *cingcis*, E. Ir. *Cingcigais* ; from the Lat. *quinquagesima* (dies, 50th day from the Passover).

cainneag, a mote :

cainneag, a hamper (Skye) :

cainnt, speech, Ir. *caint* ; from *can*, say, q.v. Stokes gives the stem as **kan(s)ti*, root *kans*, Skr. *çasti*, praise, from *çams*, speak, Lat. *censeo*.

caiptean, a captain, Ir., M. Ir. *caiptín* ; from M. Eng. *capitain*, from O. Fr. *capitaine*, Lat. *capitaneus*, *caput*, head.

càir, a blaze, sea foam, etc. ; see rather *caoir*.

càir, the gum, Ir. *cáir* (*cairib*, Fol.) :

càir, a peat moss, dry part of the peat moss (Dial.) ; from Eng. *carr*, boggy ground, Norse *kjarr*, brushwood. Also *càthar*, q.v.

cairb, the bent ridge of a cart saddle (*srathair*). Shaw gives further the meanings "plank, ship, fusee (*cairb a' ghunna* (Rob), chariot"; Ir. *corb*, coach. The word is the primary stem from which *carbad*, chariot, springs ; see *carbad*. As "fusee" or "fusil," *i.e.*, "musket," it seems a curtailed form of *cairbinn*.

cairbh, a carcase, carrion ; also **cairb** (Dial.) ; allied to *corpus ?*

cairbhist, carriage, tenants' rent service ; from M. Eng. *cariage*, in all senses (Cf. the charter terms—"Areage and cariage and all due service"), now *carriage*.

cairbinn, a carabine ; from the Eng.

cairbinneach, a toothless person (Sh.) ; from †**cairb,** a jaw, gum, Ir. *cairb*. See *cairb* above.

cairc, flesh, person :

càird, a delay, respite, Ir. *cáirde* ; cf. O. Ir. *cairde*, pactum. A special legal use of a word which originally means "friendship." See next.

càirdeas, friendship, so Ir., O. Ir *cairdes* ; from *caraid*, q.v.

càireag, a prating girl (Sh., who gives *caireog*) ; probably from *càir*, gum : "having jaw."

caireal, noise ; see *coirioll*.

†**cairfhiadh,** a hart or stag, Ir. *cáirrfhiadh* : **carbh-fhiadh*. For **carbh*, a deer ; cf. W. *carw*, hart, stag, Cor. *caruu*, Br. *caru* ; Lat. *cervus* ; Gr. κεραός, horned.

càirich, mend, Ir. *cóirighim*, E. Ir. *córaigim*, arrange, from *cóir*, q.v. Cf. *cairem*, sutor, Z. 775.

cairidh, a weir, Ir. *cora*, M. Ir. *coraidh* for *cora*, g. *corad*, W. *cored*, O. W. and O. Br. *coret*, from Celtic *korjô*, I set, put. See *cuir*.

cairgein, sea moss, Ir. moss, Eng. *carrageen*, so named from Carragheen (Waterford), in Ireland. This place name is a dim. of *carraig*, rock.

cairis, corpse, carcase ; founded on M. Eng. *cors*, Sc. *corrssys* (pl. in Blind Harry), now *corse*.

cairmeal, wild liquorice ; see *carrameille*.

cairnean, an egg-shell :

cairt, bark (of a tree), Ir. *cairt* ; Lat. *cortex* ; root *qert*, cut, Lit. *kertù*, cut, Eng. *rend*.

cairt, a cart, so Ir., W. *cart* ; from the Eng. *cart*.

cairt, a card, so Ir. ; G. is from Sc. *carte*, which is direct from the Fr. *carte*. The Eng. modifies the latter form into *card*. They are all from Lat. *charta*, paper. E. Ir. *cairt* meant "parchment."

cairt, cleanse, Ir. *cartaighim*, E. Ir. *cartaim*, W. *carthu*, purge, *kar-to-*. The root idea is a "clearing out ;" the root *ker*, *kar*, separate, is allied to *sker* in *ascart*, and especially in *sgar*.

cairteal, a quarter ; from Late Lat. *quartellus*, Norse *kvartill*, Lat. *quartus*, fourth.

caisbheart, cais'eart, foot gear (shoes or boots), Ir. *coisbheart* ; from *cas* + *beart*, q.v.

caisd, listen, Ir. *coisteacht*, listening, E. Ir. *coistim*, O. Ir. *coitsea*, auscultet : *co-étsim*, *co* and *éisd*, listen, q.v. O'R. gives the modern Ir. *cóisdeacht* with *o* long, which would seem the most natural result from *co-éisd*.

càise, cheese, Ir., E. Ir. *cáise*, W. *caws*, Br. *kaouz* ; from Lat. *cāseus*, whence Eng. *cheese*.

caiseal, bulwark, castle, Ir. *caiseal*, E. Ir. *caisel*, *caissle* ; from Lat. *castellum*.

caisean, anything curled, etc. ; from *cas*, curled, q.v.

caisg, check, stop, Ir. *coisgim*, O. Ir. *cosc*, castigare, W. *cosp*, **kon-sqo-*, **seqô*, I say ; Lat. *inseque* ; Gr. *ἔννεπε*, say, *ἔνι-σπε*, dixit ; Eng. *say*, Ger. *sagen*.

Càisg, Easter, Ir. *Cáisg*, O. Ir. *cásc*, W. *pasc* ; from Lat. *pascha*, Eng. *paschal*.

caisil-chrò, a bier, bed of blood, M. Ir. *cosair chró*, bed of blood—to denote a violent death, E. Ir. *cosair*, bed. The expression appears in the Ossianic Ballads, and folk-etymology is responsible for making G. *casair* into *caisil*, bulwark. The word *cosair* has been explained as *co-ster-*, root *ster*, strew, Lat. *sternere*, Eng. *strew*.

caisleach, a ford, footpath ; from *cas-lach*, rather than *cas-slighe*, foot-way.

caislich, stir up, **caisleachadh**, shaking up, etc. ; from *cas*, sudden.

caismeachd, an alarm (of battle), signal, march tune. The corresponding Ir. is *caismirt*, alarm, battle, M. Ir. *caismert*, E. Ir. *cosmert*.

caisrig, consecrate ; see *coisrig*.

caisteal, a castle, M. Ir. *castél*, E. Ir. *castíall* ; from Lat. *castellum*, whence Eng. *castle*.

càiteach, a rush mat for measuring corn, Ir. *cáiteach*, winnowing sheet; from *càite*, winnowed, from *càth*.

caiteag, a small bit (H.S.D.), a basket for trouts (M'A. for Islands), basket (Sh.), a place to hold barley in (M'L.). For the first sense, cf. W. *cat*, a piece, Sc. *cat*, a rag. In Irish Lat. the trout was called *catus* (Giraldus).

caiteas, scraped linen, applied for the stoppage of wounds (M'F.); from Sc. *caddis*, lint for wounds, M. Eng. *cadas*, *caddis*, cotton wool, floss silk for padding, from O. Fr. *cadas*. See G. *catas*. *caiteas* = sawdust, scrapings (M'D.).

caitein, nap of cloth, shag, Ir. *caitín*, catkin of the osier, little cat. The Eng. words *caddis*, *catkin*, and *cotton* seem to be mixed up as the basis of the G. and Ir. words. Cf. W. *ceden*, shaggy hair.

caith, spend, cast, Ir., O. Ir. *caithim*, **katjô*, I consume, castaway; Skr. *çâtayati*, sever, cast down, destroy, *çât-ana*, causing to fall, wearing out, root *çat*. Allied to the root of *cath*, war.

caithear, just, right, Ir. *caithear* (Lh.), *caithfidh*, it behoves, M. Ir. *caithfid*; from *caith*, doubtless (Atk.).

caithream, shout of joy, triumph, Ir. *caithréim*; from *cath*, battle, and *réim*, a shout, E. Ir. *rém*. This last word Strachan refers to the root *req* (**rec-m* or **rec-s-m*), Ch. Sl. *reką*, speak, Lith. *rėkiù*.

caithris, night-watching:

càl, kail, cabbage, Ir. *cál*, W. *cawl*, Cor. *caul*, Br. *kaol*; from Lat. *caulis*, a stalk, whence likewise Eng. *cole* (*cole*wort) and Sc. *kail*.

cala, caladh, a harbour, Ir. *caladh*, M. Ir. *calad*. It is usual to correlate this with It. *cala*, Fr. *cale*, bay, cove (Diez, Thurneysen, Windisch), and Stokes even says the G. and Ir. words are borrowed from a Romance **calatum*, It. *calata*, *cala*, Fr. *cale*, cove. More probably the Celtic root is *qel*, *qal*, hide, as in Eng. *hollow*, M. Eng. *holh*, hollow, cave, also Eng. *hole*, possibly. The root of *cladh*, has also been suggested.

caladair, a calendar, Ir. *calaindéir*; from M. Eng. *kalendar*, through Fr. from Lat. *calendarium*, an account-book, from *calendæ*, the Calends or first of the month.

calaman, a dove; the common form of the literary *columan*, q.v.

calanas, spinning of wool; seemingly founded on Lat. *colus*, distaff. See *cuigeal*.

†calbh, head, pate, bald, so Ir., E. Ir. *calb*; from Lat. *calva*, scalp, *calvus*, bald. H.S.D. gives as a meaning "promontory," and instances "Aoineadh a' Chailbh Mhuilich," which surely must be the Calf of Mull; and Calf is a common name for such subsidiary isles—from Norse *kálfr*, Eng. *calf*. Cognate with Lat. *calva*, *calvaria* (St. Lec.).

calbh, a shoot, osier twig, Ir. *colbha*, plant stalk, sceptre, hazel tree, E. Ir. *colba*, wand; see *colbh*.

calbh, gushing of water or blood (H.S.D.) from *above*?

calbhair, greedy of food (Suth.); from *càil*?

calc, drive, ram, caulk, Ir. *calcaim*; from Lat. *calco*, *calx*, the heel, Eng. *in-culcate*.

caldach, sharp, pointed (Sh., M'L.):

calg, awn, beard of corn, bristles, Ir. *calg*, *colg*, E. Ir. *colg*, a sword, O. W. *colginn*, aristam, W. *cola*, beard of corn, sting, *caly*, penis, Br. *calc'h* (do.), **kalgo-*, **kolgo-*; Gr. κολοβός, stunted; Got. *halks*, poor; further is Lat. *cellere*, hit, *culter*, knife; etc. The main root is *qel*, *qlâ*, hit, break; see *claidheamh*, *cladh*. The Caledonian hero *Calgacos* derives his name hence. Hence **calg-dhìreach**, direct, "sword-straight" to a place.

call, loss, Ir. *caill*, E. Ir. *coll*, W. *coll*, Cor. *colled*, jactura, M. Br. *coll*, **koldo-*; Eng. *halt*, Got. *halts*, O. H. G. *halz*, lame; root *qel*, as above in *calg*, q.v.

calla, **callda**, tame, **callaidh** (M'A., also Sh., who gives the meaning "active" to the last form); cf. W. *call*, wise; from Lat. *callidus*?

callag, **calltag**, the black guillemot, diver; compare Eng. *quail*, Fr. *caille*.

callaid, a partition, fence; the same as *tallaid*, q.v.?

callaid, a wig, cap (M'F.); from Eng. *calotte*, skull-cap.

callan, a noise, Ir. *callán*, *callóich*; from Eng. *call*?

calltuinn, hazel, Ir., E. Ir. *coll*, W. *collen*, Cor. *coll-widen*. M. Br. *quel-vezenn*, **koslo-*; Lat. *corylus*; Norse *hasl*, Eng. *hazel*. **coll* + *tann*.

Calluinn, New Year's Day, Ir. *calláin*, Calends, or first day of the month, E. Ir. *callaind*, the Calends, particularly the first Jan., W. *calan*, Calends; from Lat. *calendæ* (Eng. *Calends*).

calm, a pillar (M'A.), Ir. *columhan*, *colbh*; from Lat. *columna*, etc.

calm, **calma**, brave, Ir., E. Ir. *calma*. Cf. W. *celf*, skill, art, *celfydd*, skilled, O. Br. *celmed*, efficax. The root *cal* is to be compared with that in Ger. *held*, hero, **haleth* or **calet*. The I.E. root is *qel*, as in Lat. *celsus*, high, *columna*, column, Eng. *excel*.

calman, dove; see *calaman*.

calmarra, the pike (Wh.)?

calpa, the calf of the leg, so Ir., E. Ir. *calpda*, bonus pes (Corm.), *colpa*, tibia; from the Norse *kálfi*, whence also Eng. *calf*.

calpa, principal set to interest, Sc. *calpa,* death-duty payable to the landlord, from N. *kaup,* stipulation, pay.

calum, hardness on the skin (H.S.D.; **cathlum** in M'D.); from Lat. *callum, callus.* It is not the obsolete **caladh,** hard, E. Ir. *calad,* W. *caled,* O. Br. *calat,* **kaleto-,* root *kal,* hard; Got. *hallus,* stone, Norse *helle, hallr*; Skr. *çilâ,* stone.

cam, crooked, one-eyed, Ir. *cam,* O. Ir. *camm,* W. *cam,* Br. *kam,* Gaul. *cambo-,* root *kemb,* wind; Gr. *κόμβος,* a band, bond; Lit. *kingė,* door-bar. It has been referred to the root of Gr. *σκαμβός,* crooked (see *ceum*), and to Lat. *camera,* whence Eng. *chamber.* Hence **camag,** club, **camas,** bay.

camag-gharuidh, hollow above the eye, Ir. *camóg-ara,* "the bend of the *ara,*" O. Ir. *aire,* g. *arach,* tempus; Gr. *παρειά,* cheek.

camart, wry-neck:

camastrang, quarrelsome disputation (M'D.):

camhach, talkative; **com-ag-ach,* root *ag* in *adhan*?

camhal, a camel, Ir. *camhall,* E. Ir. *camail,* W. *camyll*; from Lat. *camelus.*

camhan, a hollow plain, Ir. *cabhán* (County *Cavan*); from the Lat. *cavus.*

camhanaich, break of day, twilight, Ir. *camhaoir*; (M'A. *sgamhanaich,* "lights"):

camlag, a curl:

camp, campa, a camp, Ir., M. Ir. *campa*; from the Eng. *camp.*

campar, vexation, grief; from Sc. *cummar,* Eng. *cumber.*

can, say, sing, Ir. *canaim,* O. Ir. *canim,* W. *cana,* sing, Br. *kana*; Lat. *cano,* sing; Gr. *κανάζω*; Eng. *hen.*

cana, porpoise, young whale, Ir. *cana* (O'R.), *cána* (O'B.), whelp, pup, M. Ir. *cana* (do.); from Lat. *canis*?

canach, mountain down, cotton, Ir. *canach,* O. Ir. *canach,* lanugo; Gr. *κνῆκος,* thistle, *κνηκός,* yellow; Skr. *kāncanas,* golden, a plant; **qonak-.* Stokes refers it to **casnaka,* Lat. *cânus,* white (**casno-*), Ag. S. *hasu,* grey, Eng. *hare.*

cànain, language, Ir. *cánamhuin.* Seemingly a long-vowel form of the root *qan,* sing, cry. See *cainnt.*

canal, cinnamon; see *caineal.*

canan, a cannon; from the Eng.

canastair, a canister; from the Eng.

cangaruich, fret; from Sc. *canker,* fret, Eng. *canker.*

cangluinn, trouble, vexation; from Sc. *cangle.*

canna, a can, so Ir., E. Ir. *cann*; from Eng. *can.*

cannach, pretty, kind; **cas-no-,* root, *qas,* Lat. *cānus,* white (*casnus*), Ag. S. *hasu,* grey, Eng. *haze*? Or it may be allied to Lat. *candidus,* white, Skr. *cand,* shine.

canntaireachd, articulate music, chanting, Ir. *cantaireachd*, singing, *cántaire*, a singer; from Lat. *cantor*, *cano*, I sing.

cànran, wrangling, grumbling, muttering, Ir. *cannrán*; from *can*, say, sing.

cantal, grief, weeping (Sh., M'L.), Ir. *cantlamh*:

caob, a clod, a bite, Ir. *caob*, clod, M. Ir. *coep*, E. Ir. *caip*, *cáep*, clot, lump, O. Ir. *caebb oo*, jecur.

caoch, empty (as a nut), blind, so Ir., O. Ir. *caech*, W. *coeg*, foolish, Cor. *cuic*, **kaiko-s*; Lat. *caecus*; Got. *haihs*, one-eyed.

caoch, caothach, rage; see *cuthach*.

caochan, a streamlet; from *caoch*, blind?

caochail, change, die, **caochladh**, a change, Ir. *caochluighim*, O. Ir. *coimchláim cóem-chlóim*: *imchloud*, *imchlóad*, inversio; for *co-imm-clóim*; from *clóim*, muto: see *claoidh*. The aspiration of the *mn* of *imb* is unusual, but the history of the word is also unusual, for it actually appears as *claemchlód* in E. Ir. oftener than once, and Ir. *claochlódh*, *claochladh*.

caod Chaluim-chille, St John's wort (Sh):

caog, wink; apparently from Eng. *cock* (the eye). Cf. Norse *kaga*, keek; Sc. *keek*; Shet. *coag*, peep slily.

caogad, fifty, so Ir., O. Ir. *cóica(t)*, **qenqekont*; Lat. *quinquaginta*; Gr. πεντήκοντα. See *cóig*.

caoidh, lamentation, Ir. *caoi*, *caoidh*, E. Ir. *cói*, *cái*, inf. to *cíim*, ploro, **keiô*, root *qei*, which appears in *caoin*, q.v., and in Eng. *whine*, *whisper*, etc. Bezzenberger suggests **keipô*, and compares Lit *szëptis*, grimace, Ch. Sl. *o-sipnąti*, raucescere. A former derivation of Stokes' is repeated by Rhys (*Manx. Pray.*², 26): **qesi*, root *qes* as in Lat. *questus*.

caoillean, a twig or osier for wicker, M. Ir. *cóelach*; from *caol*, slender.

caoimheach, a bedfellow (Sh.), Ir. *caoimhthech*, E. Ir. *com-aithech*, neighbour; see *aitheach*. Also **caomhach**, friend, bedfellow The latter seems from, or influenced by, *caomh*.

caoimhneas, kindness. This word is supposed by folk etymology to be from *caomh*, kind, whereas it is really allied to O. Ir. *coibnes*, affinitas, **co-ven-estu-*, root *ven* of *fine*, q.v.

caoin, kind, mild, so Ir., O. Ir. *càin*, kind, beautiful [W. *cain*?]: **koini-*, root *koi*, *kei* of *caomh*, q v. Stokes gives base as *kaini-*, and Bezzenberger compares Gr. καίνυσθαι, excel, Ch. Sl. *sinąti*, gleam forth. If the base idea were "beauty," Eng. *shine* might be compared.

caoin, the exterior surface of cloth, right side, rind, sward; from *caoin*, gentle, polished?

caoin, weep, so Ir., O Ir. *cóinim*, *cáinim*, O. W. *cuinhaunt*, deflebunt, Br. *couen*, *queiniff*, **koiniô* ; *qein*, *qîn* ; Eng. *whine*, Norse *hvína*, whirr ; Gr. *κινυρός*, wailing. See *caoidh*.

caoinich, dry, make dry (as hay by the sun), **caoin**, seasoned ; from the adj. *caoin* ?

caoir, a blaze, stream of sparks, a coal, Ir. *caor*, E. Ir. *cáer*, **kairo*, Eng. *hoar* (**kairo-*), Teut. root *hai* in Norse *heið*, atmospheric clearness, O. H. G. *hei*, heat, Eng. *heat* ; Skr. *kêtus*, light. More near are Gr. *κίρις* (lamp, Hes.), Skr. *kiráṇa*, a ray, *kiriká*, sparkling. The root *skei* of Eng. *shine*, Got. *skeirs*, clear, has been also suggested. **caoran**, a peat ember.

caoirean, a plaintive song ; also **caoi-ràn**, moaning (H.S.D.). The root word is *caoidh* ; possibly *ràn*, roar, forms the latter part.

caoirnean, a drop of sheep or goats' dung, a drop or globule ; cf. Ir. *caoirín*, a little berry, little sheep, from *caor*, berry, *caora*, sheep. The two ideas seem confused in Gaelic. In Argyle, *gaoirnean* ; (Arg *ao* here is northern *ao*). From *skar*, *sharn* ?

caol, slender, so Ir., O. Ir. *cóil*, W., Cor. *cul*, O. Br. *culed*, macies, **koilo-* ; Lett. *káils*, naked ; Lat. *caelebs*, single ? Gr. *κοῖλος*, hollow ? Hence **caol** ; **caolas**, a firth or Kyle.

caolan, gut, intestine, Ir. *caolán*, E. Ir. *coelán*, O. W. *coilion*, exta ; from *caol*.

caomh, tender, kind, so Ir., E. Ir. *coem*, O. Ir. *cóim*, W. *cu*, O.W. *cum*, Br. *cuff*, *cun*, debonnaire, **koimo-*, root *kei*, lie ; Gr. *κοιμάω*, put to rest, *κεῖμαι*, lie ; Got. *háims*, a village, Ag. S. *hám*. Eng. *home*. The idea is "restful."

caomhach, bedfellow, friend, Ir. *caomthach*, friend ; see *caoimheach*, and cf. Ir. *caomhaighim*, I protect, cherish, from *caomh*.

caomhain, spare, save, **caomhnadh**, sparing, Ir. *caomhnaim*, preserve, keep, protect, *caomhaighim*, *caomhnuighim*, preserve. The last form seems the most original, if we refer the root to O. Ir. *anich*, protegit, *aingim*, I protect (*a-nak*), root *nak* and *nank*, as in *adh'ac*, *thig*, etc. The form *nak* is more particularly allied to Skr *náçati*, reach, Lit. *neszù*, draw. The G. verb may have been **com-anich-*. It is possible to derive it from *caomh* with *caomhuin* as an inf. form which usurped the place of the present stem.

caonnag, strife, tumult, Ir. *caonnóg*, strife, a nest of wild bees : **kais-no-*, root *kuis*, *kai*, heat, Eng. *heat*, G. *caoir* ?

caor, berry of the rowan, a mountain berry, Ir. *caor*, O. Ir. *cáer*, bacca, W. *cair*, berries, *ceirion*, berry, **kairâ*. It is seemingly the same word as *caoir*, blaze, the idea arising probably from the *red* rowan berries.

caora, a sheep, Ir. *caora*, g. *caorach*, O. Ir. *cáera*, **cairax*, from **ka(p)erax*, allied to Lat. *caper*, a goat, Gr. *κάπρος*, a boar, Eng. *heifer*. Cf. W. *caeriwrch*, roebuck.

caorrunn, the rowan tree, Ir. *caòrthann*, E. Ir. *caerthann*, W. *cerddin*, Br. *kerzin*, **cairo-tann*, from *caor*, berry, and **tann*, tree, Br. *tann*, oak, Cor. *glas-tannen*. The connection with O. H. G. *tanna*, fir, oak, M. H. G. *tan*, wood, Ger. *tanne*, fir, Eng. *tan*, *tanner* (Gr. *θάμνος*, bush ?) is doubtful ; it would necessitate the idea of borrowing, or that the Celtic word was *dann*. Ogam *Maqui Cairatini*, McCaorthainn. Rhys says W. is borrowed from Gadelic (C.F.L. 292).

càpa a cap ; from the Eng. *cap*.

càpraid, drunken riotousness (Dial) ; from Lat. *crâpula*.

capull, a horse, mare (more commonly), so Ir., E. Ir. *capall*, Br. *caval* ; from Lat. *caballus*, whence Eng. *cavalry*, etc., *caple* (M. Eng. *capil*, from Celt.). Norse *kapall*, nag, seems borrowed from Gaelic. The W. is *ceffyl*, with remarkable vocalisation. *Capal-coille* ?

car, a turn, twist, Ir. *cor*, M. Ir. *cor* (=*cuairt* (O'Cl), O. Ir. *curu*, gyros, W. *cor-wynt*, turbo, M. Br. *coruent*, **kuro-* ; Lat. *curvus* ; Gr. *κυρτός*, curved. See *cruinn*.

càr, friendly, related to, Ir. *cára(d)*, a friend. See *caraid* for the usual root.

càradh, condition, usage ; from *càirich*, mend.

caraich, move, stir, Ir. *corruighim*, from *corrach*, unsteady. The G. confuses this with *car*, turn.

caraid, a friend, so Ir , O. Ir. *cara*, g. *carat*, **karant-* ; O. Ir. verb *carim*, *caraim*, I love, W. *caraf*, amo, Br. *quaret*, amare, Gaul. *carantus*, *Caractacus*, etc.; Lat. *cârus*, dear, Eng. *charity*, etc.; Got. *hôrs*, meretrix.

càraid, a pair, couple, Ir. *córaid*, E. Ir. *córait* :

carainnean, refuse of threshed barley, Ir. *carra*, bran ; see *carthuinnich*.

caraist, catechism ; from Sc. *carritch*, a corruption of *catechise*.

caramasg, contest, confusion (Arm. M'F.) : from *car* and *measg* ?

caramh, beside ; see *caruibh*.

càramh, **càradh**, condition, treatment :

carathaist, compulsory labour, **cairiste, cairbhist,** which last see.

carbad, a chariot, so Ir., O. Ir. *carpat*, W. *cerbyd*, O. Br. *cerpit*, Gaul. *Carpentoracte*, *Carbantia*, **karbanto-* ; Lat. *corbis*, a basket ; Norse *hrip*, pannier for peats on horse-back. Lat. *carpentum* (Eng. *carpenter*, etc.), seems borrowed from Gaulish. The root idea is " wicker," referring to the basket character of the body of these chariots.

carbad, jaw, jaw-bone, so Ir., W. *car yr ên* (car of the mouth), Br. *karvan*. The idea is "mouth chariot," from the resemblance between the lower jaw and the old wicker chariots. Loth cfs. W. *carfan*, beam, rail, row.

carbh, engrave, carve; from the English.

carbh, a particular kind of ship or boat (Islay); from Norse *karfi*, a galley for the fiords.

carbhaidh, carraway-seed; from the English.

carbhanach, a carp, Ir. *carbhán*, Manx, *carroo*; from Norse *karfi*, Eng. *carp*.

carcair, a prison, sewer in a cow-house, Ir. *carcar*, prison, E. Ir. *carcair* (do.); from Lat. *carcer*, prison, barrier. *cacair* in Glenmoriston.

carcais, a carcase; from the English.

càrd, card wool, Ir. *cardaighim*; from the Eng. *card*.

cargo, a cargo, load; from the English.

Carghus, Lent, torment, Ir. *Corghas*, M. Ir. *corgus*, W. *garawys*; from Lat. *quadragesima*.

càrlàg, a lock of wool (Sh., H.S.D.), **carla,** a wool-card (Sh. Coneys for Ir.); **card-la-*, from *card* of Eng. For phonetics, cf. *òirleach*.

càrlas, excellence, Ir. *carlamh*, excellent, **co-er-lam-*, *erlam*, clever, **air-lam*? For *lam*, see *ullamh*.

càrn, heap of stones, cairn, Ir. *carn*, E. Ir., W. *carn*, Br. *karn*, **kar-no-*, root *kar*, be hard; Gr. κραναός, rock (κρα-, καρ); further Eng. *hard*, *harsh*. See *carraig*.

càrn, a horning. The G. seems a confusion between *còrn*, horn, Eng. *horn*, put to the *horn*, and *càrn*. M'F. gives **àir chàrn** for "outlawed," **càrn-eaglais,** excommunication.

càrn, a sledge, cart, peat cart, Ir. *carr*, dray, waggon, E. Ir. *carr*, biga, W. *carr*, biga, O. Br. *carr*, vehiculum (gl.), Gaul. *carros*, Latinised into *carrus* (whence, through Fr., Eng. *chariot*, *career*, *carry*, *cargo*, *charge*); from Celt. *karso-*; Lat. *currus* (*quors-*), from *qṛs*; Eng. *horse*, *hurry*.

carnaid, red; from Eng. *carnation*.

càrnag, (1) a she-terrier, (2) a small fish found in stony shores at ebb-tide. The first meaning from *càrn*, cairn. Terriers were used for cairn hunting.

carr, the flesh of the seal and whale (Heb.; Carmichael); founded on obsolete *carn*, flesh?

càrr, the itch, mange, superficial roughness, Ir. *carr*; **carrach,** scabby, M. Ir. *carrach*, **karsâko-*, from *kars*, be rough, hard; cf. Eng. *harsh* (**horsqs*), and *hard*, Lit. *krasta*, the itch (**kors-ta-*); further root *kar*, to be hard, rough. For **càrr,** rocky shelf, Ir. *carr*, rock, see *carraig*.

carrachan, a frog-fish, called "cobler," Ir. *carrachán*, the rock fish called cobler (Coneys). From *carr*, a rock. Also the word means "the wild liquorice root"—*carra-meille*, q.v.

carragh, a pillar stone, Ir. *carrthadh*, *cartha*, E. Ir. *corthe*. The root, despite the vocalic difficulty caused by the E. Ir. form, is likely the same as in *carraig*; yet cf. *kor* of *cuir*, set.

carraid, conflict; from the root *kars* in *càrr*, "rough-work?"

carraig, rock, so Ir., O. Ir. *carric*, W. *careg*, O. W. *carrecc*, Br. *karrek*, **karsekki-* (so Rhys, R. C.[17] 102, who thinks W. borrowed), from root *kars*, hard, rough; Norwegian, *herren*, hard, stiff, *harren*, hard, Eng. *harsh*, *hard* (root *kar*). See *càrr*.

carra-meille, wild liquorice, wood pease, Ir. *carra-mhilis*. The name is explained as "knots of honey," the *carra* being the same as *càrr*, and *meille* the gen. of *mil*. Hence Sc. *carmele*, etc.

carran, spurrey, spergula arvensis, Ir. *carrán*, scurvy grass. From the root *kars* of *càrr*. **Carran** also means a "shrimp," and is of the same origin.

carran-creige, the conger; see *carran* above.

carrasan, hoarseness, wheezing, Ir. *carsán*; from the root *kars*, be rough. See *càrr*. Cf. *κόρυζα*, catarrh, *rotz*.

càrt, a quart, Ir. *cárt*; from the Eng. *quart*, Lat. *quartus*.

cartan, a small brown insect that eats into the flesh, Ir. *cartán*, a small brown insect that eats into the flesh, a crab. A Gadelicised form of *partan*, q.v.

carthannach, affectionate, charitable, Ir. *carthannach*; from Lat. *caritas*.

carthuinnich, dwell apart as in a cave, separate (M'F.). Cf. **caruinnean**, refuse of threshed corn, **caruinnich**, winnow. Possibly from the root *kar*, separate, a form of the root of *sgar*, q.v.

caruibh, an caruibh, beside, near. This is the dat. pl. of *car*.

cas, foot, leg, Ir. *cos*, O. Ir. *coss*, W. *coes*, **koksâ*; Lat. *coxa*, hip; M. H. G. *hahse*, bend of the knee; Skr. *kákshas*, armpit.

cas, steep, sudden, Ir. *casach*, an ascent, M. Ir. *cass*, rapid, **kasto-*; Eng. *haste*.

cas, curled, Ir., M. Ir. *cas*, curly, *casaim*, flecto; **qasto-*, root *qas*; Norse *haddr* (*has-da-*), hair, Eng. *hair*; Lit. *kasa*, hair-plait, Ch. Sl. *kosa*, hair (Kluge). Stokes compares it with Lat. *quasillum*, a basket, root *quas*.

cas, gnash the teeth, Ir. *cais*, hate, W. *câs*, hate, Br. *cas*, **cad-s-to-*; Eng. *hate*, Ger. *hass*, Got. *hatis*. Of the same ultimate origin as *cas*, sudden (Strachan).

cas, fire (as a stone) (Suth.), seemingly founded on Eng. *cast.* Cf. *casadh ar a chéile* = met (Ir.).

càs, a difficulty, Ir. *cás*; from Lat. *casus* (Eng. *case*).

casach, fishing tackle (part attached to hook): from *cas.*

casad, casd, a cough, Ir. *casachdach*, W. *pâs*, *peswch*, Br. *pas*, **qusto-*; Eng. *host*, Ag. S. *hvósta*, Ger. *husten*; Lit. *kósiu*; Skr. *kâsate*, coughs.

casag, a cassock, Ir. *casóg*; from the Eng. The E. Ir. word is *casal*, from Lat. *casula.*

casaid, a complaint, accusation, Ir. *casaoid*, O. Ir. *cossóit.* The word is a compound, beginning with *con*, and seemingly of the same origin as *faosaid*, q.v. Stokes thinks that the word is borrowed from the Lat. *causatio*; this is not likely, however. Root *sen*, W. *cynhenn*, quarrel.

casair, sea drift, Ir. *casair*, a shower, E. Ir. *casair*, hail, W. *cesair* (do.), Br. *kazerc'h* (do.), **kassri-*, **kad-tri-*; from root *cad* as in Lat. *cado*, fall. The Ir. and G. (?) **casáir,** phosphorescence, seems to be the same word.

casan, a path, Ir. *casán*; from *cas*, foot.

casan, a rafter, roof-tree; from *cas*?

casgair, slay, butcher, so Ir., O. Ir. *coscar*, victory, destruction; **co-scar*; see *sgar.*

casnaid, chips of wood (Arm.), Ir. *casnaidh*; **co-+snaidh*, q.v.

caspanach, parallel (Sh.), Ir. *cospanach* (O'R.); **co-spann*; see *spann.*

castan, a chestnut; from Lat. *castanea*, through M. Eng. *castane*, *chesnut.*

castaran, a measure for butter ($\frac{1}{4}$ stone); from the Eng. *castor.*

castreaghainn, the straw on a kiln below the grain (Arm., not H.S.D.):

cat, a cat, so Ir. E. Ir. *catt*, W. *cath*, Cor. *kat*, Br. *kaz*, Gaul *Cattos*; Lat. *catta*, perhaps also *catulus*; Eng. *cat*, Ger. *katze*, etc. It is a word of doubtful origin; possibly, however, Celtic, and applied first to the wild cat, then to the tame Egyptian cat introduced in the early centuries of the Christian era.

cata, càta, sheep-cot, pen; from Eng. *cot.*

catadh, catachadh, taming, **càtadh** (M'F.); cf. *tataich.*

catag, potato cellar (Dialectic); see *cata.*

catas, refuse at carding of wool, Ir. *cadás*, cotton, scraping of linen rags; from Eng. *caddis.* See further under *caiteas.*

cath, battle, Ir., O. Ir. *cath*, W. *cad*, O. W. *cat*, Cor. *cas*, Gaul. *catu-*; O. H. G. *hadu-*, fight, Ag. S. *heaðo-*, Ger. *hader*, contention; Skr. *çatru*, enemy; Gr. κότος, wrath.

càth, chaff, husks of corn, Ir., O. Ir. *cáith*, W. *coden*, a bag, husk, pod (?), **kûti-*, root *kât*, *kat*, as in *caith*, spend, cast.
cathachadh, provoking, accusing, fighting, Ir. *cathaighim*; from *cath*, fight.
cathadh, snow-drift, Ir. *cáthadh*, snow-drift, sea-drift; cf. M. Ir. *cúa*, gen. *cúadh*, W. *cawod*, O. Cor. *cowes*, nimbus, Br. *kaouad*, **kavat* (Stokes); allied to Eng. *shower*. It is possible to refer the G. word to the root of *caith*, *càth*.
cathair, a city, Ir., E. Ir. *cathair*, O. Ir. *cathir* (**kastrex*), W. *caer*, Br. *kaer*, **kastro-*; Lat. *castrum*, fort (Stokes). The root seems to be *cat*, *cats*; the phonetics are the same as in *piuthar* for the final part of the word.
cathair, a chair, Ir. *cathaoir*, E. Ir. *catháir*, W. *cadair*, Br. *kador*; from Lat. *cathedra*, whence also, through Fr., Eng. *chair*.
cathan, a wild goose with black bill (Heb.); see *cadhan*.
cathan-aodaich, a web (M'D.):
càthar, mossy ground; see *càir*.
cathlunn, a corn (Sh.; not in H.S.D,); formed on Lat. *callum*. See *calum*.
catluibh, cudwort; see *cadhluibh*.
cè, **cèath**, cream, M. Ir. *ceó*, milk; cf. Br. *koavenn*, which suggests a form *keivo-* (cf. *glé* from *gleivo-*), root *kei*, *skei*, shade, cover, as in Gr. σκιά, shadow, Ger. *schemen* (do.)? The Br. *koavenn* has been referred to **co + hufen*, W. *hufen*, cream. Cf. *ceò*, mist, "covering."
cé, the earth, used only in the phrase **an cruinne cé**, the (round) earth, Ir., E. Ir. *cé*, *for bith ché*, on this earth. The *cé* is supposed to be for "this," from the pronominal root *kei*, Gr. κεῖνος, he, Lat. *ce*, *cis*, Eng. *he*. The root *kei*, go, move (Lat. *cio*, Gr. κίω), has also been suggested.
cè, give?
cè, spouse (Carm.), Ir. *cé*:
eaba, **ceibe**, the iron part of a spade or other delving instrument; see *caibe*.
cèabhar, a fine breeze (Heb.):
ceabhar (Carm.), sky, (Prov.) *ci'ar*:
ceach, an interjection of dislike; see the next word.
ceacharra, dirty, mean, obstreperous (Carm.), Ir. *ceachair*, dirt, M. Ir. *cecharda*, **kekari-*; from *kek*, the *e* form of the root *kak* seen in *cac*, q.v.
ceachladh, digging, Ir. *ceachlaim*, O. Ir. *ro-cechladatar*, suffoderunt, **ce-clad-*, a reduplicated or perfect form of the root *clad* of G. *cladh*, q.v.
cead, permission, so Ir., O. Ir. *cet*, **ces-do-*; Lat. *cēdo*, I yield (for *ces-dô*).

ceadan, bunch of wool, Ir. *ceadach*, cloth, coarse cloth, W. *cadach*, clout. Rhys regards W. as borrowed from Ir. For all, cf. *cadadh, caiteas.*

ceadha, the part of the plough on which the share is fixed. Also **ceidhe.** Both words are used for Eng. *quay.*

ceafan, a frivolous person (Dialectic):

ceàird, a trade, E. Ir. *cerd*; see *ceàrd.*

ceal, stupor, forgetfulness, Ir. *ceal*, forgetfulness; from the root *qel* of *ceil*, conceal. Cf. E. Ir. *cel*, death. *ceal*, end (Carm.).

†ceal, same, similar hue (Carm.):

cealaich, the fire-place of a kiln:

cealaich, eat (Kirk), Ir. *cealaim*; root *qel* as in Lat. *colo?*

cealaich, conceal:

cealair, a virago (Badenoch):

cealg, guile, treachery, so Ir., E. Ir. *celg*, **kelgâ*; Arm. *keλch^c*, hypocrisy. The further root is *qel* of *ceil.*

ceall, g. **cille,** a church, so Ir., E. Ir. *cell*; from Lat. *cella*, a cell, a hermit's cell especially, whence the Gadelic use. Hence **cealloir,** superior of a cell, and the name Mackellar. "A retired spot" (Hend.).

cealtar, broad-cloth, Ir. *cealtair*, clothes, E. Ir. *celtar*, *celt*, raiment; from *qel*, cover, as in *ceil*, q.v.

ceana, whither, for *c'iona, c'ionadh?* Cf. Ir. *cá h-ionad.* See *ionadh.*

ceanalta, mild, kind, so Ir.; from **cen*, as in *cion*, *†cean*, love, desire. See *cion.*

ceangal, a tie, binding, so Ir., E. Ir., *cengal*, W. *cengl*; from Lat. *cingulum*, vb. *cingo*, I bind, Eng, *cincture.*

ceann, head, so Ir., O. Ir. *cend, cenn*, W., Br. *penn*, Gaul, *Penno-*, **qenno-*. Perhaps for *qen-no-*, root *qen* (labialised), begin, Ch. Sl. *koni*, beginning, as in *ceud*, first. The difficulty is that the other labialising languages and the Brittonic branch otherwise show no trace of labialisation for *qen.* Windisch, followed by Brugmann, suggested a stem *kvindo-*, I. E. root *kvi*, Skr. *çvi*, swell, Gr. Πίνδος, Pindus Mount; but the root vowel is not *i*, even granting the possible labialisation of *kvi*, which does not really take place in Greek. Hence **ceannag,** a bottle of hay, **ceannaich,** buy (= "heading" or reckoning by the head; cf. Dial. **ceann,** sum up), **ceannaidh,** head-wind (Hend.), **ceannas,** vaunting (Hend.).

ceannach, a purchasing, so Ir., E. Ir. *cennaigim*, I buy, O. Ir. *cennige*, lixa, *caingen*, negotium.

ceannairc, rebellion, turbulence, so Ir.; **ceann + arc*; for root *arc*, see *adharc.* For meaning cf. Eng. *head*strong, W. *pen*ffest (do.).

ceannard, commander, chief, Ir. *ceannárd*, arrogant, commanding, "high-headed," from *ceann* and *àrd*; M. *kinnoort*, Ir. *ceann-phort*, commander, authority, head post or city: *ceann+port.*

ceannrach, ceannraig (Cam.), a bridle or horse's head-gear, Ir. *ceannrach*; from *ceann + rach.* For *rach* (root *rig*), see *cuibhreach*, *àrachas.*

ceannsaich, subdue, tame, Ir. *ceannsaighim*; from *ceannas*, superiority, "head-ness," from *ceann* and the abst. termination *as.* Similarly **ceannsal,** rule.

ceap, a block, shoemaker's last, so Ir., E. Ir. *cepp*, W. *cyff*, Br. *kef*; from Lat. *cippus.*

ceap, catch, stop. This word seems borrowed from the Sc. *kep*, of like meaning, a bye-form of Eng. *keep.* The Ir. *ceap*, bound, bind, stop (?), seems from *ceap* above.

†**ceapach,** a tillage plot, Ir. *ceapach.* This Stokes refers to a Celtic *keppo-*, garden, root *kep*, *kāp*, Lat. *campus*, Gr. κῆπος, garden, Ger. *hube*, piece of land. Satisfactory though the meaning be, the derivation is doubtful as involving the preservation of *p*, even though flanked by a second *p* (or *-nó-*, i.e., *kep-nó-*, which is still more doubtful). Perhaps from *ceap*, a block, in the sense of a "holding." Hence the common place-name **Keppoch.**

ceapag, a verse, an impromptu verse, carelessly sung verse, E. Ir. *cepóc*, a chorus song: a rare word in Ir., and said to be Sc. Gaelic for Ir. *aidbsi*, great chorus. From *ceap*, catch? cf. Eng. *catch*, a chorus verse. Zimmer suggests that it stands for *Ce Póc*, "kiss here," (?) sung by the girls as a refrain at gatherings!

ceapaire, bread covered with butter, etc., Ir. *ceapaire*; from *ceap*, a block. Cf. **ceapag,** a wheel-barrow wheel.

cearb, piece, article of clothing, so Ir., E. Ir. *cerp*, cutting, *cerbaim*; **kṛbh*, *skṛbh*; Gr. κάρφος, twig, Eng. *shrub*; *(*s*)*ker*, cut, divide. Cf. W. *carp*, rag, *cerpyn.* Bezzenberger cfs. M. H. G. *herb*, asper. St. now *skerb*, Eng. *sharp.*

cearc, a hen, so Ir., M. Ir. *cerc*, **cercâ*; from I. E. *qerqo*, to sound, hence "a noise-making bird"; Gr. κέρκος, a cock, κρέξ, a fowl; Lat. *querquedula*, a teal, O. Prus. *kerko*, a diver; Skr. *kṛka-vâkus*, a cock.

cearcall, a hoop, so Ir.; from L. Lat. *circulus*, *circullus*, a hoop, from *circulus*, a circle.

ceàrd, a craftsman, Ir. *céard*, E. Ir. *cerd*, W. *cerdd*, art; Lat. *cerdo*, craftsman; Gr. κέρδος, gain.

ceàrdach, a smithy, Ir. *céardcha*, O. Ir. *cerddchae*; from *cerd+cae*, the latter word *cae* meaning a house in Ir., a Celtic *kaio-n*, allied to Eng. *home.*

ceard-dubhan, scarabæus, dung-beetle, hornet (H.S.D. for form), **ceardaman** (M'A.); see *cearnabhan*. *cearr-dubhan* (Carm.), "wrong-sided little black one."

cearmanta, tidy (Arm.); *cearmanaich*, make tidy (Perth.):

ceàrn, a corner, quarter, Ir. *cearn*, *cearna*, angle, corner, E. Ir. *cern*; evidently an *e* form of the stem found in *corn*, horn, q.v.

cearnabhan, a hornet, Ir. *cearnabhán*; from **cerno-*. Cf. Eng. *hornet* (**kr̥s-en-*), Lat. *crabro*.

ceàrr, wrong, left (hand), E. Ir. *cerr*, **kerso-*; Lat. *cerritus*, crazed; Gr. ἐγκάρσιος, slantwise; Lit. *skersas*, crooked.

ceàrrach, a gamester, Ir. *cearrbhach*, a gamester, dexterous gambler. Cf. G. **ceàrrbhag, cearrag**, the left-hand, the use of which was considered in plays of chance as "sinister."

ceart, right, so Ir., E. Ir. *cert*; Lat. *certus*, certain, sure, *cerno*, discern; Gr. κρίνω, judge, κριτής, a judge, Eng. *critic*.

ceasad, a complaint (M'F.), Ir. *ceasacht*, grumbling, M. Ir. *cesnaighim*, complain, *ces*, sorrow, **qes-to-*; Lat. *questus*, *queror*, I complain, *querela*, Eng. *quarrel*.

†**ceasg,** floss (Carm.), animal with long flossy hair or wool, Ir. *ceaslach*, long hair or wool on fleece legs. See *Ceus*.

ceasnaich, examine, catechise, Ir. *ceasnuighim*; from Lat. *quæstio*, *quæstionis*, Eng. *question*. Stokes (Bk. of Lis.) has suggested that the Lat. and Gadelic are cognate; though possible (*qais*, *qis* may become by umlaut *ces* in G.), it is improbable from the stem form in *n* persisting in the G. verb.

ceathach, mist; this is really the old stem of *ceò*, mist, E. Ir. *ciach*, q.v. Ir. *ceathach*, showery, is from *cith*, a shower.

ceathairne, yeomanry, the portion of a population fit for warfare; see *ceatharn*.

ceatharn, a troop, so Ir., E. Ir. *ceithern*, **keternâ*; Lat. *caterva*, troop, *catêna*, a chain; O. Sl. *ceta*, company (Stokes). It has also been regarded as borrowed from Lat. *quaternio*, which in the Vulg. means a "body of four soldiers," quaternion. Hence Eng. *cateran*, *kern*.

ceidhe, quay, coulter-place, Ir. *ceigh*, quay. See *ceadha*.

ceig, a mass of shag, clot, **ceigein,** a tuft, a fat man. From Scandinavian *kagge*, round mass, *keg*, corpulent man or animal, whence Eng. *keg*; Norse, *kaggi*, cask, Norwegian, *kagge*, round mass.

ceig, a kick; from the Eng.

ceil, conceal, Ir., *ceilim*, O. Ir. *celim*, W. *celu*, I. E. *qel*; Lat. *cêlo*, Eng. con-*ceal*; Ag. S. *helan*, hide, Eng. *Hell*; Gr. καλύπτω, hide; Skr. *kála*, darkness.

céile, spouse, fellow, so Ir., O. Ir. *céle*, socius, W. *cilydd* (*y gilydd* = *a chéile* of G. = *eguille* of Br.), **keiljo-*, "way-farer," from *kei*, go (Lat. *cio*, move, Gr. κίω, go, κινέω, move, *kinetics*). The idea is the same as in Ir. *sétig*, wife, from *sét*, way. Strachan thinks that G. and W. demand a stem *ceglio-*; and Dr Stokes thinks that, if *céle*, servus, is different from *céle*, fellow, it must come from *kak-lio-* (better *keklio-*), and be allied to Lat. *cacula*, a servant. Hence **céilidh**, a gossiping visit or meeting.

ceileach, martial (H.S.D.), Ir. *ceallach*, war, M. Ir. *cellach*, war; Teut. *hildi-*, war, Lat. *per-cellere*, hit.

ceileir, chirping of birds, Ir. *ceileabhar*, *ceileabhrach*, musical, M. Ir. *ceilebradh eoin*, singing of birds, E. Ir. *celebrad*, a celebrating or observance, a welcome of joy; from Lat. *celebratio.*

céillidh, wise, sober, Ir. *céillidhe*; from *ciall.*

ceilp, kelp; from Eng.

céin, remote; really the oblique form of *cian*, q.v.

céir, wax, Ir., M. Ir. *céir*, W. *cwyr*, O. W. *kuyr*, Cor. *coir*, Br. *coar*; from Lat. *cêra*, wax.

céir, céire, the buttock; see *péire.*

ceireanaich, fondle, make much of (Perth); cf. *ceirein*, plaster.

ceirein, a plaster, a "clout," Ir., M. Ir., *céirín*, a plaster; from *céir*, wax. Eng. *cerate.*

ceirtle, a clew, ball of yarn, Ir. *ceirsle* (so G. too), *ceirtlín*, O. Ir. *certle*, glomus, **kertilliâ*; from I. E. *qert*, wind, bend; Skr. *kart*, spin; Lat. *cartilago*, Eng. *cartilage*; Gr. κάρταλος, basket; Eng. *hurdle.*

céis, a case, hamper; from Eng. *case.* Ir. *ceis*, basket, M. Ir. *ceiss*, is a different word, possibly allied to, if not borrowed from, Lat. *cista* (Stokes). From Ir. *ceis* comes **ceis-chrann**, polypody, given in H.S.D. from O'R. Cf. O. Ir. *cass*, basket, Lat. *quasillus.*

ceisd, a question, so Ir., E. Ir. *ceist*; from Lat. *quœstio.* Hence **ceisdein**, a sweetheart, founded on "ceisd mo chridhe"—darling (*i.e.*, question, anxiety) of my heart.

céiseach, large, corpulent woman; see *ceòs.*

Céitein, May, O. Ir. *cétam* (g. *cétaman*), *cetsoman* (*cetshaman*) in Cor. Gl., where it is explained as *cét-sam-sín*, the first weather-motion of *sam* or summer. The word means the "first of summer"—*cét+sam-*, the *sam* of *samhradh*, q.v. The termination is possibly influenced by other time words. See *Samhainn.*

ceithir, four, Ir. *ceathair* (n.), *ceithre* (adj.), O. Ir. *cethir*, W. *pedwar*, Cor. *peswar*, Br. *pevar*, Gaul. *petor-*, **qetveres*, I. E. *qetvôr*; Lat. *quatuor*; Gr. τέτταρες; Got. *fidvôr*, Eng. *four*; Lit. *keturi*; Skr. *catvâras.*

ceò, mist, Ir. *ceó*, E. Ir. *ceó*, g. *ciach*, **cevox*, g. **cevocos*, I. E. *sqevo-*, Lat. *obscūrus*, Norse *ský*, cloud, Eng. *sky*. The idea is "covering."

ceòb, a dark nook, corner :

ceòban, small drizzle ; *ceò + boinne* or *-bainne*, "mist-drop." The Ir. is *ceóbhrán*, for *ceò + braon*. This last is G. **ciùran**, q.v. Hence **ceòpach** (for **ceòbnach** ?) Also **ceòpan**. Ir. *ciabhrán*, drizzle, fog, M. Ir. *ciabor*, mist.

ceòl, music, Ir., E. Ir. *ceól*, g. *ciúil*, **kipolo-*, a Gadelicised form of **pipolo* ; onomatopoetic root *pīp*, Lat. *pîpilo*, chirp, *pipilum*, outcry, *pîpo*, chirp, Ag. S. *pípe*, Eng. *pipe* (hence W. *pib*, G. *pìob*, etc). Stokes and Rhys have given a Celtic *qeqlo-* for stem, allied to W. *pib*, pipe. For phonetics, see *feòil*. Stokes now suggests alliance with Ger. *heulen*, hoot, howl, O. H. G. *hiuwilôn*.

ceòs, the hip, podex ; see *ceus*, poples. Hence **ceòsach**, broad-skirted, bulky, clumsy.

ceòsan, burr or light down of feathers ; see *ceus*, wool of legs, etc.

ceud, first, Ir. *céad*, O. Ir. *cét*, W. *cynt*, formerly, *cyntaf*, first, Br. *kent*, *kenta* (do.), Gaul. *Cintu-*, **kentu-* ; allied to W. *cann*, with Gr. *κατά*, down, against (= *kn̥ta*), Lat. *contra*. Further allied is possibly (*and this is the usual derivation*) I. E. *qen*, begin, Lat. re-*cens*, Eng. *recent* ; Gr. *καινός* (= *κανιός*), new ; Skr. *kaná*, young ; Ch. Sl. *koni*, beginning. Some again have compared Teut. *hind* as in Eng. *hindmost*.

ceud, a hundred, so Ir., O. Ir. *cét*, W. *cant*, Cor. *cans*, Br. *kant*, **kn̥to-n* ; Lat. *centum* ; Gr. *ἑκατόν* (= *se-kn̥ton*) ; Got. *hund*, Eng. *hund*-red ; Lit. *szìmtas* ; Skr. *çatám*.

ceudfadh, sense, Ir. *céadfadh*, O. Ir. *cétbaid*, W. *canfod*, to perceive, **cant-buti-*, "with-being," from *ceud*, with, first, and *bu*, be.

ceudna, the same, so Ir., O. Ir. *cétna*, **centinio-s* ; from *ceud*, first.

ceum, a step, Ir. *céim*, O. Ir. *ceimm*, W., Cor. *cam*, O. W. *cemmein*, gradibus, Br. *kam*, **kn̥gmen-*, verb **kengô*, I go, Ir. *cingim*, Gaul. *Cingeto*-rix, "king of marching men"—of warriors : I. E. *kheng*, limp ; Ger. *hinken*, limp ; Skr. *khañj*, limp

ceus, ham, poples : **cencso-* ; Lit. *kenkle*, hough, bend of the knee, *kinka*, knee joint ; Ag. S. *hóh* (= *hanχ*), Eng. *hough* (Strachan for Lit.). The gen. is **ceòis**, whence *ceòs*, etc.

ceus, the coarse part of the wool on sheep's legs (Heb.), M. Ir. *céslach* ; from *ceus*, ham.

ceus, crucify, Ir. *céasaim*, *ceusaim*, O. Ir. *céssaim*, suffer, **kentsô*, suffer : I. E. *qentho* ; Gr. *πένθος*, *πάθος*, suffering, Eng. *pathos* ; Lit. *kenczù*, suffering.

ceutach, becoming ; see *ciatach*.

cha, cha'n, not, Ir. *nocha n-*, O. Ir. *ní con* aspirating. The particle *no* or *nu* is no part of this negative: only *ní* and *con*, "non quod," *con* being the same as *gu'n*. Aspirating power of it is as yet unexplained. Ulster Ir. *cha*.

chaidh, went, ivit, Ir. *dochuaidh*, O. Ir. *dochóid*, he went, **coud-*; Skr. *codati*, make haste, *codayati*, drive, *códa*, a goad; Eng. *shoot*. See *deach*.

chaoidh, for ever, Ir. *choidhche*, E. Ir. *chaidche*, *coidchi*; for *co-aidche*, *gu oidhche*, "till night."

cheana, already, Ir. *cheana*, E. Ir. *chena*, in sooth, quidem, jam, *ol chena*, *ar chena*, O. Ir. *cene*, *olchene*; from *cen-é*, "without this," root in *gun*, without, *cion*, want.

chi, will see, Ir. *chidhim*, *chím*, O. Ir. *atchí*, videt, **ad-cesiô*, **kesiô*; Skr. *caksh*, see, for **ca-kas*; Lat. *canus* (**cas-no-?*), grey; Ag. S. *hasu*, grey, Eng. *hare*. See *chunnaic*, *faic*. The aspiration of *chì* is due to the lost *ad-* initial, which is confused with the verbal particle *do*, *a*.

cho, co, as, so, Ir. *comh*, W. *cyn*; from *com*, with. See *comh-*. Gaelic "Cho dubh ri feannaig" = Welsh "Cyn ddued a'r frân."

chon, to; dialectic form of *gu*. The *n* belongs to the article. Also *thun*; q.v. Compare *chugad* and *thugad* to *chon* and *thun* in phonetics.

chuala, heard, Ir. *do chuala*, O. Ir. *rochúala*, W. *cigleu*, **kuklova*; root *kleu* as in *cluinn*, q.v.

chugad, towards thee, so Ir., O. Ir. *chucut*, **cu-cu-t*, where the prep. *cu* or *gu*, to, is reduplicated. See *gu*. The *t* or *-ut* is for *tu*, q.v. So with **chuga, chuige,** etc.

chum, chùm, a chum, to, for, in order to, Ir. *chum*, *do chum*, O. Ir. *dochum n-*, *dochom n-*; an idiomatic use of *com*, side? Cf. Eng. *side*, *beside*.

chun, to, until; see *chon*.

chunnaic, saw, Ir. *choncadar*, they saw, O. Ir. *conaca*, vidi; from *con*+*faic*; for *con*, see *comh-*, and see *faic*. The old past was **chunnairc,** still used in Ir. as *chonnairc*, from *con*+*dearc*, q.v.

cia, who, what, Ir. *cia*, O. Ir. *cía*, W. *pwy*, Cor. *pyu*, Br. *piu*, **qei*; Lat. *qui* (Old Lat. *quei*). See further under *co*.

ciabh, a lock of hair, so Ir., E. Ir. *ciab*: **kes-abu-*, *kes* of *cas?*

Ciadaoin, Di-ciadaoin, Wednesday, Ir. *Céadaoin*, O. Ir. *cétáin*, first fast, "Day of the First Fast." The first weekly fast was the latter half of Wednesday, the next was Friday—*Di-h-aoine*. Thursday is the day "Between two fasts"—*Diardaoin*, q.v. See further under *Di-*.

ciagach, sly-humoured (Dialectic):

cial, side or brim of a vessel; see *ciobhull*.

ciall, sense, understanding, Ir., O. Ir. *ciall*, W. *pwyll*, Cor. *pull*, Br. *poell*, **qeislâ*: I. E. *qei*, observe, see, shine; Gr. *πινυτός*, wise; Skr. *cetati*, perceive, *cittam*, thought, *cinōti*, discover; further Ger. *heiter*, clear.

ciamhair, sad (Sh., Arm.), Ir. *ciamhair*, *ciamhaire* (O'Cl., O'Br.):

cian, remote, so Ir., O. Ir. *cían*, **keino-*; from the pronominal root *kei*, there, Gr. *κεῖνος*, ille, Lat. *cis*, *citra*, Eng. *he*. Others have referred it to root *qei*, *qi*, Skr. *ciras*, long, Got. *hveila*, time, Eng. *while*. Hence **cianail**, sad, lonesome, Ir. *cian-amhuil*.

cianog, a small measure of arable land (Heb.: H.S.D.); see *cionag*.

ciar, dusky, Ir., E. Ir. *cíar*, **keiro-s*, "shadowy"; root *sqhei*, Gr. *σκιερός*, shady, *σκιά*, shadow, Skr. *châyā́*, shadow, Ag. S. *scimo* (do.). It has been compared to Eng. *hoar*, Norse *hárr*, but the vowels do not suit.

cias, g. **ceòis**, border, skirt, fringe:

ciatach, **ciatfach**, elegant, becoming, Ir. *céadfadhach*, discreet, belonging to the senses; from *ceudfadh*, q.v.

cibein, rump (of a bird, M'D.), Ir. *cibín*, the rump (Con.). Cf. Ir. *giob*, a tail.

cibeir, a shepherd; from Sc., Eng. *keeper*.

cibhearg, a rag, a little ragged woman (Sh.):

cidhis, a mask, vizard (M'D.), **luchd cidhis**, masqueraders; from Sc. *gyis*, a mask, *gysars*, masqueraders, M. Eng. *gīsen*, to dress, Eng. *guise*, *disguise*; all from O. Fr. *guise*, modus, *desguiser*, disguise. The Sc. was directly borrowed in the Stuart period.

cigil, tickle (Sh.); see *ciogail*.

cileag, a diminutive, weakly person (Arg.):

cilean, a large codfish; from Norse *keila*, gadus longus or "long cod." Also **cilig** (Sutherland).

cill, a church; locative case of *ceall*, q.v., used for the most part in place-names.

cillein, a concealed heap, repository, Ir. *cillín*, a purse or store of hoarded cash (O'B.), dim. of *ceall*, cell, church, q.v.

cineal, offspring, clan, Ir. *cineul*, O. Ir. *cenél*, W. *cenedl*, O. W. *cenetl*, Cor. *kinethel*, **kenetlo-n*: I. E. *qen*, begin; Gr. *καινός*, new (*καvjός*); Lat. re-*cens*, Eng. *recent*; Ch. Sl. *koni*, beginning; Skr. *kaná*, young.

cinn, grow, increase, spring from, Ir., E. Ir. *cinim*, spring from, descend of; root *qen* of *cineal*, q.v. Also **cinnich**, grow, increase.

cinneadh, **cinne**, tribe, clan, Ir. *cineadh*, *cine*, E. Ir. *ciniud* (g. *cineda*); from root *qen* in *cineal*, q.v. Hence **cinnich**, gentiles, Ir. *cineadhach*, a gentile.

cinneag, a spindle (Sutherland):
cinnseal, need, desire (Arm.), contact, origin (M'A.). In the first sense, the word is from *cion*, want; in the second, from *cinn*. In the sense of "contact," as exemplified by M'A., the Sc. *kinches*, correspondence, etc. ("to kep kinches wi' one"), has to be remembered, a word apparently from *kin*.
cinnte, certain, so Ir., O. Ir. *cinnim*, definio, *écintech* infinitus; from *ceann*, head, q.v.
ciob, bite, wound (Bib. Gl.); see *caob*. *cìbidh* (Hend.).
ciob, coarse mountain grass, tow, Ir. *cíob*, coarse mountain grass, scirpus cæspitosus. Club rush, flaky peat (Carm.).
ciobhull, the jaw (M'D., who writes "na cíobhuill"), **ciobhal** (Sh.), more properly **giall** (Arm.), q.v. H.S.D. gives the pl. as **cibhlean.**
cìoch, a woman's breast, Ir. *cíoch*, E. Ir. *cích*; cf. W. *cig*, flesh, M. Br. *quic* (do.), **kîkâ* (*kêkâ*?). Bez. suggests (with query) connection with Bulg. *cica*, teat, Polish *cyc*.
cìocras, hunger, longing, Ir. *cíocras*, hunger, greed, ravenousness:
ciod, what, Ir. *cad*, O. Ir. *cate*, *cote*, lit. "quid est," *co* + *ta*, q.v. Ir. *caidé* (North *goidé*), O. Ir. *caté*, what is it, O. Ir. *ité*, it is.
ciogail, tickle, Ir. *giglim*; see *diogail*. In the Heb. **ciogailt**, tickling, also signifies terror, a crisis of timorous determination (H.S.D.).
ciom, a comb, wool-card, Ir. *ciomam*, I comb (O'B., Sh.); from M. Eng. *kemb*, to comb. H.S.D. has not the word.
ciomach, a prisoner, Ir. *cimidh*, O. Ir. *cimbid*, **kṃbiti-* (Stokes), root *kemb*, wind; Lat. *cingo*, surround; Gr. κόμβος, band, Norwegian *hempa* (do.). See *ceangal*, from the same I. E. root *qeng*.
ciombal, bell, cymbal, so Ir.; from Lat. *cymbalum*, Eng. *cymbal*.
ciomboll, a bundle of hay or straw (Heb.); from Norse *kimbill*, a bundle, *kimbla*, to truss, Sc. *kemple*, forty bottles of hay or straw, *kimple*, a piece (Banffshire).
cion, want; from the root *ken* of *gun*, without.
cion, love, esteem, Ir. *cion*, *cean*, M. Ir. *cen*, O. Ir. *fochen*, welcome; root *qino-*, *qi*, I. E. *qei*, notice, as in *ciall*. Further, Gr. τιμή, honour, τίω, honour, τίνω, pay penalty. The sense of honour and punishment is combined in the same word. See *ciont*.
cionag, a small portion of land, one-fourth of a *cleitig* or one-eighth of a "farthing" land (Heb.), Ir. *cionóg*, a small coin, a kernel; cf. W. *ceiniog*, a penny.
cionar, music (Arm.; Sh. has **cionthar**; H.S.D. has **ciòn'thar** from A. M'D., querulous music):
cionn, os cionn, etc.; this is the old dat. of *ceann*, head (**qennō*).

cionnarra, identical, idem; Ir. *cionda* (dial. Gaelic **cionda**), for *ceudna*, by metathesis of the *n*. The G. *-arra* is an adjectival form of the *-ar* in *aon-ar*, etc.

cionnas, how, Ir. *cionnus*, O. Ir. *cindas* = *co* + *indas*; see *co* and *ionnas*.

ciont, guilt, Ir. *cionnta*, O. Ir. *cintach*, injustice, *cin*, guilt (**cin-at-*), dat. pl. *cintaib*; also G. †**cion**; I. E. *qin*, Gr. τίνυμαι, punish, ποινή, punishment, Lat. *pœna*, punishment, Eng. *pain*. See *cion*.

ciora, a pet lamb or sheep, **cireag,** a petted sheep, **ciridh,** the call to a sheep to come to one: all from a shorter form of the root *ka'er* or *kair* (i.e., *kir*) of *caora*, q.v.

cioralta, cheerful, **ciorbail,** snug; from Eng. *cheerful*. Cf. *tiorail*.

ciorram, hurt, damage, wounding, Ir. *ciorrbhadh*, E. Ir. *cirriud*, *cirud*, **cir-thu-*, root *ker*, destroy, Lat. *caries*, decay, Gr. κήρ, death, Skr. *çṛnâtí*, smash. *ro cirrad*, was mutilated.

ciosaich, subdue: "make tributary;" from *cìs*, tribute, tax.

ciosan, a bread basket, corn-skep (M'D.), Ir. *cisean*, *cis*, basket, M. Ir. *ceiss*, possibly allied to (if not borrowed from) Lat. *cista* (Stokes). See *céis*. Sc. *cassie*.

ciotach, left-handed, sinister, so Ir., W. *chwith*, **sqîttu-* (Stokes), **sqit-tu-*, and *sqit* is an extension of *sqi*, *sqai* in Gr. σκαιός, Lat. *scaevas* (**sqai-vo-*), left.

ciotag, a little plaid, shawl, O. Ir. *cétaig*, acc. case (Bk. of Armagh);

cìr, a comb, Ir. *cíor*, O Ir. *cír*, **kensrâ*; cf. Gr. κτέις, g. κτενός, (from *skens*), Ch. Sl. *cesľŭ*, Lit. *kasýti*, scratch (Stokes, Strachan), root *qes*, shave, scratch; cf. Gr. ξέω, ξυρόν. Zimmer refers it to the root *qers*, to furrow, Skr. *karsha*, a scratch, etc.; but *qers* would give a G. *cerr*. A Celtic *cêra* would be the ideal form, suggesting Lat. *cêra*, wax, "honey-*comb*."

cìr, cud, Ir., E. Ir. *cír*, Manx *keeil*, W. *cil*, Br. *das-kiriat*, ruminer. Perhaps identical with the above (Windisch). *cir*, *ciridh*, sheep (Carm.).

cìs, tribute, tax, Ir. *cíos*, O. Ir. *cís*; from Lat. *census*, whence Eng. *census*.

cisd, cist, a chest, Ir. *cisde*, M. Ir. *ciste*, W. *cist*; from Lat. *cista*, Ir. *cis*, piece of basket work of osiers. Cf. O. Ir. *cass*, basket, Lat. *quasillus*.

cisean, hamper (Islay); from *céis*.

ciseart, a light tweed (N. Lochaber).

cistin, a kitchen; from the Eng.

cith, a shower, Ir. *cith*, *cioth*, g. *ceatha*, E. Ir. *cith*, O. Ir. *cithech*, flebilium; **citu-*:

cith, rage, ardour; **ketu-*, cf. *cuthach*: **an cith**, attuned, where *cith* seems from Eng. *key*, mood.

cithean, a complaining; see *caoin*.

cithris-chaithris, confusion (M'L.): "hurly-burly;" an onomatopoetic word.

ciùbhran, ciùran, ciùrach, small rain, drizzle, Ir. *ceóbhrán*. See *ceòban*. M. Ir. *ciabor*, mist.

ciuchair, beautiful, dimpling (Sh., Arm.; not H.S.D.):

ciùcharan, ciùcran, a low-voiced plaint: from Norse *kjökra*, whine, *kjökr*, a voice stifled with tears.

ciùin, mild, Ir. *ciúin*, **kivo-ni-*, I.E., *kivo-*, *keivo-*, akin, dear; Lat. *civis*, Eng. *civil*; Norse *hýrr*, mild, Ag. S. *heóre*, Ger. *ge-heuer*, safe; Ch. Sl. *po-çivŭ*, benignus; Skr *çivá*, friendly.

ciùrr, hurt, Ir. *ciorrbhaigim*, I maim, wound: see *ciorram*. Cf., however, O. Ir. *dufiurrsa*, adteram, *du-furr*, attriveris, *iúrthund*, to hurt, root *org* as in *tuargan*.

clab, an open mouth, Ir. *clab*; from Eng. *clap*, a clap, noise, the human tongue. Hence **claban**, a mill-clapper.

claban, top of the head, brain-pan (H.S.D.); cf. W. *clopen*, G. *claigionn*, q.v. Possibly Pictish?

clàbar, filth, mire, clay, Ir. *clábar* (whence Eng. *clabber*); cf. *làban*.

clabar-nasg, the clasp of wooden cow collar (Arg.):

clabog, a good bargain, great pennyworth:

clach, a stone, Ir., E. Ir. *cloch*, W. *clwg*, a rock, detached rock, *clog*, a rock, *clogan*, a large stone, **klukâ*; root *kal*, *kl-*, hard; Got. *hallus*, stone, Norse *hella*, flat stone, Skr. *çilâ*, a stone. Usually correlated with Lat. *calculus*, a pebble, Eng. *calculate*.

clachan, kirk or kirk town, Ir. *clochán*, monastic stone-cells singly or in group; also G. and Ir. "stepping stones."

clàd, comb wool, **clàd**, a wool comb; from Sc. *claut*, *clauts*, wool comb, also a "clutching hand, a hoe or scraper;" from *claw*.

cladach, a shore, beach, so Ir., **claddo-*, "a score, shore;" from *clad* of *cladh*, q.v.

clàdan, a burr, a thing that sticks, Ir. *cladán*, burr, flake; from *clàd*.

cladh, a churchyard, Ir. *cladh*, a bank, ditch, E. Ir. *clad*, a ditch, W. *cladd*, *clawdd*, fossa, Cor. *cledh* (do.), Br. *cleuz* (do.), **klado-*, **klâdo-*; root *kela*, *kla*, break, split, hit; Gr. κλαδαρός, easily broken; Lat. *clâdes*; Russ. *kladu*, cut. See further *claidheamh*, sword. Hence **cladhaich**, dig.

cladhaire, a poltroon, so Ir.; "digger, clod-hopper," from *cladh*?

clag, a bell, Ir. *clog*, O. Ir. *clocc*, W., Cor. *cloch*, Br. *kloc'h*, **klokko-*, **kloggo-*; root, *klog*, *klag*, sound; Lat. *clango*, Eng. *clang*; Gr. κλάζω, κλαγγή, clang; Lit. *klagéti*, cackle. Bez. suggests

Bul. *klŭcam*, hit, giving the stem of *clag* as **klukko-*. Hence Eng. *clock*, etc.

clàideag, a lock, ringlet; see *clàd*, *clàdan*.

claidheag, the last handful of corn cut on the farm, the "maiden" (Badenoch); Sc. *claaik-sheaf* (Aberdeen, etc.), from *claaick*, the harvest home; the state of having all the corn in.

claidheamh, a sword, Ir. *clóidheamh*, O. Ir. *claideb*, W. *cleddyf*, Cor. *cledhe*, Br. *kleze*, **kladebo-s*; root *klad*, Skr. *kladga*: Gr. κλάδος, a twig; Ch. Sl. *kladivo*, a hammer. Further root *kela*, *klâ*, hit, split; Lat. *culter*, per-*cellere*, etc. See *cladh*.

claidhean, better **clàidhean**, the bolt of a door, Ir. *claibín*; from the same source as *claidheamh*. H.S.D. gives it in supp. as *clàimhean*.

claidreach, a damaging, shattering: **claddo-*; root *clad* of *claidheamh*.

claigionn, a skull, Ir. *cloigionn*, M. Ir. *cloicend*, W. *clopen*, Br. *klopenn*, **cloc-cenn*, from *clag* and *ceann*, "bell-head, dome-head." Stokes considers the Ir. borrowed from the Welsh. Cf. *claban*.

clais, a furrow, ditch, so Ir., E. Ir. *class*, W. *clais*, **clad-s-ti-*; from **clad* of *cladh*. Br. *kleus*, pit.

clàistinn, hearing, listening; from **clôstâ*, ear; see *cluas*.

clàiteachd, gentle rain (Arran):

clambar, wrangling, Ir. *clampar*; from Lat. *clamor*.

clamhan, a buzzard:

clamhradh, a scratching, so Ir.: **clam-rad*; see *cloimh*, itch.

clamhsa, an alley, close, so Ir.; from Eng. *close*.

clàmhuinn, sleet:

clann, children, clan, so Ir., O. Ir. *cland*, W. *plant*, **qlanatâ*: I. E. root *qel*; Gr. τέλος, company; O. Slav. *celjadĭ*, family, Lit. *kiltis*=Lett. *zilts*, race, stock; Skr. *kúla*, race. Some have added Lat. *populus*. Usually regarded as borrowed from Lat. *planta*, a sprout, Eng. *plant*, whence G. **clannach**, comatus.

claoidh, vex, oppress, Ir. *claoidhim*, O. Ir. *clóim*, W. *cluddio*, overwhelm, **cloid*; I. E. *klei*, incline, as in *claon*, q.v. Windisch and Stokes refer it to **cloviô*, root *qlov*, *qlav*, *qlu*, shut in, Lat. *claudo*, close, *claudus*, lame, Gr. κλείς, κλειδός, key.

claon, inclining, squint, oblique, Ir. *claon*, O. Ir. *clóin*: **kloino-*; Lat. *clīno*, *acclīnis*, leaning, Eng. *incline*; Gr. κλίνω (ι long), incline; Eng. *lean*; Lit. *szlěti*, incline; Skr. *çrayati* (do.).

clap, **clapartaich**, clap, clapping; from the Eng. *clap*.

clàr, a board, tablet, Ir., O. Ir. *clár*, W *clawr*, O. W. *claur*.; Gr. κλῆρος (for κλᾶρος), a lot, κλάω, break; root *qela*, *qlâ*, break etc., as in *claidheamh*, *coille*, q.v. Hence, *inter alia*, **clàrach**, a woman of clumsy figure, "board-built."

clàrsach, a harp, Ir. *cláirseach*; from *clár*. Cf. for meaning *fiodhcheall*, chess-play, "wood-intelligence."

clasp, claspa, a clasp, Ir. *clasba*; from the Eng.

clàtar, mire (Dial.); from Sc *clart*.

clathnàire, bashfulness (M'D., who writes **cláthnáire**. H.S.D. gives the form in the text): *clath*+*nàire*; see *nàire*. *Clath* seems from the root *qel*, hide, as in *ceil*, q.v. (H.S.D.).

cleachd, a practice, custom, Ir. *cleachdadh*, E. Ir. *clechtaim*, I am wont, **kḷcto-*, root *qel*, as in Lat. *colo*, Eng. *cultivate*, Gr. *πέλομαι*, go, be, etc. Cf., however, *cleas*.

cleachd, a ringlet, a fillet of wool, E. Ir. *clechtaim*, I plait (Cam.), W. *pleth*; from Lat. *plecto*, Eng. *plait*.

clearc, a curl, lock of hair:

cleas, a play, trick, feat, so Ir., E. Ir. *cless*, **clessu-*, **clexu-*; root *klek*, *klok*, as in *cluich*, q.v.

cleath, concealment, hiding; also **cleith** (**kleti-s*); inf. to *ceil*, hide, q.v.

cleibe, an instrument for laying hold of fish, or of sea-fowls, Ir. *clipe*; from Eng. *clip*, a gaff or cleek, a fastener, Norse *klýpa*, to pinch, O. H. G. *chluppa*, tongs.

cléir, the clergy, Ir. *cléir*; from Lat. *clêrus*. See the next word.

cléireach, a clerk, a cleric, O. G. *clérec* (Bk. of Deer), Ir. *cléireach*, E. Ir. *clérech*, Br. *kloarek*; from Lat. *clēricus*, a clerk, cleric, from Gr. *κληρικός* (do.), from *κλῆρος*, a lot, office: "the lot (*κλῆρον*) of this ministry" (Acts i. 17).

cleit, a quill, feather, down, Ir. *cleite*:

cleit, a rocky eminence; from Norse *klettr*, rock, cliff. Common in Northern place-names.

cleit, bar, ridge (Carm.).

cleith, a stake, wattle, Ir. *cleith*, *cleath*, E. Ir. *cleth*, tignum, W. *clyd*, sheltering, M. Br. *clet*, warm (place); root *qleit*, *qlit*, O. Sax. *hhlîdan*, cover, Got. *hleiðra*, hut, Ch. Sl. *kleti*, house. Hence **cleith**, roof; the E. Ir. *cléthe*, roof, roof-pole, appears to be for *kleitio-*, the same root in its full vocalic form (Schräder).

cleith, concealing, O. Ir. *cleith*; see *cleath*.

cleitig, clitig, a measure of land—an 8th of the "penny" land:

cleòc, a cloak, Ir. *clóca*; from the Eng.

cleuraidh. one who neglects work (Arran):

clì, vigour:

clì, left (hand), wrong, Ir. *clí*, E. Ir. *clí*, *clé*, W. *cledd*, O. W. *cled*, Br. *kleiz*, **klijo*; root *klei*, incline, Got. *hleiduma*, left, etc. See further under *claon*.

cliabh, a basket, hamper, the chest (of a man), Ir. *clíabh*, O. Ir. *cliab*, corbis, **cleibo-*. Root *klei* as in *cliath*.

cliadan, a burr; cf. *clàdan*.

cliamhuinn, son-in-law, Ir. *cliamhuin*, G. and Ir. **cleamhnas**, affinity; root *klei*, lean, Lat. *cliens*, Eng. *client*, in-*cline*, *lean*.

cliar, a poet, hero or heroes, Ir., E. Ir. *clíar*, society, train, clergy; from Lat. *clērus*, as in *cléir*, q.v. Hence **cliaranach**, a bard, swordsman. The **Cliar Sheanachain** (Senchan's Lot) was the mythic bardic company, especially on its rounds (Gaelic Folk Tales). Hence **cliarachd**, singing, feats.

cliatan, a level plot of ground: **cliath-t-an*, a participial formation from *cliath*, harrow—"harrowed, level."

cliath, harrow, hurdle, Ir. *clíath*, E. Ir. *cliath*, O. Ir. Vadum *clied* (Adamnan), Dublin, W. *clwyd*, hurdle, Cor. *cluit*, Br. *kloned*, Gaul. **clêta*, whence Fr. *claie*, hurdle, **kleitâ*; root *klei*, lean; Lett. *slita*, wood fence, Lit. *szlitė́*, a rack (of a waggon).

cliath, tread hens, as cock:

cliathach, side, the side of the ribs, Ir. *cliathán*, side, breast, **kleito-*, "slope," root *klei*, incline; Norse *hlíð*, a slope, mountain side, Gr. κλιτύς (ι long), a slope, hill-side.

clibeag, a trick, wile (H.S.D.); from *cleibe*, *clip*, as *clìchd* from *cleek*.

clibist, a misadventure; see *cliob*.

clic, a hook, gaff: see the next word.

clìchd, an iron hook; from Sc. *cleik*, Eng. *cleek*, *click*.

clìchd, a cunning trick; from the above. Sc. *cleiky*, ready to take the advantage, tricky, *cleek*, inclination to cheat: "There's a *cleek* in 'im" (Banffshire).

cliob, to stumble, **cliobach**, stumbling, awkward. Cf. Sc. *clypock*, a fall. See next.

cliob, anything dangling, excrescence, **cliobain**, a dew-lap, Ir. *cliob*, *clibín*; also Ir. *cliobach*, hairy, shaggy, *cliobóg*, a (shaggy) colt, etc. Cf. Sc. *clype*, an ugly, ill-shaped fellow: origin unknown (Murray); *clip*, a colt, Ger. *klepper*, palfrey. Root *q̣lg*, stumpy, Gr. κολοβός.

cliopach, halt in speech (H.S.D.): cf. Eng. *clip* words.

cliostar, a clyster; from the Eng.

clip, a hook, clip, Ir. *clipe*, a gaff; from the Eng. *clip*. See *cleibe*.

clipe, deceit (H.S.D.); see *clibeag*.

clis, active, Ir., M. Ir. *cliste*, ready, quick. Cf. W. *clys*, impulse: **cḷ-sto-*; root, *kel*, as in Lat. *celer*, swift, etc.? **"Na fir chlis,"** the Merry Dancers. From *cleas*. Cf. Ir. and E. Ir. *deil-clis*, staff-sling.

clisbeach, unsteady of foot, cripple; from *clis*. Also **clisneach**.

cliag, start, Ir. *cliosg* (Meath Dial., *clist*); from *clis*.
clisinnean, boat ribs, *clisneach*, rib:
clisneach, the human body, carcase, outward appearance (Arm.; not H.S.D.):
clisneach, a bar-gate (H.S.D.), a rib (Wh.):
cliù, renown, praise, Ir., O. Ir. *clú*, W. *clyw*, sense of hearing, *clod*, praise; Gr. *κλέος*, fame; Skr. *çravás*, I. E. *kleu*, hear. See further under *cluinn*.
cliùchd, mend nets:
cliùd, a slap with the fingers; from the Sc. *clout*, Eng. *clout*, a cuff, "clout."
cliùd, a small or disabled hand; from Sc. *cloot*, hoof, half-hoof?
clò, clòth, broad-cloth; from Eng. *cloth*, *clothing*, etc.
clò, a print, printing press, M. G. *cló* (Carswell), Ir. *cló*, *clódh* (*clodhuighim*, Coneys; E. Ir. *clod*, mark?); cf. the next word. Also **clòdh.**
†**clò,** a nail, Ir., E. Ir. *cló*, W. *clo*, key, Br. *klao*, tool, **klavo-*; Lat. *clâvus*, nail, *clavis*, key; Gr. *κλείς*, key, etc. See *claoidh*.
clò-chadail, slumber; see *clòth*.
clobha, a pair of tongs; from Norse *klofi*, a fork (of a river), a forked mast, snuffers, *klof*, fork of the legs, "cloven, cleft." The Ir. *clobh(a)* in Con. and Fol., and the *clomh* of Lh., seems a Scottish importation, for Coneys says the vernacular is *tlobh*. In fact, the Ir. word is *tlú*, *tlúgh*: "lifter"; root *tḷ-* as in Lat. *tollo*?
clobhsa, a close, lane, farm-yard, Ir. *clamhsa*, W. *claws*; from Eng. *close*. Also, *clamhsa*, q.v.
clochranaich, wheezing in the throat (M'F.; Sh. has **clochar,** and **clochan,** respire); from Sc. *clocher*, wheezing, *cloch*, cough feebly. It is an onomatopoetic word, like Eng. *cluck*, *clock*.
clod, a clod, turf; from the Eng.
clogad, clogaid, a helmet, Ir. *clogad*, M. Ir. *clogat*, *at chluic*, E. Ir. *clocatt*; from *ad*, hat, q.v., and †**clog,** head, which see in *claigionn*.
clogais, a wooden clog; from Eng. *clogs*.
cloidhean, the pitch of the box-tree or any shrub tree (Arm.; not H.S.D.). Cf. *glaoghan*.
cloimh, scab, itch, Ir. *clamh*, scurvy, E. Ir. *clam*, leprosus, W. *clafr*, leprosy, *claf*, diseased, Cor. *claf* (do.), M. Br. *claff* (do.), Br. *klanv*, **klamo-*, sick; Skr. *klam*, weary; Gr. *κλαμαρός*, weak (Hes.); Lat. *clêmens*.
clòimh, wool, down of feathers, Ir. *clúmh*, down, feathers, E. Ir. *clúm*, pluma, W. *pluf*, plumage; from Lat. *pluma* (Eng. *plumage*).

clòimhdich, rub or scratch as itchy; same as *clamhradh* in meaning and root.

clòimhein, icicle, snot; from *clòimh.*

clois, the herb "stinking marsh, horse tail," Ir. *clóis, clo-uisge* (O'R.), "water nail" (Cameron).

cloitheag, a shrimp, prawn (M'D.), Ir. *cloitheóg.* Possibly for *claidh-, *cladi-,* root *clad* of *cladh*: "a digger." M'L. has instead *cloidheag,* a small shore-fish.

clomh, counteract, subdue (Carm.). See *caochail.*

clomhais, cloves; from the Eng.

clos, rest, sleep, stillness; **clud-to-,* root *klu, klav*; see *claoidh.*

closach, a carcase; from *clos,* q.v.

clòsaid, a closet, Ir. *closeud*; from the Eng.

clòth, mitigate, still; from the root *klav,* of *claoidh,* q.v.

cluain, a green plain, pasture, Ir. and E. Ir. *cluain*: **clopni-*; Lit. *szlapti,* become wet, *szlapina,* a wet spot; Gr. κλέπας (Hes.), a wet muddy place (Strachan).

cluaineas, cluain, intriguing, deceit, Ir. *cluainearachd, cluain, *clopni-*; Gr. κλέπτω, steal; Eng. *lift, cattle lifting* (Strachan). *Cluain* = sense (Glenmoriston).

cluaran, a thistle; cf. W. *cluro,* whisk.

cluas, ear, Ir., O. Ir. *cluas,* W. *clust, *kloustâ,* root *kleus, klus, kleu,* hear; O. Sax. *hlust,* hearing, Eng. *listen,* etc. See *cluinn.*

clùd, a patch, clout, Ir. *clúd,* W. *clwt,*; from the Eng. *clout,* Ag. S. *clút,* (Rhys, Murray).

cluich, play, Ir. *cluiche,* a game, E. Ir., *cluche,* a game, O. Ir. *cluichech,* ludibundus: **klokjo-*; Got. *hlahjan,* Eng. *laugh,* Ger. *lachen* (Windisch, Stokes). *placere?*

cluigein, a little bell, anything dangling; from *clag.*

cluinn, hear, Ir., E. Ir. *cluinim,* W. *clywed* hearing, Cor. *clewaf,* audio, Br. *klevet,* audire, **klevô,* I hear; Lat. *clueo,* am reputed, in*clutus,* famous; Gr. κλύω, hear; Eng. *loud, listen*; Skr. *çru,* hear, *crâvas,* sound. Hence *cliù, cluas,* etc.

cluip, cheat: hardly **kloppi-*; Gr. κλέπτω.

clupaid, the swollen throat in cattle:

cluthaich, cover, clothe, Ir. *cluthmhar,* sheltered, warm. Cf. E. Ir. *clithaigim,* I shelter, *clith,* clothing, W. *clyd,* sheltering; root *qel* of *ceil,* q.v. Ir. *clúdaim,* I clothe, cover, from Eng. *clothe,* has possibly influenced the vowel both in G. and Ir.

cluthaich, chase, Ir. *cluthaighim*: **kluto-, *klu*; see *claoidh?*

cnab, pull, haul; see *cnap.*

cnabaire, an instrument for dressing flax, Ir. *cnáib,* hemp; see *cainb.*

cnag, a crack, Ir. *cnag*; from the Eng. *crack.*

cnag, a pin, knob, Ir. *cnag*; from the Eng. *knag*, a peg, Dan. *knag*, a peg, Sw. *knagg*, a knag.

cnàid, a scoff, Ir. *cnáid*:

cnàimh, bone, Ir. *cnáimh*, O. Ir. *cnáim*, **knâmi-s*; Gr. κνήμη, leg; Eng. *ham*.

cnaimhseag, a pimple, bear-berry:

cnàmh, chew, digest, Ir. *cnaoi*, *cnaoidhim*, E. Ir. *cnám*, gnawing, W. *cnoi*; Gr. κνώδων, a tooth, κνάω, scrape; Lit. *kandù*, bite; Skr. *khâd*, chew. Root *qnē*, *qnā*, *qen*. Hence **cnamhuin**, gangrene.

cnàmhaiche, matured person (M'D.):

cnap, a knob, Ir. *cnap*, E. Ir. *cnapp*; from Norse *knappr*, a knob, M. Eng. *knap*. Hence also G. and Ir. **cnap**, a blow, Sc. *knap*, Eng. *knappe*, blow.

cnapach, a youngster; from *cnap*. But cf. Norse *knapi*, boy, varlet, Eng. *knave*.

†**cnarra**, a ship, Ir. *cnarra*; from Norse *knörr*, g. *knarrar*, Ag. S. *cnear*.

cnatan, a cold: **krod-to-*; Ger. *rotz*, catarrh; Gr. κόρυζα (do.). Also **cneatan**.

cnead, a sigh, groan, so Ir., E. Ir., *cnet*; from the root *can* of *can*, say, sing.

cneadh, a wound, so Ir., E. Ir. *cned*, **knidâ*; Gr. κνίζω, sting, κνίδη, nettle; Ag. S. *hnítan*, tundere. Cf. Teut. *hnit*, hit; Gr. κνιζω, stick, cut; *cneidh-ghalar*, painful complaint.

cneap, a button, bead; see *cnap*.

cneas, skin, waist, Ir. *cneas*, E. Ir. *cnes*; from *cen* of *cionn*, skin; see *boicionn*; Corn. *knes*, body, W. *cnawd*, human flesh.

cneasda, humane, modest, Ir. *cneasda*; from *cen* as in *cineal*, kin.

cnèatag, fir cone, shinty ball:

cneisne, slender (M'D.); from *cneas*.

cniadaich, caress, stroke:

cnò, a nut, Ir. *cnó*, O. Ir. *cnú*, W. *cneuen*, pl. *cnau*, Cor. *cnyfan*, Br. *knaouenn*, **knovâ*; Norse, *hnot*, Ag. S. *hnutu*, Eng. *nut*, Ger. *nuss*.

cnoc, a hillock, Ir, *cnoc*, O. Ir. *cnocc*, O. Br. *cnoch*, tumulus, Br. *kreac'h*, *krec'henn*, hill, **knokko-*; from *knog-ko-*, Norse, *hnakki*, nape of the neck, Ag. S. *hnecca*, neck, Eng. *neck*. Some have given the stem as **cunocco-*, and referred it to the root of Gaul. *cuno-*, high, W. *cwn*, height, root *ku*, be strong, great, as in *curaidh*, q.v. Cf. Ag. S. *hnoll*, O.H.G. *hnol*, vertex, head. See *ceann*.

cnòcaid, a ycung woman's hair bound up in a fillet. Founded on the Sc. *cockernonny*.

cnod, a knot, Ir. *cnota* ; from the Eng.

cnòd, a patch, piece on a shoe ; cf. Sc. *knoit*, *knot*, large piece.

cnòdaich, acquire, lay up, Ir. *cnódach*, acquiring (O'R.) ; see *cnòd*.

cnòdan, the gurnet, Ir. *cnúdán* (Fol.) ; cf. Sc. *crooner*, so-called from the *croon* or noise it makes when landed. The G. seems borrowed from Sc. *crooner*, mixed with Sc. *crout*, croak.

cnòid, a sumptuous present (Heb.) ; **cròid** :

cnoidh, tooth-ache, severe pain ; see *cnuimh*.

cnomhagan, a large whelk, buckie ; cf. *cnò*, nut.

cnot, unhusk barley ; from **cnotag**, the block or joint of wood hollowed out for unhusking barley. The word is the Eng. *knot ?*

cnuachd, head, brow, temple, Ir. *cruaic* (O'R.) ; cf. W. *cnuwch*, bushy head of hair, *cnwch*, knuckle, *cnuch*, joint, **cnoucco-*, "a prominence" ; root *kneu*, *knu* ; Norse *hnúkr*, *hnjúkr*, knoll, peak, *hnuðr*, a knob. Hence **cnuachdach**, shrewd : "having a head."

cnuas, gnash, chew, crunch ; for *cruas*, *cruais*, founded on Eng. *crush*, *crunch ?*

cnuasaich, ponder, collect, Ir. *cnuasuighim*, *cnuas*, a collection, scraping together, G. and Ir. **cnuasachd**, reflection, collection, **knousto-* ; root *knu*, *knevo*, scrape, Gr. κνύω, scratch, Norse *hnöggr*, niggard, Eng. *niggard*, Ag. S. *hneáw*, sparing. The idea is "scraping together" : a *niggard* is "one who scrapes." Stokes (Dict.) gives the root as *knup*, and compares Lit. *knupsyti*, oppress. St. now, possibly, **knoud-to*, Norse, *knúðr*, ball. Cf. *cruinnich*, for force.

cnuimh, a worm ; wrong spelling for *cruimh*, q.v.

cnumhagan, a handful (Heb.) ; for *crobhagan*, from †**crobh**, the hand ? See *cròg*.

co, **cò**, who, O. Ir. *co-te*, now G. *ciod*, q.v. ; W. *pa*, Cor. *py*, *pe*, Br. *pe*, quia, root *qo-*, *qa-*, *qe* ; Lat. *quod* ; Gr. πό-θι, etc. ; Eng. *who*.

co, **cho**, as, so ; see *cho*.

còb, plenty (Sh.) ; from Lat. *copia*. Ir. *cóib*, party, followers.

cobhair, assistance, so Ir., O. Ir. *cobir*, **cobris*, *co* + *ber*, root *bher*, carry ; see *beir* ; and cf. for meaning Gr. συμφέρει, it is of use.

cobhan, a coffer, box, Ir. *cofra* ; from Eng. *coffin*, *coffer*.

cobhar, foam, Ir. *cubhar*, E. Ir. *cobur* : *co* + *bur* ; for *bar*, see *tobar*, well.

cobhartach, spoil, booty :

cobhlach, fleet. See *cabhlach*.

coc, cock, to cock ; from the Eng.

còcaire, a cook, Ir. *cócaire*, M. Ir. *cocaire*, Cor. *peber*, pistor ; from the Lat. *coquo*, I cook.

cochull, also **coich** (Carm.), husk, hood, Ir. *cochal*, O. Ir. *cochull*, W. *cwcwll*, hood, cowl; from Lat. *cucullus*, Eng. *cowl*.

cocontachd, smartness (A. M'D.); see *coc*, *gog*.

codaich, share, divide; from *codach*, gen. of *cuid*.

còdhail, a meeting; see *comhdhail*.

cogadh, war, so Ir., O. Ir. *cocad*: **con-cath*, "co-battle"; see *cath*.

cogais, conscience, Ir. *cogus*, O. Ir. *concubus*: *con* + *cubus*; and O. Ir. *cubus*, conscience, is for *con-fis*, *co* and *fios*, knowledge, q.v.

cogan, a loose husk, covering (H.S.D.), a small vessel; see *gogan* for latter force.

cogull, tares, cockle, Ir. *cogal*; borrowed from M. Eng. *cockel*, *cokkul*, now *cockle*.

coibhneas, proper spelling of *caoimhneas*, which see.

coibhseachd, propriety, so Ir. *coibhseach*, becoming; cf. M. Ir. *cuibdes*, fittingness, from *cubaid*; see *cubhaidh*.

coicheid, suspicion, doubt:

cóig, five, Ir. *cúig*, O. Ir. *cóic*, W. *pump*, E. W. *pimp*, Cor. *pymp*, Br. *pemp*, Gaul. *pempe*, **qenqe*; Lat. *quinque*; Gr. πέντε; Lit. *penki*; Got. *fimf*; Skr. *páñca*.

coigil, spare, save, so Ir., E. Ir. *coiclim*, *cocill* (n.); **con-cel*, root *qel*, as in Lat. *colo*, etc. Also **cagail**. The E. Ir. *cocell*, concern, thought, is for *con-ciall*; *ciall*, sense.

coigreach, a stranger, Ir. *coigcrigheach*, *cóigcríoch*, **con-crích-ech*, "provincial," E. Ir. *cocrích*, province, boundary. See *crìoch*. The meaning is, "one that comes from a neighbouring province."

coilceadha, bed materials, †**coilce**, a bed, Ir. *coilce*, a bed, E. Ir. *colcaid*, flock bed, O. W. *cilcet*, now *cylched*; from Lat. *culcita*, a pillow, Eng. *quilt*.

coilchean, a little cock, water spouting; from *coileach*, q.v.

coileach, a cock, so Ir., O. Ir. *cailech*, W. *ceiliog*, Cor. *celioc*, Br. *kiliok*, **kaljákos*, the "caller"; root *qal*, call; Lat. *calare*, summon, Eng. *Calends*; Gr. καλέω, call; Lit. *kalba*, speech, etc.

coileag, a cole of hay; from the Sc. *cole*, a cole or coil of hay. See *gòileag*. **Còileag** (Perth.).

coileid, a stir, noise (Heb.); cf. Eng. *coil*, of like force. The G. seems borrowed therefrom.

coileir, a collar, Ir. *coiléar*; from the Eng.

coilionn, a candle; see *coinneal*.

coi'lige (Dial.), race, course (Hend.): *coimhliong*.

coiliobhar, a kind of gun; see *cuilbheir*.

coille, **coill**, wood, Ir. *coill*, O. Ir. *caill*, W. *celli*, Cor. *kelli*, **kaldet-*, Gr. κλάδος, a twig; Eng. *holt*, Ger. *holz*. Further root *qla*, *qela*, split, hit, as in *cladh*, *claidheamh*, q.v.

coilleag, a cockle (M'D.), Ir. *coilleóg* (O'R.), Cor. *cyligi* :
coilleag, a rural song, a young potato, a smart blow :
coilleag, coileig (accent on end syllable ; Perth.), a smart stroke :
coilpeachadh, equalizing cattle stock (Heb.) ; see *colpach.*
coilpein, a rope :
coimeas, comparison, co-equal, Ir. *coimheas,* E. Ir. *coimmeas* : *com* + *meas.* See *meas.*
coimh-, co- ; see *comh-.*
coimheach, strange, foreign, cruel, Ir. *coimhtheach, cóimhthigheach, cóimhightheach,* strange, M. Ir. *comaigthe,* foreign, O. Ir. *comaigtech,* alienigena ; for *comaitche* (Stokes). See *tathaich.*
†**Coimhdhe,** God, Ir. *Cóimhdhe,* God, the Trinity, O. Ir. *comdiu,* gen. *comded* (Bk. of Deer), Lord, **com-mediôs,* "Providence," root *med,* think, as in G. *meas,* esteem, Lat. *modus, meditor, meditate.* See *meas.* The fanciful "Coibhi, the Celtic arch-druid," is due to a confusion of the obsolete *Coimhdhe* with the Northumbrian Coifi of Bede.
coimhead, looking, watching, Ir. *cóimhéad,* O. Ir. *comét,* **com-entu-.* For *entu,* see *dìdean.*
coimhearsnach, a neighbour, Ir. *cómharsa,* gen. *cómharsan,* E. Ir. *comarse* ; from *com* and *ursainn,* a door-post (Zimmer). See *ursainn.*
coimheart, a comparison ; **com-bért,* root *ber,* of *beir.* Cf. Lat. *confero.*
coimheirbse, wrangling : *com* + *farpuis,* q.v.
coimhirp, rivalry, striving (Arg.) ; same root as *oidhirp.*
coimhliong, a race, course, also **coi'lige** (Dial.) ; Ir. *cóimhling* ; from *com* and *lingim,* I leap. For root, see *leum.*
coimsich, perceive, Ir. *coimsighim* : *com-meas* ; see *meas.*
coimirc, mercy, quarter, so Ir. ; see *comairce.*
coimpire, an equal, match ; from Eng. *compeer* or Lat. *compar.*
coimrig, trouble ; from Sc., Eng. *cumber, cumbering.*
coimseach, indifferent (Sh.) ; from *coimeas,* co-equal.
coindean, a kit (Arm. : not H.S.D.) :
còineag, a nest of wild bees (M'L.) ; from *còinneach,* moss. See *caonnag.*
coinean, a rabbit, coney, Ir. *coinín,* W. *cwning* ; from M. Eng. *cunin,* from O. Fr. *connin, connil,* from Lat. *cuniculus,* whence Eng. *coney,* through Fr.
coingeis, indifferent, same as, no matter ; *con-geas,* from *geas,* desire, etc. Cf. *àilleas,* from *ail-ges.*
coingeal, a whirlpool (H.S.D.) :
coingheall, a loan, Ir. *coinghioll,* obligation ; *con* + *giall,* q.v.
coingir, a pair (Sh.) :

coinlein, a nostril; see *cuinnean.*
coinn, fit of coughing; a nostril (Hend.):
coinne, a supper, a party to which every one brings his own provisions (Heb.). Cf. E. Ir. *coindem, coinmed,* coigny, conveth, quartering, **kond,* eat, as in *cnàmh,* q.v.
coinne, woman (Hend.); from N. *kona, kvenna* (gen. pl.), woman, Eng. *queen.*
coinne, coinneamh, a meeting, Ir. *coinne,* E. Ir. *conne, *con-nesiâ*; root *nes,* come, dwell, Gr. νέομαι, go, ναίω, dwell; Skr. *nas,* join some one. Stokes seems to think that *kon-dê-* is the ultimate form here, *dê* being the I. E. *dhê,* set, Gr. τίθημι, etc. *Coinneamh,* when used as adverb = *coinnibh,* dat. plur.?
còinneach, moss, Ir. *caonach,* M. Ir. *cúnnach,* O. Ir. *coennich,* muscosi:
coinneal, candle, so Ir., E. Ir. *candel,* W. *canwyll,* O. W. *cannuill,* Cor. *cantuil*; from Lat. *candela,* whence Eng. *candle.*
coinneas, a ferret; **con-neas,* "dog-weasel"? See *neas.*
coinnseas, conscience (Hend.):
coinnlein, a stalk, Ir. *coinlín,* M. Ir. *coinnlin,* O. Ir. *connall,* stipula, **konnallo-*; Lat., *canna,* a reed, Gr. κάννα. Stokes also joins W. *cawn,* reed, **kâno-.*
còir, just, right, Ir., O. Ir. *cóir,* W. *cywir*: **ko-vêro-,* "co-true," from *vêro-,* now *fìor,* q.v. Hence **còir,** justice, right, share. Also in the phrase **'n an còir,** in their presence; see *comhair.*
coirb, cross, vicious, Ir. *corbadh,* wickedness, E. Ir. *corpte,* wicked; from Lat. *corruptus.* Also see *coiripidh.*
coirceag, a bee-hive (Sh., O'R.):
coire, fault, so Ir., O. Ir. *caire,* O. W. *cared,* W. *cerydd,* Br. *carez,* **karjâ*; Lat. *carinare,* blame, abuse; Let. *karinât,* banter, Ch. Sl. *karati,* punish.
coire, a cauldron, so Ir., E. Ir. *core, coire,* W. *pair,* Cor., Br. *per,* **qerjo*; Norse *hverr,* kettle, Ag. S. *hwer*; Skr. *carú*; Gr. κέρνος, a sacrificial vessel.
coireal, coral, from the Eng.
coireall, a quarry, Ir. *coireul, coilér* (F. M.); from Fr. *carriere,* with dissimilation of *r*'s (Stokes).
coireaman, coriander, so Ir.; founded on the Lat. *coriandrum,* Gr. κορίαννον.
coirioll, a carol; from the Eng.
coiripidh, corruptible; from Lat. *corruptus.*
còirneil, a colonel, Ir. *curnel, corniel* (F. M.); from the Eng.
coirpileir, a corporal; from the Eng.
coiseunuich, bless (Sh.); *con + seun* or *sian,* q.v.
coisich, walk, Ir. *coiseachd* (n); from *cas, coise,* q.v.

coisinn, win ; see *cosnadh*.

coisir, a festive party, chorus, Ir. *coisir*, feast, festive party, *cóisir* (O'R., O'B., and Keat.), feasting, "coshering":

coisrigeadh, consecration, O. G. *consecrad* (Bk. of Deer), Ir. *coisreagadh*, O. Ir. *coisecrad* ; from Lat. *consecratio*.

coit, a small boat, Ir. *coit*, E. Ir. *coite*. Cf. Lat. *cotta*, species navis, Norse *kati*, a small ship, Eng. *cat*. Stokes suggests that the G. and Ir. are from the Low Lat. *cotia*, navis Indica. Hence Eng. *cot*. Now from **quontio* ; Gaul. *ponto*, whence Eng. *punt*.

coitcheann, common, public, so Ir., O. Ir. *coitchenn* : **con-tech-en* ?

coiteir, a cottar, Ir. *coiteóir* ; from the Eng. *cottar*.

coitich, press one to take something : **con-tec-*, root *tek*, ask, Eng. *thig* ; see *atach*.

col, an impediment, Ir. *colaim* ; root, *qela*, *qlâ*, break, split ? See *call* ; and cf. Gr. κωλύω, hinder, which is probably from the same root.

col, sin, Ir., E. Ir. *col*, W. *cwl*, O. Br. *col*, **kulo-* ; Lat. *culpa*, *colpa*, fault. Stokes hesitates between referring it to the root of Lat. *culpa* or to that of Lat. *scelus*, Got. *skal*, Eng. *shall*, Ger. *schuld*, crime.

colag, a small steak or collop (Arg.) ; from Eng. *collop*.

colaiste, a college, Ir. *colaisde* ; from the Eng.

colamoir, the hake (Sh., O'B.), Ir. *colamóir* ; cf. Sc. *coalmie*, *colemie*, the coal-fish.

còlan, a fellow-soldier, companion ; cf. *còmhla*, together. The Ir. *cómhlach* is for *com-lach*, the *lach* of *òglach*.

colann, colainn, a body, so Ir., O. Ir. *colinn*, gen. *colno*, W. *celain*, carcase, O. W. *celein*, cadaver, **colanni-* (Brugmann) ; root *qela*, break, the idea being "dead body" ? Cf. for meaning Gr. νέκυς, corpse, from *nek*, kill.

colbh, pillar, Ir., *colbh*, E. Ir. *colba*, W. *celff*, Br. *kelf* ; Lat. *columna*, Eng. *column* ; root *qel*, high. G. **colbh**, plant stalk, Ir. *colmh*, is allied to Lat. *culmus*. The Celtic words, if not borrowed from, have been influenced by the Lat.

colc, an eider duck (Heb.) ; from Sc., Eng. *colk*, E. Fris. *kolke*, the black diver.

colg, wrath, Ir., *colg* ; a metaphorical use of *calg* (i.e. *colg*), q. v.

colg, sword (ballads). See *calg*.

collachail, boorish (H.S.D. ; O'R. quoted as authority), Ir. *collachamhuil* ; from Ir. *collach*, boar. See *cullach*.

collaid, a clamour, Ir. *collóid* ; see *coileíd*.

collaidh, carnal, sensual, so Ir., E. Ir. *collaide* ; for *colnaide*, from *colann*, body, flesh.

collaidin, codalan, white poppy (H.S.D.; O'R. only quoted), Ir. *collaidín, codalán*; from *colladh, codal*, sleep.
collainn, a smart stroke; also **coilleag.**
colman, a dove; see *calman.*
colpach, a heifer, steer, Ir. *colpach*, M. Ir. *calpach*; apparently founded on Norse *kálfr*, a calf. Hence Sc. *colpindach.*
coltach, like; for *co-amhuil-t-ach.* See *amhuil, samhuil.*
coltar, a coulter, Ir. *coltar*, E. Ir. *coltar*; from M. Eng. *cultre*, Lat. *culter.*
columan, a dove, Ir. and O. Ir. *colum*, W. *colomen, cwlwm*, Corn. *colom*, Br. *coulm*; from Lat. *columbus, columba.*
còm, the cavity of the chest, Ir. *com, coim*, chest cavity, waist, body. The G. is allied to W. *cwm*, a valley, "a hollow," **kumbo-*; Gr. κῦφος, a hump, Lat. *cumbere*; Ger. *haube*, hood; root *kûbho-*, bend. The O. Ir. *coim*, covering, is from the root *kemb*, wind, as in *càm*, q.v.
coma, indifferent, so Ir., E. Ir. *cuma*, O. Ir. *cumme*, idem, *is cumma*, it is all the same; from root *me*, measure: "equal measure."
comaidh, a messing, eating together, E. Ir. *commaid*, **kom-buti-s*, "co-being," from **buti-s*, being. See *bì*, be.
comain, obligation, Ir. *comaoin*, O. Ir. *commáin*: **com-moini-*; Lat. *communis.* See *maòin.*
†comairce, protection; see *comraich.*
comanachadh, celebration of the Lord's Supper; from *comann* or *comunn*, society, Lat. *communio*, Eng. *communion.*
comannd, a command; from the Eng.
†comar, a confluence, Ir. *comar, cumar*, E. Ir. *commar*, W. *cymmer*, Br. *kemper*, confluent, **kom-bero-*; Lat. *con-fero.* Root *bher*, as in *beir.*
comas, comus, power, Ir. *cumas*, E. Ir. *commus*, **com-mestu-*, **mestu-*, from *med*, as in *meas* (Zimmer, Brugmann).
combach, a companion; a shortened form of *companach.*
combaid, company (Dial.):
combaiste, compaiste, a compass, Ir. *compás*; from the Eng.
comh-, prefix denoting "with, com-, con-," Ir. *comh-*, O. Ir. *com-*, **kom-*; Lat. *cum, com-, con-*, Eng. *com-, con-*, etc. It appears as *coimh-, com-* (before *m* and *b*), *con-* (before *d, g*), etc.
comhach, prize, prey: **com-agos-*; root *ag*, drive?
comhachag, owl, W. *cuan*, Br. *kaouen*, O. Br. *couann*; L. Lat. *cavannus* (from the Celtic—Ernault), Fr. *chouette*, O. Fr. *choue.* Cf. Ger. *schuhu, uhu.* An onomatopoetic word originally.
co had, a comparison (Sh.); *comh+fada*, q.v.
co haib, contention about rights (M'A.):

comhaich, dispute, assert, contend:

comhailteachd, a convoy, Ir. *comhailtim*, I join; from **comhal**, a joining, so Ir., E. Ir. *accomallte*, socius, O. Ir. *accomol*, conjunctio, W. *cyfall*, **ad-com-ol*. For *ol*, see under *tional*, *alt*.

comhair, presence, e regione, etc., Ir. *cómhair*, E. Ir. *comair*, W. *cyfer*, O. W. *civer*: *com+air*, the prep. *comh* and *air*, q.v. (Asc.). Cor. *kever*. Cf. *comhghar* of Ir.

comhairc, an outcry, appeal, forewarning, Ir. *cómhairce*, E. Ir. *comaircim*, I ask: *com+arc*. For *arc*, see *iomchorc*.

comhairle, advice, Ir. *cómhairle*, O. Ir. *airle*, counsel, *air+le*. This *le* is usually referred to the root *las*, desire, Skr. *lash*, desire, Lat. *lascivus*, wanton. Ascoli suggests the root *lā* of O. Ir. *láaim*, mittere, Gr. ἐλαύνω.

comhal, a joining—an Ir. word; see *comhailteachd*.

comhalta, a foster-brother, Ir. *cómhalta*, E. Ir. *comalta*, W. *cyfaillt*, friend, **kom-altjos*, root *al*, rear, Lat. *alo*, etc. See *altrum*.

comharradh, a mark, Ir. *cómhartha*, O. Ir. *comarde*; from *com* and O. Ir. *airde*, signum, W. *arwydd*, M. Br. *argoez*, **are-vidio-*; root *vid*, as in Lat. *video*, here *prœ-video*, etc.

comhart, the bark of a dog; from *comh* and *art*, O. Ir. *artram*, latratus, W. *cyfarth*, *arthio*, to bark, O. Br. *arton*. Cf. Ir. *amhastrach*, barking.

còmhdach, clothing, covering, Ir. *cúmhdach*, veil, covering, defence, E. Ir. *comtuch*, *cumtach*, covering, "shrine": **con-ud-tog*; root *teg*, *tog*, as in *tigh*, q.v. Cf. *cúintgim*, peto: **com-di-segim*.

còmhdaich, allege, prove: **com-atach*; see *atach*?

còmhdhail, a meeting, Ir. *cómhdháil*, E. Ir. *comdál*: *com+dàil*; see *dàil*.

còmhla, together, Ir. *cómhlámh*: *com+làmh*, "co-hand, at hand." See *làmh*.

còmhla, door, door-leaf, Ir. *cómhla*, E. Ir. *comla*, gen. *comlad*: **com-lā-*, root (*p*)*lā-*, fold, groove (cf. Lat. *sim-plu-s*, O.H.G. *zwîfal*, two-fold); root *pal*, *pel*, as in *alt*, joint.

comhlann, a combat, Ir. *cómhlann*, E. Ir. *comlann*: **com+lann*; see *lann*.

comhluadar, conversation, colloquy, Ir. *cómhluadar*, company, conversation; from *luaidh*, speak (**com-luad-tro-*). See *luaidh*.

còmhnadh, help, Ir. *cúngnamh*, O. Ir. *congnam*, inf. to *congniu*, I help: *com+(g)nì*, "co-doing." See *nì*, do, *gnìomh*, deed.

còmhnard, level, Ir. *cómhárd*: *com+àrd*, "co-high, equally high."

còmhnuidh, a dwelling, Ir. *cómhnuidhe*, a tarrying, dwelling, E. Ir. *comnaide*, a waiting, delay, (also *irnaide*): **com-naide*; root *nes*, *nas*, dwell ; Gr. *ναίω*, dwell, *νέομαι*, go, *ναέτης*, inhabitant ; Skr. *nas*, join any one.

còmhradh, conversation, Ir. *cómhrádh* ; *com* + *ràdh* ; see *ràdh*.

còmhrag, a conflict, Ir. *cómhrac*, E. Ir. *comrac*, battle, O. Ir. *comracc*, meeting, W. *cyfrang*, rencounter, **kom-ranko-* ; root *renk*, assemble ; Lit. *rìnkti*, assemble, *surinkìmas*, assembly.

comhstadh, a borrowing, loan : **com-iasad-* ; see *iasad ?* Cf. E. Ir. *costud*, consuetudo.

compàirt, partnership, Ir. *cómpártas* ; from *com-* and *pàirt*, q.v.

companach, companion, Ir. *cómpánach*, M. Ir. *companach* ; from E. Eng. *compainoun*, through Fr., from L. Lat. *compâniô*, "*co-bread-man*," from *pânis*, bread. Dialectic **combach.**

comradh, aid, assistance :

comraich, protection, sanctuary, Ir. *cómairce*, *comruighe*, E. Ir. *comairche*, M. Ir. *comairce* ; from the root *arc*, defend, as in *teasairg*, q.v.

comunn, society, company, Ir. *cumann* ; from Lat. *communio*, Eng. *communion*.

con-, with ; see *comh-*.

cona, cat's tail or moss crops (Sh.) ; see *canach*. Cf. *gonan*, grass roots.

conablach, a carcase, so Ir. ; for *con-ablach* ; see *con-* and *ablach*. "Dog's carcase" (Atkinson).

conachag, a conch (M'A.) ; from the Eng.

conachair, a sick person who neither gets worse nor better (M'A.), uproar (M'F.) :

cona-ghaothach, tempest, raging gale (Hend.) :

conair, a path, way (Sh., O'B.), so Ir., O. Ir. *conar* :

conaire, the herb "loose-strife," Ir. *conair* (O'R.) ; see *conas*.

conal, love, fruitage (Carm.) :

conalach, brandishing (Sh. ; not H.S.D.) ; cf. the name *Conall*, **Cuno-valo-s*, roots *kuno* (see *curaidh*) and *val*, as in *flath*, q.v.

conaltradh, conversation, Ir. *conaltra* (O'R. ; Sh.) : **con-alt-radh ?* For *alt*, see *alt*, joint.

conas, a wrangle, so Ir. (O'R., Sh.) ; from *con-*, the stem of *cù*, dog : "currishness"?

conas, conasg, furze, whins, Ir. *conasg* (O'R., Sh.) : cf. *conas* above. Manx *conney*, yellow furze.

condrachd, contrachd, mischance, curse, E. Ir. *contracht* ; from Lat. *contractus*, a shrinking, *contraction*.

confhadh, rage, Ir. *confadh*, M. Ir. *confad* : *con*+*fadh* ; for *fadh*, see *onfhadh*.

cònlan, an assembly, Ir. *conlán*. H.S.D. gives as authorities for the Gaelic word "Lh. et C. S."

conn, sense, so Ir., E. Ir. *cond* : **cos-no-*, root *kos*, *kes*, as in G. *chì*, see; Gr. κοννέω, understand, κόσμος, array ("what is seen"), world. See further under *chì* for *kes*. Stokes equates *cond* with Got. *handngs*, wise; but this is merely the Eng. *handy*. It has been suggested as an ablaut form to *ceann*, head. Got. *hugs*, sense, has also been compared; **cug-s-no-* is possible.

connadh, fuel, so Ir., O. Ir. *condud*, W. *cynnud*, Cor. *cunys*, **kondutu-*; root *kond*, *kn̥d*; Lat. *candeo*, *incendo*; Gr. κάνδαρος, coal.

connan, lust :

connlach, straw, stubble, so Ir., O. Ir. *connall*, stipula : *konnallo-*; Lat. *cannula*, *canna*, a reed, *canalis*, Gr. κάννα, reed. See *coinnlein*.

connsaich, dispute; see under *ionnsaich*.

connspair, a disputant : **con-deasbair*; see *deasbair*.

connspeach, a wasp, Ir. *coinnspeach* (Fol.); see *speach*, wasp.

connspoid, a dispute, Ir. *conspóid*; from a Lat. **consputatio*, for **condisputatio*. See *deasbud*.

connspunn, conspull, cònsmunn, a hero, Ir. *conspullach*, heroic (O'R.) :

constabal, the township's bailiff (Heb.); from Eng. *constable*.

contraigh, neaptide, O. Ir. *contracht*; from Lat. *contractus*, shrinking (Zeuss, Meyer). See **condracht** and **traogh**.

contran, wild angelica, Ir. *contran* (O'R.) :

conuiche, a hornet (H.S.D.), **cònuich** (Arm.), **conuibhe, connuibh** (M'L., M'A.); used by Stewart in the Bible glosses. Same root as *conas*.

cop, foam, M. Ir., E. Ir. *copp*; from Ag. S., M. Eng. *copp*, vertex, top, Ger. *kopf*, head.

copag, docken, Ir. *copóg*, *capóg*; M. Ir. *copóg*. Founded on the Eng. *cop*, head, head-dress, crest, tuft; W. *copog*, tufted. The same as *cop*, q.v.

copan, a boss, shield boss, cup; from the Norse *koppr*, cup, bell-shaped crown of a helmet, Eng. *cup*.

copar, copper, Ir. *copar*; from the Eng.

cor, state, condition, Ir. *cor*, O. Ir. *cor*, positio, "jactus," **koru-*, vb. **koriô*, I place. See *cuir*.

còram, a faction, a set (M'A.); from the Eng. *quorum*.

corc, a cork, so Ir.; from the Eng.

corc, a knife, gully, dirk, Ir. *corc* : **korko-*, **qor-qo-*, root *qor*, *qer*, cut; Lit. *kirwis*, axe; Gr. κέρμα, a chip, κείρω, cut. Allied to the root *sqer* of *sgar*, q.v.

corc, oats, Ir. *coirce*, M. Ir. *corca*, W. *ceirch*, Br. *kerc'h*, **korkjo-*. Bezzenberger suggests connection with Lettic *kurki*, small corn. Possibly for *kor-ko-*, where *kor*, *ker* is the root which appears in Lat. *Ceres*, Eng. *cereal*, Gr. κόρος, satiety, Lit. *szérti*, feed. The meaning makes connection with Gr. κόρκορος, pimpernel, doubtful.

corcur, crimson, Ir. *corcur*, scarlet, O. Ir. *corcur*, purple, W. *porphor*; from Lat. *purpura* (Eng. *purple*).

còrd, a rope, Ir. *corda*; from Eng. *cord*, Lat. *corda*.

còrd, agree, Ir. *cord*; from obsolete Eng. *cord*, agree, bring to an agreement, from Lat. *cord-*, the stem of *cor*, heart, whence Eng. *cordial*, etc. The Sc. has the part. as *cordyt*, agreed.

cordaidhe, spasms (Sh.): "twistings," from *còrd*.

còrlach, bran, refuse of grain (M'D.; O'R. has *corlach*), **còrrlach**, coarsely ground meal, over-plus. A compound of *còrr*, "what is over"?

còrn, a drinking horn, Ir., E. Ir. *corn*, W. *corn*, Br. *korn*, **korno-*; Lat. *cornu*; Eng. *horn*; Gr. κέρας, horn.

còrnuil, retching, violent coughing: **kors-no-*? For *kors*, see *carrasan*.

coron, a crown, Ir., E. Ir. *coróin*, *corón*, W. *coron*; from Lat. *corona* (Eng. *crown*).

corp, a body, Ir., O. Ir. *corp*, W. *corff*, Br. *korf*; from Lat. *corpus* (Eng. *corpse*, Sc. *corp*).

corpag, tiptoe (Arm.); seemingly founded on *corr* of *corrag*.

corr, a crane, Ir., E. Ir. *corr*, W. *crychydd*, Cor. *cherhit*, O. Br. *corcid*, ardea, **korgsá*, *korgjo-s*; Gr. κέρχω, be hoarse, κερχνη, a hawk, O. Sl. *kraguj*, sparrow-hawk. Cf. W. *cregyr*, heron, "screamer," from *cregu*, be hoarse; Ag. S. *hrágra*, Ger. *reiher*, heron, Gr. κρίζω, κρίκε, screech.

còrr, excess, overplus, Ir. *corr*; G. **corr**, odd, Ir. *cor*, *corr*, odd; also Ir. *corr*, snout, corner, point, E. Ir. *corr*, rostrum, corner. The E. Ir. *corr*, rostrum, has been referred by Zimmer and Thurneysen to *corr*, crane—the name of "beaked" bird doing duty also for "beak." The modern meanings of "excess, odd" (cf. *odd* of Eng., which really means "point, end") makes the comparison doubtful. Refer it rather to *kors-*, stick out, point, head; Gr. κόρση, head; stem *keras-*; Lat. *crista*, Eng. *crest*; further is Gr. κέρας, horn, Lat. *cerebrum*, Norse *hjarsi*, crown of the head; and also *corn*, horn, q.v. Hence **corran**, headland.

corra-biod, an attitude of readiness to start; from *còrr*, point, and *biod* = *biog*, start. **corra-beaga** (M'A.).

corrach, abrupt, steep, Ir., M. Ir. *corrach*, unsteady, wavering; "on a point," from *corr*, point, odd?

corra-chagailt, glow-worm-like figures from raked embers, Ir. *corrchagailt*; from *còrr*, a point, and *cagailt*.

corradhuil, first effort of an infant to articulate. An onomatopoetic word.

corrag, a forefinger, finger; from *còrr*, point, etc.

corra-ghriodhach, a heron, crane, Ir. *corr-ghrian*, heron; from *còrr*, and (E. Ir.) *grith*, a cry, scream, **gṛtu-*, root *gar*, of *goir*, q.v.

corran, a sickle, Ir. *corrán*, *carrán*, M. Ir. *corrán*, **korso-*, root *kors*, *kers*, an extension of I. E. *qero*, Gr. κείρω, etc., as in *corc*, q.v. Cf. I. E. *qerpo*, cut, from the same root, which gives Lat. *carpo*, cull, Gr. καρπός, fruit (Eng. harvest), Lit. *kerpu*, cut, Skr. *kṛpana*, sword. G. may be from a *korpso-*, *korso-*. The Gaelic has also been referred to the root *kur*, round, as in *cruinn*, Ir. *cor*, circuit (O'Cl.).

corran, headland; see *còrr*.

corran, a spear, barbed arrow (Ossianic Poems); from *corr*, a point, q.v.

corranach, loud weeping, "coronach," Ir. *coránach*, a funeral cry, dirge: *co* + *ràn-ach*, "co-weeping"; see *rán*.

corrghuil, a murmur, chirping (Heb.); see *corradhuil*.

còrrlach, coarsely ground meal, overplus; see *còrlach*.

corruich, anger, rage, Ir. *corruighe*, vb. *corruighim*, stir, shake; from *corrach*. The striking resemblance to M. Eng. *couroux*, O. Fr. *couroux* (from Lat. *corruptus*), has been remarked by Dr Cameron (Rel. Celt. II., 625).

còrsa, a coast; from the Eng. *course*. Cf. **còrsair**, a cruiser.

cor-shìomain, thraw-crook; from *cor* or *car*, q.v., and *sìoman*, q.v.

cos, a foot, leg; see *cas*.

còs, a cave, Ir. *cuas*, topographically *Coos*, *Coose*, M. Ir. *cuas*, a cave, hollow: **cavosto-*, from *cavo-*, hollow; Lat. *cavus*. It is possible to refer it to **coud-to*, *koudh*, hide, Gr. κεύθω, Eng. *hide*, *hut*. The Norse *kjós*, a deep or hollow place, is not allied, but it appears in Lewis in the place-name *Keose*.

cosanta, industrious; see *cosnadh*.

cosd, cost, Ir. *cosdus* (n), M. Ir. *costus*, W. *cost*; from O. Fr. *cost*, Eng. *cost*.

cosgairt, slaughtering; see *casgairt*.

cosgaradh, valuation of the sheep and cattle which a crofter is entitled to; Norse *kost-gorð*, state of affairs (Lewis).

cosgus, cost; a by-form of *cost*.

coslach, like, **coslas**, likeness, Ir., *cosmhuil*, like, O. Ir. *cosmail*, *cosmailius* (n.): *con* + *samhail*, q.v.

cosmhail, like; see the above.

cosmal, rubbish, refuse of meat, etc. (M'A.):

cosnadh, earning, winning, Ir. *cosnamh*, defence, O. Ir. *cosnam*, contentio, **co-sen-*, root *sen*, Skr. *san*, win, *saniyas*, more profitable, Gr. ἔναρα, booty. M. Ir. *aisne*, gain, **ad-senia*, Skr. *sanati*, Gr. ἄνυμι.

costag, costmary ; from the Eng.

cot, a cottage ; from Eng. *cot*.

còta, a coat ; Ir. *cóta* ; from the Eng.

cota-bàn, a groat :

cotan, cotton, Ir. *cotún* ; from the Eng.

cothachadh, earning support, Ir. *cothughadh*, M. Ir. *cothugud*, support ; from *teg*, *tog*, as in *tigh ?*

cothaich, contend, strive ; from *cath*, battle ?

cothan, pulp, froth ; see *omhan*.

cothar, a coffer, Ir. *cófra* ; from the Eng.

cothlamadh, things of a different nature mixed together :

cothrom, fairplay, justice, Ir. *cómhthrom*, equilibrium, E. Ir. *comthrom*, par : *com + trom*, q.v.

cràbhach, devout, Ir. *crábhach*, O. Ir. *cráibdech*, *crabud*, fides, W. *crefydd*, **krab*, religion ; Skr. *vi-çrambh*, trust.

crabhat, a cravat, Ir. *carabhat* ; from the Eng.

cracas, conversation ; from Sc., Eng. *crack*.

cràdh, torment, Ir. *crádh*, E. Ir. *crád*, *cráidim* (vb.). Ascoli has compared O. Ir. *tacráth*, exacerbatione, which he refers to a stem *acrad-*, derived from Lat. *acritas*. This will not suit the *à* of *cràdh*. Possibly it has arisen from the root *ker*, cut, hurt, (*ker*, *krâ*).

crà-dhearg, blood-red, E. Ir. *cró-derg* ; see *crò*.

crag, **crac**, a fissure ; from the Eng. *crack*.

crag, knock ; from the Eng. *crack*.

craicionn, skin, Ir. *croiceann*, O. Ir. *crocenn*, tergus, Cor. *crohen*, Br. *kroc'hen*, **krokkenno-*, W. *croen*, **krokno-* (?). From **krok-kenn* : *krok* is allied to Ger. *rücken*, back, Eng. *ridge*, Norse *hryggr* ; and *kenn* is allied to Eng. *skin*. For it, see *boicionn*.

craidhneach, a skeleton, a gaunt figure, **craidhneag**, a dried peat ; for root, see *creathach*, *crìon*, (**krat-ni-*).

cràigean, a frog, from *cràg*, *cròg*, q.v. : "the well-pawed one."

craimhinn, cancer, Ir. *cnamhuinn* ; from *cnàmh*, q.v.

cràin, a sow, Ir. *cráin*, M. Ir. *cránai* (gen. case) : **crācnix*, "grunter," root *qreq*, as in Lat. *crōcio*, croak, Lit. *krõkti*, grunt.

cràiteag, a niggard woman ; likely from *cràdh*.

cràlad, torment ; for *cràdh-lot*, *cràdh* and *lot*, q.v.

cramaist, a crease by folding (Skye) :

cramb, a cramp-iron, Ir. *crampa*; from the Eng.

crambadh, crampadh, a quarrel:

cràlaidh, crawl, crawling; from the Eng.

crann, tree, a plough, Ir. *crann*, a tree, lot, O. Ir. *crann*, W. and Br. *prenn*: **qrenno-*; cf. Gr. *κράνον*, cornel, Lat. *cornus*, Lit. *kéras*, tree stump, O. Pruss. *kirno*, shrub (Bezzenberger). Windisch correlated Lat. *quernus*, oaken, but this form, satisfactory as it is in view of the Welsh, rather stands for *quercnus*, from *quercus*, oak.

crannadh, withering, shrivelling, Ir. *crannda*, decrepit; from *crann*: "running to wood."

crannag, a pulpit, a wooden frame to hold the fir candles, Ir. *crannóg*, a hamper or basket, M. Ir. *crannoc*, a wooden vessel, a wooden structure, especially the "crannogs" in Irish lakes. From *crann*; the word means many kinds of wooden structures in Gadelic lands.

crannchur, lot, casting lots, Ir. *crannchar*, O. Ir. *cranchur*; from *crann* and *cuir*.

crannlach, the teal, red-breasted merganser; from *crann* and *lach*, duck, q.v.

craobh, tree, so Ir., E. Ir. *cróeb*, *cráeb*, **croib*? "the splittable," root *krei*, *kri*, separate; as *tree* of Eng. and its numerous congeners in other languages is from the root *der*, split; and some other tree words are from roots meaning violence of rending or splitting (*κλάδος*, *twig*, e.g.). For root *kri*, see *criathar*.

craoiseach, a spear, E. Ir. *cróisech*; from *craobh*?

craoit, a croft; see *croit*.

craos, a wide, open mouth, gluttony, so Ir., E. Ir. *cróes*, *cráes*, O. Ir. *crois*, gula, gluttony. Zimmer cfs. W. *croesan*, buffoon. Possibly a Celtic k^{r}*apestu-*, allied to Lat. *crāpula*, or to Gr. *κραιπάλη*, headache from intoxication.

crasgach, cross-ways, **crasg,** an across place; for *crosg*, from *cros* of *crois*, a cross, q.v.

crasgach, corpulent (Sh.; H.S.D. for C. S.); from obsolete *cras*, body (O'Cl.), Ir. *cras*, for **crapso-*, **kṛps*, root *kṛp* of Lat. *corpus*?

cratach, back of person, side (Skye): *crot*?

crath, shake, Ir. *crathadh*, O. Ir. *crothim*, **kṛto-*; perhaps allied to Lit. *kresti*, *kratýti*, shake. But it may be allied to *crith*, q.v. It has been compared to Gr. *κραδάω*, brandish, which may be for *σκαρδάω*, root *sker* in *σκαίρω*, spring, Ger. *scherz*, joke. This would suit G. *crith*, W. *cryd* and *ysgryd*.

crè, clay, Ir., O. Ir. *cré*, g. *criad*, W. *pridd*, Cor., Br. *pry*. Its relation to Lat. *crêta*, which Wharton explains as from *crêtus*, "sifted," from *cerno*, is doubtful. If *cerno* be for **crino*, Gr. *κρίνω*, we should have the root *kri*, *krei*, separate, as in *criathar*, and it is not labialised in any language (not *qrei*). The Celtic phonetics are not easily explained, however. Stokes gives the stem as *qreid-*, but the modern G. has the peculiar *è* sound which we find in *gnè*, *cè*. This points to a stem *qrē-jâ*, root *qrê*, which is in agreement with Lat. *crêta* without doing the violence of supposing *crino* to give *cerno*, and this again *crêtus*. Cf. O. Ir. *clé*, left.

crè, creubh, body ; see *creubh*.

crèabag, a ball for playing, fir cone :

creach, plunder, so Ir., E. Ir. *crech*, plundering, hosting ; cf. Br. *kregi*, seize, bite, catch (as fire). From the root *ker*, cut, ultimately. See *corc*, knife, and *creuchd*.

creachag, a cockle, Ir. *creach*, scollop shell (O'R.) ; cf. W. *cragen*, a shell, Cor. *crogen*, Br. *krog*.

creachan, creachann, bare summit of a hill wanting foliage, a mountain : "bared," from *creach ?*

creachan, pudding made with a calf's entrails (M'L.) :

creadhonadh, a twitching, piercing pain (Heb.) ; possibly for *cneadh-ghonadh*, "wound-piercing."

creag, a rock, so Ir. ; a curtailed form of *carraig*. Also (Dialectically) **craig**. Hence Eng. *crag*.

creamh, garlic, Ir. *creamh*, earlier *crem*, W. *craf* ; Gr. *κρόμυον*, onion ; Ag. S. *hramse*, Eng. *ramsons* ; Lit. *kermúszė*, wild garlic.

crean, crion, quake, tear up (Carm.) :

creanair, sedition (Arm. ; not H.S.D.), so Ir. (O'R.) :

creanas, whetting or hacking of sticks (M'F. ; H.S.D. considers it Dialectic), neat-handed (M'L.) :

creapall, entangling, hindering, so Ir. ; it is an Ir. word evidently, from Lh. ; founded on Eng. *cripple*.

creapall, a garter, **creapailld** (Skye) ; (Arm. *creapull*) :

creathach, (faded) underwood, firewood, Ir. *creathach*, hurdle, brushwood, faggots (O'R.) : **kṛto-* ; cf. *crìon*.

creathall, cradle, from Northern M. Eng. *credil*, Sc. *creddle*, Eng. *cradle*, Ag. S. *cradol*. Further derivation at present uncertain (Murray).

creathall, a lamprey :

creatrach, a wilderness, so Ir. (Lh., etc.) ; M'A. gives the word, but it is clearly Ir. Cf. *creathach*.

creic, sell, M. Ir. *creicc*, sale, E. Ir. *creic*, buying, O. Ir. *crenim*, I buy, W. *prynn*, buy; Skr. *krînami* (do.). There seems a confusion in G. and E. Ir. with the word *reic*, sell, q.v.

creid, believe, Ir. *creidim*, O. Ir. *cretim*, W. *credu*, Cor. *cresy*, Br. *cridiff*, **kreddiô*; Lat. *credo*; Skr. *çrad-dadhâmi*. From *cred-dô*, "I give heart to."

creigeir, a grapple (M'D.); from some derivative of Norse *krækja*, to hook, *krækill*, a crooked stick, Eng. *crook?*

creim, creidhm, gnaw, chew, nibble, Ir. *creimim*, *creidhmim*, M. Ir. *créim*. Ir. is also *creinim*, W. *cnithio*, *cnoi* (which also means "gnaw"): from *knet*, *knen*, *knō*, *ken*, bite, scratch, as in *cnàmh*, q.v. The *n* of *kn* early becomes *r* because of the *m* or *n* after the first vowel.

crein, suffer for (W. H.). Allied to the O. Ir. *crenim*, buy: "You will *buy* for it!" See under *creic*.

créis, grease; from Sc. *creische*, from O. Fr. *craisse*, *cresse*, from Lat. *crassa*, *crassus*, thick. Eng. *grease* is of like origin.

creithleag, a gadfly, so Ir. (Fol.), M. Ir. *crebar*, W. *crëyr*, root *creb*, scratch? Cf. Lett. *kribinát*, gnaw off. Ir. *creabhar*, horse-fly.

creòth, wound, hurt (Dialectic), Ir. *creo*, a wound (O'R.); **creonadh**, being pained: **krevo-* as in *crò*, blood.

creubh, creubhag, cré, the body; cf. M. Ir. *crí*, **kreivio-*, flesh, body; Got. *hraiva-*, Norse *hrae*, body, O. H. G. *hreô*, corpse. It is possible to refer *crí*, *cré* to **krepi-*, Lat. *corpus*, O. H. G. *href*, Ag. S. *hrif*, body, Eng. mid-*riff*. Stokes: *crí*, *kṛpes*.

creubh, dun, crave; from the Eng. *crave*.

creubhaidh, tender in health; seemingly from *creubh*.

creuchd, wound, Ir. *créachd*, O. Ir. *crécht*, W. *craith*, scar, *creithen*, M. Br. *creizenn* (do.), **crempto-*; root *kerp*, *ker*, Lit. *kerpù*, cut, Skr. *kṛpana*, sword (Strachan). Stokes gives the Celtic as *krekto-s*, and Bez. cfs. Norse *hrekja*, worry. This neglects the *é* of Gadelic.

creud, what, Ir. *creud*, *créad*, E. Ir. *crét*; for *ce rét*. See *co* and *rud*.

creud, creed, Ir. *créidh*, M. Ir. *credo*, W. *credo*; from Lat. *credo*, I believe; the first word of the Apostles' *Creed* in Lat.

creutair, creature, Ir. *créatúr*, W. *creadur*; from Lat. *creatura*.

criadh, clay, so Ir. Really the oblique form of *crè*, q.v.

criathar, a sieve, Ir., O. Ir. *criathar*, O. W. *cruitr*, Cor. *croider*, M. Br. *croezr*, **kreitro-*; Ag. S. *hridder*, *hriddel*, Eng. *riddle*, Ger. *reiter*; further Lat. *crîbrum* (**kri-θro-n*); root *kri*, *krei* separate, whence Gr. *κρίνω*, Eng. *critic*, etc.

criachadh, proposing to oneself; from *crìoch*, end. Cf. Eng *define*, from *finis* and *end*, used for "purpose."

cridhe, heart, Ir. *croidhe*, O. Ir. *cride*, W. *craidd*, Br. *kreis*, middle, **kṛdjo-n*; Gr. κραδία, καρδία; Lat. *cor*, *cordis*; Eng. *heart*, Ger. *herz*; Lit. *szirdis*.

crilein, a small creel (M'E.), a box, small coffer (H.S.D.), **crilein** (Arm., M'L.), a box, Ir. *crilín*, E. Ir. *criol*, coffer, **krêpolo*. **criol** (Arran, Perth). Stokes gives the stem as *krêpo-*, and Bez. adds Skr. *çûrpa*, winnowing basket (Cf. for phonetics *lìon*, and Skr. *pûrna*, full). Sc., Eng. *creel*, which appears about 1400, is usually derived hence; but as the G. form itself is doubtful, and, from all appearance, taken from Lh., it is best to look elsewhere for an etymology for *creel*, as, through Fr., from Lat. *craticula*. The G. *criol* exists only in Sh., who found it in Lh. See *croidhleag*.

crioch, end, Ir. *críoch*, O. Ir., *crích*, **krîka*, from the root *krei*, separate, as in *criathar*, q.v. Stokes and Bezzenberger join W. *crip*, a comb, and compare Lit. *kreikti*, strew, and, for sense, appeal to the Ger., Eng. *strand*, "the strewed," O. Slav. *strana*, side. It has also been referred to the root of Lat. *circus*, circle, Gr. κρίκος.

criom, nibble, **criomag**, a bit; see *creim*.

crion, little, withered, Ir. *críon*, E. Ir. *crín*, W. *crin*, fragile, dry, Br. *krin*, **krēno-s*; the root *krē* appears to belong to root *kēr*, *kera*, destroy, Skr. *çṛṇâmi*, break, rend, Lat. *caries*, decay, Gr. ἀκήρατος, pure, untouched, Got. *hairus*, sword. Stokes allies it to Skr. *çrâṇa*, cooked, *çrâ*, cook, possibly a form of the root *kera*, mix, Gr. κέραμαι, mix.

crioncanachd, a strife, quarrelsomeness, Ir. *críoncánachd*: an Ir. word from Lh., apparently. Perhaps *críon-cán*, "small reviling."

crionna, attentive to small things, prudent, so Ir. (*críonna*, Con.); also dialectic **crionda**, which shows its connection with *crìon*. Cf. W. *crintach*, sordid.

criopag, a wrinkle, Ir. *criopóg*; founded on Eng. *crimp*, *crumple*. M'A. has **criopag**, a clew of yarn.

crios, a belt, girdle, so Ir., O. Ir. *criss*, *fo-chridigedar*, accingat, W. *crys*, shirt, E. W. *crys*, belt, M. Br. *crisaff*, succingere, Br. *kreis*, middle. Bez. suggests comparison with Lit. *skritulýs*, circle, knee-cap, *skreistė*, mantle. It has been referred also to the root *krid* of *cridhe*, heart.

Criosdaidh, a Christian, Ir. *Criosduighe*, M. Ir. *cristaige*; from the G. *Crìosd*, Ir. *Críosda*, Christ; from Lat. *Christus*, Gr. Χριστός, the Anointed One.

criostal, a crystal, so Ir; from the Eng.

criot, an earthen vessel (Dialect, H.S.D.), Ir. *criotamhail*, earthen, made of clay (O'B.), *criot*, an earthen vessel (O'R.):

criotaich, caress; see *cniadaich*.
criplich, a cripple; from the Eng. *cripple*.
crith, shake, quiver, Ir., E. Ir. *crith*, W. *cryd*, O. W. *crit*, **kritu-*; Ag. S. *hriða*, fever, Ger. *ritten*, fever. See *crath*, to which *crith* has been suggested as cognate (root *kr̥t*, *krot*, *kret*).
critheann, critheach, the aspen tree, Ir. *crann-critheach*; from *crith*.
crò, a sheep cot, pen, Ir. *cró*, M. Ir. *cró caerach*, ovile, *crò na muice*, pig-stye, W. *craw*, hovel, pig-stye, Br. *kraou*, *crou*, stable, **krâpo-s*, a stye, roof; Ag. S. *hróf*, Eng. *roof*, Norse *hróf*, a shed (Stokes). The Norse *kró*, small pen, Sc. *croo*, seem borrowed.
crò, the eye of a needle, Ir., E. Ir. *cró*, W. *crau*, M. Br. *cräo*, Br. *kraouenn*.
†**crò**, blood, E. Ir. *cró*, *crú*, W. *crau*, Cor. *crow*, **krovo-s*; Lat. *cruor*, gore; Lit. *kraújas*, blood; Skr. *kravis*, raw flesh; Gr. *κρέας*, flesh; Eng. *raw*.
†**crò**, death, Ir., E. Ir. *cró*. From the same origin as *crò*, blood. This is the Sc. *cro*, the weregild of the various individuals in the Scoto-Celtic Kingdom, from the king downwards.
cròc, beat, pound (Dialectic, H.S.D.):
cròc, a branch of a deer's horn; cf. Norse *krókr*, Eng. *crook*.
cròcan, a crook; from the Norse *krókr*, Eng. *crook*.
croch, hang, Ir. *crochaim*, *croch*, a cross, gallows, E. Ir. *croch*, cross, W. *crog*; from the Lat. *crux*, *crucis*.
cròch, saffron, Ir. *cróch*; from Lat. *crocus*, from Gr. *κρόκος*, crocus, and its product saffron.
crodh, cattle, Ir. *crodh*, a dowry, cattle, M. Ir. *crod*, wealth (cattle): **krodo-*, I. E. *qordh*, *qerdh*; Eng. *herd*, Ger. *herde*; Lit. *kerdžus*, herd (man), Ch. Sl. *creda*, a herd; Skr. *çardhas*, a troop.
cròdha, valiant, Ir. *cródha*, E. Ir. *cróda*, valiant, cruel, **croudavo-s*, "hardy"; root *croud* of *cruaidh*, q.v.
crodhan, hoof, parted hoof, Ir. *crobhán*, a little hoof or paw. See *crubh*.
crog, an earthen vessel, **crogan**, a pitcher, Ir. *crogán*, pitcher, E. Ir. *crocann*, olla, W. *crochan*, **krokko-*; Gr. *κρωσσός*, pitcher (**κρωκjος*); to which are allied, by borrowing somehow, Eng. *crock*, Ag. S. *crocca*, Norse *krukka*, Ger. *krug*. G. and W. phonetics (G. *g* = W. *ch.*) are unsatisfactory. Schrader derives these words from O. Ir. *crocenn*, skin—a "skin" vessel being the original.
crog, an aged ewe; from the Sc. *crock*; cf. Norw. *krake*, a sickly beast, Fries. *krakke*, broken-down horse, etc.

cròg, large hand, hand in paw form, ***crobhag**, Ir. *crobh*, hand from wrist to fingers, paw, hoof, O. Ir. *crob*, hand. See *crubh*.
crogaid, a beast with small horns (M'A.); from *crog ?*
crogan, a gnarled tree (Arg.); cf. *cròcan*.
crògan, thornbush (Arg), from *cròg*, W. *crafanc*, claw.
cròic, foam on spirits, rage, difficulty, cast sea-weed:
croich, gallows, Ir. *croch*, gallows, cross, E. Ir. *croch*, cross, W. *crogbren*, gallows; from Lat. *crux*, *crucis*.
cròid, a sumptuous present (Heb.); see *cnòid*.
cròidh, pen cattle, house corn; from *crò*. Dialectic for latter meaning is **cródhadh**.
croidhleag, a basket, small creel; see *crìlein*.
cròilean, a little fold, a group; from *crò*.
crois, a cross, so Ir., E. Ir. *cross*, W. *croes*; from Lat. *crux*.
croistara, cranntara, also **-tàra, -tarra**, the fiery cross: *crois* + *tara*; see *crois* above. As to *tara*, cf. the Norse *tara*, war (Cam.).
croit, a hump, hillock, Ir. *croit*, W. *crwth*, a hunch, harp, *croth*, a protuberant part (as calf of leg), **crotti-*; from *krot*, *kurt*, root *kur*, round, as in *cruinn*, *cruit*, q.v.
croit, a croft; from the Eng. *croft*. In the sense of "vulva," cf. W. *croth*, Br. *courz*, which Stokes refers to *cruit*, harp; but the G. may be simply a metaphorical use of *croit*, croft.
cròlot, wound dangerously; *crò* + *lot*, q.v.
cròm, bent, Ir., E. Ir. *crom*, O. Ir. *cromm*, W. *crwm*, Br. *krom*, O. Br. *crum*, **krumbo-*; from the same root as *cruinn ?* The Ag. S. *crumb*, crooked, Eng. *crumple*, Ger. *krumm*, have been compared, and borrowing alleged, some holding that the Teutons borrowed from the Celts, and *vice versa*. Dr Stokes holds that the Celts are the borrowers. The Teutonic and Celtic words do not seem to be connected at all in reality. It is an accidental coincidence, which is bound to happen sometimes, and the wonder is it does not happen oftener.
cromadh, a measure the length of the middle finger, Ir. *cruma*, *cromadh*; from *crom*.
croman, kite, hawk, from *crom*.
cron, fault, harm, Ir. *cronaim*, I bewitch; cf. M. Ir. *cron*, rebuking. The idea is that of being "fore-spoken" by witchcraft. See next.
cronaich, rebuke, Ir. *cronuighim*, M. Ir. *cronaigim*, *cron*, rebuking, E. Ir. *air-chron* (do.), **kruno-*; cf. Teut. *hru*, noise, Norse *rómr*, shouting, Ag. S. *hréam*, a din.
crònan, a dirge, croon, purring, Ir., E. Ir. *cronán*. O'Curry (Mann. and Cust. III., 246) writes the Ir. as *crónán*, and defines it as the low murmuring or chorus to each verse of

the *aidbsi* or choral singing. Sc. *croon*, *croyn* (15th century), corresponds to Du. *kreunen*, groan, M. Du. *krönen*, lament, M. Low G. *kronen*, growl, O. H. G. *chrônan*, M. L. G. *kroenen*, chatter (Murray, who thinks the Sc. came from Low Ger. in M. Eng. period). It seems clear that the Gadelic and Teutonic are related to each other by borrowing; seemingly the Gadelic is borrowed.

cropan, deformed person (Suth.); from Norse *kroppinn*, deformed. See under *crùb*.

crosach, crossing, thwarting, Ir. *crosanta*; also G. **crosan** (and **crostan**), a peevish man; all from *cros*, the basis of *crois*, cross, q.v.

crosanachd, from *crosan*, poet, chorister.

crosda, perverse, irascible, so Ir.; from the G. base *cros* of *crois*, cross.

crotal, lichen, especially for dyeing, cudbear: **crottal*; **krot-to-*, from *krot*; cf. Gr. *κροτώνη*, an excrescence on a tree. Hence Sc. *crottle*. M. Ir. *crotal* means "husk" (which may be G. **crotal** above), "kernel, cymbal." In the last two senses the word is from the Lat. *crotalum*, a rattle; the Irish used a small pear-shaped bell or rattle, whence the Ir. Eng. *crotal* (Murray).

cruach, a pile, heap, Ir., E. Ir. *cruach*, W. *crug*, Cor. *cruc*, O. Br. *cruc*, **kroukâ*; Lit. *kráuti*, to pile, *krúvi*, heap; Norse *hrúga*, heap. Others have compared the Norse *hraukr*, a small stack, Ag. S. *hreác*, Eng. *rick*.

cruachan, cruachainn, hip, upper part of the hip, E. Ir. *cruachait*; from *cruach*, heap, hump. Stokes translates the Ir. as "chine," and considers it, like the corresponding Ger. *kreuz*, derived from Lat. *crûcem*, cross. The Gaelic meaning is distinctly against this.

cruaidh, hard, Ir. *cruaidh*, O. Ir. *cruaid*, **kroudi-s*; root *kreva*, to be bloody, raw, whence *crò*, blood, q.v.; Lat. *crûdus*, Eng. *crude*. Hence **cruailinn**, hard, rocky.

crùb, squat, crouch, Ir. *crúbadh*, to bend, crook; also G. **crùbach**, cripple, Ir. do.; from Norse *krjúpa*, to creep, kneel (Eng. *creep*, etc.), *kroppinn*, crippled, root *kreup*, *krup*, as in Eng. *cripple*, Sc. *cruppen thegether*, contracted, bowed. Cf. W. *crwb*, bent.

crùb, bed recess (Carm.):

crùban, the crab-fish, Ir. *crúban*, W. *crwban*. From *crùb* above.

crubh, a horse's hoof, Ir. *crobh*, paw, hoof, E. Ir. *crù*, **kruvo-*, hoof; Zend *çrva*, *çruva*, nail, horn; further Gr. *κέρας*, horn, and *corn*, q.v. (Stokes).

crudha, horse shoe, Ir. *crúdh*: seemingly from the above word.

crùidein, the king-fisher, Ir. *cruidín* :

cruidhean, paw (Arm.) = *crùibhean.*

cruimh, a worm, Ir. *cnuimh,* O. Ir. *cruim,* W., Cor. *pryf,* Br. *prenv,* **qṛmi-* ; Lit. *kirmis,* Lett. *sérms* ; Skr. *kṛmis, krímis.*

cruinn, round, so Ir., O. Ir. *cruind,* W. *crwn,* Br. *krenn,* **krundi-s* ; root *kuro-,* circle, turn, as in *car,* q.v. Cf. Lat. *curvus* ; Gr. κυρτός, bent, κορώνη, ring, Lat. *corona,* Eng. *crown.* Bezzenberger cfs. the form *crundi-* from *kur* to Lat. *rotundus* from *rota.*

crùisgein, a lamp, jug, Ir. *crúisgín* ; from M. Eng. *cruskyn,* from O. Fr. *creusequin,* from Teut. *krûs,* whence Eng. *cruse.*

crùisle, crùidse, mausoleum, hollow vault of a church ; from M. Eng. *cruddes,* vault, crypt, *crowd,* by-form of Eng. *crypt.*

cruit, a harp, so Ir., O. Ir. *crot,* W. *crwth,* fidicula, Late Lat. (600 A.D.) *chrotta,* **krotta* : *krot-ta-,* from *krot, kurt,* root *kur,* as in G. *cruinn,* round, q.v., Gr. κυρτός (do.): "the curved instrument." Stokes refers it to the root *krot,* strike, as in Gr. κροτέω, rattle, clap. Hence Eng. *crowd.*

cruithneachd, cruineachd, wheat, Ir. *cruithneachd,* O. Ir. *cruithnecht* : **kṛt-on-,* root *kert, ker,* cut, "that which is cut" ; Lit. *kertù,* cut ; Gr. κείρω, Lat. *curtus,* etc. (Rhys). It has been compared to the Lat. *Ceres,* Eng. *cereal,* and Lat. *cresco, creo,* as in *cruth.*

crùlaist, a rocky hill (H.S.D., from MSS.) ; from *cruaidh ?* Cf. *cruailinn.*

crumag, the plant skirret ; Sc. *crummock.* From Gaelic *crom* (Cameron).

cruman, the hip bone, Ir. *crumán,* hip bone, crooked surgical instrument ; from *crom.*

crùn, crown, Ir. *crún* ; from M. Eng. *crune,* from O. Fr. *coronne,* from Lat. *corona.*

crunnluadh, a quick measure in pipe music : *cruinn + luath.*

crup, crouch, contract, Ir. *crupaim* ; founded on the M. Eng. *cruppel,* cripple, a root *crup,* appearing in Sc. *cruppen,* contracted. See *crùbach.*

crùsbal, crucible (Hend.).

cruscladh, wrinkling :

cruth, form, figure, Ir., O. Ir. *cruth,* W. *pryd,* **qṛtu-s,* root *qer,* make ; Lat. *cerus,* creator, *creo,* Eng. *create* ; Lit. *kuriù,* build ; Skr. *kar,* make, *kṛtas,* made.

cruthach, placenta of mare :

cù, a dog, Ir., O. Ir. *cú,* g. *con,* W. *ci,* pl. *cwn,* Cor., Br. *ki,* pl. Br *koun,* **kuô,* g. **kunos* ; Gr. κύων ; Lat. *canis* ; Eng. *hound* Skr. *çvá,* g. *çúnas.*

cuach, a cup, bowl, Ir. *cuachóg,* O. Ir. *cúach*: Lat. *caucus,* Gr. *καῦκα*; Skr. *koça.* It is generally held that *cuach* is borrowed from the Lat., though phonetically they may be cognate. The W. *cawg* is certainly borrowed.

cuach, curl, so Ir.; from the above.

cuag, an awkward curve, kink, an excrescence on the heel; also **guag** (Dialectic): **kouggâ,* **kouk-gâ*; root *qeuq,* bend; Skr. *kuc,* bend. Lit. *kuku,* hook?

cu'ag, cubhag, cuckoo, Ir. *cuach,* O. Ir. *cúach,* W. *côg,* of onomatopoetic origin—from the cuckoo's cry of *kuku,* whence Eng. *cuckoo,* Lat. *cucûlus,* Gr. *κόκκυξ,* Skr. *kôkilas, koka.*

cuailean, the hair, a lock, curl, Ir. *cuailen* (Stokes). This Stokes refers to a stem **koglenno-,* and cfs. Gr. *κόχλος,* a spiral-shelled shell-fish, *κοχλίας,* spiral-shelled snail, Lat. *cochlea.* As the Gr. may be for *χόχλος,* the derivation is uncertain. Ir. *cuailín,* a bundle, faggot, suggests that a similar derivation from *cual* was used metaphorically for a "bundle or cord of hair."

cuaille, a club, bludgeon, Ir., E. Ir. *cuaille,* **kaullio-*; Gr. *καυλός,* stalk; Lat. *caulis,* stalk; Lit. *káulas,* a bone (Stokes). It may, however, be for **coud-s-lio-,* from *qoud,* Lat. *cûdo,* strike.

cuairsg, roll, wreathe, so Ir.; from *cuairt,* with the termination *-sqô.*

cuairt, circuit, so Ir., O. Ir. *cúairt.* Stokes gives the stem as *kukṛti-,* from *kur,* circle, as in *cruinn.*

cual, a faggot, burden of sticks, Ir. *cual,* M. Ir. *cual,* heap, **kuglo-,* root *kug, qeug*; Eng. *heap*; Lat. *cumulus* (= *cub-lus*?); Lit. *kúgis,* heap.

cuallach, herding or tending cattle:

cuallach, society, family, Ir *cuallaidheachd,* society, *cuallaidhe,* a companion:

cuan, the ocean, Ir., M. Ir. *cuan,* harbour, **copno-*; Norse *köfn,* Ger. *hafen,* Eng. *haven.*

cuanal, cuantal, a company, a band of singers, flocks (Carm.), E. Ir. *cúan,* host, **koupn-,* Lit. *kupa,* heap, Eng. *heap* (?).

cuanna, cuannar, handsome, fine, Ir. *cuanna*; also **cuanta,** robust, neat: **kaun-navos,* from *kaun, skaun*; Ger. *schön.*

†**cuar,** crooked, Ir. *cuar,* E. Ir. *cúar,* **kukro-,* root *kuc,* bend; Skr. *kucati,* bend, Lit. *kukŭ,* hook (Strachan). But cf. *cuairt.*

cuaradh, paining, tormenting; cf. W. *cur,* pain, care, *curio,* beat. The Dictionaries refer the word to *ciùrr,* as a Dialectic form.

cuaran, a brogue, sock, Ir. *cuaróg,* M. Ir. *cúarán,* W. *curan,* a covering for the foot and leg, **kourano-,* "mocassin": **keuro-*; root *keu, ku,* as in Lat. *cu-tis,* skin, Eng. *hide,* Ag. S. *hýd* (**kûtí-*).

cuartach, a fever (Arg.); from *cuairt.*
cuartag, ringworm (Hend.):
cuas, a cave; see *còs.*
cuat, sweetheart (Carm.):
cùb, a tumbril, box-cart; from Sc. *coop, coup,* box-cart, etc., probably the same as Eng. *coop,* basket. Dialectic **coba.**
cùb, crouch, Ir. *cúbaim*; founded on Lat. *cubo,* lie.
cùbaid, pulpit; ultimately from Lat. *pulpitum,* a speaking platform, whence Eng. *pulpit,* Sc. *poopit.* Dialectic **bùbaid.**
cùbair, a cooper; from the Eng.
cubhag, cuckoo; see *cu'ag.*
cubhaidh, fit, so Ir., O. Ir. *cobaid,* fit, *cubaithiu,* concinnior: **con-vedo-,* "suiting"; root *ved,* bind, as in *feadhainn.*
cùbhraidh, fragrant, Ir. *cumhra, cúmhra,* M. Ir. *cumra, cumrae,* E. Ir. *cumrai* (i n-aballgort chumrai); **com-rae*:
cubhraig, cubhrainn, a coverlet; founded on the Eng. *cover, coverlet.* Dialectic **cuibhlig.**
cuchailte, a residence (Arm.; not H.S.D.), Ir. *cuclaidhe*; **con-cladh-*; from *cladh,* q.v.
cudaig, the fish cuddy, young of the coalfish, Ir. *cudóg, códog,* haddock, **cod-do-*; Eng. *haddock?* Sc. *cuddy, cudden,* may be of G. origin (Murray). Also **cudainn.**
cùdainn, a large bushel or tub; cf. Norse *kútr,* cask, Sc. *coodie, quiddie,* small tub. M. Ir. *cuidin, coithin,* catînus, is probably from a Celt. *kotîno-,* Gr. κοτύλη, cup, Lat. *catînus,* a deep vessel.
cudrom, cudthrom, weight: **con-trom-,* "co-heavy"; O. Ir. *cutrumme,* similis. See *trom.* Dialectic **cuideam.**
cugainn, delicacy, "kitchen," E. Ir. *cuicen*; from Lat. *coquina.*
cugan, food (Carm.):
cugar, mab, or wild cat (Carm.):
cugullach, precarious, unstable (Carm.):
cuibheas, sufficiency:
cuibheasach, tolerable, middling, Ir. *cuibheasach,* decent, pretty good, fairly good (in health), *cuibheas,* decency, *cuibhe,* decent. See *cubhaidh* for stem. The Ir. *cuibhe* shows that it is possible to derive the word from **con-vesu-,* root *vesu* of *feabhas.*
cuibhle, cuibhill, a wheel; from Eng. *wheel.*
cuibhne, deer's horn (Arm., M'L.), deer's tibia (H.S.D.):
cuibhreach, a bond, chain, so Ir., O. Ir. *cuimrech,* vb. *conriug,* ligo, W. *rhwym,* vinculum, Br. *rum, kevre,* **kom-rigo-n*; *rigo-,* a bond; Lat. *corrigia,* shoe-lace; M. H. G. *ric,* band, string.

Stokes (rightly) now gives root as *rek*, bind, Skr. *raçana*, cord, rope, *raçmi* (do.).

cuibhrig, cover, coverlet; see *cubhraig*.

cuibhrionn, portion, so Ir., E. Ir. *cuibrend*, W. *cyfran*: **com-rann*; see *rann*.

cuicheineach, coquetting, secretly hobnobbing (Arg): *co-ceann*.

cuid, share, part, Ir. *cuid*, g. *coda*, O. Ir. *cuit*, W. *peth*, res, pars, Cor. *peth*, Br. *pez*, **qezdi-*, **qozdi-*; *qes*, *qos*, seemingly from the pron. root *qo*, *qe* (see *co*). Cf. Lat. *quotidie*, *quota*, Br. *ped*, how much. Bezzenberger compares Lit. *kedėti*, burst, Sl. *cęsti*, part; root *qed*. Hence Eng. *piece*. Some have suggested comparison with Lat. *costa*, rib, Eng. *coast*.

cuideachd, company, Ir. *cuideachda*, O. Ir. *cotecht*, coitio, conventus: **con-techt*; see *teacht*.

cuideag, a spider (H.S.D.), Ir. *cuideog* (O'R.):

cuideal, pride (Arm.), **cuidealas** (M'A.); from *cuid*?

cuideam, weight; see *cudrom*.

cuidh, **cuith**, inclosure (Barra); from Norse *kví*, Orkney *quoy*, a pen, Orkney and Shetland *quey*, *quay*, enclosed land.

cuidhe, wreath of snow; see *cuith*.

cuidhtich, quit, requite, Ir. *cúitighim*; from Eng. *quit*?

cuidich, assist, Ir. *cuidighim*, M. Ir. *cuitigim*, share; from *cuid*.

cuidridh, common (Sh.; not H.S.D.), Ir. *cuidri(dh)*, entertainment, commons: **con-trebi-*, as in *caidreabh*?

cuifein, the wadding of a gun; from Sc. *colfin*.

cuigeal, a distaff, so Ir., M. Ir. *cuigel*, W. *cogail*, Corn. *cigel*, Br. *kegel*; from M. Lat. *conucula*, for *colucula*, from *colus*. From Lat. *conucula* comes Ger. *kunkel*, Fr. *quenouille*.

cùil, corner, recess, Ir. *cúil*, O. Ir. *cuil*, W. *cil*, **kûli-* See *cùl*.

cuilbheart, a wile, trick; from *cùil* + *beart*.

cuilbheir, a gun; from the Eng. *culverin*.

cuilc, reed, cane, Ir. *cuilc*, **kolki-*; root *kol*, as in Lat. *culmus*, stalk, Gr. *κάλαμος*, reed, Eng. *haulm*.

cuile, an apartment where stores are kept, O. Ir. *cuile fínda*, vinaria, **koliâ*; Gr. *καλία*, hut, Skr. *kulâya*, hut, nest (Stokes); from **kol-io-*, root *qel* of *ceil*.

cuileag, a fly, Ir. and E. Ir. *cuil*, W. *cylion*, flies, Cor. *kelionen*, Br. *quelyenen*, **kuli-s*, *kuliâno-s*; Lat. *culex*.

cùileagan, feast (in a corner) (Carm.).

cuilean, a whelp, Ir. *cuileán* (O'B.), *cuileann* (O'R.), E. Ir. *culén*, W. *colwyn*, Cor. *coloin*, catulus, Br. *kolenn*, young of quadrupeds; Gr. *κύλλα*=*σκύλαζ*, whelp (Bez.). It may be from *cù*, **kun*, dog. Ernault, **culenos*: root of *κύος*; M. Br. *colen*, so D'Arbois. Rhys says W. borrowed.

cuilidh, cellar, secret place, treasury ; see *cuile.*

cuilionn, holly, so Ir., E. Ir. *cuilenn,* W. *celyn,* Cor. *celin,* Br. *kelenn* (pl.), **kolenno-* ; Eng. *holly,* Ag. S. *holegn.*

cuilm, a feast ; Dialectic for *cuirm,* q.v.

cuimein, the plant cumin, Ir. *cuimín* ; from Lat. *cuminum,* Eng. *cumin.*

cuimhne, remembrance, so Ir., O. Ir. *cuman, cuimnech,* memor, W. *cof,* Cor. *cov,* M. Br. *couff,* **co-men* ; root *men,* as in Lat. *memini,* I remember, Eng. *mention, mind,* etc.

cuimir, brief, handsome, so Ir., E. Ir. *cumbair,* **com-berro-* ; for *berr,* see *bearr.*

cuimrig, trouble ; see *coimrig.*

cuimse, a mark, aim, moderation, Ir. *cuimse* ; from *com + meas* ; see *meas.* Cf. *eirmis.*

cuin, when, E. Ir. *cuin,* W., Br. *pan* ; Lat. *quum* ; Eng. *when* ; see *co.* The Ir. *can* (O'Cl.) is allied to Lat. *quando,* and more nearly than *cuin* to W., Br. *pan.*

cuing, a yoke, Ir., E. Ir. *cuing* : **con-jungi-,* root *jung, jug,* as in Lat. *jungo,* Eng. *joke.* For phonetics, see next. Stokes since gives the stem as *ko-jungi-.*

cuinge, narrowness, O. Ir. *cumce* ; see *cumhang.*

cùinn, coin ; from the Eng.

cuinneag, a pail, milk pail, Ir. *cuinneóg,* M. Ir. *cuindeog,* W. *cunnog, cynnog* ; cf. Lat. *congius,* a quart.

cuinnean, a nostril :

cuinnlein, a stalk of corn, a nostril ; for the first meaning, see *connlach* ; for the second, *cuinnean* above.

cuinnse, a quince ; from the Eng.

cuinnsear, a dagger, sword ; from the Eng. *whinger.*

cuip, a whip ; from Eng. *whip.*

cuir, put, Ir., E. Ir. *cuirim,* O Ir. *cuiriur,* W. *hebyor,* put aside, **koriô,* I put. The root is likely *ker, kor,* of *cruth,* q.v. For meaning cf. Lat. *facio* and Gr. *τίθημι.* Bezzenberger compares it to Skr. *kaláyati,* drive, bear, do, Lit. *karta,* position, lie.

cuircinn, a particular kind of head-dress for women, Ir. *cuircín,* head, crest, comb (O'R.) ; from *currachd ?* Sc. *courche, curges* (pl.), a covering for a woman's head, Eng. *kerchief.* E. Ir. *cuirce,* bow, knot ; which makes the Sc. and Eng. comparison doubtful.

cuireadh, an invitation, so Ir. ; from *cuir,* q.v.

cuireall, a kind of pack-saddle (H.S.D. from MSS.) :

cuireid, cuirein, turn, wile ; from *car,* q.v.

cuirinnein, the white water-lily (H.S.D., which quotes only O'R.), Ir. *cuirinín* (O'R.) :

cuirm, a feast, so Ir., E. Ir. *coirm*, *cuirm*, M. W. *cwrwf*, W. *cwrw*, beer, Cor. *coref*, Gaul. *κοῦρμι*, *cervisia* **kurmen*; Lat. *cremor*, broth (Eng. *cream*); Gr. *κεράννυμι*, mix; Skr. *çrâ*, *çṛ*, cook; I. E. *kera*, *kra*, mix.

cuirnean, a small heap of stones, dew-drop, ringlet, Ir. *cuirneán*, head of a pin, brooch, ringlet. In the first sense, it is from *càrn*, and possibly also in the other two senses, the idea being "cluster, heap."

cuirpidh, wicked, corrupt; see *coirbte*, *coirb*.

cùirt, court, Ir. *cúirt*; from the Eng.

cùirtein, a curtain, **cùirteir**, plaiding (Dialectic); formed on Eng. *curtain*.

cùis, cause, matter, Ir., E. Ir. *cúis*, O. Ir. *cóis*; from Lat. *causa*.

cuisdeag, the little finger (Sh., H.S.D.), Ir. *cuisdeog* (O'R.):

cuiseag, a stalk, kind of grass, Ir. *coisín*, a stem, stalk, little foot; from *cas*, foot. But see next. *di fetchoisig*, "by piping."

cuisle, pulse, vein, pipe, Ir. *cuisle*, E. Ir. *cuisli*, g. pl. *cuislend*, a pipe for music, O. Ir. *cusle*, g. *cuslen*, *cuislennach*, a piper. It has no connection with Lat. *pulsus*, and its etymology is obscure (Stokes). Cf. Eng. *hose*.

cuiste, a couch, Ir. *cúiste*, *cuiste* (O'B.); from Eng. *couch*.

cuith, a wreath of snow, a pit, Ir., E. Ir. *cuithe*, a pit, W. *pydew*; from Lat. *puteus*, Eng. *pit*.

cuithe, pen for sheep (Carm.); see *cuidh*.

cùitich, quit, requite; see *cuidhtich*.

cùl, back, Ir., O. Ir. *cúl*, W. *cil*, Cor. *chil*, Br. *kil*, **kûlo-*; Lat. *cûlus*. Hence *cùlaist*, recess.

culadh, a good condition of the body, **culach**, fat, sleek: "well-covered," from *cul* of *culaidh*?

culaidh, apparel, so Ir.; root *qel*, *qol*, cover; Ger. *hülle*, a covering, Lat. *occulo*. See *ceil*.

culaidh, boat (Suth.):

cùlag, turf for the back of the fire, sitting behind another on horseback, a collop; all from *cùl*.

cùlan, tresses, hair; from *cùl*.

cùlaobh, behind, the back; E. Ir. *cúlaib* (dat. pl.), *cúlu* (acc. pl.); from *cùl*. The dat. (and acc.) pl. of *cùl* used locatively—for rest (and motion). Compare *beulaobh*.

cularan, a cucumber, Ir. *cularán*, W. *cylor*, earth nuts, Br. *coloren*, earth nut. Ernault makes the Celtic word to be **carul-an-*, and compares Gr. *κάρυον*, nut.

cullach, a boar, Ir., E. Ir. *cullach*, O. Ir. *callach*, *cullach*, *caullach*, Br. *kalloc'h*, "entire," *qellecq*, epithet for stallions and boars, **kalluâko-s*, from **kalljo-*, testicle, W. *caill*, testiculus, M. Br.

quell; root *kal*, hard, as in *clach*, q.v., Norse *hella*, flat stone, etc. (Bezzenberger). Cf. Lat. *culleus*, bag, scrotum, whence O. Fr. *couillon*, Eng. *cullion*, testicles, Sc. *culls*. Hence **cullbhoc**, wether-goat, Ir. *culbhoc*.

cullachas, impotence, **cullach**, eunuch; from *coll*, *call*; see *call*.

culraoinidh, goal-keeper (Suth.); from *cùl* and *raon*?

culuran, birth-wort, cucumber; see *cularan*.

cum, keep, hold, Ir. *congbhaighim*, inf. *congmhail*, O. Ir. *congabin*; from *con* and *gabh*, take. The G. *cum* is for *congv* or *congbh*, and the *gv* becomes *m* as in *ìm*, *ciomach*, *tum*, etc.

cuma, cumadh, shape, form, Ir. *cuma*, E. Ir. *cumma*, vb. *cummaim*:

cumail, keeping, Ir. *cumail*, *congmhail*; inf. to *cum*, i.e., *cum-gabhail*.

cuman, a milking pail; Gr. κύμβη, κύμβος, cup; Ger. *humpen*, bowl.

cumanta, common, Ir. *cumann*; from the Eng. *common*.

cumha, mourning, so Ir., E. Ir. *cuma*: I. E. root *qem*, *qom*; Eng. *hum*, Ger. *hummen*.

cumha, a stipulation, Ir. *cumha*, E. Ir. *coma*, bribe, gift, condition: **com-ajo-*, "co-saying," O. Ir. *ái*, a saying, Lat. *ajo*? See *adhan*. Cf. *cunnradh*.

cumhachd, power, so Ir., O. Ir. *cumachte*, W. *cyfoeth*, power, riches, **kom-akto-*, root *ag*, drive, carry, Lat. *ago*, Gr. ἄγω, Eng. *act*, etc. (Stokes). The O. Ir. *cumang*, potestas, is doubtless a nasalised form of the root *ag* (=*ang*); it has been referred to the root *ang*, Lat. *angere*, etc., as in *cumhang* below, but the meaning is unsatisfactory. The word *cumhachd* has also been analysed as *co-mag-tu-*, where *mag* has been variously referred to I. E. *meg*, great (G. μέγας, Eng. *much*), or I. E. *mēgh* (Eng. *may*, Lat. *machina*, *machine*).

cumhang, narrow, Ir. *cúmhang*, O Ir. *cumang*, W. *cyfyng*, **kom-ango-s*; root *ang*; Gr. ἄγχω, choke, ἄγχι, near; Lat. *ango*, *angustus*; Ger. *eng*.

cùmhlaidean, stipulations (Hend.):

cùmhnant, covenant; from M. Eng., Sc. *conand*, *couenant*, Eng. *covenant*, from O. Fr. *convenant*, Lat. *convenire*. M. Br. has *comanant*, W. *cyfammod*. Dial. plurals are **cùmhlaichean** and **cùmhlaidean**.

cumraich, cumber; from the Eng.

cunbhalach, constant, steady, Ir. *cungbhailteach*, firm, miserly; from *cungbhail*, keeping, Ir. inf. of *cum*, q.v.

cungaidh, instrument, accoutrements: **con-gen-*, root *gen* of *gnìomh*, deed. See next.

cungaisich, help, co-operate, Ir. *cunghas*, co-operation, vb *cungnaighim*, I help, *cungantach*, helpful, E. Ir. *cungnam*, assistance: **con + gníom*; see *còmhnadh*.

cunnart, danger, M. G. *cunntabhart* (M'V.), Ir. *cuntabhairt*, *contabhairt*, danger, doubt, O. Ir. *cumtubart*, *cundubart*, *contubart*, doubt, **con-to-bart*, root *ber*, of *beir*, q.v. (Cam.).

cunnradh, cùnradh, bargain, covenant, Ir. *connradh*, *cunnradh*, O. Ir. *cundrad*, *cunnrath*, Manx *coonrey*: **con-ràdh*; see *ràdh*, say. Corm. derives from *ráth*, surety.

cunnt, count, Ir. *cunntas*, *cuntas*, reckoning, *cuntaim*, I count; from the Eng.

cunnuil, an objection (Sh.), Ir. *cunuil* (Lh.):

cùp, box-cart, coup; see *cùb*.

cupa, a cup, Ir. *cúpán*, W. *cib*; from Lat. *cûpa*, tub, Eng. *cup*, *coop*, etc.

cupull, a couple, Ir. *cúpla*, *cupall*, W. *cwpl*; from M. Eng. *couple*.

cur, a placing, setting; inf. to *cuir*, q.v.

curach, a boat, coracle, Ir., E. Ir. *curach*, Irish Lat. *curucis*, dat. pl. (Adamnan), W. *corwc*, *cwrwg*, *cwrwgl*, **kuruko-* (Stokes); Armen. *kur*, a boat, O. Sl. *korici*, a kind of vessel. The Lat. *carina* has been compared, but the vowels are unsuitable. Hence Eng. *coracle*.

cùradh, affliction, obstacle, **curabh** (Lh.), obstacle. In the sense of affliction, cf. *cuaradh*.

curaideach, frisky, cunning; see *cuireid*.

curaidh, a champion, Ir. *curadh*, E. Ir. *cur*, g. *curad*, *caur*, W. *cawr*, Cor. *caur*, gigas, Gaul. Καύαρος (Polyb.), *Cavarillus*, etc., **kavaro-s*, a hero, mighty, root *keva*, *kû*, be strong; Skr. *çavîra*, mighty, *çûra*, hero; Gr. κύριος, lord, κῦρος, might.

cùraing, cùrainn, a coverlet (Dialectic, H.S.D.); founded on Eng. *covering*. M'A. has **cùrainn**, plaiding (felt); of the same origin.

cùram, care, Ir. *cúram*; from Lat. *cura*.

curcag, sandpiper, M. Ir. *cuirrcech*, plover; from *currech*, a marsh (K. Meyer). See next.

curcais, bulrush, so Ir. (O'B., etc.), E. Ir. *curcas*, O. Ir. *curchas*, O. W. *cors*, cannulos, W. *corsen*, reed, Br. *corsenn*, reed, **korokasto-*, *korkasto*; Lat. *cârex* (Stokes, Ernault). The E. Ir. *currech*, a marsh, is allied, **gr̥siko-*, Gaul. **parriko-*, A. S. *pearroc*, Fr. *parc* (St.), Lat. *cursus*. Perhaps Eng. *hurst* (St.).

cùrr, corner, pit, Ir. *curr*, Keat. *curr*, pit, *corr*, well, cistern; cf. W. *cwr*, corner.

curracag, a bubble on the surface of liquids; see *curracbd*.

currachd, hood, cap, night-cap, Ir. *currach* (O'R.), M. Ir. *curracach*, cuculatus (Stokes, Ir. Gl. 598, who suggested connection with W. *pyrchwyn*, crest of a helmet). Sc. *curch*, *courchie*, Eng. *kerchief*, seem to be the origin of the G. word.

currachdag, peat-heap (M'A.); cf. *gurracag*.

curradh, a crowding together (Macpherson's *Ossian*):

curraidh, exhausted (H S.D.), **currtha** (Sh., O'B), Ir. *currtha*; cf. *ciùrr*.

curran, curral, a carrot, root, radish, Ir. *currán*, any kind of tap-rooted plant (O'R., Sh.): **cors*, head, as in *corr*? Cf. Eng. *carrot*, ultimately from Gr. καρωτόν, carrot, from κάρα, head, top; **cors* and *kar* of κάρα are ultimately from the same source.

curran, curral, horse-panniers for heavy loads; cf. Sc. *currack*, *corrack* (do.), Eng. *crooks*.

currucadh, cooing of pigeons, Ir. *currúcadh* (O'R.), Sc., Eng. *curr*, *curring*. The word is onomatopoetic.

currucag, the lapwing: see *curcag*

currusan, a milk-pail:

cùrsa, course, manner, Ir. *cúrsa*, from the Eng. *course*.

curta, bad (Sh.; not H.S.D.), *curtsa* (O'R); from Eng. *curst*, *cursed*.

cus, sufficiency, overplus:

cusag, a wild mustard (Sh., Arm.; not H.S.D.):

cusp, a kibe:

cuspair, an object, mark, Ir. *cuspóir*, M. Ir. *cuspóir* (Keat., Oss.[3] 296). Dialectic **cuspair**, a customer (see *cuspunn*).

cuspunn, custom, tribute, also **cusmunn**; founded on Eng. *custom*.

cut, hank of yarn, Ir. *cuta*, one-twelfth of a hank of yarn; from Eng. *cut*.

cut, to gut (fish); from Eng. *gut*.

cutach, bobtailed, so Ir., E. Ir. *do-chotta*, they cut short, W. *cwta*. The relationship, if any, existing between *cut*, *cutach*, and Eng. *cut*, is one of borrowing; the history of Eng. *cut* is obscure, and the Celtic words mean "short, shorten," not "to cut" with a knife. Besides, the E. Ir. appears a century and a half earlier than the Eng. (1139 *v.* 1275). Stokes has suggested a borrowing from Fr. *couteau* (= *cultellus*, knife) for the E. Ir. form. Rhys says W. is Eng. *cutty*, borrowed.

cuthach, caothach, rage, Ir. *cuthach*, **koti-aca-*; root *kot*, Gr. κότος, wrath. See *cath*. Stokes says Pict. Skr. *kváthati*, seethe, Got. *hvapjan*, foam.

D

dà, two, Ir. *dá*, O. Ir. *dá* (m.), *dí* (f.), *da n-* (n.), W. *dau* (m.), *dwy* (f.), Cor. *dou*, *diu*, Br. *daou*, *diou*, (f.), **dvâ*, **dvâu* (m.), *dvei* (f.), *dvabin* (dat.); Skr. *dvau*, *dvâ*, *dve* (f., n.); Gr. δύω; Lat. *duô*: Got. *tvai*, Eng. *two*.

dabhach, a vat, a measure of land (either one or four plough-gates, according to locality and land), O. G. *dabach* (Bk. of Deer), Ir. *dabhach*, a vat, **dabâkâ*; Gr. θάπτω, bury, τάφος, grave; root *dhabh*, *dhôbh*, deepen, dig out. Cf. Lit. *dûbiù*, hollow out. Bezzenberger suggests alliance with Eng. *top*, Ger. *topf*. Eng. *tub*, if allied to the Ger. *zuber*, is from the root of *two*, "a two-eared" vessel. Also **dabhoch**, and in place-names **Doch-**.

dàcha, more likely; see *dòcha*.

dachaidh, home (adverb), a home, Ir. *do thigh*, M. Ir. *dia tig*, home, E. Ir. *dia thaig*; from *do* and *tigh*. In Ir. the phrase is a prepositional adverb; in Gaelic it ceases to be a phrase and becomes a welded noun.

dad, anything, aught, tittle, M. G. *dad*, mote (in sunbeam), Ir. *dadadh*, *dadamh*, aught, a jot, etc., **da-z-dho-*, root *da*, divide, Lit. *dalìs*, part, Gr. δασμός, division? See † *dàil*. Hence **dadmun**, a mote, and **dadum** = *dad*.

dag, a pistol; from M. Eng. *dag*, a pistol, from Fr. *dague*, a dagger, whence Br. *dag*. The change of meaning from "dagger" to "pistol" is one which occurs in the history of "pistol" itself, for it originally meant "dagger." Eng. *dagger* is allied.

daibhir, poor, Ir. *daidhbhir*, M. Ir. *daidber*: **do-adberi-*, from *do-* and *adber*, **ád-bherô*, Lat. *adfero*. See *saoibhir*.

dàicheil, handsome, Ir. *dóigheamhuil*, well appointed, decent; see *dàcha*, *dòcha*, *dòigh*.

daidein, daddy, Ir. *daidín*, *daid*, M. Ir. *datán*, foster-father, *datnait*, foster-mother, W. *tad*, Cor. *tat*; Lat. *tata*; Gr. τέττα; Lit. *tetýtis*, Ch. Sl. *teta*; Skr. *tatás*. Eng. *dad* is borrowed from the Welsh (Skeat).

daigeil, firm or well-built (of a man)—Arg. Cf. *daingean*.

dail, a wooden collar for cattle; cf. W. *dal*, a hold, catch, Br. *dal*, a holding; root *dhê*, *dhô*, set? Cf. Gr. θήκη, repository, τίθημι, place, Lat. *facîo*, etc. But see *dàil*, delay.

dail, a dale, meadow, from Norse *dalr*, Eng. *dale*.

dàil, delay, credit, Ir. *dáil*, M. Ir. *dál*, gen. *dála*, respite, **dâli-*; from *dvôl*, *dvel*, whence Eng. *dwell*, Norse *dvöl*, delay.

dàil, a meeting, so Ir., O. Ir. *dál*, O. W. *datl*, forum, W. *dadl*, sermo, O. Br. *dadlou*, curiæ, Br. *dael*, **datlâ*, root *dha*, *dhê*, set, as in *dail* (Ernault). Stokes suggests connection with O. Sl. *dê-*, dicere.

† **dàil**, † **dàl**, portion, tribe, Ir. and O. Ir. *dáil*, *dál*, Bede *daal* = part, *Dalreudini*, later *Dál-riata*, *Dalriada*, the early Scotic kingdom of Argyle, etc : **dâlo-*, root *dâ*, divide, Gr. δατέομαι, divide, δασμός, division, Lit. *dalis*, a part, Skr. *dắti*, cut off, *dalas*, part. The verb **dailich**, distribute, is given in H.S.D. as a dialectic form ; the Ir. is *dáilim*. Zimmer thinks *dàil*, meeting, and *dàil*, part, are originally the same.

dailgneachd, prophetic vision. See *tairgneachd*.

dàimh, relationship, Ir. *dámh*, tribe, family, E. Ir. *dám* : **dâmâ*, tribe, company ; Gr. δῆμος, Dor. δᾶμος, people, tribe, Eng. *demo*cracy. It is usual to compare O. W. *dauu*, cliens, W. *daw* (*dawf*), son-in-law, M. Br *deuff*, Br. *den* (do.) ; but these words may be allied to Gr. δάμαρ, spouse, and be from the root *dam*, *dom*, house.

daingean, strong, firm, so Ir., O Ir. *daingen*, W. *dengyn*, barbarous, **dangeno-*, firm, hard, verb **dengô*, E. Ir. *dingim*, press. Bezzenberger compares Norse *tengja*, fasten, tie together, Ag. S. *tengan*, press, O. H. G. *gi-zengi*, conjunctus. Thurneysen compares W. *tengyn*, obstinate, and Fr. *tangoner*, press. It is possible to connect *daingean* with Norse *dyngja*, heap, women's apartment, Ag. S. *ding*, carcer, Lit. *dengiu*, cover ; perhaps O. H. G. *tunc*, earth-house, Eng. *dung*.

dàir, inire vaccam, Ir. *dáir*, M. Ir. *dair*, **dârô*, root *dhṝ-*, *dhoro*, Gr. θρώσκω, spring, θορός, semen viri, Skr. *dhắra*, stream, seed.

dairireach, rattling noise, E. Ir. *der-drethar*, cries, W. *dâr*, noise, *daredd*, tumultuous noise, root *der*, *dher*, as in Gr. θρῆνος, dirge, Skr. *dhraṇ*, sound, Eng. *drone*. See *dùrd* and *stairirich*.

dais, a heap of hay or peats, O. Ir. *dais*, a heap, W. *dâs*, O. W. *das*, M. Br. *dastum*, to mass, **dasti-* (for G. and W.) ; Ag. S. *tass* (whence Fr. *tas*). Bezzenberger and Stokes correlate it with Norse *des*, hay heap, Sc. *dass*.

dais, **dois**, a blockhead (H.S.D.), **daiseachan**, insipid rhymer (Arm). ; seemingly borrowed from the Sc. *dawsie*, stupid, *dase*, stupefy. For root, see *dàsachd*. Norse *dasi*, lazy fellow.

dais, a musical instrument :

daithead, a diet ; from the Eng. See *dìot*.

dala, one of two ; see under *dara*.

dall, blind, Ir., E. Ir. *dall*, W., Br. *dall*, Cor. *dal*, **dvalno-*, I. E. *dhvḷ-no-*; Got. *dvals*, foolish, Eng. *dull*; Lat. *fallo*, cheat, (=*dhalnó*); Gr. *θολερός*, turbid. Hence *inter alia*, **dallag**, a field shrew, a mole, Ir. *dallóg*.

dallanach, a winnowing fan; from *dall*.

dalma, bold, forward, obstinate: "vigorous?" root *dhḷ* in *duille*.

dalta, foster-son, god-son, O. G. *dalta* (Bk. of Deer), Ir. *dalta*, O. Ir. *dalte*, **daltaio-s*, root *dhê*, *dhêl*, suck; Gr. *θῆλυς*, female; Lat. *fêlo*, suck, *femina*; etc. (Stokes, Strachan). See *deoghail*. It has been usual to refer *dalta* to the root *al* of *altram*, the *d* being considered as the remains of *de*, the prepositional prefix (**de-altjo-s*).

dàm, a dam; from the Eng.

dàmais, draughts, **bord dàmais**, draught board; from the Sc. *dams*, *dambrod*, Ger. *dambrett*, from Fr. *dame*, dame, draughts, Lat. *domina*.

damh, ox, stag, so Ir., O. Ir. *dam*, Cor. *da*, dama, M. Br. *daunt*, sheep, Br. *danvad*, sheep, *demm*, roe, **damo-s*; Lat. *dâma*, *damma*, deer; Gr. *δαμάλης*, a stier, *δάμαλις*, a calf; Skr. *damya*, untamed stier. Allied is Eng. *tame*, Lat. *domare*, Eng. *domestic*, etc.

dàmhair, rutting time; for *damh-dhàir*, from *damh* and *dàir* (H.S.D.).

dàmhair (H.S.D.), **damhair** (Sh., Arms.), earnest, keen:

damhan-allaidh, spider, Ir. *damhán-alla*, O. Ir. *damán n-allaid* (g. pl.), "wild little deer"; see *damh* and *allaidh*.

damnadh, cursing, condemnation, so Ir., M. Ir. *damnad*; from Lat. *damnatio*.

dàn, fate, destiny, Ir. *dán*; cf. M. Ir. *dán*, gift, W. *dawn*, gift, talent, Lat. *dônum*, root *dó*, Gr. *δίδωμι*, give, Skr. *dâ-*, give.

dàn, a poem, Ir. *dán*, song, O. Ir. *dán*, g. *dáno*, ars, **dâsnu-*, root *dâs*, know; Gr. *δήνεα*, plans, arts, *δαήμον*, skilful; Ch. Sl. *danhanh*, wisdom; Skr. *damsána*, miracle (Stokes).

dàn, bold, Ir. *dána*, O. Ir. *dáne*, *dána*, **dâsnavo-s*, from the root of *dàn* above (Stokes).

danns, dance (thou), **dannsa**, **damhsa**, a dance, Ir. *damhsa*, W. *dawns*; from the Eng.

dao, obstinate, O. Ir. *doe*, g. *doi*, tardus, **dausio-s*; Ag. S. *dysig*, foolish, Eng. *dizzy*, O. H. G. *tusîc*, stultus, Ger. *thor*, foolish (Stokes, Windisch).

daobhaidh, wicked, perverse (Heb.); see *dao*.

daoch, strong dislike, horror, **daochan**, anger (Sh.):

daoi, wicked, a wicked man, Ir. *daoi*, a wicked or foolish person; opposite of *saoi* (with *do-*, **du-*), which see for root.

daoimean, a diamond; from the Eng.
daol, daolag, a beetle, Ir. *daol*, E. Ir. *dael, doel, dail*: **doilo-*, root *dei, di*, as in *dian*, q.v. Stokes connects with M. Ir. *dael*, frightsomeness, root *dvei*, fright, Gr. δέος, a fright, Skr. *dvis*, hate.
daolair, a lazy man, a niggard, Ir. *daol*, lazy (O'R.):
daonnan, daondan, continually, always, **d' aon-tan* (?), "from one time." Cf. *greis*.
daor, enslaved, so Ir., O. Ir *dóir*; opposite of *saor* (with negative *do-*, **du-*), which see for root.
daor, dear, Ir. *daor, daoradh*, making dear (Four Masters); from M. Eng. *deere, deore*, dear (Stokes).
daorach, intoxication; cf. Sc. *deray*, mirthful noise at a banquet, M. Eng. *derai*, disorder, from Fr. *desroi*, dis-*array*.
dar, when (conj.), Northern form for **'n uair**; probably *d' uair* = *do-uair*.
dara, second, so Ir.; M. G. *darle* (Oss. Ballad, Fernaig MS), **ind-araile*, "the other," from *ind*=*an*, the, and O. Ir. *araile*, alius = *ar* + *aile*, *air* + *eile*, q.v., *alalijos*, Br. *arall*. Also **an dala,** the one of two, O. Ir. *indala*, from *ind* and *aile*, that is, *an* and *eile*. Further, **dàrna** (= *dala*), E. Ir. *indarna*, **ind-araile n-ai*, the one of them (two), O. Ir. *indala n-ai*, where *ái*, eorum, is the pl. of *a*, his.
darach, oak, Ir. *dair, darach*, E. Ir. *dair*, gen. *darach*, W., Cor. *dar*, **darik-*; Lat. *larix*, Eng. *larch*; Gr. (Maced.) δάρυλλος, oak, δρῦς (do.), δόρυ, spear; Eng. *tree*, etc. Hence **darach,** body of a boat.
darcan, the hollow of the hand (Dialectic, H.S.D.); cf. *deàrna*.
darcan, a teal:
dàrna, one of two; see under *dara*.
darnaig, darn, darning; from the Eng. *darning*, which is itself from W. *darn*, piece, patch (root *dera*, split, Eng. *tear*).
dàsachd, rage, madness, M. G. *dásacht* (M'V.), Ir. *dásachd*, O. Ir. *dásacht*, insania; Ag. S. *dwáes*, foolish, Sc. *dawsie*, Du. *dwaas*, senseless (Strachan).
dath, colour, Ir., E. Ir. *dath*, **datu-*; from the root *dha, dhê*, place, as in *dail*, etc. ?
dàth, singe, Ir. *doghaim*, E. Ir. *dóthim*, inf. *dóud*, *daif* (n.), Br. *deuiff*, to burn, **daviô*, I burn; Gr. δαίω, burn; Skr. *du*, *dunóti*, burn, *davas*, a brand.
dathas, fallow deer; **damhasg, dabhasg**; from *damh* + *seasg* (?).
de, of, Ir. *de*, O. Ir. *de, di*, O. W. *di*, W. *y*, Cor. *the*, Br. *di*, **de*, **di*, **dê*; Lat. *dê*; from *dvê*, a case-form from *dvô*, two. Gaelic and Irish confuse this prep. with *do*, to; a confusion

which even extends to O. Ir. in pre-accentual *de* compounds. Hence **do** of the past tenses: *do chaidh*, went, i.e., *deach*; *do rinn*, did, from *do-gníu*, I do, etc.

dé, what; also **gu dé**; a curtailed form of *ciod è*, "what is it"; from *ciod* and *è*, q.v. Ir. *caidé*, Galway *godé*.

dé, **an dé**, yesterday, Ir. *ané*, (*andé*), O. Ir. *indhé*, W. *y ddoe*, Br. *deac'h*, M. Br. *dech*, **sendi-gesi*, art. *an* and **gesi*; Lat. *heri* (=**hesî*); Gr. χθές; Eng. *yesterday*. The Celtic forms are all influenced by the word for "to-day," G. *an diu*, O. Ir. *indiu*, W. *heddyw*, *dyw*; from *diu*, **divo*, day, q.v. Zimmer in fact refers the word to the root of *diu* (Zeit.[30] 17). **jesi*, *ghjesi*, *heri*, etc. (St.).

dé: **teine dé**, M. Ir. *tene díait*, lightning; **deia*, shine with *-anti* or *-anta* (n.) (St.).

dèabh, drain, dry up, **dèabhadh** (pronounced *dè-u*), shrinking (as the staves of a wooden vessel), Dialectic **deò'**; I. E. *dhevo-*, run, Eng. *dew*, Gr. θέω, run, Skr. *dhav*, run, flow.

deacaid, boddice, jacket; from Eng. *jacket*.

deacair, difficult, surly, Ir. *deacair*, O. Ir. *deccair*; for *di-acar*: prep. *de* and *acar*, as in *socair*, q.v.

deach, went; the post-particle or enclitic form of *do chaidh*, q.v., Ir. *deachaidh*, O. Ir. *dechud*.

deachd, dictate, so Ir., *deachdadh* (n.); from Lat. *dicto*, *dictatio*, whence Eng. *dictation*.

deadhan, a dean; from the Eng.

deagh, good, Ir. *deagh*, O. Ir. *deg-*, *dag-*, W. *da*, Cor. *da*, bonum (gl.), Gaul. *Dago-*, **dago-*, **dego-*, "good, acceptable;" Gr. δέχεσθαι, receive. Further allied to Gr. δεξιός, right, δέκομαι, receive; Lat. *dexter*, right, *decus*, *doceo*; Gaelic *deas*, O. Ir. *dech*, best (superlative to *deagh* or *maith*).

deaghad, living, diet, morals (Uist); see *dìot*.

deaghaidh: see *déidh*.

deal, friendly (H.S.D., M'E.); see *dìleas*.

deal, **deala**, a leech, Ir. *deal*, a blood-sucker (O'R.); from I. E. root *dhê*, suck, as in *deoghail*, q.v. Cf. Lit. *dėlė*, leech; also Ir. (and G. in Dict. therefrom) **deala**, teat, E. Ir. *del*.

dealaich, separate, Ir. *dealuighim*, E. Ir. *deligim*, *deil*, separation; I. E. *delo-*, to split, Skr. *dalítas*, split, Gr. δέλτος, tablet, Lit. *dalis*, part. Cf. †*dàil*, part.

dealan, **dealanach**, lightning, Ir. *dealán*, a spark, flaming coal, **dilo-*: root *di*, *dei* (*dêi*), *deya* (Fick), shine; Gr. δέελος (=δέj-ελος), conspicuous, δῆλος, clear; Skr. *dî*, shine; further is **dei-vo-s*, whence G. *dia*, etc. M. Ir. *tene-gelain*, "lightning," now "will o' the wisp"; *tene-gelan*, fireflaught.

dealan-dé, butterfly, Ir. *dalán-dé*, *dealán-dé*. The G. also means the phenomenon observed by whirling a stick lighted at the end. Apparently the meaning is "God's fire." For *dé*, see *dia*.

dealan-doruis, door-bolt (Sh., O'R.) ; see *deil*.

dealas, zeal, **dealasach**, zealous ; from the Eng. *zeal*, *zealous*.

dealbh, form, so Ir., O. Ir. *delb*, W. *delw*, Br. *-delu*, **delvo-*, root *del* ; Lat. *dolare*, hew, *dolo*, a pike ; Gr. δαιδάλλω, embellish, work cunningly ; O. H. G. *zol*, log ; Ch. Sl. *dely*, vat.

dealg, a pin, skewer, so Ir., O. Ir. *delg*, M. W. *dala*, sting, fang, W. *dal*, a catch, Cor. *delc*, monile, **delgos* ; Ag. S. *telgan*, virgultum, twig, Du. *telg*, M. H. G. *zelge*, Norse *tjálgr*, a prong ; Lit. *dalgís*, scythe (?). Bezzenberger compares Norse *dálkr*, a cloak pin ; cf. Ag. S. *dalc*, buckle.

dealradh, brightness, so Ir., E. Ir. *dellrad*, jubar ; from *deal-*, as in *dealan*, q.v.

dealt, dew, Ir. *dealt*, M. Br., Br. *delt*, moist, damp :

dealunn, loud barking (H.S.D.) ; see *deileann*.

deamhan, a demon, so Ir., O. Ir. *demon* ; from Lat. *daemon*, from Gr. δαίμων, Eng. *demon*.

deamhais, deimheis, shears, Ir. *deimheas* (pronounced *díos*), E. Ir. *demess*, **di-mess*, "two-edged"; from *di* of *da*, two, and E. Ir. *mess*, edge (Cormac's Gl.), "cutter," from root *met*, mow, cut, as in *meath*, *meith*, cut, prune, Lat. *meto*. Cf. Gaul, *mataris*.

dèan, do, Ir. *déan* (imper.), O. Ir. *dén*, *dénim* : enclitic or post-particle form of O. Ir. *dogníu*, G. *nì*, I do ; from *de*, of, and *gnî* of *gnìomh*, q.v. Inf. **dèanamh** (=*de-gnîmu-*).

deann, haste, speed ; cf. E. Ir. *denmne*, haste, which Cormac explains as *di-ainmne*, "non-patience," from *ainmne*, patience ; root *men*, wait (Lat. *maneo*, etc.).

deannag, a small pinch, a grain, **deannach**, mill dust, Ir. *deanóg*, a pinch, grain :

deannal, conflict, stir, so Ir. (O'R.) ; from *deann*. In the sense of "flash" (H.S.D.), **deannal** seems a metathetical form of *dealan*.

deanntag, a nettle, Ir. *neantóg*, M. Ir. *nenntóg*, E. Ir. *nenaid*, **nenadi-*, for **ne-nadi-*, a reduplicated form ; Ag. S. *netele*, Eng. *nettle* ; Lit. *néndré*, pipe, tube. The *t* of G. and Ir. is due to the same phonetic law that gives *teine* the pl. *teintean*.

dearail, poor, wretched, Ir. *dearóil*, E. Ir. *deróil*, feeble, O. Ir. *deróil*, penuria, from *der-*, privative prefix (see *deargnaidh*), and *óil*, abundance, which Windisch has referred to **pḷli-*, a form of the root *pḷ*, *pel*, full, as in *lán*.

dearbadan, dearbadan-dé, butterfly (M'D., H.S.D.) :

dearbh, certain, so Ir., O. Ir. *derb*, **dervo-* ; I. E. *drevo-*, whence Ag. S. *treówe*, Eng. *true*, Ger. *treu*.

dearc, dearcag, a berry, so Ir., O. Ir. *derc*, **derkes-*, Skr. *drâkshâ*, grape, vine (Stokes); root *derk*, see, the idea being "conspicuous." Cf. Gr. δράκων, dragon, δορκάς, gazelle, from the root *derk*, see. See *dearc*, behold. The O. Ir. *derucc*, g. *dercon*, glans, is, like Ger. *eichel*, glans (from *eiche*, oak), from the root of *darach*, oak (Zimmer).

dearc, dearc-luachrach, a lizard, Ir. *earcluachra*, the "*earc* of the rashes," M. Ir. *erc*, speckled, red, Ir. *earc*, salmon, W. *erch*, fuscus, darkish, **erko-s*, for **perko-* ; Gr. περκνός, dark-blue, πέρκη, a perch ; Skr. *pṛçnis*, speckled ; Ger. *forelle*, a trout, O. H. G. *forhana*. For meaning, cf. *breac*, a trout, "the speckled one." The *d* of G. *dearc* belongs to the article.

†**dearc,** an eye, a cave, hole, Ir. *dearc* (do.), O. Ir. *derc* (do.); from the root *derk*, behold. See verb *dearc*: "eye-pit" gives the meaning "cave." Shaw has *deirc* for "pit" in Engl.-Gael. section.

dearc, behold, see, Ir. *dearcaim*, O. Ir. *dercaim*, video, *derc*, eye, **derkô*, I see, perfect **dedorka* (cf. *chunnairc*=*con-darc*); I. E. *derk*, see ; Gr. δέρκομαι, δέδορκα, have seen ; O. H. G. *zoraht*, bright ; Skr. *darç*, see.

dearg, red, so Ir., O. Ir. *derg*, **dhergo-s* ; Eng. *dark*, Ag. S. *deorc*.

deargad, deargant, a flea, Ir. *deargán*, *dreancuid*, *deargnuid*, E. Ir. *dergnat* : **derg-nat*, "reddener," from *dearg*, red?

deàrgnaidh, unlearned (Arm.; M'A. says "Irish"), Ir. *deargnaidh*, **der-gnadi-* ; from *der-*, privative prefix (*di*+*air*, see *de* and *air*), and root *gnâ*, *gen*, know, as in *aithne*.

deàrlan, brimful ; **der-lán* ; from intensive prefix *der* (=*de*+*ro*) and *làn*, full.

dearmad, neglect, forgetfulness, so Ir., O. Ir. *dermet*, **der-mét* ; from *der-*, priv. particle (see *deàrgnaidh*) and *mét*, **mento-*, mind ; root *men*, think ; Lat. *mens*, *mentio*, *commentum* ; Eng. *mind* ; etc.

dearmail, anxiety (M'D.), anxious (H.S.D.) :

deàrn, do, Ir. *deárnaim*, O. Ir. *derninn*, facerem, **di-ro-gnî-*, a side form of *dèan* with infixed *ro*. See *dèan*.

deàrna, the palm of the hand, Ir. *déarna*, E. Ir. *derna* ; cf. Gr. δῶρον, palm, handbreadth, δάρις, the distance between the thumb and little finger, a span (Hes.), δαρείρ, the distance between the big and little fingers (Hes.). It is further referred to the I. E. root *der*, split, open (Fick, Prellwitz). Hence **deàrnagan,** a small oaten or wheaten cake, a hand.

dearras, keenness, obstinacy ; see *diarras*.

deàrrsach, a swig of liquor (Wh.):

deàrrsadh, radiance, effulgence, Ir. *dearsgaim*, *dearsgnaim*, I polish, burnish, M. Ir. *derscnaigim*, explain, make clear, **de-ro-sec-*, root *sec*, see, Eng. *see?* Hence **deàrrsgnuidh,** burnished, brilliant. The word †**deàrsgnaidh,** excellent, is allied to O. Ir. *dersigem*, præcellimus, *dirósci*, excels, *doroscai*, præstet, **di-roscag-* (Thur.), **roscag*=*ro-od-sec-*, root *sec*, pass, as in *seach?* E. Ir. *dersciagthech*, splendid.

deas, right, south, Ir. *deas*, O. Ir. *dess*, W. *deheu*, Cor. *dyghow*, M. Br. *dehou*, **dekso-s*, **deksivo-s* (Stokes); Lat. *dexter*; Gr. δεξιός; Got. *taihsva*; Lit. *desziné* (n.), Ch. Sl. *desĭnŭ*, right; Skr. *daksina-s*.

deasbair, a disputant, **deasbaireachd,** disputation, Ir. *deaspoirim* (O'R., Sh.); cf. *cuspair*.

deasbud, a dispute; from the Eng. *dispute*, Lat. *disputo*.

deasgainn, rennet, barm, **deasgadh,** lees, yeast, Ir. *deasgadh*, lees, O. Ir. *descad*, faex, fermentum, leaven, **desc-âtu* (Z. 803): **disc-atu-*; cf. Lat *faex*, for *ðaix*. Gaelic root *dik*, whence *dik-sko*, then *desc-*.

deasgraich, a heterogeneous mass (=*dreamsgal*, H.S.D.):

deasmaireas, curiosity, **deasmas** (Sh.), Ir. *deismireach*, *deismis*, curious (O'B., O'R.):

deasoireach, spicy (Sh., H.S.D.):

deat, an unshorn year-old sheep or wedder, **deathaid,** **det-anti-*, "sucking one"; from *det*, *de*, suck. See *deoghail*.

deatam, anxiety; cf. O. Ir. *dethitiu*, *dethiden*, care. For root, see *dìdean*. M'A. has also **deatamach,** necessary, which seems allied.

deathach, deatach, smoke, Ir., M. Ir. *deatach*, O. Ir. *dé*, g. *diad*, E. Ir. *dethach*, *detfadach*, smoky, W. *dywy*, vapour. From I. E. root *dhêu*, *dheu*, *dhu*, *dhve*, smoke, air; Lat. *fûmus*, smoke; Gr. θυμιάω, to smoke; Ch. Sl. *dymŭ* (n.); Skr. *dhûmás*. Ir. *dé* is for *dīvâ*, from *dhêu* or *dhêv*; the gen. *diad* is phonetically like the nom. *biad*, food (**bivoto-n*). The form *deatach* is probably for **dett-acos*, *dett* being from *dhve* (cf. Gr. θεός, for θεσ-ός, from *dhve-s-*). The *t* (=*tt*) of *deatach* is difficult to account for. For phonetics cf. *beathach*.

déibhleid, a feeble or awkward person, M. Ir. *déblén*, E. Ir. *dedblén*, weakling, from *dedbul*, weak; the opposite of *adhbhal*, q.v. (*di-adbul*). Stokes allows the alternate possibility of its being from Lat. *dêbilis*; see *dìblidh*.

deic (cha deic), convenient; cf. O. Ir. *tecte*, becoming, *anas tecte*, quod decet:

deich, ten, so Ir., O. Ir. *deich n-*, O. W. *dec*, W. *deg*, Cor. *dek*, Br. *dec*, **dekn̥*; Lat. *decem*; Gr. δέκα; Got. *taihun*, Eng. *ten*; Skr. *dáçan*. **Deicheamh,** tenth, O. Ir. *dechmad*, W. *decvet*, Cor. *degves*, Br. *decvet*, **dekm̥meto-s* (Brug.), an extension (by the superlative suffix *-to-*) of **dekm̥mo-s*, Lat. *decimus*.

déide, déideadh, toothache, Ir. *déideadh*. See *deud*.

déideag, a pebble, toy; cf. *éiteag*.

déidh, desire; a noun formed from the adverbial phrase *an déidh*, after.

déidh, an déidh, after, Ir. *a n-diaigh*, O. Ir. *i n-dead*, post, E. Ir. *i n-diaid*, from O. Ir. *déad*, finis, W. *diwedd*, finis, Cor. *deweth*, Br. *diuez*, **dê-ved-on* (Stokes); from the root *ved*, lead, as in *toiseach*, q.v. (Stokes prefers *ved* of *feadhainn*). Also **deidh, déigh,** the latter a bad form etymologically. The O. Ir. had also the form *degaid* (=*di-agaid*), the opposite of *i n-agid*, now *an aghaidh*, against, adversus.

deidhinn, mu dheidhinn, concerning, of; cf. E. Ir. *dágin*, *daigind*, *im dágin*, because of, because, *dáig*, *déig*, for the sake of, because (prep. and conj.), O. Ir. *dég*, quia. See *dòigh*.

deifir, haste, speed, Ir. *deifir*, *deithfir*, M. Ir. *deithbhireach* (O'Cl.), speedy, busy; to which Stokes and Ernault compare W. *difrif*, serious, M. Br. *adevry*, seriously.

deigh, ice, Ir. *oighear*, snow, *leac-oighir*, ice, O. Ir. *aig*, g. *ega*, *aigred*, W. *ia*, Cor. *iey*, glacies, Br. *yen*, cold, **jagi-*, ice; Norse *jaki*, piece of ice, *jökull*, iceberg, Ag. S. *gicel*, piece of ice, Eng. *icicle* (=*ís-gicel*); Lit. *iżas*, ice lump. The *d* of G. is prothetic, arising from the art.: O. Ir. *ind-aig*.

deighlean, a quire of paper (Sh., O'B.), Ir. *deighleán*:

deil, an axle, Ir. *deil*, an axle, rod, turner's lathe, O. Ir. *deil*, rod, Cor. *dele*, antempna, O. Br. *deleiou*, antemnarum, Br. *delez*, **deli-*, **deljo-*; I. E. root *del*, split. See *dealaich*. Stokes refers it to the root *dhel*, whence Ger. *dolde*, umbel, O. H. G. *tola*, racemus, Gr. θάλος, a short twig; as in *duileag*, q.v.

deil, dil, keen, diligent (Arg.); formed from *dealas*, zealous.

deil, leech; Dialectic for *deal*.

deilbh, a forming, warping (for weaving), so Ir.; see *dealbh*.

déile, a plank, deal; from the Eng. *deal*.

deileann, loud, sharp barkings, E. Ir. *deilm*, stem *delmen*, noise, alarm:

deileas, a grudging, eagerness; see *dealas*.

deilgneach, thorny, prickly, Ir. *deilgneach*, thorns; from *dealg*. **Cadal-deilgneach,** the prickly sensation in a numbed limb.

déilig, deal with, a dealing; from Eng. *dealing*.

deillseag, a slap with the open hand, **déiseag**:

deiltreadh, gilding, lacquering; **deilt-rad*, from †**deilt**, separation, root *del* of *dealaich?*
deimheis, a shears; see *deamhais.*
deimhinn, certain, Ir. *deimhin*, O. Ir. *demin*, *demnithir*, certius, **demeni-*, I. E. root *dhê*, set, fix, *dhemen-*, setting, Gr. θέμεναι, set, θέμα, a pledge, theme, θέμις, law, "something laid down"; Eng. *doom*, *deem*; etc.
déine, eagerness; see *dian.*
deir, a deir, says (said), inquit, Ir. *deirim*, O. Ir. *adbeir*, dicit; *deir* is the root-accented form (**ad-béró*) of *abair* (the prepositional accented form, **ád-berô*). See *abair.* The *a* of *a deirim* belongs to the *ad-*, while the *d* of it takes the place of *b* in the root (*ber*).
déirc, alms, so Ir., M. Ir. *déarc*, *desheirc*, O. Ir. *dearc*, *deircc*, *desercc*, (caritas), for *de-shercc*; see *searc*, love.
deireadh, end, so Ir., O. Ir. *dered*, O. G. *derad* (Bk. of Deer): **der-vedo-n*, root *ved* as in *déidh*, q.v.? Ascoli suggests that *der* is the basis, the opposite of *er*, front, from the proposition *air* (**pare*). Hence **deireas**, injury.
déis, an déis, after, so Ir., O. Ir. *di éis*, retro, O. G. *daneis*, after them (**di-an-éis*), O. Ir. *éis*, footstep, track, **in-sti*, root *sto*, *sta*, stand, Lat. *instare?* Strachan gives the stem as **encsi-*, from *eng*, footstep, as in *eang*, q.v.; Stokes takes it from **pend-ti-*, root *ped*, as in *eadh*, Eng. *foot.*
deis-dé, a sanctuary, halting place, halt (Wh.); *dess dé*, "God's right hand" (K. Meyer in "King Eochaid").
deisciobul, a disciple, Ir. *deisciobal*, O. Ir. *descipul*, W. *dysgybl*, Br. *diskibil*; from Lat. *discipulus.*
deise, a suit of clothes; from *deas.* Ir., M. Ir. *deise*, a robe; E. Ir. *deis*, entourage of chief. Cf. for meaning Eng. *suit.*
déiseag, a slap; see *deillseag.*
deiseil, southward, sun-ward, E. Ir. *dessel*; from *deas* and *sel* (**svel*), W. *chwyl*, versio. See *deas* and *seal.*
deismireach, curious; see *deasmaireas.*
déistinn, déisinn, disgust, Ir. *déistion*, edge (set the teeth on edge), disgust. Cf. M. Ir. *déistiu*, refuse of everything, posterity, from *déis?*
deithneas, deithneamhach, etc.; from *déine*, from *dian.*
deò, breath, Ir. *deó* in *gu deo*, ever, **dveso-*; I. E. *dhves*, breathe; W. *dywy?* Lit. *dvėsti*, breath, *dvásė*, spirit, breath, Russ. *dvochati*; Gr. θεός, god (= θεσ-ός); M. H. G. *getwâs*, ghost.
deoch, a drink, Ir. *deoch*, g. *dighe*, O. Ir. *deug*, g. *dige*, **degu-*. To *degu-* Bezzenberger cfs. Lit. *dažýti*, dip, wet, tinge. W.

diod, M. Br. *diet*, are referred by Stokes to the root *dhê*, suck, as in *deoghail*, or to **dê-patu* (Lat. *potus*).

deòdhas, deòthas, eagerness, desire (**deothas,** M'F., O'R.); from *dhevo-*, Gr. *θέω*, run, *θυμός*, soul, etc. See *deathach*.

deoghail, suck, Ir. *diuilim*, *deolaim*, M. Ir. *diul* (n., dat.), **delu-*, root *del* as in *deal*, leech; I. E. *dhê*, suck; Lat. *fêlare*, suck, *fêmina*, woman, "suck-giver"; Gr. *θῆλυς*, female, *θηλή*, teat, *θηλάζω*, suck; Skr. *dháyati* (do.). The Breton forms show *n*; Br. *dena*, suck. See *dìonag*.

deòidh, fa dheòidh, at last, finally, Ir. *fá dheoidh*, O. Ir. *fo diud*, postremo; dat. case of O. Ir. *déad*, end. See *déidh* for derivation.

deòin, assent, Ir., E. Ir. *deóin*, **degni-*; I. E. root *dek*, *degh*; Gr. *δοκέω*, seem, *δόξα*, opinion, *διδαχή*, teaching, Lat. *doceo*, *doctrina*, etc. See *deagh*, good.

deòradh, an alien, Ir. *deóraidh*, a stranger, exile, M. Ir. *deorad*. Stokes thinks the word is borrowed from Brittonic—Br. *devroet*, depaysé, "dis-countrified" (*di-brog-*, see *brugh*), Cor. *diures*, exul. *deòradh*: opposite of *urradh*, guarantor, =*di-urradh* (Jub.). *air-rad* (Meyer). Hence the name *Dewar*.

detheine, a heated boring iron: **dé-théine*, the accent being on the second portion *teine*, fire. For *dé*, see *dealan-dé*.

detheoda, henbane (M'D.):

detìach, deteigheach, the gullet, weasand (M'D., Sh., etc.): peculiar as accented on *iach*, properly *det-íach*; Dial. **it-ioch,** epiglottis (Arg.).

deubh, shrink; see *dèabh*.

deubhann, a fetter for a horse:

deuchainn, diachainn, a trial, attempt, Ir. *d' fhéachain*, to see. See *feuch*, *feuchainn*.

deud, a tooth, Ir. *déad*, O. Ir. *dét*, W. *dant*, Cor. *dans*, Br. *dant*, *dn̥tâ* (Stokes); Lat. *dens* (*dentis*); Gr. *ὀδούς* (g. *ὀδόντος*); Eng. *tooth*, Got. *tunþus*; Lit. *dantìs*; Skr. *dant-*.

deug, diag, -teen, e.g., **cóig-deug,** fif-teen, Ir. *déag*, O. Ir. *déc*, *deac*, W. *deng*, ten (?). The exact relationship of *deug* to *deich* is difficult to decide. The other I. E. languages, as a rule, make 13 to 19 by combining the unit numeral with 10, as Ger. *drei-zehn*, Ag. S. *ðríténe*, Lat. *tridecim*. **dvei-penge* (St.).

deur, diar, a tear, drop, Ir. *déar*, *deór*, O. Ir. *dér*, W., Cor, *dagr*, O. Br. *dacr*, M. Br. *dazrou*, tears, **dakru*; Gr. *δάκρυ*; Lat. *lacrima*, for *dacrima*; Eng. *tear*, Got. *tagr*.

Di-, -day; the prefix in the names of the days of the week, Ir., O. Ir. *dia*, *die* (O. Ir.), W. *dydd*, Cor. *det* (for *dedh*), Br. *dez*, *dijas (*dejes- ?); Lat. *diês*; Skr. *dyáús*, day, sky; Gr. Ζεύς, Διός, Jove. Allied to *dia*, god. **Di-dòmhnuich,** Sunday, Ir. *Domhnach*, E. Ir. *domnach*, from Lat. (dies) *dominica*, Lord's day—*dominus*, lord; **Di-luain,** Monday, Ir. *Dia-luain*, M. Ir. *luan*, W. *Dydd Llun*, from Lat. dies *Lunæ*, "day of the moon"; **Di-màirt,** Tuesday, Ir. *Dia-mairt*, E. Ir. *máirt*, W. *Dydd mawrth*, from Lat. dies *Martis*, "day of Mars"; **Di-ciaduinn, Di-ciadaoin,** Wednesday, Ir. *Dia-céadaoine*, O. Ir. *cétáin, cétóin, de cétain* (*de* = *dia* = Lat. *die*), *dia cetáine*, from *ceud*, first, and *aoine*, fast, q.v., E. Ir. *áine*: "day of the first fast," Friday being the second and chief day; **Diardaoin,** Thursday, Ir. *Dia-dhardaoin*, E. Ir. *dardóen*=*etar dá óin*, "between two fasts"—the day between the two fasts of Wednesday and Friday; **Di-haoine,** Friday, Ir. *Dia-aoine*, *Dia-haoine*, E. Ir. *áine, dia áine*, O. Ir. *dia oine dídine* (day of the last fast): "day of the fast," from *aoin*, fast, q.v.; **Di-sathuirn,** Saturday, Ir. *Dia-sathuirn*, M. Ir. *satharn*, *dia sathairn*, from Lat. dies *Saturni*, day of Saturn. The days of the week were originally named (in Egypt) after the seven planets of the ancients—Sun, Moon, Mars, Mercury, Jove, Venus, Saturn.

di-, negative prefix, Ir. *dí-*, *dío-*, O. Ir. *dí-*, W. *di*, **dê*; Lat. *dê*, of. See *de*. Also **dim-, diom-**(*dìmeas, dimbrigh, diombuaidh, diomal*).

dia, a god, so Ir., O. Ir. *día*, W. *duw*, O. W. *duiu*, Cor. *duy*, Br. *doe*, Gaul. *dêvo-*, Δειονονα=Dîvona, **deivo-s*; Lat. *dîvus* (for *deivos*), deified one, *deus*; Gr. δῖος, divine; Norse *tívar*, gods, Eng. *Tues*-day, "day of *Tiw*," the war-god; Lit. *dêvas*, Pruss. *deiwas*; Skr. *devá*. Hence **diadhaidh,** pious, Ir. *diadha*, O. Ir. *diade*, divinus.

diabhol, devil, Ir. *diabhal*, O. Ir. *diabul*, W. *diawl*, Br. *diaoul*; from Lat. *diabolus*, whence also Eng. *devil*.

diachadaich, especially (Heb.):

diallaid, a saddle, so Ir., M. Ir. *diallait*, cloak, O. Ir. *dillat*, clothes, W. *dillad*, M. Br. *dillat*.

dialtag, a bat, Ir. *ialtóg*. See *ialtag*.

diamhain, idle; see *dìomhain* rather.

diamhair, secret, Ir. *diamhair*, M. Ir., E. Ir. *diamair*, O. Ir. *diamair, dimair*. Root *mar*, remain; *dí-mar*, disappear?

dian, keen, hasty, so Ir., O. Ir. *dían*, **deino-s*; root *dei*, *dî*, hasten; Gr. δίεμαι, hasten; Skr. *dî*, *dîyati*, hurry, allied to the root *dî*, *div*, shine.

dianag, a two-year-old sheep; cf. O. Ir. *dínu*, lamb, from the root *dhê*, suck. See *deoghail*. But Sc. *dinmont*?

Diardaoin, Thursday; see *Di-*.

diardan, anger, Ir. *díardain*, E. Ir. *diartain*; from *di-*, intensive prefix (E. Ir. *dí-*, as in *dímór*, excessively great), from *de*, and *ardan*, pride. Cf. *andiaraid*, wrathful.

diarras, dìorras, stubbornness, vehemence, Ir. *díorruisg*, fierceness, rashness: *dí-réidh?*

dias, an ear of corn, so Ir., O. Ir. *días*, W. *twys* (pl.): **steipsâ*, root *steip*, stiff, Lat. *stipes*, stake, stipula, Eng. *stiff?* Cf. *geug* and W. *cang*, *ysgainc*, for phonetics.

dibheach, an ant (H.S.D. quotes only O'R., while Arms. makes it obsolete; M'A. has it), Ir. *dibheach*: **de + beach?*

dibhfhearg, vengeance, indignation, Ir. *dibhfhearg*, *díbhfearg* (Keat.), E. Ir. *díbérg*; from *dim* and *fearg*; see *di-* of *diardan*.

dibhirceach, diligent (Sh.; H.S.D., which refers to C. S., but neither in M'A. nor M'E.), Ir. *dibhirceach*, diligent, violent (O'B., etc.):

dìbir, forsake; see *dìobair*.

dibith, dimbith, luckless, lifeless (Carm):

dìblidh, abject, vile, Ir. *díbligh*, O. Ir. *diblide*, senium; seemingly from Lat. *dêbilis*, weak, feeble (Eng. *debilitate*, etc.). Zim. (Zeit. [24]) has suggested **dí-adbul*, "un-great," from *adbul*, i.e. *adhbhal*, q.v.

dìbrigh, dimbrigh, contempt, Ir. *dimbrigh*; from *dim-*, *dí-*, and *brìgh*, q.v.

dìchioll, diligence, Ir. *díthchioll*: **dí-cell-*; for *cell*, see *timchioll*. Or from *ciall*, sense; "attention to"?

Di-ciadaoin, Wednesday; see *Di-*.

did, a peep; an onomatopoetic word.

dìdean, protection, a fort, Ir. *dídean*, O. Ir. *dítiu*, g. *díten*, **di-jemtion-* (Stokes); root *jem*, cover, protect, Lett. *ju'mju*, *ju'mt*, cover a roof. The O. Ir. verb is *do-emim*, tueor. Ascoli makes the root *em*, as in Lat. *emo*, buy. Cf. *eiridinn*.

Di-dòmhnuich, Sunday; see *Di-*.

difir, difference, Ir. *difir*, *dithfir*, M. Ir. *dethbir*; from Lat. *differo*, Eng. *differ*.

dìg, a wall of loose stones, a dike; from the Sc. *dike*, Eng. *dike*.

dil, eager, keen. See *deil*.

dìl, dìle, dìlinn, a flood, Ir. *díle*, pl. *díleanna*, E. Ir. *díli*, g. *dílenn*, diluvium; from Lat. *diluvium* (Stokes), whence Eng. *deluge*.

dile, dill (M'D.); from the Eng.

dìleab, a legacy, Ir. *dilb* (O'R.):

dìleag, a small drop; from *dìle*, flood.

dìleas, dear, faithful, Ir. *díleas*, O. Ir. *díles*, proprius, own, **dêlesto-*, *dêl*, I. E. *dhêl*, *dhê*, suck, Lat. *filius*, *femina*, etc. See *deoghal*. Zeuss has suggested *dí* + *les*, from *leas*, advantage.

dìleigh, digest, **dìleaghadh,** digesting, Ir. *dìleaghadh*, from *di-leagh*, root of *leagh*, melt.

dileum (accent on *leum*), a shackle; *di* + *leum*, q.v.

dìlinn, leac dhìlinn, a stone *in situ*, a rock appearing above ground: "natural," from *dìl-* as in *dìleas*.

dìlleachdan, an orphan, Ir. *dílleachda*, O. Ir. *dilechtu*, orfani: "der*e*lict," from *di-* and *leig*, let go (*di-lēc-*, let go).

dimbrigh, contempt; see *dìbrigh*.

dìmeas, contempt, Ir. *dímheas*, O. Ir. *dímess*; from *dí-*, *dím-*, and *meas*.

dinn, press, force down, squeeze, Ir. *dingim*, *ding*, a wedge, E. Ir. *dingim*, perf. *dedaig*, **dengô*; Ag. S. *tengan*, press, Norse *tengja*, fasten (Bezzenberger). See *daingean*. Brugmann refers it to **dhinghô*, Lat. *fingo*, mould, feign, I. E. *dheigh*, Eng. *dough*.

dinnein, a small heap, Ir. *dinn*, a hill, fortified hill, E. Ir. *dinn dind* (do.), **dindu-*; Norse *tindr*, spike, peak, Ger. *zinne*, pinnacle, Eng. *tine*. But cf. Gr. *θίς*, *θινός* (*ι* long), a heap, Skr. *dhanvan*.

dìnneir, a dinner, Ir. *dinnéar*; from the Eng.

dinnsear, ginger, Ir. *gingsear*, M. Ir. *sinnsar*; from M. Eng. *ginger*, Lat. *zingiber*.

dìobair, forsake, Ir. *dìbirim*; for *dì* + *ìobair*, q.v. *di-ud-ber* (St).

diobhail, loss, Ir. *díoghabhail*, O. Ir. *dígbail*, deminutio; *dì-* and *gabhail*, q.v.

dìobhargadh, persecution, **dìobhargach,** fierce, keen, Ir. *dibheargach*, vindictive; see *dibhfhearg*.

diobhuir, vomit: **de* + *beir*, Lat. *defero*; from *de* and *beir*.

diocail, lower, diminish (H.S.D., which quotes MSS. only); *dí* + *ad-cal*; from *càil ?*

dìochain, forgetfulness; Dialectic for *dichuimhne*, that is *di-* and *cuimhne*.

diod, diodag, a drop; from the Eng. *jet ? jot ?*

diog, a syllable, Ir. *digim*, *diugam*, cluck as a hen: G. **diug,** the call to hens. Onomatopoetic.

diogail, tickle, Ir. *giglim*, O. Ir. *fogitled* (for *fogicled ?*). The G. seems borrowed from the Eng. *tickle*, *kittle*; and possibly all are onomatopoetic, and reshaped in later times. Cf. Eng. *giggle*, Lat. *cachinnus*.

diogair, eager, Ir. *díogar* (O'R.), E. Ir. *dígar* (?):

dìogan, revenge, Ir. *díogan* (O'B., etc.); the word is Irish (not in M'A.; M'E. marks it doubtful):

dìoghail, dìol, avenge, pay, Ir. *díoghalaim, díolaim,* O. Ir. *dígal* (n.), W., Cor. *dial, *dê-galâ.* See *gal,* valour, etc.

dìoghluim, glean, **dìoghluim,** a gleaning, Ir. *díoghluim* (n.): **de-gluim*; for *gluim,* see *foghlum.*

dìol, pay, Ir. *díolam,* M. Ir. *dílaim*; see *dìoghail.*

dìolan, illegitimate, M. G. *diolain* (M'V.), Ir. *díolanlas,* fornication (O'B.): **dí-lánamnas,* "non conjugium"? See *lànain.*

diomadh, discontent, pain, Ir. *diomadh, diomdha*; see *diùmach.*

diomarag, clover seed:

diomasach, proud, Ir. *díomus,* pride, M. Ir. *díumus,* pride, "too great measure": *dí-od-mess,* root *mess* of *comus* (Zimmer).

diombach, diombuidheach, displeased, Ir. *diombuidheach,* unthankful; from *diom-, dim-,* un-, and *buidheach,* thankful, q.v. Confused with *diùmach,* q.v.

diombuaidh, unsuccessfulness, **diombuan,** transitory: negative compounds of *buaidh* and *buan,* q.v.

dìomhain, idle, Ir, *díomhaoin,* O. Ir. *dímáin*; from *dí-* and *maoin,* "office-less"; see *maoin.*

dìomhair, secret; see *diamhair.*

dìon, protection, Ir. *díon,* E. Ir. *dín,* g. *dína, *dênu-*; root *dhê,* set?

diong, match, equal, pay, E. Ir. *dingbain,* ward off, *dingbála,* worthy: **din-gab,* "off-give." See *gabh.*

diongmhalta, perfect, Ir. *díongmhalta,* perfect, sure. See *diong* above.

dionnal, a shot, fight; see *deannal.*

diorachd, ability (H.S.D.): Cf. Ir. *dír,* proper, **dêr.*

dìorras, vehemence, vehement anger; see *diarras.*

diosd, a jump, kick with the heels (Dialectic); from Sc. *jisk,* caper.

dìosg, barren, **dìosgadh,** barrenness, not giving milk, Ir. *díosc, díosg*: *dī-sesc-*; see *seasg.* For its composition, see *déirc.*

diosg, a dish; from Lat. *discus,* Norse *diskr,* Ag. S. *disc,* Eng. *dish.*

dìosgan, a creaking or gnashing noise, Ir. *díosgán.* See *gìosgan.*

dìot, a meal, **dìot mhór,** dinner, M. Ir. *diet, diit,* E. Ir. *díthait*; from Lat. *diaeta,* Eng. *diet*; *dithit,* feast during day (Meyer), *dithait* (ĭ) (Táin).

dìpin, a deepening (in a net), a certain measure of a net; from Sc. *deepin,* a net, Eng. *deep.*

dìr, ascend; curtailed from *dìrich.*

dìreach, strait, Ir. *díreach,* O. Ir. *dírech, *dê-reg,* root *reg,* stretch; Lat. *rego, directus,* Eng. *direct,* etc. The root is found also in *éirigh, rach,* etc. Hence **dìrich,** straighten, ascend.

dìs, susceptible to cold, Ir. *dís,* poor, miserable, E. Ir. *diss, dis,* weak, **de-sti-*? Root *sta.*

dìsleach, stormy, uncouth, straggling, Ir. *dísligheach*, deviating, *dí-slighe*, *slighe*, path, q.v. In the sense of "stormy," the derivation is doubtful.

dìsne, a die, dice, Ir. *dísle*; from M. Eng. *dys*, dice.

dìt, condemn, Ir. *díotach*, condemnatory, *díotáil*, an indictment; from the M. Eng. *dîten*, indict, Sc. *dite*—a parallel form to *indict*, *endite*, from Lat. *indicto*, *dicto*, dictate, *dico*, say. Further Sc. *dittay*.

dith, press together, **dithimh**, a heap (Sh.):

dìth, want, defeat, Ir. *díth*, O. Ir. *díth*, destruction, **dêto-*, from *dê* (as in *de*, of, *dì-*, un-); Lat. *lêtum* (=*dêtum*), death (Stokes).

dìthean, daisy, darnel, blossom, M. Ir. *dithen*, darnel, Manx *jean* (do.):

dithis, a pair, two, Ir. *dís*, O. Ir. *dias*, g. *desse*, dat. and acc. *diis* (also *días*, *díis*), duitas, **dveistâ*, from the fem. **dvei*, O. Ir. *dí*, two. See *dà*. O. Ir. *dias*, **dveiassa*: cf. Lat. *bes*, *bessis*, from **bejess* (St.).

dìthreabh, a desert, Ir. *díthreabh*, O. Ir. *dithrub*; from *dí-* and *treb*; see *treabh*, *aitreabh*.

diu, **diugh** (to)-day, **an diu**, to-day, Ir. *andiu*, *aniu*, O. Ir. *indiu*, W. *heddyw*, M. Br. *hiziu*, Br. *hirio*, **divo-* (Stokes); Skr. *divâ*; Lat. *diû*. See *Di-*, day. The **an** (O. Ir. *in*) is the article.

diù, worth while: **do-fiù*; see *fiù*.

diùbhaidh, **diùgha**, refuse, the worst, **diu** (M'F., M'E.), Ir. *díogha*; opposite of *rogha*. See *roghainn*.

diùbhail, mischief, loss; see *dìobhail*.

diùbhras, difference, **diubhar** (Arm.): **divr*, **difr*, from *differ* of Lat. *differo*. See *difir*.

diuc, the pip, a sickness of fowls:

diùc, a duke, Ir. *diubhce*, *diúic* (Keat.); from the Eng. *duke*.

diùcair, a ducker, a bladder for keeping nets at the proper depth under water; from the Eng. *ducker*.

diuchaidh, addled:

diùdan, giddiness, **diudan** (Arm.):

diug, an interjection to call hens, cluck, Ir. *diugam*, cluck: onomatopoetic. See *diog*.

diugan, mischance (H.S.D., which marks it as Dialectic):

diugh, to-day; see *diu*.

diùid, tender-hearted, a spiritless person, Ir. *diúid*, O. Ir. *diuit*, simplex:

diùlanas, bravery, Ir. *díolúntas*, earlier *diolmhaineach*, soldier, mercenarius; from *dìol*, pay.

diùlt, refuse, Ir. *diúltaim*, E. Ir. *díultaim*, O. Ir. *díltuch*, refusing, *doríltiset*, negaverunt, **di-îlt* (Thu.). Zimmer suggests the root of Lat. *lateo*, lurk, Stokes gives **de-laudi* ("Celt. Dec."), and Ascoli hesitates between **di-la-* (*la*, throw, Gr. ἐλαύνω) and **di-shlond*. Possibly an active form of *till*, return. *díltud*, v. n. of *do-sluindi*.

diùmach, displeased, Ir. *díomdhach*, M. Ir. *dímdach*, *dimmdach*: **dim-med-*, root *med*, mind, as in *meas*.

dleas, dleasnas, duty, Ir. *dlisdeanas*, legality, E. Ir. *dlestanas* (do.), **dlixo-*, **dl̥g-so-*, right; see *dligheadh*.

dligheadh, law, right, Ir. *dlígheadh*, O. Ir. *dliged*, W. *dyled*, *dled*, debt, **dligeto-n*, Cor. *dylly*, debere, Br. *dle*, debt, **dl̥gô*, I owe; Got. *dulgs*, debt; Ch. Sl. *dlugu* (do.).

dlo, a handful of corn, **dlò** (M'L., M'E.), Ir. *dlaoigh*, a lock of hair or anything, E. Ir. *dlai*, a wisp; cf. W. *dylwf*, wisp, and Lat. *floccus*?

dluigheil, handy, active (Dial.), Ir. *dlúigh*, active (O'B.), M. Ir. *dluigh*, service, E. Ir. *dluig*, service, **dlogi-*; same root as *dligheadh*.

dlùth, close, Ir. *dlúth*, E. Ir. *dlúith*, O. Ir. *dlútai*, (pl.), *dlúthe*, adhaerendi, **dlûti-*. Cf. Gr. θλάω, crush. *dru*?

dlùth, the warp of a web, Ir., O. Ir. *dlúth*, stamen, W. *dylif* (**dlû-mi-*?); from the above root (*dlû*).

do, to, Ir. *do*, O. Ir. *do*, *du*, Cor. *dhe*, O. Br. *do*, Br. *da*; Eng. *to*, Ag. S. *tó*, Ger. *zu*; Lat. *-do* (*endo*, *indu*); Gr. -δε. Stokes derives the prep. *do* from the verbal particle *do*, *to*. See the next word.

do, a verbal particle denoting "to, ad," Ir. *do*, O. Ir. *do-*, *du-*, also *to-*, when it carries the accent (e.g. *dobiur*, I give, **do-bérô*, but *tabair*, give, **tó-bere*); W. *du-*, *dy-*, *y*. Cf. Got. *du*, to prep. and prefix, for **þu*?

do, thy, Ir. *do*, O. Ir. *do*, *du*, W. *dy*, E. W. *teu*, Cor. *dhe*, Br. *da*, **tovo*; Lat. *tuus*; Skr. *táva*, etc. See *tu*.

do-, du-, prefix of negative quality, Ir. *do-*, *dó-*, O. Ir. *do-*, *du-*, **dus-*; Skr. *dus-*; Gr. δυσ-; Got. *taz-*, Ger. *zer-*. Its opposite is *so*, q.v. Following the analogy of *so*, it aspirates the consonants though originally it ended in *s*.

dobair, a plasterer (M'D.), Ir. *dóbadóir*, W. *dwbiwr*; from M. Eng *dauber*, Eng. *daub*.

dòbhaidh, boisterous: **du-vati-*, root *vet*, as in *onfhadh*, q.v.

†**dobhar**, water, Ir. *dobhar*, E. Ir. *dobur*, W. *dwfr*, Cor. *dofer*, Br *dour*, Gaul. *dubrum*, **dubro-n*, **dub-ro-*, root *dub*, deep, as in *domhain*, q.v. Cf. Lit. *dumblas*, mire, Lett. *dubli* (do.); Lit *duburys*, a place with springs, *dumburýs*; Ger. *tümpel*, a dee

place in flowing or standing water. Hence **dobharchu** ("water-dog") and **dobhran,** the otter.

docair, grievous, hard, trouble, E. Ir. *doccair*, uneasiness, trouble. See *socair.*

docha, preferable, **is docha,** prefer; see *toigh.*

dòcha, more likely, Ir. *dócha*, O. Ir. *dochu*; comparative of *dóigh*, O. Ir. *dóig*, likely, **dougi-*, **douki-*; Gr. δεύκει, thinks, ἀδευκής, unseemly; Ger. *zeuge*, witness; further allied is Lat. *dûco.* Connection with Gr. δοκέω has been suggested, and Zimmer has analysed it into **do-ech*, **do-sech*, root *sec*, say (as in *casg*, etc.: Cam.), citing the by-form *toich* (G. **toigh**), which is a different word. Hence **dòchas, dòigh.**

dochair, dochar, hurt, damage, so Ir., E. Ir. *dochor*; from *do-* and *cor-*, i.e., *cor*, state: *dochar*, "bad state." See *cor*, *sochair.* Hence **dochartach,** sick.

dochann, injury, hurt, M. Ir. *dochond*, ill-fortune, O. Ir. *conaichi*, felicior, from **cuno-*, high, root *ku* (as in *curaidh*)?

dòchas, hope, Ir. *dóchas*, M. Ir. *dóchus*; see *dòcha.*

docran, anguish (Sh., Arm.; not H.S.D.); cf. *docrach*, hard, from *docair.*

dod, a tantrum, fret, Ir. *sdoid* (n.), *sdodach* (adj.), *dóiddeach*, quarrelsome (Con.). Cf. Sc. *dod.*

dòdum, a teetotum (Dialectic); from the Eng.

dog, a bit; from the Eng. *dock.*

dogadh, mischief (Sh.), O. Ir. *dodcad* (Str.).

dogail, cynical, **doganta,** fierce; from the Eng. *dog.*

dògan, a sort of oath (Dialectic, M'L.); Sc. *daggand*, Eng. *doggonit*, Amer. *doggond.*

dogha, a burdock, Ir. *meacan dogha*; Eng. *dock*, Ag. S. *docce.*

doibhear, rude, uncivil, so Ir. (Lh., which H.S.D. quotes, O'B., etc.): "ill-bearing"; from *do-* and *beir?*

doibheas, vice, Ir. *dóibheus*; from *do-* and *beus.*

doicheall, churlishness, Ir. *doicheall*, g. *doichle*; E. Ir. *dochell*, grudging, inhospitality: opposed to E. Ir. *sochell*, meaning "kindness," *soichlech.* Root is that of *timchioll.* Gaul. *Sucellos*, a god's name.

dòid the hand, grasp, Ir. *dóid*, E. Ir. *dóit*, O. Ir. *inna n-doat*, lacertorum, **dousenti-*; Skr. *dos* (**daus*), *doshan*, fore-arm, Zend *daosha*, shoulder. Strachan, who cites the meanings "hand, wrist," suggests a stem **doventi-*, from I. E. *dheva* (move violently), comparing Gr. καρπός, wrist, from *qrp*, turn. Hence **dòideach,** muscular.

dòid, a small farm: "a holding"; from *dòid*, hand. Cf. **dòideach,** firmly grasping.

dòideach, frizzled up, shrunk (of hair); from *dàth*, singe.
dòigh, manner, trust, Ir. *dóigh*. For root, see *dòcha*.
doilbh, difficult (H.S.D.), dark (Sh., O'B.), Ir. *doilbh*, dark, gloomy: cf. *suilbh*.
doileas, injury; from *do-* and *leas*.
doilgheas, sorrow, so Ir.; from *doiligh*, sorry, the Ir. form of *duilich*, q.v.
doilleir, dark, Ir. *dóiléir*; see *soilleir*.
doimeag, a slattern; cf. Ir. *doim*, poor, and for root, see *soimeach*.
doimh, bulky, gross; see *dòmhail*.
doimh, doimheadach, vexing, galling: **do-ment-*, "ill-minded."
doimheal, stormy (Sh.; not H.S.D.):
dòineach, sorrowful, baneful (Arm., who has *doineach* with short *o*), O. Ir. *dóinmech*, *dóinmidh*. Dr N. M'L. "fateful." *dàn?*
doinionn, a tempest, Ir. *doineann*, O. Ir. *doinenn*. See *soineann*.
doirbeag, a minnow, tadpole, Ir. *dairb*, a marsh worm, murrain caterpillar, E. Ir. *duirb* (acc.), worm, **dorbi-*: I. E. *derbho-*, wind, bend, Skr. *darbh*, wind, M. H. G. *zirben*, whirl.
doirbh, hard, difficult, so Ir., O. Ir. *doirb*; see *soirbh*.
doire, grove, Ir. *doire*, *daire*, O. Ir. *daire* (Adamnan), *Derry*, W. *deri*, oak grove; see *darach*.
doireagan, peewit; Dialectic form of *adharcan*.
doireann, doirionn (Arg.), tempestuous weather; see *doinionn*. For phonetics, cf. *boirionn*.
doirionta, sullen, so Ir.; cf. the above word.
dòirling, dòirlinn, isthmus, beach, Ir. *doirling*, promontory, beach: **do-air-líng-* (for *ling*, see *leum*)? For meaning, see *tairbeart*.
dòirt, pour, Ir. *doirtim*, *dórtadh* (inf.), E. Ir. *doirtím*, O. Ir. *dofortad*, effunderet, *dorortad*, was poured out, **fort-*, root *vor*, *ver*, pour, E. Ir. *feraim*, I pour, give; Lat. *ûrina*, *urine*; Gr. *οὖρον*; Norse *úr*, drizzling rain, Ag. S. *vär*, sea; Skr. *vā́ri*, water. To this Stokes refers *braon* (for *vroen-*, *veróenâ ?*).
doit, foul, dark (H.S.D. only):
dòit, a small coin less than a farthing; from the Sc. *doit*.
dol, going, Ir. *dul*, O. Ir. *dul*, inf. to *doluid*, *dolluid*, ivit, from *luid*, went, **ludô*, from I. E. *leudho*, go, Gr. *ἐλεύσομαι*, will come, *ἤλυθον*, came. Stokes and Brugmann refer *luid* to *(*p*)*ludô*, root *plu*, *plou* of *luath*, q.v.
dòlach, destructive: "grievous"; from †**dòl**, grief, Sc. *dool*, from Lat. *dolor*.
dolaidh, harm, so Ir., E. Ir. *dolod*, O. Ir. *dolud*, damnum, O. G. *dolaid*, burden, charge; its opposite is E. Ir. *solod*, profit: **do-lud*, "mis-go"; from *lud* of *luid*, go (Ascoli).

dòlas, grief, Ir. *dólas*: formed from *sòlas*, consolation, on the analogy of other *do-* and *so-* words. See *sòlas*.

dòlum, mean, surly, wretchedness, poverty. Cf. *dòlach*.

dom, the gall, gall-bladder; see *domblas*.

domail, damage; apparently founded on Lat. *damnum*.

domblas, gall, bile, Ir. *domblas*, M. Ir. *domblas ae*, i.e., "bitterness of the liver"; from M. Ir. *domblas*, ill-taste; from *do-mlas*. See *blas*.

domhach, a savage; see *doimh*.

dòmhail, bulky: M. Ir. *derg-domla*, pl., from **domail*, root of *meall*: **do-fo-mell ?*

domhain, deep, so Ir., O. Ir. *domain*, W. *dwfn*, Br. *don*, **dubni-s*, **dubno-s*; Eng. *deep*, Got. *diups*; Lit. *dubùs*, deep, *dumburýs*, a hole in the ground filled with water, *dauba*, ravine, Ch. Sl. *dŭbrĭ*, ravine: I. E. *dheub*. See also *dobhar*.

domhan, the Universe, so Ir., O. Ir. *domun*, Gaul. *Dubno-*, *Dumno-* (in many proper names, as *Dubnotalus*, *Dumnorix*, "World-king," Gaelic *Domhnall*, **Dumno-valo-s*, W. *Dyfnual*), Celtic **dubno-*, the world, the "deep"; another form of *domhain* above. Cf. Eng. *deep* for the "sea." D'Arbois de Jubainville explains *Dubno-* of Gaulish names as "deep," *Dumnorix*, "deep king," "high king"; and he has similarly to explain *Biturix* as "king for aye," not "world king": all which seems a little forced.

Dòmhnach, Sunday, so Ir., E. Ir. *domnach*; from Lat. *dominica*, "the Lord's." See under *Di-*.

don, evil, defect, Ir. *don*; see next word.

dona, bad, so Ir., E. Ir. *donae*, *dona*, wretched, bad; opposite to *sona*, *son*, happy. See *sona*.

dongaidh, moist, humid; from the Sc. *donk*, Eng. *dank*.

donn, brown, Ir., O. Ir. *donn*, W. *dwn*, Gaul. *Donnus*, *Donno-*; **donno-s*, **dus-no-*; Lat. *fuscus*; Eng. *dusk*, *dust*. Eng. *dun* may be hence.

donnal, a howl, complaint; **don-no-*, I. E. *dhven*, whence Eng. *din*, Skr. *dhvana*, sound. Meyer says: "Better *donal*, fem." G. is masc.

dorbh, dorgh, a hand-line, Ir. *dorubha*; also **drogha,** q.v.

dorc, a piece (Dialectic): **dorco-*, root *der*, split, Eng. *tear*; N. *dorg*.

dorch, dark, Ir. *dorcha*, O. Ir. *dorche*; opposed to *sorcha*, bright, **do-reg-io-*, root *reg*, see, Lit. *regiù*, I see. See *rosg*. The root *reg*, colour, Gr. ῥέζω, colour, ἔρεβος, Erebus, Norse *rökr*, darkness, *Ragna-rökr*, twilight of the gods, is allied. Ascoli and Zimmer refer it to the Gadelic root *rich*, shine, O. Ir. *richis*, coal, Bret. *regez*, glowing embers, Skr. *ric*, *ṛc*, shine.

dòrlach, a handful, quantity : **dorn-lach*, from *dòrn*, a fist.

dòrn, a fist, Ir. *dorn*, O. Ir. *dorn*, W. *dwrn*, Cor. *dorn*, O. Br. *dorn*, Br. *dourn*, hand, Gaul. *Durnacos*, **durno-* ; Gr. δῶρον, palm, δάρειρ, δάριν, a span ; Lettic *dúrc*, fist ; I. E. root *der*, split. **dver*, **dur*, strong.

dorra, more difficult, Ir. *dorrach*, harsh, M. Ir. *dorr*, rough, **dorso-* ; Czech *drsen*, rough (Stokes, Strachan).

dorran, vexation, anger, Ir. *dorrán*, M. Ir. *dorr*, **dorso-* ; see above word.

dòruinn, pain, anguish, Ir. *dóghruing*. Cf. E. Ir. *dogra*, *dógra*, lamenting, anguish, *dogar*, sad, from *do-* and *gar*, q.v.

dorus, a door, Ir., O. Ir. *dorus*, W. *drws*, Cor. *daras*, O. Cor. *dor*, Br. *dor*, **dvorestu-* ; Lat. *fores* ; Gr. θύρα ; Eng. *door* ; Lit. *dùrys* ; Skr. *dvā́r*.

dos, a bush, tuft, Ir. *dos*, O. Ir. *doss*, **dosto-*, root *dus* ; Lat. *dumus* (= *dus-mus*), thicket ; Eng. *tease*, *teasel*.

dosdan, a kind of food given to horses ; from Eng. *dust*.

dosgadh, dosgainn, misfortune ; cf. Ir. *dósgathach*, improvident. From *do-* and *sgath*, q.v. Ir. *dosguidhtheach*, morose, extravagant.

dotarra, sulky ; see *dod*.

doth, a doating on one ; cf. Sc. *daut*, dote, M. Eng. *doten*.

dràbach, dirty, slovenly, Ir. *drabaire*, *drabóg*, slut, *drab*, a stain ; from Eng. *drab*. See *drabh*. Hence **drabasda,** obscene.

drabh, dissolve, **drabhag,** dregs, **drabhas,** filth, E. Ir. *drabar-slog*, rabble ; from Eng. *draff*, allied to Ger. *treber*, Norse *draf*. Stokes thinks that the G. is allied to, not derived from, the Eng. The Eng. word *drab* is allied to *draff*, and so is *dregs*.

dràbh, scatter, dissolve (M'A., Arg.), not **drabh** (H.S.D., which, however, has **drabhach,** rifted). **dràbhach,** wide-sutured, rifted (Arg.) :

dràc, a drake ; from the Eng. See *ràc*.

dragh, trouble, O. Ir. g. *mor-draige*, roughness : **drago-*, I. E. *dregho-*, Ag. S. *trega*, vexation, Norse *tregr*, dragging, slovenly, *trega*, grieve ; Skr. *drâgh*, pain ; Gr. *ταραχή, τρᾱχύς (St.).

dragh, pull, draw, Ir. *dragáil* ; from the Eng. *drag*, *draw*, Norse *draga*.

dràgon, a dragon, Ir. *dragún*, E. Ir. *drac*, g. *dracon* ; from Lat. *draco(n)*, Eng. *dragon*.

dràichd, a slattern (Arm.) :

draighlichd, a trollop, draggle-tail (Arg.) ; from Eng. *draggle-tail ?* Cf. *draghlainn* under *draoluinn*.

draillsein, a sparkling light (Sh., H.S.D.) ; see *drillsean*.

draimheas, a foul mouth; cf. Ir. *drabhas*, a wry mouth, *dramhaim*, I grin. The G. seems from *drabh* above.
draing, a snarl, grin; see *dranndan*.
dràm, dram, a dram, Ir. *dram*; from the Eng.
dramaig, a foul mixture, crowdie (Sh., H.S.D.); from the Sc. *dramock*.
drannd, dranndan, a hum, snarl, Ir. *draint*, *dranntán*, M. Ir. *drantaigim*, I snarl; from a Celtic **dran*, I. E. *dhreno-*, sound, drone; Eng. *drone*; Gr. θρῆνος, dirge; Skr. *dhraṇ*, sound, murmur.
drann, dranna, a word (M'A., Arg.); same as *drannd*.
draoch, a fretful or ghastly look, hair standing on end, Ir. *driuch*, fretfulness, angry look: root *dhrigh*; Gr. θρίξ, τριχός, hair. For meaning, cf. *snuadh*, hue, hair.
draoi, draoidh, druidh, a magician, druid, Ir. *draoi*, gen. pl. *druadh*, E. Ir. *drai*, *drui*, g. *druad*, Gaul. *druides* (Eng. *druid*). Its etymology is obscure. Stokes suggests relationship with Eng. *true*, G. *dearbh*, q.v., or with Gr. θρέομαι, cry (as in *drannd*, *dùrd*), or Gr. ἀθρέω, look sharp, Pruss. *dereis*, see. Thurneysen analyses the word as *dru*, high, strong, see *truaill*. Brugmann and Windisch have also suggested the root *dru*, oak, as Pliny did too, because of the Druids' reverence for the oak tree. Ag. S. *drý*, magus, is borrowed from the Celtic. *draoineach*, *druineach*, artisan, "eident" person (Carm.); *draoneach*, "any person that practices an art" (Grant), agriculturist; *druinneach*, artist (Lh.). Ir. *druine*, art needlework; θρόνα, flowers in embroidery, drugs.
draoluinn, delay, tediousness, drawling; from the Eng. *drawling*, Sc. *drawl*, to be slow in action, *drawlie*, slow and slovenly. Dialectic **draghlainn,** a slovenly person, a mess.
drapuinn, tape; from the Eng. *drape*.
draos, trash, filth, Ir. *draos*. Cf. Eng. *dross*.
dràsda, an dràsda, now, Ir. *drásda*, M. Ir. *trasta*, for *an tràth sa*, this time.
drathais, drawers; from the Eng.
dreach, aspect, Ir. *dreach*, E. Ir. *drech*, W. *drych*, M. Br. *derch*, **dṛkâ*, **dṛkko-*, root *derk* as in *dearc*, q.v.
drèachd, dreuchd, duty, office, Ir. *dréacht*, song, O. Ir. *drécht*, portio, **drempto-*, root *drep*, Gr. δρέπω, pluck, cull (Strachan).
dreag, drèag, a meteor or portent; from the Ag. S. *dréag*, apparition, Norse *draugr*, ghost. Also **driug.**
dreall, dreoll, door-bar, **dreallag,** a swingle-tree: *dṛs-lo-*, root *der*, split, Eng. *tree?* Cf. W. *dryll*, **dhruslo*, θραυω.

dreallaire, an idler; see *drollaire.*

dreallsach, a blazing fire; see *drillsean.*

dream, a tribe, people, Ir. *dream,* E. Ir. *dremm*; from **dream,** bundle, handful, manipulus, Br. *dramm,* a sheaf, **dregsmo-*; Gr. δράγμα, a handful, δράσσομαι, grasp; Ch. Sl. *drazhaiti,* grasps; Skr. *darh,* make fast, I. E. *dergho-,* fasten. Hence **dreamsgal,** a heterogeneous mass. *dreg*: *dreng,* tramp? Cf. *drong.*

dreamach, peevish, **dream,** snarl; cf. Ir. *dreamhnach,* perverse, E. Ir. *dremne,* fierceness, from *dreamh,* surly, **dremo-,* from *drem, drom,* rush, Gr. δρόμος, a race. G. *dreamach* may be for **dregsmo-,* root *dreg* as in *dreangan.*

dreangan, a snarler, Ir. *drainceanta,* snarling, *drainc,* a snarl, also *draint,* W. *drengyn,* a surly chap, *dreng,* morose, **drengo-,* root *dreg,* from *dhre* of *dranndan.*

dreas, bramble, bramble-bush, Ir. *dreas*; see *dris.*

dreasair, a dresser (house-furniture).

dreathan-donn, wren, Ir. *dreaán, drean,* W. *dryw,* **drivo-,* **dr̥-vo-,* root *der, dher,* jump? See *dàir.* Cf. for sense Gr. τρόχιλος. Or from *dhrevo,* cry, Gr. θρέομαι, G. *drannd,* q.v.?

dreigeas, a grin, peevish face, E. Ir. *dric,* wrathful; **dreggo-,* root *dreg* as in *dreangan.*

dreimire, a ladder, Ir. *dréimire,* E. Ir. *dréimm,* ascent, vb. *dringim,* W. *dringo,* scandere, **drengô.* Bezzenberger compares the Norse *drangr,* an up-standing rock (cf. *cliff* and *climb*). The root *dreg* of *dreimire* has also been compared to Ger. *treppe,* staircase, Eng. *tramp.* See *dream,* people, "goers." Ir. *ag dreim,* advancing.

dréin, a grin: **dreg-ni-,* root *dreg* of *dreangan.*

dreòchdam, the crying of the deer; from *dhrevo, dhre,* cry.

dreòlan, a wren, Ir. *dreólán*: **drivolo-*; see *dreathan.*

dreòlan, a silly person, Ir. *dreólán,* W. *drel,* a clown; from Eng. *droll*? Thurneysen prefers to consider these words borrowed from Eng. *thrall,* Norse *þræl.* The word appears as **dreòlan, dreallaire, drollaire.** In the sense of "loiterer," these words are from the Norse *drolla,* loiter, Eng. *droil.*

dreòs, a blaze:

dreugan, a dragon (Dialectic); see *dràgon.*

driachan, plodding, obstinacy, Ir. *driachaireachd*: **dreiqo-*; cf. Eng. *drive,* from *dhreip.*

driamlach, a fishing line, Manx *rimlagh,* E. Ir. *ríamnach*: **reimmen-*; see *réim.*

driceachan, tricks (M'D.).

drifeag, hurry (Heb.); see *drip.*

dril, a spark, sparkle, Ir. *dril*, *drithle*, pl. *drithleanna*, M. Ir. *drithle*, dat. *drithlinn*, also *drithre*, **drith-renn-* (for *-renn-*, see *reannag*), **drith*. Hence **drillsean**, sparkles, from *drithlis*, a spark. *Drìllsean*, rushlight, rush used as wick.

driodar, dregs, lees, Ir. *dríodar*, gore, dregs: **driddo-*, **dṛd-do-*, root *der*, Eng. *tear*. Cf. Sc. *driddle*.

driog, a drop, Ir. *driog* (*dríog*, Con.), *driogaire*, a distiller; seemingly borrowed from Norse *dregg*, M. Eng. *dreg*, dregs.

driongan, slowness, Ir. *driongán*, a plaything, worthless pastime:

drip, hurry, confusion, Ir. *drip*, bustle, snare: **drippi-*, **dhribh*, Eng. *drive?* N. *drepa*, hit.

dris, a bramble, brier, Ir. *dris*, O. Ir. *driss*, O. W. *drissi*, W. *dryssien*, Cor. *dreis*, Br. *drezen*, **dressi-*. Bezzenberger suggests a stem **drepso-*, M. H. G. *trefs*, Ger. *trespe*, darnel, M. Eng. *drauk* (=*dravick* of Du.), zizanium. It must be kept separate from *droighionn*, O. Ir. *draigen*, Celtic root *dṛg*, though G. *dris* might be for **dṛg-si-*, for the W. would be in *ch*, not *s*. See *droighionn*.

drithlean, a rivet:

drithleann, a sparkle, Ir. *drithlinn*; oblique form of *dril*.

driubhlach, a cowl, so Ir. (O'R.); Sh. has *dribhlach*.

driùcan, a beak, Ir. *driuch*. M'A. gives also the meaning, "an incision under one of the toes." See *draoch*.

driuch, activity (M'A.):

driuchan, a stripe, as in cloth (M'A.):

driug, a meteor, portent; see *dreag*.

dròbh, a drove; from the Eng.

drobhlas, profusion, so Ir.:

droch, evil, bad, Ir. *droch*, O. Ir. *droch*, *drog*, W. *drwg*, Cor. *drog*, malum, M. Br. *drouc*, **druko-*. Usually compared to Skr. *druh*, injure, Ger. *trug*, deception. Stokes has suggested *dhruk*, whence Eng. *dry*, and Bezzenberger compares Norse *trega*, grieve, *tregr*, unwilling (see *dragh*).

drochaid, a bridge, Ir. *droichiod*, O. Ir. *drochet*:

drog, a sea-swell at its impact on a rock (Arg.):

drogaid, drugget, Ir. *drogáid* (O'R.); from the Eng.

drogha, a hand fishing line; also **dorgh, dorbh**, Ir. *dorubha*, *drubha*; Norse *dorg*, an angler's tackle.

droich, a dwarf, Ir. *droich*, **drogi-*, allied to Teut. *dwergo-*, Ger. *zwerg*, Norse *dvergr*, Eng. *dwarf*.

droigheann, bramble, thorn, Ir. *droigheann*, O. Ir. *draigen*, W. *draen*, Cor. *drain*, *drein*, Br. *drean*, **dragino-*: cf. Gr. τραχύς, rough, θράσσω, confuse, Eng. *dregs*. Bezzenberger compares Lit. *drìgnės*, black henbane, Gr. δράβη, a plant. Ebel referred it to the same origin as Gr. *τέρχνος*, twig. Also **droighneach,** (1) thorn, (2) lumber, "entanglement."

droinip, tackle :

drola, a pot-hook, Ir. *drol*, *droltha*, M. Ir. *drol*, *drolam*, handle, E. Ir. *drolam*, knocker, ring :

droll, an animal's tail, a door bar, unwieldy stick ; cf. *dreallag* for the last two meanings.

droll, drollaire, a lazy fellow ; see *dreòlan.*

droman, the alder tree ; see *troman.*

drong, droing, people, tribe, Ir. *drong*, E. Ir. *drong*, O. Br. *drogn*, *drog*, factio, Gaul. *drungus*, whence Lat. *drungus*, a troop (4th century), **drungo-* ; Got. *driugan*, serve as a soldier, Ag. S. *dryht*, people, Norse *drótt*, household, people.

drongair, a drunkard ; from the Eng.

dronn, the back, Ir. *dronnóg* : **dros-no-*, root *dros* of *druim*, q.v.

dronng, a trunk ; from the Eng.

drothan, a breeze (M'D.) :

druabag, a small drop, **druablas,** muddy water, **druaip,** dregs, lees. The first is from Eng. *drop* ; *druablas* is from M. Eng. *drubli*, turbid, Sc. *droubly* ; and *druaip* is from Norse *drjúpa*, drip. *drubhag* and *drùigean* (Wh.).

drùb, a wink of sleep, a mouthful of liquid ; from Norse *drjúpa*, drip. See the above words.

drùchd, dew, Ir. *drúchd*, E. Ir. *drúcht*, **drūb-tu-*, root *dhreub* ; Ag. S. *dréapian*, trickle, Eng. *drip*, *drop*, Norse *drjúpa*, drip, Ger. *triefen.*

drùdh, penetrate, pierce, **drùidh** ; see the next.

drùdhadh, oozing, soaking ; cf. Skr. *dru*, *dráva*, melt, run, Got. *ufar-trusian*, besprinkle. Cf. Gaul. *Druentia* (Gaelic *Druie*, a river in Strathspey).

drugair, a drudge, Ir. *drugaire* ; from M. Eng. *druggar*, a dragger, Eng. *drudge.*

druid, close, Ir. *druidim*, E. Ir. *druit*, close, firm, trustworthy : **druzdo-*, **drus*, W. *drws*, door. See *dorus.* Stokes now refers **druzdi-* to the same source as Eng. *trust.*

druid, a starling, Ir. *druid*, E. Ir. *truid*, Manx *truitlag*, W. *drudwy*, Br. *dred*, *dret* : **struzdi* ; Lat. *turdus*, thrush ; Lit. *strázdas* (Bohemian *drazd*), thrush, Eng. *throstle.*

druidh, a magician ; see *draoi.*

drùidh, penetrate ; see *drùdh.* Cf. Ir. *treidhim* ; *treaghaim* (Sh.).

druim, back, ridge, so Ir., O. Ir. *druimm*, pl. *dromand*, W. *trum*, **drosmen-* ; Lat. *dorsum.*

drùis, lust, **drùiseach, drùth,** lecherous, Ir. *drúis*, adultery, E. Ir. *drúth*, lewd, a harlot, **drūto-.* Cf. M. Eng. *drüð*, darling,

O. Fr. *drūd* (do.), *druerie*, love, whence M. Eng. *druerie*, Sc. *drouery*, illicit love. Mayhew refers the Fr. and Eng. to O. H. G. *drût*, dear (also *trût*, *drûd*): a Teut. *dreuð?* Cf. Ger. *traut*, beloved (Kluge).

druma, a drum, Ir., M. Ir. *druma;* from the Eng.

druman, elder; see *troman.*

drumlagan, a cramp in back, wrists, etc. (M'D.):

dù, meet, proper, Ir., E. Ir. *dú.* This Stokes regards as borrowed from O. Fr. *dû* (= *debntus*), whence Eng. *due.* But see *dùthaich*, *dual.*

du-, do-, prefix denoting badness of quality, Ir., O. Ir. *du-*, *do-*, **dus*; Gr. δυς-; Got. *tuz-*, Norse *tor-*; Skr. *dus-*. See *do-*.

duaichnidh, gloomy, ugly, Ir. *duaichniúghadh*, to disfigure. See *suaicheantas.*

duaidh, a horrid scene, a fight, Ir. *dúaidh*, evil (O'B.): **du-vid?*

duairc, uncivil, Ir., E. Ir. *duairc*: opposite of *suairc*, q.v.

duaireachas, a squabble, slander: *du-aireachas.* See *eireachdail.*

duairidh, dubharaidh, a dowry; from the Eng.

duais, a reward, so Ir., E. Ir. *duass*, gift: **dovestâ*; Gr. δοῦναι, to give (= *dovénai*): Lit. *dûti* (do.), *dovanà*, a gift; Lat. *duint* (= *dent*). Root *dô*, give.

dual, a lock of hair, Ir., E. Ir. *dual*, **doklo-*; Got. *tagl*, hair, Ag. S. *taegl*, Eng. *tail*, Norse *tagl*, horse's tail.

dual, hereditary right, so Ir., M. Ir. *dúal*, **dutlo-*; see *dúthaich.* Stokes refers it to Fr. *dû*, as he does *dù*, q.v. Ir. *dúal*, just, proper, might come from **duglo-*, root *dhugh*, fashion, Gr. τεύχειν, Got. *dugan*, Eng. *do.*

duan, a poem, song, so Ir., E. Ir. *dúan*, **dugno-*; Lettic *dugát*, cry as a crane (Bez.) Stokes derives it from *dhugh* above under *dual.*

duarman, a murmur; cf. *torman* from *toirm.*

dùbailte, double, Ir. *dubâilte*; from M. Eng. *duble*, O. Fr. *doble*, Lat. *duplex.*

dubh, black, Ir. *dubh*, O. Ir. *dub*, W. *du*, O. W. *dub*, Cor. *duv*, Br. *du*, **dubo-*; Gr. τυφλός (= θυφ-λός), blind; Got. *daubs*, deaf, Ger. *taub*, Eng. *deaf*, also *dumb.* Cf. Gaul. river name *Dubis*, now *Doubs.*

dubhach, sad, Ir. *dúbhach*, O. Ir. *dubach;* see *subhach.*

dubhailc, wickedness, Ir. *dúbhailce*; see *subhailc.*

dubhailteach, sorrowful; founded on *dubh.*

dubhairt, said; see *thubhairt.*

dùbhaith, a pudding:

dubhan, a hook, Ir. *dubhán*, M. Ir. *dubán*:

dubhchlèin, the flank (H.S.D. from MSS.):

dùbhdan, a smoke, straw cinders, soot; from *dubh*. Cf. Ir. *dúbhadán*, an inkstand.

dùbhlaidh, gloomy, wintry; cf. **dubhlá**, a dark day, day of trial. From *dubh*.

dùbhlan, a challenge, Ir. *dubhshlán;* from *dubh* and *slàn;* Ir. *slán*, defiance.

dubhliath, the spleen, O. Ir. *lue liad*, *lua liath*, Cor. *lewilloit*, W. *lleithon*, milt of fish. Cf. Lat. *liēn*.

dubhogha, the great grandson's grandson; from *dubh* and *ogha:* *dubh* is used to add a step to *fionnogha*, though *fionn* here is really a prep., and not *fionn*, white. See *fionnogha*.

dùc, **dùcan** (Perth), a heap (Arm.); **dumhacán*, E. Ir. *duma*, mound, heap. Root of *dùn*.

dùchas, hereditary right; see *dúthaich*.

dud, a small lump (M'A); see *tudan*.

dùd, a tingling in the ear, ear, Ir. *dúd*. See next word.

dùdach, a trumpet, M. G. *doytichy* (D. of Lis.), Ir. *dúdóg*: onomatopoetic. Cf. Eng. *toot*.

dùdlachd, depth of winter:

duidseag, a plump woman of low stature (Perth); "My old Dutch;" *dúitseach* (Arm.). *Dutch*man, docked cock.

dùil, expectation, hope, Ir. *dúil*, **dûli-*, root *du*, strive, Gr. θυμός soul; Lit. *dumas*, thought (Stokes for Gr.)

dùil, an element, Ir. *dúil*, O. Ir. *dúil*, *dúl*, **dûli-*; Skr. *dhûli-*, dust; Lit. *dulkės* (do.); Lat. *fuligo*, soot. Stokes (Dict.) refers it to **dukli-*, root *duk*, fashion; Ger. *zeugen*, engender; further Lat. *duco*. Hence dialectic **Na dùil**, poor creatures! Ir. *dúil* means "creature" also. Hence also **dùileag**, a term of affection for a girl.

duileasg, dulse, Ir. *duileasg*, M. Ir. *duilesc*, W. *dylusg*, what is drifted on shore by floods. Hence Sc. *dulse*. Jamieson suggests that the G. stands for *duill' uisge*, "water-leaf."

duilich, difficult, sorry, Ir. *doiligh*, E. Ir. *dolig*; cf. Lat. *dolor*, grief.

duille, a leaf, Ir., M. Ir. *duille*, W. *dalen*, M. Br. *del*; Gr. θύλλα, leaves, θάλλω, I bloom; Ger. *dolde*, umbel: root *dhḷ*, *dhale*, bloom, sprout. Gaul. πεμπε-δουλα, "five leaved," is allied.

duillinnean, customs, taxes (M'D.):

dùin, shut, Ir. *dúnaim*, "barricading;" from *dùn*, q.v.

duine, a man, Ir., O. Ir. *duine*, pl. *dóini* (= **dváñji*), W. *dyn*, pl. *dyneddon*, Cor., Br. *den*, *dunjó-s*: "mortal;" Gr. θανεῖν, die, θάνατος, death, θνητός, mortal; Eng. *dwine*; Skr. *dhvan*, fall to pieces.

duircein, the seeds of the fir, etc., **duirc-daraich**, acorns. See *dorc.* O. Ir. *derucc*, glans, is referred by Windisch to the root of *darach*, q.v.

duiseal, a whip; from M. Eng. *duschen*, strike, of Scandinavian origin, now *dowse.*

dùiseal, dùsal, slumber; from Norse *dúsa*, doze, Eng. *doze.*

duisleannan, ill-natured pretences, freaks (Dialectic, H.S.D.), **dùisealan** (M'E.); from *dúiseal*: "dreaming?"

dùisg, awake, Ir. *dúisgim*, *dúisighim*, O. Ir. *diusgea*, expergefaciat, **de-ud-sec-*, root *sec* as in *caisg*, q.v.

dul, dula, a noose, loop, Ir. *dul*, *dol*, snare, loop, W. *dôl*, noose, loop, *doli*, form a ring or loop; Gr. δόλος, snare; Lat. *dolus*, etc.

dula, a pin, peg, Ir. *dula*; cf. Lat. *dolo*, a pike, M.H.G. *zol*, a log.

dùldachd, a misty gloom; see *dúdlachd.*

dùmhlaich, increase in bulk; see *dòmhail.*

dùn, a heap, a fortress, Ir., O. Ir. *dún*, W. *din*, Gaul. *dûnum*, -δουνον, **dûno-n*, **dûnos-*; Ag. S. *tún*, Eng. *town*, Ger. *zaun*, hedge, Norse *tún* (do.); Gr, δύνασθαι, can. Root *deva*, *dû*, to be strong, hard, whence also *dùr.*

dunach, dunaidh, woe; from *dona?*

dùr, dull, stubborn, Ir., E. Ir. *dúr*, W. *dir*, force, Br. *dir*, steel, Gaul. *dûrum*, fortress, **dûro-*, Lat. *dûrus.* For further connections see *dûn.*

dùrachd, dùthrachd, good wish, wish, diligence, Ir. *dúthrachd*, O. Ir. *dúthracht*, **devo-traktu-s-*, **trakkô*, press; Ag. S. *thringan*, Ger. *dringen*, press forward, Eng. *throng* (Stokes). Windisch has compared Skr. *tark*, think, which may be the same as *tark* of *tarkus*, spindle, Lat. *torqueo.* Verb **dùraig**.

dùradan, durradan, an atom, mote, Ir. *dúrdán*; from the root *dûr* as in *dùr* above: "hard bit?"

durc, a lumpish person:

durcaisd, turcais, pincers, nippers, tweezers; from Sc. *turkas*, from Fr. *turquoise*, now *tricoises*, "Turkish" or farrier's pincers.

dùrd, a syllable, sound, humming, Ir., E. Ir. *dórd*, *dordaim*, mugio, W. *dwrdd*, sonitus, *tordd*, **dordo-s*, root *der*, sound, I.E. *dher*; Lettic *dardėt*, rattle. Further Gr. θρῆνος, dirge, τονθρύς, muttering, Norse *drynr*, roaring, Eng. *drone*; root *dhre.*

durga, surly, sour, Ir. *dúrganta.* Cf. Ir. *dúranta*, morose. G. seems to be from Norse *durga*, sulky fellow, Eng. *dwarf.*

durlus, water-cress; from *dur* = *dobhar* and *lus*, q.v.

durraidh, pork, a pig, **durradh!** grumphy! Cf. *dorra.*

durrag, a worm:

durrghail, cooing of a dove, Ir. *durdail*; also **currucadh,** q.v. Onomatopoetic.
durrasgach, nimble (Dial., H.S.D.):
dursann, an unlucky accident, Ir. *dursan*, sorrowful, hard (O'R.); from the stem of *dorra*.
dus, dust, **duslach**; from Eng. *dust*.
dùsal, a slumber; from the Eng. *doze*. See *dùiseal*.
dùslainn, a gloomy, retired place:
dùth, hereditary; see *dù*.
dùthaich, a country, district, Ir. *dúthaigh*, O. Ir. *duthoig*, hereditary (M. Ir. *dúthaig*), G. **dùthchas,** hereditary right: root *dû* as in *dùn?* Cf. *dù*.
duthaich, great gut (M'Lagan):
duthuil, fluxus alvi = **dubh-ghalar**; from *dubh* and *tuil*.

E

e, accented **è,** he, it, Ir. *é*, O. Ir. *é*, **ei-s*: root *ei*, *i*; O. Lat. *eis* (= *is*, he, that), *ea*, she (= *eja*); Got. *is*, Ger. *er*, *es*; Skr. *ayam*. The O. Ir. neuter was *ed*, now **eadh** (as in **seadh, ni h-eadh**).
ea-, èa-, privative prefix; see *eu-*.
eabar, mud, puddle, Ir. *abar*, marshy land, Adamnan's *stagnum Aporicum*, Loch-aber, E. Ir. *cann-ebor* (see *Innear*), **ex-bor*, **ad-bor*, the *bor* of *tobar*, q.v.
eabon, ebony, so Ir.; from Lat. *ebenum*, Eng. *ebony*.
eabur, ivory, so Ir.; from Lat. *ebur*.
each, a horse, so Ir., O. Ir. *ech*, W. *ebol*, colt, Br. *ebeul*, Gaul. *Epo-*, **ekvo-s*; Lat. *equus*; Ag. S. *eoh*, Got. *aihva-*; Skr. *açva-s*.
eachdaran, eachdra, a pen for strayed sheep; see *eachdranach* for root.
eachdraidh, a history, Ir. *eachdaireachd*, history, *eachdaire*, historian, E. Ir. *echtra*, adventures; from E. Ir. prep. *echtar*, without, **ekstero*, W. *eithr*, extra; Lat. *extra*, *externus*; from *ex* (see *a*, *as*).
eachdranach, a foreigner, Ir. *eachdrannach*, O. Ir. *echtrann*, exter; Lat. *extraneus*, Eng. *strange*. From *echtar*, as in *eachdraidh*.
eachrais, confusion, mess; cf. Ir. *eachrais*, a fair, E. Ir. *echtress*, horse-fight. See *each* and *treas*.
èad, jealousy; see *eud*.
eadar, between, Ir, *eidir*, O. Ir. *eter*, *iter*, *etar*, W. *ithr*, Cor. *yntr*, Br. *entre*, Gaul, *inter*, **enter*, i.e., *en-ter*, prep. *en*; Lat. *inter*; Skr. *antár*, inside.
†**eadh,** it, **seadh,** yes, O. Ir. *ed*; see *e*.

eadh, space, E. Ir. *ed*, root *ped*; Gr. πεδίον, a plain; Lat. *oppidum*, town; Ch. Sl. *pad*, tread. Root *pedo*, go, as in Eng. *foot*, Lat. *pes*, *pedis*, etc.

eadha, the letter *e*, an aspen tree, Ir. *eadhadh* :

eadhal, a brand, burning coal (Bibl. Gloss.); see *éibheall*.

eadhon, to wit, namely, viz., so Ir., O. Ir. *idón*, **id-souno-*, "this here"; for *id*, see *eadh*, and *souno-* is from **sou*, **so* as in *so*. Cf. Gr. οὗ-τος. Stokes (*Celt. Decl.*) takes *id* from *it*, is, goes, root *i*, go, of Lat. *eo*, Gr. εἶμι, etc.; he regards *id* as part of the verb substantive.

eadradh, milking time, Ir. *eadarthra*, noon, milking time; from *eadar* + *tràth*.

eadraig, interpose, **eadragainn,** interposition, Ir. *eadargán*, separation; from *eadar*.

eag, a nick, notch, Ir. *feag*, Manx *agg*, W. *ag*, cleft, **eggâ-* : *peg ?*

eagal, feagal, fear, Ir. *eaguil*, *eagla*, E. Ir. *ecla*, O. Ir. *ecal* (adj.), **ex-gal*; see *gal*, valour.

eagan, perhaps; Dialectic for *theagamh*.

eagar, order, row, so Ir., E. Ir. *ecor*, **áith-cor*; from *aith-* and *cuir*.

eaglais, a church, Ir. *eagluis*. O. Ir. *eclais*, W. *eglwys*, Br. *ilis*; from Lat. *ecclêsia*, Eng. *ecclesiastic*.

eagna, wisdom, so Ir., O. Ir. *écne*, **aith-gen-*; see *aith-* and *gen* of *aithne*. In fact *aithne* and *eagna* are the same elements differently accented (**aith-gén-*, *áith-gen-*).

eàirlig, want, poverty, **airleig**; cf. *airleag*, lend, borrow.

eàirlin, keel, bottom, end : **air-lann*; see *lann*, land.

eàirneis, furniture; see *airneis*.

eala, a swan, so Ir., M. Ir. *ela*, W. *alarch*, Corn. *elerhc*, **elaio*, **elerko-s*; Gr. ἐλέα, reedwarbler, ἐλασᾶς, grosbeak, ἐλεᾶς, owl, ἐλειός, falcon; Lat. *olor*, swan. Gr. πέλεια, wild dove, Lat. *palumba*, dove, O. Prus. *poalis* (do.), have been suggested.

ealach, ealachainn, a peg to hang things on, E. Ir. *alchuing*, *elchuing*, dat. *alchaing*, pl. *alchningi*.

ealadh, learning, skill, **ealaidh,** knack, Ir. *ealadh*, E. Ir. *elatha*, gen. *elathan*, W. *el*, intelligence : root *el* : : *al* (of *eilean*) ?

èaladh, euladh, a creeping along (as to catch game), Ir. *euloighim* steal away, E. Ir. *élaim*, I flee, O. Ir. *élud*, evasio; Ger. *eilen*, hasten, speed; root *ei*, *i*, go, Lat. *i-re*, etc. Hence *èalaidhneach*, creeping cold. Strachan derives it from **ex-lâjô*, root *lâ*, *ela*, go, Gr. ελαύνο (as in *eilid*, etc.). Stokes now **ass-lúim*.

ealag, a block, hacking-stock; see *ealach*.

ealaidh, an ode, song, music; see *ealadh*.

ealamh, eathlamh, quick, expert, Ir. *athlamh*, E. Ir. *athlom*, *athlam*, **aith-lam*; **lam* is allied to *làmh*, hand ("handy" is the idea). See *ullamh* for discussion of the root *lam*.

ealbh, a bit, tittle, Ir. *ealbha*, a multitude, a drove, W. *elw*, goods, profit, **elvo-*; cf. Gaul. *Elvetios*, *Elvio*, etc.; **pel-vo-*, root *pel*, full?

ealbhar, a good for nothing fellow (Suth.); from Norse *álfr*, elf, a vacant, silly person.

ealbhuidh, St John's wort, Ir. *eala bhuidh* (O'R.):

†**ealg,** noble, so Ir., E. Ir. *elg*: *Innis Ealga* = Ireland. Cf. *Elgin*, Glen-*elg*.

ealla, nothing ado ("Gabh *ealla* ris"—have nothing ado with him):

eallach, a burden, so Ir., M. Ir. *ellach*, trappings or load; cf. Ir. *eallach*, a drove, O. Ir. *ellach*, conjunctio, **ati-slogos* (Zimmer), from *sluagh*. See *uallach* and *ealt*.

eallach, cattle (Arran), so Ir.: cf. O. Ir. *ellach*, conjunction, **ati-slôgos* (Zimmer).

eallsg, a scold, shrew:

ealt, ealta, a covey, drove, flock, Ir. *ealta*, E. Ir. *elta*: **ell-tavo-*, from *peslo-*, a brute, Cor. *ehal*, pecus; O. H. G., *fasal*, Ag. S. *fäsl*, proles (Stokes for Cor.). See *àl*. Ascoli joins O. Ir. *ellach*, union, and Ir. *eallach*, a drove, cattle, with *ealt*. See *eallach*.

ealltuinn, a razor, Ir. *ealtín*, O. Ir. *altan*, W. *ellyn*, O. Cor. *elinn*, O. Br. *altin*, Br. *aotenn*, **(p)altani*; Ger. *spalten*, cleave; Skr. *pat*, split; Old. Sl. ras-*platiti*, cut in two.

eaman, tail; see *feaman*, q.v.

eanach, honour, praise, E. Ir. *enech*, honour, also face; hence "regard" (Ascoli): **aneqo-*, W. *enep*; root *oq* of Lat. *oc-ulus*, etc.

eanach, dandriff, scurf, down:

eanach-gàrraidh, endive, Ir. **eanach-garraidh**; evidently a corruption of Lat. *endiva* (Cameron).

eanchaill, eanchainn, brains, Ir. *inchinn*, E. Ir. *inchind*, W. *ymmenydd*, Cor. *impinion* (= *in* + *pen-*), *in* + *ceann*, "what is in the head."

eang, foot, footstep, track, bound, Ir. *eang*, E. Ir. *eng*, track; cf. root *ong* given for *theagamh*.

eang, a gusset, corner; cf. Lat. *angulus*, Eng. *angle*.

eangach, a fetter, net, Ir. *eangach*, a net, chain of nets. From *eang*, foot.

eangarra, cross-tempered (H.S.D.): "having angles"; from *eang*.

eangbhaidh, high-mettled, M. Ir., *engach*, valiant; from *eang*, a step.

eangladh, entanglement; possibly from the Eng. *tangle*; not likely founded on *eangach*.

eanghlas, gruel, milk and water, Ir. *eanghlais*, E. Ir. *englas* (fem. *a* stem), milk and water, green water (Corm.), from *in* and M. Ir. *glas*, milk, **glagsa*; Gr. γλάγος, γάλα(κτος), milk, Lat. *lac* (= **glak-t*). Cormac says it is from *en*, water, and *glas*, grey. *en* = water, **pino* (St.).

eanntag, nettles; see *deanntag*.

eanraich, eanbhruith, soup, juice of boiled flesh, Ir. *eanbhruithe*, E. Ir. *enbruthe*, from *in* and *bruith*, boil. Corm. and O'Cl. have an obsolete *broth*, *bruithe*, flesh, and explain it as "water of flesh." For *en*, water, see *eanghlas*. Most dialects make it "chicken-soup," as from *eun* + *bruith*.

ear, an ear, the east, from the east, Ir. *soir*, eastern, *anoir*, from the east, O. Ir. *an-air*, ab oriente; really "from before," the prep. *an* (**apona*) of *a nall* (see *a*, from), and *air* (= **ari*), before. The observer is supposed to face the sun. The opposite is **iar, an iar**, from *iar*, behind, q.v.

earail, an exhortation, O. Ir. *eráil*, *iráil*, **air-áil*; from *àill*, desire. Hence **earal**, provision, caution.

earar, an earar, the day after to-morrow, Ir. *oirthior*, eastern, day following, day after to-morrow, O. Ir. *airther*, eastern, **ariteros*, **pareiteros* (Gr. παροίτερος), comparative of *air*, before.

eararadh, a parching of corn in a pot before grinding: **air-aradh*, root *ar*, as in Lat. *aridus*, arid?

earasaid, a square of tartan worn over the shoulders by females and fastened by a brooch, a tartan shawl: **air-asaid?* Cf. *asair* for root.

earb, a roe, so Ir., E. Ir. *erb*. O. Ir. *heirp*, **erbi-s*, Gr. ἔριφος.

earb, trust (vb.), **earbsa** (n.), Ir. *earbaim*, O. Ir. *erbaim*, *nom-erpimm*, confido, **erbiô*, let, leave; M. H. G. *erbe*, bequeath, Ger. *erbe*, heir, Got. *arbja*, heir: all allied to Lat. *orbus*, Eng. *orphan*.

earball, a tail, so Ir., E. Ir. *erball*, **áir-ball*; from *air* (= **ari*) and *ball*, q.v. *urball* in Arran and the West.

earc, heifer (Carm.), cow, Ir. *earc*, E. Ir. *erc*, cow (Corm.):

earchall, earachall, misfortune: **air-càll*; from *air* and *call*, q.v.

earghalt, arable land; *air* + *geadhail*, which see.

eargnaich, inflame, enrage: **áir-gon-*; from *air* and *gon?* Also *feargnaich*, which suggests *fearg* as root.

earlachadh, preparing food (Suth.); from old adj. *erlam*, ready. See *ullamh*.

eàrlaid, expectation, trust: **ari-lanti-*, root *lam* of *lamh*.

eàrlas, earnest, arles; see *airleas*.

eàrnach, murrain, bloody flux in cattle:

eàrr, end, tail, Ir. *earr*, E. Ir. *err*, **ersâ*; Gr. ὄρρος, rump; Ag. S. *ears*, Eng.

earr, a scar (Lewis); Norse *örr*, *arr* (do.).

earrach, spring, so Ir., O. Ir. *errech*, **persâko-*, from *pers*, which is from *per*, as *eks*, (=*ex*) is from *ek*; *per*, before, Lat. *per*, *prœ*, Eng. *for*, *fore*, ; as in *air*, (=*ari*). The idea is the "first of the year." Cf. Ger. *frühling*, spring, of like descent. Such is Stokes' derivation. Another view is that *earrach* is from *eàrr*, end (cf. for form *tòs* and *toiseach*, and *earrach*, lower extremity) meaning the "end of the year," the *céitein*, May, "first of summer," being the beginning of the year. Not allied to Lat. *ver*.

earradh, clothes, so Ir., E. Ir. *errad*, *eirred*, **áir-rêd*, **ari-reido-n*; from *reid* of *réidh*. Eng. *array* comes from the Gaul. equivalent (**ad-rêdare*), and Eng. *ready* is allied. Hence **earradh**, wares.

earradhubh, the wane, the wane of the moon: *earr+dubh ?*

earrag, a taunt (a blow, Arms.):

earrag, a shift, refuge, attempt (H.S.D., from MSS.):

earraghlòir, vain glory: **er-glòir*; the *er* is the intensive particle; Lat. *per*.

earraid, a tip-staff, **tearraid, tarraid** (Dial.): from Eng. *herald ?*

earraigh, a captain (H.S.D.); see *urra*.

earrann, a portion, Ir. *earrunn*, M. Ir. *errand*, **áir-rann*; from *rann*, portion.

earras, wealth; see *earradh*.

earrlait, ground manured one year and productive next (Carm):

eàrr-thalmhuinn, yarrow; see *athair-thalmhuinn*.

eas, a waterfall, Ir. *eas*, g. *easa*, E. Ir. *ess*, g. *esso*, **esti-* **pesti*; Skr. *â-patti*, mishap ("mis-fall"); Lat. *pessum*, down, *pestis*, a pest; Slav. *na-pasti*, casus (Bez.).

eas-, privative, prefix, Ir. *eas-*, O. Ir. *es-*, W. *eh-*, Gaul. *ex-*, **eks*. See *a*, *as*, out.

easach, thin water-gruel; from *eas*.

easag, a pheasant, a squirrel (M'D.), Ir. *easóg*, pheasant (Fol.), weasel, squirrel. For the "squirrel-weasel" force, see *neas*, *nios*. As "pheasant," it may be founded on the M. Eng. *fesaunt*, O. Fr. *faisan*.

easaraich, boiling of a pool, ebullition, bustle; from G. and Ir. **easar**, a cataract, from *eas*. **ess-rad-?*

easar-chasain, thorough-fare; cf. *aisir*.

easbalair, a trifling, handsome fellow (M'A.):

easbaloid, absolution, Ir. *easbalóid*; from Lat. *absolutio*.

easbhuidh, want, defect, so Ir., E. Ir. *esbuid*, **ex-buti-s*, "being out" of it; from roots of *as* and *bu*, q.v.

easbuig, a bishop, Ir. *easbog*, O. Ir. *espoc*, *epscop*, W. *esgob*, Br. *eskop* ; from Lat. *episcopus*, whence Eng. *bishop*.

†**easg,** a ditch, fen, Ir. *easgaidh*, quagmire, *easc*, water, E. Ir. *esc*, water, fen-water, O. British Ἴσκα, the *Exe*, [Scotch *Esks*], **iskâ*, water, **(p)idskâ* ; Gr. πῖδαξ, well, πιδύω, gush. The W. *wysg*, stream, O. W. *uisc* requires, **eiskâ*, from *peid*, *pîd*.

easg, easgann, eel, Ir. *eascu*, g. *eascuinne*, O. Ir. *escung*, "fen-snake," i.e., *esc*, fen, and *ung*, snake, Lat. *anguis*. See *easg*, ditch.

†**easga,** the moon (a name for it surviving in Braemar last century), O. Ir. *ésca*, *ésce*, *æsca*, **eid-skio-* ; from root *eid*, *îd*, as in Lat. *idus*, the *ides*, "full light," i.e., full moon (Stokes) : **encscaio-*, Skr. *pñjas*, light, Gr. φέγγος, light (Strachan).

easgaid, hough ; better *iosgaid*, q.v.

èasgaidh, ready, willing, Ir. *éasguidh*, E. Ir. *escid*, W. *esgud*, Br. *escuit* ; from *eu-* and *sgìth*, q.v.

easgraich, a torrent, coarse mixture ; see *easg*.

easp, door latch (Lewis) ; Norse, *hespa* (do.).

easradh, ferns collected to litter cattle, E. Ir. *esrad*, strewing, **ex-sratu-*, root *ster*, strew, Lat. *sternere*, etc. See *casair*, bed, under *caisil-chrò*.

easraich, boiling of a pool, bustle ; see *easaraich*.

eathar, a boat, Ir. *eathar*, ship, boat, O. Ir. *ethar*, a boat, **itro-*, "journeyer" ; from *ethaim*, I go, **itâo*, go, root *ei*, *i* ; Lat. *eo* ; Gr. εἶμι ; Lit. *eimi* ; Skr. *émi*.

eatorra, between them, so Ir., O. Ir. *etarro*, **etr̥-so*, **enter-sôs*. For *sôs*, see *sa*.

éibh, cry ; see *éigh*.

eibheadh, the aspen, letter *e*, Ir. *eadha* ; also *eadhadh*, q.v.

éibheall, éibhleag, a live coal, spark, Ir. *eibhleóg*, E. Ir. *óibell*, spark, fire, W. *ufel*, fire, **oibelos*, fire, spark (Stokes).

éibhinn, joyous ; see *aoibhinn*.

eibhrionnach, eirionnach, a young gelded goat ; from Sc. *aiver* (do.), with G. termination of *firionnach*, etc. *Aiver* is also *aver*, worthless old horse, any property, Eng. *aver*, property, from Lat. *habere*.

éideadh, éididh, clothing, a suit ; see *aodach*.

eidheann, ivy, Ir. *eidhean*, E. Ir. *edenn*, W. *eiddew*, Cor. *idhio*, **(p)edenno-*, root *ped*, fasten, hold on ; Lat. *pedica*, a fetter ; Eng. *fetter*, etc. For sense, cf. Lat *hedera*, ivy, from *ghed*, catch, *prœhendo*, Eng. *get*.

eididh, a web ; apparently a shortened form of *éideadh*.

éifeachd, effect, so Ir. ; from Lat. *effectus*.

eige, a web, **eididh** (on analogy of **éididh**), **veggiâ*, root of *figh*.

eigh, ice ; see *deigh*. Hence **eighre, oighre**, Ir. *oidhir*, E. Ir. *aigred*, W. *eiry*, snow.

eigh, a file, Ir. *oighe* : **agiâ* ; root *ag* of Eng. *axe*, Got. *aqizi*.

éigh, a cry, Ir. *éigheamh*, O. Ir. *égem*, Celtic root *eig* ; Lettic *ígt*. Cf. also Lat. *aeger* (Stokes, Zim.).

eighreag, a cloudberry ; see *oighreag*.

éiginn, necessity, Ir. *éigin*, O. Ir. *écen*, W. *angen*, **enknâ* (Stokes) ; Gr. ἀνάγκη (=ἀν-άγκη). Allied by root (*ank : enk*) to *thig*, etc.

eildeir, an elder ; from the Scotch, Eng. *elder*.

eile, other, another, Ir. *eile*, O. Ir. *aile*, W. *aill*, *all*, Br. *eil*, *all*, Gaul. *allo-*, **aljo-*, **allo-* ; Lat. *alius* ; Gr. ἄλλος ; Eng. *else*.

eileach, mill-race, mill-dam, embankment ; from *ail*, stone, "stone-work."

eilean, an Island, Ir. *oilean*, E. Ir. *ailén* ; from Norse *eyland*, Eng. *island*.

eilean, training ; see *oilean*.

eileir, the notch on the staves of a cask where the bottom is fixed. (In Arg. *èarrach*) :

eileir, a deer's walk, **eileirig**, where deer were driven to battue them. Hence the common place-name *Elrick*. Bk. of Deer *in d-elerc* ?

eileir, sequestered region, etc. ; see *eilthir*.

eilgheadh, levelling of a field for sowing, first ploughing ; cf. Ir. *eillgheadh*, burial, to which Stokes cfs. Umbrian *pelsatu*, Gr. θάπτειν, *pelsans*, sepeliundus. H. Maclean compared the Basque *elge*, field.

eilid, a hind, so Ir., O. Ir. *elit*, W. *elain*, cerva, **elinti-s*, **elanî*, Gr. ἐλλός, fawn, ἔλαφος (=ἔλνφος), stag ; Lit. *élnis*, stag ; Arm. *eλn* ; etc.

eilig, willow-herb, epilobium ; from Lat. *helix*.

eilitriom, a bier (H.S.D. for Heb.), Ir. *eletrom*, *eleathrain*, M. Ir. *eilitrum* ; from Lat. *feretrum* (Stokes).

eilthir, a foreign land, **eilthireach**, a pilgrim, Ir. *oilithreach*, O. Ir. *ailithre*, pilgrimage ; from *eile* and *tìr*, q.v.

eiltich, rejoice :

eineach, bounty, Ir. *oineach*. Cf. O. Ir. *ainech*, protectio, root *nak*, attain, as in *tiodhlac*. Hence the H.S.D. **eineachlann**, protection (from Ir.).

eirbhe, dyke or wall between crop-land and hill-land (M'F.). :

eirbheirt, moving, stirring ; E. Ir. *airbert*, use, *airbiur*, dego, fruor : *air* and *beir*, q.v.

eirbhir, asking indirectly : "side-say" ; *air* + *beir* ; cf. *abair*.

eirbleach, slack-jointed or crippled person; cf. Sc. *hirplock*, lame creature, *hirple*. The possibility of *air-ablach* (cf. *conablach*) should be kept in view.

eirc-chomhla, portcullis (M'D.):

eire, a burden, Ir. *eire*, E. Ir. *ere*, O. Ir. *aire*: **pario*, root of *air*. Cf. Lat. *porto*.

eireachd, an assembly, Ir. *óireachdus*, E. Ir. *airecht*, O. Ir. *airect*, **air-echt*, *echt* being from the root of *thig*. Stokes refers it to the same origin as W. *araeth*, speech, root *req*, as in O. Slav. *reka*, speak, Lat. *raccare*, cry as a lion.

eireachdail, handsome, O. Ir. *airegde*, præstans, from *aire*(*ch*), primas. See *airidh*.

eireag, a pullet, young hen, Ir. *eireog* (Fol., O'R.), M. Ir. *eirin*, W. *iaren*, Cor. *yar*, gallina, Br. *iarik*, **jari-*, hen; Lit. *jerubė*, heathcock, N. Slav. *jertŭ*, nuthatch (Bez.).

eireallach, a monster, clumsy old carle (Dial., H.S.D); from *eire*.

eiriceachd, heresy, so Ir., E. Ir. *éres*, O. Ir. *heretic*, hereticus; from the O. Ir. form somehow, which itself is from Lat. *hœreticus*.

éirich, rise, **éirigh,** rising, Ir. *éirighim*, *éirghe*, E. Ir. *érigim*, *éirgim*, inf. O. Ir. *éirge*, *érge*, **eks-regô*; Lat. *ērigo*, erect, Eng. *erect*, *rego*, I govern; Gr. *ὀρέγω*, extend; Eng. *right*; I. E. root *reg*. See *rach*.

eiridinn, attendance, patience, O. Ir. *airitiu*, g. *airiten*, reception, *airema*, suscipiat, **ari-em-tin-*, root *em*, grasp, take; Lat. *emo*, buy; Lit. *imù*, hold.

éirig, ransom, Ir. *éiric*, E. Ir. *éric*, *éiricc*: **es-recc*, "buying or selling out," from *reic*. Vb. *as-renim*, reddo, enclitic *érnim*, impendo.

eirmis, hit, find out, O. Ir. *ermaissiu*, attaining, *irmadatar*, intelligunt, *irmissid*, intelligatis, **air-mess-*, **air-med-*; root, *med*, as in *meas*, judgment, q.v.

éis, delay, impediment; founded on *déis?*

éisd, listen, hear, Ir. *éisdim*, O. Ir. *étsim*. Ascoli analyses it into **étiss*, **aith-do-iss*, animum instare; the *iss* he doubtless means as from the reduplicated form of the root *sta* (cf. O. Ir. *air-issim*, I stand). *an-tus-*, great silence! Cf. Ir. *éist do bhéal* = hush! Root of *tosd*.

eisg, eisgear, satirist, Ir. *eigeas*, pl. *eigse*, a learned man, E. Ir. *écess*: **ád-gen-s-to?* See *eagna*.

eisimeil, dependence, obligation, M. Ir. *esimol*, *an esimul*, **ex-em-mo-lo*, root *em* of *eudail*. Cf. Lat. *exemplum*.

eisiomplair, example, Ir. *eisiompláir*, M. Ir. *esimplair*; from Lat. *exemplar*.

eisir, eisiridh, oyster, Ir. *eisir*, *.oisre*; from M. Eng. *oistre*, from Lat. *ostrea*.

eisleach, the withe that ties the tail-beam to the pack-saddle, crupper:

éislean, grief: **an-slàn*; cf. Ir. *eislinn*, weak, E. Ir. *eslinn* (do.): **ex-slàn*; see *slàn*.

eislinn, boards on which the corpse is laid, a shroud (H.S.D., from MSS.; M'E.):

eite, unhusked ear of corn (M'E.):

éite, éiteadh, stretching, extending:

eiteach, burnt roots of heath:

éiteag, white pebble, precious stone; from Eng. *hectic*, lapis *hecticus*, the white hectic stone, used as a remedy against dysentery and diarrhœa (Martin, *West. Isles*, 134). See *eitig*.

eitean, a kernel, grain, Ir. *eitne*, *eithne*, E. Ir. *eitne* (n.).

eithich, false, perjured, Ir. *eitheach*, a lie, perjury, O. Ir. *ethech*, perjurium; root *pet*, fall? Cf. Ir. *di-thech*, denial on oath, *for-tach*, admission on oath, *di-tongar i. séntar*, *fortoing*, proved by oath: **tongô*, swear. See *freiteach* for root.

eitich, refuse, Ir. *eitighim*. For root, etc., see under *freiteach*.

éitigh, fierce, dismal, O. Ir. *étig*, turpe, *adétche*, abomination. Scarcely **an-teg-*, "un-wonted, un-*house*-like" (Zim.), for G. would be *éidigh*. This Stokes (Bez. Beit [21]) makes **an-teki-s*, not fair, W. *têg*, fair, Gr. τίκτω, produce, τέκνον, child, Eng. *thing*. Still G. should be *éidigh*.

eith, go (Sutherland), **dh' eithinn,** would go, Ir. *eathaim*, E. Ir. *ethaim*, **itâô*; root *ei*, *i*; Lat. *ire*, *itum*; Gr. εἶμι, etc.

eitig, consumption; from Sc. *etick*, from Fr. *étique*, *hectique*, Eng. *hectic*.

eitreach, storm, sorrow: **aith-ter-*? See *tuirse*.

eòisle, a charm; a metathesis of *eòlas*.

eòl, eòlas, knowledge, Ir. *eól*, *eólas*, E. Ir. *eólas*, O. Ir. *heulas*, *d-eulus*: **ivo-lestu*?

eòrna, barley, Ir. *eórna*, E. Ir. *eorna*, **jevo-rnıo-*, **jevo-*; Gr. ζειά, spelt; Skr. *yáva*, corn, barley; Lit. *jawai*, corn.

eothanachadh, languishing (H.S.D. gives it as Dial.; M'E.); see *feodhaich*.

eu-, negative prefix, Ir. *ea-*, *éu-*, O. Ir. *é-*. It stands for *an-* before *c*, *t*, *p*, and *s*. See *an-*.

eucail, disease: *an* + *cáil*, q.v.

euchd, a feat, exploit, Ir. *éachd*, feat, covenant, condition; E. Ir. *écht*, murder, slaughter, from *éc* (St.).

euchdag, a fair maid, a charmer: "featsome one," from *euchd*.

eud, jealousy, zeal, Ir. *éad*, O. Ir. *ét*, W. *addiant* (= *add-iant*), longing, regret, Gaul. *iantu-* in Iantumarus, **jantu-*; Skr.

yatná, zeal; Gr. ζητέω, seek, ζῆλος, zeal, Eng. *zeal*; root *jâ*, *jat*, strive.

eudail, treasure, cattle, Ir. *éadáil*, *eudáil*, profit, prey, E. Ir. *étail*, treasure, booty, E. Ir. *ét*, herds, riches: **em-tâli-*, root *em*, hold, as in Lat. *emo* (see *eiridinn*). Also **feudail.** *éd* = *áirneis no spréidh*, O'Cl.

eug, death, Ir. *eug*, O. Ir. *éc*, W. *angeu*, Cor. and O. Br. *ancou*, **enku-s*, **enkevo-*; Lat. *nex*, death; Gr. νέκυς, corpse; Skr. *naç*, perish.

eugail, disease; see *eucail.*

eugais, eugmhais, as eugais, without, Ir. *éagmhuis*, want, dispensation, E. Ir. *écmais*: **an-comas*, "non-power"?

eug-, negative prefix, as in **eugsamhuil** = *an-con-samuil*; see *cosmhail.*

euladh, creeping away; see *èaladh.*

eumhann, a pearl (H.S.D. from MSS.), O. Ir. *ném*, g. *némann*, pearl, *níam*, sheen, *níamda*, bright, W. *nwyf*, vigour, *nwyfiant*, brightness, vigour: **neim*. Cf. *neamhnuid.*

eun, a bird, Ir. *eun*, O. Ir. *én*, O. W. *etn*, W. *edn*, Cor. *hethen*, Br. *ezn*, **etno-s*, **petno-*, root *pet*, fly; Gr. πέτομαι, fly, πετηνά, fowls; Lat. *penna*, wing; Eng. *feather*; Skr. *pátati*, fly. Hence **eunlaith**, birds, E. Ir. *énlaith.*

eur, refuse, Ir. *eura*, refusal, E. Ir. *éra*, *eraim*, **ex-rajo-* (n.), root *râ*, give, W. *rhoi*, give, Cor. *ry*, Br. *reiff*, give; Skr. *ráti*, give, Zend *râ*. See *rath*, luck, favour.

F

fa, under, Ir. *fa*, E. Ir. *fa* (as in distributive numbers); a side form of *fo*, q.v., used in adverbial expressions.

†**fa**, was (past of **is**), M. G. *fa* (D. of Lis.), Ir. *fa*, *fa h-* (Keat.), M. Ir. *fa h-*, E. Ir. *ba h-*, **bât*, *(*e*)*bhv-â-t*; Lat. *-bat*, *-bamus*, of *rege-bam*, etc.; root *bheu*, to be. See *bu*, the form now used.

fabhairt, fadhairt, forging, moulding (better **faghairt,** "tempering" (Wh.), which suits the pronunciation best); Ir. *faghairt*, tempering (Keat.); founded on Lat. *faber*, smith, whence, through Fr., Eng. *forge.*

fàbhar, favour, Ir. *fábhar*, W. *ffafr*; from Lat. *favor.*

fabhd, a fault; from Sc. *faut*, from Fr. *faute.*

fabhra, fabhrad, abhra, eyelid, eyebrow, Ir. *abhra*, *fabhra*, eyelid, E. Ir. *abra*, n. pl. *abrait*, Cor. *abrans*, Br. *abrant*, eyebrow, Mac. Gr. ἀβροῦτες; further ὀφρύς, brow, Eng. *brow*. There is an E. Ir. *bra*, pl. *brói*, dual *brúad*, **bruvat-*. The phonetics are not clear. Stokes has suggested Lat. *frons*, *frontis*, as allied, **bhront-* with the prep. *a*(*p*)*o* (= E. Ir. *-a-*), ab.

fabhradh, swirl, eddy (Carm.). Cf. O. Ir. *fobar* (St.).

facal, focal, word, Ir. *focal,* O. Ir. *focul,* from Lat. *vocabulum* (through **focvul,* Güterbock). Stokes and Wind. take it from Lat. *vocula.*

fachach, the puffin—a water fowl (Sh.); root *va,* blow? Onomatopoetic: *f-ah-ah,* call of bird?

fachail, strife (Sh.; H.S.D. marks it Dialectic); cf. Ir. *fachain,* striving.

fachant, puny (H.S.D. for N. High.):

fachaint, ridicule, scoffing; from *fo-cainnt,* "sub-speaking." Cf. W. *gogan,* satire, Br. *goge,* **vo-can,* root *can,* sing, say.

fad, fada, long, Ir. *fada,* O. Ir. *fota,* longus, *fot,* length, **vad-dho-* or *vaz-dho-,* Lat. *vastus,* vast? Hence **fadal,** delay, desiderium, Keat. *faddáil,* "long delay," from *fad* and *dáil.*

fàdadh, fadadh, kindling, Ir. *fadadh, fadaghadh, fadógh* (Keat.), Mid. Ir. *fatód,* E. Ir. *átúd,* which Zimmer analyses as **ad-soud* (*soud* of *iompaidh*), but unsatisfactorily; E. Ir. *adsúi* tenid, kindles, *adsúithe,* kindled (Meyer). Cf. *fód.*

fadharsach, trifling, paltry, **fagharsach**:

fadhbhag, cuttle-fish:

fafan, a breeze:

fàg, leave, Ir. *fágaim,* O. Ir. *foacbaim, fácbaim,* **fo-ad-gab-*; root *gab* of *gabh,* q.v.

fagus, faisg, near, Ir. *fogus,* E. Ir. *focus, ocus,* O. Ir. *accus,* W. *agos,* Br. *hôgoz,* **aggostu-.* See *agus.*

faic, see, Ir. *faic,* O. Ir. *im-aci,* vides-ne, **ád-cî-,* see *chì.* The *f* is prothetic.

faich, faiche, a green (by the house), Ir., E. Ir. *faithche,* the field nearest the house, E. Ir. *faidche,* **ad-cáio-,* "by the house," Celtic *kaio-n,* house; see *ceardach.* Ascoli refers it to O. Ir. *aith,* area (an imaginary word), and Jubainville allies it with W. *gwaen,* plain, Ger. *weide* (see *bhàn* for W.).

faiche, a crab, or lobster's, burrow (M'A.); see *aice*:

faichd, hiding place, den, mole's burrow; see *aice.*

faicheil, stately, showy; cf. Ir. *faicheallach,* luminous:

faicill, caution, guard, E. Ir. *accill,* preparation, watch: **ád-ciall*; from *ciall,* sense? Cf. *dìchioll.*

fàidh, a prophet, Ir. *fáidh,* O. Ir. *fáith,* **vâti-s*; Lat. *vates*; Norse *óðr,* sense, song, M. Eng. *wood,* Sc. *wud* (=mad), Ger. *wuth,* rage. W. has *gwawd,* carmen: **vâto-.*

faidhbhile, a beech, Ir. *feagha, fagh-vile* (Lh., *Comp. Voc.*), W. *ffawydden,* Br. *fao*; from Lat. *fagus.* G. adds the old word *bile,* a tree, which is the same in origin as *bile,* leaf.

faidhir, a fair, Ir. *faidhrín*; founded on Eng. *fair*, *faire* (from Lat. *feria*). For phonetics, cf. *paidhir* from *pair*, and *staidhir* from *stair*.

faidseach, lumpish (Sh.); **faidse**, lump of bread (M'A.):

faigh, get, Ir. *faghaim*, E. Ir. *fagbaim*, O. Ir. *ní fogbai*, non invenis, from *fo-gabim*, root *gab* of *gabh*, q.v.

faighe, begging, etc.; see *faoighe*.

faighnich, **foighnich**, ask: **vo-gen-*, root *gen*, know, as in *aithne*. Cf. E. Ir. *imma foacht*, asked. Windisch refers to *iar-faigim*, *iarfacht*, I asked, =*iarmifoacht*, root *ag*, say. *iarmi-fo-siag* (St. R.C.[19] 177).

fail, **foil**, corrupt, putrefy, parboil; root *vel*, bubble, boil; Norse *vella*, boil, Eng. *well*, Ger. *wallen*, bubble.

fail, **foil**, a stye, Ir. *fail*, O. Ir. *foil*, *mucc-foil*, hara, *trét-fhoil*, W. *gwâl*, couch, **vali-*, root *vel*, cover, encircle; Gr. εἰλύω, envelop (**velu-*), εἶλαρ, shelter; Skr. *valá*, cave, *vali*, projecting thatched roof. In the sense of "encircling, rolling," add Lat. *volvo*, *volumen*, Eng. *volume*, *wallow*, etc. Further allied is G. *olann*, wool, Eng. *wool*, Lat. *lâna*, etc.

fail, **fàil**, a ring, Ir. **fáil**, O. Ir. *foil*, g. *falach*, **valex*; Gr. ἕλιξ, a twist, spire, vine-tendril; root *vel*, "circle," as above in *fail*. Cf. for vowel *fàl*, dike; Br. *gwalen*, "bague sans chaton." Also **failbhe**, Ir. *failge*, for **failghe**; from the stem *falach* or *falagh* condensed to *falgh*.

failc, bathe, lave, Ir. *folcadh*, O. Ir. *folcaim*, W. *golchi*, Br. *goalc'hi*, wash, **volkô*; Lettic *wa'lks*, damp, *wa'lka*, flowing water, swampish place. Further allied is G. *fliuch*, q.v. Possibly here place *Volcae*, the Rhine Gauls, after whom the Teutons named the Celts; whence *Wales*, *Welsh*, etc.

failcin, pot-lid (Arran), **failceann** (Rob.); from *fail*, ring (Rob.).

fàile, smell, savour; see *àile*.

fàileag, dog-brier berry (=*mucag*):

faileagan, little lawns (Carm.): cf. *àilean*.

faileas, shadow, **aileas** (Dial.); from *fo-leus*? or allied to *ail*, mark?

failleagan, **ailleagan**, **faillean**, root or hole of the ear, **faillean**, sucker of a tree: **al-nio-*, root *al*, nourish?

fàillig, **fàilnich**, fail, **fàillinn**, failing, Ir. *faillighim*, E. Ir. *faill*, failure, W. *gwall*, Br. goall, **valni-*; root *val* of *feall*, q.v. Borrowing from Eng. *fail*, from Lat. *fallo*, is, however, possible in the modern languages.

failm, a helm; from the Norse *hjálm*, Eng. *helm*.

failmean, kneepan (M'A.); from *fail*, ring (Rob.). See *falman*.

fàilt, **fàilte**, welcome, hail! Ir., O. Ir. *fáilte*, **vâletiâ*, root *vâl*, *vel*, glow; W. *gwawl*, lumen; Gr. ἀλέα, warmth, sun's heat; Got.

vulan, be hot, O. H. G. *walm*, heat (Bez.). Cf. Cæsar's *Valetiacus*. Borrowing from Lat. *valête* seems to be Zimmer's view (Zeit. [30] 28). Rhys suggests W. *gwell*; Hend., Eng. *wealth*.

fainear, under consideration, Ir. *fa deára*, remark, *fé ndeár*, *fé ndeara* (Munster). Foley gives *tabhair fa d' aire* = "observe." "Thoir fainear" = observe, consider. The above may be a fixed *fa d' aire* = *fa-deara*, with *n* from the plural *an*, their.

fainleag, ainleag, a swallow, Ir. *áinleóg*, O. Ir. *fannall*, W. *gwennol*, Cor. *guennol*, Br. *gwenneli*, **vannello-*. Cf. Fr. *vanneau*, lapwing, It. *vannello*, Med. Lat. *vannellus*, which is usually referred to Lat. *vannus*, fan. **vat-n-allo-s* (Holden).

fàinne, a ring, Ir. *fáinne*, *áinne*, O. Ir. *ánne*, **ânniâ*; Lat, *ânus*, Eng. *annular*.

fair, fàir, far, fetch, bring; a curtailed form of *tabhair* through *thabhair* or (*tha*)*bhair* ? Cf. *thoir*.

fàir, dawn, E. Ir. *fáir*, W. *gwawr*, Br. *gouere-*, morning, *gwereleuen*, morning-star, **vâsri-*, Lit. *vasará*, summer, Skr. *vâsará*, early shining, morning (adj.), Lat. *ver*, spring, Gr. *ἔαρ*, spring (Stokes).

fàir, fàire, ridge, sky-line; from **fàir,** dawn? Cf., however, Ir. *faireóg*, hillock, and *fàireag*, below.

fairc, bathe; see *fathraig*.

fairc, links, lands sometimes covered by the sea (M'A., who says that in Islay it means "hole"); from Eng. *park* ?

fairce, fairche (M'D.), a mallet, Ir. *farcha*, *farcha*, *farca*, M. Ir. *farca*, E. Ir. *forcha tened*, thunderbolt; root *ark* as in *adharc* ?

faircill, a cask or pot lid, E. Ir. *farcle* : **vor-cel-*, root *cel*, cover.

faire, watching, Ir., E. Ir. *faire*; see *aire*.

fàireag, a gland, swollen gland, Ir. *fáireóg* (Fol., O'R.); cf. W. *chwaren*, gland, blotch, root *sver*, hurt, Ger. *schwer*, difficult. The W. precludes comparison with Lat. *vărus*, pimple, *varix*, dilated vein, Eng. *varicose*.

fairge, the ocean, Ir. *fairrge*, O. Ir. *fairgge*, Ptolemy's *Vergivios*, the Irish Atlantic; from the same root as *fearg*. In Sutherland *fairge* means the "ocean in storm." Usually pronounced as if *fairce*. W. *Môr Werydd*, the Atlantic.

fairgneadh, hacking, sacking:

fairich, perceive, feel, Ir. *airighim*, O. Ir. *airigur*, sentio; same root as *faire* (Stokes, Beit. [8] 341).

fairleas, an object on the sky-line (H.S.D. from MSS.); **f-air-leus*; from *leus*, light.

fairmeil, noisy: allied to *seirm*. See *foirm* ?

fairsing, wide, Ir., O. Ir. *fairsing*, W. *eang* (= **ex-ang*, *ehang*), **f-ar-ex-ang* : "un-narrow," root *ang*, narrow (Stokes for W.).

fairtlich, fairslich, baffle; **vor-tl̥-*, "over-bear," root *tel*, *tol*, bear (Lat. *tolero*, Eng. *tolerate*)?
faisg, pick off vermin: for root see *caisg*
faisg, near: see *fagus*.
fàisg, squeeze, wring, Ir. *fáisg*, E. Ir. *faiscim*, W. *gwasgu*. premere, O. Br. *guescim*, Br. *goascaff*, stringere, **vakshô*; Skr. *vâhate*, press; Eng. *wedge*; further Lat. *vexo*. **fo-ad-sech* (Asc.).
fàisne, a pimple, weal (H.S.D., Dial.):
fàisneachd, fàistine, prophecy, omen, Ir. *fáisdineachd*, *fáisdine*, O. Ir. *fáitsine*; for *fáith-sine*, where *th* is deaspirated before *s*; from *fáith*, with the termination *-sine* (*-stinet*) Zeuss² 777.
faisneis, speaking, whispering, Ir. *fáisnéis*, rehearsal, M. Ir. *faisnéis*, E. Ir. *aisnéis*, vb. *aisnédim*, narrate, **as-in-feid-*, *infiadim*, root, *veid*, *vid*, know; see *innis*.
fàite, a smile, Ir. *faitbe* (O'R.), laugh, O. Ir. *faitbim*, I laugh, **fo-aith-tibim*, *tibiu*, I laugh, **stebiô*; Lit *stebiûs*, astonish.
faiteach, fàiteach, timorous, shy, Ir. *fáiteach*, *faitcheas*, fear (Keat.), O. Ir. *faitech*, cautus: **f-ad-tech*, "home-keeping"?
fàitheam, a hem, Ir. *fáithim*, *fathfhuaim*; *fo* and *fuaim*. See *fuaigh*.
fàl, turf, sods, dike, Ir. *fál*, hedge, fold, O. Ir. *fál*, saepes, W. *gwawl*, rampart, Pictish *fahel*, murus, **vâlo-*; Lat. *vallum*, Eng. *wall*. See further under *fail*, stye.
fàl, a spade, peat spade, Manx *faayl*, W. *pâl*, Cor. *pal*; from Lat. *pâla*. Also "scythe" (Wh.).
falach, a hiding, covering, Ir., E. Ir. *folach*, W., Br. *golo*, **vo-lugô*, **lugô*, hide, lie; Got. *liugan*, tell a lie, Eng. *lie* (Stokes). Ernault refers it to the root *legh*, *logh*, lie, as in G. *laighe*: "under-lie," in a causative sense.
falachd, spite, malice, treachery, Ir. *fala*. See *fàillig*, *feall* for root.
faladair, orts (M'D.):
fàladair, a scythe, really "man who works the scythe," a turfer, from *fàl*: "scythe" properly is *iarunn fàladair*.
fàladair, bare pasture (H.S.D. for Heb.): "turf-land," from *fàl*.
fala-dhà, a jest, irony, fun; see *fealla-dhà*.
falair, an interment, funeral entertainment (Stew.) =*farair*?
fàlaire, an ambler, mare, Ir. *falaire*, ambling horse; seemingly founded on Eng. *palfrey*. The form **àlaire** exists, in the sense of "brood-mare" (M'Dougall's *Folk and Hero Tales*), leaning upon *àl*, brood, for meaning. Ir. *falaradh*, to amble.
falaisg, heath-burning, Ir. *folosg* (do.), E. Ir. *foloiscim*, I burn slightly; from *fo* and *loisg*, q.v.

falamh, empty, Ir. *folamh*, M. Ir. *folum*, E. Ir. *folom*, *folomm*; cf. O. W. *guollung*, M. Br. *gollo*, Br. *goullo*. Windisch derives the G. from *lom*, bare, but the modern aspiration of *folamh* makes this derivation doubtful. Ernault refers the Br. to the root of Lat. *langueo*.

falbh, go, **falbhan**, moving about, walking, waving, Ir. *foluamhain*, bustling, running away, E. Ir. *folúamain*, flying; see *fo* and *luainech*. O. Ir *fulumain*, volubilis, allied to Lat. *volvo*, Eng. *wallow*, would suit the phonetics best, but it does not appear in the later dialects. The verb *falbh* is made from *falbhan*. Hennessey referred the G. to *falamh*, empty. Cf. E. Ir. *falmaigim*, empty, quit (Zim.).

falbhair, the young of live stock, a follower as a calf or foal; from the Sc. *follower*, a foal, Eng. *follower*.

falcag, common auk, **falc** (Heb.); from Norse *álka*, Eng. *auk*.

fallaid, dry meal put on cakes:

fallain, healthy, Ir. *fallάin*, E. Ir. *follán*; for *fo* + *slàn*, q.v.

fallsa, false (M'D.), Ir., M. Ir. *fallsa*; from the Lat. *falsus*.

falluing, a mantle, so Ir., M. Ir. *fallaing*, Latinised form *phalingis* (Geraldus), dat. pl., W. *ffaling*; from Lat. *palla*, mantle, *pallium*. Cf. O. Fr. *pallion*, M. Eng. *pallioun*. M.E. *falding*, sort of coarse cloth (Hend.).

fallus, sweat, Ir. *fallus*, *allus*, O. Ir. *allas*: **jasl*, root *jas*, *jes*, seethe, yeast, W. *jas*, what pervades, Br. *goell* (= *vo-jes-l*), leaven; Eng. *yeast*, *zeal*; Gr. ζέω, boil.

falmadair, the tiller: "helm-worker," from **falm**, helm, from Norse *hjálm*, helm. See *failm*.

falmair, a kind of fish (H.S.D. for Heb.), **falmaire**, herring hake:

falman, kneepan:

falt, hair, Ir. *folt*, O. Ir. *folt*, W. *gwallt*, Cor *gols*, caesaries, O. Br. *guolt*, **valto-s* (Stokes), root *vel*, cover; Lat. *vellus*, fleece, *lána*, wool, Gr. λάσιος, hairy (= *vlatios*); Eng. *wool*; Lit. *velti*, hairs, threads. Stokes compares only Russ. *volotĭ*, thread, Lit. *waltis*, yarn, Gr. λάσιος. Same root as *olann*, wool, **vel*, **vol*, **ul*.

faltan, a tendon, snood; for *altan*, from *alt*.

famhair, a giant, Ir. *fomhor*, pirate, giant, E. Ir. *fomór*, *fomórach*, a Fomorian, a mythic race of invaders of Ireland; **fo-mór*, "sub-magnus" (Zimmer). Stokes refers the *-mor*, *-morach*, to the same origin as *mare* of night*mare*, Ger. *mahr*, nightmare. Rhys interprets the name as "sub-marini," taking *mor* from the root of *muir*, sea. The *ó* of *mór*, if it is long (for it is rarely so marked) is against these last two derivations.

famhsgal, **fannsgal**, hurry, confusion (Arg.):

famh-thalmhainn, fath, a mole, **fadhbh** (Lh.), W. *gwadd*, Corn. *god*, Br. *goz* ; M. Eng. *wont*, talpa. Dialectic **ath-thalmhain.**

fan, stay, Ir. *fanaim*, O. Ir. *anaim* ; root *an*, breathe, exist, as in *anam*, *anail* : "gabhail anail" = taking rest. Stokes suggests *an* = *m̥n*, root *men*, remain, Lat. *maneo*, Gr. *μένω*, a phonetic change not yet proved for Gaelic. W. *di-anod*, without delay.

fanaid, mockery, Ir. *fonomhad*, E. Ir. *fonomat* : **vo-nom-anto-*, root *nem*, take, for which see *nàmhad.*

fanaigse, dog violet (H.S.D. quoting O'R.), Ir., *fanaigse* (O'R.) : from *pansy ?*

fànas, a void space ; from Lat. *vanus.*

fang, a sheep-pen, fank ; from Sc. *fank.*

fang, a vulture, Ir. *fang*, raven.

fann, faint, Ir. E Ir. *fann*, W., Br. *gwan*, Cor. *guan*, debilis, **vanno-s*, root *vâ*, *ven*, spoil, wound ; Got. *wunns*, affliction, *winnan*, to suffer, Eng. *wound*, *wan* ; Gr *ἄτη*, infatuation, etc. Others have connected it with Lat. *vanus* and with Eng. *want.* *Fannan-feòir*, weak breeze (M'D.).

fannadh, fishing with a feathered hook (H.S.D. for Heb.) :

faob, an excrescence, knob, piece, Ir. *fadhb* (Lh.†), O. Ir. *odb*, obex, W. *oddf*, : **ud-bhv-o-*, "out-growth," root *bhu*, be (see *bu*). Stokes gives a Celtic **odbó-s*, from *eðgo-s*, *ozgo-s* (?), allied to Gr. *ὄσχη*, twig ? Lat. *obex* ; or to Lit. *ůdega*, tail. Lidén equates, Lat. *offa*, a ball. Stokes now *ὀσφύς.*

faobh, booty, Ir. *fadhbhaim*, I despoil, O. Ir. *fodb*, exuvias : **vodvo-*, from I. E. *vedh*, slay, thrust ; Skr. *vadh*, slay ; Gr. *ὠθέω*, push. The root may be *vedh*, pledge, Gr. *ἄεθλον*, war prize, Eng. *wager.*

faobhag, the common cuttle-fish (Heb.).

faobhar, edge, so Ir., E. Ir. *faebur*, O. Ir., *faibur*, machera, sword, **vaibro-s*, Lat. *vibro*, vibrate, brandish, Lit. *wyburti*, wag (Stokes). Cf. further W. *gwaew*, pl. *gweywyr*, a lance.

faoch, faochag, a periwinkle, Ir. *faochóg*, M. Ir. *faechóg* ; cf. W. *gwichiad.*

faoch, curve (Carm.) :

faochadh, a favourable crisis in sickness, relief ; see *faothaich.*

faochainn, entreat earnestly, strive, inf. **faochnadh** (M'A., Arg.) :

faochaire, knave (Carm.) :

faod, feud, may, Ir. *féadaim*, I can, E. Ir. *fétaim*, can, *sétar*, *seitir*, potest, **sventô* ; Got. *swinþs*, strong, Ag. S. *swíð* (do.), Norse, *svinnr*, clever, Ger. *geschwind*, swift (Stokes).

faodail, goods found by chance or lost, waif : "foundling," E. Ir. *étaim*, I find, **pentô*, Eng. *find.* See *eudail.*

faodhail, a ford, a narrow channel fordable at low water, a hollow in the sand retaining tide water : from N. *vaðill*, a shallow, a place where straits can be crossed, Shet. *vaadle*, Eng. *wade.*

faoghaid, faghaid, faodhailt, starting of game, hunting :

faoghar, a sound ; see rather *foghar.*

faoighe, faighdhe, begging, asking of aid in corn, etc., M. Ir. *faigde,* O. Ir. *foigde,* mendicatio, **fo-guide* ; from *fo* and *guidhe,* beg, q.v.

faoilidh, liberal, hospitable, Ir. **faoilidh,** joyful, O. Ir. *fáilidh,* blithe, **vâleti-s,* allied to *fáilt,* welcome (Stokes). Hence **faoilte,** welcome, delight. Root, **vil,* Gr. ἱλαρός, gay ?

faoileag, faoileann, a sea-gull, Ir. *faoileán,* O. Ir. *foilenn,* W. *gwylan,* Br. *gwelan,* whence Fr. *goëland* and Eng. *gull.* For root, Stokes compares Eng. *wail.*

faoilleach, faoillteach, the month extending from the middle of January to the middle of February, Ir. *faoillidh* (do.), *faoilleach* (do.), holidays, Carnival. The idea is "Carnival" or month of rejoicing ; from *faoilidh.* Usually referred to *faol,* wolf : "wolf-month." Cf. *féill.* February in Ir. = *mí na Féile Brighde.*

faoin, vain, void, Ir. *faon,* M. Ir. *faen,* weak :

faoisg, unhusk, **faoisgeag,** a filbert, unhusked nut, O. Ir. *áesc,* concha, *aesc,* classendix, Lat. *aesculus* ? (Stokes). Cf. W. *gweisgion,* husks, *gweisgioni,* to husk.

faoisid, faosaid, confession, Ir. *faoisidin,* O. Ir. *fóisitiu,* **vo-sestamtion-* (Stokes), *furoissestar,* confessus : *fo* and *seasamh,* q.v. Cf. Gr. ὑφίστημι, submit.

† **faol, faolchu,** a wolf, so Ir., E. Ir. *fáel, fael-chú,* W. *gweilgi,* the sea ("wild dog"), **vailo-s* ; Arm. *gail.*

faolainn, a stony beach (Heb.) : "the beach," *vaðlinn.*

faolum, learning ; see *foghlum.*

faomadh, fainting from closeness or excitement, falling (Lewis) ; from *aomadh.*

faondradh, wandering, exposure, O. Ir. *airndrethach,* errantia (= *air-ind-reth-*) ; G. is for *fo-ind-reth-,* root *ret,* run, of *ruith,* q.v. For *ind,* see *ionn-.*

faotainn, getting, E. Ir. *foemaim,* I receive, root *em,* grasp, hold, Lat. *emo.* G. is for **vo-em-tin-.*

faothaich, relieve, be relieved from fever, etc., Ir. *faothamh,* recovery after a crisis, alleviation : **fo-thàmh ?*

far, upon, **far an (am),** where, Ir. *mar a n-,* where ; from *mar* and rel., not from *for.*

far, with, **far rium,** with me, Ir. *a bh-farradh,* with (lit. "in company of," with gen.). See *farradh* and *mar ri.*

far, freight (a ship), Ir. *faraim, faraighim, farthadh* or *faradh,* a freight :

far, bring ; see *fair.*

far-, over; see *far*, upon, and *air* (b). **Far-ainm**, nick-name; **far-cluais**, listening; etc.

farachan, death watch beetle: "hammerer"; from *fairche*, hammer, Ir. *farachan*, a hammer (also Gaelic, Wh.). The possibility of its being from *faire* must not be overlooked.

faradh, a roost, Ir. *faradh* (do.), E. Ir. *forud*, a bench, seat, shelf: **for-sud*, root, *sed*, seat, as in *suidhe*, q.v. Cf. W. *gor-sedd*, a seat. E. Ir. *forad*, platform, **ver-podo-*.

faraich, a cooper's wedge; see *fairce*.

farail, a visit, inquiry for health; from *far* or *for* and *-ell-*, *-eln-*, go, root, *el*, as in Lat. *amb-ulare*, Gr. ἐλθεῖν. See further under *tadhal*.

faraire; see *forair*.

faraire, lykewake:

farasda, easy, gentle, Ir. *farasda*, *forasda*, solid, reasonable, "staid": **for-asda*; for *asda*, see *fasdadh*. *Farasda* is confused with *furasda*, q.v.

farbhail, a lid; from *far-bheul*, "super-os," from *beul*, mouth.

farbhalach, a stranger; for *falbhalach*, from *falbh*?

farbhas, a surmise; **far-meas*, from *meas*, judge. Cf. *eirmis*.

farbhas, noise:

fàrdach, a mansion, hearth, home; cf. *dachaidh*.

fàrdadh, alder bark for dyeing black (H.S.D., Dial.), lye, or any colour in liquid (M'A.); from *far* and *dath*?

fàrdal, delay, M. Ir. *fordall*, staying, E. Ir. *fordul*:

fardan, a farthing, Ir. *fardín*; from the Eng.

fàrdorus, lintel, Ir. *fárdorus*, E. Ir. *fordorus*, porch, W. *gwarddrws*, lintel; from *for*, *far* and *dorus*.

farfonadh, a warning (H.S.D.); see root in *fathunn*: **vor-svon*.

fargradh, a report: **vor-gar*, root *gar* as in *goir*.

fàrlus, chimney or roof-light, E. Ir. *forlés*; from *for* and *leus*, q.v. Cf. *àrlas*.

farmachan, a sand lark (H.S.D., Dial.):

farmad, envy, Ir. *formad*, O. Ir. *format*: **for-mad*, the *mad* being for *mento-* (**ver-mento-*, Stokes), root *men*, Lat. *mens*, Eng. *mind*. See *dearmad*.

farmail, a large pitcher (Heb.):

farpas, refuse of straw or hay (H.S.D., M'E.); cf. *rapas*.

farpuis, strife, **co-fharpuis**:

fàrr, off! be off!

farrach, violence, Ir. *farrach*, *forrach*; see *farran*.

†**farradh**, company, vicinity, M. G. *na warri* (D. of L.), Ir. *farradh*, E. Ir. *farrad*, *i fharrad*, near, O. Ir. *in arrad*; from *ar-sod-*, "by-seat," root *sod*, *sed*, sit, as in *suidhe*. Hence Ir. compound, prep. *a bh-farradh*; and from the same source comes the G. *mar ri*, q.v.

fàrradh, litter in a boat:
farragan, a ledge (Arran), =*faradh*, *dh* hardened.
farraid, ask, inquire; **faghairt** (Perth), which suggests *fo-gar-t*, root, *gar*, speak. Cf. *iarr*.
farral, farran, anger, force, Ir. *farrán*, vexation, anger, *forrán*, oppression, M. Ir. *forrán*, destruction, E. Ir. *forranach*, destructive. Hence G. **farranta,** great, stout, Ir. *farránta* (O'B.). Also **farrach.** The root seems to mean "superiority;" root *vers*, *vors*, as in *feàrr*, q.v. ?
farrusg, a peeling, inner rind; M. Ir. *forrusc*; from *for* and *rùsg*, q.v.
farruinn, pinnacle; from *far* and *rinn*.
farsaing, wide; better *fairsing*, q.v.
farspach, farspag, arspag, a seagull:
farum, noise, Ir. *fothrum*, E. Ir. *fothrom*, *fothrond*, W. *godornn*, tumultuous noise (Hend.); for *fo-thoirm*, from *toirm*. Stokes suggests *fo-thrond*, from *torann*. The roots are allied in either case
fàs, grow, Ir. *fásaim*, O. Ir. *ásaim*, *fásaim*, root *aux*, *aug*, increase, Lat. *augeo*, Gr. *αὔξω*, Eng. *eke*, *wax*. Stokes and Strachan refer *fás* to a stem *(p)ât-to-*, *pát*, *pat*, eat, feed, Gr. *πατέομαι*, eat, Eng. *feed*, *food*. Lat. *pasco*, *pastum*.
fàs, empty, waste, **fàsach,** a desert, Ir. *fás*, *fásach*, O. Ir. *fás*, *fáas*, vanus, *fásach*, desert: **vâsto-s*, a waste; Lat. *vastus*, vastare; Eng. *waste*, Ger. *wüste*. Hence **fàsan,** refuse of grain: "waste." *fásach*, desert, is neuter, see M'A. pref. VIII.
fasair, harness, girth-saddle; see *asair*.
fasan, fashion; from the Eng.
fasdadh, hiring, binding, Ir. *fastogh*, hiring , see *foisteadh*.
fasdail, astail, a dwelling, E. Ir. *fastud*, holding fast, vb. *astaim*, *fastaim*, O. Ir. *asstai*, moratur, *adsaitis*, residentes, **ad-sod-*, root, *sed*, *sod* of *suidhe* (Thur.). W. *eistedd*, sitting, is for **ex-sod-ijo*. It is possible to refer *astaim* to **ad-stâ-*, root *sta*, stand, Lat. *sto*; the *-asda* of *farasda*, "staid," seems from it (cf. *tairis*).
fasgadh, shelter, Ir. *fosgadh*, O. Ir. *foscad*, umbra: **fo-scáth*, "sub-umbra"; see *sgàth*, shade.
fasgaidh, a picking or cleansing off of vermin. See *faisg*. *fasgnadh* ?
fasgnadh, winnowing, **fasgnag, asgnag,** corn-fan, Ir. *fasgnaim*, I purge.
faspan, difficulty, embarrassment:
fath, a mole; see *famh*.
fàth, vista (Carm.):

fàth, a cause, reason, Ir. *fath, fáth*, E. Ir. *fáth*, : **vât-u-* ; root *vât* as in *fàidh ?* See next.
fathamas, a degree of fear, awe, a warning ; also **fothamas** : **fo-ted-mess-*, root of *meas, tomhas*, etc.
fathamas, occasion, opportunity : **fo-tad-mess-*, see *amas*.
fathan, athan, coltsfoot, Ir. *fathán* (O'R.) :
fathanach, trifling, silly :
fathraig, fothraig, bathe, Ir. *fothrugaim*, O. Ir. *fothraicim, fothaircthe*, balnearum, *fothrucud*, a bath, **vo-tronkatu-* (Stokes), W. *trochi*, mergere, balneare, Br. *go-zronquet* ; Lit. *trinkti*, wash, bathe (Bez.).
fathast, yet, M. Ir., E. Ir. *fodesta, fodechtsa*, for *fo-fecht-sa*, the *d* being otiose and caused by analogy (Zim., Zeit.[30] 21). Atkinson suggests with a query *fo'nd(fh)echt-sa*. The root word is *fecht*, time: "under this time, sub hoc tempus." See *feachd*, time. Hence also **feasd** (= *i fecht-sa*).
fathunn, news, floating rumour, **fabhunn** (Dial.) : **vo-svon*, root *sven*, sound (see *tabhann*), or root *bon, ban*, Eng. *ban*, O. Ir. *atboind*, proclaims ?
fè, fèath, (fèith, fiath), a calm, M. Ir. *feith*, E. Ir. *féth*, O. Ir. *féth*, Gadelic root *vei*, **ve-jo-*, root *ve, vê*, blow, Gr. ἀήρ, air, (whence Eng. *air*), Ger. *wehen*, to blow, Eng. *wind*, especially *weather* (root *vet*) for the G. sense.
feabhas, feobhas, goodness, "betterness," Ir. *feabhus*, O. Ir. *febas*, superiority, *feib*, distinction, **visus*, g. *vesv-iás* (Thur., Zeit.[28] 149, and Brug.), from *vesu-* or *vesv-*, as in *fiù*, q.v. Stokes doubtfully compares Lat. *vigeo*, Eng. *vigour* (Bez. Beit.[19] 75).
feachd, an army, host, expedition, Ir. *feachd*, an expedition, E. Ir. *fecht* (*ar fecht 7 sluagad*), W. *gwaith*, action, work. This Zimmer refers to O. Ir. *fichim*, I fight (Lat. *vinco*, Got. *veihan*, root *viq*), as well as †**feachd**, time, Ir. *feachd*, E. Ir. *fecht*, *oenfhecht*, once, W. *gwaith*, turn, *vicem*. Stokes separates the latter (**feachd**, time, E. Ir. *fecht*, journey), giving as stem *vektâ*, root *vegh* (Lat. *veho*, Eng. *waggon*) ; for *fecht*, campaign, hosting, he gives the Celtic *viktâ*, root *viq*, as Zimmer does. The words seem, as Stokes has it, from two roots, but now they are indistinguishably mixed. Osthoff regards *feachd*, time, as allied to Lat. *vices* ; see *fiach*.
fead, a whistle, Ir. *fead*, M. Ir. *fet-, fetán*, a flute, a whistle, W. *chwythell*, a whistle, *chwyth*, a blast, breath, **sviddo-*, **svizdo-*, Lat. *sibilus*, Eng. *sibilant*. See further under *séid*.
feadh, length, extent, so Ir. ; see *eadh*.
feadhainn, people, some people, troop, Ir. *feadhainn*, E. Ir. *fedain*, company, *cobeden* conjugatio, W. *gwedd*, team, yoke, root *ved*, I. E. *vedh*, Eng. *wed*, Lat. *vas, vadis*, surety, Skr. *vi-vadhá*, shoulder-yoke.

fealan (M'A. **feallan**), itch, hives; it also means "worm" (see *fiolan*), M. Ir. *filún*, glandular disease, *fiolún saith*, anthrax, malignant struma, all which Stokes takes from L. Lat. *fello*, strumae.

feall, treachery, Ir. *feall*, E. Ir. *fell* (*velno-), W. *gwall*, defect, Br. *goall* (do.), Cor. *gal*, malus, malum, Br. *gwall* (do.), root *vel*, cheat; Lit. *ap-vilti*, *vilióti*, cheat, Lett. *wilát*, deceitful; Norse *vél*, a deceit, wile, Eng. *wile*; Zend *vareta*, error. Stokes hesitates between the above and *vel* from *u(p)el*, Got. *ubils*, Eng. *evil*.

fealla-dhà, joking, irony: **feall+dhá*, "double-dealing."

feallsanach, philosopher, Ir. *feallsamhnach*, *feallsamh*, philosopher, O. Ir. *felsub*; from Lat. *philosophus*.

feamach, gross, dirty (Sh., O'R.): from *feam*, tail, as in *feaman*.

feamainn, sea-weed, Ir. *feamuin*, E. Ir. *femnach*, W. *gwymon*, Fr. *goëmon*, **vit-s-máni-*, root, *vi*, *vei*, wind, as in *fèith*, vein? Stokes gives the stem as *vemmâni-* (*vembani-* ?), which suggests **vegvo-*, root *veg*, as in *feur*.

feaman, a tail, Ir. *feam*, M. Ir. *feam*, mentula, Manx *famman*; also G. **eaman**, **engvo-*, Lat. *inguen*, groin.

feann, flay:

feannadh, skinning, excessive cold; see *fionnadh*. The idea of "cold" is metaphorical. E. Ir. *fennaim*, I skin, is referred by Stokes to the root of Eng. *wound*: he gives the stem as **venvo-*.

feannag, hooded crow, Ir. *feannóg*, *fionnóg*: cf. *fionna*, pile, for root: "piled crow"?

feannag, a lazy-bed; older *fennoc*, trench: from *feann*, flay.

fear, a man, Ir. *fear*, O. Ir. *fer*, W. *gwr*, O. W. *gur*, Corn. *gur*, Br. *gour*, **viro-s* (Rhys thinks the Celtic start was *ver*: cf. W. *gwr=ver*, super, and G. *eadh*, O. Ir. *ed*=Lat. *id*, etc.): Lat. *vir*; Ag. S. *wer*, Norse *verr*, Eng. *werwolf*; Lit. *wýras*; Skr. *vîra*.

fearann, land, so Ir., E. Ir. *ferand*, also *ferenn*, a girdle, garter, root *vera*, enclose, look after; Skr. *varaṇá*, well, dam, *vṛṇoti*, cover, enclose; Gr. ἔρυσθαι, draw, keep; Ch. Sl. *vrěti*, claudere: further Lat. *vereor*, Eng. *ware*.

fearg, wrath, so Ir., E. Ir. *ferg*, O. Ir. *ferc*, *ferg*, **vergâ*; Gr. ὀργή; root *vergo*, swell, be puffed up. Hence **feargnadh**, provocation.

feàrna, alder tree, Ir. *fearn*, *fearnóg*, E. Ir. *fern*, *fernog*, W. *gwern*, Corn. *gwernen*, Gaul. *verno-*, Fr. *verne*, **verno-*; Gr. ἔρνια, wild figs (? Bez.).

feàrr, better, Ir. *feárr*, O. Ir. *ferr*, **vers*, **ver(i)s*, a comparative in *-is* from the prep. *ver* (=G. *far*, *for*, super); now comparative for *math*, but evidently once for *fern*, good, **verno-s*, Lat. *supernus* (cf. *-no-* of *magnus* disappearing in *major*, and *-ro-* of Celtic *mâros* in G. *mò*). Stokes refers *ferr* to *vers*, raise, **uersos-*, height, top; Lat. *verruca*, steep place, Lit. *wirzùs*, top, Skr. *varshman-*, height, *várshîyas*, higher. Cf. W. *goreu*, best (= Lat. *supremus*).

feàrsaid, a spindle, Ir *fearrsaid*, M. Ir. *fersaid*, **versatti-* **verttati-*, W. *gwerthyd*, Cor. *gurthit*, O. Br. *guirtilon*, fusis, M. Br. *guerzit*, root *vert*, turn; Lat. *vertô*, *vortex*; Ger. *werden*, to be, Eng. *worth*, be, M.H.G. *wirtel*, spindle ring. Skr. *vártate*, turn, roll, *vartulâ*, spindle ball.

fearsaideag, thrift or sea gilly-flower; from obs. **fearsad**, estuary, sand-bank, passage across at ebb-tide, whence place-name *Fersit*, and in Ireland *Belfast*; for root see *feart*.

feart, attention, notice; Br. *gortos*, to attend, root *vert*, *vort*; Ger. *warten*, attend, Eng. *ward*, from *ware*, Nor. *varða*, ward. An extension of root *ver*, watch, Lat. *vereor*, etc.

feart, a virtue, efficiency, deed, Ir. *feart*, O. Ir. *firt*, pl. *ferta*, W. *gwyrth*; from Lat. *virtus* (Windisch, Stokes).

†**feart**, a grave, Ir. *feart*, O. Ir. *fert*, tumulus, **verto-*; root *ver*, cover, enclose, which see under *fearann*. Cf. Skr. *vṛti*. enclosure, hedge.

fearthuinn, rain, Ir. *fearthuinn*, E. Ir. *ferthain*, inf. to *feraim*, I pour, give, **veraô*, rain: Lat. *ûrína*, urine, Gr. οὖρον (do.): Norse *úr*, a drizzle, Ag. S. *wär*, sea; Skr. *vâri*, water, Zend, *vâra*, rain. See *dòirt*.

feascradh, shrivelling, so Ir. (O'R.):

feasd, am feasd, for ever, Ir. *feasda*, henceforward, E. Ir. *festa*, *ifesta*, now, from this point forward, *i fecht-sa*; from *feachd* by metathesis of the *s*. See *fathast*.

feasgar, evening, Ir. *feascar*, O. Ir. *fescor*, **vesqero-*, W. *ucher*, **uksero-* for **usqero-*; Lat. *vesper*; Gr. ἑσπέρος.

feathachan, slight breeze; see *feothachan*.

fèile, generosity, hospitality, Ir. *féile*, E. Ir. *féle*; from *fial*, q.v.

†**féile**, charm, incantation, E. Ir. *éle*, *héle*, *mo fhele*; from Norse *heill*, auspice, omen, Eng. *hale*, etc.; allied to O. Ir. *cél*, augurium, W. *coel*, omen, O. W. *coil* (Zim., Zeit. [33] 147). For G. *féile*, see *Inv. Gaelic Soc. Tr.*[17] 243. Stokes regards Zimmer's derivation from N. a failure, and compares W. *wylo*, wail, weep, as Ir. *amor*, music = W. *afar*, grief, and G. *ceòl* = Ger. *heulen*, howl. Rhys cfs. W. *eli*, oil, ointment.

fèile, fèileadh, a kilt, E. Ir., O. Ir. *fial*, velum: O. Ir. *ronfeladar*, he might clothe us; from Lat. *vêlum*, a covering, *vêlare*, Eng. *veil*. In Islay, Jura, etc., it is *an t-sibhleadh*. McL. and D.

also gives *éibhleadh*. Hend. questions if Lat. See *uanfebli* in Fled. Br. 68. Root *sveil* as in *fill*, *spaoil*, etc.?

féill, a fair, feast, Ir. *féil*, festival, holiday, O. Ir. *féil*, W. *gwyl*, festum, Br. *goel*, **vegli-* ; Lat. *vigilia*, Fr. *veille*, a watch, vigil, Eng. *vigil*, *wake*. The Celtic words are borrowed from Lat. (Windisch, Stokes). Hence *féillire*, an almanack.

féin, self, Ir., O. Ir. *féin*, **sve-j-sin*, "self there," **sve-j*, **sve*, Pruss. *swais*, Ch. Sl. *svojĭ* ; Lat. *suus*, *sē* ; Gr. ἕ, ὅς. Zeuss explains *féin* as *bé-shin*, "quod sit hoc," *bé* being the verb to be. This explanation is due to the divers forms of the O. Ir. word for "self, selves": *fésine* (=*bé-sin-é*, sit id hoc), *fésin*, *fadesin* (= *bad-é-sin*), *fodén*, etc.

Féinn, g. **Féinne**, the Fingalians, Ir. *Féinne*, *Fiann*, E. Ir. *fíann*, **veinnâ*, also E. Ir. *fían*, a hero, **veino-s*, root, *vein*, strive ; Lat. *vênari*, hunt ; Skr. *vénati*, go, move, desire. Zimmer takes the word from Norse *fjándi*, an enemy (Eng. *fiend*), which he supposes the Irish troops called themselves after the Norsemen.

feirm, a farm, Ir. *feilm* ; from M. Eng. *ferme*, Eng. *farm*.

féisd, **féis**, a feast ; better *feusd*, q.v.

feith, wait, Ir. *feithim*, E. Ir. *fethim*, inf. *fethem* (=G. **feitheamh**), **vetô*, root *vet* ; Lat. *vetus*, old, Eng. *veteran* ; Gr. ἔτος, year ; Eng. *wether* ("yearling").

féith, a sinew, a vein, Ir., O. Ir. *féith*, fibra, **veiti-s*, root *vei*, *vi*, wind, bend ; Lat. *vîmen*, withe, *vîtis*, a vine ; Gr. ἰτέα (long ι), willow ; Eng. *withe* ; Lit. *výtis*, willow-wand, Ch. Sl. *viti*, res torta ; Skr. *vayati*, weave, flecto. The W. shows a stem **vittâ*, vein, W. *gwythen*, Br. *gwazen*, Cor. *guid-* ; cf. Lat. *vitta*, fillet. Hence **féith**, a bog channel (Ir. *féth*, a marsh, bog-stream), and **feithleag**, honeysuckle, M. Ir. *feithlend*, woodbine, W. *gwyddfid* (do.).

feitheid, a bird or beast of prey (M'A.), Ir. *feithide*, a beast :

feochadan, corn-thistle, thistle (Arm., H.S.D.), Ir. *feochadan* (O'R.), *feóthadán* (O'B.), and *feóthán*. Cf. *fobhannan*.

feòcullan, the pole-cat, Ir. *feochullan* (Fol., O'R. has *feocullan* like Sh.). Cf. Sc. *fethok*, *fithowe*, pole-cat, M. Eng. *ficheu*, now *fitchew*.

feobharan, pith, puff (**feo'ran**)—Dial. ; *feodharan*, root, **vet*, *vetu-*?

feobhas, goodness ; see *feabhas*.

feòdar, pewter, Ir. *péatar*, W. *ffeutar* ; from the Eng. *pewter*.

feodhaich, decay, Ir. *feodhaim*, M. Ir. *feodaigim*, wither : "senesco ;" **vetu-*, root *vet*, as in Lat. *vetus*, G. *feith*? O. Ir. *feugud*, W. *gwyw*, Lat. *vietus* ; **vivagatu*?

feòil, flesh, Ir. *feoil*, E. Ir. *feóil*, O. Ir. *feúil*, **vepoli-s* ; Skr. *vapâ*, fat, *vápus*, body, form?

feòirlig, a farthing land, **feòirling**; from Ag. S. *feorþling*, Eng. *farthing*.

feòirne, chess, Ir. *feoirne* (Sh., O'R., Fol.):

feòrag, a squirrel, Ir. *feoróg* (Sh., O'R., Fol.), W. *gwiwer*, Br. *gwiber*; Lit. *vovere*, Lettic *wâweris*, Pruss. *weware*; Lat. *viverra*, ferret (Pliny).

feòraich, inquire, **fiafraigh** (Kintyre Dial.), Ir. *fiafruighim*, O. Ir. *iarfaigim*: **iar-fach*, prep. *iar* and *fach*, E. Ir. *faig*, dixit, **vakô*, say; Lat. *vocô*, call, *vox*, voice; Skr. *vac*, say. The *r* of G. and modern Ir. has shifted to behind the *f*, while a prothetic *f* is added.

feòrlan, a firlot; see *feòirling*.

feothachan, feothan (Arran), a little breeze; root *vet*, as in *onfhadh*.

feuch, fiach, behold, see, try, Ir. *feuch*, *féach*, E. Ir. *féchaim*, *fégaim*, **veikô*; Gr. εἰκών, image (Eng. *iconoclastic*), ἔοικα, I seem, εἰκάζω, conjecture; Skr. *viç*, appear, arrive.

feud, may, can; see *faod*.

feudail, cattle; usual spelling of *eudail*, q.v.

feudar, 's fheudar, it is necessary, M. Ir. *is eidir*, it is possible, for *is ed fhétir*, it is what is possible. *Feudar* is the pres. pass. of *feud*, may. In G. the "may" has become "must." The negative, **cha 'n fheudar**, is common in E. Ir. as *ni fhétir*, *ni étir*, cannot be.

feum, use, need, Ir. *feidhm*, pl. *feidhmeanna*, need, use, duty, need-service of a vassal, E. Ir. *feidm*, effort, **védes-men-*, "need-service;" root *ved*, as in *feadhainn*. Hence **feumannach**, a steward: "a servitor."

feun, a waggon, wain, O. Ir. *fén*, W. *cywain*, vehere, **vegno-*, root *vegh*, carry; Lat. *veho*, *vehiculum*, vehicle; Gr. ὄχος, chariot; Eng. *waggon*, *wain*; Skr. *vahati*, carry.

feur, fiar, grass, Ir. *feur*, O. Ir. *fér*, W. *gwair*, Cor. *gwyr*, **vegro-*, I.E. root *veg*, increase, be strong; Lat. *vegeo*, quicken, *vigor*, vigour, Eng. *vegetation*; Ag. S. *wacan*, nasci, Eng. *waken*. Strachan and Stokes refer it to the root *veg*, *ug*, be wet, moist, Lat. *uvidus*, moist, Eng. *humour*, Gr. ὑγρός, wet, Norse *vökr*, moist; but judged by the Latin, the Celtic should be *vebro-*, which would not give W. *gwair*.

feursa, a canker, **feursann**, a worm in the hide of cattle:

feusag, fiasag, a beard, Ir. *féusóg*, *féasóg*, E. Ir. *fésóc*, beard, *fés*, hair, **vanso*, O. Pruss., *wanso*, first beard, Ch. Sl. *vasŭ* beard.

feusd, feusda, (féisd, féis), a feast, Ir. *féis*, *feusda*, E. Ir. *feiss*; from Lat. *festia*, Eng. feast.

feusgan, fiasgan, a mussel :

fhuair, found, invenit, Ir. *fuair*, O. Ir. *fúar*, inveni, *frith*, inventus est, **vovora*, root *ver* ; Gr. εὗρον, I found, εὕρηκα (Strachan, Prellwitz). The root *ver* is likely that found in Gr. ὁράω, I see, Lat. *vereor*, Eng. *ware*.

fiabhras, a fever, Ir., M. Ir. *fiabhrus* ; from Lat. *febris*.

fiacaill, a tooth, Ir., O. Ir. *fiacail*. There is an E. Ir. *fec* for *féc*, a tooth, a stem **veikkâ* :

fiach, value, worth ; see next.

fiach, fiachan, debt, value, Ir. *fiach*, O. Ir. *fíach*, **veico-*, Lat. *vices*, change, Ger. *wechsel*, exchange, Skr. *vishtí*, changing, in turn (Osthoff). This is the right derivation.

fiadh, a deer, Ir. *fiadh*, E. Ir. *fíad*, O. Ir. *fíadach*, venatio, W. *gwydd*, Br. *guez*, *goez*, savage, **veido-s*, wild ; O. H. G. *weide*, a hunt, Ger. *weide*, pasturage, Norse *veiðr*, hunting ; further is G. *fiodh*, wood, Eng. *wood*. Hence **fiadhaich,** wild.

fiadhaich, invite, welcome (Skye) :

fiadhair, lay or fallow land ; from the above root of *fiadh*. Cf. Ger. *weide*, pasture. Also G. **fiadhain,** wild, Ir. *fiadháin*, wild, uncultivated.

fial, generous, Ir. *fial*, E. Ir. *fíal*, modest, W. *gwyl*. Bez. suggests **veiplo-*, Teutonic *vîba-*, Ger. *weib*, Eng. *wife*. Cf. Ir. *fialus*, relationship. The underlying idea is "kindness, relationship."

fiamh, awe, reverence, Ir. *fiamh*, fear, reverence, ugly, horrible, E. Ir. *fiam*, horrible :

fiamh, aspect, appearance, trace, Ir. *fiamh*, track, trace, chain, *fíamh* (O'Cl.) = lorg, E. Ir. *fiam*, a chain, **veimo-*, root *vei*, wind, as in *féith*. **Fiamh ghàire, fèath ghaire** (Arg.), a slight smile, is in Ir. *fáetheadh an gháire*, appearace of a smile, E. Ir. *féth*, aspect.

fianaidh, peat cart ; *carn-fianaidh* (Ross) ; see *feun*.

Fiann, the Fingalians ; see *Féinn*. This is the real nom. case.

fiantag, the black heath-berry ; root *vein* as in the above word.

fianuis, witness, a witness, Ir. *fiadhnuise*, *fiadhan*, a witness, O. Ir. *fiadnisse*, testimony, *fiadu*, acc. *fiadain*, testem, **veidôn-*, I. E. root *veid*, *vid*, know, see, as in *fios*, q.v. ; Ag. S. *witta*, a witness, Eng. *witness*, root, *wit*, know.

fiar, crooked, Ir. *fiar*, E. Ir. *fíar*, W. *gwyr*, Br. *goar*, *gwar*, **veiro-*; root *vei*, wind as in *féith* ; Eng. *wire*, Ag. S. *wîr*, wire.

fiat, fiata, wild ; a participial formation from *fiadh*. Also **fiadhta,** so Ir.

fiatach, quiet and sly (Skye) :

fiathail, calm ; see *fè*.

fich, an interjection denoting "nasty!" Eng. *fie*, Norse *fý*, Ger. *pfui*. Also Dial. **fuich, fuidh,** which leans on Norse *fúi*, rottenness ("Cha bhi fuidh ach far am bi fàile").

fichead, twenty, Ir. *fiche*, *ar fhichid*, O. Ir. *fiche*, g. *fichet*, W. *ugeint*, *ugain*, Cor. *ugens*, *ugans*, Br. *ugent*, **vikn̥s*, **vikn̥tos*; Lat. *vîginti*; Gr. εἴκοσι; Zend *vîçaiti*.

fideadh, a suggestion (H.S.D.): **vid-dho-*, root *vid*, wit.

fideag, a small pipe, reed, flute, Ir. *fideóg*; for root, see *fead*. Shaw also gives the meaning "small worm." M'L. has **fìdeag.**

fidean, a green islet or spit uncovered at high tide, web of sea-clam (Isles); from the N. *fit*, webbed foot of waterfowl, meadow land on the banks of firths or rivers, *fitja*, to web, Eng. *fit*.

fìdhleir, a fiddler; from *fiodhull*. Ir. *fidiléir* is Eng. *fiddler* directly borrowed. Hence G. **fidleireachd**, restlessness; "fiddling" about.

fidir, know, consider, Ir. *fidir*, knows, O. Ir. *fetar*, scio, *fitir*, novit, **viddetor*, **vid-dho-* (the *-dho-* as in *creid*, Windisch); root *vid*, see, as in *fios*. Thurneysen explains it as **videsar* (aorist stem *vides-*) becoming *vid-shar*, but *d-sh* does not produce *t* or *d* without an *n* before it.

fige, figis, a fig, Ir. *fíge*; from Lat. *fîcus*, Eng. *fig*.

figh, weave, Ir. *fighim*, E. Ir. *figim*, O. W. *gueig*, testrix, W. *gweu*, to weave, Cor. *guiat*, tela, Br. *gwea*, M. Br. *gweaff*, **vegiô*; Ger. *wickeln*, roll, wind, curl, *wieche*, wick, Eng. *wick*. Ag. S. *wecca* (Stokes). Usually referred to the root *vei*, *vi*, wind.

file, filidh, a poet, Ir. *file*, g. *filidh*, O. Ir. *fili*, g. *filed*, **velet-*, "seer"; W. *gwelet*, to see, Br. *guelet*, sight, **velô*. Cf. Norse *völva*, prophetess, sibyl. Old Germanic *Veleda*, a prophetess (Tacitus).

fill, fold, Ir. *fillim*, fold, return, O. Ir. *fillim*, flecto, **velvô*; Lat. *volvo*, roll, *volumen*, Eng. *volume*; Gr. εἰλύω, envelop; Got. *af-valvjan*, roll away, Eng. wallow. Cf. W. *olwyn*, a wheel (Stokes). Windisch (*Curt. Et.*) suggests *vald* as root, allied to Norse *velta*, roll, Got. *valtjan*, Eng. *welter*, Ger. *walze*, roll, waltz. See especially *till*.

fillein, a collop: a "roll"; from *fill*.

fine, a tribe, kindred, Ir., O. Ir., *fine*, O. Br. *coguenou*, indigena, **venjâ*, kinship; Norse *vinr*, a friend, Ag. S. *wine*, O. H. G. *wini* (do.); I. E. root *ven*, love, Lat. *Venus*, *veneror*, Eng. *venerate*, Skr. *van*, love

fìnealta, fine, elegant, Ir. *fínealta*; cf. M. Ir. *fín-* in *Fínscothach*, fair-flowered, *Fin-shnechta*, bright-snow, root *svén*; Gr. ἦνοψ, bright (Stokes for M. Ir.).

finiche, jet (M'D., M'A.), **finichd,** black as jet (M'E.) :
finid, end ; from Lat. *finit,* the colophon of so many tales when written.
finideach, wise, so Ir. (Lh., Sh., H.S.D., which gives C. S. as authority) :
finne, a maiden (Arm., M'A., M'E.) : "fairness, beauty" ; from *fionn* (**vindiâ*).
finnean, a buzzard :
†**fioch,** wrath, Ir. *fíoch,* E. Ir. *fích,* feud, I. E. **veiqo-,* fight ; Got. *veihan,* strive, O. H. G. *wîgan,* fight ; Lat. *vinco.* Hence **fiochdha,** angry.
fiodh, wood, so Ir., O. Ir. *fid,* W. *guid, gwydd, gwydden* (sing.), Corn. *guiden,* Br. *gwezenn,* tree, *gwez,* trees, Gaul. *vidu-, *vidu-;* Eng. *wood,* Ag. S. *wudu,* O. H. G. *witu.* Hence †**fiodhcheall,** chess play, E. Ir. *fidchell,* W. *gwyddbwyll,* "wood-sense," from *fiodh* and *ciall.* Also **fiodhag,** wild fig, **fiodhan,** cheese-vat.
fiodhradh, an impetuous rush forward (Heb) :
fiodhull, a fiddle, E. Ir. *fidil,* from Low Lat. *vitula,* whence Fr. *viola,* Eng. *viol, violin.* Cf. Eng. *fiddle,* from Med. Lat. *fidula,* Lat. *fidis.*
fioghuir, a figure, Ir. *fíoghair,* M. Ir. *figur* ; from Lat. *figura.*
fiolagan, a field-mouse (Arran) :
fiolan, fiolar, an earwig, nesscock, W. *chwil,* beetle, *chwiler,* maggot, Br. *c'houil* ; Gr. *σίλφη,* cockroach, Eng, *sylph.* Cf. *feallan.*
fiomhalach, a giant (Sh.) ; from *fiamh.*
fìon, wine, Ir. *fíon,* O. Ir. *fín,* W., Cor., Br. *gwin* ; from Lat. *vinum.*
fìonag, a mite, insect, a miser, Ir. *fineóg,* a mite in cheese, etc. :
fionn, white, Ir. *fionn,* O. Ir. *find,* W. *gwyn,* Corn. *guyn,* Br. *gwenn,* Gaul. *vindo-, *vindo-,* a nasalised form of root *vid, veid,* see, as in *fios.* Cf. Servian *vidný,* clear.
fionn-, to, against, Ir. *fionn-, ionn-,* O. Ir. *ind-* ; see *ionn-.*
fionna, fionnadh, hair, pile, Ir. *fionnadh,* E. Ir. *finda, findfad,* O. Ir. *finnae,* pilorum, **ves-niâ,* root *ves,* clothe, Lat. *vestis,* Eng. *vestment.* Stokes has compared it to Lat. *villus,* hair, which he takes from **vin-lus,* but which is usually referred to the root *vel* of *vellus, lana,* etc. The *-fad* of E. Ir. is for **vida,* aspect, W. *gwedd,* root *vid,* see.
fionnachd, refreshment : "coolness," **ionn-fhuachd* : cf. *fionnar.*
fionnan-feòir, grasshopper, Ir. *finnín feoir* (O'R.) :
fionnairidh, a watching : **ind-faire* ; see *fionn-,* to, and *faire.*
fionnar, cool, Ir. *fionnfhuar,* M. Ir. *indfhuar* ; from *fionn-* and *fuar.*
fionnas-gàrraidh, parsley (M'L.) :

fionndairneach, rank grass, downy beard (H.S.D.) :

†**fionndruinne**, (white) bronze, E. Ir. *findruine*, white bronze : **find(b)ruine* (Hend.) Eng. *bronze*.

fionnogha, grandson's grandson, Ir. *fionnúa* ; from *fionn-*, ad-, and *ogha*.

fionnsgeul, a romance, Ir. *finnsgeul* ; from *fionn-* and *sgeul* : *ande-sqetlon*.

fìor, true, Ir. *fíor*, O. Ir. *fír*, W. *gwir*, O. W. *guir*, Br. *gwir*, **vêro-*; Lat. *vêrus* ; Ger. *wahr*. Root *ver*, *vor*, *var*, see, as in Eng. *beware*, *ward*. Before the noun the word is **fìr**. Hence **fìrean**, righteous man, O. Ir. *fírian*, W. *gwirion*, **vêriâno-s*.

fios, knowledge, Ir. *fios*, O. Ir. *fiss*, **vid-tu-*, root *vid*, *veid*, know ; Lat. *video*, see ; Gr. εἶδον, ἰδεῖν, saw, οἶδα, know, Got. *vitan*, watch, Eng. *wit* ; Skr. *vid*, know, *vetti*, to know. Hence **fiosrach**, knowing.

fir-chlis, the northern lights ; see *fear* and *clis*.

fir-chneatain, backgammon men :

fire faire, interjection—"what a pother ;" from the Sc. *fiery-fary*, bustle.

fireach, hill ground, mountain : cf. *fearann*, root **ver*.

firead, a ferret, Ir. *firéad* ; from the Eng.

fireun, an eagle, Ir. *fír-én* : "true-bird ;" from *fìor* and *eun*. So in E. Ir. *fír-iasc* is the salmon. So in Reay Country (Rob.).

firionn, male, so Ir. ; E. Ir. *firend* ; from *fear*.

fise faise, interjection—noise of things breaking, talking secretly.

fitheach, a raven, Ir., O. Ir. *fiach* ; this is a dissylable, **vivo-ko-*; the phonetics being those of *biadh*. Stokes gives **veijako-s* or **veivako-s*. It is still distantly allied to Ger. *weihe*.

fithreach, dulse, so Ir. (Lh., O'B., etc.) :

fiù, worthy, Ir. *fiú*, O. Ir. *fiú*, W. *gwiw*, Cor. *guiu*, O. Br. *uuiu*, Gaul. *vesu-*, **vesu-*, *vêsu-*, good ; Skr. *vásu*, good ; root *ves*, be, Eng. *was*. Some give **visu* (**vîsu-*) as the stem, Gr. ἴσος, like (= *visvo-s*), Skr. *vishu*, æque. Hence **fiùbhaidh**, a prince, valiant chief, Ir. *fiúbhas*, dignity ; also **fiùghanta**, generous, Ir. *fiughantach*, *fiúntach* (Keat.), worthy.

fiughair, expectation, E. Ir. *fiugrad*, praedicere ; from Lat. *figura*. Ir. has *fíoghair*, figure, fashion, sign.

fiùran, a sapling, Ir. *fiúrán* (Sh., O'R., Fol.) :

fiùthaidh (fiùbhaidh), an arrow ; see *iùthaidh*.

flaiche, a sudden gust of wind (Sh., O'R.) :

flaitheanas, heaven, glory, **flaitheas**, sovereignty, Ir. *flaith-eamhnus*, O. Ir. *flaithemnas*, gloria ; from *flaithem*, lord, g. *flaitheman* ; see *flath*.

†**flann**, red, blood-red, so Ir., E. Ir. *fland*, blood, red : *vl-ando-*, root, *vol* of *fuil*, q.v.

flasg, a flask, W. *fflasg*; from the Eng.

flath, a chief, prince, Ir. *flaith*, O. Ir. *flaith*, chief, dominion, *flaithem(an)*, chief (**vlatimon-*), W. *gwlad*, region, M. W. *gulatic*, rex, Corn. *gulat*, patria, Br. *gloat*, realm, Gaul. *vlatos*, **vlato-s*, **vlati-s*, root *vala*, *vla*, be strong; Lat. *valere*, Eng. *valid*; Got. *valdan*, Ger. *walten*, rule, Eng. *weild*, *Walter*; Ch. Sl. *vladą*, rule, Russ. *vladiete*, rule, O. Pruss. *waldnika-*, king. Also **valo-s* as the final element of certain personal names—**Domhnall**, **Dumno-valo-s* (see *domhan*), **Conall**, **Kuno-valo-s* (**kuno-s*, high, root *ku*, as in *curaidh*, q.v., Teutonic *Hûn-*, Humbold, Humphrey, Hunwald, etc.), **Cathal**, **Katu-valo-s* (see *cath*), etc.

fleachdail, flowing in ringlets (H.S.D., from MSS.); from Lat. *plecto*, plait.

fleadh, a feast, Ir. *fleadh*, O. Ir. *fled*, W. *gwledd*, O. W. *guled*, pompae, **vḷdâ*, root *vel*, wish; Gr. εἰλαπίνη, feast, ἔλδομαι, wish, ἐλπίς, hope; Lat. *voluptas*; Eng. *will*, *well*.

fleadhadh, brandishing; Eng. *wield*; see *flath*.

fleasg, a rod, wreath, Ir. *fleasg*, garland, wand, sheaf, O. Ir. *flesc*, rod, linea, **vleska*, from **vledska*, root *vḷd*; Ger. *wald*, wood, Eng. *wold*; Gr. ἄλσος, grove; Ch. Sl. *vladi*, hair. From the Celtic comes the Fr. *flèche*, arrow, whence Eng. *Fletcher*, arrow-maker. See *fleisdear*.

fleasgach, young man, bachelor, so Ir., M. Ir. *flesgach*: "wand-bearer." From *fleasg*, above. The Ir. *fleasgaigh ealadhna*, itinerant medicine men, carried *fleasgan* to denote their profession.

fleasgairt, a barge or boat hung with festoons; from *fleasg*.

fleisdear, arrow-maker; from Sc. *fledgear*, M. Eng. *flecchere*, now *fletcher*, from O. Fr. *flechier*. See *fleasg* further.

fleodradh, floating (Heb.), **fleodruinn**, a buoy; from Norse *fljóta*, to float, Eng. *float*.

fleogan, an untidy, flabby person, a flat fish (Arms.), **fleoidhte**, flaccid (Sh.):

fliodh, chickweed, a wen, Ir. *fliodh*, *fligh*, chickweed, W. *gwlydd*, chickweed, soft stems of plants, **vḷdu-*. Same root as in *fleasg*.

fliuch, wet, Ir., O. Ir., *fliuch*, W. *gwlyb*, O. W. *gulip*, Corn. *glibor*, humor, Br. *gloeb*, wet, **vḷqu-s*, wet; Lat. *liquidus* (= *vliquidus*); Lit. *wa'lks*, wet, *wa'lka*, swampy place. See *failc*.

flò, hallucination (H.S.D. for N.H.):

flod, a state of floating; from Eng. *float*, Norse *floti*, a raft.

flodach, lukewarm; see *plodadh*.

flùr, **plùr**, flower, Ir. *plúr*, M. Ir. *plúr*; from the M. Eng. *flour*, O. Fr. *flour*, Lat. *florem*. G. **flùr** is from the Scotch.

fo, under, Ir., O. Ir. *fo*, W. *go-*, O. W. *guo-*, Cor. *go-*, Cor., Bret. *gou-*, Ganl. *vo-*: **vo*, for **u(p)o*; I. E. *upo*; Gr. ὑπό, ; Lat. *s-ub*; Got. *uf*; Skr. *upa*, hither.

fò, brink (Carm.):

fobhannan (fòthannan), a thistle, Ir. *fóbhthán. fóthannán*, E. Ir. *omthann*, **omo-tanno-*, "raw or rough twig"? See *amh* and *caorrunn*. Dial. **fonntan** (Arran).

focal, word; see *facal*.

fochaid, scoffing, Ir. *fochmhuid*, *fochuidbheadh*, M. Ir. *fochmaid*, E. Ir. *fochuitbiud*, **fo-con-tib-*, root *teb*, smile, O. Ir. *tibiu*, laugh; Lit. *stebiûs*, be astonished.

fochair, presence, **am fochar,** coram, Ir., M. Ir. *fochair*: **fo-char*, *car* being *cor*, put.

fochann, young corn in the blade, Ir. *fochan*, M. Ir. *fochon*; **vo-kuno*? Root *kun*, *ku*, increase, Gaul. *cuno-*, high, etc. See *curaidh*.

fód, a peat, turf, Ir. *fód*, O. Ir. *fót*: **vonto-*?

fodar, fodder, Ir *fodar*; from the Eng. *fodder*.

fògair, expel, banish, Ir. *fógair*, command, proclaim, O. Ir. *fócairim* (do.), *fócre*, monitio: **fo-od-gar-*; root *gar* of *goir*.

†**fogh,** quiet, careless (Stew.):

foghail, a hostile incursion, Ir. *foghail*, E. Ir. *fogal*; **fo-gal*: root *gal*, valour, war. See *gal*.

foghail, fòghail, noise, bustle, merriment; for first sense, see *foghair*, for second, see *othail*.

foghainteach, valorous, Ir. *fóghainteach*, good, fit, serviceable, *fóghaint*, ability: "capable"; from *foghainn*, suffice. See *fòghnadh*. Ir. *foghaintidhe*, a servant.

foghair, a sound, tone, so Ir., O. Ir. *fogur*, sonus: **fo-gar-*; root *gar* of *goir*. Strachan makes the root part *fog*, and refers it to *fuaim*, q.v.

foghar, harvest, Ir. *fóghmhar*, M. Ir. *fogamur*, autumn, E. Ir. *fogamur*, *fogomur*, last month of autumn: **fo-gamur*, the *gamur* being from the root of *geamhradh*, winter, q.v. The idea is "sub hiemem." Cf. W. *cynauaf*, harvest, O. W. *kynnhaeaf*, from *cyn*, before, and *gauaf*, winter.

fòghlum, learning, Ir. *fóghluim*, O. Ir. *foglaim*, vb. *fogliunn*: **vo-glendô*, **glendô*, make clear; Eng. *glance*, Ger. *glanz*, splendour; Ch. Sl. *gl̨edati*, show.

fòghnadh, sufficiency, service, Ir. *foghnamh*, O. Ir. *fognam*, service; from *fo* and *gnìomh*, deed.

foichein, a wrapper, infant's clout:

foichlean, a sprout, young corn (Arm.), **faichean** (Arg.), Ir. *foichnín*; see *fochann*.

fóid, a peat; see *fód.*

fòidheach, a beggar; see *faoighe.*

foidhearach, naked (H.S.D., Dial.):

foidhidinn, patience, Ir. *foighid,* O. Ir. *foditiu,* toleratio (**vo-dam-tin-*), vb. *fodamim,* patior, root *dam*; Lat. *domo,* I tame, subdue; Gr. *δαμάω* (do.); Eng. *tame*; Skr. *dâmyati,* tame.

foighnich, ask; see *faighnich.* Also, more Dialectic, **foinich.**

foil, macerate, broil; see *fail.* Hence **foileag,** a cake suddenly and imperfectly toasted.

foil, pig-stye; see *fail.*

fòil, slow, stately, **fòill,** composure, Ir. *fóil, fóill,* softly! a while, M. Ir. *co fóill,* slowly, for a while, E. Ir. *co foill,* slowly:

foileadh, slow development:

foill, treachery, O. Ir. *foile,* astutia. G. is for **volni-,* Ir. for **voliâ,* both side-forms to *feall,* treachery, q.v.

foillsich, reveal, O. Ir. *foillsigim,* **svolnestikiô*; see *follus.*

foinich, ask; see *faighnich.*

foinne, a wart, Ir. *faine, faithne,* W., Cor. *gwenan,* blister, Br. *gwennhaenn,* a wart; Eng. *wen,* Ag. S. *wenn* (Ern.).

foinneamh, foinnidh, handsome, genteel; cf. next word, also Lat. *vinnulus,* delightful, root *ven,* as in G. *fine,* etc.

foinnich, temper, Ir. *foinnim,* temper, knead, *foinnighte,* tempered, kneaded. Cf. above word.

foir-, prefix meaning "super," same as **for-**: see *far, air(b).*

fòir, help, Ir. *fóir* (vb. and n.), E. Ir. *foriuth,* I help, O. Ir. *don-fóir,* to help us: **vo-ret-*; root *ret* of *ruith,* run. For force, cf. *furtachd.* The W. *gwared,* release, Br. *goret,* are of like elements. Similarly **foirbheart** (an Ir. word really), assistance, is from *foir-* and *beir.*

foirbhillidh, acceptable (M'D.); from *for* and *bail,* good?

foirceadal, foircheadal, instruction, catechism, Ir. *foircheadal,* O. Ir. *forcital,* doctrina, vb. *forchun,* doceo: **for-can-*; root *can,* say, sing. See *can.*

foireann, foirionn, a band, crew, Ir. *fuirionn,* E. Ir. *fairenn,* O. Ir. *foirinn,* O. W. *guerin,* W. *gwerin,* people, M. Br. *gueryn,* **vorênâ, *vorinni-,* multitude, root *ver,* enclose; Ag. S. *vorn,* multitudo, caterva; Lit. *worà,* long row in Indian file; Skr. *vrấ,* troop, company See *fearann.*

foirfe, perfect, Ir. *foirfe,* complete, old, O Ir. *foirbthe,* perfectus, *forbe,* perfectio, vb. *forbanar,* perficitur, *forfenar,* consummatus: **for-ben-*; root *ben, ba,* go (Lat. *venio,* Gr. *βαίνω,* *ἔβην,* etc.), practically a verb "to be" (Stokes *Neo-Celtic Verb Subst.*).

fòirin, assistance, E. Ir. inf. dat., *foirithin*; see *fòir.*

foirinn, border land (Cam.):

foirm, noise; side form of toirm?
fòirmeil, brisk, lively (Sh., etc.): from Eng. *formal* (Rob.).
foirmeilich, formalists.
fòirne, a band, dwellers, Ir. *foirne* (O'B.); an **oblique form** of *foireann*, g. *foirne*.
fòirneadh, intruding; see *teirinn*, *teàrnadh*.
fòirneis, a furnace; see *fùirneis*.
foirneata, conspicuously brave; see *niata*.
fois, rest, Ir. *fois*, O. Ir. *foss*, residence, remaining, rest, W. *ar-os*; **vosso-*; root *ves*, be, rest; Gr. ἄστυ, city (**vastu*); Skr. *vástu*, place; Lat. *Vesta*; Eng. *was*, Ger. *wesen*, be, Got. *visa*, remain. So all etymologists till Windisch (1892) suggested the root *stâ*, that is **vo-sto-*. Stokes still holds by old (1903). Hence **foisdin**, taciturnity, Ir. *foisdine*.
foisteadh, wages, hire, Ir. *foistighim*, I hire; M. Ir. *foss*, servant, W. *gwas* (Eng. *vassal*); from the same root as *fois*. Also **fasdadh**.
folach, covering, hiding; see *falach*.
fòlach, rank grass growing on dunghills; **vog-lo-*, root, *vog*, *veg* of *feur*.
folachd, a feud, bloodiness; see *fuil*.
folachdain, water-parsnip (H.S.D. quotes only O'B.), Ir. *folachtain*:
follas, publicity, **follaiseach**, public, Ir. *follus*, public, manifest, O. Ir. *follus*, clear, shining, manifest, **svolnestu-s*; see *solus*.
fonn, land, Ir. *fonn*, E. Ir. *fond*; from Lat. *fundus*, which, again, is connected with G. *bonn*, q.v.
fonn, a tune, Ir. *fonn*, tune, desire, delight, M. Ir. *adbonn*, a strain; **svonno-*, root *sven*, sound, Lat. *sonus*, Eng. *sound*. See *seinn*.
fonnsair, a trooper (M'A.):
for-, super-, Ir., O. Ir. *for-*; prep. *for*, for which see *far*, *air* (*b*).
forach, **forch**, projection into the sea (Carm.):
forail, command, Ir. *fordilim*. See *earail* for formation and root.
forair, watch, Ir. *foraire*; from *for* and *aire*.
forasda, sedate, so Ir.; see *farasda*, in the sense of "staid."
forbhas, ambush (Sh., H.S.D., which quotes Lh. and C.S.), Ir. *forbhas*, E. Ir. *forbas*, siege:
forc, a fork, Ir. *forc*, E. Ir. *forc* (= *gobul*); for Lat. *furca*, Eng. *fork*.
forc, push (especially if legs are forked), pitch with a fork; from *forc*, fork.
forfhais, **foras**, information, inquiry, Ir. *foras*, E. Ir. *foras*, *forus*, true knowledge: **for-fiss*, from *fiss* or *fios*, knowledge, q.v. *Foras feasa*, "Basis of knowledge."
forgan, keenness, anger; from a side-form *forg* (**vorg*) of *fearg*?

fòrlach, a furlough; from the Eng.
forluinn, spite, hatred (H.S.D.), Ir., M. Ir. *forlonn*; from *for* and *lonn*, fierce.
forman, a mould, Ir. *formán*; from Lat. *forma*.
forradh, gain (H.S.D.), excrescence, shift (M'E.); from *for* and *rath?* See *rath*.
forsair, a forester; from the English.
fortail, strong, hardy, (an Ir. word clearly), Ir. *foirteamhail, fortail*, brave, stout, E. Ir. *fortail*, predominant, strong; from Lat. *fortis*.
fortan, fortune, Ir. *fortún*; from Lat. *fortuna*.
fortas, litter, refuse of cattle's food, orts; from the Eng. *orts*. Lh. has an Ir. *fortas*, straw.
fòs, yet, still, Ir. *fós*, M. Ir. *fós, beos*, O. Ir. *beus, beius*. Stokes makes it a comparative in *s* form *beo-*, allied to Lat. *beô*, gladden, *be*-ne, well.
fosg, fosgag, the lark (Carm.):
fosgail, open, so Ir., E. Ir. *oslaicim*: **f-od-as-leig*; Gaelic root *leic* or *leig*, let. See *leig* and cf. *tuasgail*.
fosgarach, open, frank:
fosglan, porch (Carm.):
fosradh, pounded bark (or anything) to stop leaks; cf. Ir. *fosradh*, scattering, from **vo-ster-*, root *ster*, strew.
fosradh, hand feeding of cattle (Heb.):
fothach, the glanders in horses, Ir. *fothach, fóthach*:
fòtus, a flaw, refuse (M'A. says "rotten pus," and gives **fòt,** rotten earth): from Sc. *faut*, as in *fabhd*.
frabhas, refuse, small potatoes (Arg.):
frachd, freight; from Sc. *fraught*, Eng. *freight*.
fradharc, vision, sight, Ir. *rádharc*, E. Ir. *rodarc*: **ro-darc*; root *derk*, see, as in *dearc*, q.v.
fraigein, a brisk, warlike fellow; see *frogan*.
fraigh, wattled partition, E. Ir. *fraig*: **vragi-*, root *verg*; Skr. *vraja*, hurdle; Gr. εἴργω, shut in.
fraileach, sea-weed (Sh., O'R.):
frangalus, tansy; **lus na Fraing** (Cameron), the French herb; from *Fraing*, France. Ir. *lus na bhfhrancach*; M. Ir. *frangcan*, tansy (St.).
fraoch, heather, Ir. *fraoch*, O. Ir. *froech*, W. *grug*, Cor. *grig*, M. Br. *groegon*, **vroiko-*; Gr. ἐρείκη. Hence G. **fraoch,** wrath, Ir. *fraoch*, E. Ir. *fraech*, furor.
fraochan, toe-bit of shoe; "heather-protector," from *fraoch?*
fraoidhnidh, flourishing:
fraoidhneis, froinis, a fringe; from the Eng.
fraoileadh, a flustering by liquor; Dial. **sraoileadh**:

fraon, a place of shelter in the mountains (Sh., O'R.), *fraoinibh* (D. Bàn.):

fras, a shower, Ir. *fras*, E. Ir. *frass*, **vrastâ* ; Gr. ἕρση, dew ; Skr. *varsham*, rain.

freagair, answer, Ir. *freagairim*, E. Ir. *frecraim* : **frith-gar-*, root *gar* of *goir*.

freasdal, serving, attending, Ir. *freasdail*, O. Ir. *frestal*, *fresdel* : **fris-do-el-* ; for root see *fritheil*. Dr Cameron referred it to *fris* and *tal*, which see in *tuarastal*.

freiceadan, a guard, watch : **frith-coimhead-an* ; from *coimhead*, guard, look, q.v.

freiteach, a vow, interdictory resolution, E. Ir. *fretech*, *fristoing*, repudiation, renunciation, O. Ir. *fristossam*, renuntiaverimus ; root *tong*, *tog*, swear, Lat. *tongeo*, think, Eng. *think*. Stokes gives the final root as *tag*, take, Lat. *tangere*. Ir. *tong*, swear, is allied to W. *tyngu*.

freòine, fury, rage :

freothainn, bent-grass (Arg.):

freumh, friamh, a root, Ir. *fréamh*, E. Ir. *frém*, W. *gwraidd*, *gwreiddyn*, Cor. *grueiten*, Br. *grisienn*, **vṛd-mâ*, **vṛdjo-*, **vṛdnu-* : Lat *radix*, root ; Gr. ῥίζα ; Got. *vaurts*, Eng. *wort*, *root*.

frìde, a tetter, ring-worm, M. Ir. *frigde*, flesh-worm, E. Ir. *frigit*, W. *gwraint*, M. Br. *gruech*, **vṛgṇtiâ*, root *verg* ; Eng. *wriggle*.

frìdeam, support, attention :

frighig, fry ; from the Eng. *frying*.

friochd, a second dram, a nip :

friochdan, a frying pan, Ir. *friochtán* ; cf. Ir. *friochtalaim*, I fry. From *fry* of the Eng.

frioghan, friodhan, a bristle, pig's bristle ; M. Ir. *frighan* i. *guairech muc* ; root *vṛg* as in *fraigh*? Cf. W. *gwrych*, hedge, bristles, **vṛg-ko-*. Hence **frioghail**, sharp, keen.

frionas, fretfulness : **friogh'n-as*, "bristliness ;" from *frioghan*.

friotach, fretful (Stew.) ; see *frith*, sour look.

†**frith**, an incantation to discover if far-away persons live (Heb.), fate (Sh., O'R.) ; from the Norse *frétt*, enquiry of the gods about the future, Sc. *fret*, *freit*.

frith, frioth, small, trifling (Sh. O'R.), which M'A. says antecedes the noun, is the prep. *frith* or *ri*.

frith, a sour or angry look (A. M'D.), **frithearachd**, peevishness, Ir. *frithir*, peevish : **vṛti-* ; root of *ri* "against"?

frìth, a forest, deer forest, Ir. *frith*, wild, mountainous place, W. *ffridd*, forest ; from M. Eng. *frið*, deer park, Ag. S. *frið*.

frith-, fre-, freas-, prefix = prep. *ri* by force and derivation ; which see.

fritheil, attend, Ir. *friotholaim* (Con. *friothólaim*), E. Ir. *frithailim*, root *-al-* (Ascoli), go; root *al*, *el*, *eln* of *tadhal*, q.v.

frithir, earnest, eager (Stew.), Ir. *frithir*, earnest, peevish; cf. *frith*, sour look.

fròg, a hole, fen, den, **ròg** (Suth.).

frogan, liveliness, a slight degree of drunkenness:

froighnighe, a dampness oozing through the wall; from *fraigh* and *snighe*.

froineadh, a sudden tugging, rushing at (M'D.):

froinis, a fringe; see *fraoidhneis*.

fròmhaidh, hoarse, rough:

fruan, acclivity (Carm.):

fuachd, cold, so Ir., O. Ir. *uacht*, *ócht*, **aukto-*; Lettic *auksts*, cold (adj.), Lit. *áuszti*, cold, be cold.

fuadaich, drive away, Ir. *fuadaighim*, drive away, snatch away, E. Ir. *fúataigm*: **fo-od-tech (?)*; see *teich*. Hence **fuadan**, wandering.

fuadarach, hasty, in a hurry (Stew., Arm. and H.S.D.), Ir. *fuadar*, haste; from *fuad-* of *fuadaich*? Cf. Sc. *foutre*, activity.

fuagarthach, exiled; see *fògair*.

fuaidne, loose pins of warping stakes. Cf. O. Ir. *fuat*.

fuaigh, stitch, **fuaigheal**, sewing, so Ir., E. Ir. *fúagaim*, *úagaim*, O. Ir. *úaimm* (n.): **oug-s-men-*; root *poug*, *pug*, stitch, stick; Lat. *pungo*, Eng. *punch*. Zimmer (in 1882), referred it to the root of *òigh*, the idea being "integrate," from *óg*, *uag*, "integer." O. Ir. *óigthidi*, sartores.

fuaim, noise, so Ir., E. Ir. *fúaimm* (pl. *fuamand*). Neither **vog-s-men* (Strachan; root *vog* of Skr. *vagnú*, sound, Got. *vôpjan*, cry, Eng. *whoop*) nor **voc-s-men* (Stokes; root *voq*, voice, Lat. *voco*) can give *ua*, only *ŏ* or *ă*.

fuaithne, loom posts (Uist), Ir. *uaithne*, pillar, post, E. Ir. *úatne*, a post (bed post). So Henderson; *fùidne* (Wh.):

fual, urine, so Ir., O. Ir. *fúal*: **voglo-* or **voblo-*; root *vog*, *veg*, *ug*, be wet,; Gr. *ὑγρός*, wet, Eng. *hygrometer*; Lat. *humidus*, *uveo*, (for *ugveo*), be moist, Eng. *humour*; Norse *vökva*, moisture.

fuar, cold, Ir. *fuar*, E. Ir. *uar*, W. *oer*, Cor. *oir*: **ogro-*, root *ug*, *aug* of *fuachd*, q.v. Stokes refers it to the root *veg*, *ug*, discussed under *fual*, especially Gr. *ὑγρός*, wet; a root which would rather be *vob* in Celtic (cf. Lat.), and this would not give W. *oer*. Strachan suggests either Ch. Sl. *ognĭ*, fire (Lat. *ignis*) or Gr. *πάγος*, frost (root *pâg*, fix, fit). Hence **fuaradh**, windward side, **fuaran**, a well, **fuarraidh**, damp, **fuarralanach** (Ir. *fuarálach*, chill), cold feeling, etc.; *fuar bhalla*, an outside wall; *fuar-shlat*, the rough strong hoop used to bend in staves at the ends of casks (Wh.).

fuasgail, loose, untie, so Ir., E. Ir. *fuaslaicim*; see *tuasgail*.
fuath, hatred, so Ir., M. Ir. *fúath*; cf. E. Ir. *uath*, awe, terror, terrible, and see *uath* for root.
fuath, a spectre, so Ir., O. Ir. *fúath*, figura, forma:
fùcadh, fulling cloth, M. G. *owkkit* (D. of L.), Ir. *úcaire*, fuller; cf. *pùc*.
fudag, a shoe-strap (H.S.D. says Dial.):
fudaidh, mean, vile; from Sc. *footy*, *fouty*.
fùdar, powder, Ir. *púdar*; from the Eng.
fùdraic, smart, in good condition:
fuidh! an interjection. See *fich*.
fuidheall, remainder, Ir. *fuigheall*, O. Ir. *fuidell*, W. *gweddill*; also G. **fuidhleach**, remains, E. Ir. *fuidlech*: **vodilo-*, *dîl* allied to Eng. *deal*, *dole*, Ger. *teil* (St. with query).
fuidir, a fool (Carm.):
fùidreadh, commixing, pulverising; from *fùdar*. Dial. **fùdradh**, turning hay in the sunshine to dry it.
fùidsidh, craven; from Sc. *fugie*, one who flies from the fight.
fuigheag, a thrum, Ir. *fughóg*; from a short vowel form of root of *fuaigh*.
fuil, blood, Ir., O. Ir. *fuil*, gen. *fola*, *folo*: **voli-*, root *vol*, *vel*, well; Eng. *well*. Stokes agrees
fuilear, cha 'n fhuilear dhomh, I need, must; for *furail*, O. Ir. *foráil*, excessive injunction, infliction, same root as *earail*.
fuilig, fuiling, fulaing, suffer (thou), Ir. *fulangaim*, E. Ir. *fulangim*, O. Ir. *fuloing*, sustinet, inf. *fulang*: "under-go"; from *fo* and **long*, going, root *leng*, spring, go, as in *leum*, q.v. Further allied is Ger. *verlangen*, desire, Eng. *long*, Lat. *longus*.
fuin, bake, Ir. *fuinim*, I knead, bake, boil, E. Ir. *fuinim*, bake, cook. Zimmer takes the word to mean "to fire, bake," from the Norse *funi*, flame, fire, E. Ir. *oc-fune* = Norse *við funa*, a-roasting; but unlikely. Possibly **voni-*, "dress," root *ven*, *von*, Lat. *Venus*, Eng. *venerate*.
fuirbidh, a strong man, also **fuirbearnach**; compounds of *bì* and *beir*, with *for*, super.
fuirearadh, a parching of corn; see *eararadh*.
fuirich, stay, Ir. *fuirighim*, E. Ir. *fuirigim*, noun *fuirech*, O. Ir. *fuirset* (*s* future): **vo-reg*; root *reg*, stretch, go; Lat. *porrigo*, *rego*. See *rach*.
fuirm, stools, a form, Ir. *fuirm*, W. *ffurf*; from Eng. *form*.
fùirneis, fòirneis, a furnace, Ir. *furnéis*; from the Eng.
fuithein, fuifein, a galling, taking off the skin by riding (M'D.): *fo-bian*?
fulaing (vb.), **fulang** (n.); see *fuilig*.

fulaisg, rock ; from *fo* + *luaisg,* q.v.
fulbh, gloom (Arg.) ; see *suilbh.*
fulmair, a species of petrel, fulmar ; from Sc., Eng. *fulmar.*
fulpanachd, articulation, jointing (Sh., O'R., H.S D.) ; cf. *alp.*
funntainn, benumbment by cold ; see *punntuinn.* Sc. *fundy.*
furadh, parching corn (Carm.), also *furaradh.* See *fuirearadh.*
furail, incitement, command, Ir. *furáil,* E. Ir. *uráil, furáil,* O. Ir. *iráil* ; the same as *earail,* q.v.
furan, a welcome, Ir. *furán, foran* (Connaught) ; root *ver,* as in E. Ir. *feraim fáilti,* I welcome. The root means in E. Ir. "give rain" (see *fearthuinn*). The root of *fhuair* seems mixed with that of *fearthuinn.* See *fearthuinn.*
furas, patience : **f-air-asta, asta* (standing, staying) being for *ad-sta-, ad* and *sta,* stand.
furasda (furas), easy, easier, Ir. *furas, furasda,* E. Ir. *urusa* : **air-usa,* from *usa,* easier, q.v.
furbaidh, wrath (Sh., O'R.), **furban** (H.S.D., from MSS.) ; see *fuirbidh.*
furbhailt, furailt, courtesy, kindly reception ; also **furmailt.** For the latter Armstrong gives "ceremony" as force, which may be from Eng. *formality.* The words, otherwise, seem from *for-fàilte.*
furm, a stool ; see *fuirm.*
fùrlaich, hate, detest (Arms.), revolt against (Rob.) :
furtachd, relief, help, so Ir., O. Ir. *fortacht* (gen. in *-an*) : **for-tiacht* ; for Gaelic root *tiagh, tigh,* see *tighinn.*
fusgan, a heather brush ; cf. Sc. *whisker,* a bunch of feathers for sweeping, Eng. *whisk.*
futhar, the dog-days ; from Sc. *fure*-days.

G

gab, a tattling mouth ; from Sc. *gab* (do.), M. Eng. *gabben,* to chatter, mock, Norse *gabb,* mockery, O. Fris. *gabbia,* accuse.
gàbairt, a transport vessel (Heb.) ; from Sc. *gabert,* a lighter, from Fr. *gabarre,* storeship, lighter.
gabh, take, Ir. *gabhaim,* O. Ir. *gabaim, gaib,* capit, inf. *gabáil,* W. *gafael,* prehensio (Eng. *gavel*kind), Cor. *gavel* : **gabô,* capio, do, **gabagli* ; Got. *giban,* give, Ger. *geben,* Eng. *give* ; Lit. *gabénti,* bring.
gàbhadh, danger, peril, Ir. *gábha(dh),* E. Ir. *gába, gábud* : cf. E. Ir. *gád,* danger, Gr. χάζω, retire, χζίος, want, χωρίς, Lat. *hē-res.*
gabhagan, a titlark (Sh., O'R., H.S.D.) :
gabhal, fork ; see best G. form in *gobhal.*

gabhann, flattery (Kirk, etc. ; O'R.), gossip (Perth) ; from *gabh* : "take in" ?

gabhar, goat ; see best G. form in *gobhar*.

gabhd, a crafty trick ; from Sc. *gaud*, a trick. Cf. M. E. *gaude*, specious trick (Chaucer), from Lat. *gaudium*, Eng. *gaud*.

gabhlan, a wandering, a man devoid of care (H.S.D., which makes it Dial. ; M'E.) :

gach, each, every, Ir. *gach*, O. Ir. *cach*, *cech*, omnis, quivis, W. *pob*. O. W., Cor. *pop*, Br. *pep*, *pob* : **qo-qa*, **qe-qa*, root *qo*, *qe*, of interrogative *co* ; Lat. *quisque* ; Skr. *kaç-ca* ; etc.

gad, a withe, switch, Ir. *gad*, E. Ir. *gat* : **gazdo-* ; Got. *gazds*, goad, O. H G. *gart*, sting, rod, Norse. *gaddr*, sting, Eng. *yard* ; Lat. *hasta*, spear (from *ghaz-dhâ* ?)

gàd, **gàt**, an iron bar ; from Sc. *gad*, a bar of metal, Eng. *gad*, wedge of steel, M. Eng. *gad*, spike, bar, Norse, *gaddr*, as under *gad*.

gadaiche, thief, Ir. *gaduigh*, E. Ir. *gataige* ; see *goid*.

gadair, tie the fore feet of a horse, etc. (H.S.D., Dial) ; from *gad*.

gadhar, **gaothar**, lurcher dog, Ir. *gadhar*, mastiff, hunting dog, M. Ir. *gadar*, mastiff, E. Ir. *gagar* ; from Norse *gagarr*, dog (K. Meyer) ? The Norse has *gagg*, the fox's cry, *gagl*, a wild-goose ; this seems to prove that the Norse has a root *gag*, howl, and is likely the original source of *gagar*.

gadluinne, a slender, feeble fellow, a salmon after spawning (Sh.) : **gad* + ?

gadmunn, hair insect, nit (H.S.D., M'A.) :

gàdraisg, tumult, confusion (H.S.D., Dial.) :

gafann, henbane (Sh., O'B., H.S.D.), Ir. *gafann*, Cor. *gahen* :

gàg, a cleft, chink, Ir. *gág* : **gâggâ*, *gâs-g*, I. E. root *ghâg*, further *ghô*, *gha* ; Eng. *gap*, *gape* ; Gr. χάσκω, yawn, χάος, abyss, Eng. *chaos* ; Lat. *fauces*, throat. Cf. W. *gag*. Skeat takes hence Eng. *jag*.

gagach, stuttering (Sh., O'R.), Br. *gak* ; an onomatopoetic word. Cf. Eng. *gag*, which Skeat queries if from G.

gagan, a cluster :

gaibhteach, a person in want, craver ; from *gabh*.

gailbheach, stormy, prodigious, E. Ir. *gailbech*, blustering ; cf. Eng. *gale*, of Scandinavian origin, Dan. *gal*, furious, Norse *galinn* (do.). Also **gailbhinn**, a storm at sea, a storm of snow.

gailbhinn, a great rough hill (Sh., "gailebhein," H.S.D.) :

gaile, excitement (M'D.) :

gaill, surly look, etc. ; see *goill*.

gàilleach, gailleach, the gum, a swelling of the gum (in cattle), seam of shoe uppers, or junction of inner and outer barks of trees, Ir. *gailleach* (O'B.):

gailleag, a blow on the cheek, Ir. *gailleóg*; from *gaill*. Cf. *sgailleag*.

gaillionn, a storm; cf Norwegian *galen*, wind-storm, Norse *galinn*, furious, Eng. *gale*.

gaillseach, an earwig, so Ir.:

gaillseach, a mouth overcharged so that the cheeks swell out, a mouthful of flesh. See *goill*.

gaineamh, sand, so Ir., E. Ir. *ganem*; root *gâ* of Gr γαῖα, earth? Stokes gives the stem as *gasnimâ*, root *ghas*, Lat *harēna*, sand. But *gasn-* should give G. *gann*. Also **gainmheach,** E. Ir *ganmech*,

gainisg, gainisgeag, sedge, a small divinity in marshes and sedges by water, moaning for deaths to come (Carm.):

gainne, a dart, arrow (Sh., O'B., H.S.D., M'E.), **gàinne,** arrow-head (Arg.), Ir. *gainne*: *gasniâ*; root *gas* of *gad*, q.v.

gainntir, a prison, Ir. *gaintir* (Fol.):

gair, near; see *gar*.

gair, call, crow; see *goir*.

gàir, a shout, outcry, Ir., E. Ir. *gáir*, W. *gawr*, clamor: **gâri-*; Gr. γῆρυς (Dor. γᾶρυς), voice; root *gar*, *ger*, as in *goir*, q.v.

gàir, laugh, **gàire,** a laugh, Ir. *gáirim*, *gáire*, E. Ir. *gáire* (n.); from root *gar*, as in the foregoing word. Stokes gives the stem as **gâsriâ*, and cfs. Skr. *hasrá*, laughing, *has*, laugh.

gairbh, a greedy stomach, deer's paunch:

gairbheil, gaireal, freestone, gravel, Ir. *gairbhéal*, pron. *grabheal*; from Eng. *gravel*.

gairbhtheann, a species of wild grass (H.S.D.):

gàirdeachas, rejoicing, Ir. *gáirdeachas*, M. Ir. *gáirdechad*, delighting; from *gàir*, laugh. K. Meyer regards this as from older **gartiugud*, shortening or whiling time, from *goirid*, E. Ir. *urgartiugud*, while time, amuse; with a leaning on *gàir*, laugh. Cf. W. *difyru*, amuse, divert, from *byr*, short.

gàirdean, gaoirdean, an arm; from Sc. *gardy*, arm, *gardis*, yards, same as *yard*.

gairgean, garlic; from Eng. *garlic* and G. *garg*, bitter, by popular etymology.

gairgein, stale wine, Ir. *gairgín*, dung; from *garg*.

gaireas, goireas, convenience; see *goireas*.

gairisinn, disgust, Ir. *gairseamhuil*, obscene, wanton:

gairm, a call, office, Ir. *gairm*, pl. *garmanna*, O. Ir. *gairm*, W., Br. *garm*, a shout: **garsmen-*; root *gar* of *goir*, q.v.

gàirneal, a meal chest, Ir. *gairnéal*, a meal magazine, garner; from Sc. *garnell*, *girnell*, Eng. *garner*, from O. Fr. *gernier*, from Lat. *granarium*, granary.

gàirneilear, a gardener; from the English.

gais, a torrent (H.S.D. and Ir.), surfeit; from Eng. *gush* ?

gàis, wisdom, lance, plenty (Carm):

gais, shrivel up; from *gas*, twig ? For sense, cf. *crannadh*.

gaisde, a trap (Sh., O'B., H.S.D.), Ir. *gaisde*, O. I. *goiste*, noose; from *gaoisd*, horse hair ?

gaisde, a wisp of straw (H.S.D.); cf. *gaoisd*.

gaise, a daunting (M'A.); cf. *gais*, shrivel.

gaisge, valour, Ir. *gaisge*, bravery, E. Ir. *gaisced*, *gasced*, bravery, feats of arms, armour, weapons; the idea seems to be "feats" and the root the same as in *gasda*, q.v.

gal, weeping, Ir. *gul*, E. Ir. *gol*, I. E. *gel*, pain; Ger. *qual*, pain, *quälen*, torment; Lit *gélti*, to smart. Cf. *galar*.

†**gal**, valour, war, E. Ir. *gal*, O. Br. *gal*, puissance, **galâ*, W. *gallu*, posse, Br. *galloet* (do.), Cor. *gallos*, might: **galno-*; Lit. *galiu*, I can, Ch. Sl. *golemŭ*, great. Hence the national name *Galatae*, Galatian, also *Gallus*, a Gaul (but see *Gall*).

galad, good girl, brave girl, fem. for *laochan*, used in encouraging address: **a ghalad.** Root is *gal* (**galnat*), brave.

galan, a gallon, Ir. *galun*; from the Eng.

galar, a disease, Ir, O. Ir. *galar*, W. *galar*, grief, Br. *glar*, *glachar* (do.); **galro-n*. Bez. suggests as allied Norse *galli*, flaw, Umbr. *holtu*, Ch. Sl. *zŭlŭ*, bad, sore. But cf. *gal*, weep.

galc, thicken cloth, fulling; from the Eng. *walk*, *waulk*.

Gall, a Lowlander, stranger, Ir. *Gall*, a stranger, Englishman, E. Ir. *gall*, foreigner; from *Gallus*, a Gaul, the Gauls being the first strangers to visit or be visited by the Irish in Pre-Roman and Roman times (Zimmer). For derivation see *gal*, valour. Stokes takes a different view; he gives as basis for *gall*, stranger, **gallo-s*, W. *gal*, enemy, foe: **ghaslo-* ? root *ghas*, Lat *hos-tis*, Eng. *guest*. Hence he derives *Gallus*, a Gaul, so named from some Celtic dialect.

galla, a bitch; cf. W. *gast*, a bitch. G. is possibly for **gas-liâ*. Pott has adduced Spanish *galgo*, greyhound, which, however, is founded on *Canis Gallicus*. See *gasradh* for root.

gallan, a branch, a youth (fig.): **gas-lo-*, root *gas* of *gas*, q.v. Cf. W. *gelin*, a shoot.

galluran, wood angelica, so. Ir.: *gal* + *flùran*.

galuban, a band put upon the dugs of mares to prevent the foal sucking (H.S.D., Dial.):

gàmag, a stride, Ir. *gámus*, proud gait or carriage: **gang-mo-* (?); Sc. *gang*, Ger. *gang*, gait. Cf. *gòmag*.

gamhainn, a year-old calf, a stirk, Ir. *gamhuin*, a calf, E. Ir. *gamuin*, pl. g. *gamna*, year-old calf; from *gam*, winter: "winter-old." For root, see *geamhradh*. Confirmed by the proverb: "Oidhche Shamhna, theirear gamhna ris na laoigh" —On Hallowe'en the calves are called stirks. Similarly and from the same root are Norse *gymbr*, a year-old ewe lamb, Sc. *gimmer*, Gr. *χίμαρος*, a yearling goat (Dor.). Hence **gamhnach,** farrow cow.

gamhlas, malice, **gannlas, ganndas** (Dial.); from *gann ?*

ganail, rail, fold (Sh., O'B., H.S.D.), Ir. *ganail*: cf. gunwale.

gangaid, deceit (Sh., O'B., etc.), bustle, light-headed creature (Sh.), Ir., M. Ir., *gangaid*, deceit, falsehood:

gann, scarce, Ir. *gann*, O. Ir. *gann*, *gand*: **gando-s*; Skr. *gandháyate*, hurt; Lit. *gendù*, be injured (Stokes).

gànradh, a gander, Ir. *gandal*; from the Eng.

gànraich, roaring noise as of billows or birds:

gaog, a lump as in yarn or cloth; cf. *goigean*.

gaoid, a blemish, Ir. *gaoid*, a stain; cf. E. Ir. *góet*, a wound: **gaizdo-*; Lit. *żaizda*, a wound.

gaoir, a noise, a cry of pain or alarm, sensation or thrill of pain (Perth.); from *gàir*, shout?

gaoisd, gaoisid, horse hair, M. Ir. *goisideach*, crinitus, O. Ir. *goiste*, suspendium, laqueus: **gaissinti-*, **gait-tinti*; Gr. *χαίτη*, mane, flowing hair.

gaoistean, a crafty fellow (H.S.D. from MSS.), Ir. *gaistín*; cf. *gaisde*, a trap.

gaoithean, a fop, empty-headed fellow; from *gaoth*, wind.

gaol, love, Ir. *gaol*, kin, family, E. Ir. *gáel*, relationship: **gailo-*; Lit. *gailùs*, compassionate; Got. *gailjan*, gladden, Ger. *geil*, wanton; Gr. *φίλος*, friendly. Stokes and Strachan agree.

gaorr, fæces, ordure in the intestines, gore, Ir. *garr*; probably from Eng. *gore*, Ag S *gor*, dirt. Hence **gaorran,** big belly, a glutton. In Arg. pronounced with Northern *ao* sound; in North, pronounced with *ao* broad as in Arg. Consider *skar* in sharn (Sc.); cf. *caoirnean* or *gaoirnean*.

gaorsach, a bawd, slut: "dirty wench;" from *gaorr* and the female termination *-sach ?* Cf. *siùrsach*.

gaort, giort, a saddle girth; from the Eng.

gaoth, wind, so Ir., E. Ir. *gaeth*, *goeth*, O. Ir. *gáith*: **gaito-*, from root *gai*, I. E. *ghai*, *ghei*, *ghi*, drive, storm, as in G. *geamhradh*, q.v. Eng. *ghost* (I. E. *ghoizdo-s*) is allied. Stokes refers it to the root of *gath* solely, which is *ghai* as above.

gar, warm, Ir. *goraim*, O. Ir. *gorim*, Br. *gor*, burning, W. *gwrês*, heat: **gorô*, I warm; Gr. *θερος*, summer heat, *θερμός*, warm, Eng. *thermo*-meter; Lat. *furnus*, oven, furnace; Ch. Sl.

gorêti, burn; further Eng. *warm* (I. E. **ghᵘormo-*, Teut. *gwarm*.

gar, gair, gaire, near proximity, Ir. *gar*, near (adj. and adv.), M. Ir. *gar*, shortly, W. *ger*, *gar*. near. See *goirid* for root.

gar, although (Dial.): **ga-ro*. For *ga*, see *ge; ro* is the verbal particle.

gàradh, gàrradh, a garden, Ir. *gardhadh*, M. Ir. *garrda*; from the Norse *garðr*, a yard, M. Eng. *gard*, *garþ*, Eng. *yard*, *garden*.

garadh, garaidh, a den, copse, **garan,** thicket, Ir. *garán*, underwood, thicket, *garrán*, grove, root *gar*, bristle, be rough, I. E. *gher*, stand stiff, tear, scratch; Gr. χάραξ, a stake, χαράδρα, ravine; Lat. *hir-sutus*, hirsute, *hēr*, hedge-hog, *furca*, a fork; Lit. *żeriù*, scrape, etc. See *garbh*.

garbh, rough, so Ir., O. Ir. *garb*, W. *garw*, Br. *garu*, hard, cruel: **garvo-*; I. E. *gher*, scratchy, rough, tearing; Gr. χήρ, hedgehog, Lat. *hēr* (do.), *hirsutus*, hirsute, Skr. *hárshati*, be stiff. See *garadh* further. Some join it with Lat. *gravis*, but as this is allied to Gr. βαρύς, heavy, the G. would rather be *barbh*. Lat. *horreo ?*

garbhag, sprat, garvie (Dial.); from the Sc. *garvie*. In Arran, **garbhanach** is the sea-bream, but this is from G. *garbh*.

garbhan, the gills of a fish (N. H.). See *giùran*.

gàrcan, a hen's complaint; onomatopoetic. See *gràchdan*.

garg, fierce, angry, bitter, Ir. *garg*, O. Ir. *garg*, *gargg*: **gorgo-s*; Gr. γοργός, rough, frightsome. There is an obsolete M. Ir. *gearg*, **gergo-s*.

gàrlach, a screaming infant, little villian, vagabond, Ir. *garlach*; from *gar*, cry, with the termination *-lach* (see *òglach*).

garluch, a mole (Sh., O'B., H.S.D.), Ir. *garluch*: **gar-luch*; *luch* and *gar* (?).

garmainn, garman, a weaver's beam, Ir., E. Ir. *garmain*, O. Ir. gen. *garmne*, W. *carfan*; from the root of *cuir*, put ? **ger*, **gher*, spear ?

garrach, a glutton, gorbelly, dirty creature, Ir. *garrfhiach*, a glutton (O'B.); allied to Eng. *gorbelly*, *gore*, by borrowing (?).

gàrradh, a garden; better spelling than *gàradh*, q.v.

garrag, a young crow; cf. Eng. *gorcrow*, root *gor* of Eng. *gore*, as in *garrach*.

garrag, a sudden yell, Ir. *gartha*, clamour, roaring; from *gar* of *goir*.

gart, surly aspect, gloom; cf. *goirt*, sore, sour.

gart, standing corn, Ir. *gort*, cornfield, O. Ir. *gort*, seges; Gr. χόρτος, fodder. See *goirtean* further.

gartan, a garter; from the Eng.

gas, twig, a stalk, Ir. *gas* : **gastâ* ; Lat. *hasta* (see *gad*). Bez. queries if not from **gaksâ*, Lit. *zagarai*, brushwood.

gàsaid, fray (Dial.) :

gasda, excellent, Ir. *gasda*, clever, ingenious, E. Ir. *gasta* (do.) : **gassavo-s*, **gas-tavo*, root *gad* (*gad-s*) ; Gr. ἀγαθός, Eng. *good*, Lat. *habilis ?*

gasg, a tail : **gad-sko-* ; Zend *zadhañh*, podex, Gr. χέζω, cacare.

gasgag, a step, stride : **gad-sko-*, root *gad*, go, M. Ir. *gaid*, goes ; Eng. *gait*, Ger. *gasse*, way.

gasradh, salacity in female dogs, W. *gast*, a bitch ; root *gas*, *gat-s*, M. Br. *gadales*, meretrix, Fr. *gouïne*, O. Ir. *goithimm*, futuo.

gasraidh, rabble, mercenary soldiers, Ir. *gasradh*, band of domestic troops, "youths," from *gas*, military servant ; borrowed from the W. *gwas*, whence Eng. *vassal*. See *fasdadh*.

gàt, an iron bar ; see *gàd*.

gath, a dart, sting, Ir. *gath*, E. Ir. *gai*, *gae*, Gaul. *gaiso-n* ; Norse *geirr*, spear, Ag. S. *gâr*, Eng. *gar*-lic ; Gr. χαῖος, shepherd's crook ; Skr. *héshas*, missile.

ge, whoever, **ge b' è**, whatever, whoever, Ir. *gibé*, E. Ir. *cé bé* ; for *ge*, see *co*, the interrogative pronoun ; *bé* is the subj. of *bì*.

ge, though, Ir. *gidh*, O. Ir. *ce*, *ci*, *cía* ; same root as above. See also *ged*.

geacach, sententious, pert ; from Sc. *geck*, to sport, to deride, Ger. *gecken*, hoax.

gead, a spot of arable land, a garden bed, a spot in a horse's forehead, Ir. *gead* :

gead, a lock of hair (H.S.D.) ; also "to clip" :

geadas, a pike, Ir. *geadus* ; from Norse *gedda*, Sc. *ged*, allied to Eng. *goad*.

gèadh, a goose, Ir. *géadh*, E. Ir. *géd*, W. *gwydd*, O. Cor. *guit*, auca, Cor. *goydh*, goose, Br. *goaz*, *gwaz* : **gegdo-*, root *geg*, cry like a goose ; Norse *gagl*, wild goose, M. H. G. *gage*, *gige*, cry like a goose, *gigze*, produce inarticulate sound ; Lit. *gagónas*, goose-like, Servian *gagula*, a water-fowl, Russ. *gagara*, silver-diver (Stokes). It cannot be referred to the roots of Eng. *goose* and *gander* (*ghans-*, *ghandro-*).

geadhail, a ploughed field, park (Arg., M'A.) ; hence **earghalt**, arable land : same root as **gead**, viz., *ged*, hold, Eng. *get*.

geal, a leech, E. Ir. *gel*, W. *gel*, Cor. *ghel*, Br. *gelaonen* ; Gr. βδέλλα, βλέτυες, leeches (Hes.) ; Skr. *jalûka*, blood-leech ; I. E. root *gel*, devour, Lat. *gula*, throat, Eng. *gullet*, etc.

geal, white, Ir. *geal*, E. Ir. *gel* : **gelo-*, I. E. root *ghel*, clear, shine, glow ; Lit. *geltas*, pale-yellow ; Eng. *gleam*, glow ; Gr. χλίω, be warm, χάλις, unmixed wine ; etc. Stokes connects it with Lit. *żila-s*, grey ; the usual derivation joins it with Lat.

helvus, light bay, Eng. *yellow*, Lit. *żélti*, grow green, Ch. Sl. *zelenŭ*, green. Hence **gealach**, the moon, so Ir.; **gealan**, a linnet.

gealbhan, a fire, little fire: **gelvo-*, I. E. *ghel*, glow; Eng. *glow*, *gleam*; Gr. χλίω, be warm. See *geal*.

gealbhonn, a sparrow, so Ir., M. Ir. *gelbund*, W. *golfan*, Cor., Br. *golvan*; from *geal*, white. Cf. Gr. χελιδών, swallow, Norse *gal* (do.).

geall, a pledge, Ir. *geall*, O. Ir. *gell*, pignus: **gis-lo-*, root *gis*, *geis*, of *giall*, hostage, q.v. Stokes derives it thus: **geldo-s*, **geldo-n*, now **gelno-n*, *gislo-n-*, Got. *gild*, tribute, Ger. *geld*, money, Eng. *yield*, *guild*; Gr. ὀφέλλω, owe, τέλθος (Hes.), debt.

geall, desire, longing, Ir. *geall*: in the G. phrase, **an geall air**, Keating's *i ngeall*, in need of; from *geall* above.

gealtach, cowardly, Ir. *gealtach*, fearful; see *geilt*.

geamhradh, winter, Ir. *geimhreadh*, E. Ir. *gemred*, O. Ir. *gaimred*, O. W. *gaem*, W. *gauaf*, Cor. *goyf*, Br. *goam*, M. Br. *gouaff*: **gimo-* (for Gadelic), **gaiamo-*, **gaimo-* (for Brittonic, Stokes); I. E. *ghim*, *gheim*, *ghiem*; Skr. *himá*, cold, Zend *zima*, winter; Ch. Sl. *zima*; Gr. χειμών; Lat. *hiems*. The O. Ir. *gam*, for *gem*, has its vowel influenced by the analogy of *samh* of *samhradh* (Thur.). Thur. now suggests Celt. **giamo*; cf. Gaul. *Giamillus*.

geamhta, geamhd, anything short and thick, Ir. *geamhdóg*, a little cake of bread (O'R.); for root, cf. *geimheal*. Cf. Ir. *giobhta*, *giota*, a piece.

geamnaidh, chaste, Ir. *geanmnuidh*, E. Ir. *genmnaid*, O. Ir. *genas*, castitas; from the root *gen*, birth, Eng. *genteel*, *gentle*. See *gin*.

gean, mood, humour, good humour, Ir. *gean*, favour, approval, affection; cf. Lat. *genius*, *ingenium*, root *gen*, Eng. *kin*, *kind*. E. Ir. *gen*, laugh, may be compared to Gr. γάνος, joy (Bez.); Stokes suggests **gesno-*, Skr. *has*, laugh.

geangach, crooked, thick and short; see *gingein*.

geanm-chnò, chesnut, Ir. *geanmchnú*: "chastity tree;" a mistaken translation of Lat. *castanea*, chesnut, as if from *castus*, chaste.

geannair, a hammer, wedge, Ir. *geannaire*; see *geinne*.

gearan, a complaint, Ir. *gearán*, M. Ir. *gerán*, root *ger*, cry; O. H. G., *quëran*, sigh, *chara*, weep, Ag. S. *cearu*, sorrow, Eng. *care*; further allied is root *gar*, sound, as in *goir*. Cf. W. *gerain*, cry, squeak, and Gr. δύρομαι, lament.

gearasdan, a garrison, Ir. *gairision*; from the Eng.

geàrnal, girnell; see *gàirneal*.

geàrr, short, cut (vb.), Ir. *geárr*, *geárraim*, E. Ir. *gerr*, *gerraim*: **gerso-s*. Stokes cfs. Gr. χερείων, χείρων, worse, Skr. *hrasva*, short. Cf. M. Eng. *garsen*, gash, O. Fr. *garser*.

geàrr, a hare, Ir. *geirrfhiadh*: "short deer;" from *geàrr* and *fiadh*, the latter word being omitted in G.

geàrrach, diarrhœa, bloody flux:

gearraidh, the pasture-land between the shore-land and the moorland (Heb.); from N. *gerði*, fenced field, garth. Shet. *Gairdie*.

gearran, a gelding, Ir., M. Ir. *gearrán*; from *geàrr*, cut.

Gearran, the 4 weeks dating from 15th March onwards (H.S.D.). This forms a part of the animal nomenclature given to the several periods of Spring-time: first the **Faoilleach**, explained as "Wolf-month"; then the **Feadag**, or Plover, a week's length; then the **Gearran**, or Gelding, variously estimated as to length and time; then came the **Cailleach**, or Old Woman, a week's time; then perhaps the three days of the **Oisgean**, or ewes. See Nich. pp. 412-414.

geas, spell, taboo, charm, Ir., E. Ir. *geis*, taboo, *gessim* (vb.): **gessô*, **ged-to*, root *ged* of *guidhe*, q.v.

geata, gate, so Ir., M. Ir. *geta*; from Ag. S. *geat*, Eng. *gate*.

ged, although: **ge-ta*; same as *ciod*.

geil, a bubble, well (Carm.); also *boil*:

géill, yield, submit, Ir. *géillim*, E. Ir, *gíallaim*, O. Ir. *geillfit*, dedentur; from *giall*, hostage.

geilt, terror, fear, Ir. *geilt*, a distracted person, wild, M. Ir. *geltacht*, flying, E. Ir. *geilt*, mad by fear; Norse *verða at gjalti*, to turn mad with terror (borrowed from Celtic, Stokes, Thurneysen; borrowed into Celtic, Zimmer). Stokes refers it to a root *ghel*, fly, suggested by Gr. χελιδών, a swallow.

geimheal, a fetter, chain, Ir. *géimhiol*, E. Ir. *geimel*, *gemel*: **gemelo-*, root *gem*, fasten; Gr. γέντο, grasped (*γέμ-το), γάμος, marriage; Lat. *gemini*, twins; Ch. Sl. *żimą*, com primere.

geimhleag, **gèimhleag** (Wh.), a crow-bar, lever; from Sc. *gaveloch*, a spear, *javelin*, Ag. S. *gafeloc*, spear, possibly from an early form of W. *gaflach*, a dart, the root being that in *gobhal*, fork.

geinn, a wedge, so Ir., E. Ir. *geind*, W. *gaing*, Br. *genn*, O. Br. *gen*, M. Br. *guenn*: **genni-*, root *gen*, as in Lettic *dfenis*, the wood wedged into the fork of the ploughshare, *dfenulis*, sting, Ch. Sl. *żęlo* (do.). N. *gand*, *gann*, a peg, stick, Lat. *offendo*, **fendo*, Eng. *offend* (Stokes and Liden). Cf. Ir. *ding*.

geintleach, a heathen, Ir. *geinteach*, M. Ir. *genntlige* (adj.), *gennti*, gentiles; from the Lat. *gens* (*gentis*), *gentilis*.

geir, tallow, Ir., E. Ir. *geir*, W. *gwer*, *gired*, grease. Cf. Gr. χρίω, anoint, Scr. *gharsati* (do.), **ghrsjô*.

geis, gestation, gestators ; milk (Carm.) :

géisg, creaking noise ; see *gìosgan*.

geòb, a wry mouth ; from the Eng. *gape*, Ag. S. *geapian*.

geòc, **geoic**, a wry neck ; formed on Eng. *cock ?* Cf. Sc. *gekk*, grimace.

geòcaire, a glutton, Ir. *geócaire*, a glutton, stroller, parasite, M. Ir. *geocach*, mimus ; formed on Lat. *jocosus* (Stokes).

geòdh, **geodha**, a creek : from the Norse *gjá*, a chasm, whence N. Scotch *geo*.

geòla, ship's boat, yawl ; from the Scandinavian—Mod. Norse *jula*, Swedish *julle*, Dan. *jolle*, Sc. *yolle*, Eng. *yawl*, *jolly*-boat.

geòlach, a wooden bier, the shoulder-bands of the dead ; for root, see *giùlan ?*

geòpraich, a torrent of idle talk ; cf. *geòb* above.

geolan, a fan, **geulran** (Sh.), Ir. *geóilrean* ; from the root of *giùlan ?*

geòtan, a spot of arable ground (H.S.D.), a driblet or trifling sum (M'A.) :

geuban, **giaban**, the craw or crop of a bird ; see *geòb*.

geug, a branch, Ir. *geug*, *géag*, E. Ir. *géc* : **gn̥kâ*, *kn̥kâ*, W. *cainc*, *ysgainc* ; Skr. *çañkú*, twig, stake ; Ch. Sl. *sąkŭ*, surculus.

geum, a low, Ir. *geim*, a lowing, roar, E. Ir. *géim*, shout, *géssim*, I low : **gengmen-* ; Lit. *żvengiu*, neigh ; Ch. Sl. *zvęgą*, sound. Cf. Eng. *squeak*. Cf. Ch. Sl. *gangnati*, murmur.

geur, **giar**, sharp, Ir. *geur*, O. Ir. *gér* :

gheibh, will get, Ir. *gheibhim* ; root-accented form of *faigh*, q.v.

giaban, gizzard ; see *geuban*.

giall, a jaw or cheek, jowl, Ir., M. Ir. *giall*, faucibus ; the G. form **ciobhall** seems borrowed from Ag. S. *ceafl*, Eng. *jowl* ; perhaps all are from the Eng.

†**giall**, a hostage, pledge, Ir. *giall*, O. Ir. *giall*, W. *gwystl*, hostage, Cor. *guistel*, obses, Br. *goestl*, Gaul. *Co-gestlos*, **geislo-*, **geistlo-* ; O. H. G. *gîsal*, Ger. *geisel*, Norse *gísl*, Ag. S. *gîsel*.

giamh, **giomh**, a fault, blemish :

gibeach, hairy, **gibeag**, a rag, bundle, Ir. *giobach*, *giobóg*, and *giob*, tail, rag, O. Ir. *gibbne*, cirrus :

gibeach, neat ; for *sgibeach ?* See *sgiobalt*.

gibein, a piece of flesh (M'E.) ; from *gib* of *giblion*.

giblean, April :

giblion, entrails of a goose, **gibean** (St Kilda), grease from the solan goose's stomach :

gibneach, cuttle-fish : **gebbi-* ; Ger. *quappe*, turbot ?

gidheadh, nevertheless, Ir. *gidheadh*: for an older *cid + ed* "though it (is)"; Lat. *quid id*. See *co* and *eadh*.

gigean, geigean, master at death revels (Carm.):

gigean, a diminutive man, little mass; native form of *ceig*, q.v.

gighis, a masquerade, so Ir.; from Sc. *gyis*, a mask, *gysar*, a harlequin, one that disguises himself at New Year, *gys*, to disguise, M. Eng. *gîsen*, dress, prepare, from O. Fr. (*de*)*gviser* Eng. dis-*guise*.

gilb, a chisel: **gḷbi-*; cf. Gr. γλάφω, carve. But cf. W. *gylyf*, sickle, O Cor. *gilb*, foratorium, allied to G. *guilbneach*, q.v.

gille, lad, servant, Ir. *giolla*, E. Ir. *gilla*; cf. Eng. *child*, Ag. S. *cild*. Zimmer thinks it is borrowed from the Norse *gildr*, stout, brawny, of full worth, Eng. *guild*, Ag. S. *gild*, payment (see *geall*), *gilda*, fellow, used in the names of Norsemen converted to Christianity instead of *maol*, slave. *Gille-foluinn*, sea-grass (Wh.).

gilm, a buzzard:

gilmean, a fop, flatterer; see *giolam*,

gimleid, a gimlet, Ir. *gimléad*; from the English.

gin, beget, Ir. *geinim*, M. Ir. *genar*, was born, O. Ir. *ad-gainemmar*, renascimur, *gein*, birth, W. *geni*, nasci, Br. *ganet*, born, **genô*, nascor; Lat. *gigno*, *genui*, begat; Gr. γίγνομαι, become, γένος, race; Eng. *kin*; Skr. *jána*, race, stock, *jánâmi*, beget. Hence **gin**, anyone.

gineal, offspring, W. *genill*; Ir. *ginealach*, a generation, G. **ginealach**, M. Ir. *genelach*, genealogy, from Lat. *genealogia*, root *gen* as in *gin*.

gingein, a cask, barrel, thick set person (not H.S.D.):

giobag, gibeag, fringe, rag, Ir. *giobóg*. See *gibeach*.

gioball, vesture, cast clothes, Ir. *giobál*; see *gibeach*.

gioball, a chap, odd fellow; a bad fellow (Perth); a metaphoric use of *gioball* above.

giodaman, a perky fellow:

giodar, dung, ordure (H.S.D. for C.S.), Ir. *giodar* (do.), *geadan*, buttock: **geddo-*, root *ghed*, cacare; Gr. χέζω, cacare, χόδανος, the breech; Skr. *had*, cacare, Zd. *zadhañh*, podex.

giodhran, a barnacle (bird), Ir. *giodhrán*, O. Ir. *giugrann*, W. *gwyrain*: **geguranná*; root *geg* as in *gèadh*, q.v. Fick has compared Lat. *gingrum*, goose. Also **giùran**. In Is. of Arran, *giúraing*, a shell fish that bores holes in wreckage.

giog, cringe; also "peep" (M'A.):

giogan, a thistle (Sh., O'R. *giogun*):

giolam, gileim, tattle, Ir. *giolmhaim*, solicit:

†**giolc**, reed, Ir. *giolcach*, E. Ir. *gilcach*:

giolc, stoop, aim at (M'A):
giolcair, a flippant fellow:
giolcam-daobhram, animalcule (H.S.D.):
giomach, a lobster, Ir. *giomach*, *gliomach* (?), W. *ceimwach*:
giomanach, a hunter; from the Eng. *game*.
gionach, greed, M. Ir. *ginach*, craving; from †**gin**, mouth, O. Ir. *gin*, W. *gên*, gena, mentum, Cor. *genau*, os, Br. *guen*, cheek: **genu-*; Gr. γένυς, chin; Lat. *gena*, cheek; Eng. *chin*.
giorag, panic, apprehension, noise, Ir. *giorac*, noise (*gíorac*, Con.):
giort, a girth, Ir. *giorta*; from the Eng.
gìosgan, creaking, gnashing, Ir. *gíosgán*; also Ir. *díoscán*.
giseag, a fret or bit of superstition, a charm; see *geas*.
gith, a shower, series (H.S.D.); cf. E. Ir. *gith*, way of motion, Skr. *hi*, set in motion, impel, *hiti*, impelling.
githeilis, running to and fro on trifling errands, trifling, E. Ir. *gith*, way, motion. See above word.
githir, **gìr**, corn-reapers' wrist pain:
giùd, a wile:
giugas, refuse of fish left on shore:
giùig, a drooping of the head, languor:
giùlan, a carrying: **gesu-lo-*, root *ges*, carry, Lat. *gero*, *gestum*.
giulla, **giullan**, a lad, boy, Ir. *giolla*, servant, footman. From the same source as *gille*.
giullaich, prepare, manage well; from *giulla*, the idea being "serving;" cf. Ir. *giolla* above, and Ir. *giollas*, service.
giùmsgal, flattery:
giùram, complaining, mournful noise (H.S.D.); cf. I. E. *gevo-*, cry, as in *guth*, q.v.
giùran, gills of a fish, **garbhan**,: **gober-*, root of *gob*?
giùran, barnacle goose; see *giodhran*.
giuthas, fir, Ir. *giumhas*, E. Ir. *gius*: **gis-usto*, root *gis*; Ger. *kien*, resinous wood, *kien-baum*, Scotch fir, *kiefer* (*kien-föhre*), pine, Ag. S. *cén*, fir-wood, **kiz-n* (Schräder). Cf. root *gis* of *gaison*, O. Ir. *gae*. Ag. S. *gyr*, abies.
glac, take, seize, Ir., M. Ir. *glacaim*, *glaccad*, grasping, E. Ir. *glace*, hand, handful: **glapko-* (?), Eng. clasp. See *glas*.
glag, noise of anything falling, noise, horse-laugh, Ir. *glagaire*, a babbler, *glagan*, mill clapper: **glag-ko-*; Gr. γλαζω (**glagjô*), sing, noise; Eng. *clack*, M. Eng. *clacke*, mill clack, Norse *klaka*, chatter bird-like; also Eng. *clap*. There is a degree of onomato-poesy about these words. Cf. *clag*.
glàib, dirty water, puddle, Ir. *gláib*; cf. *láib*.
glaim, complaint, howling, Ir. *gláim*, M. Ir. *gláimm*: **glag-s-mâ-*; Ger. *klagen*, weep (Stráchan, Stokes).

glainne, glaine, a glass, Ir. *gloine*, E. Ir. *gloine*, *glaine*, W. *glain*, a gem, what is pure; from *glan*, clean.

glaiseach, foam (M'A.), **glais-sheile,** water-brash, from obs. *glais*, stream, E. Ir. *glaiss*, same root as *glas*.

glaisleun, lesser spear-wort (Sh.), Ir. *glaisleun*; from *glas* and *leun* or *lèan*, a swamp (Cameron).

glaistig, water imp; from *glas*, water. So Carm. Manx *glashtyn*, kelpie, etc.

glàm, devour, Ir. *glámaim*, devour, gobble, *glámaire*, glutton: **glad-s-mo-*; Ch. Sl. *gladu*, hunger. Sc. *glam*.

glamair, a smith's vice; from the Norse *klömbr*, a smith's vice, Ger. *klemmem*, pinch, jam.

glamhsa, a snap as by a dog; for form, compare Ir. *glamhsan*, a murmur, which is an aspirated form of *glaim*, howling. The G is similarly from *glàm*, devour, with possibly a leaning on the idea of noise as in *glaim*. H.S.D. has **glamhus,** open chops. **Glomhas,** open chasm (Wh.).

glan, clean, pure, Ir., O. Ir. *glan*, W. *glain*, Br. *glan*, Gaul. river name *Glana*: **glano-s*, root, *glê*, *gel*, *gla*, shine; Gr. γλήνεα, shows, γλήνη, eyeball, γελεῖν, shine (Hes.), and γλαινοί, bright ornamentation (Hes.), from root *glai*, from which Eng. *clean* comes (thus: *glê*, *gla*: *glêi*, *glai*).

glang, a ringing noise; see *gliong*.

glaodh, a cry, call, Ir. *glaodh*, M. Ir. *gloed*, a shout; cf. O. Ir. *adgládur*, appello, Skr. *hrā́date*, sound, Gr. γλῶσσα, tongue (*γλωθια ?), Ir. and G. would then be from an O. Ir. **gláid*, from **glâdi-*. Hence **glaodhar, glaoran,** a noise, prating. O. Ir. *gloidim*, ringo.

glaodh, glue, Ir. *glaodh*, M. Ir. *glóed*, E. Ir. *gláed*; **gloi-do-*, from I. E. *gloi*, *glei*, be sticky; Gr. γλοιά, γλία, γλίνη, glue: Lat. *gluten*; Ch. Sl. *glénu*, mucus; Eng. *clay*, Ger. *klei*, slime. W. *glud* and M. Br. *glut* are from the Lat.

glaodhan, pith of wood; from *glaodh*, the idea being "resinous or gluey stuff."

glaomar, a foolish person (Dial.): "noisy one;" from *glaodh*.

glaoran, blossom of wood-sorrel: **gloiro-*, "bright," root *glei* of *glé*?

glas, a lock, Ir., O. Ir. *glas*: **glapsâ*; Eng. *clasp*.

glas, grey, Ir. *glas*, green, pale, E. Ir. *glass*, W., O. W., Br. *glas*, green: **glasto-*, green; Ger. *glast*, sheen (Bez.), root *glas*, to which Ger. *glass*, Eng. *glass*, are probably allied.

glé, very, Ir. *glé*, very, pure, O. Ir. *glé*, bright, W. *gloew*, bright, O. W. *gloiu*, liquidum: **gleivo-*, I. E. *ghlei-*, shine; Eng. *gleam*, *glimmer*, Ger. *glimmen*; Gr. χλίω, χλιαρός, warm (Kluge). Bez. refers it to the root of Eng. *clean* (see *glan*).

gleac, a wrestle, fight, Ir., E. Ir. *gleic* : **glekki-*, **gleg-ko-*, I. E. *gleghô*, wager ; Ag. S. *plegen*, Eng. *pledge*, *play* ; Skr. *glah*, play at dice, cast in wappenshaw.

gleadh, an onset, deed (H.S.D.) ; cf. Ir. *gleó*, g. *gliadh*, tumult, E. Ir. *gliad*, battle :

gleadh, tricks (Sh., O'B. *gleádh*, H.S.D.) ; Ir *gleadh* (O'R.) ; for *gleagh*, *gleg*, root of *gleac* ?

gleadhraich, gleadhair, noise, rattling, clang of arms, Ir. *gleaghrach*, shout, noise ; cf. Norse *gleðir*, Christmas games, *gleðr*, merriment, Eng. *glad*. Ir. *gliadrach*, loquacious. If E. Ir. *glechrach* means "noisy," the stem is *glegar*, which also appears (*Mart. Gorman*, edited by Stokes).

gleann, a glen, so Ir., E. Ir. *glenn*, *glend*, W. *glan*, brink, shore, M. Br. *glenn*, country, Br. *glann*, river bank : **glennos* (a neuter *s*-stem). Stokes compares M. H. G. *klinnen*, Swiss *klänen*, to climb, Norse *klunna*, cling to. Norse *gil* ?

glèidh, preserve, keep, Ir. *gléithim*, keep, clear up, cleanse, E. Ir. *gléim*, make clear, put in order, lay by. See *glé* for root, and also *gleus*.

gleithir, a gadfly (M'D., Sh., O'R.) : **glegh-* ; cf. Sc. *cleg*, Norse *kleggi*, gadfly.

gleò, dazzling haziness about the eyes :

gleog, a drooping, silly look ; cf. *sgleogair*.

gleòid, a sloven, Ir. *gleoid*. See *sgleòid*.

gleòisg, gleosg, a vain, silly woman, Ir. *gleosg*. See next word.

gleòman, a silly, stupid fellow, Ir. *gleodhmán* :

gleòrann, cresses, wild angelica, Ir. *gleórann*, wild angelica ; cf E. Ir. *gleóir*, sheen, M. Ir. *gleordha*, bright ; root is likely that of *glé* (**glivo-ro-*).

gleus, order, trim, tune, Ir. *gleus*, E. Ir. *glés* ; for root, see *glèidh* and *glé*. Strachan adduces E. Ir. *glése*, brightness, and takes it from **glent-t-*, allied to Ger. *glanz*, splendour, Eng. *glance*. Cf. W. *glwys*, fair, pleasant. Hence **gleusda,** diligent.

† **glib**, a lock of hair, Ir. *glib* : **g̣lb-bi* ; cf. Eng. *clip*. Hence Eng. *glib*.

glìb, sleet, **glibshleamhuinn**, slippery with sleet (Sh., who gives **glib**, slippery) ; from Sc. *glib*, slippery, Eng. *glib*.

glic, wise, Ir. *glic*, O. Ir. *glicc* : **g̣lkki-*. Stokes compares Gr. καλχαίνω, ponder, and takes from G. the Sc. *gleg*.

glidich, move, stir :

glinn, pretty, (Strathspey and Lochbroom Dialects for **grinn**), Ir. *glinn*, bright ; Eng. *glint*, *gleam*, *glance*.

gliog, gliogar, a tinkling, clink, Ir. *gliogar* ; Eng. *click*, *clack* : an onomatopoetic root.

gliogram, a staggering; from *gliogar*, the idea being "noise-making"? Cf. Ir. *glingin*, drunkenness. Also G. **gliogach,** clumsy, unstable.

gliomach, slovenly, long-limbed fellow; cf. Ir. *gliomach*, a lobster.

gliong, ringing noise, Ir. *glionc* (O'R.); allied to, or from, the Eng. *clink*, Teut. *kling*.

gliostair, a clyster; from the Eng.

gliùchd, a blubbering, crying:

gloc, the clucking of a hen, noise, loud note; Eng. *clock*, *cluck*, W. *clwc*; Lat. *glocire*; etc. Onomatopoetic.

gloc, swallow greedily, **glochdan,** a wide throat; from the Sc. *glock*, gulp, *glog*, swallow hastily, E. Eng. *glucchen*, *gulchen*, swallow greedily, Ger. *glucken*, *gulken*, *klucken*.

glochar, a wheezing, difficult respiration, Ir. *glocharnach*; cf. Sc. *glag*, *glagger*, make a noise in the throat as if choking, *glugger*, to make a noise in the throat swallowing. Allied to *gloc*, etc.

gloc-nid, a morning dram taken in bed; from *gloc* and *nead*.

glodhar, ravine, chasm (Kintyre); in Lewis names N. *gljúfr*.

glog, a soft lump, **glogair,** a stupid fellow: "unstable one"; from *glug*, *gluig*.

glog, a sudden, hazy calm, a dozing (M'A.):

glòic, having hanging cheeks, as in hens:

gloichd, gloidhc, gloibhc (Wh.), a senseless woman, an idiot; from the Sc. *glaik*.

gloin, gloine, glass; see *glain*.

glòir, glory, Ir., E. Ir. *glóir*, Br. *gloar*; from Lat. *gloria*, whence, Eng. *glory*.

glòir, speech, Ir. *glór*, E. Ir. *glórach*. noisy; same as *glòir*, glory.

glòirionn, spotted in the face (H.S.D.), drab-coloured (M'A.):

glòmadh, glòmainn, the gloaming; from the Eng.

glomhar, a muzzle, an instrument put into a lamb or kid's mouth to prevent sucking, E. Ir. *glomar*, bridle; root, *glom*, *glem*. Ger. *klemmen*, jam, M. H. G. *klammer*, tenaculum, Lat *glomus*, a clew.

glomhas, a rock, cleft, chink:

glong, a slimy substance; root *glen*, be slimy, Gr. *βλέννα*, slime, snot, O. H. G. *kleban*, cleave. See *sglongaid*.

glonn, a deed of valour, Ir. *glonn*, E. Ir. *glond*, a deed: **gl-onno-*, root of *gal*?

glonn, loathing, qualm, Ir. *glonn*, E. Ir. *glonn*, crime: "facinus"; extended use of the above word.

glothagach, frog's spawn (Sh., O'R.):

gluais, move, Ir., E. Ir. *gluaisim*, O. Ir. *gluas-*; **gl-eusso-*, from root *gel*, Lat. *volo-*, fly, Gr. *βάλλω*? So Dr Cameron.

gluc, socket of the eye:

glug, noise of liquid in a vessel when moved, Ir. *glug* (do.), *glugal*. clucking of a hen; Eng. *cluck*. All are onamatopoetic. See *gloc*. Also **glugach**, stammering: "clucking." Cf. Sc. *glugger*, to make a noise in the throat by swallowing any liquid.

gluig, addled (of an egg); from the above word. Cf. W. *clwc*, soft, addled (of an egg).

glumadh, a great mouthful of liquid, **glumag**, a deep pool; allied to *glug* above.

glumraidh, hungriness, devouring (as sea waves) (Hend.):

glùn, the knee, Ir., O. Ir. *glún*, W., Br. *glin*: **glûnos*. Stokes compares Albanian *ǵu* (*ǵuri*, *ǵuni*), knee. Possibly by dissimilation of the liquids for **gnûnos*, from **gnû*, **gneu*, allied to Eng. *knee*, Gr. γνύξ, on the knee.

glupad, dropsy in throat of cattle and sheep (Carm.):

glut, voracity, **glutair**, a glutton, W. *glwth* (do.), Br. *glout* from Lat. *glutire*, swallow, Eng. *glutton*; M. Ir. *glota*, belly.

gnàithseach, arable land under crop (M'A.):

gnamhan, periwinkle (Sh., O'B., H.S.D.), Ir. *gnamhan*:

gnàth, custom, usual, Ir. *gnáth*, O. Ir. *gnáth*, solitus, W. *gnawd*, custom: **gnâto-*; Lat. (*g*)*nôtus*, known; Gr. γνωτός (do.); Skr. *jnâta* (do.); root *gnô*, *gnâ*, *gen*, know, Eng. *know*, etc.

gnè, nature, kind, Ir. *gné*, O. Ir. *gné*, gen. *gnée*, pl. *gnéthi* (neuter *s*-stem): **gneses-*; root *gen*, beget, Lat. *genus*, Gr. γένεσις genesis, γενος, Eng. *kind*.

gnìomh, a deed, Ir. *gníomh*, O. Ir. *gním*: **gnêmu-*; root *gnê*, do, from *gen*, beget, as in *gin*. Hence **dèan, nì, rinn.**

gnò, **gnodh**, gruff (Arm.); cf. Ir., E. Ir. *gnó*, derision.

gnob, a bunch, tumour: from the Eng. *knob*.

gnog, a knock; from Eng. *knock*.

gnogach, sulky (Sh., O'R., etc.), **gnoig**, a surly frown (H.S.D.); cf. *gnù*, *grùig*.

gnoigean, ball of rosin put on horns of vicious cattle (Skye):

gnoimh, visage, grin (Arm., M'D., M'A.); **gnòimh** (Rob.); cf. *gnùis*.

gnoin, shake and scold a person (M'A.):

gnomh, grunt of a pig (M'A.), for *gromh*, Ir. *grossachd*: an onomatopoetic word, allied to Lat. *grunnire*, grunt, Gr. γρῦ, swine's grunt, Eng. *grunt*, *grumph*. See *gnòsd*.

gnòmhan, groaning (of an animal), grunting; a long-vowel form of *gnomh?*

gnos, a snout (especially of a pig), Ir. *gros*, *grossach*, having a large snout: **grupso-*; Gr. γρύψ, a griffin, "hook-nosed," γρυπός, bent, Ger. *krumm*.

gnòsd, gnòsad, gnùsd, low noise of a cow, Ir. *gnúsachd* ; **grum-so* ; see *gnomh*, grunt, and *gnòmhan*. Aran Ir. *gnosacht*, grunt of pig.

gnothach, business, Ir. *gnóthuig* (pron. *gnathuigh*), *gnó* (pl. *gnóthaidhe*) : **gnavo-*, active, Lat. *gnavus*, active, Eng. *know*. See *gnìomh* and *gnàth*, for root.

gnù, gnò, surly, parsimonious, **gnùgach,** surly. See *gnò* and *grùig*.

gnùis, the face, countenance, Ir., O. Ir. *gnúis*, (fem. *i*-declension ; **gnûsti-* ; root *gen*, know, Eng. *know*, etc.

gnùth, a frowning look ; see *gnù*.

gò, a lie, fault, Ir. *gó*, lie, fraud, O. Ir. *gó*, *gáo*, *gáu*, W. *gau*, Br. *gou*, *gaou* : **gavo-*. Cf. Gr. γαυσός, crooked, γαυσάδας, a liar (Ernault). Bezzenberger gives several alternatives ; Lit. *pri-gáuti*, deceive, or Persian *zûr*, false, or Gr. χαῦνος, spongy, χάος, abyss.

gob, a beak, bill, Ir. *gob*, bill, mouth, E. Ir. *gop-chóel*, lean-jawed ; **gobbo*, root *gobh*, *gebh* ; Gr. γαμφηλαί, γαμφαί, jaws ; Ch. Sl. *ząbu*, tooth, *zobati*, eat ; Skr. *jambhas*, a tooth. Stokes compares it (**gobh-nó-*) to Zend. *zafan*, mouth The relationship to Eng. *gobbet*, *gobble*, Fr. *gobet*, O. Fr. *gober*, devour, is not clear. But cf. also Eng. *gab*, *gabble*, G. *gab*.

gobha, gobhainn, a smith, Ir. *gobha*, g. *gobhann*, O. Ir. *goba*, g. *gobann*, O. W. *gob*, W. *gof*, pl. *gofion*, Cor. *gof*, Br. *go*, Gaul. *Gobann-* : **gobân-* ; root *gobh*, as in Gr. γόμφος, a bolt, Eng. *comb* (Windisch), for which see *gob*. Lat. *faber* may, however, be allied, and the root then be *ghob*. *Gobha-uisge*, water ousel ; also *gobha-dubh*.

gobhal, a fork, Ir. *gabhal*, fork, gable, O. Ir. *gabul*, W. *gafl*, Br. *gaol* : **gabalu-* ; Eng. *gable*, Ger. *gabel*, fork ; Gr. κεφαλή, head.

gobhar, a goat, Ir. *gabhar*, O. Ir. *gabor*, W. *gafr*, Corn. *gauar*, Br. *gabr*, *gaffr*, Gaul. *gabro-* : **gabro-* ; root *gab* of *gabh*, take, as Lat. *caper* is allied to *capio*, take (Loth)? Stokes gives the stem as **gam-ro*, root *gam* of *geamhradh*, winter, and *gamhuinn*, I. E. *ghim* ; but *im* of *ghim* could not change to Gaul. *ab* in *gabro-*.

goc, a tap, cock ; from the Eng. *cock*.

gocaman, an usher, attendant, sentinel, or look-out man ; Martin's (*Western Isles*, p. 103) *gockmin*, *cockman* ; from Scandinavian *gok-man*, look-out man (Arms. ; Mackinnon says it is Danish). For root, cf. Ger. *gucken*, peep. Norse, *gauksman* ; *gauk maðr*, cuckoo man. Norse *gaukr*, cuckoo ; Sc. *gowk*.

gòdach, giddy, coquettish (Sh., etc.) ; cf. *gabhd*. *Godadh nan ceann*, tossing of one's head (Wh.).

godsag, a titbit :

gog, a nod, tossing of the head, Ir. *gog* ; from Eng. *cock*. **godadh** (Arg.).

gogaid, a giddy female, Ir. *gogaide* ; from Eng., Fr. *coquette*.

gogail, cackling, noise of liquor issuing from a cask, Ir. *gogallach* ; Eng. *cackle*. The words are onomatopoetic. Also **goglais**.

gogan, a wooden milk-pail, also **cogan** ; from Sc. *cogue*, *cog*, apparently allied to M. Eng. *cog*, ship, Norse *kuggi*, a small ship, Teutonic *kuggon-*, ship.

goic, a tossing of the head in disdain, a scoff, Ir. *goic* ; founded on the Eng. *cock*, like *gog*, q.v.

goid, steal, Ir. *goidim*, E. Ir. *gataim* : **gad-dô* , root *gad*, *ghad*, *ghed*, seize ; Gr. χανδάνω, ἔχαδον, hold, contain ; Lat. *prehendo*, seize, *praeda*, booty, *hedera*, ivy ; Eng. *get*. Thur. has compared the Lat. *hasta*, spear, giving a stem **ghazdho-*.

goigean, a bit of fat meat, cluster, thread tangle or kink ; cf. *gagan* : **gaggo-* ; cf. Gr. γαγγλίον, ganglion, a "knot," Eng. *kink*.

goil, boil, Ir. *gailim*, seethe, boil : **gali-* ; I. E. *gel*, well, Ger. *quellen*, gush. See next.

goile, a stomach, appetite, Ir. *goile*, *gaile*, stomach, appetite, throat, M. Ir. *gaile* ; also O. Ir. *gelim*, I consume ; Lat. *gula*, throat (Eng. *gullet*), *glutire*, swallow (Eng. *glutton*) ; Skr. *gilati*, swallow ; I. E. *gel*, allied to root of *goil*.

gòileag, a haycock, cole ; from the Sc. *cole*, Eng. *coll*.

goileam, tattle, chattering, also **gothlam** (*l* = *le*) ; see *gothlam*.

goileam, fire (kindling) (Carm.) :

goill, distorted face, angry face, grin, blubber lip ; cf. Ir. *gailleóg*, a blow on the cheek, G. *gailleag*. Cf. for root Gr. χεῖλος, lip, *χεσλος = Skr. *ghas*, eat, swallow.

goillir, a Lewis bird of the size of the swallow, which comes to land in winter (Arms.) :

goimh, anguish, pain, Ir. *goimh* : **gomi-*, root *gom*, *gem*, press, Lat. *gemo*, groan, Ch. Sl. *žimą*, compress.

goin, gointe ; see *gon*.

goir, call, cry, crow, Ir. *goirim*, E. Ir. *gairim*, O. Ir. *adgaur*, convenio : **garô*, speak, I. E. *ger*, cry ; Gr. γέρανος, crane, δειριᾶν, abuse ; Skr. *járate*, cry, crackle ; further Lat. *garrio*, chatter (**gars-*) ; Eng. *garrulous*, Lit. *garsas*, noise ; also root *gâr*, as in Gaelic *gàir*, Gr, γῆρυς, voice, etc.

goireas, convenience, apparatus ; from *gar*, near, and *goirid*.

goirid, short, Ir. *gairid*, O. Ir. *garit*. For root, see *geàrr* (Skr. *hrasva*, short, etc.), from which comes the comparative **giorra**. Also *gar*, near, q.v.

goirt, sore, sour, Ir. *goirt*, sore, salt, E. Ir. *goirt*, bitter : **gorti-*, I. E. *gher*, be rough, as in *garbh*.

goirtean, a little field of corn, croft, Ir. *goirtín*, *gort*, garden, corn-field, O. Ir. *gort*, seges, W. *garth*, enclosure, Br. *garz* (do.) : **gorto-* ; Lat. *hortus* ; Gr. χόρτος, straw-yard ; Eng. *garden*, *garth*, etc.

goisear (pl. **-an**), guisers, waits, singers about Christmas, etc. (Carm.) :

gòisinn, gòisne, a snare, Ir. *gaisde*, O. Ir. *goiste*, suspendium. Cf. *gaoisid*.

goisridh, company, people ; see *gasraidh*.

goisdidh, gossip, godfather, M. Ir. *goistibe*, godfather ; from M. Eng. *godsibbe*, now *gossip*.

golag, a budget : **gulo-* ; Gr. γύλιος, wallet, O. H. G. *kiulla*.

gòlanach, two-headed (H.S.D.) : "forked," from *gobhlan ?*

gomag, a nip, pinch (M'L., **gòmag**), *gàmag*, large bite (Skye) :

gon, wound, bewitch, Ir. *gonadh*, wounding, E. Ir. *gonim* : **gonô*, I wound, I. E. *ghen* ; Gr. φόνος, slaughter, θείνω, hit ; Norse, *gunnr*, battle, O. H. G. *gundea* (do.) ; Skr. *han*, strike, slay.

gonan, grass roots ; cf. *cona*.

gòrach, silly, Ir. *gorach* ; Gr. γαῦρος, exulting, skittish, haughty ; root *gau*, be free, Lat. *gaudium*, Eng. *joy*.

gorm, blue, green, Ir., E. Ir. *gorm*, blue, W. *gwrm*, dusky : *gorsmo-*, root *gor*, warm (" warm colour "), as in G. *gar* (Stokes).

gòrsaid, a cuirass, gorget ; from Eng. *gorget*.

† **gort**, a field, standing corn, Ir. *gort* ; see *gart*, *goirtean*.

gort, goirt, famine, Ir. *gorta*, O. Ir. *gorte* ; I. E. *gher*, desire, want ; Gr. Χρέος, necessity, χρηΐζω, wish ; Eng. *yearn*.

goth, toss the head contemptuously or giddily (M'A.) ; **gòth**, airy gait (Arm., **gothadh**, Sh., O'R.) : possibly from Eng. *go*. Cf. W. *goth*, pride.

gothlam, prating noise, M. Ir. *gothach*, noisy ; from *guth*.

grab, interrupt, **grabadh**, hindrance, Ir. *grabadh* ; apparently from Eng. *grab*. Cf. W. *crap*, prehensio, Romance *graffo*.

grabh, abhorrence :

grabh, grabhail, engrave, Ir. *grabháil* ; from Eng. *grave*, engrave.

gràchdan, querulous noise of hens, Ir. *gràgoill*, clucking of a hen, crow's crowing. See *gràg*.

grad, sudden, Ir. *grad*, *grod* : **groddo-*, root *grod*, *gred*, as in *greas*, q.v.

gràda, ugly ; usual form of *grànda*, q.v.

gradan, snuff, corn kilned by burning its straw, the meal derived from the foresaid corn, Ir. *gradán*. Cf. *greadan*.

gràdh, love, Ir. *grádh*, E. Ir. *grád*: **grâdo*-, **grâ-dho*-, root *grâ*; Lat. *grātus*, Eng. *grateful*; Skr. *gûrdháya*, praise; Gr. *γέρας*, honour.

gràdran, complaining noise of hens; onomatopoetic. See *gràg*.

gràg, croaking of crows, Ir. *grág*; Eng. *croak*, *crake*. Onomatopoetic words. Cf. I. E. *grâq*, Lat. *graculus*, *gracillare*, hen's cry, M. H. G. *kragelen*, cackle.

gragair, glutton (Sh., O'B., etc.), Ir. *gragaire* (O'B.), *grágaire* (Con.):

graigh, stud, flock of horses; see *greigh*.

gràin, abhorrence, disgust, Ir. *gráin*, E. Ir. *gráin*, W. *gruen*, grief, rough: **gragni*- (Strachan, Stokes). Ch. Sl. *groga*, horrible.

gràineag, a hedgehog, Ir. *gráineóg*: the "horrent one"; from *gráin*, above.

graing, disdain, a frown, Ir. *grainc*. Cf. *sgraing*.

gràinne, a grain, small quantity, Ir. *gráinne*, O. Ir. *gráinne*, granulum, *grán*, granum, W. *grawn*, Cor. *gronen*, Br. *greun*, (pl.): **grâno*-; Lat. *grânum* (**gr̥̄no*-); Eng. *corn* (Stokes). Some hold that the Celtic is borrowed from the Latin.

grainnseach, a grange, Ir. *gráinseach*; from the Eng.

grainnseag, a cracknel (M'F.), bear berry (H.S.D. for N.H.):

gràis, prosperity, blessing (N.H.); from *gràs*.

gràisg, a rabble, Ir. *gráisg*, *gramhaisg*, *gramaisg*:

gramaich, hold, keep fast, Ir. *gramuighim*; see *greim*.

gramur, refuse of grain (H.S.D.):

gràn, kiln-dried grain, Ir. *grán*, corn, O. Ir. *grán*; see *gràinne*.

grànda, **gràda**, ugly, Ir. *granda*, *granna*, E. Ir. *gránde*, *gránna*, teter, dirus; from *gràin*, q.v.

gràpa, a graip, dung fork, Ir. *grápa*; from Sc. *graip*.

gràs, grace, Ir., M. Ir. *grás*, W. *gras*; from Lat. *gratia*.

grath, terror (Dial., H.S.D.):

grathuinn, a while; for **tràthain*, from *tràth*, influenced by *greis*?

gread, wound, whip, burn, Ir. *greadaim*; cf. W. *greidio*, scorch: **greddo*-; root *ghredh*; cf. Eng. *grind*, Lat. *frendo*, **ghrendho* (St.). Cf. also Eng. *grist*, Lat. *hordeum*. Swedish *grädda*, bake, may be compared.

greadan, a considerable time with all one's might at anything (M'A.); from *gread*.

greadan, parched corn; from *gread*. Cf. *gradan*. Ir. *greadóg* means "griddle." Eng. *griddle*, W. *greidell*, are allied. Cf. *grist*, *hordeum*, *κριθή*.

greadhan, **greadhuinn**, a convivial party, happy band. Ir. *greadhanach*, drolling, G. **greadhnach**, joyful; root *gred*, go, as in *greas*, q.v.? M. Ir. *gredan*, exulting shouts. Root *χαρ*?

grealach, greallach, entrails: **gre-lach,* root *gṛ,* I. E. *ghṛ,* gut; Gr. χορδή, gut, Eng. *cord*; Lat. *haru-spex,* diviner, "entrails-inspector," *hernia,* rupture. Shaw has **greathlach.** Hence **greallach,** dirty, Ir. *greallach,* clay, dirty. Cf. Eng. *gore.*

greallag, a swingle-tree:

greann, hair, bristling of hair, surly look, also "cloth," "rough piled clothing," Ir. *greann,* beard, fair hair, E. Ir. *grend,* beard, W., Br. *grann,* eyelid, cilium: **grendâ*; Ger. *granne,* beard of corn or cat, Norse *grön,* moustache, Span. *greña,* tangled hair, Prov. Fr. *gren,* O. Fr. *grenon,* beard of cheek and lip; Albanian *kryande.* **greanndag,** rag, tatter. Hence **greannar.**

greas, hasten, urge, Ir. *greasuighim,* M. Ir. *gressim*: **gred-to-*; I. E. *ghredh,* step out, go; Lat. *gradior, gradus,* step; Got. *grids,* a step; Ch. Sl. *gręda,* stride, come; Skr. *gṛdhyati,* step out. The E. Ir. *grísaim,* I incite, is a different word, coming from *grís,* fire.

greidil, a gridiron, Ir. *greidil, greideal,* M. Ir. *in t-slissin gretli,* Sean. Mor. *gretel,* W. *greidel, gradell,* O. W. *gratell*; from Late Lat. *graticula,* from *cratis,* wicker-work, Eng. *crate, grate, grill, hurdle.* Eng. *griddle,* M. Eng *gredel,* are the same as the Celtic words. Skeat has suggested *gread* above as the origin of the Celtic forms; cf. Ir. *greadóg,* a griddle. Hence **greidlean,** an instrument for turning the bannocks on the griddle.

gréidh, prepare, dress, Ir. *gréasaim*; see *gréis.* *Gréidhear, gré'ar,* grieve (N. Gael.).

greigh, a stud of horses, Ir., M. Ir. *groigh,* E. Ir. *graig,* W. *gre*: **gragi-*; Lat. *grex,* flock; Gr. γαργαρα, heaps; O. H. G. *quarter,* herd.

greim, a hold, a morsel, so Ir., O. Ir. *greim, greimm,* a hold, strength, W. *grym,* force, strength: **gredsmen-*; root *gher,* hold, Gr. χείρ, hand, Skr. *háras,* grip. Stokes separates *greim,* morsel, from *greim,* hold, strength. *Greim,* morsel, he refers to **gresmen,* a bite, Skr. *grásati,* devour, Gr. γράω, eat, Norse *krás,* a dainty.

greis, prowess, onset, slaughter, a champion, E. Ir. *gress, gréss,* attack; from the root of *greas* above (Stokes).

greis, a while, Ir. *do ghréas,* always, O. Ir. *do grés, do gress,* semper, M. Ir. *do-gres*: **grend-to-,* going on, root *grend, gred,* I. E. *ghredh* as in *greas.* Strachan gives **grencs-,* and compares Norse *kringr,* round, Ger. *kring.* See **treis.**

gréis, greus, embroidery, needle-work, Ir. *obair-ghréis,* from *gréas,* E. Ir. *gréss,* any work of art or trade; see *greusaich.*

greód, a crowd (Arg.); from Eng. *crowd.*
greòs, expansion of the thighs, **greòsgach**, grinning (H.S.D.): **grencs-*; Norse *kringr*, round, Ger. *kring.*
greusaich, griasaich, shoemaker, any worker in embroidery or furniture, Ir. *gréasaidhe*, shoemaker: **greid-to-*; Gadelic *greid*, dress, broider, I. E. *ghrei*, rub; Gr. χροιά, χρῶμα, hide, skin, colour, χρίω, anoint (Christus).
grian, sun, Ir., O. Ir. *grían*: **greinâ, ghr-einâ*, root *gher*, warm, as in *gar*. Cf. Skr. *ghṛṇis*, sunshine, *ghramsa*, heat; W. *greian*, what gives heat, sun. See further under *grìos*. Hence **grianan**, sunny place, summer house, *solarium* of Lat., from *sol*, sun.
griasaich, a species of aculeated fish: "cobbler" fish; from *griasaich*, shoemaker.
grid, substance, quality; from Sc. *grit*, grain of stones, grit, grain, Eng. *grit*. Hence **grìdeil**, industrious (M'A.).
grigirean, the constellation of Charles' wain, **grigleachan**, a constellation; see *grioglachan.*
grìleag, a grain of salt, any small matter: **gris-il-*, root *greis*, gravel, as in *grinneal.*
grìmeach, grim, surly; from Eng. *grim*, Norse *grimmr.*
grìmeil, warlike (H.S.D.), Ir. *grimeamhuil* (Lh., O'B.), *grim*, war; from the Norse *grimmr*, fierce, wroth?
grinn, pretty, Ir. *grinn*, E. Ir. *grind*: **gṛnni-*, "bright"; root *gher*, as in *grian, grìos*. Cf. *glinn.*
grinneal, bottom of the sea, gravel, Ir. *grinnioll*, channel, bed of a river, sand of the sea, sea bottom, M. Ir. *grinnell*: **gris-ni-*, root, *greis, gris*, gravel, E. Ir. *grían*, gravel (**greisano-*), W. *graian*, gravel, *greienyn*, a grain of gravel. Rhys (Hib. Lect., 571) refers these words to the root of *grian*, sun, the particle of gravel being supposed to be "a shining thing." This view is supported by **grioglachan** and **griogag**, q.v.
griob, nibble (Heb.); from Sc. *gnip*, gnaw, eat, Eng. *nip, nibble.*
griobh, a pimple (M'A.):
griobhag, hurry:
grìoch, a decaying or lean young deer, **grìochan**, consumption (Dial., H.S.D.):
griogag, grìogag (Glen-Urquhart), a pebble, bead: **grizgu-*, root *gris, greis*, gravel, as in *grinneal.*
grioglachan, Pleiades, **grigleachan**, a constellation, Ir. *griogchán*, constellation. For root, see *griogag.*
griomacach, thin-haired, **griomagach**, shrivelled grass (H.S.D.):
grioman, a certain species of lichen, malt bud (H.S.D.):
grios, entreat, pray, Ir. *gríosaim*, encourage, incite, rake up a fire; from earlier *grí·s*, heat, which see in *grìosach.*

grìosach, burning embers, Ir. *gríosach*, coals of fire, burning embers, M. Ir. *grìssach*, E. Ir. *grís*, fire, embers, Br. *groez*, heat: **grens*, **gr̥ns*, heat; Skr. *ghraṁsa*, sun, heat, sunshine; root *gher* of *gar*, q.v. Hence **grìs**, inflammation; Ir. *grís*, pimple.

grìs, horror; from Sc. *grise*, to shudder, M. Eng. *grīs-*, horror, *grīseful*, *grīse*, horrible, Eng. *grisly*.

grìsionn, brindled, **grìs-fhionn**, "gray-white," **grìs** (Sh. *gris*), gray; from M. Eng. *grīs*, gray fur.

griùrach, the measles, **griuthach** (do.), **grìobhach** (M'A.), **griùragan**, indefinitely small particle, pustules on the skin; root *ghru*, as in *grothlach*; *grúlach* (Skye) = *griobhlach*.

gròb, join by indentation, serrate; cf. M. Eng. *grōpin*, to groove, also *groupe* and *grave*. A borrowed G. word.

gróbag, a poor shrivelled woman; from *gròb*.

groban, top or point of a rock, hillock:

gròban, mugwort (N.H.):

gròc, croak, frown on; from Eng. *croak*.

grod, rotten, E. Ir. *grot*, *gruiten*, stale butter, small curds in whey; a metathesis of *goirt*?

groganach, wrinkled (as heather), Ir *grug*, a wrinkle; cf. *grùig*.

gròig, awkwardness, perverseness, **gròigean**, awkward man; see *grùig*.

gròiseid, a gooseberry; from the Sc. *groset*, from O. Fr. **grose*, *grosele*, goose-berry, whence Eng. *gooseberry* for *grooseberry*.

gròmhan, a groaning, growling; the same as *gnòmhan*.

gros, snout; correct spelling of *gnos*, q.v.

gròta, a groat; from the Eng.

grothlach, a gravel pit, abounding in gravel (O'B., Sh., etc.), Ir. *grothlach*, W. *gro*, pebbles, Cor. *grow*, gravel, Br. *grouan*. From these come Eng. *gravel*, O. Fr. *gravele*. Cf. Norse *grjot*, stones, Ag. S. *greót*, Eng. *grit*, root *grut*, Lit. *grústi*, pound, bray, Gr. χρυσός gold (= χρυδ-σός).

grotonach, corpulent (O'B., Sh., etc.), so Ir.: "heavy-breeched" (Arms.)—**grod-tónach*.

gruag, hair of the head, a wig, Ir. *gruag*: **grunkâ*, root *gru*, Eng. *crumple*? Hence **gruagach**, a maiden, brownie.

gruaidh, cheek, brow, Ir. *gruaidh*, cheek, E. Ir. *gruad*, W. *grudd*, Cor. *grud*, maxilla: **groudos*. Bez. suggests the root *ghrud*, *ghreud*, as in *grothlach*, above, the idea being "pounding, mashing" (Lit. *grústi*, bray, pound), and the original force "jaw": cf. Lat. *maxilla* and *macero*, macerate. Stokes queries if it is from the root of Eng. *great*. Eng. *proud*?

gruaigean, a species of sea-weed (H S.D. for Heb.), birses (M'A.); "little hairy one" (Carm.), from *gruag*. *Miorcan* in Lewis.

gruaim, gloom, surly look, Ir. *gruaim*: **grousmen-*; root *greut*, *grût*, Lat. *brûtus*, dull, Eng. *brute*, Lettic *grûts*, heavy, Stokes cfs. only Ch. Sl. *sŭ-grustiti sę*, grieve over.

grùdair, a brewer, Ir. *grúdaire*, *grúid*, malt: **grûddi-*; Ang. Sax. *grût*, coarse meal, Ger. *grütze*, groats, Dan. *gröd*; Lit. *grúdas*, corn. Eng. *grit*, *groats* are allied Hence **grùid,** lees.

grùig, a drooping attitude, churlishness, churlish, Ir. *grúg*, a grudge, anger, *gruig*, churlishness (O'R.), *gruc*, sulky (O'Cl.); cf. Eng. *grudge*, M. Eng. *grucchen*, O. Fr. *grouchier*, *groucier*. Also **grùgach,** wrinkled.

gruilleamach, prancing, leaping suddenly (H.S.D.):

grunnaich, sound, fathom; see *grunnd*.

grunn, grunnan, a handful, lot, crowd (Dial. **grainnean),** O. Ir. *grinne*, fascis, fasciculum, Br. *gronn*, a heap: **grendio-*, **grondo-*; Gr. γρόνθος, closed fist, Skr. *grantha*, bind, etc. (Stokes for O. Ir.). Cf. for root *bréid*.

grunnasg, groundsel; formed on the Eng.

grunnd, bottom, ground, thrift; from Sc. *grund*, bottom or channel in water, Norse *grunnr*, bottom of sea or river, Eng. *ground*. Hence **grunndail,** steadfast, solid, sensible.

grùnsgul, a grunting; from **grunn*, grunt, Lat. *grunnire*, Eng. *grunt*.

gruth, curds, Ir., M. Ir. *gruth*: **grutu-*; Eng. *curds*, M. Eng. *crud*, Sc. *crowdie*, *croods*; Gr. γρύσει, will melt, γρύτη (υ long), frippery; I.E. *gru*, Eng. *crumb*, Ger. *krauen*, Gr. γρῦ, morsel. Hence **gruitheam,** curds and butter: *gruth* + *ìm*.

grùthan, grùan, liver, Ir. *aev. grúan* (Lh. *Comp. Voc.* sub "jecur"): **grûso-*: root *ghru*, gritty, of *grothlach*.

gu, to, ad, Ir. *go*, *gu*, O. Ir. *co*, *cu*, W. *bw* in *bwy gilydd*, to its fellow: **qos*; Ch. Sl. *kŭ*, to; cf. Lat. *usque* for **quos-que*? (Bez.). Used adverbially in *gu math*, *gu h-olc*. Cf. Gr. κας, καὶ, Skr. *-ças*.

guag, a giddy, whimsical fellow, Ir. *gúag*, *guaigín*, folly, silly one; from M. Eng. *gowke*, *gōki*, a fool, Sc. *gowk*, Eng. *gawky*.

guag, a splay-foot; see *cuag*.

guaigean, thick, little and round: **goug-go-*, root *gu*, bend.

guailisg, false, falsity (Carm.):

guaillean, a coal of fire; see *gual*. Cf. *caoirean*, a peat, cinder, ember.

guaillich, go hand in hand: "shoulder to shoulder;" see *guala*.

guaimeas, quietness; see *guamach*.

guaineas, briskness, liveliness; see *guanach*.

guairdean, vertigo; cf. Ir. *gúairdeán*, whirlwind; from *cuairt*?

guairsgeach curled, crinitus, Ir, *gúaire*, hair of the head; from I.E. *gu*, bend, as in *guala*.

†**guais**, danger, **guaiseach**, dangerous, Ir. *guais*, O. Ir. *gúassacht*:

guait, leave ("Gabh no guait e"--Take or leave it); from Eng. *quit*? *g-uait*?

gual, coal, Ir. *gual*: **goulo-*, **geulo-*; root *geul*, *gul*; Teutonic **kola-*, Norse *kol*, coals, Ger. *kohle*, Eng. *coal*. W. *glo*, Br. *glaou*, **glôvo-* (Stokes), is allied to the Eng. *glow*.

guala, gualann, shoulder, Ir. *guala*, g. *gualann*, E. Ir. *gualu*, g. **gualand*: **goulôn-*, root *geu*, *gu*, *gu*, bend; Gr. γυῖον, limb, γύαλον, a hollow, γύης, ploughtree (Lat. *bura*); Old Bactrian =Zend, *gāo*, hand. Strachan and Stokes give the root *gub*, bend, stem **gublôn-*, I.E. *gheubh*, bend, Gr. κυφός (υ long), bent, stooping; Lettic *gubt*, stoop.

guamach, neat, snug, smirking; also "plentiful" (Sh., O'R.), careful, managing (Arran):

guanach, light, giddy, Ir. *guanach*, *guamnach*, M. Ir. *guamnacha*, active (O'Cl.); root *guam* of *guamach* above.

gucag, a bubble, bell, globule, bud: **gukko-*, Ger. *kugel*, ball.

gùda, a gudgeon, Ir. *guda*; formed on Eng. *gudgeon*, M. Eng. *gojon*.

gudaleum, gudarleum, a bound, wild leap (Arg.):

guga, the solan goose, a fat, silly fellow, Ir. *guga*. See next word for root.

gugail, clucking of poultry, Ir. *gugailim*: an onomatopoetic word. Cf. Eng. *chuck*. See also *gogail*.

gugairneach, a fledgling:

guidh, pray, **guidhe**, a prayer, wish, Ir. *guidhim*, *guidhe*, O. Ir. *guidiu*, *gude*, *guide*: **godio-*, root *ged*, *god*, I.E. *ghedh*, ask; Gr. πόθεω, desire, θέσσασθαι, pray for; Got. *bidjan*, ask, Ag. S. *biddan*, Eng. *bid*.

guil, weep, Ir., E. Ir. *guilim*; see *gal*.

guilbneach, the curlew: "beaked one," E. Ir. *gulbnech*, beaked, O. Ir. *gulban*, beak, O. W. *gilbin*, acumine, W. *gylf*, bill, beak, *gylfant*, Cor. *gilb*, foratorium, *geluin*, rostrum: **gulbano-*; Ger. *kolben*, piston, knob, gun-stock. Bez. compares only N. Slovenic *golbati*, gnaw. Cf. Lit. *gulbė*, swan.

guileag, the swan's note, warbling (Sh. has **guillag**, chattering of birds, O'R. *guilleog*); root *gal*, cry, call, Lat. *gallus*, cock, Eng. *call*?

guileagan, custom of boiling eggs outside on Easter Sunday = *latha guileagan* (M'D.):

guim, cuim, conspiracy (Carm.):

guin, a wound, O. Ir. *guin*: **goni-*; see *gon*.

guir, hatch, lie on eggs, **gur**, hatching, Ir. *gur*, W. *gori*, to brood; from the root *gor*, *gar*, warm. See *gar*.

guirean, a pimple, **gur,** a festering, Ir., M. Ir. *guirín*, pustule, E. Ir. *gur*, pus, W. *gôr*, pus, *goryn*, pustula : **goru-*, fester, "heat"; root *gor*, *gar*, warm, as in *gar*.
guisead, a gusset; from the Eng.
guit, a corn-fan, unperforated sieve : *gottiá* :
guitear, a gutter, kennel; from Eng. *gutter*.
gulm, a gloom, forbidding look; from the Eng. ?
gulmag, sea-lark (H.S.D.) :
gun, without, Ir. *gan*, O. Ir. *cen*; Gr. κενεός, empty; root, κενο-. So O.H.G. *hina*, *hinweg*, Ag. S. *hin-*.
gu'n, gu'm, that, Gr. ὅτι, Ir. *go*, O. Ir. *co*, *con*. Windisch considers this the prep. *con*, with, and *co*, to; Zim. and Thur. regard it as from *co*, to (see *gu*). The latter explains the *n* as the relative: **co-sn*, a view supported by the verbal accent being on the first syllable and by the occasional form *conn* (?) See *cha'n*.
gùn, gown, Ir. *gúna*; from the Eng. *gown*, from W. *gwn* (**gwun*). from Celtic **vo-ouno-*, root in Lat. *ex-uo*, doff, *ind-uo*, don, Lit. *aunù*, put on shoes, *áuti*.
gunna, a gun, Ir., M. Ir. *gunna*; from M. Eng. *gunne*, Eng. *gun*.
gur, that, Ir. *gur*: **co-ro*; see *gu'n* for *co*. Uses are: *Gur cruaidh e*=O. Ir. *corrop cruaid é*: *corrop* is now Ir. *gurab*, that is *co-ro-bi* (*ba*, verb "to be"). *Gur*=*gun ro*, *con ro-* (St.).
guraiceach, a blockhead (Sh., H.S.D.) :
guraiceach, unfeathered bird, lump (Arg.), from *gur*.
gurpan, crupper; from Sc. *curpon*, Eng., O. Fr. *croupon*.
gurracag, a blot (Arg.) :
gurrach, gurraban, crouching, crouching on the hunkers: **gurtha-*, from *gur*, brooding as in *guir*? Cf. Sc. *curr*, to "hunker," *currie*, a stool, Eng. *cower*. The Perthshire **curraidh,** hunkering, is from Scotch.
gurrach, fledgling, **gurach** (Arg.):
gurt, fierceness, sternness of look; also *gart*, q.v.
gus, to, Ir. *gus*, O. Ir. *cossin*, to the, to which; prep. *gu*, *co*, and the article or relative. The *s* of the article is preserved after the consonant of *co* (=*qos*).
gus, anything (Arg.):
gusair, sharp, keen, strong, Ir. *gusmhar*, strong; from *gus*, force, smartness: **gustu-*, "choice," root *gu*, Eng. *choose*.
gusgan, a hearty draught:
gusgul, refuse, dirt, idle words, roaring:
guth, voice, Ir., O. Ir. *guth*: **gutu-*; I.E. *gu*; Gr. γόος, groan; Skr. *hu*, call, cry, *havatē*, calls; Ch. Sl. *zovą*, to call. This is

different from I.E. *gu*, Gr. *βοή*, shout, Lat. *bovare*, cry (Prellwitz, Osthoff).

I

i, she, Ir. *í*, *sí*, O. Ir. *í*, *hí*, *sí*, W., Br. *hi*: **sî*; Got. *si*, ea, Ger. *sie*, they; Skr. *syá*: I. E. *sjo-*, *sjā-* (Brug.). See *sa*, *so*, *sin*.

iach, a yell, cry, Ir. *íachdadh*, O. Ir. *iachtaim*: **eicto-*, **eig-to-*, from *eig* of *éigh*.

† **iach,** a salmon, E. Ir. *eó*, g. *iach*, W., Br. *eog*, W. *ehawc*, Cor. *ehog*: **esax*; Lat. *esox*: Basque *izokin* (borrowed from Celtic).

iad, they, Ir. *iad*, E. Ir. *iat*, O. Ir. only in *olseat-som*, say they, W. *hwynt*: confusion of roots *ei*, *sjo* with the 3rd plur. in *nt*. Of E. Ir. *iat*, *siat*, Brugmann says :—"These have the ending of the 3rd plur. of the verb; later on *iat*, *siat* were detached, and began an independent existence." Stokes similarly says they are *se* and *hwy* with the *nt* of the verbal 3rd pl. added.

iadach, jealousy, Ir. *éad*; see *eud*.

iadh, encompass, Ir. *iadhaim*, join, shut, surround, E. Ir. *iadaim*: **eidâô*, **ei-dho-*, root *ei*, go? Stokes analyses it into **ei-dâmô*, for **epi-dâmô*, Skr. *api-dā́nā*, a lock: for *epi*, see Gr. *ἐπί* under *iar*; and *dâmô* is from *dhô*, *dhê*, place, Gr. *τίθημι*, Lat. *facio*. It has also been correlated to Gr. *πιέζομαι*, press, Skr. *pîdayti*, press (**pisdā*), from *pise*, stamp, press, Lat. *pistor*, etc.

ial, moment, season, gleam of sunshine; a poetic word, seemingly a metaphoric use of *iall*. Galway Ir. *iall*, moment, *iall deireannach dá shaoghal*.

iall, a thong, Ir. *iall*, E. Ir. *íall*: **peisla*; cf. *pileus*, felt, etc.

† **iall,** a flock of birds, Ir. *iall*, a flock of birds, E. Ir. *iall*, grex; **eisla*, Gr. *ἴλη*. Hence *eallach* (St.). Cf. Ir. *éilín sicini*, brood or clutch of chickens.

iallach, jaunty, lithe; cf. *uallach*.

ialtag, a bat, Ir. *ialtóg*, E. Ir. *iathlu* (*iatlu*, O'Cl.), W. *ystlum*: **isatal-* (Ascoli). Dial. **dealtag anmoch**; Lat. *vesper-tilio*.

ian, a bird; see *eun*.

iar, after, Ir. *iar*, O. Ir. *iar n-*, post: **e(p)eron*; Skr. *aparam*, afterwards; Got. *afar*, post; further Gr. *ὄπιθεν*, behind, *ἐπί*, to, on, Skr. *ápi*, Lit. *apė*, to, on, Lat. *ob*. See *air*(c).

iar, an iar, siar, west, Ir. *iar*, *siar*, O. Ir. *íar*, occidens, *aníar*: a special use of the prep. *iar* above. See *ear* for force.

iarbhail, anger, ferocity; from *air* and *boile*?

iarbhail, a consequence, remains of a disease:

iargainn, pain, Ir. *iargan*, groans of a dying man (O'B.); from *air* and *gon*.

iargail, the west, evening twilight, Ir. *iargúl*, remote district, *iargcúl* (Con.); from *iar* and *cúl*, back: "behind," west. **iargalta**, churlish, inhospitable, surly, turbulent (M'A.), Ir. *iarcúlta*, churlish, backward.

iargall, battle, contest, so Ir., O. Ir. *irgal*: *air* + *gal*, the *air* being *air*(a). See *gal*.

iarghuil, sound, noise; see *uirghioll*.

iarla, an earl, Ir. *iarla*, M Ir. *íarla*; from Norse *jarl*, Eng. *earl*. W. has *iarll*.

iarmad, offspring, remnant, Ir. *iarmat*, offspring (O'B.), *iarmart*, consequences of anything, *iarmhar*, remnant; root *mar*, remain. See *mar*.

iarmailt, the firmament, for **fiarmaint*, Ir. *fiormaimeint*, M .Ir. *firmeint*, E. Ir. *firmimenti* (g.); from Lat. *firmamentum*. Cf. *Tormailt*, Norman.

iarna, a hank of yarn, Ir. *íarna*, a chain or hank of yarn; from Eng. *yarn*.

iarnaich, smooth with an iron; from *iarunn*.

iarogha, great grandson, O. Ir. *iarmui*, abnepotes; from *iar* and *ogha*: "post-nepos."

iarr ask, Ir., E. Ir. *iarraim*, I seek, ask, *iarrair*, a seeking, *iarair*: **iarn-ari-*, "after-go," root *(p)ar*, *per*, go, seek, bring, through, Gr. *πεῖρα*, experience, Lat. *ex-perior*, try, Eng. *experience*, etc. (Stokes). See *aire* further for root.

iarunn, iron, Ir. *iarann*, M. Ir. *iarund*, O. Ir. *iarn*, W. *haiarn*, *hearn*, Corn. *hoern*, O. Br. *hoiarn*, Br. *houarn*, Gaul. *isarnodori*, ferrei ostii: **eisarno-*; Got. *eisarn*, O. H. G *isarn*, Ger. *eisen*, Eng. *iron* (all borrowed from Celtic according to Brugmann, Stokes, etc.). Shräder regards the *eis* or *îs* of *eisarno-* as only a different vowel-scale form of I. E. *ayos*, *ayes-*, metal, whence Lat. *aes*, Eng. *ore*.

iasachd, iasad, a loan, Ir. *iasachd*, E. Ir. *iasacht*:

iasg, fish, Ir. *iasg*, O. Ir. *íasc*, *æsc*, g. *éisc*; **eisko-*, **peisko-*; Lat. *piscis*, fish; Got. *fisks*, Eng. *fish*.

†**ibh**, drink, M. G. *ibh* (M'V), Ir. *ibhim* (Con. *íbhim*), O. Ir. *ibim*, O. W. *iben*, bibimus, Cor. *evaf*, Br. *eva*: **ibô*, **pibô*; Lat. *bibo*; Skr. *pibamî*.

ic, cure, heal, so Ir.; see *ioc*.

ìc, an addition, *eke*, frame put under a beehive (Carm.); Sc. *eik*.

idir, at all, Ir. *idir*, O. Ir. *itir*, *etir*: **enteri*, a locative case of *enter*, the stem of the prep. *eadar*, q.v.

ifrinn, hell, Ir. *ifrionn*, E. Ir. *ifern(d)*, O. Ir. *ifurnn*; from Lat. *infernum*, adj. *infernus*, Eng. *infernal*.

igh, tallow (Sh.), fat (H.S.D., which marks it as obsolete), M. Ir. *íth*, g. *itha*, Manx *eeh*: root *pi*, *pei*, Gr. *πίων*, Skr. *pínas*, fat.

igh, ì, a burn, a small stream with green banks (Suth.). This is the Suth. pronunciation of *ùidh*, a ford, etc.

ilbhinn, a craggy mountain ("Mar ilbhinn ailbhein craige," Oss. Ballad); if not mere jingle, it means "many peaked": *iol* + *beann*.

ileach, variegated, Ir. *ile*, diversity; see *iol*-.

ìm, butter, Ir. *im* (g. *íme*, Coneys), E. Ir. *imb*, W. *ymenyn*. Cor. *amenen*, Br. *amann*, *amanen*: **emben*- or **m̥ben*-; Lat. *unguen*, Eng. *unguent*, vb. *unguo*, I smear: Ger. *anke*, butter; Skr. *áñjas*, a salve, ointment.

im-, about, also with intensive force, Ir. *im*-, O. Ir. *im*-, *imm*-; it is the prefixive form of prep. *mu*, q.v. Also **iom-**.

imcheist, anxiety, doubt, O. Ir. *imchesti*, contentiones; from *im*- and *ceist*.

imeachd, journeying, **imich**, go, Ir. *imtheachd*, *imthighim*, O. Ir. *imthecht*; from *im*- and *teachd*, *tighinn*: **imich**, is for *im-thigh*, root *tig*, *teig* of *tighinn*, q.v.

imisg, a sarcasm, scandal: **im-isc*; for *isc*, see *inisg*.

imleag, navel, Ir. *imleacan*, *imlinn*, E. Ir. *imbliu*, acc. *imblind*, *imlec*, *imlecán*: **embiliôn*-, **embilenko*-; Lat. *umbilîcus*; Gr. ὀμφαλός; Eng. *navel*; Skr. *nā́bhi*, *nâbhîla*; I. E. *onbhelo*-, *nobhelo*-.

imlich, lick, Ir. *imlighim*, *lighim*; *im-lighim*. "about-lick." With *lighim* is cognate O. Ir. *lígim*, I lick, W. *llyaw*, *llyad*, licking, Br. *leat* (do.): **leigô*, **ligo*; Lat. *lingo*; Gr, λείγω; Eng. *lick*; Ch. Sl. *lizati* (to lick); Skr. *lihati*.

imnidh, care, diligence, Ir. *imnídhe*, O. Ir. *imned*, tribulatio: **m̥bi-men-eto*-, root *men* of *menmna*. Ascoli analyses the O. Ir. as **imb-an-eth*, root *an*, breathe.

impidh, a prayer; see *iompaidh*.

impis, **imis**, imminence, **an impis**, about to, almost, M. Ir. *imese catha*, imminence of battle, root *ved* of *tòiseach* (Stokes).

imreasan, controversy, Ir. *imreasán*, O. Ir. *imbresan*, altercatio, *imbresnaim*, I strive, W. *ymryson*, contention, dispute: **imbi-bres*-, root *bres* of M. Ir. *bressa*, contentions, battles, Br., Cor. *bresel* (from *bris*, break)? Windisch suggests for Gadelic **imm-fres-sennim* (prep. *imm* or *im* and *fris*, *frith*), from O. Ir. *sennim*, I drive, **svem-no*-, allied to Eng. *swim*.

imrich, remove, flit, Ir. *imircim*, E. Ir. *immirge*, journey, expedition: **m̥bi-reg*-, root *reg*, go, stretch (as in *rach*). Windisch suggests *imm-éirge*, from *éirigh*.

in-, **ion-**, **ionn-**, a prefix of like force as Lat. *in*-, used especially before medials, liquids, and *s* (*ionn*- only before *s*), Ir. *in*-, *ion*-, *inn*-, *ionn*- (before *s*), O. Ir. *in*-; it is the Gadelic prep. *in*, *ind*, now *an*, *ann*, in (q.v.), used as a prefix.

inbhe, quality, dignity, rank, Ir. *inmhe*, patrimony, estate, M. Ir. *indme*, rank: **ind-med-*, prep. *ind* (*ann*) and root *mē*, *med* of *meas*? Ir. *inme*, wealth, better *indme* or *indbe* (St.).

inbhir, a confluence of waters, Ir. *innbhear*, *inbhear*, E. Ir. *indber*, *inbir*, *inber*, W. *ynfer*, influxus: **eni-bero-s* (Stokes), from *eni* or modern *an*, in, and *bero-*, stem of *beir*, Lat. *fero*. The combination is the same as Lat. *infero*, Eng. *inference*.

inghean, a daughter, Ir. *inghean*, O. Ir. *ingen*, Ogam *inigena*: **eni-genâ*; root *gen*, beget (see *gin*) and prep. *an*; Lat. *indigena*, native; Gr. ἐγγόνη, a grand-daughter. Also **nighean**, q.v. Lat. *ingenuus*?

inich, neat, tidy, lively:

inid, Shrove-tide, Ir. *inid*, E. Ir. *init*, W. *ynyd*, Br. *ened*; from Lat. *initium* [*jejunii*], beginning of Lent.

inisg, a reproach; cf. M. Ir. *indsce*, O. Ir. *insce*, speech: **eni-sqiâ*, root *seq*, say, as in *sgeul*, q.v. Gr. ἔνισπε, Lat. *inseque*, say, are exactly the same as Ir. in root and prefix.

inn-, **ionn-**, (**innt-** before *s*), prep. prefix of like force with *frith*, *ri*, against, to, Ir. *inn-*, *ionn-*, O. Ir. *ind-* (*int-* before *s*), *inn-*, *in-*: **n̥de*, Gaul. *ande-*: **ande*, from *n̥dh*, Goth. *und*, for, until, O. H. G. *unt-as*, until; Skr. *ádhi*, up to (*n̥dhi*).

inndrich, originate, incite:

inne, a bowel, entrail, gutter, sewer, kennel (M'A.), Ir. *inne*, *innighe*, M. Ir. *inne*, *inde*, a bowel, viscera (pl.), E. Ir. *inne*, *inde*, O. Ir. *inna*, d. pl. *innib*, viscus, viscera: prep. *in* + ? Cf. Gr. ἔντερον, a bowel, Ger. *innere*, Skr. *antaram*; also Dial. Eng. *innards* (for *inwards*).

inneach, woof, so Ir., E. Ir. *innech*: *(*p*)*n̥-niko-*, root *pan*, thread, Lat. *pannus*, cloth, Gr. πηνός, woof thread on the bobbin? See further under *anart*. A compound with *in* or *ind* is possible: *in-neg-*, Lat. *in-necto*?

inneadh, want (M'F.):

inneal, an instrument, arrangement, Ir. *inneal*, arrangement, dress, E. Ir. *indell*, yoke, arrangement; G. **innil**, prepare, ready, Ir. *inniollaim*, arrange, E. Ir. *indlim*, get ready: **ind-el-*, root *pel*, join, fold, as in *alt*, q.v. Ascoli joins O. Ir. *intle*, insidiæ, *intledaigim*, insidior, and G. **innleachd**, q.v.; but gives no root.

innean, an anvil, Ir. *inneóin*, E. Ir. *indeóin*, O. Ir. *indéin*, W. *einion* [*engion*?], Cor. *ennian*, Br. *anneffn*: **ande-bnis*, "on-hit," from *inn-* and *benô*, hit, as in *bean*, q.v. Osthoff gives the stem **endivani-*, "on-hit," Zd. *vaniti*, hit.

innear, dung, M. Ir. *indebar*: **ind-ebar*; cf. E. Ir. *cann-ebor* (= *cac*, O'Cl.), on the analogy of which Stokes suggests that *ind-* of *indebar* is for *find*, white, but G. is against this. O'Dav. has *find-ebor*, dung; so Meyer, but not O'Dav.!

innil, prepare, ready; see *inneal*.

innis, an island, Ir. *inis*, O. Ir. *inis*, W. *ynys*, Cor. *enys*, Br. *enez*, pl. *inisi*: **inissî*, from *ṇss*, Lat. **inssa*, *insula*, Gr. *νῆσος* (Dor. *νᾶσος*). The connection of the Celtic, Lat., and Gr. is almost certain, though the phonetics are not clear. Strachan suggests for Celtic **eni-stî*, "in-standing," that is, "standing or being in the sea."

innis, tell, Ir. *innisim*, E. Ir. *innisim*, *indisim*: **ind-fiss-*, from *fiss*, now *fios*, knowledge; root *vid*. Cf. *adfíadim*, narro (**veidô*), *infíadim*. *vet* (St.)?

innleachd, device, mechanism, Ir. *inntleachd*, device, ingenuity: **ind-slig-tu-*, root *slig* of *slighe*, way? Ascoli joins O. Ir. *intle*, insidiæ, *intleduigim*, insidior, and W. *annel*, a gin, Cor. *antell*, ruse, Br. *antell*, stretch a snare or bow, and Ir. *innil*, a gin, snare. The O. Ir. *intliucht*, intellectus (with *sliucht*, cognitio), is considered by Zimmer to be a grammatical word from Lat. *intellectus*. Stokes disagrees. Hence **innlich**, aim, desire.

innlinn, provender, forage: "preparation," from *innil*, prepare.

innsgin, mind, courage (H.S.D. from MSS.), also in A. M'D.'s song, "*Am breacan uallach*"; *innsgineach*, sprightly (Sh., O'R.):

inntinn, mind, Ir. *inntinn*: **ind-seni-*; root *sen* or *senn*, as in Ger. *sinn*, sense? Kluge, however, gives **sentno-* as the earliest form of the Ger. Possibly it may be a plural from O. Ir. *inne*, sensus, meaning the "senses" originally. The Gadelic words can scarcely be from a depraved pronunciation of Lat. *ingenium*.

inntreadh, **inntreachduinn**, a beginning, entering; from Eng. *entering*.

iob, a raw cake, lump of dough (H.S.D. for N.H.); also **uibe**, q.v.

ioba, pl. **iobannan**, tricks, incantations (Arg.); see *ubag*.

iobairt, an offering, sacrifice, Ir. *íodhbuirt*, M. Ir. *édpart*, O. Ir. *edpart*, *idpart*: **aith-od-bart-*, root *bert*, *ber* of *beir*, q.v. Cf. W. *aberth* (= *ad-bert*), a sacrifice.

ioblag, a victimised or depised female, a trollop (Glenmoriston):

ioc, pay, remedy, **iocshlaint**, a cure, salve, remedy, Ir. *íocaim*, pay, remedy, *íocshláinte*, a cure, remedy, E. Ir. *ícaim*, heal, pay, O. Ir. *íccaim*, heal, W. *iachäu*, to cure, *iach*, sound, Cor. *iach*, sanus, Br. *iac'h*, healthy, O. Br. *iac*: **jakko-*, sound; Gr. *ἄκος*, a cure; Skr. *yaças*, grandeur. The long vowel of the Gadelic forms is puzzling, and these have been referred to **isacco-*, from, *iso-*, *eiso-*, Gr. *ἰαομαι*, heal, Skr. *ishayati*, refresh.

iochd, clemency, humanity, Ir. *iochd*, clemency, confidence, M. Ir. *icht*, protection, E. Ir. *icht*, progeny, children : **pektus*, root *pek*, *pak*, Lat. *pectus*, breast, *paciscor*, paction ; allied to *uchd*. For *iochd*, progeny, cf. Norse *átt*, family (Rhys). See *aicme*.

ìochdar, the lower part, bottom, Ir. *íochdar*, O. Ir. *íchtar*. It is formed from *ìos*, *ís*, down, on the analogy of *uachdar*. See *ìos*.

iod, alas ! Cf. Eng. *tut*. Also **ud**, oh dear !

iodhal, an image, Ir. *íodhal*, O. Ir. *ídal* ; from Lat. *idolum*, Eng. *idol*.

iodhlann, a cornyard, Ir. *iothlann*, granary, O. Ir. *ithla*, g. *ithland*, area, W. *ydlan*, O. W. *itlann*, area : **(p)itu-landâ*, "corn-land" ; O. Ir. *ith* (g. *etho*), corn, W., Cor. *yd*, Br. *ed*, *it* ; Skr. *pitu*, nourishment, eating, Zend *pitu*, food. For further connections, see *ith*, eat. For *-lann*, see *lann*.

iodhnadh, pangs of child-birth, Ir. *iodhana*, pangs, E. Ir. *idu*, pl. *idain* : **(p)idôn-* ; Got. *fitan*, travail in birth.

ìogan, deceit, fraud :

ioghar, ioghnadh ; see *iongar*, *iongnadh*.

iol-, prefix denoting "many," Ir. *iol-*, O. Ir. *il*, multus : **elu-*, **pelu-*, many ; Got., O. H. G. *filu*, Ger. *viel*, many ; Gr. *πολύς*, many ; Skr. *purú*. The root is *pel*, *plâ*, *plê*, as in G. *làn*, *lìon*, Eng. *full*, etc.

iola, a fishing station, fishing rock, fishing bank (Heb. and N.H.) ; Shet. *iela*.

iolach, a shout, pæan, Ir. *iolach*, merriment, O. Ir. *ilach*, pæan ; W. *elwch*, a shout. **elukko*, root *pel*, roar ; *πελαγος* ? (St). Cf. Ag. S. *ealá*, oh, alas.

iolair, eagle, Ir *iolar*, M. Ir. *ilur*, for *irur*, **eruro-s*, W. *eryr*, Cor., Br. *er* ; Got. *ara*, O. H. G. *aro*, Ger. *aar*, Ag. S. *earn* ; Lit. *erélis*, Prus. *arelie* ; also Gr. *ὄρνις*, a bird.

iolar, down (Perthshire), also **urlar** : a degraded adverbial form of *urlar* ? Or for **ior-ar*, **air-air*, "on-by" ?

iolla, view, glance ; *gabh iolla ris*, just look at it ; cf. *ealla*.

iollagach, frolicsome ; see *iullagach*.

iollain, expert (H.S.D. ; Sh., O'R. **iollan**) ; from *ealaidh*.

iom-, the broad-vowel form of the prefix *im-*, q.v.

ioma, iomadh, many, many a, Ir. *ioma*, *iomdha*, E. Ir. *immad*, multitudo, O. Ir. *imbed*, copia, *immde*, multus (**imbde*), *immdugud*, exuberantia : **imbeto-*, from the prep. *imbi*, *embi*, now *im-*, *mu*, about (Z.[2] 64). Bez. queries if allied to Lat.

pinguis, thick, Gr. *παχύς*, but *gh*, *ghv* gives in Gadelic a simple *g* (Ost. *Ind. For.*[4]). Also G. **iomad**, many, **iomaididh**, superabundance, Ir. *iomad*, a multitude, much, For *d* cf. *liuthad*.

iomadan, concurrence of disasters, a mourning :

iomagain, iomaguin, anxiety : **imb-ad-goni-*, root *gon* of *iargain*?

iomain, a driving (of cattle, etc.), Ir. *iomáin*, tossing, driving, E. Ir. *immáin*, a driving (**embi-agni-*), inf. to *immagim*, circumago ; Lit. *ambāges*, going round, windings ; root *âg*, *ag*, drive ; Lat. *ago*, Gr. *ἄγω*, etc.

iomair, a ridge of land, Ir. *iomaire*, E. Ir. *immaire*, *imbaire* : **embi-ario-*, root *ar*, plough ; see *ar*.

iomair, need, behove : "serve"; Ir. *timthire*, servant, O. Ir. *timmthirim*, I serve. For force, cf. *feum*. The root is *tìr*, land?

iomair, employ, exercise, play, noun **iomairt**, Ir. *imirt*, a game, E. Ir. *imbert*, O. Ir. vb. *imbrim*, infero, etc. : for *imb-berim*, root *ber* of *beir*, q.v.

iomall, a border, limit, Ir. *imiol*, E. Ir. *imbel*, W. *ymyl* : **imb-el*, "circuit," root *el*, go, Lat. *amb-ulare*, walk, which reproduces both roots. See further under *tadhal*. Hence **iomallach**, remote.

iomarbhaidh, a struggle, Ir. *iomarbhaidh*, E. Ir. *immarbág* : **imm-ar-bág-* ; root *bâg*, strive, Norse *bágr*, strife, O. H. G. *bâga*, vb. *pâgan*. See *arabhaig*. M'A. gives **iomarbhuidh**, hesitation, confusion.

iomarcach, very numerous, superfluous (Carswell's **imarcach**), Ir. *iomarcach*, M. Ir. *imarcraid*, superfluity (also "carrying," from *immarchor*, *cor*, place, as in *iomarchur*). M'A. gives the meaning as "in many distresses, distressed," and the root as *arc* of *airc*.

†**iomarchur**, a rowing, tumbling, straying, Ir. *iomarchur* (O'B.), E. Ir. *immarchor* (=*imm-ar-cor*, from *cor* or *cuir*, put), carrying, errand.

iomchan, carriage, behaviour :

iomchar, carriage, behaviour, Ir. *iomchar*, E. Ir. *immchor* ; from *imm-* and *cuir*, q.v.

iomchoire, blame, a reflection ; from *iom-* and *coire*.

iomchorc, regards, salutation, petition, also G., Ir. **iomchomharc**, O. Ir. *imchomarc*, interrogatio, salutatio : **imm-com-arc-*, from *arc*, ask, W. *archaff*, I ask, *erchim*, Cor. *arghaf*, M. Br. *archas*, will command : **(p)arkô*, ask, root *perk*, *prek*, *pr̥k* ; Lat. *precor*, Eng. *pray*, *posco* (=*porcsco*), demand; Ger. *frage*, *forschung*, question, inquiry ; Lit. *praszýti*, beg ; Skr. *pracnas*, question.

iomchuidh, proper, Ir. *iomchubhaidh,* M. Ir. *immchubaid;* from *iom-* and *cubhaidh,* q.v.

iomhaigh, an image, Ir. *iomhaigh,* M. Ir. *iomáig, imagin,* Cor. *auain;* from Lat. *imago.*

iomlag, the navel; see *imleag.*

iomlaid, an exchange, Ir. *iomlut;* possibly from the G. root *lud,* go (see *dol*).

iomlan, whole, E. Ir. *imshlán,* quite whole.

iompaidh, a turning, conversion, Ir. *iompógh,* O. Ir. *impúd, impúth,* W. *ymod,* a turn: **imb-shouth,* O. Ir. *sóim,* averto: **soviô,* root *su, sou,* Lat. *sucula,* windlass. It has also been referred to the root *sup,* Lat. *dissipo,* Lit, *supù,* swing.

iomradh, fame, report, Ir. *iomrádh,* O. Ir. *immrádud,* tractatio, cogitatio; from *iom-* and *ràdh,* say.

iomrall, an error, wandering, Ir. *iomrolladh, iomrulladh,* E. Ir. *imroll,* mistake: **ambi-air-al,* root *al, el,* go, as in *iomall.*

iomram, iomramh, rowing, Ir. *iomramh, iomrámh* (O'B.), E. Ir. *immram,* vb. *immráim;* from *iom-* and *ràmh.*

ion, fit, **ion-,** prefix denoting fitness, Ir. *ion-,* prefixed to passive participles, denotes fitness (O'D., who quotes *inleighis,* curable, *inmheasta,* believable): a particular use of *in-,* in-, which see. *ion is iomlan,* almost perfect (Hend.).

ion-, negative prefix *an* before *b, d, g,* Ir. *ion-,* O. Ir. *in-;* see *an* for derivation. The primitive *ṇ* before *b, d, g,* becomes *in* in Gadelic.

ionad, a place, Ir. *ionad, ionnad;* the E. Ir. has *inad* only, pointing to modern *ionadh:*

iona(dh), in **c'iona, c'ionadh,** whether: *co* and *ionadh* or *iona,* E. Ir. *inad,* place. See above. The Modern Ir. is *ca hionad.*

ionaltair, a pasturing, pasture; from *in-* and **altair,* a shorter form of *altrum.* Cf. for form Ir. *ingilim,* I pasture, from *in-* and *gelim,* I eat (root *gel,* as in G. *goile*). *iomair ionailt,* browsing rig (Carm.).

ionann, alike, Ir. *ionnan,* O. Ir. *inonn, innon, inon.* Possibly for **sin-ôn, *sin-sôn,* "this-that;" see *sin,* and *són* of O. Ir. is for **sou-n, *sou,* hoc, Gr. οὗ-τος (for root, see *sa*). Cf. for form Lat. *idem = is-dem,* Gr. ὁ αὐτός.

ionbhruich, broth; see *eanraich.*

ionga, g. **ingne,** pl. **ingnean, inean,** a nail, Ir. *ionga,* g. *iongan,* O. Ir. *inga,* g. *ingen,* W. *ewin,* Cor. *euuin,* Br. *ivin:* **engînâ* (Stokes); Lat, *unguis;* Gr. ὄνυξ, g. ὄνυχος; Got. *nagljan,* Eng. *nail;* Skr. *nakhá.* Fick gives the I. E. root as *nogh, ṇgh,* with stems *noghlo-, ṇghlo-.*

iongantach, wonderful, so Ir., *ingantach*; formed from the noun *iongnadh*, wonder.

iongar, ioghar, pus: **in-gor*, root *gor* of *guirean*, q.v. Dr Cam. compared Gr. ἴχωρ, blood of the gods (Gael, No. 548). **ping-aro-*, *pi*, swell?

iongnadh, wonder, so Ir., O. Ir. *ingnád*, *ingnáth* (adj. and n.); for *in-gnáth*, "not wont"; see *ion-* (neg. prefix) and *gnàth*.

ionmhas, treasure, Ir. *ionmhas*, *ionnmhus*, E. Ir. *indmass*; from *in-* and *-mass* of *tomhas*, measure, q.v. Ascoli connects it with O. Ir. *indeb*, lucrum, M. Ir. *indbas*, wealth.

ionmhuinn, dear, Ir. *ionmhuin*, O. Ir. *inmain*: **eni-moni-*, root *mon*, *men*, mind, remember, for which see *cuimhne*. See *muinighin*.

ionn-, prefix of the same force as *fri*, *ri*; see *inn-* further.

ionnairidh, a watching at night; from *ionn-* and *aire*.

ionnaltoir, a bath, Ir. *ionnaltóir* (O'R.), bather (Con.); see *ionnlad*.

† **ionnas**, condition, status, **ionnas gu**, insomuch that, so that, **cionnas**, how, Ir. *ionnus*, so that, O. Ir. *indas*, status: **ind-astu-*, "in adstatu," from *ad-sta*, root *sta*, stand. Zeuss[2] derives it from *ind* and the abstract termination *-assu* (*-astu-*), seemingly giving it the idea of "to-ness."

ionndruinn, missing: **ind-reth-in*, "wandering"; see *faondra*.

ionnlad, washing, Ir. *ionnlat*, O. Ir. *indlat*, Ir. vb. *innuilim*, M. Ir. *indalim*. There is also an E. Ir. *indmat*, washing of the hands. From **ind-lutto-*, **lutto* from *lu*, *lov*, bathe, Lat. *lavo*, etc.?

ionnsaich, learn, E. Ir. *insaigim*, seek out, investigate, noun *saigid*, seeking out, *saigim*: *in-* and *sag*, root *sag*, seek; Lat. *sāgio*, am keen, *sagax*, acute; Gr. ἡγέομαι, lead; Got. *sôkjan*, seek, Eng. *seek*; I. E. *sâg*, *sag*. The G. **connsaich** is from *co-in-saigim*, *sagim*, say, dispute; Got. *sakan*, dispute, Eng. *forsake*, *sake*.

ionnsuidh, attempt, approach, Ir. *ionnsuigh*, E. Ir. *insaigid*, a visit; from *in-* and *saigid*, seeking out, visiting. See *ionnsaich*. Hence the prep. *dh'ionnsuidh*.

ionntag, a nettle; see *deanntag*.

ionntlas, delight (H.S.D.); from *in-* and *tlàth*?

ionntraich, miss (Dial.); see *ionndruinn*.

ionraic, righteous, Ir. *ionnruic*, O. Ir. *inricc*, dignus: **ind-rucci-* (Ascoli); possibly **rucci-* is for **rog-ki*, root *rog*, *reg* of *reacht*.

ioraltan, harmless tricks: **air + alt*.

ioras, down; from *air* and *ìos*. Dial. **uireas**.

iorbhail, infection, taint: **air + bail*, "on-issue."

iorcallach, a robust man: "Herculean"; from **Iorcall,** Hercules, a Gaelic word formed from the Latin one.

iorghuil, fray, strife, so Ir., O. Ir. *irgal*; from *air* and *gal*, q.v. Also **iorgull.**

iorrach, quiet, undisturbed:

iorram, a boat song: **air-rám*, "at oar" song. Cf. *iomram* for phonetics.

† **ìos,** down, Ir. † *íos*, in phrases **a nìos,** from below, **sìos,** to below, so Ir.; O. Ir. *ís*, *íss*, infra, W. *is*, comp *isel*, sup. *isaf*, Br. *is*, *iz*, *isel*, comp. *iseloch*: **enso* or **endso*, from *en*, now *an*, in; Lat. *īmus*, lowest, from **ins-mus*, from *in*. Stokes cfs. rather Skr. *adhás*, under (*ṇdhas*), Eng. *under*, giving the prehistoric form as **insô*; and there is much in favour of this view for the meaning's sake, though most philologists are on the side of *en* or *end*, now *an*, being root. Lat. *imus* or *infimus* would then follow the Celtic.

ìosal, low, Ir. *iosal*, O. Ir. *ísel*: **endslo-s*; see *ìos* above.

iosgaid, hough, poples, Ir. *ioscaid*, M. Ir. *iscait*, E. Ir. *escait*:

iosop, hyssop, Ir. *íosóip*; from Lat. *hyssopum*, whence Eng.

ìotadh, thirst, Ir. *íota*, O. Ir. *ítu*, g. *ítad*: **isottât-*, root *is*, desire, seek; Gr. *ἰότης*, wish, *ἵμερος*, desire; Ch. Sl. *iskati*, seek; Skr. *ish*, seek, Zend. *ish*, wish.

iothlann, cornyard; see *iodhlann*.

ìre, progress, state, degree of growth, O. Ir. *hire*, *ire* (*íre*), ulterior: **(p)ereio-*, from *per*, through, over; Gr. *περαῖος*, on the other side. Stokes makes the proportional comparison of these forms thus:—*(p)ereios* : *περαῖος* = *(p)arei* (now *air*) : *παραί*.

iriosal, humble: **air-ìosal*, q.v.

iris, hen-roost, basket or shield handle, M. Ir. *iris*, pl. *irsi*, suspender, shield handle, satchel strap: **are-sti-*, from *air* and *sta*, stand. See *ros*, *seas*.

is, is, Ir., O. Ir. *is*, O. Ir. *iss*, O. W. *iss*, *is* = Gr. *ἐστὶ*; Lat. *est*, is; Eng. *is*, etc.

is, and, Ir., E. Ir. *is*; seemingly an idiomatic use of *is*, is. Consider the idiom; "Nì e sin is mise an so"—"He will do it and I here"; literally: "He will do it, I am here." It is usually regarded as a curtailment of *agus*, and hence spelt variously as **a's, 'us.**

isbean, a sausage; from Norse *íspen*, a sausage of lard and suet (= *í-spen*, from *speni*, a teat).

isean, a chicken, young of any bird, Ir. *iséan*, E. Ir. *essíne*, O. Ir. *isseniu*, pullo: **ex(p)et-nio-*? Root *pet*, fly; that is, **ex-én-*, *én* being *eun*, bird,

isneach, a rifle gun; from *oisinn*, corner? Meyer suggests from *isean*, young of birds, comparing "fowling-piece."

ist! whist! Eng. *whist! hist!* Lat. *st!* Onomatopoetic.

ite, a feather, Ir. *iteóg*, O. Ir. *ette*: **ettiâ*, **pet-tiâ*, root *pet*, fly; Gr. πέτομαι, I fly; Lat. *penna*, a wing (**pet-na*), Eng, *pen*; Eng. *feather*, Ger. *fittich*; etc. See *eun*. W. *aden*, wing, is near related. **iteachan,** a spool, weaver's bobbin.

iteodha, hemlock. Cameron (29) suggests a derivation from *ite*, the idea being "feather-foliaged."

ith, eat, Ir., O. Ir. *ithim*: **itô*, **pitô*, I eat; Ch. Sl. *pitati*, feed: Skr. *pitu*, nourishment, Zend *pitu*, food; further Gr. πίτυς, pine. Also †**ith,** †**ioth,** corn, as in *iodhlann*, q.v.

iubhar, yew, Ir. *iubhar*, E. Ir. *ibar*, Gaul. *Eburos*; Ger. *eberesche*, service-tree (**ebarisc*). So Schräder. It does not seem that Ir. *eó*, W. *yw*, Br. *ivin*, **ivo-*, Eng. *yew*, can be allied to *iubhar*. Hence **iubrach,** a yew wood, stately woman, the mythic boat of Fergus Mc Ro in the Deirdre story. *Eboracum?*

iùc, corner, slit. See *niùc*.

iuchair, a key, Ir. *eochair*, E. Ir. *eochuir*, Manx *ogher*, W. *egoriad*, key, *egor*, *agor*, opening: **ekûri-*; root stem *pecu-*, fastening, whence Lat. *pecu*, cattle, Eng. *fee*. Cf. W. *ebill*, key, auger.

iuchair, the roe, spawn, Ir., M. Ir. *iuchair*: **jekvuri-*, Lat. *jecur*, liver?

iuchar, the dog-days:

iugh, a particular posture in which the dead are placed:

iùl, guidance, Ir. *iul*; cf. *eòlas*.

iullag, a sprightly female, **iullagach,** sprightly:

iùnais, want, E. Ir. *ingudáis*, O. Ir. *ingnais*, absence: **in-gnáth*, from *gnáth*, known, custom; see *gnàth*. Also **aonais.**

iunnrais, stormy sky:

iunntas, wealth:

iurpais, fidgeting, wrestling; cf. *farpuis*.

†**iursach,** suspensory (Oss. Ballads), applied to the mail-coat. From *iris*. H.S.D. gives the meaning as "black, dark."

iuthaidh, fiuthaidh, iùthaidh, arrow, gun, etc.:

iutharn, hell; for **ifhern*, a side-form of *ifrinn*.

L

là, latha, day, Ir. *lá*, g. *laoi*, O. Ir. *lathe*, *laithe*, *lae*, g. *lathi*, d. *lau*, *lóu*, *ló*: **lasio-*, root *las*, shine; Skr. *lásati*, shines; Gr. λάω, behold.

làban, làpan, mire, dirt, Ir. *lábán*; also **làib.** Cf. for root *làthach* (**làth-bo-*).

labanach, a day-labourer, plebeian, Ir. *labánach* (O'B., etc.; Sh.); from Lat. *labor?*

labhair, speak, Ir. *labhraim*, E. Ir. *labraim*, O. Ir. *labrur*, *labrathar*, loquitur, W. *llafar*, vocalis, *lleferydd*, voice, Corn. *lauar*, sermo, Br. *lavar*, Gaul. river *Labarus* : **labro-*, speak ; Gr. λάβρος, furious, λαβρεύομαι, talk rashly. Bez. prefers the root of Eng. *flap*. Others have compared Lat. *labrum*, lip, which may be allied to both Celtic and Gr. (λαβρεύομαι). Hence G. and Ir. **labhar**, loud, O. Ir. *labar*, eloquens, W. *llafar*, loud, Gr. λάβρος.

la-bhallan, water shrew (Suth.), **la-mhalan** (Forbes) :

lach, a wild duck, Ir., E. Ir. *lacha* ; cf. the Lit. root *lak*, fly.

lach, reokoning, contribution per head ; from the Sc. *lauch*, tavern reckoning, *lawing* (do.), from the root of Eng. *law*.

lachan, a laugh ; from the Sc., Eng. *laugh*.

lachduinn, dun, grey, tawny, Ir., M. Ir. *lachtna*, grey, dun ; cf. Skr. *rakta*, coloured, reddened, *rañj*, dye, whence Eng. *lake*, crimson.

làd, **lòd**, a load, Ir. *lád* ; from the M. Eng. *laden*, to lade.

lad, a mill lead ; from the Eng. *lead*, *lade*. For the N.H. meaning of "puddle," see **lod**.

ladar, a ladle ; from the Eng. *ladle* by dissimilation of the liquids.

ladarna, bold, so Ir., M. Ir. *latrand*, robber, W. pl. *lladron*, thieves ; from Lat. *latro*, *latronis*, a thief.

ladhar, a hoof, fork, so Ir., E. Ir. *ladar*, toes, fork, branch : **plaðro-n*, root *pla*, extend.

lag, a hollow, Ir. *log*, a pit, hollow : **luggo-*, root *lug*, bend ; Gr. λυγίζω, bend ; Lit. *lugnas*, pliant. Stokes gives the basis as **lonko-*, root *lek*, *lenk*, bend, Lit. *lànkas*, a curve, *lanka*, a mead, Ch. Sl. *lakŭ*, bent ; but this would give *à* in G. ; Ger. *lücke*, gap, blank.

lag, weak, Ir. *lag*, E. Ir. *lac*, M. Ir. *luice* (pl.), W. *llag*, sluggish : **laggo-s*, root *lag* ; Lat. *langueo*, Eng. *languid* ; Gr. λαγγάζω, slacken, λαγαρός, thin ; Eng. *slack*, also *lag*, from Celtic. Cf. λάκκος.

làgan, sowens : **latag-ko-* ? Root *lat*, be wet, Gr. λαταξ, drop, Lat. *latex*. See *làthach*.

lagh, law, Ir. *lagh* (obsolete, says Con.) ; from the Eng. The phrase **air lagh**, set in readiness for shooting (as of a bow) is hence also.

laghach, pretty, Ir. *lághach*, *laghach* (Donegal) ; cf. M. Ir. *lig*, beauty, root *leg*, Lat. *lectus*, chosen, Eng. *election* ? Cf. O. W. *lin*, gratia. Kluge says Eng. *like*.

làidir, strong, Ir., E. Ir. *láidir* :

laigh, **luigh**, lie, Ir. *luigh*, E. Ir. *laigim*, O. Ir. *lige*, bed, W. *gwe-ly*, bed (Cor. *gueli*, Br. *guele*), Gaul. *legasit* (=posuit ?) : **logô*, *legô*, to lie, **legos*, bed, I. E. root *legh*, lie; Gr. λεχος, bed, λέχεται, sleeps (Hes.); Got. *ligan*, Ger. *liegan*, Eng. *lie*, etc.

laimhrig, landing place, harbour: from N. *hlað-hamarr*, pier or loading rock, Shet. *Laamar*. Also *lamraig*.

laimhsich, handle, Ir. *laimhsighim*: **lám-ast-ico-*, from **lamas*, handling, from *làmh*, q.v.

lainnir, brightness, polish, E. Ir. *lainderda*, glittering, glancing; also **loinnear**, bright, q.v.

lainnir, a falcon (Carm.):

laipheid, an instrument for making horn-spoons:

làir, a mare, Ir. O. Ir. *láir*, g. *lárach*: **lârex*. Stokes suggests connection with Alban. *pelé*, *pēlé*, mare.

lairceach, stout, short-legged, fat, **lairceag**, a short, fat woman:

làirig, a moor, sloping hill, a pass; cf. M. Ir. *laarg*, fork, leg and thigh, O. Ir. *loarcc*, furca. Often in place names:

laisde, easy, in good circumstances; cf. Ir. *laisti*, a heavy, stupid person; from *las*, loose?

laisgeanta, fiery, fierce; from *las*, q.v.

laithilt, a weighing as with scales, Ir. *laithe*, scales: **platio-*, root *plat*, *plet*, as in *leathan*.

lamban, milk curdled by rennet (Dial.); see *slaman*.

lamh, able, dare, Ir. *lamhaim*, E. Ir. *lamaim*, O. Ir. *-laimur*, audeo, W. *llafasu*, audere, Cor. *lavasy*, Br. *lafuaez*: **plamô*, a short-vowel form of the root of *làmh*, hand, the idea being "*manage* to, dare to?" Stokes says it is probably from **tlam*, dare, Gr. τόλμα, daring, Sc. *thole*; see *tlàth*. Windisch has compared Lit. *lemiù*, *lemti*, fix, appoint.

làmh, hand, Ir. *lámh*, O. Ir. *lám*, W. *llaw*, Cor. *lof*, O. Br. *lau*; **lâmâ*, **plâmâ*; Lat. *palma*, Eng. *palm*; Gr. παλάμη; Ag. S. *folm*, O. H. G. *folma*. Hence **làmhainn**, glove, E. Ir. *lámind*. *làmh*, axe (Ross), *làmhaidh* (Suth.); *làmhag*, a small hatchet (Arg.), M. Ir. *laime*, axe; Ol. Slav. *lomiti*, break, **lam*, Eng. *lame* (St.).

lamhrag, a slut, awkward woman, **lamhragan**, awkward handling; from *lámh*: "underhand."

làn, full, Ir., O Ir. *lán*, W. *llawn*, O. W. *laun*, Cor. *leun*, *len*, Br. *leun*: **lâno-*, **plâno-*, or *pl̥̄-no-* (Brug.), root *pl̥̄*, *plâ*, *pel*; Skr. *pûrṇás*, full; further Lat. *plênus*; Gr. πλήρης, πολύς, many; Eng. *full*, etc. See also *iol*, *lìon*, *lìnn*.

lànain, a married couple, Ir. *lánamhain*, E. Ir. *lánamain*, O. Ir. *lánamnas*, conjugium: **lag-no-*, root *log*, *leg*, lie, as in *laigh*? Stokes divides the word thus: *lán-shamain*. For *samhain*, assembly, see *samhainn*.

lànan, rafter beam, from *lànain*.

langa, a ling; from Norse *langa*, Sc. *laing*, Eng. *ling*.

langadar, seaware with long leaves (Lewis):

langaid, a fetter, fetters (especially for horses), **langar,** Ir. *langfethir* (O'B.; Lh. has † *langphetir*), E. Ir. *langfiter* (Corm. Gl., "English word this"), W. *llyfethar,* M. W. *lawhethyr*; from Eng. *lang* (long) and *fetter*. The Sc. has *langet, langelt,* which is the origin of G. *langaid.*

langaid, the guillemote (Heb.); from Sc. (Shetland) *longie,* Dan. *langivie* (Edmonston).

langaiseachadh, pulling a boat along by a rope from the bank:

langan, lowing of the deer; from the Sc., Eng. *lowing?*

langasaid, a couch, settee; from Sc. *langseat, lang-settle,* "long seat."

lann, a blade, sword, Ir. *lann,* also "a scale, scale of a fish, disc" (Arg., M'A.): **lag-s-na?* Root *lag,* as in E. Ir. *laigen,* lance, W. *llain,* blade, Lat. *lanceo,* Gr. λόγχη, lance-point. Thur. (*Zeit.* 28) suggests **plad-s-na,* "broad thing"; Gr. πλαθάνη, Ger. *fladen,* flat cake, further G. *leathann,* broad, etc. O. Ir. *lann,* squama, is referred by Stokes to **lamna,* allied to Lat. *lamina, lamna*; which would produce rather O. Ir. **lamn,* Modern *lamhan.* Ir. *lann,* gridiron, is doubtless allied to O. Ir. *lann.*

lann, an inclosure, land, Ir. *lann,* E. Ir. *land,* W. *llan,* O. W. *lann,* area, ecclesia, Br. *lann*: **landâ*; Teut. *land,* Eng. *land.* See *iodhlann.*

lannsa, a lance, Ir. *lannsa*; from the Eng.

lanntair, a lantern, Ir. *laindéar*; from the Eng.

laoch, a hero, Ir. *laoch,* a soldier, hero, E. Ir. *láech,* a hero, champion: **laicus,* soldier, "non-cleric," E. Ir. *láech,* laicus, W. *lleyg*; all from Lat. *laicus,* a layman, non-cleric.

laogh, a calf, so Ir., E. Ir. *lóeg,* W. *llo,* Cor. *loch,* Br. *leué,* M. Br. *lue*: **loigo-s,* calf, "jumper," root *leíg,* skip Got. *laikan,* spring, Lit. *láigyti,* skip, Skr. *réjati,* skip (see *leum* further). It is possible to refer it to root *leigh,* lick: "the licker."

laodhan, pith of wood, heart of a tree, Ir. *laodhan, laoidhean*; also G. *glaodhan,* q.v.

laoighcionn, lao'cionn, tulchan calf, calf-skin; from *laogh* and †*cionn,* skin, which see under *boicionn.* *Crann-laoicionn,* wooden block covered with calf-skin (Wh.).

laoidh, a lay, so Ir., E. Ir. *láed, láid,* O. Ir. *lóid*: **lûdi-?* Alliance with Teutonic *liuþ,* Eng. *lay,* Fr. *lai,* Ger. *lied,* is possible if the stem is *lûdi-*; cf. for phonetics *draoidh* and ancient *drûis, drûidos,* Druid, Gaul. Lat. *druidæ* (Stokes).

laoineach, handsome; cf. *loinn.*

laoir, drub lustily (M'A.), **laoireadh,** rolling in the dust (H.S.D.). Cf. *léir.*

laoiscionn, thin membrane inside of sheep and cattle (Lewis); N. *lauss-skin*, loose skin ?

laoisg, a group, crowd (disparagingly) (Skye):

laom, a crowd, lodge (as corn), Ir. *laomdha*, bent, M. Ir. *loem*, crowd, heap :

laom, a blaze, Ir. *laom* ; from Norse *ljómi*, ray, Ag. S. *léoma*, Sc. *leme*, to blaze.

laom, go to shaw (as potatoes) (Skye):

laom-chrann, main beam of a house (Wh.):

laosboc, a castrated goat:

laoran, a person too fond of the fire-side:

lapach, benumbed, faltering; cf. *lath*. *Lapanaich*, bedraggle (Perth).

làr, the ground, Ir., O. Ir. *lár*, W. *llawr*, O. Cor. *lor*, O. Br. *laur*, solum, Br. *leur*: **lâro-*, **plâro* ; Eng. *floor*, Ag. S. *flór*, Norse *flór*, Ger. *flur* ; root *plâ*, broad, broaden, Lat. *plânus*, Eng. *plain*, etc.

làrach, a site, Ir. *láithreach*, O. Ir. *láthrach* ; from *làthair*, q.v.

las, loose, slack, W. *llaes* ; from Lat. *laxus*, Eng. *lax*.

las, kindle, **lasair**, flame, so Ir., E. Ir. *lassaim*, *lassair*, W. *llachar*, gleaming: **laksar-* ; Skr. *lakshati*, see, show, O. H. G. *luogên* (do.). Also by some referred to **lapsar-*, Gr. *λάμπω*, shine, Eng. *lamp*, Pruss. *lopis*, flame. See *losgadh*. Windisch has compared Skr. *arc*, *ṛc*, shine. Hence **lasgaire**, a youth, young "spark"; **lastan**, pride, etc.

lasgar, sudden noise:

lath, benumb, get benumbed. Cf. W. *llad*.

làthach, mire, clay, Ir., E. Ir. *lathach*, coenum, W. *llaid*, mire, Br. *leiz*, moist: **latákâ*, **latjo-*, root *lat*, be moist; Gr. *λάταξ*, *λάταγές*, drops; Lat. *latex*, liquid.

lathailt, a method, a mould (Wh.):

làthair, presence, Ir. *láthair*, O. Ir. *láthar*, *lathair* : **latri-*, **lâtro-*, root *plât*, *plâ*, broad; Lettic *plât*, extend thinly; further in G. *làr* above. Asc. refers it to the root of O. Ir. *láaim*, I send, which is allied to Gr. *ἐλαύνω*, I drive, etc. Hence **làrach**.

le, by, with, Ir. *le*, O. Ir. *la*, rarer *le* : **lẹt* ; from *leth*, side.

lèabag, a flounder; see *leòb*. Also **leòbag**.

leabaidh, a bed, **leabadh**, Ir. *leaba*, *leabuidh*, E. Ir. *lepaid*, *lepad*, g. *leptha* : **lebboti-*, **leg-buto-* "lying-abode," from root *leg*, *λεχ*, lie, as in *laigh* ? W. *bedd*.

leabhar, a book, so Ir., O. Ir. *lebor*, W. *llyfr* ; from Lat. *liber*.

leabhar, long, clumsy, M. Ir. *lebur*, O. Ir. *lebor*, long: **lebro-*, root *leg*, hanging, Gr. *λοβός*, a lobe; Eng. *lappet* ; also Lat. *liber*, book.

leac, a flag, flag-stone, so Ir., E. Ir. *lecc*, W. *llech* : **liccâ*, **ḷp-kâ*, root *lep*, a shale; Gr. λέπας, bare rock; Lat. *lapis*, stone. Stokes and Strachan refer it to the root *pḷk*, flat, Lat. *planca*, Eng. *plank*, Gr. πλάξ, plain.

leac, a cheek, **leacainn**, a hill side, Ir. *leaca*, cheek, g. *leacan*, E. Ir. *lecco*, g. *leccan*: **lekkôn-*; O. Pruss. *laygnan*, Ch. Sl. *lice*, vultus. Root *liq*, *lig*, appearance, like, Gr. -λίκος, Eng. *like*, *lyke*-wake, Ger. *leichnam* body.

leadair, mangle, so Ir., E. Ir. *letraim*, inf. *letrad*, hacking: **leddro-* :

leadan, flowing hair, a lock, teasel, Ir., *leadán*, M. Ir. *ledán*, teasel. Root *li*, stick; see *liosta*.

leadan, notes in music, Ir. *leadán*, musical notes, litany; from Lat. *litania*, litany.

leag, throw down, Ir. *leagaim*, inf. *leagadh* : **leggô*, from *leg*, root of *laigh*, lie (cf. Eng. *lay*)? The preserved *g* may be from the analogy of *leig*, let; and Ascoli refers the word to the O. Ir. root *leg*, *lig*, destruere, sternere: *foralaig*, straverat, *dolega*, qui destruit.

leagarra, self-satisfied, smug (Arg.):

leagh, melt, so Ir., O. Ir. *legaim*, *legad*, W. *llaith*, moist, *dad leithio*, melt, Br. *leiz* : **legô*; Eng. *leak*, Norse *leka*, drip, Ger. *lechzen*.

leamh, foolish, insipid, importunate, Ir. *leamh*; cf. E. Ir. *lem*, everything warm (?) and soft (Corm. sub *lemlacht*, new milk, W. *llefrith*, sweet milk, Corn. *leverid*, *liuriz*; O. Ir. *lemnact*, sweet milk); consider root *lem*, break, as in Eng. *lame*, etc.

leamhan, elm, Ir. *leamhann*, *leamh*, M. Ir. *lem* : **ḷmo-*; Lat. *ulmus*, Eng. *elm*: **elmo-*. W. *llwyf* (**leimá*) is different, with which is allied (by borrowing ?) Eng. *lime* in *lime-tree*.

leamnacht, tormentil, Ir. *neamhain* :

leamhnad, **leamhragan**, stye in the eye, W. *llefrithen*, *llyfelyn* : **limo-*, "ooze"? Cf. Lat. *līmus*, mud, *lino*, smear, Eng. *loam*.

lèan, **lèana**, a lea, swampy plain, Ir. *léana* (do.): **lekno-*? Cf. Lit. *lëkns*, *lëkna*, depression, wet meadow (cf. Stokes on *lag* above); this is Mr Strachan's derivation. The spelling seems against referring it, as Stokes does, to the root *lei*, Gr. λειμών, meadow, Lit. *léija*, a valley; though W. *llwyn*, grove, favours this. Cf. W. *lleyn*, low strip of land.

lean, follow, Ir. *leanaim*, O. Ir. *lenim*, W. *can-lyn*, *dy-lyn*, sequi: **linami*, I cling to; Skr. *linâmi*, cling to; Lat. *lino*, smear; Gr. ἀλίνω (do.); **lipnâmi*, Lit. *lipti*, cleave to; root *lî*, *li*, adhere. Inf. is **leanmhuinn**.

leanabh, a child, Ir. *leanbh*, E. Ir. *lenab* : **lenvo-* ; from *lean* ? Corm. gives also *lelap*, which, as to termination, agrees with G. **leanaban.** Cf. αλοφυρμοαι.

leann, ale, see *lionn*.

leannan, a sweetheart, Ir. *leannán*, a concubine, E. Ir. *lennan*, *lendan*, concubine, favourite : *lex-no-*, root *leg*, lie, as in *laigh* ? From *lionn* ; cf. *òlach* ?

lear, the sea (poetical word), Ir. *lear*, E. Ir. *ler*, W. *llyr* : **liro-*, root *li*, flow, as in *lighe*, flood. Stokes gives the Celtic as *lero-s*, but offers no further derivation.

learag, larch ; from Sc. *larick*, Eng. *larch*, from Lat. *larix* (**darix*, as in *darach*, q.v.).

learg, leirg, plain, hillside, Ir. *learg*, E. Ir. *lerg*, a plain ; cf. Lat. *largus*, Eng. *large*.

learg, diver bird (Carm.) :

leas, advantage, Ir. *leas*, O. Ir. *less*, W. *lles*, Cor. *les*, Br. *laz* : **lesso-*, root *pled*, fruit ; Slav. *plodŭ*, fruit (Stokes, Bez.).

leas-, nick-, step-, Ir. *leas-*, O. Ir. *less-*, W. *llys-* (W. *llysenw* = G. *leas-ainm*), Br. *les-* ; same as *leas* above : "additional." Cf. Fr. use of *beau*, *belle* for *step-*. Stokes suggests **lisso-*, blame, root *leid*, Gr. λοιδορέω, revile (Lat. *ludere* ?) ; others compare *leas-* to Ger. *laster*, vice (see *lochd*) ; Bez. queries connection with Ag. S. *lesve*, false, Norse *lasinn*, half-broken.

leasg, leisg, lazy, Ir. *leasg*, O. Ir. *lesc*, W. *llesg* : **lesko-s* ; Norse *löskr*, weak, idle, O. H. G. *lescan*, become extinguished, Ger. *erloschen* (Stokes). Brugmann and others give stem as **led-sco-*, comparing Got. *latz*, lazy, Eng. *late*, to which Norse *löskr* may be referred (**latkwa-z*) ; root *lêd*, *lad*. ἐλιννυω, rest (Zeit.[34], 531).

leasraidh, loins, Ir. *leasruigh*, pl. of *leasrach* ; see *leis*.

leathad, declivity, hillside ; cf. Ir. *leathad*, breadth. See *leud*.

leathan, broad, so Ir., O. Ir. *lethan*, W. *llydan*, O. W. *litan*, Br. *ledan*, Gaul. *litano-s* : **l̥tano-s*, Gr. πλατύς, broad ; Skr. *práthas*, breadth ; Lat. *planta*, sole of the foot, sprout : root *plet*, *plat*, extend.

leathar, leather, so Ir., E. Ir. *lethar*, W. *lledr*, M. Br. *lezr*, Br. *ler* : **letro-* ; Eng. *leather*, Ger. *leder*, Norse *leðr*. To prove that the Teutons borrowed this word from the Celts, it is asserted that the original Celtic is **(p)letro-*, root *pel* of Gr. πελλα, hide, Eng. *fell*.

leatrom, burden, weight, **leatromach,** pregnant, Ir. *leathtrom*, burden, pregnancy ; from *leth* and *trom*.

leibhidh, race, generation (Mc Ithich, 1685) ; from Eng. *levy* ?

leibhidh, amount of stock (Carm.) :

leibid, a trifle, dirt, **leibideach,** trifling, Ir. *libideach*, dirty, awkward :

léideach, strong, shaggy, Ir. *léidmheach*, strong (O'B.), O. Ir. *létenach*, audax :

leig, let, Ir. *léigim*, O. Ir. *léiccim*, *lécim* : **leinqiô* ; Lat. *linquo* ; Gr. λείπω : Got. *leihvan*, Eng. *loan*.

léigh, a physician, **leigheas**, a cure, Ir. *léigheas*, M. Ir. *leges* ; see *lighiche*.

léine, a shirt, so Ir., E. Ir. *léne*, g. *lénith*, pl. *lénti* : **leinet-*, from *lein*, *lîn* ; Lat. *lînum*, flax, Eng. *linen*, Sc. *linder* ; Gr. λῖτα, cloth, λίνον, flax. See *lìon*. Strachan refers it, on the analogy of *deur* = *dakro-*, to *laknet-*, root *lak*, of Lat. *lacerna*, cloak, *lacinia*, lappet.

léir, sight, Ir. *léir*, sight, clear, O. Ir. *léir*, conspicuous. If Strachan's phonetics are right, this may be for **lakri-*, root *lak*, see, show, W. *llygat*, eye, Cor. *lagat*, Br. *lagad*, eye, Skr. *lakshati*, see, show, O. H. G. *luogên* (do.), as in *las*, q.v.

léir, gu léir, altogether, Ir. *léir*, M. Ir. *léir*, complete, W. *llwyr*, total, altogether : **leiri-s* :

léir, torment, to pain : **lakro-*, root *lak*, as in Lat. *lacero*, lacerate ?

leirg, a plain ; see *learg*.

leirist, a foolish, senseless person, slut (**leithrist**) :

leis, thigh, Ir. *leas*, *leis*, hip, O. Ir. *less*, clunis ; **lexa*, root *lek* ; Eng. leg, Gr. λάξ, kicking (St.). Nigra connects it with *leth*, side. See *slios*.

leisdear, arrow-maker ; from the Eng. *fletcher*, from Fr. *flèche*, arrow. See *fleasg*.

leisg, laziness, lazy, Ir. *leisg* (n.) ; see *leasg*.

leisgeul, excuse ; from *leth* and *sgeul*, "half-story."

leithid, the like, so. Ir., E. Ir. *lethet* ; from *leth*, half, side.

leithleag, léileag, print for frocks :

leitir, a hillside, slope, E. Ir. *lettir*, g. *lettrach*, W. *llethr*, slope : **lettrek-*. It may be from **leth-tír*, "country-side," or from *let* of *leathan* ; cf. W. *lleth*, flattened, "broadened."

leòb, a piece, shred, Ir. *léab*, a piece, *leadhb*, a patch of old leather, M. Ir. *ledb* : **led-bo-* ; for root *led*, cf. *leathar* ? Hence **leòb**, a hanging lip, **leòbag, lèabag**, a flounder. Cf. Norse *leppr*, a rag (Craigie).

leobhar, long, clumsy ; see *leabhar*.

leòcach, sneaking, low :

leòdag, a slut, prude, flirt :

leog, a slap in the head (M'D.) :

leogach, hanging loosely, slovenly :

leòir, enough, Ir., E. Ir. *leór*, *lór*, O. Ir. *lour*, W. *llawer*, many : **lavero-*, root *lav*, *lau*, gain, Lat. *lûcrum*, gain, *Laverna*, Skr. *lóta*, booty, Eng. *loot*, etc. Stokes refers W. *llawer* to the comparative stem of *plê*, full ; see *liuth*.

leòm, conceit, **leòmais**, dilly-dallying; cf. Ir. *leoghaim*, I flatter, *leom*, prudery.

leómann, moth, Ir. *leomhan*, *léamhann*, E. Ir. *legam*.

leómhann, leoghann, lion, Ir. *leomhan*, O. Ir. *leoman*; from Lat. *leo*, *leonem*.

leòn, wound, Ir. *leónaim*, E. Ir. *lénaim*, wound, *lén*, hurt; this Strachan refers to **lakno-*, root, *lak*, tear, as in Lat. *lacero*, lacerate, Gr. λακίς, a rent. But cf. *leadradh*, E. Ir. *leod*, cutting, killing, **ledu*, root *led*, *ledh*, fell, Lat. *labi*, Eng. *lapse*.

leth, side, half, Ir., O. Ir. *leth*, W. *lled*, O. Br. *let*: **letos*; Lat. *latus*. Brugmann refers it to the root *plet*, broad, of *leathan*.

leth-aon, twin, **leth-uan**: E. Ir. *emuin*, twins, **jemnos*:

lethbhreac, a correlative, equal, match; from *leth* and *breac* (?).

lethcheann (pron. **lei'chean**), the side of the head, cheek; from *leth* and *ceann*, with possibly a leaning on the practically lost *leac*, *leacann*, cheek.

leud, lèad, breadth, Ir. *leithead*, O. Ir. *lethet*; see *leathan*.

leug, a precious stone, Ir. *liag*, a stone, M. Ir. *lég*, *lég-lógmar*, O. Ir. *lia*, g. *liacc*: **lêvink-*; Gr. λᾶιγξ, g. λάιγγος, a small stone, λᾶας, stone; Ger. *lei*, stone, rock, Ital. *lavagna*, slate, schist.

leug, laziness, lazy, slow; see *sléig*.

leugh, lèagh, read, Ir. *léaghaim*, M. Ir. *légim*, O. Ir. *legim*, *rolég*, legit, *legend*, reading; from Lat. *lĕgo*, I read, Eng. *lecture*, etc.

leum, a jump, Ir., O. Ir. *léim*, *léimm*, W. *llam*, Br. *lam*, O. Br. *lammam*, salio: **lengmen-*, O. Ir. vb. *lingim*, I spring, root *leg*, *leng*; Skr. *langhati*, leap, spring; M. H. G. *lingen*, go forward, Eng. *light*, etc. The O. Ir. perfect tense *leblaing* has made some give the root as *vleng*, *vleg*, Skr. *valg*, spring, Lat. *valgus*, awry, Eng. *walk*; and some give the root as *svleng*, from *svelg*. It is difficult to see how the *v* or *sv* before *l* was lost before *l* in *leum*.

leus, lias, a torch, light, Ir. *leus*, E. Ir. *lés*, *léss*, O. Ir., *lésboire*, lightbearer: **plent-to-*, from *plend*, *splend*, Lat. *splendeo*, Eng. *splendid* (Strachan). Cf. W. *llwys*, clear, pure.

lì, colour, O. Ir. *lí*, *líi*, W. *lliw*, Cor. *liu*, color, Br. *liou*, O. Br. *liou*, *liu*: **lîvos-*; Lat. *lîvor*, *lividus*, Eng. *livid*.

† **lia**, a stone, O. Ir. *lia*, g. *liacc*; see *leug*.

liagh, a ladle, Ir., M. Ir. *liach*, O. Ir. *liag*, trulla, scoop, W. *llwy*, spoon, spattle, Cor. *loe*, Br. *loa*: *leigâ*, ladle, root *leigh*, *ligh*, lick (as in *imlich*, q.v.); Lat. *ligula*, spoon, ladle.

liath, gray, so Ir., E. Ir. *líath*, W. *llwyd*, canus, O. Br. *loit*, M. Br. *loet*: **leito-*, **pleito-*, for **peleito-*; Gr. πελιτνός, livid; Skr. *palitá*, gray; Lat. *pallidus*; Eng. *fallow*, Ag. S. *fealo*, yellow. Cf. O. Fr. *liart*, dark grey, Sc. *lyart* (**leucardus ?*).

liathroid, a ball (M'D., *liaroid*) :
liatrus, blue-mould, **liathlas, liatas** : *liath* + ?
lid, liod, a syllable, lisp, **lideach, liotach**, lisping, Ir. *liotadh*, a lisp (Fol.) ; cf. Gr. λιτή, prayer, Lat. *lito*, placate.
lidh, steep grassy slope : N. *hlið* ?
ligeach, sly ; from the Sc. *sleekie, sleekit*, sly, smooth, Eng. *sleek*.
lighe, a flood, overflow, Ir., E. Ir. *lia*, O. Ir. *lie*, eluvio, W. *lli*, flood, stream, *lliant*, fluctus, fluentum, Br. *livad*, inundation ; root *lî*, *leja*, flow ; Skr. *riyati*, let run ; Lit. *lëti*, gush ; Gr. λίμνη, lake, λεῖος, smooth, Lat. *levis*, level, *lîmus*, mud ; etc. Stokes hesitates between root *li* and roots *pleu* (Eng. *flow*) and *lev*, *lav*, Lat. *lavo*, *luo*.
lighiche, a physician, Ir. *liaigh*, g. *leagha*, E. Ir. *liaig*, O. Ir. *legib*, medicis : Got. *leikeis*, Eng. *leech*.
linig, lining ; from the Eng.
linn, an age, century, offspring, Ir. *linn*, O. Ir. *línn*, *lín*, pars, numerus : **lênu-*, from *plên*, as in *lìon*, fill (Brug.), q.v.
linne, a pool, linn, Ir. *linn*, E. Ir. *lind*, W. *llyn*, M. W. *linn*, Cor. *lin*, Br. *lenn* : **linnos*, root *li*, *lî*, flow ; Gr. λίμνη, lake, etc. ; see *lighe*.
linnean, shoemaker's thread ; from Sc. *lingan*, *lingel*, from Fr. *ligneul*, Lat. **lineolum*, *linea*, Eng. *line*.
linnseag, shroud, penance shirt ; founded on the Eng. *linsey*.
liobarnach, slovenly, awkward, so Ir. ; founded on Eng. *slippery* ?
liobasda, slovenly, awkward, so Ir. ; see *slibist*.
liobh, love (Carm.) :
liod, lide, syllable ; see *lid*.
liomh, polish, Ir. *líomhaim*, *liomhaim*, M. Ir. *límtha*, polished, sharpened, W. *llifo*, grind, whet, saw ; Lat. *lîmo*, polish, whet, *lîmatus*, polished, root, *lî*, *lei*, smooth, flow.
lion, flax, lint, Ir. *líon*, E. Ir. *lín*, W. *llin*, Cor., Br. *lin* : **lînu-* ; Lat. *lînum*, flax ; Gr. λίνον, flax, λῖτα, cloth ; Got. *lein*, O. H. G. *lîn* ; Ch. Sl. *lĭnŭ* ; root *lei*, *li*, smooth, flow.
lion, a net, Ir. *líon*, O. Ir. *lín* ; from the above word.
lion, fill, Ir. *líonaim*, O. Ir. *línaim* : **lênô*, **plênô* ; Lat. *plênus*, full ; Gr. πλήρης, full ; root *plê*, *plâ*, as in *làn*, q.v. Hence **lionar, lionmhor**, numerous.
lion, cia lion, how many ; same as *linn*, O. Ir. *lín*.
lionn, leann, ale, so Ir., O. Ir. *lind*, M. Ir. *lind dub*, W. *llyn* : **lennu-* ; same root and form (so far) as *linne*, q.v. This is proved by its secondary use in G. and Ir. for "humours, melancholy." Stokes suggests for both connection with Gr. πλαδαρός, moist.
lionradh, gravy, juice ; from *lìon*, "fullness" ?

lios, a garden, Ir. *lios*, a fort, habitation, E. Ir. *liss*, *less*, enclosure, habitation, W. *llys*. aula, palatium, Br. *les*, court, O. Br. *lis*: **l̥sso-s*, a dwelling enclosed by an earthen wall, root *plet*, broad, Eng. *place*, Gr. πλατύς, broad; O. H. G. *flezzi*, house floor, Norse *flet*, a flat. For root, see *leathan*.

liosda, slow, tedious, importunate, so Ir., M. Ir. *liosta*, *lisdacht*, importunity, E. Ir. *lista*, slow: **li-sso-*, root *li*, smooth, Gr. λισσός, smooth, λεῖος, as in *lighe*.

liosraig, smooth, press (as cloth after weaving), dress, **sliosraig** (Badenoch); compare the above word for root and stem.

liotach, stammering, lisping. See *lid*.

lip, liop, liob, a lip, Ir. *liob*; from Eng. *lip*.

lipinn, lìpinn, a lippie, fourth of a peck; from Sc. *lippie*.

lìrean, a species of marine fungus (H.S.D.):

lit, porridge, M. Ir. *lité*, E. Ir. *littiu*, g. *litten*, W. *llith*, mash: **littiôn-* (Stokes), **pl̥t-tiô*, from *pelt*, *polt*, Gr. πόλτος, porridge, Lat. *puls*, *pultis*, pottage.

litir, a letter, so Ir., E. Ir. *liter*, W. *llythyr*, Br. *lizer*; from Lat. *litera*.

liubhar (H.S.D. **liùbhar**), deliver; from the Lat. *libero*, Eng. *liberate*.

liùg, a lame hand or foot, sneaking look, Ir. *liug*, a sneaking or lame gait, *liugaire*, cajoler, G. **liùgair** (do.):

liuth, liutha, liuthad, many, many a, so many, Ir., O. Ir. *lia*, more, O. W. *liaus*, Br. *liez*: *(*p*)*lêjôs*, from *plê*, full, Gr. πλείων; Lat. *plus*, *plûres*, older *pleores*; Norse *fleiri*, more.

liùth, a lythe; from the Sc.

liuthail, liuil, bathing, from *liu*, *li*. water (Carm.); M. Ir. *lia*, flood (Stokes, 249).

loban, lòban, lòpan, a creel for drying corn, basket, wooden frame put inside corn-stacks to keep them dry, basket peat-cart, peat-creel; from N. *laupr*, basket, timber frame of a building, Shet. *loopie*, Ag. S. *léap*.

lobanach, draggled, **lobair**, draggle; from **lob**, puddle (Armstrong): **loth-bo-*, *loth* of *lòn*, q.v.?

lobh, putrefy, Ir. *lobhaim*, O. Ir. *lobat*, putrescant, inf. *lobad*, root *lob*, wither, waste; Lat. *lâbi*, to fall, *lâbes*, ruin, Eng. *lapse*.

lobhar, a leper, so Ir., O. Ir. *lobur*, infirmus, W. *llwfr*, feeble, O. W. *lobur*, debile, M. Br. *loffr*, leprous, Br. *laour*, *lovr*, *lor*, leper. For root see above word.

lobht, a loft, Manx *lout*, Ir. *lota* (Connaught); from Norse *lopt*, Eng. *loft*.

locair, plane (carpenter's), Ir. *locar*; from Norse *lokar*, Ag. S. *locer*.

loch, a lake, loch, Ir., E. Ir. *loch*: **loku-*; Lat. *lacus*; Gr. λάκκος, pit.
lochd, a fault, so Ir., O. Ir. *locht*, crimen: **loktu-*, root *lok*, *lak*, Gr. λακ-, λάσκω, cry; O. H. G. *lahan*, blame, Ag. S. *leahan*, Ger *laster*, a fault, vice, Norse *löstr*. Eng. *lack*, *leak*, **lak*?
lochdan, a little amount (of sleep), Ir. *lochdain*, a nap, wink of sleep (Arran and Eigg, *lochd*):
lòchran, a torch, light, Ir. *lóchrann*, O. Ir. *lócharn*, *lúacharn*, W. *llugorn*, Cor. *lugarn*: **loukarnâ*, root *louq*, *leuq*, light; Lat. *lŭcerna*, lamp, *lux*, light; Gr. λευκός, white.
lod, lodan, a puddle, Ir. *lodan*: **lusdo-*, **lut-s*, root *lut*, *lu*, Lat. *lutum*, mud, Gr. λῦμα, filth.
lòd, a load, Ir. *lód*; from the Eng.
lodhainn, a pack (of dogs), a number: "a leash;" see *lomhainn*.
lodragan, a clumsy old man, plump boy:
logais, logaist, awkward, unwieldy person, loose slipper or old shoe (Arg.); from Eng *log*. Cf. Sc. *loggs*. Eng. *luggage*?
logar, sea swash (Lewis):
logh, pardon, Ir. *loghadh* (n.), E. Ir. *logaim*, O. Ir. *doluigim*. Stokes refers it to the root of *leagh*, melt.
lòghar, excellent:
loguid, a varlet, rascal, soft fellow, M. Ir. *locaim*, I flinch from:
loibean, one who works in all weathers and places; cf. *làib*, under *làban*.
loiceil, foolishly fond, doting, Ir. *loiceamhlachd*, *lóiceamhlachd* (O'B.), dotage:
loigear, an untidy person, ragged one:
lòine, a lock of fine wool, tuft of snow: Cf. λαχνη;
loinid, churn staff, Ir., M. Ir. *loinid*. Stokes takes from N. *hlunnr*. O'R. has *lunn*, churn-dasher.
lòinidh, rheumatism, **greim-lòinidh**:
loinn, good condition, charm, comeliness, joy, Ir. *loinn*, joy, M. Ir. *lainn*, bright; from *plend*, Lat. *splendeo*, Eng. *splendid*. Hence **loinnear,** bright. So Stokes.
loinn, glade, area; oblique form of *lann*, the locative case in place names.
loinn, a badge; a corruption of *sloinn*?
loinnear, bright, elegant, E. Ir. *lainderda*, glittering: **lasno-*, from *las* flame, q.v.? Cf. *lonnrach*. See *loinn*.
loinneas, a wavering:
loirc, wallow, **loir** (Perth):
loirc, a deformed foot, **lorcach,** lame; cf. *lurc*, *lorc*.
loireag, a beautiful, hairy cow; a plump girl, pan-cake, water-nymph (Carm.); cf. *lur*, *lurach*.

loireanach, male child just able to walk; cf. *luran.*

lòiseam, pomp, show:

loisneach, cunning: "foxy;" Ir. *loisi, los,* a fox: **luxo-*; Gr. λύγξ, lynx, O. H. G. *luhs,* Ang. S. *lox,* lynx.

loistean, a lodging, tent, Ir. *lóistín*; from the Eng *lodging.*

loithreach, ragged (Hend.):

lom, bare, Ir. *lom,* O. Ir. *lomm,* W. *llwm*: **lummo-, *lups-mo-,* root *lup,* peel, break off; Lit. *lupti,* peel, Ch. Sl. *lupiti,* detrahere; Skr. *lumpami,* cut off. Hes. has Gr. λυμνός = γυμνός, which Stokes suggests alternately. Hence **lomradh,** fleecing, O. Ir. *lommraim,* tondeo, abrado, *lommar,* bared, stripped; which last Stokes compares rather to Lat. *lamberat,* scindit ac laniat.

lombair, bare; cf. O. Ir. *lommar,* bared (see *lom*). Possibly the *b* is intrusive, as in Eng. *number, slumber.*

lomchar, bare place; from *lom* and *cuir, cor.*

lomhainn, a leash, Ir. *lomna,* a cord (O'Cl.), O. Ir. *loman,* funis, lorum, W. *llyfan,* Cor. *louan,* Br. *louffan,* tether: **lomanâ.*

lomhair, brilliant:

lomnochd, naked, so Ir., E. Ir. *lomnocht*; from *lom* and *nochd,* naked.

lompair, a bare plain; see *lombair,* which is another spelling of this word.

lompais, niggardliness, Ir. *lompais*; from **lommas,* from *lom.*

lòn, food, Ir., M. Ir. *lón,* O. Ir. *lóon,* adeps, commeatus, O. Br. *lon,* adeps: **louno-.* Strachan and Stokes cf. O. Sl. *plŭti,* caro, Lit. *plutà,* a crust, Lettic *pluta,* a bowel. Bez. queries if it is allied to L. Ger. *flôm,* raw suet, O. H. G. *floum.* It was usual to refer it to the same root as Gr. πλοῦτος, wealth; and Ernault has suggested connection with *blonag* (**vlon*), which is unlikely.

lòn, marsh, mud, meadow (Arg.), water (Skye): **lut-no-,* root *lut,* muddy, O. Ir. *loth,* mud, Lat. *lutum*; further root *lu, lou,* as in *lod.* It may be from **louno-,* with the same root; cf. M. Ir. *conluan,* hounds' excrement.

lon, lon-dubh, the blackbird, Ir., M. Ir., O. Ir. *lon.* Stokes refers it to **lux-no-* (root *leuq,* light, Lat. *lux,* etc.), but this in the G. would give *lonn.*

lon, elk, M. G. *lon* (D. of L.), Ir. *lon*: **lono-*; cf. O. Slav. *lani,* hind, and, further, Celtic **elanî,* roe (see *eilid*).

lon, a rope of raw hides (St Kilda): possibly a condensation of *lomhainn.*

lon, lon-chraois, gluttony, M. Ir. *lon cráis.* Kuno Meyer, (*Vision of M'Conglinne*) translates *lon* separately as "demon." For *craois* see *craos.* *lon,* water (Carm.) + *craos*?

lon, prattle, forwardness, Ir. *lonaigh*, a scoff, jest, W. *llon*, cheerful: **luno-*, root, *lu*, *lav*, enjoy, win, W. *llawen*, merry; Gr. ἀπολαύω, enjoy; Got. *laun*, reward. See further under *luach*. *làn-aighear*, boisterous mirth (Wh.)?

long, a ship, Ir. *long*, E. Ir. *long*, vessel (vas), ship, W. *llong*, ship: **longâ*; Norse *lung*, ship (Bez.); cf. Lat. *lagena*, flagon (Stokes). Usually supposed to be borrowed from Lat. (navis) *longa*, war ship. Cf. Ptolemy's River Λόγγος, the Norse *Skipafjörðr*, now Loch Long. **plugnâ*? Eng. *fly*?

longadh, a diet, so Ir., E. Ir. *longad*, eating; a side form of *slug*, which see for root.

longphort, harbour, camp, palace, Ir. *longphort* (do.); from *long* + *port*. Hence **lùchairt**, palace; *longart*, *lunkart*, in place-names.

lonn, timber put under a boat for launching it; from Norse *hlunnr*, a roller for launching ships.

lonn, anger, fierce, strong, Ir. *lonn*, O. Ir. *lond*, wild. Stokes (*Zeit.*[30], 557) doubtfully suggests connection with Skr. *randhayati*, destroy, torment.

lonnrach, glittering, so Ir.; cf. *loinnir*. *lònrach*, well fed (Hend.).

lòpan, soft, muddy place (Suth.): see **làban**.

lorc, shank (Carm.):

lorg, a staff, Ir., E. Ir. *lorg*, Cor. *lorc'h*, baculus, Br. *lorc'hen*, temo: **lorgo-*, Norse *lurkr*, a cudgel (Bez., Cam.).

lorg, track, footstep, Ir., E. Ir. *lorg*, O. Ir. *lorc*, trames, *lorgarecht*, indago, W. *llyr*, course, duct, Cor. *lergh*, *lerch*, Br. *lerc'h*, track: **lorgo-*. Bez. compares L. Ger. *lurken*, creep. Rhys adds W. *llwrw*, direction (*Manx Pray.*[2], 127).

los, purpose, sake, Ir., E. Ir. *los*, sake, behalf, part, M. Ir. *los*, growth; *a los*, "about to" (Wh.); *in dobhran losleathan*, beaver (otter of broad tail), Ir. *los*, tail, end (O'Cl.), W. *llost*, Br. *lost*, **losto-*, *lostâ*:

losaid, a kneading trough, Ir. *losad*, E. Ir. *lossat*: **lossantâ*, **lok-s-*, root *lok*, *lek*; Gr. λέκος, a dish, pot; Lit. *lekmenė*, a puddle; Lat. *lanx*, dish.

losgadh, a burning, Ir. *loscadh*, E. Ir. *loscud*, W. *llosg*, urere, Cor. *losc* (n.), Br. *losk*: **loskô*, I burn, **lopskô*, root, *lop*, *lap*; Gr. λάμπω, shine; O. Pruss. *lopis*, flame, Lett. *lapa*, pine-torch (Stokes). See *lasair*, to whose root it is usually referred.

losgann, a toad, Ir. *loscain*, E. Ir. *loscann*; from *losg* above, so named from the acrid secretions of its skin.

lot, wound, so Ir., E. Ir. *lot*, damage, *loitim*, laedo: **lottô*, **lut-to-*, root *lut*, *lu*, cut; Skr. *lû-*, cut; Gr. λύω, loose; Eng. *loss*, *lose*; Pruss. *au-laut*, die. Stokes refers it to a stem **lud-nó-*, root *lud*, Teut. root, *lut*, Eng. *lout*, *little*, Norse *lúta*, to lout, bow, Ag. S. *lot*, dolus, etc.

lot, share, etc., one's croft (Lewis) :

loth, a colt, Manx, *lhiy*, W. *llwdn*, young of deer, sheep, swine, hens, etc., Cor. *lodn* (do.), M. Br. *lozn*, beast, Br. *loen*, animal: **pluto-*, **plutno-* ; cf. Lat. *pullus*, foal, Eng. *filly*.

loth, marsh (Suth.) O. Ir *loth*, mud ; see further under *lòn*. Hence *Loth* parish.

lothail, the plant brook-lime, Ir. *lothal* (O'B.), *lochal* :

luach, worth, value, Ir. *luach*, O. Ir. *lóg*, *luach* : **lougos*, root *lou*, *lû*, gain ; Lat. *lûcrum*, gain, *Laverna*, the thieves' goddess ; Got. *laun*, a reward, Ag. S. *léan* (do.) ; O. Slav. *lovŭ*, catching.

luachair, rushes, Ir., E. Ir. *luachair* : "light-maker," from *louk*, light (Lat. *lux*, etc.), M. W. *lleu babir*, rush-light.

luadh, fulling cloth ; cf. Ir. *luadh*, motion, moving, root *ploud* (Lit. *plaudżu*, wash, Eng. *fleet*), a side-form of the root of *luath*. But compare *dol*.

luaidh, mention, speaking, Ir. *luadh*, O. Ir. *luad* : **laudo-* ; Lat. *laus*, *laudis*, praise. Hence **luaidh**, beloved one : "spoken or thought of one."

luaidh, lead, Ir., M. Ir. *luaidhe* : **loudiâ* ; Eng. *lead*, Ag. S. *léad* (**lauda-*), Ger. *loth*.

luaimear, a prattler, Ir. *luaimearachd*, volubility ; see next word.

luaineach, restless, Ir. *luaimneach*, E. Ir. *luamnech*, volatile (as birds), *lúamain*, flying ; root *ploug*, fly ; Eng. *fly*, Ger. *fliegen*, Norse *fljúga*.

luaireagan, a grovelling person, a fire-fond child ; from *luaith*, ashes : "one in sackcloth and ashes"?

luaisg, move, wave, **luasgadh** (n.), Ir. *luasgaim*, M. Ir. *luascad*, O. Br. *luscou*, oscilla, Br. *luskella*, to rock: **louskô*, **ploud-sko-*, root *ploud* or *plout*, *plou*, go, flow, move, as in *luath*, q.v. Bez. queries connection with Lit. *plúskát*, *plúkt*, pluck, tear.

luan, moon, Monday, so Ir. ; M. Ir., O. Ir. *luan*, moon, Monday : **loukno-*, Lat. *lux*, *luceo*, *lûna*, moon. The Gadelic is possibly borrowed from Lat. Ir. *go lá an Luain*, till doomsday.

luaran, a dizziness, faint :

luath, ashes, Ir. *luaith*, E. Ir. *lúaith*, W. *lludw*, Cor. *lusu*, Br. *ludu* : **loutvi-*. Bez. queries if it is allied to Ger. *lodern*, to flame.

luath, swift, Ir. *luath*, O. Ir. *lúath* : **louto-*, root *plout*, *plou*, go, flow, be swift ; Eng. *fleet*, Norse *fljótr*, swift (root *pleud*) ; Gr. πλέω, I sail ; Lat. *pluit*, it rains ; Skr. *plavate*, swim, fly.

lùb, bend, Ir., M. Ir. *lúbaim*, E. Ir. *lúpaim* (*ro·lúpstair*, they bent, L. Leinster) : *lúbbô*, root *leub*, *lub* ; Eng. *loop*, M. Eng. *loupe*, noose ; λυγίζω, see *lag*. Skeat regards the Eng. as borrowed from the Celtic. Hence **lùib**, a fold, creek, angle.

luch, a mouse, Ir., O. Ir. *luch*, g. *lochat*, W. *llyg*, *llygoden*, Corn. *logoden*, Br. *logodenn*, pl. *logod* : **lukot-*, **pluko-*, "gray one"; Lit. *pilkas*, gray, *pele*, mouse; root *pel*, *pol*, gray, as under *liath*. Stokes refers it to the Gadelic root *luko-*, dark (read *lauko-* or *louko-*), whence E. Ir. *loch* (read *lóch*), which he takes from I. E. *leuq*, shine (Lat. *lux*, etc.), comparing W. *llwg*, livid, blotchy, to which add W. *llug*, blotch, dawning. From this obsolete G. word *lóch*, dark, comes the name of the rivers *Lòchaidh*, Adamnan's *Nigra Dea* or *Loch-dae*, which we may take as the G. form of it from another of his references.

lùchairt, a palace, castle; see *longphort*.

luchd, people, Ir. *luchd*, O. Ir. *lucht*, W. *llwyth*, tribe: **lukto-*, from *plug*, *pulg*, Eng. *folk*, Ger. *volk*, whence O. Slov. *pluku*, a troop.

luchd, a burden, Ir. *luchd*, E. Ir. *lucht*, W. *llwyth*, a load: *lukto-*. The O. W. *tluith* (or *maur-dluithruim*, multo vecte) has suggested **tlukto-*, allied to Lat. *tollo*, raise (Stokes). Eng. *flock*?

lùdag, the little finger, Ir. *lughadóg*, O. Ir. *lúta*, dat. *lútain* : **lûddôn-*, root *lûd*, *lud*, Eng. *little*, Ag. S. *lýtel*, O. H. G. *luzil*; root *lu*, *lû*, Eng. *loss*, *-less*, Gr. λύω, etc.

lùdag, **lùdan**, **lùdnan**, a hinge, **ludanan**, hinges, Ir. *lúdrach* (Fol.), *ludach*, *ludann* (O'R.) :

ludair, a slovenly person, **ludraig**, bespatter with mud, **luidir**, wallow, Ir. *ludar* (n), *ludair* (vb.); two words from *lod*, mud, and *luid*, rag.

ludhaig, permit, allow: from the Eng. *'lowing*, *allowing*. *lughaic*, stipulate for (Hend.).

lùgach, having crooked legs, **lùgan**, a deformed person, **lùigean**, a weakling: **lûggo-*, root *leug*, *lug*, bend, Gr. λυγίζω, bend, Lit. *lugnas*, pliant.

lugh, swear, blaspheme, O. Ir. *luige*, oath, W. *llw*, Br. *le* : **lugio-n*, oath, "binding"; Got. *liugan*, wed, O. H. G. *urliugi*, lawless condition, Ag. S. *orlege*, war.

lugh, a joint (M'A.), **luighean**, a tendon, ankle, Ir. *luthach*, joints, *luighéan*, a nave, M. Ir. *luíthech*, sinew.

lugha, less, Ir. *lugha*, O. Ir. *lugu*, *laigiu*, positive, *lau*, *lú*, little, W. *llai*, less, from *llei*, Br. *lei*, from *lau* : **legiôs*, from **legu-s*, little: Lat. *levis*; Gr. ἐλαχύς, little; Skr. *laghá-s*, light, Eng. *light*.

luibh, an herb, Ir. *luibh*, O. Ir. *luib*, *lubgort*, herb-garden, garden, W. *lluarth*, garden, Cor. *luvorth*, Br. *liorz*, garden: **lubi-*, herb; Norse *lyf*, herb, Got. *lubja-leisei*, witchcraft, "herb-lore," O. H. G. *luppi*, poison, magic, Ag. S. *lyb* (do.).

luid, luideag, a rag, a slut, Ir. *luid*: **luddi*, root *lu*, cut, lose, as under *lot*.

luidhear, a vent, chimney, louvre, W. *llwfer*; from M. Eng. *louere, lover*, smoke-hole, O. Fr. *lover*. The Norse *ljóri*, a louvre or roof-opening, is from *ljós*, light.

luidse, a clumsy fellow; from the Sc. *lotch*, lout, *louching*, louting.

lùigean, a weak person; see *lúgach*.

luigh, lie; see *laigh*.

luighean, an ankle: cf. E. Ir. *lua*, foot, kick, O. Ir. *lue*, heel:

luighe-siùbhladh (laighe-siùbhladh), child-bed, Ir. *luidhsiúbhail* (Fol.), M. Ir. *ben siuil*, parturient woman, *luige seola*, child-bed. Stokes refers *siuil* to M. Ir. *siul*, bed, and compares the Eng. phrase *to be brought a-bed*. The G. and Ir. seem against this, for the idea of *luighe-siùbhladh* would then be "bed-lying"; still worse is it when *leabaidh-shiùladh* is used. Consider *siubhal*, bearing.

luigheachd, requital, reward: **lugi-*, root *lug*, *loug*, as in *luach*.

luim, a shift, contrivance:

luimneach, active (Smith's *S. D.*); cf. *luaineach*.

luinneag, a ditty, Ir. *luinnioc*, chorus, glee, M. Ir. *luindiuc*, *luindig*, music-making; **lundo-*, root *lud*, as in *laoidh*, Eng. *lay*?

luinneanach, tossing, floundering, paddling about; see *lunn*, a heaving billow.

luinnse, luinnsear, a sluggard, lazy vagrant, Ir. *lunnsaire*, idler, watcher; from Eng. *lungis* (obsolete), *lounger*.

lùir, torture, drub (M'A); see *laoir*.

lùireach, a coat of mail, Ir. *lúireach*, E. Ir. *lúirech*, W. *llurig*; from Lat. *lôrîca*, from *lôrum*, a thong. Hence **lùireach,** a patched garment, an untidy female.

luirist, an untidy person, tall and pithless:

lum, part of the oar between the handle and blade; from N. *hlumr*, handle of an oar.

luma-làn, choke-full, also **lom-làn** and **lumha-lan** (Hend.); from *lom* + *làn*.

luman, a covering, great-coat, Ir. *lumain*, E. Ir. *lumman* (g. *lumne*, M'Con.). In some dialects it also means a "beating," that is a "dressing."

lùnasd, lùnasdal, lùnasdainn, Lammas, first August, Ir. *lughnas*, August, E. Ir. *lúgnasad*, Lammas-day: "festival of Lug"; from *Lug*, the sun-god of the Gael, whose name Stokes connects with Ger. *locken*, allure, Norse *lokka* (do.), and also *Loki* (?). E. Ir. *nassad*, festival (?), is referred by Rhys to the same origin as Lat. *nexus*, and he translates *lúgnasad* as "Lug's wedding" (*Hib. Lect.*, 416).

lunn, a staff, oar-handle, lever; from Norse *hlunnr*, launching roller. See *lonn*. Dial. **lund.**

lunn, a heaving billow (not broken); also **lonn.** See *lonn*, anger.

lunndair, a sluggard; cf. Fr. *lendore*, an idle fellow, from M.H.G. *lentern*, go slow, Du. *lentern*. Br. *landar*, idle, is borrowed from the Fr.

lunndan, a smooth grassy plot (possibly "marshy spot," Rob.). Hence place-name *An Lunndan*.

lunndraig, thump, beat; from the Sc. *lounder*, beat, *loundering*, a drubbing.

lur, delight, **lurach**, lovely, **luran**, darling, a male child; **luru-*, root *lu*, *lau*, enjoy, as in *lon*.

lurc, a crease in cloth; from Sc. *lirk*, a crease, M. Eng. *lerke*, wrinkle.

lurcach, lame in the feet; see *loirc*.

lùrdan, cunning, a sly fellow; from Sc. *lurdane*, worthless person, M. Eng. *lourdaine*, lazy rascal, from O. Fr. *lourdein* (n.), *lourd*, dirty, sottish, from Lat. *luridum*.

lurg, lurgann, a shank, Ir., E. Ir. *lurgu*, g. *lurgan*; W. *llorp*, *llorf*, shank, shaft.

lus, an herb, plant, Ir. *lus*, E. Ir. *luss*, pl. *lossa*, W. *llysiau*, herbs, Cor. *les*, Br. *louzaouen*: **lussu-*, from **lubsu-*, root *lub* of *luibh*.

luspardan, a pigmy, sprite, Martin's *Lusbirdan*; from *lugh*, little (see *lugha*), and *spiorad*.

lùth, strength, pith, Ir. *lúth*, E. Ir. *lúth*; cf. O. Ir. *lúth*, velocity, motion, from the root *pleu*, *plu* of *luath*. Or *tlúth*, from *tel*?

M

ma, if, Ir. *má*, O. Ir. *má*, *ma*, Cor., Br. *ma* (also *mar*); cf. Skr. *sma*, *smâ*, an emphatic enclitic (= "indeed") used after pronouns, etc., the *-sm-* which appears in the I. E. pronoun forms (Gr. ἀμμε = *ṇs-sme*, us).

mab, a tassel; a side-form of *pab*, q.v.

màb, abuse, vilify:

mabach, lisping, stammering; cf. M. Eng. *maflen*, Du. *maffelen*, to stammer.

mac, a son, Ir. *mac*, O. Ir. *macc*, W. *mab*, O, W. *map*, Cor. *mab*, Br. *map*, *mab*, Ogam gen. *maqvi*: **makko-s*, **makvo-s*, son, root *mak*, rear, nutrire, W. *magu*, rear, nurse, Br. *maguet*: I. E. *mak*, ability, production; Gr. μακρός, long, μάκαρ, blessed; Zend *maçanh*, greatness; Lettic *mázu*, can, be able. Kluge compares Got. *magaths*, maid, Ag. S. *magþ*, Eng. *maid*, further Got. *magus*, boy, Norse *mögr*, which, however, is allied to O. Ir. *mug* (pl. *mogi*), slave. The Teut. words also originally come from a root denoting "might, increase," Gr. *μῆχος*, means, Skr. *mahas*, great. Hence **macanta,** mild: "filial."

macamh, a youth, generous man, Ir. *macamh*, *macaomh*, a youth, E. Ir. *maccoem*: from *mac* and *caomh*.

mach, a mach, outside (motion to "out"), Ir. *amach*, E. Ir. *immach*; from *in* and *magh*, a field, *mach* being its accusative after the prep. *in*, into: "into the field." Again **a muigh,** outside (rest), is for E. Ir. *immaig*, *in* with the dat. of *magh*: "in the field." See *an*, *ann* and *magh*.

machair, a plain, level, arable land, Manx *magher*, Ir., M. Ir. *machaire*, *macha*; **makarjo-*, a field; Lat. *mâceria*, an enclosure (whence W. *magwyr*, enclosure, Br. *moger*, wall). So Stokes. Usually referred to **magh-thìr*, "plain-land," from *magh* and *tìr*.

machlag, matrix, uterus, Ir. *machlóg* (O'B., etc.), M. Ir. *macloc*; cf. Ger. *magen*, Eng. *maw*.

macnas, sport, wantonness, Ir. *macnas* (do.), *macras*, sport, festivity; from *mac*.

mactalla, macalla, echo, Ir., M. Ir. *macalla*; from *mac* and obsolete *all*, a cliff, g. *aille* (**allos*), allied to Gr. *πέλλα*, stone (Hes.), Norse *fjall*, hill, Eng. *fell*. See also **†ail,** which is allied.

madadh, a dog, mastiff, so Ir., M. Ir. *madrad*: E. Ir. *matad* (McCon.), *maddad* (Fel.), W. *madog*, fox (cf. W. *madryn*, reynard): **maddo-*, **mas-do-*, the *mas* possibly being for *mat-s*, the *mat* of which is then the same as *math-* of *mathghamhuin*, q.v. Connection with Eng. *mastiff*, Fr. *mâtin*, O. F. *mestiff*, from **mansatinus*, "house-dog," would mean borrowing.

madadh, mussel:

màdog, madog, a mattock, W. *matog*; from M. Eng. *mattok*, now *mattock*, Ag. S. *mattuc*.

màdar, madder, Ir. *madar* the plat madder; from the Eng.

madhanta, valiant, dexterous in arms, Ir. *madhanta*: "overthrowing," from the E. Ir. verb *maidim*, overthrow, break, from **matô*, Ch. Sl. *motyka*, ligo, Polish *motyka*, hoe (Bez.).

maduinn, morning, Ir. *maidin*, O. I. *matin*, mane, *maten*; from Lat. *matutina*, early (day), Eng. *matin*.

màg, a paw, hand, lazy bed, ridge of arable land, E. Ir. *mác*,: **mankâ*, root *man*, hand, Lat. *manus*, Gr. *μάρη*, Norse *mund*, hand. Sc. *maig* is from Gaelic.

magadh, mocking, Ir. *magadh*, W. *mocio*; from the Eng. *mock*.

magaid, a whim; from Sc. *maggat*, *magget*.

magairle(an), testicle(s), Ir. *magairle*, *magarla*, E. Ir. *macraille* (pl.): **magar-aille*, "*magar* stones;" *magar*, and *all* of *mactalla*: *magar* = **maggaro-*, root *mag*, *meg*, great, powerful, increase? Cf., however, *mogul*.

màgan, toad; properly **mial-mhàgain**, "squat beast;" from *màg* above.

magh, a plain, a field, Ir. *magh*, O. Ir. *mag*, W. *ma*, *maes* (**magestu-*), Cor. *mês*, Br. *maes*, Gaul. *magos*: **magos*, **mages-*, field, plain, "expanse," from root *magh*, great, Skr. *mahî*, the earth, *mahas*, great; G. *μῆχος*, means, Lat. *machina*, machine; Got. *magan*, be able, Eng. *may*.

maghan, stomach: N. *magi*.

maghar, bait for fish, so Ir., E. Ir. *magar* (Corm.), small fry or fish:

maibean, a cluster, bunch; see *mab*.

maide, a stick, wood, Ir., E. Ir., *matan*, a club: **maddio-*, **mas-do-*; Lat. *malus* (= **mâdus*), mast; Eng. *mast*.

màidhean, delay, slowness:

màidse, a shapeless mass:

màidsear, a major; from the Eng.

Màigh, May, E. Ir. *Mái*; from Lat. *Maius*, Eng. *May*.

màigean, a child beginning to walk, a fat, little man: from *màg*.

maighdeag, concha veneris, the shell of the escallop fish; from *maighdean*? Cf. *madadh*, mussel.

maighdean, a maiden, so Ir., late M. Ir. *maighden* (F. M.); from M. Eng. *magden*, *maiden*, Ag. S. *mægden*, now *maiden*.

maigheach, a hare, Ir. *míol bhuidhe* (for *míol mhuighe*), E. Ir. *míl maige*, "plain beast"; from *mial* and *magh*. The G. is an adj. from *magh*: **mageco-*, "campestris."

maighistir, maighstir, master, Ir. *maighisdir*, M. Ir. *magisder*, W. *meistyr*, Cor. *maister*; from Lat. *magister*, Eng. *master*.

màileid, a bag, wallet, knapsack, Ir. *máiléid*, *máilín*; see *màla*.

maille ri, with, Ir. *maille re*, O. Ir. *immalle*, *malle*; for *imb-an-leth*, "by the side," *mu an leth* now.

màille, mail armour; from the Eng. *mail*.

mainisdir, a monastery, so Ir., E. Ir. *manister*; from Lat. *monasterium*.

mainne, delay, Ir. *mainneachdna*; cf. O. Ir. *mendat*, residence, O. G. *maindaidib* (dat. pl.), Skr. *mandiram*, lodging, habitation; Lat. *mandra*, a pen, Gr. *μάνδρα* (do.).

mainnir, a fold, pen, goat pen, booth, Ir. *mainreach*, *mainneir*, M. Ir. *maindir*, ; Lat. *mandra*, Gr. *μάνδρα*, pen, as under *mainne*. K. Meyer takes it from early Fr. *maneir*, dwelling, Eng. *manor*.

mair, last, live, Ir. *mairim*, O. Ir. *maraim*: **marô*; Lat. *mora*, delay (**mr̥-*).

màireach, to-morrow, Ir. *márach*, E. Ir. *imbârach*, to-morrow, *iarnabárach*, day after to-morrow, W. *bore*, *boreu*, morning, *y fory*, to-morrow, M. W. *avory*, Br. *beure*, morning, **bârego-* (Stokes, Zimmer): **mṝ-ego-*, root *mṝgh*, *mṛgh* (*mṛg* ?); Got. *maurgins*, morning, *da maurgina*, to-morrow, Eng. *morrow*, Ger. *morgen*, etc.

mairg, pity! Ir. *mairg*, E. Ir. *mairg*, vae: **margi-*; Gr. *μάργος*, mad, Lat. *morbus* (?). Usually referred to **mo-oirc*, **mo oirg*, "my destruction," from *org*, destroy, (See *tuargan*).

mairiste, a marriage; from the Eng.

màirneal, a delay, Ir. *mairneulachd*, tediousness, a sailing:

mairtir, a martyr, so Ir., E. Ir. *martir*, W. *merthyr*; from Lat. *martyr*, from Gr. *μάρτυς*, *μάρτυρος*, a witness.

maise, beauty, so Ir., E. Ir. *maisse*, from *mass*, comely; root *mad*, *med*, measure, Eng. *meet*, Ger. *mässig*, moderate; further Eng. *mete*, etc.

maistir, urine, so Ir.; **madstri*, root *mad*, Lat. *madeo*.

maistreadh, churning, so Ir.; root *mag*: Gr. *μαγίς*, *μάσσω*, Ch. Sl. *masla*, butter.

maith, **math**, good, Ir., O. Ir. *maith*, W. *mad*, Cor. *mas*, M. Br. *mat*: **mati-s*, root *mat*, *met*, measure, I. E. *mê*, measure, as in *meas*, q.v. ? Bez. suggests as an alternative Skr. *úpa-mâti*, affabilis, Gr. *ματίς* (= *μέγας*, Hes.).

maith, **math**, pardon, Ir. *maitheam* (n.), E. Ir. *mathem*, a forgiving, W. *maddeu*, ignoscere, root *mad*, "be quiet about," Skr. *mádati*, linger, *mandas*, lingering, Got. *ga-môtan*, room; see *mainnir*. Rhys regards the W. as borrowed from Ir.; if so, G. is same as *maith*, good.

màl, rent, tax, M. Ir. *mál*, W. *mâl*, bounty; from Ag. S. *mál*, tribute, M. Eng. *māl*, now *mail* (black-*mail*), Sc. *mail*.

màla, a bag, budget, Ir. *mála*; from the M. Eng. *māle*, wallet, bag (now *mail*), from O. Fr. *male*, from O. H. G. *malha*.

mala, pl., **malaichean** (*mailghean* in Arg., cf. *duilich*, *duilghe*), eyebrow, Ir. *mala*, O. Ir. *mala*, g. *malach*, M. Br. *malvenn*, eyelash: **malax*; Lit. *blakstėnai*, eyelashes, *blakstini*, wink, Lettic *mala*, border, Alban. *mal'*, hill, border.

malairt, an exchange, so Ir., M. Ir. *malartaigim*, I exchange, also "destroy": in E. Ir. and O. Ir. *malairt* means "destruction," which may be compared to Lat. *malus*, bad.

malc, putrefy: **malqô*; Lit. *nu-smelkiù*, decay, Servian *mlak*, lukewarm (Strachan), O. H. G. *mola(h)wên*, tabere (Bez.). It has also been referred to the root *mel*, grind.

màlda, gentle, Ir. *málta*; Gr. *μαλθακός*, soft (see *meall*).

mall, slow, Ir., O. Ir. *mall* (W. *mall*, want of energy, softness ?); Gr. *μέλλω*, linger (**melno-*); Lat. *pro-mello*, litem promovere.

It has also been referred to the root of Gr. *μαλθακός*, soft (see *meall*), and to that of Lat. *mollis*, soft, Eng. *mellow*.

mallachd, a curse, so Ir., O. Ir. *maldacht*, W. *mellith*, Br. *malloc'h*; from Lat. *maledictio*, Eng. *malediction*.

màm, large round hill, Ir. *mam*, mountain, M. Ir. *mamm*, breast, pap (O'Cl.): "breast, pap," Lat. *mamma*, mother, breast, Eng. *mamma*, etc. Hence **màm**, an ulcerous swelling of the armpit.

màm, a handful, two handfuls, Ir., M. Ir. *mám*, handful, W. *mawaid*, two handfuls: **mâmmâ* (Stokes), from **manmâ*, allied to Lat. *manus*, hand? Cf., however, *màg*.

màn, a mole on the skin, arm-pit ulcer; side form *màm*.

manach, a monk, Ir., E. Ir. *manach*, M. Ir. *mainchine*, monkship, monk's duties (cf. *abdaine*), W. *mynach*, Br. *manac'h*; from Lat. *monachus*, Eng. *monk*. Hence **manachainn**, a monastery.

manach, the angel fish:

manachan, the groin:

manadh, an omen, luck, E. Ir. *mana*, omen; Lat. *moneo*, warn, advise; Ag. S. *manian*, warn, exhort.

mànas, the portion of an estate farmed by the owner, a large or level farm; from the Sc. *mains*, Eng. *manor*.

mandrag, mandrake, Ir. *mandrác*; from the Eng. W. *mandragor* is from M. Eng. *mandragores*, Ag. S. *mandragora*.

mang, a fawn, M. Ir. *mang*, E. Ir. *mang* (Corm.): Celtic root *mag* (*mang*), increase, Eng. *maiden*, Got. *magus*, boy (see *mac*).

mangan, a bear; see *mathghamhain*.

mannda, manntach, lisping, stammering, Ir. *manntach*, toothless, stammering, E. Ir. *mant*, gum, O. Ir. *mend*, dumb, etc., Ir. *meann*, dumb (O'Br.), W. *mant*, jaw, *mantach*, toothless jaw: **mandəto-*, jaw; Lat. *mandere*, eat, *mandibula*, a jaw; further is Eng. *meat*, Gr. *μασάομαι*, chew, eat, root *mad*.

mànran, a tuneful sound, a cooing, humming, Ir. *manrán*:

maodail, a paunch, stomach, ruminant's pouch, Ir. *méadail*, *maodal*, *meadhail* (Lh.), M. Ir. *medhal* (Ir. Gl., 235), *métail*: **mand-to-*? Root *mad*, *mand*, eat, as under *mannda*?

maoidh, grudge, reproach, Ir. *maoidhim*, grudge, upbraid, brag, E. Ir. *máidim*, threaten, boast, O. Ir. *móidem*, gloriatio: **moido-*; root *moid*, *meid*; M. H. G. *gemeit*, grand, O. H. G. *kameit*, jactans, stolidus, O. Sax. *gemêd*, stupid, Got. *gamaids*, bruised. See *miadh*.

maoidhean, personal influence, interest; from Sc. *moyen* (do.), Fr. *moyen*, a mean, means, Eng. *means*, from Lat. *medianus*, median, middle.

maoile, brow of a hill ; see *maol*.

maoim, terror, onset, eruption, surprise, Ir. *maidhm*, a sally, eruption, defeat, E. Ir. *maidm*, a breach or breaking, defeat: **matesmen-* (Stokes), **matô*, break ; Ch. Sl., Pol. *motyka*, a hoe. Some give the root as allied to Skr. *math*, stir, twirl, Lit. *mentùris*, whorl.

maoin, wealth, Ir. *maoin*, O. Ir. *máin*: **moini-* ; Lat. *mūnus*, service, duty, gift (Eng. *munificence*), *communis*, common ; Got. *ga-mains*, common, Eng. *mean* ; Lit. *maínas*, exchange.

maoineas, slowness ; see *màidhean*.

maoirne, a bait for a fishing hook (N.H.), **maoirnean**, the least quantity of anything ; cf. *maghar*, root *mag*, grow.

maois, a large basket, hamper, **maois-eisg**, five hundred fish, Ir. *maois*, W. *mwys*, hamper, five score herring, Cor. *muis*, *moys* ; Sc. *mese*, five hundred herring, Norse *meiss*, box, wicker basket, *meiss síld*, barrel-herrings, O. H. G. *meisa*, a basket for the back ; Lit. *maiszas*, sack, Ch. Sl. *mèchŭ*. The relationship, whether of affinity or borrowing, between Celtic and Teutonic, is doubtful. The Brittonic might come from Lat. *mensa*, a table, and the Gadelic from the Norse.

maoiseach, maoisleach, a doe, heifer: *maol-sech* (*maol*, hornless) ; see *mìs*.

maol, bald, Ir. *maol*, O. Ir. *máel*, *máil*, W. *moel*, Br. *maol* : **mailo-s* ; Lit. *mailus*, something small, smallness, Ch. Sl. *mèlŭkŭ*, small ; further root *mei*, lessen (see *maoth*). The Ir. *mug*, servant, has been suggested as the basis : **mag(u)lo-*, servile, "short-haired, bald"; but this, though suitable to the W., would give in G. *mál*. Cf. Ir. *mál*, prince, from **maglo-*. Hence **maol**, brow of a hill or rock, W. *moel*, a conical hill ?

maolchair, the space between the eyebrows ; from *maol*.

maol-snèimheil, lazy, careless, indifferent (H.S.D.), *maol-snè(imh)*, *maol-snìomh* (Rob.), a lazy one :

maor, an officer of justice or of estates, Ir. *maor*, an officer, O. G. *mœr*, *máir* (B. of Deer), W. *maer*, steward ; from Lat. *major*, whence Eng. *mayor*.

maorach, shell-fish, Ir. *maorach* ; cf. Gr. *μύραινα* (*υ* long), lamprey, *σμῦρος*, eel.

maoth, soft, Ir. *maoth*, E. Ir. *móeth*, O. Ir. *móith* : **moiti-s* ; Lat. *mîtis*, mild ; further root *mei*, lessen (see *mìn*).

mar, as, Ir., M. Ir. *mar*, E. Ir., O. Ir. *immar*, quasi : **ambi-are*, the prepositions *imm* (now *mu*) and *air* ? W. *mor*, as, Corn., Br. *mar*, is explained by Ernault as unaccented Br. *meur*, G. *mòr*, big.

mar ri, M. G. *far ri* (D. of L.) : from *mar* and *ri*.

màrach, a big, ungainly woman (Arg.); from *mór*, with neuter termination *ach*. Also **màraisg**.

marag, a pudding, M. Ir. *maróc*, hilla, E. Ir. *mar*, sausage; from the Norse *mörr*, dat. *mörvi*, suet, *blóð-mörr*, black pudding.

marasgal, a master, regulator, Ir., M. Ir. *marascal*, regulator, marshal; from M. Eng. and O. Fr. *marescal*, now *marshal*.

marbh, dead, Ir. *marbh*, O. Ir. *marb*, W. *marw*, Cor. *marow*, Br. *maro*, M. Br. *marv*; **marvo-s*, root *mṛ*; Lat. *morior*, die; Lit. *mirti*, die; Gr. *μαραίνω*, destroy; Skr. *mar*, die.

marc, a horse, G. and Ir. **marcach**, a horseman, E. Ir. *marc*, horse, W., Cor., Br. *march*, Gaul. *μαρκα-ν* (acc.): **marko-s*, **markâ*; O. H. G. *marah*, mare, *meriha*, horse, Norse *marr*, mare, Ag. S. *mearh*, Eng. *mare* and *marshal*.

marg, a merk: from the Eng. *mark*, Sc. *merk*, Norse *mörk*, g. *markar*.

margadh, a market, so Ir., M. Ir. *margad*, *marcad*, E. Ir. *marggad* from M. Eng. *market*, from Lat. *mercatus*.

màrla, marl, Ir. *márla*, W. *marl*; from Eng. *marl*. The G. has the sense of "marble" also, where it confuses this word and Eng. *marble* together.

marmor, marble, Ir. *marmur*; from Lat. *marmor*. A playing marble is in the G. dialects **marbul**, a marble.

màrrach, enchanted castle which kept one spell-bound, labyrinth. thicket to catch cattle (M'A.). Root *mar*, *mer*, deceive, as in *mear*, *brath*.

marrum, **marruin**, cream, milk, and their products (Carm.). Cf. *marag*.

màrsadh, marching, Ir. *marsáil*; from the Eng.

mart, a cow, Ir. *mart*, a cow, a beef, E. Ir. *mart*, a beef; hence Sc. *mart*, a cow killed for family (winter) use and salted, which Jamieson derives from *Martinmas*, the time at which the killing took place. The idea of *mart* is a cow for killing: **martâ*, from root *mar*, die, of *marbh*?

Màrt, March, Ir. *Márt*, E. Ir. *mairt*, g. *marta*, W. *Mawrth*; from Lat. *Martius*, Eng. *March*.

martradh, maiming, laming, Ir. *mairtrighim*, murder, maim, martyrise, O. Ir. *martre*, martyrdom; from Lat. *martyr*, a martyr, whence Eng

màs, the buttock, Ir. *más*, E. Ir. *máss*: **mâsto-*; Gr. *μήδεα*, genitals, *μαστός*, *μαζός*, breast, cod, *μαδάω*, lose hair; Lat. *madeo*, be wet; root *mâd*, *mad*.

mas, before, ere: see *mus*.

màsan, delay, Ir. *masán* (O'B., etc.):

masg, mix, infuse; from the Sc. *mask*, Swed. *mäske*, to mash, Fries. *mask*, draff, grains, Eng. *mash*.

masgul, flattery:
masladh, disgrace, Ir. *masla, masladh,* despite, shame, disgrace:
math, good, Ir. *math*; see *maith.* This is the commonest form in G., the only Northern Dialect form.
math, forgive: see *maith.*
mathaich, manure land; from *math*?
màthair, mother, Ir. *máthair,* O. Ir. *máthir,* W. *modryb,* dame, aunt, O. Br. *motrep,* aunt: **mâtêr*; Lat *mâter*; Gr. *μήτηρ,* Dor. *μάτηρ* (*α* long); Norse, *móðir,* Eng. *mother*; Skr. *mâtár.*
mathghamhuin, a bear, Ir. *mathghamhuin,* E. Ir. *mathgaman,* from *math-* and *gamhainn*; with *math,* bear (?), cf. W. *madawg,* fox, and possibly the Gaul. names *Matu-genos, Matuus, Teuto-matus,* etc.
meacan, a root, bulb, Ir. *meacan,* any top-rooted plant, O. Ir. *meccun, mecon,* Gr. *μήκων,* poppy; O. H. G. *mági,* Ger. *mohn*; Ch. Sl. *maku*: **mekkon-,* root *mek, mak* of *mac*?
meachainn, mercy, an abatement, **meachair,** soft, tender, **meachran,** hospitable person, Ir. *meach,* hospitality:
meadar, a wooden pail or vessel, Ir. *meadar,* a hollowed-out drinking vessel, churn, M. Ir. *metur*; from Lat. *metrun,* measure, metre, meter.
meadar, verse, metre; for root, etc., see above word.
meadhail, joy; see *meadhrach.*
meadh-bhlàth, luke-warm: "mid-warm;" O. Ir. *mid-,* mid-, root *med, medh,* as in next.
meadhon, the middle, so Ir., O. Ir. *medón, im-medón,* M. W. *ymeun,* W. *mewn,* within, Br. *y meton,* amidst; cf. for form and root Lat. *mediânum,* the middle, Eng. *mean,* further Lat. *medius,* middle; Gr. *μέσος*; Eng. *middle*; etc.
meadhrach, glad, joyous, Ir. *meadhair,* mirth, *meadhrach,* joyous, E. Ir. *medrach*: **medro-*; Skr. *mad,* rejoice, be joyful, *máda,* hilarity. But *medu,* ale?
mèag, whey, Ir. *meadhg,* E. Ir. *medg,* W. *maidd* (**meðjo-*), Cor. *maith,* O. Br. *meid,* Gallo-Lat. *mesga,* whey, whence Fr. *mègue*: **mezgâ,* whey; O. Slav. *mozgu,* succus, marrow (Thurneysen), to which Brugmann adds O. H. G. *marg,* marrow (Eng. *marrow*), Lit. *mazgoti,* wash, Lat. *mergo,* merge.
meaghal, barking, mewing, alarm; see *miamhail.*
meal, possess, enjoy, Ir. *mealadh* (n.), M. Ir. *melaim,* I. enjoy: possibly from the root *mel, mal,* soft, as in *mealbhag.* Cf. O. Ir, *meldach,* pleasant, Eng. *mild.*
mealasg, flattery, fawning, great rejoicing; see *miolasg.*
mealbhag, corn poppy; cf. Lat. *malva,* mallow, whence Eng. *mallow*; Gr. *μαλάχη,* root *mal, mel,* soft, "emollient," Gr. *μαλακός.* soft, Lat. *mulcere.*

mealbhan, sea bent (Suth.), sand dunes with bent (W. Ross):

mealg, milt of fish; for ***fealg** = **sealg**?

meall, a lump, hill, Ir. *meall*, lump, knob, heap, E. Ir. *mell*, Br. *mell*, joint, knot, knuckle, Gaul. *Mello-dunum* (?), now *Melun*: **mello-*, from **melno-*; O. Slav. *iz-molêti*, just out, protuberate (Bez. with query); **mḷso*; cf. Gr. μέλος, limb, part.

meall, deceive, entice, Ir. *meallaim*, M. Ir. *mellaim*, deceive, E. Ir. *mell*, error: *melsô* (Stokes), root *mel*, *mal*, bad; Lat. *malus*; Lit. *mìlyti*, mistake, *mélas*, lie; Gr. μέλεος, useless; Armen. *meλ*, peccatum. O. Ir. *meld*, pleasant (?), Gr. ἀμαλός, root *mela*, grind.

meallan, clach-mheallain, hail, Ir. *meallán* (Fol., O'R.); from *meall*, lump?

meambrana, parchments, Ir. *meamrum*, O. Ir. *membrum*; from Lat, *membrana*, skin, membrane, from *membrum*.

meamhair, meomhair, memory, Ir. *meamhair*, O. Ir. *mebuir*, W. *myfyr*; from Lat. *memoria*, Eng. *memory*.

meamna, meanmna, spirit, will, Ir. *meanma* (n.), *meanmnach* (adj.), O. Ir. *menme*, g. *menman*, mens; **menmês*, g. *menmenos*, root *men*, mind, think; Skr. *mánman*, mind, thought, *manye*, think; Lat. *memini*, remember, *mens*; Gr. μέμονα, think, μνῆμα, monument; Eng. *mean*, *mind*; etc.

mean, meanbh, small, E. Ir. *menbach*, small particle: **mino-*, **minvo-*, root *min*; Lat. *minus*, Eng. *diminish*, Lat. *minor*, *minutus*, minute; Gr. μινύθω, lessen; Got. *mins*, less: root *mi*, *mei*. See *mi-*. Stokes gives also an alternate root *men*, Skr. *manâk*, a little, Lat. *mancus*, maimed, Lit. *mènkas*, little.

meanachair, small cattle, sheep or goats (Dial.); for **meanbh-chrodh**.

mèanan, a yawn, Ir. *méanfach*, E. Ir. *mén-scailim*, I yawn, "mouth-spread," *mén*, mouth, *ménogud*, hiatus; cf. W. *min*, lip, edge, Cor. *min*, *meen*, Br. *min*, snout. Strachan and Stokes suggest the stem **maknâ*, **mekno-*, root *mak*; Ag. S. *maga*, stomach, Ger. *magen*, Eng. *maw*.

meang, guile, Ir. *meang*, E. Ir. *meng*: **mengâ*; Gr. μάγγανον, engine (Eng. *mangle*), μαγγανεύω, juggle; Lat. *mango*, a dealer who imposes. Cf. N. *mang*, traffic, *monger*.

meang, whey; Dial. for *mèag*.

meangan, meanglan, a twig, Ir. *meangán*, *beangán*: **mengo-*, Celtic root *meg*, *mag*, increase; see under *maighdean*, *mac*. Cf. M. Ir. *maethain*, sprouts.

meann, a kid, Ir. *meannán*, *meann*, W. *myn*, Cor. *min*, Br. *menn*: **mendo-*, kid, "suckling"; Alban. *ment*, suck; O. H. G. *manzon*, ubera; perhaps Gr. μαζός, breast (Stokes, Strachan)

It may be from the root *min*, small (**minno-*), a form which suits the W. best.

meannd, mint; from the Eng.

meantairig, venture; from Eng. *venturing*. W. *mentra*.

mear, merry, Ir. *mear*; cf. Eng. *merry*, Ag. S. *merge*, *myrige*, O. H. G. *murg*, *murgi* (root *mṛgh*). The E. Ir. *mer*, mad, is allied to *mearachd*. O. Ir. *meraigim*, prurio. Lat. *meretrix*.

mearachd, error, Ir. *mearaighim*, I err, *mearughadh*, a mistaking, erring, M. Ir. *merugud*, wandering, root *mer*, *mṛ*; Gr. ἁμαρτανω, miss (see *brath*); Eng. *mar*, Got. *marzian*, cause to stumble. Cf. E. Ir. *mer*, mad, *meracht*, mad act, O. Ir. *meraige*, a fool, O. Br. *mergidhaam*, I am silly, which Loth joins to Gr. μάργος, mad.

mearcach, rash; from the root of *mear*.

mearganta, brisk, lively, **meargadaich**, be impatient (Suth), Ir. *mearganta*, brisk; from *mear*.

mèarsadh, marching; see *màrsadh*.

mearsuinn, vigour, strength; cf. *marsainn*, abiding, from *mar*, remain.

meas, fruit, Ir. *meas*, fruit, especially acorns, *measog*, acorn, E. Ir. *mess*, fruit, W. *mes*, acorns, Cor. *mesen*, glans, Br. *mesenn*, acorn: **messu-*, root, *med*, *mad*, eat (see *manntach*), and, for force, cf. Eng. *mast*, fruit of forest trees, Ag. S. *maest*, fruit of oak or beech, Ger. *mast*.

meas, judgment, opinion, respect, Ir. *meas*, O. Ir. *mess*, **messu-*, root *med*; Lat. *meditari*, think, *modus*, method; Gr. μέδομαι, think of; Got. *mitan*, measure, Eng. *mete*: further root *mê*, measure, Eng. *metre*, *meter*, etc.

measan, a lapdog, Ir. *measán*, E. Ir. *mesan*, *meschu*:

measair, a tub, measure; see *miosar*.

measarra, temperate, modest, Ir. *measarrdha*, O. Ir. *mesurda*: "measured"; probably borrowed from the Lat. *mensuratus*, *mensura* (Stokes). But it may be from *meas*, judgment.

measg, am measg, among, Ir. *measg*, *a measg*, among, W. *ym mysg*, M. Br. *e mesg*: **med-sko-*, root *med*, *medh*, as in *meadhon*, middle.

measg, measgach, mix, Ir. *measgaim*, E. Ir. *mescaim*, W. *mysgu*: **miskô*, **mig-skô*, root, *mig*, *mik*; Gr. μίγνομι, μίσγω; Lat. *misceo*; Eng. *mix*, Ger. *mischen*; Lit. *maiszýti*; Skr. *miksh*.

measgan, a dish to hold butter, Ir. *míosgan*; see *miosgan*. But cf. E. Ir. *mescan*, a lump of butter, M. Ir. *mesgan*, massa; from *measg*, mix?

meat, meata, feeble, soft, cowardly, Ir. *meata*, E. Ir. *meta*, cowardly: **mit-tavo-*; see *meath*. W. has *meth*, failure. **mettaios* (St.)

meath, fail, fade, become weak, dishearten, Ir. *meathaim*, fail, droop, soften, E. Ir. *meth*, failure, decay : **mitô*, root *mit*, the short form of root *meit*, *moit* (see *maoth*).

meidh, a balance, Ir. *meadh*, O. Ir. *med*, d. *meid*, W. *medd*, centre of motion: **medâ*, root *med*, mete; Lat. *modius*, a peck: Gr. *μέδιμνος*, a measure (6 *modii*); Eng. *mete*. See *meas* further. Hence **meidhis,** a measure, instalment (Arg., M'A).

meidhinnean, mèigean, hip-joints :

meigead, the bleating of a goat or kid, Ir. *meigiodaigh*; Gr. *μηκάομαι*, bleat, *μήκας*, she-goat, "bleater"; Ger. *meckern*, bleat; Skr. *makakas*, bleating; root *mêk*, *mek*, *mak*, an onomatopoetic syllable.

mèil, bleat, Ir. *méidhlighim*, M. Ir. *meglim*, I bleat, *megill*, bleating; Ger. *meckern* : see *meigead*. G. is for **megli-* or **mekli*.

meil, beil, grind, Ir. *meilim*, O. Ir. *melim*, W. *malu*, Br. *malaff*: **melô*; Lat. *molo*; Gr. *μύλλω*; O. H. G. *malan*, grind, Eng. *meal*, *mill*; Lit. *málti*, molo. Hence **meildreach, meiltir, a** quantity of corn sent to grind, **meiltear,** miller.

meilcheart, chilblain (Arg.), Ir. *miolcheárd* (Kerry), *miolchartach*, *miolcartán*, *milchearta* (Tirconnell); root in *meilich*.

meile, the thick stick by which the quern is turned, a quern, Ir. *meile*, hand-mill: "grinder"; from *meil*?

meilearach, long sea-side grass; from Norse *melr*, bent.

meilich, become chill with cold, be benumbed; from the root *mel*, crush, grind. See *meil*.

meiligeag, pea-pod, husk of peas, etc. :

meill, the cheek, Ir. *meill*; G. **méill,** blubber-lip (M'L., M'E.), **méilleach, beilleach,** blubber-lipped (**meilleach,** H.S.D.); see *béilleach*.

méilleag, beilleag, outer rind of bark :

mèin, mèinn, ore, mine, Ir. *méin*, *mianach*, E. Ir. *míanach*, W. *mwyn* : **meini-*, *meinni-*, root *mei*, *smei*, *smi*; O. Sl. *mêdi*, aes; O. H. G. *smîda*, metal, Eng. *smith* (Schräder).

mèin, meinn, disposition, Ir. *méin*, M. Ir. *mèin*, mind, disposition : "metal, mettle"; seemingly a metaphoric use of the foregoing word. A root *mein*, mind, mean, appears to exist in Eng. *mean*, Ger. *meinen*; cf. W. *myn*, mind. Thurneysen compares Eng. *mien*.

mèineil, flexible, sappy, substantial; from *mèin*, ore : "gritty"?

meirbh, spiritless, delicate, so Ir., E. Ir. *meirb*, W. *merw* : **mervi-*; O. H. G. *maro*, soft, mellow, Ger. *mürbe*, Ag. S. *mearo*, Norse *merja*, crush; Gr. *μαραίνω*, destroy, *μάρναμαι*, fight; Lat. *martus*, hammer, "crusher;" etc. See *marbh* from the same root ultimately (*mer*, *mar*). Hence **meirbh,** digest.

meirean nam magh, agrimony, Ir. *meirín na magh (*O'B., *méirín* (Con.):

meirg, rust, Ir. *meirg*, O. Ir. *meirg*, *meirc*, Br. *mergl*: **mergi-*, "red, dark;" Eng. *murk*, Ag. S. *mirce*, Norse *myrkr* (cf. G. *dearg* and Eng. *dark*). Ernault compares Gr. μάργος, senseless; and it has been joined to O. W. *mergid*, debilitas, O. Br. *mergidhehan*, evanesco, root *mar*, *mer*, fade, die.

meirghe, a banner, Ir. *meirge*, E. Ir. *mergge*; from the Norse *merki*, a banner, mark, Eng. *mark* (Zimmer).

meirle, theft, **meirleach,** thief, Ir. *meirleach*, E. Ir. *merle*, theft, *merlech*, thief; root *mer*, *mra* (as in *bradach*); see *mearachd*. Stokes compares G. ἀμείρω, deprive; but this is likely ṇ-μερjω, privative ṇ or *a* and root *mer* (μέρος, share).

meirneal, a kind of hawk; from the Eng. *merlin*.

meiteal, metal, Ir. *miotal*; from the Eng. *metal*, Lat. *metallum*.

mèith, fat, sappy, Ir. *méith*, *méath*, O. Ir. *méth*, W. *mwydo*, soften: **meito-*; the *e* grade of the root seen in **moiti-* (in *maoth*, q.v.), the root being *mit*, *meit*, *moit* (*meath*, *mèith*, *maoth*).

meòg, whey; better than *mèag*.

meòraich, meditate, remember, Ir. *méamhruighim*, M. Ir. *mebrugud*, rehearsing, remembering; from Lat. *memoria*. See **meamhair,** also spelt **meomhair,** with the verb **meomhairich** = **meòraich.**

meuchd, mixture (Dial.): **meik-tu*, root *meik*, *mik*, as in *measg*.

meud, miad, size, Ir. *méid*, *méad*, W. *maint*, Cor. *myns*, Br. *meñt*: **mṇti-*, *ment*, "measure," a nasalised form of the root *met*, measure, Lat. *mensus*, having measured, *mētior* (vb.), Gr. μέτρον, measure; etc. Bez. queries its alliance only with Norse *munr*, importance. Usually referred to the root *mag*, *meg* (**maganti-*), great, or to that of *minig*, q.v.

meur, miar, a finger, Ir. *meur*, O. Ir. *mér*. Strachan suggests the stem **makro-*, root *mak*, great, mighty, Gr. μακρός, long, Lat. *macer*, lean, *macte*, good luck, Zend. *maç*, great. Brugmann has compared it to Gr. μόκρωνα (Hes.), sharp (Lat. *mucro*).

mhàin, a mhàin, only, Ir. *amháin*, E. Ir. *amáin*. It has been divided into a prefix and root form: *a-máin*, the latter being parallel to Dor. Gr. μῶνος, Gr. μόνος, alone. Cf. O. Ir. *nammá*, tantum, "ut non sit magis" (*na-n-má*, Zeuss).

mi, I, Ir., O. Ir. *mé*, W. *mi*, Cor. *my*, *me*, Br. *me*: **mê*, **me*; Lat. *mê*; Gr. με; Eng. *me*; Skr. *mâ*.

mi-, un-, mis-, Ir., O. Ir. *mí-*, root *mî*, *mei*, *mi*, lessen; Gr. μείων, less; Lat. *minus*, less; Eng. *mis-*, Got. *missa-* (**miþto-*). See *maoth*, *mìn*. Stokes makes *mí-* a comparative like μείων, and rejects the Teutonic words.

miadan, miadar, miad, a meadow, mead ; from the Eng. *meadow.*

miadh, respect, esteem, so Ir., O. Ir. *míad,* fastus, dignity, O. Br. *muoet,* fastu : **meido-,* fame : O. H. G. *kameit,* jactans, stolidus, M. H. G. *gemeit,* bold, O. Sax. *gemêd,* haughty (Bez.) ; allied to Eng. *meed,* Gr. μισθός, pay, Lat. *miles,* soldier. Cf. Gr. τιμή, fame, price.

mial, louse, animal, Ir. *míol,* animal, whale, louse, E. Ir. *míl,* W. *mil,* beast, Cor., Br. *mil* : **mêlo-n,* animal : Gr. μῆλον, sheep ; Norse, *smali,* sheep, Eng. *small.* Hence G. **mial-chu,** greyhound, W. *milgi,* Cor. *mylgy.*

mialladh, bad fortune (N. H.) :

mialta, pleasant (H.S.D.), O. Ir. *meld, melltach,* pleasant ; Eng. *mild* ; G. μαλθακός, soft. See *malda.*

miamhail, mewing (of cat), Ir. *miamhaoil* ; Eng. *mewl,* from O. Fr., Fr. *miauler* : an onomatopoetic word.

miann, desire, Ir. *mian,* O. Ir. *mían* : **meino-* ; Eng. *mean,* Ger. *meinen,* to mean ; O. Slov. *měnją* (do.). Cf. W. *myn,* desire, Br. *menna,* to wish, which may be from the short form *min* beside *mein.* (Otherwise Loth in *Voc. Vieux-Br.,* 145).

mias, a dish, Ir. *mías,* a dish, mess, platter, E. Ir. *mias* ; from L. Lat. *mêsa, mensa,* a table, whence Ag. S. *mýse,* table, Got. *mes,* table, dish.

mil, honey, Ir. *mil,* O. Ir. *mil,* g. *mela,* W. *mêl,* Cor., Br. *mil* : **meli-* ; Lat. *mel* ; Gr. μέλι, ; Got. *miliþ* ; Arm. *meλr.*

milc, meirc, sweet, sweetness (Carm.) :

milcean, solid warm white whey (Carm.) :

mile, a thousand, a mile, Ir. *míle,* O. Ir. *míle,* a thousand, W., Br. *mil,* Cor. *myl, myll* ; Lat. *mîle* (whence Eng. *mile*), *mille.* The Celtic words are borrowed doubtless.

mileag, a melon ; from the Eng.

mileart, honey dew (N. H.) :

milidh, a champion, Ir. *mileadh, mílidh* (O'B.), E. Ir. *mílid* ; from Lat. *miles, militis,* soldier.

milis, sweet, Ir., O. Ir. *milis,* W. *melys* : **melissi-* ; from *mil.*

mill, destroy, Ir., O. Ir. *millim* : **mel-ni-,* root *mele,* fail, miss ; Lit. *mìlyti,* fail ; Gr. μέλεος, useless, wretched, ἀμβλίσκω, cause miscarriage. The root of Eng. *melt* (**meld,* Gr. ἀμαλδύνω, destroy) has been suggested, the *mel* of which is the same as above. It may be root *mel,* crush, mill.

millteach, mountain grass, good grass ; Norse *melr,* bent grass.

min, meal, Ir. *min,* g. *mine,* O. Ir. *men* : **miná,* root *min,* lessen. Strachan suggests two derivations ; either allied to (1) Lit. *mìnti,* tread, Ch. Slav. *męti,* crush, Gr. ματέω, tread on, from root *men,* tread, or from (2) **mecsn,* root *meq, menq,* grind,

Ch. Slav. *mąka*, meal, Gr. *μάσσω*, knead. But *mexn-* would give G. *menn*.

min, soft, delicate, Ir., E. Ir. *mín*, W. *mwyn*, gentle, Cor. *muin*, gracilis, Br. *moan*, fine : **mîno-*, *meino-*, root *mei*, lessen ; Gr. *μείων*, less, *μινύθω*, lessen ; Lat. *minor*, less, *minister*. Hence **minich**, explain. Stokes has apparently two derivations for *mìn*—the one above and **mêno-*, allied to Gr. *μανός* (*α* long), thin.

minidh, an awl, Ir. *meanadh*, E. Ir *menad*, W. *mynawyd*, Br. *minaoued*, M. Br. *menauet* : **minaveto-* ; Gr. *σμινύη*, mattock, *σμίλη* (*ι* long), chisel.

minicionn, kid's skin ; from *meann* and **cionn* (see *boicionn*).

minig, minic, often, Ir. *minic*, O. Ir. *menicc*, W. *mynych*, Cor. *menough* : **menekki-s* ; Got. *manags*, many, Ger. *manch*, Eng. *many*.

minis, degree, portion (M'A.), root of *mion*.

ministear, a minister, Ir. *mínistir* ; from Lat. *minister*, servant, whence Eng. *minister*.

miobhadh, ill-usage, as by weather ; from *mi-bhàidh*.

miobhail, unmannerly (Arg.) ; *mi* + *modhail*.

miodal, flattery, Ir. *miodal* :

miodhoir, a churl, niggard one ; see *miùghair*

miog, miog (H.S.D.), a smile, sly look, Ir. *míog* : **smincu-*, root *smi*, smile, Eng. *smile*, Gr. *μειδάω*, Skr. *smayate*, laughs.

miolaran, low barking or whining of a fawning dog : see next word.

miolasg, flattery, fawning (as a dog), keen desire ; from the root *smi*, smile ? See *mìog*.

mion, small, so Ir. ; root *min*, Lat. *minor*, etc. Also *mean*, *meanbh*, q.v.

mionach, bowels, so Ir., E. Ir. *menach* ; cf. W. *monoch*.

mionaid, a minute, Ir. *minuit* (dat.) ; from the Eng.

mionn, an oath, Ir. *mionn*, g. *mionna*, E. Ir. *mind*, oath, diadem ; the *mind* was the "swearing reliques" of a saint, O. Ir. *mind*, a diadem, insignia, O. W. *minn*, sertum : **menni-* ; cf. O. H. G. *menni*, neck ornament, Ag. S. *mene*, neck chain, Lat. *monile*. See *muineal* further. Stokes gives the stem as **mindi-*, but no etymology. Windisch (Rev. Celt.[5]) equates *minn* with Lat. *mundus*, ornament, world.

miontan, a titmouse, Ir. *miontán* ; from *mion*, small, **minu-*, Lat. *minor*, etc., as under *mìn*.

miorbhuil, a miracle, Ir. *míorbhuil*, E. Ir. *mírbail* ; from Lat. *mīrabile*, Eng. *marvel*.

miortal, myrtal, Ir. *miortal* (Fol.) ; from the English. W. has *myrtwydd*, myrtle trees.

mìos, a month, Ir. *mí*, *míos*, g. *míosa*, O. Ir. *mí*, g. *mís*, W. *mis*, Cor. *mis*, Br. *mis*, *miz* : **mêns*, g. **mênsos* ; Lat. *mensis* ; Gr. *μήν* : Skr. *mâs* ; further Eng. *month*.

mios, miosa, worse, Ir. *measa*, O. Ir. *messa* : **missôs* ; Got., O. H. G. *missa-*, mis-, Eng. *mis-*, *miss*. See *mi-*.

mìosach, fairy flax, purging flax, Ir. *míosach* : "monthly ;" from *mìos*, "from a medicinal virtue it was supposed to possess" (Cameron).

miosar, a measure (as of meal), Ir. *miosúr*, E. Ir. *messar*, phiala, O. Ir. *mesar*, modus, W. *mesur* ; from the Lat. *mensura*, Eng. *measure*.

miosgan, butter kit, Ir. *míosgán* ; from *mias*, a dish.

miosguinn, envy, malice, Ir. *mioscuis* (*míoscuis*, Con.), E. Ir. *miscen*, hate, O. Ir. *miscuis* ; Gr. *μῖσος* (= *mītsos*) ; Lat. *miser*, wretched (= *mit-s-ro-s*) ; root *mit*, *mi*.

miotag, a mitten, Ir. *miotóg*, *mitín*, mittens ; from Eng. *mitten*, O. Fr. *mitaine*.

mìr, a bit, piece, Ir., O. Ir. *mír*, pl. *mírenn* : **mêsren-*, piece of flesh ; Skr. *mâmsá*, flesh ; Got. *mimz* (do.) ; Lit. *mėsà*, flesh (Stokes, Thur., Brug.). Allied also is Lat. *membrum*, member ; I. E. *mêmso-m*, flesh.

mircean, kind of sea-weed ; cf. N. *máru-kjarni*, fucus vesiculosus (Lewis).

mire, pastime, Ir. *mire*, sport, madness, M. Ir. *mire*, madness ; see *mear*.

mirr, myrrh, Ir. *miorr*, E. Ir. *mirr*, W. *myr* ; from Lat. *myrrha*, Eng. *myrrh*.

mìs, mìseach, maoilseach, goat, doe (Carm.) = *maoisleach*.

misd, the worse for, Ir. *misde*, *meisde*, M. Ir. *meste*, E. Ir. *mesaidie* = *messa-de*, "worse of ;" from *mios* and *de*, of.

misg, drunkenness, Ir. *meisge*, *misge*, E. Ir. *mesce*, O. Ir. *mescc*, drunk : **mesko-*, **meskjâ*, from **med-sko-*, also E. Ir. *mid*, g. *meda*, mead, W. *medd*, hydromel, O. Cor. *med*, sicera, Br. *mez*, hydromel : **medu-* ; Gr. *μέθυ*, wine ; Eng. *mead* ; Ch. Slav. *medŭ*, honey, wine ; Skr. *mádhu*, sweet, sweet drink, honey.

misimean-dearg, bog-mint, Ir. *misimín dearg* :

mìslean, a mountain grass, sweet meadow grass (Cameron) ; for *milsean*, from *milis*, sweet ; cf. Ir. *milsean mara*, a sort of sea-weed ; *mìsleach*, sweetness (Hend.).

misneach, misneachd, courage, Ir. *meisneach*, M. Ir. *mesnech* : **med-s-*, root *med* of *meas* : "think, hope."

mistear, a cunning, designing person ; from *misd*.

mith, an obscure or humble person ; from the root *mi*, *mei* as in *mi-*, *miosa*.

mithear, weak, crazy, Ir. *mithfir*, weak; see *mith*.

mithich, proper time, tempestivus, Ir. *mithid*, O. Ir. *mithich*, tempestivus: **meti-*, Lat. *māturus*, Eng. *mature*.

mithlean, sport, playfulness:

miùghair, niggardly; from *mi* and *fiù* or *fiù-mhor*? cf. *miodhoir*.

mnathan, wives, Ir., E. Ir. *mná*, wives: **bnâs*; see *bean*.

mo, my, O. Ir. *mo*, *mu*, W. *fy*, M. W. *my* (from *myn*), Corn., Br. *ma* (which aspirates): **mou*, **movo*: formed on the analogy of *do*, *du*, from the pronominal root *me* (see *mi*). W. *myn* or *my n-* is allied to Zend *mana*, Lith. *manè* (for *me-né*), Ch. Slav. *mene*.

mò, greater, Ir. *mó*, O. Ir. *móa*, *máo*, *máa*, *móo*, *mó*, W. *mwy*, O. W. *mui*, Corn. *moy*, Br. *mui*: **mâjôs*; Lat. *mâjor*, greater (Eng. *major*); Got. *mais*, more (adv.), *maiza*, greater, Eng. *more*: root *mâ* of *mór* q.v.

mobainn, maltreating, handling roughly; see *moibean*.

moch, early, Ir. *moch*, early, O. Ir. *moch*, mane: **moq-*; also O. Ir. *mos*, soon, W. *moch*, early, ready, Corn. *meugh*: **moqsu*; Lat. *mox*, soon; Zend. *moshu*, Skr. *makshú*, soon: also Gr. *μάψ*, idly, rashly. See *mus*. Hence **mocheirigh**, early rising, **mochthrath**, early morning, M. Ir. *mochthrath*, O. Ir. *mochtratae*, matutinus

mochd, move, yield (Oss. Ballads); cf. M. Ir. *mocht*, gentle, weak, W. *mwytho*, soften, pamper, Eng. *meek*, Norse *mjukr*, soft, meek.

mòd, a court, trial, meeting; from the Norse *mót*, meeting, town-meeting, court of law, Ag. S. *mót*, *gemót*, Eng. *moot*, *meet*.

modh, manner, Ir. *modh*, O. Ir. *mod*, W. *modd*; from Lat. *modus*. Hence **modh**, respect, E. Ir. *mod*; cf. Eng. *manners* for sense.

modhan, the sound of a bagpipe or other musical instrument (H.S.D., also **moghun**):

mòdhar, soft, gentle (**modhar**, M'A.); from *modh*.

mòg, clumsy hand or foot; see *màg*, *smòg*.

mogach, shaggy, hairy:

mogan, a footless stocking; from the Sc. *moggan*, *moggans*.

mogan, spirits from oats (Uist):

mogul, a husk, mesh (of a net), Ir. *mogal*, cluster, mesh of a net, husk, apple of the eye, E. Ir. *mocoll* (do.), O. Ir. *mocol*, subtel: **mozgu-*, I. E. *mozgho*, knot, mesh; Lit. *mázgas*, knot, mesh; O. H. G., *mascâ*, Ger. *masche*, Eng. *mesh*; Gr. *μόσχος*, sprout, calf. Lat. *macula*, a mesh, is not allied. Dialect G. **mugairle**, bunch of nuts (Glenmoriston).

mogur, bulky, clumsy:

moibean, **moibeal**, a mop, broom, Ir. *moipal*; from Eng. *mop*.

moibleadh, a gnawing, half-chewing: "making a mop of;" from above.

móid, a vow, Ir. *móid*, M. Ir. *móit*, E. Ir. *moit* (Corm.): **monti-*, W. *gofuno*, to vow, O. Br. *guomonian*, polliceri, which Bugge and Stokes connect with W. *mun*, hand (cf. Ag. S. *mund*, Lat. *manus*). But see *bóid*. Stokes now says *votum*.

mòid, the greater, Ir. *móide*, more, M. Ir. *móti*: **mò* + *de*. Cf. *misd*.

moighre, robust, handsome:

moil, matted hair; see *molach* (**mḷ-*).

moilean, a fat, plump child, a lump; cf. Ir. *moil*, *molan*, a heap. To this Lat. *môles* may be compared.

mòin, **mòine**, peat, moss, Ir. *móin*, g. *móna*, E. Ir. *móin*, pl. *móinte*, W. *mawn*, peat, turf: **mân-*; Lat. *mâno*, flow, Eng. *emanate*. Strachan takes it from **mokni-*, root *mok*, *mak*, Ch. Slav. *mokrŭ*, wet, Lit. *makone*, puddle; Stokes agrees, giving Celtic as **mâkni-*, *môkni-*. It is doubtful if W. *k* would disappear before *n* (cf. *deur*). W. has also a form *migen*, *mign*, a bog.

moineis, false delicacy (M'A.), **moinig**, vanity, boasting; from root *mon*, *men*, mind?

moire, **a moire**, certainly, hercle, Ir. *iomorro*, indeed, however, O. Ir. *immurgu*, autem.

moirear, a lord, O. G. *mormær* (Book of Deer), M. G. *morbhair* (M'V.), M. Ir. *mormhaer* (Muireach Albanach), *murmor* (M'Firbis); from *mór* and *maor*, "great steward."

mòirneas, great cascade, streams (Oss. Ballads); from *mór* and *eas*?

moit, pride, sulkiness, Ir. *moiteamhuil*, sulky, nice, pettish (Con., O'R., M'F.); cf. E. Ir. *mochtae*, magnified, **mog-tio-s*, root *mog*, *mag*, great. O. Ir. *móidem*, boasting, praise.

mol, praise, advise, Ir. *molaim*, O. Ir. *molid*, laudat, W. *moli*, *mawl*, laus, Br. *meuli*: **molô*, **mâlô*, "magnify;" root *mōl*, *mel*, be strong; Gr. *μάλα*, very; Lat. *melior*, better; Lit. *milns*, very many, Ch. Slav. *iz-molêti*, eminere (Stokes). Windisch has compared it to Ch. Sl. *moliti*, ask, Lit. *myleti*, love, Gr. *μέλε*, friend, *μείλιχος*, gentle.

mol, **mal**, a shingly beach; from Norse *möl*, g. *malar*, pebbles, bed of pebbles on the beach; root *mel*, grind.

molach, hairy, rough, Ir. *mothlach*, rough, bushy (O'R.), *muthalach*, shaggy (Fol.). If the Irish form is right, it cannot be allied to I. E. *mḷo-s*, wool, Gr. *μαλλός*, wool, tuft, Lit. *millas*, woollen stuff.

moll, chaff, Ir. *moll* (O'R.), W. *mwl*: **muldo-*; Eng. *mould*, Got. *mulda*, dust, O. H. G. *molt*, dust, mould; root *mel*, grind. Borrowed from Welsh?

mollachd, a curse; the Northern form of *mallachd*, q.v.

mòlltair, a mould; from Eng. *moulter*, *mould*.

molltair, miller's share of the grain or meal (Lewis) = *multure*:

monadh, a mountain range, W. *mynydd*, mons, Cor. *menit*, *meneth*, O. Br. *-monid*, M. Br. *menez*, mountain: **monijo-*, **menijo-*, root *men*, eminere, Eng *eminent*. Cf. Welsh Inscription *Monedorigi*, "mountain-king"; also middle G. name of St Andrews—*Rig-monath* (Chronicles). The Ir. *monadh* appears only in Lh.; O'Br. gives *mónadh*. The G. word may have been borrowed from the Picts along with the place-names in which it appears: it is rare in Argyle topography.

monaid, heed:

monais, slowness, negligence; root *men*, stay, Gr. μένω.

monar, a dimunitive person or thing, **monaran**, a mote; see *munar*.

monasg, chaff, dross; from the root of the above.

monmhur, **monaghar**, a murmuring noise, Ir. *monmhar*, *monbhar*, murmuring, *monghair*, *monghar*, roaring: **mon-mur*; cf. Lat. *murmur*.

mór, great, Ir *mór*, O. Ir. *mór*, *már*, W. *mawr*, O. W., Cor. *maur*, Br. *meur*, Gaul. *-mâro-s*; Gr. -μωρος, great, famed (ἐγχεσί-μωρος, in spear-throw great; Got. *-mêrs*, famed, *mêrian* proclaim, O. H. G. *mâri*, famed, *-mar* in Germanic names Ger. *märchen*, a tale, Norse *mœrr*, famous; Slav. *-meru* (*Vladimir*, etc.); Lat. *merus*, Eng. *mere*. A shorter form of the stem (**mâro-*) appears in *mò*, greater (*mâ-*), q.v.

morbhach, land liable to sea flooding, Ir. *murbhach*, M. Ir. *murmhagh*; from *muir* and *magh*. Hence the locative **A' Mhor'oich**, the G. name of Lovat. Aran Ir. *muirbheach*, sandy soil by the seaside.

morghath, a fishing spear; "sea-spear," from *muir* and *gath*? M. Ir. *murgai* (B. of Lis.).

mòrnan, a small timber dish, Ir. *mórnán*:

mort, murder, Ir. *mort*, M. Ir. *martad*, slaughtering; from Lat. *mort-* of *mors*, *mortis*, death.

mortar, mortar, Ir. *mortaoil*; from the Eng.

mosach, nasty, dirty; see *musach*.

mosgail, waken, arouse, Ir. *músguilim*, *músglaim*, M. Ir. *romuscail*, he awoke, *musclait*, they wake: **imm-od-sc-al*, root *sec* of *dùisg*.

mosradh, coarse dalliance, **mosraiche**, smuttiness; from *mos* with suffix *radh*. See *musach* for root.

mothaich, perceive, Ir. *mothuighim*, M. Ir. *mothaigim*, perceive, O. Ir. *mothaigid*, stupeat (?); root *mot*, *met*, Lit. *matyti*, see, Lettic *matít*, perceive, Ch. Slav. *motriti*, spectare, Gr. ματεύω, seek.

mothan, bog violet:

mòthar, loud noise, swelling of the sea, **mothar**, noise as from a cave (M'A.):

mothar, a park, clump of trees (Arm.), M. Ir. *mothar*, enclosure, a place studded with bushes:

mu, about, Ir. *um*, *im*, O. Ir. *imb*, *imm-*, W. *am*, Cor., Br. *am-*, *em*, Gaul. *ambi*: **ambi*, **m̥bi*; Lat. *ambi-*; Gr. *ἀμφί*; Ag. S. *ymb*.

muc, a pig, Ir. *muc*, O. Ir. *mucc*, W. *moch*, pigs, Br. *moc'h*, pigs: **mukku-*; Lat. *mūcus*, *muccus*, mucus; Gr. *μύξα*, phlegm, *ἀπομύσσω*, wipe the nose, *μυκτήρ*, nose; Skr. *muñcáti*, let loose.

mucag, a hip or hep, fruit of the dog-rose, M. Ir. *mucóra*; from *muc* above. Cf. Gr. *μύκης*, a mushroom, from the same root.

mùch, smother, press down, Ir., O. Ir. *múchaim*, also E. Ir. *múch*, smoke, W. *mwg*, smoke, Cor. *mok*, *megi*, stifle, Br. *mik*, suffocation, *miga*, be suffocated, *moguet*, smoke: **mūko-*, root *smūk*, *smūg* (*smūgh*, *smaugh*), Eng. *smoke*, Gr. *σμύχω*, smoulder (*υ* long). Stokes suggests old borrowing from the Ag. S. Hence **mùchan**, a vent or chimney, Ir. *múchán* (O'B.).

mùdan, a covering, covering for a gun:

mugha, destruction, decay, Ir. *múgha*, a perishing, straying, M. Ir. *mugud*, slaying, *mogaim*, I slay:

mugharn, ankle, so Ir.; cf. W. *migwrn*, ankle, joint, Br. *migorn*, cartilage, which Stokes compares to Lat. *mucro*, point.

muidhe, a churn, E. Ir. *muide*, a vessel, *buide*, a churn, W. *buddai*, churn. Stokes compares *buide* and *buddai* to Gr. *πίθος*, jar, Lat. *fidelia*, pot, which is related to Eng. *body*. The form *muidhe* has been compared to Lat. *modius*, a peck, Fr. *muid*, hogshead.

muidse, a mutch; from the Sc. *mutch*, Ger. *mütze*.

mùig, **mùg**, cloudiness, gloom, surliness, Ir. *múig*: **munki-*, root *muk*, smoke, as in *mùch*? Or **mūggi-*, allied to Eng. *muggy*?

muigh, **a muigh**, outside; see *mach*.

muilceann, fell-wort, Ir. *muilcheann*:

muileach, dear, beloved: **molico-*, from *mol*, praise?

muileag, a cranberry:

muileann, a mill, so Ir., O. Ir. *mulenn*, *muilend*, W., Corn., Br. *melin*; from Lat. *molīna*, a mill, *molo*, grind (see *meil*). G. **muillear**, miller, E. Ir. *muilleóir*, is for **muilneóir*.

muileid, a mule, Ir. *múille*; from Lat. *mulus*.

muillean, a husk, particle of chaff; from *moll*.

muillean, a truss (of hay or straw): cf. Sc. *mullio* (Orkney), and see under *mul*, heap.

muillion, a million, Ir. *milliun*; from the L. Lat. *millionem*, coined from *mille*, a thousand.

muilteag, a certain small red berry (Dial. H.S.D.). See *muileag*.

muime, a step-mother, nurse, Ir. *buime*, *muime*, a nurse, E. Ir. *mumme*, nurse, stepmother: **mud-s-mjâ*, nurse, "suckler," root *mud*, suck; Lat. *mulier*, woman; Gr. *μύζω*, suck, *μύδος*, damp; Lit. *máudyti*, bath. It has also been paralleled to Lat. *mamma*, Ger. *muhme*, mother's sister, stepmother.

muin, teach, instruct, Ir. *múinim*, O. Ir. *múnim*:

muin, the back, Ir. *muin*, E. Ir. *muin*, back, neck, W. *mwn*, neck: **moni-*, neck; Skr. *mányâ*, neck; Lat. *monile*, necklace; O. H. G. *menni*, neck ornaments, Ag. S. *mene*, neck-chain; Ch. Slav. *monisto*, necklace. See *muineal*, *muing*. Gaulish had also *μανιάκης*, collar or torque.

mùin, micturate, Ir. *mún*, urine, E. Ir. *mún*, root *meu*, *mû*, befoul; Skr. *mûtra*, urine; possibly also Lat. *mûto*, *mutto*, penis, E. Ir. *moth*, ball ferda.

muineal, the neck, Ir. *muineul*, E. Ir. *muinél*, W. *mwnwgl*: **moniklo-*; from **moni-* of *muin*, back, q.v.

muineasach, depressed (Glenmoriston):

muing, a name, Ir. *muing*, O. Ir. *mong*, W. *myng* (m.), M. Br. *móe*, Br. *moue*: **mongâ*, **mongo-*, root *mon* of *muin*, back, q.v. Further is Eng. *mane*, Norse *mön*, Ger. *mähne*; Swed. and Dan. *manke* is especially close to Gaelic.

muinichill, muilichinn (Arg.), a sleeve, Ir. *muinichille*, *muinchille*, E. Ir. *munchille*; from Lat. *manicula*, *manica*, long sleeve, from *manus*, hand.

muinighin, confidence, trust, so Ir., E. Ir. *muinigin*; from **moni-* love, desire, Norse *munr*, love, O. Sax. *munilîk*, lovable; root *men*, think (Lat. *mens*, Eng. *mind*, etc.).

muinne, stomach (Arg.). Cf. *mionach*.

muinnte, munnda, beauteous; cf. Lat. *mundus*.

mùinnteachd, disposition (Dial.); for root see *muinighin*, and cf. O. Ir. *muiniur*, I think.

muinntir, household, people, Ir. *muinntir*, O. Ir. *muinter*, *muntar*. This is regarded by Stokes, Zimmer, and Güterbock as an early borrowing from the Lat. *monasterium*, monastery; the word *familia* is often applied to monasteries by Irish writers.

muir, the sea, Ir. *muir*, O. Ir. *muir*, gen. *mora*, W. *môr*, Cor., Br. *mor*, Gaul. *mori-*: **mori-*, sea; Lat. *mare*; Eng. *mere*, Ger. *meer*; Ch. Slav. *morje*.

mùire, leprosy; from *mùr*, a countless number, q.v.

muirgheadh, a fishing spear; see *morghath*.

muirichinn, children, family, Ir. *muiridhin*, a charge, family: **mori-*, care, charge, root *mer*, *smer*, remember; Lat. *memoria*, memory; Gr. *μέριμνα*, care; Skr. *smarati*, think, mind, **mori-gen-*.

mùirn, joy, affection, Ir. *múirn*, *múirnín*, darling (Eng. *mavourneen*, my darling), M. Ir. *múirn*, *muirn* : **morni-*, root *mor*, *mer*, *smer*, as in *muirichinn* above.
mùiseag, a threat, **muiseag** (Arm.); from *mus* of *musach*.
muisean, a mean, sordid fellow; see *musach* for the root.
mùisean, a primrose, Ir. *múiseán* (O'B.):
muiseal, a muzzle, Ir. *muisiall*; from the Eng.
muisginn, an English pint, mutchkin; from the Sc. *mutchkin*, Dutch *mutsje*, an eighth part of a bottle.
mul, a conical heap, mound, Ir. *mul*, *moil*, E. Ir. *mul-*, eminence : **mulu-*; cf. Norse *múli*, jutting crag, "mull," Ger. *maul*, snout. Cf. Fr. *mulon*, little heap of dried grass. *mul-conain*, conical suppurating sore.
mul, axle, Ir *mul*, *mol*, E. Ir. *mol*, shaft; cf. Gr. *μελίη*, ash, spear.
mulachag, a cheese, Ir., M. Ir. *mulchán* :
mulad, sadness; root *mu*, mutter?
mulart, dwarf elder, Ir. *mulabhúrd*, *malabhúr*, *mulart* (O'B.):
mulc, push, butt; cf. Lat. *mulceo*, *mulco*, stroke, beat.
mulc, a shapeless lump, lump; **mulcan**, a pustule; cf. *meall*:
mullach, the top, Ir., O. Ir. *mullach* : **muldâko-*, **muldo-*, top, head; Ag. S. *molda*, crown of the head; Skr. *mûrdhán*, top, head.
mult, a wedder, Ir., O. Ir. *molt*, W. *mollt*, Cor. *mols*, vervex, Br. *maout*, a sheep (mas.): **molto-*, root *mel*, *mol*, crush, grind, "mutilate;" Russ. *molitĭ*, cut, cut up, O. H. G. *muljan*, triturate. Hence M. Lat. *multo*, whence Fr. *mouton*, a sheep, Eng. *mutton*.
munar, a trifle, a trifling person, **monar**, diminutive person or thing:
munganachd, bullying:
mùnloch, a puddle, Ir. *múnloch*, gen. *múnlocha*; from *mún* and *loch*.
mur, unless, Ir. *muna* (Donegal Ir. *mur*; Monaghan has *amur* = *acht muna*, unless), M. Ir. *mun*, *moni*, *mona*, E. Ir., O. Ir. *mani*; from *ma*, if, and *ni*, not: "if not." The G. *r* for *n* is possibly due to the influence of *gur* and of the verbal particle *ro-* (in *robh*); *mun-robh* becoming *mur-robh*.
mùr, a wall, bulwark, palace, Ir., E. Ir. *múr*, W. *mur*; from Lat. *mûrus*, a wall.
mùr, countless number (as of insects), E. Ir. *múr*, abundance; Gr. *μυρίος* (*υ* long), countless, ten thousand; Skr. *bhûri*, many. Stokes compares rather Gr. -*μυρα* of *πλήμμυρα* (*υ* long), *πλημυρίς* (*υ* short or long), flood tide, flood. **Mùr**, leprosy = countless number.

muran, sea-bent, Ir. *muraineach*, bent grass; from *muir*, the sea. Norse has *mura*, goose-grass.

murcach, sorrowful, Ir. *murcach*, *múrcach*; cf. M. Br. *morchet*, anxiety, now *morc'hed*, Cor. *moreth*, chagrin. Eng. *murky*, Norse *myrkr* could only be allied by borrowing. Cf. Lat. *marceo*, droop.

mùrla, a coat of mail:

murlach, the king-fisher:

murlag, murluinn, a kind of basket, **murlach**, fishing basket (M'A.), Ir. *muirleog*, a rod basket for sand eels and wilks (Donegal). Cf. Sc. *murlain*, a narrow-mouthed basket of a round form.

murlan, rough head of hair:

murrach, able, rich, *murrtha*, successful, M. Ir. *muire*, *muiredach*, lord, Murdoch; Ag. S. *maere*, clarus, Norse *maerr*, famous (Stokes), same root as *mór*.

murt, murder; see *mort*.

murtachd, sultry heat, wearinesss produced by heat:

mus, before, ere; cf. O. Ir. *mos*, soon, mox, used as a verbal particle; it is allied to *moch*, being from **moqsu*, Lat. *mox*.

musach, nasty, Ir. *mosach* (O'R., Sh.), W. *mws*, effluvia, stinking, Br. *mous*, muck, *mouz*, crepitus ventris: **musso-*, **mud-so-*, root *mud*, be foul or wet; Gr. μύσος (=μύδ-σος), defilement, μύδος, clamminess, decay; Lit. *mudas*, dirty sea-grass: root *mu* (*mū*), soil, befoul, G. *mùin*, Eng. *mud*, etc.

musg, a musket, Ir. *músgaid*, L. M. Ir. *muscaed* (F. M.); from the Eng.

mùsg, rheum about the eyes, gore of the eyes; from the root *mū*, befoul, be wet, as discussed under *musach*, *mùin*.

musgan, dry-rot in wood, Ir. *musgan*, mustiness, mouldiness; Lat. *muscus*, moss; Eng. *moss*, *mushroom*; Lit. *musai* (pl.), mould. This word is not in H.S.D., but it is implied in Arm. and is in M'E.; also in common use.

mùsgan, pith of wood, porous part of a bone (H.S.D.). Armstrong gives also the meanings attached to **musgan** above; the words are evidently the same.

mùsgan, the horse fish:

mùsuinn, confusion, tumult, Ir. *múisiún*, codlata, hazy state preceding sleep. From Eng. *motion*?

mutach, short, E. Ir. *mut*, everything short: **mutto-*, root *mut*, dock; Lat. *mutilus*, maimed (Eng. *mutilate*), *muticus*, docked; Gr. μίτυλος, hornless.

mùtan, mutan, a muff, fingerless glove, also **mutag** (Arms.); from *miotag*, with a leaning on *mutach*, short. Thurneysen takes it from *mutach* without reference to *miotag*. Ir. has *muthóg* (Con.).

mùth, change, M. W. *mudaw* ; from Lat. *mûto*, I change.

N

n-, from, in **a nuas, a nìos,** Ir., O. Ir. *an-* ; see *a* number 5.

na, not, ne, Ir., O. Ir. *na* : used with the imperative mood solely. It is an ablaut and independent form of the neg. prefix *in* (see *ion-*, *an-*), an ablaut of I. E. *nê*, Lat. *nê*, Gr. *νη-* ; shorter form Lat. *nĕ-*, Got. *ni*, Eng. *not* (*ne-á-wiht*), etc. ; further I.E. *n̥-*, Gr. *ἀν-*, Lat. *in-*, Eng. *un-*, Gaelic *an-*. See *nach*, which is connected herewith as Gr. *οὐκ*, *οὐ* ; the W. is *nac*, *nag*, with imperative, Br. *na*.

na, or, vel, Ir. *ná*, E. Ir., O. Ir. *nó*, W. *neu* : **nev* (Stokes, who allies it to Lat. *nuo*, nod, Gr. *νεύω*, Skr. *návate*, go, remove ; but, in 1890, Bez. Beit.[16] 51, he refers it to the root *nu*, Eng. *now*). It can hardly be separated from *neo*, otherwise, q.v. Strachan agrees.

na, than, Ir. *ná*, M. Ir. *iná*, E. Ir. *inda*, *indás*, O. Ir. *ind as*, *indás*, pl. *indate* (read *indáte*) ; from the prep. *in* and *tá*, to be (Zeuss[2], 716-7, who refers to the other prepositional comparative conjunction *oldaas*, from *ol*, de) The use of *in* in O. Ir. as the relative locative may also be compared.

na, what, that which, id quod, M. Ir. *ina*, *ana*, *inna n-*, E. Ir. *ana n-* ; for *an a*, O. Ir. rel. *an* (really neuter of art.) and G. rel. *a*, which see. Descent from *ní* or *ni*, without any relative, is favoured by Book of Deer, as *do ni thíssad*, of what would come. Possibly from both sources.

'na, 'na-, in his, in her, in (my) ; the prep. *an* with the possessive pronouns : **'nam, 'nar, 'nad** (also **ad,** E. Ir. *at*, *it*), **'nur, 'na 'nan.**

nàbaidh, nàbuidh, a neighbour ; from the Norse *ná-búi*, neighbour, "nigh-dweller," the same in roots as Eng. *neighbour*.

nach, not, that not (conj.), that not = quin (rel.), nonne ? Ir., E. Ir. *nach*, W. *nac*, *nag*, not, Br. *na* : **nako*, from *na*, not, which see above, and *ko* or *k* as in Gr. *οὐκ* against *οὐ* (Stokes). The *ko* has been usually referred to the same pronominal origin as *-que* in Lat. *neque* ; it does appear in *neach*.

nàdur, nature, Ir. *nádúr*, W. *natur* ; from Lat. *natura*.

naid, a lamprey (Sh., O'B.), Ir. *naid* :

naidheachd, news, Ir. *núaidheachd*, W. *newyddion* ; from *nuadh*, new.

nàile, yea ! an interjection :

nàird, a nàird, upwards, Ir. *andírde,* E. Ir. *i n-ardi, i n-airddi* ; prep. *in* (now *an*) into, and *àirde,* height: "into height." This adverb is similar in construction to *a bhàn, a mach, a steach,* etc., for which see *a* number 6.

nàire, shame, Ir. *náire,* E. Ir. *náre* : **nagro-,* shameful, root *nagh,* be sober, Gr. νήφω (do.), Ger. *nüchtern,* fasting, sober.

nàisneach, modest ; compare the next word.

nàistinn, care, wariness ; from Norse *njósn,* spying, looking out, Got. *niuhseini,* visitation (ἐπισκοπή), Ag. S. *neósan,* search out.

naitheas, harm, mischief :

nall, from over, to this side, Ir., O. Ir. *anall* ; from *an* (see *a* 5) and *all* of *thall,* q.v.

nàmhaid, an enemy, Ir. *námhaid,* g. *namhad,* O. Ir. *náma,* g. *námat,* pl. n. *námait* : **nâmant-,* root *nôm, nem,* seize, take ; Gr. νέμεσις, wrath, nemesis, νωμάω, νέμω, distribute ; O. H. G. *nâma,* rapine, Ger. *nehmen,* take, Eng. *nimble* ; Zend. *nemanh,* crime, Alb. *namε,* a curse. Cf. W., Corn., and Br. *nam,* blame.

na'n (na'm), if (with false supposition), M. G. *dane, da n-, da m-* (D. of Lis.), Ir. *da, dá* (for *da n-,* eclipsing), E. Ir. *dá n-, día n-,* O. Ir. *dian* : the prep. *di* or *de* and rel. *an* ; Manx *dy.* The G. form with *n* for *d* is puzzling, though its descent from *da n-* seems undoubted.

naoi, nine, so Ir., O. Ir. *nói n-,* W., Corn. *naw,* Br. *nao* : **nevn̥* ; Lat. *novem* ; Gr. ἐν-νέα ; Eng. *nine,* Ger. *neun* ; Skr. *návan.*

naoidhean, an infant, so Ir., O. Ir. *nóidiu,* gen. *nóiden* : **ne-vid-,* "non-witted"? Cf. for force Gr. νήπιος, infant (=νη-πιος, not-wise one), from -πιϝος, wise, πινυτός (do.), root *qei* of *ciall,* q.v. So Stokes in Celt. Ph.[2] ; now **no-vidiôn* (*no=ne*) ; cf. Gr. νήπιος.

naomh, holy, Ir. *naomh,* E. Ir. *nóem, nóeb,* O. Ir. *nóib* : **noibo-s* ; O. Pers. *naiba,* beautiful, Pers. *nîw* (do.). Bez. suggests the alternative of Lettic *naigs,* quite beautiful.

naosga, a snipe, Ir. *naosga* : **snoib-sko-,* root *sneib, snib* of Eng. *snipe* ?

nar, negative particle of wishing : **ni-air,* for not ; *air* and *nì.*

nàsag, an empty shell :

nasg, a band, tieband, collar, Ir., E. Ir. *nasc* : **nasko-* ; O. H. G. *nusca,* fibula, Norse *nist,* brooch : **n̥dh-sko-,* root *n̥dh* (Brug.). The verb *nasg,* O. Ir. *-nascim,* appears in Br. as *naska.* The root *nedh* is in Skr. *nahyati.* Others make the root *negh* of Lat. *nexus,* etc., and the root *snet* of *snàth,* q.v., has been suggested. See *snaim* further.

nasgaidh, gratis, free, Ir. *a n-aisge,* freely, *aisge,* a gift. See *asgaidh.*

natar, nitre; from Eng. *natron, nitre*.

nathair, a serpent, so Ir., O. Ir. *nathir*, W. *neidr*, Corn. *nader*, M. Br. *azr*: **natrîx*; Lat. *natrix*, water snake; Got. *nadrs*, Norse *naðr*, Eng. *adder*. The Teutonic words are regarded by Kluge as scarcely connected with Lat. *natrix*, whose root is *nat*, swim.

-ne, emphatic participle added to the pl. of 1st pers. pron. *sin-ne*, *ar n-athair-ne*, "our father"; O. Ir. *ni*, *-ni*, used independently (= *nos*) and as a suffix. See further under *sinne*.

neach, anyone, Ir. *neach*, O. Ir. *nech*, aliquis, W., Cor., Br. *nep*, *neb*, quisquam: **neqo-*, *ne-qo-*; Lit. *nekàs*, something, *nekùrs*, quidam, Lett. *ká ne ká*, anyhow. Stokes takes the *ne* from the negative root *ne* (see *na*); the *qo* is the pronominal stem of the interrogative (cf. Lat. *-que*, *neque*).

nead, a nest, Ir. *nead*, E. Ir. *net*, W. *nyth*, Corn. *neid*, Br. *nez*, *neiz*: **nizdo-s*; Lat. *nîdus*; Eng. *nest*; Skr. *nîdas*. Supposed to be from **ni-sed-*, "sit down."

nèamh, heaven, Ir. *neamh*, O. Ir. *nem*, W., Corn. *nef*, M. Br. *neff*, now *env*: **nemos*; Skr. *námas*, bowing, reverence; Lat. *nemus*, grove; Gr. νέμος, pasture: root *nem*, distribute, Gr. νέμω (do.), Ger. *nehmen*, take. Gaulish has νεμητον or νεμετον, O. Ir. *nemed*, sacellum. Often, and lately (1895) by Prof. Rhys, referred to the root *nebh*, be cloudy, Gr. νέφος, cloud, Lat. *nebula* (see *neul*); but the Gaelic nasalized *èa* is distinctly against this, as also is the Br. *env* (Stokes).

neamhnuid, a pearl, Ir. *meamhunn*, M. Ir. *niamnuid*, pearl, E. Ir. *nemanda*, pearly, O. Ir. *ném*, onyx (for *nem*?); root *nem* of *nèamh*.

neanntag, nettle, Ir. *neantóg*, E. Ir. *nenntai*, nettles, *nenaid*. See *deanntag*.

neapaicin, a napkin, Ir. *naipicín*; from Eng.

nèarachd, happiness, usually **mo nèarachd**, lucky to, Ir. *moigheanéar*, happy is he (O'B.), *is meunar duit-se*, happy is it for you (O'Growney), M. Ir. *mo ghenar duit*, good luck to you (F. M.), *mongenar* (L. B.), E. Ir. *mogenar*. The root seems to be *mag* (I. E. *magh*), increase (see *mac*); cf. Lat. *macte*, root, *mak*, great.

nearag, a daughter (Oss. Ballads); if a word properly handed down, it is interesting to compare it with the root of the following.

neart, strength, Ir. *neart*, O. Ir. *nert*, W., Corn. *nerth*, Br. *nerz*, Gaul. *nerto-*, root *ner*; Skr. *nár*, man; Gr. ἀνήρ (root *ner*); Lat. Umbr. *nerus*, viros, Sab. *Nero*, fortis; Teut. *Nerthus*, Norse *Njörðr*; Lit. *noréti*, to will.

neas, weazel; see *nios.*

neasg, neasgaid, a boil, Ir. *neascóid,* E. Ir. *nescoit*: **ness-conti-*, from E. Ir. *ness,* wound (**snit-so-*, root *snit,* cut. Ger. *schneide,* Sc. *sned*), and *-conti-* found in *urchoid*? Stokes regards E. Ir. *ness,* wound, as from **nekso-*, root *neg.*

neimh, poison, Ir. *nimh, neimh,* O. Ir. *nem,* pl. *neimi*: **nemes-*, "something given," root *nem-*, distribute (as in *nèamh*)?

nèip, a turnip; from the Sc. *neep,* M. Eng. *nēpe,* from Lat. *nâpus.*

neo, air neo, otherwise, alioquin (conj.); see next.

neo-, un-, Ir. *neamh-, neimh-*, M. Ir. *nem,* O. Ir. *neb-, neph-*: **ne-bo-*; the *ne* is the negative seen in *na, ni,* but the *bo* is doubtful. Zimmer suggests that *b* is what remains of the subj. of *bu,* be: "be not."

neòinean, neònan, the daisy, Ir. *nóinin*: "noon-flower," from *nòin,* noon. Cf. the Eng. *daisy* for force.

neònach, eccentric, curious: **neo-gnàthach,* "unwont."

neonagan, a stye in the eye (Arg.); cf. *leamhnad.* Also *steònagan*; cf. Sc. *styen.*

neoni, nothing, a trifle, O. Ir. *nephní*; from *neo-* and *ni,* thing.

neul, nial, a cloud, Ir. *neul,* O. Ir. *nél.* pl. acc. *níula,* W. *niwl,* mist: **neblo-s*; Lat. *nebula*; Gr. *νεφέλη*; Ger. *nebel,* mist; O. Slav. *nebo,* sky; Skr. *nabhas,* mist.

ni, not, Ir. *ní,* O. Ir. *ní, ni,* W. *ni*: **nei*; O. Lat. *nei,* Lat, *ni-, nê*; O. H. Ger. *ni,* Ger. *nein*; O. Slav. *ni,* neque; Zend *naê-*; Gr. *νη-*. Thur. says **ne-est = *nést,* Celtic *níst, nìs, ni h-* non-aspirating.

ni, a thing, Ir. *nidh,* O. Ir. *ní,* res, probably a curtailed form of O. Ir. *aní,* id quod, from the art. neut. and the pronominal suffix *ei,* which Zimmer compares to Got. *ei,* that (conj.), *sa-ei, that-ei,* which is either the locative of pronominal *o-* (Gr. *εἰ,* I. E. *ei-so,* this here), or the particle seen in Gr. *οὑτοσ-ί* (*ι* long), an instrumental of Lat. *is,* Gaelic *e,* he. Some have regarded *ni* as from **gnithe,* factum, which see in *ní,* will do.

nì, cattle; this is the same as *ni,* thing.

nì, will do, Ir. *gním,* I do, O. Ir. *dogní,* facit; see *dèan, gnìomh.*

niata, courageous, Ir. *nia,* gen. *niadh,* a champion, *niadhas,* valour, M. Ir. *forniatta,* brave, E. Ir. *nia,* g. *níath,* possibly Ogam *neta, netta* (**nêta*?): **neid-*, Gr. *ὄνειδος,* revile, Lit. *náids,* hatred, Skr. *nind,* mock, or **ni-sed-*, down-setter? Rhys (*Lect.*) cfs. the Teut. *nanþ,* venture, strive; this would give Gaelic preserved *d.*

nic, female patronymic prefix, M. Gaelic *nee* (D. of L.), Ir. *ní,* M. Ir. *iní,* an abbreviation of O. Ir. *ingen,* now *inghean* or *nighean* and *ui*, nepotis (Stokes). The G. *nic*, really "grand-daughter," stands for *inghean mhic* or *ní mhic*; we have recorded in 1566 *Ne V^c Kenze* (M'Leod Charters).

nigh, wash, Ir. *nighim*, E. Ir. *nigim*, O. Ir. *dofonuch*, lavo, *nesta*, laveris: **nigô*, I. E. *neigô*; Gr. *νίζω*, *νίπτω*; Eng. *nick*, *Auld Nick*, a water power, Ger. *nix*; Skr. *nij*, clean.

nighean, a daughter; a corruption of *inghean*, q.v.

nimh, poison, Ir. *nimh*; see *neimh*.

nior, not (with perfect tense), Ir. *níor*, E. Ir. *nír* = *ní-ro*; *ro* is the sign of past tenses.

nios, **neas**, a weazel, Ir. *neas*, *eas*(*óg*), O. Ir. *ness*:

nìos, from below, up, Ir. *aníos*, E. Ir. *anís*; from *an* (see *a* number 5) and *ìos*.

nis, now, Ir. *anois*, M. Ir. *anosa*, E. Ir. *innossai*, O. Ir. *indossa*; *ind* (now *an*) of the article and G. *fois*, rest. The word appears in **a bhos**, q.v. The form *indorsa*, this hour (= now), is rejected by Ascoli as a misspelling for *indossa*.

ni 's, id quod, the usual classical Gaelic with the verb substantive to denote comparative state: **tha i ni's fheàrr**, she is better, Ir. *nios*, M. Ir. *ní is*: "thing that is," from *ni* and *is*. The usual and true Gaelic form **na 's** is not a degraded form of Ir. *ni 's*. The G. *na* of *na 's* is simply **na** = id quod (see **na**); the Ir. is some mediæval development with *ní*, for old *ana*, id quod, was lost, the simple *a* (art.) being used now in its stead, as in O. Ir. As it was impossible to use *a* in the comparative construction with clearness, recourse was had to *ní is*. Thus Ir.: An tan do thógradh ní ba mó do dheunamh = G. An *tan* a thogradh e na bu mhò a dhèanamh. Hence **ni 's** should never have been used in Sc. Gaelic.

niùc, a corner; from the Sc. *neuk*, M. Eng. *nōk*. Dial. **iùc**. Skeat thinks the Eng. is the borrower.

no, or, vel, Ir. *ná*, E. Ir., O. Ir. *nó*, W. *neu*; see *na*.

nochd, to-night, Ir. *anochd*, O. Ir. *innocht*, hac nocte: the art. and *nochd*, night, W. *henoeth*, Corn. *neihur*, Br. *neyzor*, *nos*: **nokti-*; Lat. *nox*, *noctis*; Gr. *νύξ*, *νυκτός*; Got. *nahts*, Eng. *night*; Lit. *naktìs*; Skr. *nákti*.

nochd, naked, Ir. *nochdadh*, manifestation, O. Ir. *nocht*, W. *noeth*, Corn. *noyth*, Br. *noaz*: **noqto-*; Got. *naqaþs*, O. H. G. *nacot*, Eng. *naked*; further cf. Lat. *nūdus* (**nogvidus*); Slav. *nagŭ*; Skr. *nagná*.

nodadh, a nod, suggestion; from the Eng.

nodha, new; see *nuadh*.

noig, the anus:

noig, old-fashioned face; *noigeiseach*, snuffy; *noigeanach* (D. Bàn):

noigean, a noggin, Ir. *noigin*; from the Eng. *noggin.* Skeat thinks the Eng. are the borrowers; but this is unlikely.

nòin, noon, Ir. *nóin,* g. *nóna,* evening, noon, E. Ir. *nóin, nóna,* W. *nawn*; from the Lat. *nôna* hora, ninth hour of the day, or 3 o'clock.

noir, the east, Ir. *anoir,* O. Ir. *anair,* "from before," if one looks at the morning sun; from *an* (see *a* number 5) and *air.*

nollaig, Christmas, Ir. *nodlog,* E. Ir. *notlaic,* W. *nadolig*; from Lat. *natalicia,* the Nativity.

norra, a wink of sleep (Arran), **norradh** (M'Rury):

nòs, a custom, Ir., E. Ir. *nós,* W. *naws,* M. Br. *neuz*: **nomzo-,* Gr. νομος, law, Lat. *numerus.* Thurneysen thinks the Gadelic words are borrowed from the Welsh *naws,* from *gnaws* (see *gnàth*). Stokes gives **nomso-* as stem for Gadelic alone; the W. he regards as from *gnâ,* as above. The ideal stem would be **nâsto-,* root *nâd.*

nòs, a cow's first milk, E. Ir. *nus*; from *nua,* new, and *ass,* milk.

nòtair, a notary, Ir. *nótadóir,* O. Ir. *notire*; from Lat. *notarius.*

nothaist, a foolish person:

nuadarra, angry, surly; see *nuarranta.*

nuadh, new, Ir. *núadh,* O. Ir. *nue, núide,* W. *newydd,* O. Br. *nouuid,* Br. *neuez,* Gaul. *novio-*: **novio-s*; Lat. *novus, Novius*; Gr. νέος, young, new; Got. *niujis,* Eng. *new*; Lit. *naújas*; Skr. *navya.*

'nuair, when, "the hour that," Ir. *anuair,* E. Ir. *innúair*: the art. and the word *uair,* q.v.

nuall, nuallan, a howling, cry, Ir. *nuaill,* E. Ir. *núall*: **nouslo-n*; Skr. *nu,* cry, *navati*; Lettic *nauju,* cry; O. H. G. *niumo,* praise, rejoicing.

nuarranta, sad, surly; cf. the Ir. interjection *mo nuar,* my woe, root *nu* as above.

nuas, down, from above, Ir. *anuas*; see *a* number 5 and *uas.*

nuig, as far as, O. G. *gonice* (B. of Deer), Ir. *nuige, go nuige,* E. Ir. *connici*: **con-do-icci*; see *thig,* come.

nuimhir, number, so Ir.; from Lat. *numerus.* Usually *uimhir,* q.v.

'n uiridh, last year, Ir. *'nuraidh,* E. Ir. *innuraid*; the art. and O. Ir. dat. *urid.* See *uiridh.*

null, over, to beyond; for *nunn* on the analogy of *nall,* and for dissimilation of the *ns.* See *nunn,* the only Argyllshire form.

nunn, over, beyond, Ir. *anonn,* O. I. *inunn*; from the prep. *an* (see *a* 5) and *sund,* here ("from here"), W. *hwnt,* Br. *hont*: **suno-to-,* pronominal roots *sou* and *to*; for both cf. Gr. οὗτος (= *so-u-to-s*), this. The pronominal forms beginning in *so* and *to,* or *s* and *t* without *o,* are all from the roots *so* and *to* ultimately.

O

o, the interjection "O! oh!" Ir. *o*; see vocative *a*.

o, from, ab, Ir. *ó*, O. Ir. *ó*, *ua* (*hó*, *hua*): **ava*; Skr. *áva*, away, off; Lat. *au-*, as in *aufero*, take away; Ch. Sl. *u-*, Pruss- *au-*. Also **bho**, q.v.

o, since, when, with the rel. as **o 'n**, Ir. *ó*, O. Ir. *ó*, ex quo; it is merely the prep. *o* used as a conjunction.

ob, refuse, Ir. *obaim*, O. Ir. *obbaim*, *obbad* (inf.); referred to *ud-bad*, "out-speak," the prefix *ud-*, out (allied to Eng. *out*, Skr. *ud*, out, of) and *ba*, speak, I. E. *bha*, Lat. *fari*, Gr. *φα* in *φημί*. Ascoli gives the root as *ben* (see *bean*), repellere.

òb, a creek; from Norse *hóp*, small land-locked bay, Sc. *hope*, Ag. S. *hóp*, valley.

obaidh, a charm; see *ubag*.

obair, a work, so Ir., E. Ir. *opair*, *oper*, O. Ir. *opred*, operatio; from Lat. *opus* (g. *operis*), *opera*.

† **obair**, a confluence; the usual pronunciation of the *Aber-* in place names. See *abar*.

obann, sudden, Ir. *obann*, E. Ir. *opond*: **od-bond*, e vestigio, from *bonn*? Stokes refers it to the root of Gr. *ἄφνω*, O. Slav. *abije*, immediately, suggesting **ob-nó-*. W. *buan* also suggests itself.

ocar, interest on money, Ir. *ocar*, W. *ocr*; from Norse *okr*, usury, Ag. S. *wocer*, Got. *wokrs*, Ger. *wucher*; root *veg*.

och, an interjection, alas! Ir. *och*, *uch*, O. Ir. *uch*, vae, *ochfad*, sighing: **uk*; Got. *aúhjôn*, make a noise, Norse *ugla*, Eng. *owl*; Let. *auka*, stormwind, Serb. *uka*, a cry.

ochd, eight, Ir. *ochd*, O. Ir. *ocht n-*, W. *wyth* (**okti*), Br. *eiz*: **oktô*; Lat. *octo*; Gr. *ὀκτώ*; Got. *ahtau*; Skr. *ashtaú*.

ochòin, alas, Ir. *och ón*; literally "alas this!" From *och* and the old pronoun *ón*, discussed under *eadhon*.

ocras, hunger, Ir. *ocrus*, *ocarus*, E. Ir. *accorus*. See *acras*. The Lat. *careo*, want, may be suggested as allied; root *ker*, *kor*.

od, yonder, yon; see *ud*.

oda, tongue of land; N. *oddr*.

oda, horse-race (Uist), race, race-course (Carm.); cf. N. *at*, horse-fight.

odhar, dun, so Ir., E. Ir. *odar*: **odro-s*, for **odh-ro-*, shady, Lat. *umbra* (=**o-n-dhra*), *âter*, dark, Umbrian *adro*, atra. Bez. suggests, with query, **jodros*, allied to Lit. *jûdas*, dark. Thurneysen has referred **odro-s* to I. E. *udro-*, otter, hydra, watery, the idea being "otter-like" or "water-like" (Gr. *ὕδωρ*, Eng. *water*).

ofrail, an offering, Ir. *ofráil*, M. Ir. *offráil*, E. Ir. *oifrend*; from Lat. *offerendum*.

òg, young, Ir. *óg*, O. Ir. *óc*, *óac*, W. *ieuanc*, Corn. *iouenc*, Br. *iaouank*, Gaul. *Jovinc-illos*: **jovn̥ko-s*, comparative *jovôs*; Lat. *juvenis*, *juvencus*; Eng. *young*, Got. *juggs*; Skr. *yuvaçá*, juvenile, *yúvan*, young.

ogha, a grandchild, Ir. *ó*, *ua*, g. *ui*, a grandson, descendant, O. Ir. *ua*, *aue*, *haue*, g. *haui*: **(p)avio-s*; Gr. *παίς*, for *παϝίς*, boy; further Lat. *puer*, for *pov-er*; W. *wyr*; root *pu*, *pav*, *pov*, beget. Brug. (*Grund.*[2] 122) refers it to **avio-s*, an adj. from *avo-s*, grandfather, etc., Lat. *avus*. Eng. *eame*.

† **oghum**, the "Ogam" writing, so Ir., E. Ir. *ogum*, *Ogma mac Elathan* (son of knowledge), the Hercules of the Gaelic gods, Gaul. *Ogmios*, the Gaul. Hercules and god of eloquence: **Ogambio-s*. Cf. Gr. *ὄγμος* (**γ-μος*?), a furrow, line, Skr. *ájmas*, course, run, root *ag*: the comparison is very doubtful. See *oidheam*.

òglach, a youth, servant, Ir. *óglach*, O. Ir. *óclach*; from *òg* and suffix *-lach* (see *teaglach*).

ogluidh, gloomy, awful, bashful, Ir. *ogluidh*, bashful; from Norse *uggligr*, fearful, Eng. *ugly*.

oich, interjection of pain, Ir., O. Ir. *uch*. See *och*.

oide, foster-father, step-father, Ir. *oide*, O. Ir. *aite*: **attio-s*; Gr. *ἄττα*, father; Got. *atta*, father; Ch. Sl. *otĭcĭ*, father; Skr. *attá*, mother.

oidhche, oiche, night, Ir. *oidhche*, O. Ir. *aidche*, later *oidche*, also *adaig*: **ad-aqiâ*, **ad-aqî*, root *aq*, dark; Lat. *aquilus*, dark; Lit. *aklas*, blind; Gr. *ἄκαρον*, blind (Hes.). Skr. *andhas*, darkness, with root *andh*, *adh*, Lat. *ater*, etc., have been suggested, the *ad* of **ad-aqia* being made the root and not the *aq* (see *odhar*).

† **oidheadh**, tragical death, so Ir., E. Ir. *oided*, *aided*; root *pad*, *ped*, fall, Lat. *pestis* (Stokes). See *eas*.

oidheam, a secret meaning, inference, idea (M'A., M'E.), a book (M'F., H.S.D.). Properly *oigheam*, the same as *ogham* above (Zeuss, Rhys' *Hib. Lect.*).

oidheirp, oirpe, an attempt: **ad-erb-*, root *erb* of *earb*, q.v.?

oifig, an office, Ir. *oifig*, M. Ir. *oifficc*; from Lat. *officium* (Eng. *office*).

òigeach, a stallion, young horse; from *òg* and *each*. Commonly **àigeach**, q.v.

òigh, a virgin, Ir. *óigh*, E. Ir., O. Ir. *óg*, *uag*, integer: **augi-*, root *aug*, increase; Lat. *augeo*; Got. *áukan*, increase; Lit. *áugu*, (Brug.). Bez. (in Stokes' *Urkel. Spr.*) suggests Czech *pouhý*, pure, and a stem **pougo-s*.

oigheam, obedience, homage; cf. *taidhe.*

oighionnach, aigheannach, a thistle (Perth, according to M'A.): see *fobhannan.*

oighre, ice, Ir. *oidhir*, M. Ir. *óigred*, E. Ir. *aigred*, snow; see *deigh.*

oighre, an heir, so Ir., M. Ir. *oigir*; founded on Lat. *heres*, possibly on M. Eng. *heir* rather, which is from *heres.*

oighreag, cloudberry; founded on Sc. *averin.*

oil, vexation, offence, Ir. †*oil*. The E. Ir. *áil* has *a* long, and is for *agli-*, Got. *agls*, disgraceful (Strachan). The G. is perhaps from the root of *oillt.*

oil, rear, educate, Ir. *oilim*, O. Ir. *ailim*; root *al* as in *altrum.*

oilbheum, offence, stumbling-block, Ir. *oilbhéim*, M. Ir. *ailbéim*: "stone-dashing," "stone-stumbling"; from *ail*, rock, and *beum*, blow, q.v. (Atk.).

oilean, eilean, training, nurture, Ir. *oileamhuin*, nurture, M. Ir. *oilemain*, inf. to *ailim*, I rear; root *al*, as in *altrum*, q.v.

oillt, horror, disgust, Ir. *oilt*: **aleti-*, root *pal*, strike, whence Lat. *palma*, palm, *palpo*, palpitate, etc.?

oineach, liberality, Ir. *oineach*, mercy, liberality. See *eineach.*

òinid, a fool, Ir. *óinmhid*, E. Ir. *óinmit*, *ónmit*; from *ón-*, foolish, and *ment*, mind. See next.

òinnseach, a foolish woman, Ir. *óinseach*; from *ón-*, foolish, and the feminine termination *-seach.*

oir, edge, border, Ir., E. Ir., O. Ir. *or*, W. *gor-or*, ora superior: **oro-*. Cf. Lat. *ōra*, coast, from which Thur. regards it as borrowed; it is not allied to Ger. *ufer*, coast.

oir, for, O. Ir. *ar*, *air*; the prep. *air* (**are*) used as a conj. The Ir. *óir*, because, for, O. Ir. *óre*, *úare*, abl. of O. Ir. *uar*, *huar*, is from Lat. *hōra*, Gaelic *uair.*

oir-, prefix denoting "ad" or "on," Ir. *oir-*, O. Ir. *air-*, *ar-*; this is the prep. *air* (**are*). Hence **oirbheart**, a good deed, Ir. do., from *beart*; **oirbheas**, act of charity, from *beus*, conduct, etc. Sometimes confused with **òr-**, gold, as prefix; cf. *óirdheirc.*

oircheas, pity, charity, Ir. *oircheasachd*, need, charitableness; cf. O. Ir. *airchissecht*, gratia, indulgentia, vb. *airchissim*, parcit, indulget: *air* + *cess*; root of *cead*?

òirde, a piece or lump of anything; see *ord.*

òirdheirc, glorious, Ir. *óirdhearc*, O. Ir. *airdirc*, *erdirc*; from *air* and *dearc*, see: "con-spicuous." See *oir-* for the *òir-.*

oirfeid, music, Ir. *oirfid*, E. Ir. *air-fitiud*, playing, inf. to *arbeitim*, *arpeitim*; from *air* and *peitim*, M. Ir. *peiteadh*, music; *peit* or *pet* is from *svettâ*, whistle, pipe, G. *fead*, q.v.

òirleach, an inch, Ir. *órlach*, *ordlach*, M. Ir. *ordlach*, *tri hordlaighe*, three inches; from *ordu*, thumb, now G. *òrd-ag*, q.v.

oirthir, the east, so Ir., O. Ir. *airther*; comparative of *air*, ante—"in front," as one faces the sun in the morning.

oirthir, border, coast, so Ir., M. Ir. *airer*; from *air* and *tìr*.

òisg, a sheep, yearling ewe, E. Ir. *óisc*; for *ói-shesc*, *ói*, sheep, and *seasg*, barren, q.v. The word *ói* is from **ovi-s*; Lat. *ovis*; Gr. *οἶς*; Lit. *avis*; Skr. *ávis*.

oisinn, a corner, Ir. *isinn*, the temple, *fán na hoisean*, along the temple, E. Ir. *na-h-usine*, the temples: **od-stani-*, "outstanding" (?). See *ursainn*, *tarsainn*.

oisir, an oyster, Ir. *oisre*; from M. Eng. *oistre*, from Fr. *oistre*, from Lat. *ostrea*.

oistric, ostrich, Ir. *ostrich*; from the Eng.

oit, an interjection to denote the sense of burning heat; cf. O. Ir. *uit mo chrob*, alas for my hand!

oiteag, a breeze, puff of wind, Ir. *oiteóg*: **atti-*, root *at*, as in Gr. *ἀτμός*, vapour, Eng. *atmosphere*; Ag. S. *aeðm*, breath; Skr. *âtmán*, breath, soul.

oitir, a ridge or bank in the sea, a low promontory, Ir. *oitír*: **ad-tír*, from *tír*, land, "to-land."

òl, drink, drinking, Ir. *ól*, *ólaim*, E. Ir. *ól*, inf. to *ibim*, O. Ir. *oul*, **povolo* (St.), drinking: **potlo-*, root *po*, *pô*, drink; Lat. *pôto*, Eng. *potate*, etc.; Skr. *pâ-*, drink. Zimmer considers it borrowed from Norse *öl*, Eng. *ale*. The root *pele*, *plê*, full, has also been suggested; but it is unlikely here.

ola, oil, Ir., O. Ir. *ola*, W. *olew*, O. W. *oleu*, Br. *eol*; from Lat. *oleum*, Eng. *oil*.

òlach, a hospitable person: "boon-companion;" from *òl*.

olann, wool, so Ir., E. Ir. *oland*, O. W. *gulan*, W. *gwlan*, Corn. *gluan*, Br. *gloan*: **vlanâ*, **vlano-*; Lat. *lâna*; Gr. *λᾶνος*, *λῆνος*; Eng. *wool*, Got. *vulla*; Lit. *wilna*; Skr. *ûrnâ*; I.E. *vl̥nâ*, *vl̄nâ*.

olc, bad, Ir. *olc*, O. Ir. *olcc*, *olc*; cf. Lat. *ulciscor*, revenge, *ulcus*, wound, Eng. *ulcer*; Gr. *ἕλκος*, wound. Bez. suggests O.H.G. *ilki*, hunger, Lit. *alkti*, Ch. Sl. *alkati*, hunger.

ollabhar, a great army (M'F.), Ir. *ollarbhar*: *oll* + *arbhar*. For *oll*, see next word; E. Ir. *arbar*, a host, is from *ber* (see *beir*).

ollamh, a learned man, a doctor, so Ir., O. Ir, *ollam*, g. *ollaman*; from Ir. *oll*, great (root *pol*, *pel*, *plê*, full, fill).

òmar, amber, Ir. *omra*, W. *amfer*; from the Eng.

omhail, attention, heed, Ir. *úmhail*; cf. G. *umhal*, obedient.

omhan, othan, froth of milk or whey, whey whisked into froth (Carm.), Ir. *uan*, E. Ir. *úan*, froth, foam, W. *ewyn*, Br. *eon*: **oveno-*, **poveno-*; Lit. *putà*, foam, Lettic *putas*.

onagaid, confusion, row (Dial.); cf. *aonagail*.

onfhadh, a blast, storm, raging of the sea, Ir. *unfadh*, E. Ir. *anfud*, for *an-feth*, "excess-wind," *feth*, aura; root *vê*, *ven*, blow; Skr. *vâta*, wind; Gr. *ἄημι*, blow, *ἀήρ*, Lat. *aer*, Eng. *air*; Lit. *vėjas*, wind; further Lat. *ventus* and Eng. *wind*.

onnchon, a standard (M'F., O'B.), so Ir., also Ir. *onchú*, leopard, E. Ir. *onchú*, banner, leopard; the idea of "leopard" is the primary one. From Fr. *onceau*, *once*, Eng. *ounce*, leopard.

onoir, respect, honour, Ir. *onóir*, E. Ir. *onóir*, *onoir*: from Lat. *honor*.

ònrachd, solitude, Ir. *aonarachd*; from *aonar*, *aon*.

òr, gold, Ir., O. Ir. *ór*, W. *aur*, Cor. *our*, Br. *aour*; from Lat. *aurum*.

òr-, prefix *air*, *oir*, confused often with the prefix **òr-,** gold; *e.g.* **òrbheart,** good (golden!) deed, which is for *oirbheart* (see *oir-*).

òrag, sheaf of corn (H.S.D.), *orag* (M'F., Arm.):

oragan, an organ, Ir., M. Ir. *organ*, E. Ir. *organ*, W. *organ*; from Lat. *organum*, Eng. *organ*.

òraid, a speech, Ir. *óraid*, prayer, oration, E. Ir. *orait*, prayer, orate; from Lat. *orate*, pray ye, *oratio*, speech.

òran, a song; this is for **auran*, from the correct and still existing form **amhran,** Ir. *amhrán*, M. Ir. *ambrán*, Manx *arrane*; from *amb*, *i.e. mu*, about, and *rann*? Ir. *amhar*, E. Ir. *amor*, music. Cf. Ir. *amhra*, eulogy, especially in verse. Cf. *amra* (Cholumcille), panegyric.

orair, a porch, (**orrar,** M'D.): "front," from *air-* or *ar-* and *air*, a reduplication really of *air*, "on-before."

òrais, a tumultuous noise (H.S.D. from MSS.):

òrd, a hammer, Ir., M. Ir. *ord*, O. Ir. *ordd*, W. *gordd*, O. Cor. *ord*, Br. *orz*, *horz*, Gallo. Brit. *Ordo-vices* (?): **ordo-s*, **urdo-s*, root *verdh*, *urdh*, raise, increase, whence or allied are Gr. *ὀρθός*, Lat. *arduus*, G. *àrd*, etc.; especially Skr. *vardhate*, raise, increase, grow. See *òrdag*. Thur. thinks it perhaps possible that Romance *urtare*, hit, thrust, Fr. *heurter*, Eng. *hurt*, are hence, and Ascoli that Fr. *ortail*, big toe (*orddu* = *ortu*), is from *òrd*, the basis of *òrdag*, q.v.

òrd, a mountain of rounded form (topographical only); from above.

òrdag, thumb, Ir. *ordóg*, O. Ir. *orddu*, g. *ordan*: **ordôs*, **urdôs*; same root as *òrd* above.

òrdugh, order, Ir. *ord*, *ordughadh*, O. Ir. *ord*, *ordaad*, ordination, W. *urdd*, *urddawd*, ordaining, Br. *urz*; from Lat. *ordo*.

organ, organ; see *oragan*.

orra, ortha, orr', or, a charm, incantation, Ir. *orrtha* (*órrtha*, Con.), *ortha*, prayer, charm (in this last sense pronounced *arrtha*), E. Ir. *ortha*, acc. *orthain*, prayer (especially in verse); from Lat. *ôrâtionem*, Eng. *oration*.

orrais, squeamishness, nausea:

os, above, Ir. *os*, *ós*, *uas*, O. Ir. *os, uas*, W. *uch*, Br. *a*, *us*; see *uasal* for root.

os, an elk, deer, Ir. *os* (O'B.), E. Ir. *os*, *oss*, W. *uch*, pl. *uchen*, bos, Corn. *ohan*, boves, Br. *oc'hen* (do.), O. Br. *ohen*, boum: **ukso-s* (for G.), **uksen-* (for Brittonic); Got. *auhsa(n)*, Eng. *ox*, *oxen*; Skr. *ukshán*, bull.

os, quoth; for *ors'*, from *or*, *ar*, say; see *arsa*.

òs, mouth of a river, harbour bar; from Norse *ôss*, river mouth; Lat. *ostium*.

osadh, desisting, Ir. *osadh*, truce, E. Ir. *ossad* (do.): **ud-sta-* "stand out"; root *sta*, stand.

osag, a blast, breeze: **ut-sâ*, root, *ut*, *vet*, *ve*, blow, as in *onfhadh*.

osan, a hose, stocking, Ir. *assan*, caliga, O. Ir. *ossa*, *assa*, soccus, W. *hosan*, Cor. *hos*; from Ag. S. *hosa*, g. *hosan*, now *hose*, *hōsen*, Norse *hosa*.

oscach, eminent, superior (Sh., O'B.), Ir. *oscách*; from *os* and *cách*.

oscarach, oscarra, bold, fierce, Ir. *oscar*, champion; from the heroic name **Oscar,** son of **Oisian** (Ir. *Oisín*, little deer or *os*, q.v.) Possibly **Oscar** stands for **ud-scaro-*, "out-cutter," root *scar* of *sgar*, q.v. Zimmer derives it from Norse *'Asgeirr*. spear of the Anses or gods, and *Oisian* from the Saxon *'Oswine*, friend of the Anses; which should give respectively *'Asgar* and *'Oisine*, but the initial vowels are both *o* short in Oscar and Oisian. Doomsday Book has Osgar.

òsd, òsda, tigh òsda, an inn, Ir. *tigh ósda*; from M. Eng. *ooste*, *hóst*, hotel, house, hospitium, through Fr. from Lat. *hospitium*. Stokes takes it direct from O. Fr. *oste*.

osnadh, a sigh, so Ir., O. Ir. *osnad*, W. *uchenaid*, *uch*, Br. *huanad*. Zimmer has analysed this into *os*, up, and *an* (root of *anail*), breath: "up-breath"; cf. Lat. *suspirium*, from *sup-spírium*, "up-breath." But consider **ok-s*, from *uk* of **och.** Cf. E. Ir. *esnad*, M. Ir. *easnadh*, song, moaning.

ospag, osmag, a gasp, sob, sigh, pang, Ir. *ospóg*, *uspóg*, *osmóg*; cf. *osnadh*. Aso *uspag*, q.v.

ospairn, gasping quickly, sobbing, sighing; from *os* and *spairn*, q.v. Cf. *uspairn*.

othail, odhail, confusion, hubbub, also (Dial., where pronounced *ow-il*), rejoicing; spelt also **foghail, fòghail**; root *gal*, as in *gal*? For *odhail*, rejoicing, cf. M. Ir. *odhach*, ceolmar, also *uidheach*, *od*, music; root *ved*; Gr. ὑδέο, sing, praise, Skr. *vadati*, sing, praise; Lit. *vadinu*, rufe, root, *ved*, *vad*, *ud*, rufen.

othar, ulcer, abscess, Ir. *othar*, sick: **putro-*; Lat. *puter*, Eng. *putrid*; root *pû*, *pu*, Eng. *foul*, etc.

òtrach, dunghill, Ir., M. Ir. *otrach*, dunghill, O. Ir. *ochtrach* (= *othrach?*), excrement: **puttr-*, root *put*, *pu*, Lat. *pûteo*, *puter*, as under *othar*. Ir. *othrach*, dung, **putr*.

P

pab, shag, refuse of flax, woolly hair, and (M'A.) tassel (= **bab**), M. Ir. *papp*, *popp*, sprig, tuft, E. Ir. *popp*, bunch, which Stokes refers to a Celtic **bobbú-*, **bhobh-nú-*, from **bhobh*, **bhabh*, Lat. *faba*, bean, Gr. πομφός, blister, πέμφιξ, bubble, Lettic *bambu*, ball, I. E. *bhembho-*, inflate. Eng. *bob*, cluster, bunch, appears in the 14th century, and Sc. has *bob*, *bab* correspondingly; the Gadelic and Eng. are clearly connected, but which borrowed it is hard to say. The meaning of **pab** as "shag, flax refuse" appears in the Sc. *pab*, *pob*. Borrowing from Lat. *papula*, pimple, root *pap*, swell, has been suggested.

pac, a pack, Ir. *paca*; from Eng. *pack*. Hence **pacarras**, a mass of confusion.

pacaid, a packet; from the Eng.

padhadh, thirst, Manx *paa*; seemingly formed by regressive analogy from the adjective **pàiteach**, thirsty, a side-form of **pòiteach**, drinking, bibulous, from **pòit**, Lat. *pôtus*, drunk. M. Ir. *paadh* is explained by Stokes as **spasâtu-*, root *spas* or *spes*, Lat. *spiro*, breathe, W. *ffun*, breath, from **sposnâ*. For phonetics see *piuthar*.

padhal, ewer, Ir. *padhal*, ewer, pail, W. *padell*, pan; from Eng. *pail*; cf. *adhal*, *paidhir*, *staidhir*, *faidhir*, *rathad*.

pàganach, heathen, Ir. *páganach*, *págánta*, M. Ir. *pagánta*; from Lat. *paganus*, villager, pagan, whence Eng. *pagan*.

pàidhneachas, a penalty, pledge; from *pàigh*, with leaning on *peanas*.

paidhir, a pair; from English *pair*, M. Eng. *peire*, Fr. *paire*, from Lat. *par*. Cf., for phonetics, *faidhir* (fair) and *staidhir* (stair).

paidir, the Lord's prayer, so Ir., M. Ir. *paiter*, O. Ir. *pater*, W. *pater*; from Lat. *pater* in *Pater noster*, etc., which begins the prayer.

paidreag, a patch, clout:

paidrean, a cluster of grapes, posy, string of beads, Ir. *paidirín*, rosary, necklace; from *paidir*.

pàigh, pàidh, pay, Ir. *paidhe*, payment; from Eng. *pay*.

pail-chlach, pavement, Ir. *páil-chlach*, stone pavement, *páil*, *pabhail*, pavement; formed from the Eng. *pave*, *pavement*.

pailleart, a box on the ear, a blow with the palm: **palm-bheart*, "palm-action," from Lat. *palma*, palm; cf. W. *palfad*, stroke of the paw, Br. *palfod*, blow on the cheek.

pàilliun, a tent, Ir. *pailliún*; from M. Eng. *pailyoun* (Barbour), *pavilon*, Fr. *pavillon*, from Lat. *papilionem*, a butterfly—tents being called after the butterfly because spread out like its wings. Stokes takes it direct from the Fr.

pailm, palm tree, Ir., M. Ir. *pailm*; from Lat. *palma*, whence Eng. *palm*.

pailt, plentiful, **pailteas,** plenty, Manx *palchys*, Cor. *pals*, plenteous, M. Br. *paout*, numerous, Br. *paot*, many, much; the G. is in all likelihood a Pictish word—a root *qalt*, I.E. *qel*, company, collection, as in *clann*, q.v.

paindeal, a panther; founded on the Eng. *panther*, M. Eng. *pantere*.

painneal, a panel, Ir. *paineul*, W. *panel*; from the Eng., M. Eng., Fr. *panel*.

painnse, a paunch; from the Sc *painch*, *pench*, Eng. *paunch*.

painntear, a snare, Ir. *painteur*, M. Ir. *painntér*; from M. Eng. *pantere*, snare for birds, O. Fr. *pantiere*. Hence Eng. *painter*, boat rope.

pàipeir, paper, Ir. *pâipeur*, W. *papyr*; from Lat. *papyrus*, whence Eng. *paper*.

paipin, poppy, Ir. *paipín*, W. *pabi*; from Lat. *popaver*, whence Eng. *poppy*.

pàirc, a park, Ir. *páirc*, W. *parc*, *parwg*; from M. Eng. *park*, *parrok*, now *park*.

pairilis, palsy, Ir., M. Ir. *pairilis*, W. *parlys*; from Lat. *paralysis*, whence Eng. *palsy*.

pàirt, a share, part, Ir. *páirt*, E. Ir. *pairt*, W. *parth*; from Lat. *pars*, *partis*, a part, whence Eng. *part*. M. Ir. *pars*, point of time less than a minute.

pàisd, a child, Ir. *páisde*; formed from M. Eng. *páge*, boy, Sc. *page*, boy, now Eng. *page*.

paisean, a fainting fit, Ir., M. Ir. *páis*, E. Ir. *paiss*, passio, suffering; from Lat. *passionem*, *patior*, suffer.

paisg, wrap; see *pasgadh*.

pait, a hump, lump, Ir. *pait*, M. Ir. *pait*, mass; also Ir. *paiteóg*, small lump of butter; from Eng. *pat*. Skeat thinks the Eng. is from the Gaelic, but the *p* is fatal to the word being native Gadelic.

pàiteag, a periwinkle (H.S.D., for Heb.):
palla, green shelf in a rock (Lewis); N. *pallr*, step, dais.
palmair, a rudder, Ir. *palmaire*; see *falmadair*.
pàlas, a palace, Ir. *pálas*, W. *palas*; from Lat. *palatium*, whence Eng. *palace*.
panna, a pan; from M. Eng. *panne*, now *pan*.
pannal, **pannan**, a band or company, also, **bannal**, q.v.; from Eng. *band*.
pàp, the pope, Ir. *pápa*, O. Ir. *papa*, W., Br. *pab*; from Lat. *papa*, father, pope, Eng. *pope*.
paracas, a rhapsody (M'A.):
paradh, pushing, brandishing; cf. *purr*.
pàrant, a parent; from Eng. *parent*.
pardag, a pannier (Arm.):
pàrlamaid, parliament, Ir. *pairliméid*, M. Ir. *pairlimint*; from Eng. *parliament*.
parraist, a parish, Ir. *parraisde*; from Eng. *parish*, M. Eng. *parische*.
pàrras, paradise, Ir. *parrthas*, O. Ir. *pardus*, W. *paradwys*, Br. *baradoz*; from Lat. *paradisus*.
partan, a crab, **portan** (Skye), Ir. *partán*, *portán*, M. Ir. *partan*; Sc. *partan*. E. Ir. *partar*, *partaing*, ruby?
pasgadh, a wrapping, covering, **pasgan**, a bundle, **pasg**, a faggot; cf. Ir. *faisg*, a pen, W. *ffasg*, bundle, which last is certainly from Lat. *fasces*,
pasmunn, expiring pang (H.S.D.); from Eng. *spasm*? H.S.D. gives also the meaning "cataclysm applied to the sores of a dying person."
peabar, **piobar**, pepper, Ir. *piobar*, W. *pubyr*; from Lat. *piper*, Eng. *pepper*, Norse *piparr*.
peacadh, sin, so Ir., O. Ir. *peccad*, g. *pectho*, W. *pechod*, Br. *pechet*; from Lat. *peccatum*, *pecco*, Eng. *peccant*.
péa-chearc, pea-hen: from the Eng. *pea*. See *peucag*.
peall, skin, hide, E. Ir. *pell*; from Lat. *pellis*, hide, allied to Eng. *fell*.
peallach, shaggy, matted in the hair, from **peall**, mat, hairy skin; see *peall* above.
peallaid, sheepskin; from Scotch *pellet*, a woolless sheepskin, Eng. *pelt*, from Lat. *pellis* through Fr.
peanas, punishment, Ir. *píonús*; from Lat. *poena*, with possibly a leaning on the English *punish*.
peann, a pen, so Ir., E. Ir. *penn*, W. *pin*; from Lat. *penna*.

pearluinn, fine linen, muslin; from Sc. *pearlin*, lace of silk or thread, Eng. *purl*, edging of lace, from Fr. *pourfiler*, Lat. *filum*, thread.

pearsa, a person, Ir. *pearsa*, g. *pearsan*, O. Ir. *persa*, g. *persine*; from Lat. *persona*, Eng. *person*.

pearsail, parsley, Ir. *pearsáil*; from M. Eng. *persil*, Eng. *parsley*.

peasair, pease, Ir. *pis*, a pea, pl. *piseanna*, W. *pys*, Br. pl. *piz*; from Lat. *pisum*, Eng. *pease*.

peasan, impudent fellow, varlet; from Eng. *peasant*.

peasg, gash in skin, chapped gashes of hands, cranny, W. *pisg*, blisters; G. is possibly of Pictish origin. The Sc. *pisket* shrivelled, has been compared.

peata, a pet, Ir. *peata*, E. Ir. *petta*; Eng. *pet*. Both Eng. and Gadelic are formed on some cognate of Fr. *petit*, little, Eng. *petty* (Stokes).

peic, a peck, Ir. *peic*, W. *pec*; from Eng. *pec*.

peighinn, a penny, Ir. *pighin*, E. Ir. *pinginn*; from Ag. S. *pending*, Norse *penningr*, now Eng. *penny*.

peilig, a porpoise; from Sc. *pellack*.

peileasach, frivolous; cf. Sc. *pell*, a soft, lazy person.

peileid, cod, husk, bag:

peileid, a slap on the head, the skull or crown of the head; in the last sense, cf. Sc. *pallet*, crown of the head, M. Eng. *palet*, head-piece. In the sense of "slap," cf. Eng. *pelt*.

peileir, a bullet, Ir. *peileur*, L. M. Ir. *pelér*: from some French descendant of Lat. *pila*, ball, and allied to Eng. *pellet*, O. Fr. *pelote*, ball, Sp. *pelote*, cannon ball.

peilisteir, a quoit, flat stone; formed from the above stem?

peillic, a covering of skins or coarse cloth, Ir. *peillic*, a booth whose roof is covered with skins, E. Ir. *pellec*, basket of untanned hide; from Lat. *pelliceus*, made of skins, from *pellis*.

peinneag, a chip of stone for filling crevices in wall; from Sc. *pinning*, *pinn* (do.), allied to Eng. *pin*.

peinnteal, a snare; another form of *painntear*, q.v.

peirceall, the jaw, lower part of the face, corner, Ir. *peirciold*, cheekblade, corner: **for-ciobhull*, "on-jaw"? See *ciobhull*.

peirigill, danger, Ir. *peiriacul*; from Lat. *periculum*.

péire, the buttocks, Ir. *péire* (O'R.); cf. Cor. *pedren*, buttock, W. *pedrain*. The word **peurs,** lente perdere (M'A.), is doubtless connected.

peireid, ferret (M'A.).

péiris, testiculi (H.S.D.); apparently from Fr. *pierre*.

peiteag, waistcoat, short jacket; from Sc. *petycot*, a sleeveless tunic worn by men, Eng. *petticoat*. Manx has *pettie*, flannel waistcoat, *peddee*, waistcoat.

peithir, a forester (**pethaire**, M'D.), **peithire**, a message boy (M'A.); cf. Sc. *peddir*, a pedlar, Eng. *pedlar*.

peithir, beithir, thunderbolt; a mythic and metaphoric use of *beithir*, q.v.

peitseag, a peach; Ir. *peitseóg*; from the Eng.

peòdar, pewter, Ir. *péatar*, W. *ffeutar*; from Eng. *pewter*. Also **feòdar**, q.v.

peucag, pea-hen, Ir. *pêacóg*, peacock (Fol.); from Eng. *peacock*.

peur, a pear, Ir. *piorra*, *péire* (O'R.), W. *peran*; from Eng. *pear*.

peurda, flake of wool off the cards in the first carding:

peurdag, piartag, a partridge, Ir. *pitrisg* (Fol.); G. is from Sc. *pertrik*, a side form of Eng. *partridge*, Lat. *perdic-em*.

peursair, perchman, shore herd (Carm.):

pian, pain, Ir. *pian*, O. Ir. *pían*, poena, W. *poen*, pain, Cor. *peyn*, Br. *poan*; from Lat. *poena*, Eng. *pain*.

pibhinn, lapwing; from Sc. *peeweip*, Eng. *peewit*. The true G. is **adharcan**, "horned one" (from *adharc*, because of the appearance of its head).

pic, pitch, Ir. *pic*, W. *pyg*; from M. Eng. *pik*, now *pitch*.

pìc, a pike, Ir. *pice*, W. *pig*, from the Eng.

piceal, pike, Ir. *picill* (Fol.); from the Eng.

pigeadh, pigidh, earthen jar, Ir. *pigín*, W. *picyn*; from Eng., Sc. *piggin*, *pig*, which is a metaphoric use of Eng. *pig*, sow.

pighe, pigheann, a pie, Ir. *píghe*; from the Eng.

pigidh, robin redbreast (H.S.D.); a confused use of Eng. *pigeon*?

pilig, peel, peeling (Dial.); from the Eng. See *piol*.

pill, a sheet, cloth, the cloth or skin on which corn is winnowed; a particular use of the oblique form of *peall*, q.v. M. Ir. *pill* or *pell* means "rug."

pill, turn, Ir. *pillim*, better *fillim* (O'B.); see *till* for discussion of the root.

pillean, pack-saddle, pillion, Ir. *pillín*, W. *pilyn*; Eng. *pillion* is allied, if not borrowed, according to Skeat. All are formed on Lat. *pellis* (see *peall*). Sc. has *pillions* for "rags"; Br. *pill* (do.).

pinne, a pin, peg, Ir. *pionn* (Lh.), W. *pin*; from M. Eng. *pinne*, now *pin*.

pinnt, a pint, Ir. *piúnt* (Fol.); from the Eng.

pìob, a pipe, a musical instrument, Ir. *píob*, E. Ir. *píp*. pl. *pipai* (Lib. Leinster), (music) pipe; from Med. Lat. *pîpa*, whence Ag. S. *pîpe*, Eng. *pipe*, Ger. *pfeife*, Norse *pípa*. W., Cor., and Br. have *pib*, pipe, similarly borrowed.

piobar, pepper; see *peabar.*

pìobull, the bible (Dial.): see *bìobull.*

pioc, pick, Ir. *piocaim*; from Eng. *pick.* Thur. thinks that W. *pigo* is ultimately from the Romance *picco* (point), Fr. *pique,* or allied thereto. Skeat takes the Eng. from Celtic; but see Bradley's *Stratmann.*

piocach, a saith, coalfish (Wh.):

piocaid, pickaxe, Ir. *piocóid*; from *pioc,* Eng. *pick,* a pickaxe, from Fr. *pic* (do.). Whether the termination is Gadelic or the Fr. word *piquet,* little pickaxe, Eng. *picket,* was borrowed at once, it is hard to say.

pìochan, a wheezing, Manx *piaghane,* hoarseness, Ir. *spiochan*; Sc. *pech, pechin,* panting, *peught,* asthmatic. Onomatopoetic. Cf. Lat. *pipire,* chirp, pipe. W. has *peuo,* pant.

pioghaid, pigheid, a magpie, Ir. *pioghaid* (Fol.), *pighead* (O'R.); from Sc. *pyat, pyet,* diminutive of *pie,* M. Eng. *pye,* now usually *mag-pie.*

piol, nibble, pluck; from Eng. *peel,* earlier, *pill, pyll,* peel, pluck, ultimately from Lat. *pellis.* Also **spiol,** q v. W. has *pilio,* peel, strip.

piollach, (1) neat, trim (M'F., H.S.D., Arm.), (2) hairy (= **peallach,** of which it is a side form, H.S.D., etc.), fretful, curious-looking (M'A.). The second sense belongs to *peallach,* the first to *piol*: "pilled."

piollaiste, trouble, vexation: "plucked" state, from *piol*?

pioraid, hat, cap; see *biorraid.*

piorbhuic, piorrabhuic, periwig, Ir. *peireabhuic*; from the Eng.

piorr, scrape or dig (H.S.D.), stab, make a lunge at one (M'A.); the first sense seems from Sc., Eng. *pare*; for the second, see *purr.*

piorradh, a squall, blast; from L. M. Eng. *pirry,* whirlwind, blast, Sc. *pirr,* gentle breeze, Norse *byrr,* root *bir, pir,* of onomatopoetic origin (Skeat, sub *pirouette,* for Eng.).

pìos, a piece, Ir. *píosa*; from Eng. *piece,* Fr. *pièce,* Low Lat. *pettium,* from Gaulish **pettium,* allied to G. *cuit,* Pictish *pet* (see *pit*).

pìos, a cup, Ir. *píosa*; from Lat. *pyxis,* box (Stokes).

piostal, a pistol, so Ir.; from Eng.

pipheanaich, giggling (M'D.):

piseach, prosperity, luck, Manx *bishagh,* Ir. *biseach,* M. Ir. *bisech.* Cf. Ir. *piseóg,* witchcraft, M. Ir. *pisóc,* charm, Manx *pishag,* charm, Cor. *pystry,* witchcraft, M. Br. *pistri,* veneficium, which Bugge refers to Lat. *pyxis,* medicine box (see *pìos*).

piseag, a kitten, Ir. *puisín*; from Eng. *puss.* Aran Ir. *piseóg,* sea bream.

pit, hollow or pit (Dict. only), κύσθος, M. G. *pit* (D. of L.), Manx *pitt*, Ir. *pit*; from Ag. S. *pyt*, pit, well, now *pit*, from Lat. *puteus*, well. For force, cf. Br. *fetan*, fountain, *fete*, κύσθος. The non-existent Dict. meaning is due to the supposed force of topographic *pit* discussed in the next article.

Pit-, prefix in farm and townland names in Pictland, meaning "farm, portion"; O. G. *pet*, *pett*, g. *pette* (B. of Deer), a Pictish word allied to W. *peth*, part, Gaelic *cuid*. See further under *cuid* and *pìos*.

piùg, a plaintive note (H.S.D); cf. W. *puch*, sigh. Onomatopoetic?

piuthar, sister, Ir. *siur*, E. Ir. *siur*, *fiur*, g. *sethar*, *fethar*, O. Ir. *siur*, W. *chwaer*, Corn. *huir*, Br. *hoar*: **svesôr*, g. *svestros* (Stokes); Lat. *soror* (= *sosor*); Eng. *sister*; Lit. *sesũ*; Skr. *svâsar*.

plab, soft noise as of a body falling into water; from Sc. *plope*, Dial. Eng. *plop*: onomatopoetic like *plump*. Skeat compares Eng. *blab*. See *plub*.

placaid, a wooden dish; through Sc. (?) from Fr. *plaquette*, *plaque*, a plate, whence Eng. *placard*, Sc. *placad*. M'A. gives also the meaning "flat, broad, good-natured female," which is a metaphoric use.

plaibean, a lump of raw flesh, a plump boy; founded on Sc. *plope*, as in *plab* above. Cf. Eng. *plump*.

plaide, a blanket, Ir. *ploid*; Eng. *plaid*, Sc. *plaiden*, coarse woollen cloth, like flannel, but twilled: all are founded on Lat. *pellis*, but whether invented by Gadelic or English is at present doubtful. Skeat says it is Celtic, a view which, as the case stands, has most to say for it; cf. G. **peallaid**, sheepskin. Dunbar's "Hieland *Pladdis*."

plàigh, a plague, Ir. *pláigh*, E. Ir. *plág*, W. *pla*; from Lat *plâga*, disaster, M. Eng. *pláge*, Eng. *plague*.

plais, a splash; from Sc. *plash*, to strike water suddenly, Eng. *plash*, *splash*.

plam, anything curdled: cf. Br. *plommein*, a clot, as of blood. See *slaman*. M'A. gives it the meaning of "fat blubber cheek." Arg. has "**bainne plumaichte**," curdled or soured milk.

plang, a plack—a Scots coin; from Sc. *plack*, a copper coin equal to four pennies Scots, which came with the Flemish, etc., and is allied to Fr. *plaque*, used of coin, though really a "metal dish, etc." See *placaid*.

plangaid, a blanket; Ir. *plainceud* (Fol.); from the Eng.

plannta, a plant, Ir. *planda*; from Eng. *plant*, Lat. *planta*.

plaosg, a husk, shell, Manx *pleayse*, Ir. *plaosg*, W. *plisg* (pl.), Br. *pluskenn*. This Ernault considers borrowed from Romance—Fr. *peluche*, shag, plush, Eng. *plush*, from Lat. **pilucius*, hairy, *pilus*, hair: an unlikely derivation. Seemingly **blaosg** is another form (Manx *bleayst*, M. Ir. *blaesc*, W. *blisg*): **bhloid-sko-*, root *bhlōi*, *bhlē*, *bhel*, swell, etc.; Gr. φλοιός (**bhlovio-* ?), bark, shell, φλέδων, bladder.

plàsd, a plaster, Ir. *plasdruighim*; from the Eng.

plàt, a sort of cloth made of straw; from Sc. *plat*, plait, Eng. *plait*. M'A. has the meaning "thrust, clap on," from Sc. *plat*, a stroke to the ground, blow with the fist, M. Eng. *platten*, strike, throw down, Ag. S. *plaettan*.

plath, pladh, a flash, glance, puff of wind; from **svḷ-*, root *svel* of *solus* ?

pleadhag, a dibble, paddle; also **bleaghan, spleadhan**, q.v.

pleadhart, a buffet, blow; from *pailleart* ?

pleasg, a noise, crack, Ir. *pléasg* (*pleasg* Lh.)—an Ir. word (M'A.), Ir. *pleasgan* or *pléascán*, noise: cf. Sc. *pleesk*, *plesk*, plash, *pleesh-plash*, dabbling in water or mud.

pleasg, a string of beads:

pleat, a plait; from Sc. *plett*, Eng. *plait*.

pleid, solicitation; see *bleid*.

pleigh, quarrel, fight, Ir. *pléidh*, debate; Sc. *pley*, quarrel, debate, all from M. Eng. *pleie*, *plege*, Ag. S. *plega*, game, fight, Eng. *play*.

pleoisg, plodhaisg, a booby, simpleton; cf. W. *bloesg*, a stammerer (*mlaisqo-*), Skr. *mlecchati*, talk barbarously, *mleccha*, foreigner, Lat. *blaesus*, Gr. βλαισός.

pleòdar, pewter; from Eng. *spelter*, with leaning on *peòdar*.

pliad (H.S.D., Dial.), a plot of ground; of Scandinavian origin—Swed. *plaetti*, a plot of ground, Eng. *plot*, *plat* (Dr Cameron).

pliadach, flat, as of foot (Carm.):

pliadh, a splay foot; from Eng. *splay*.

pliaram, babbling (H.S.D.); for **bliaram*, ; see *blialum*, from Sc. *blellum*.

plionas, a hypocritical smile (Wh.):

pliotair (**pliodaire** M'A.), a fawner, cajoler; cf. Ir. *pleadail*, pleading; from Eng. *plead*.

pliut, a clumsy foot; cf. Sc. *ploots*, the feet when bare (Shet.), *plootsacks*, feet. Hence **pliutach**, a seal. See *spliut*.

ploc, a round mass, clod, block (rare), Ir. *bloc*, a block, W. *ploc*, block, plug, Br. *bloc'h*, block, mass: Gadelic and W. are from Eng. *block*, from Fr. *bloc*, of German origin—Ger. *block*, clod, lump, from the root of Eng. *balk*.

plod, a clod; from Sc. *plod*, *ploud*, a green sod (Aberdeen).
plod, a fleet, Manx *plod*; from Norse *floti*, Eng. *fleet*, *float*, etc.
plod, a pool of standing water, Manx, Ir. *plod*; from M. Eng. *plodde*, a puddle, Eng. *plod*, originally "to wade through water," *ploud*, wade through water (Grose), Sc. *plout*, *plouter* (do.).
plodadh, parboiling; from Sc. *plot*, to scald or burn with boiling water, *plottie*, a rich and pleasant hot drink made of cinnamon, cloves, etc. Also "floating" wood down river.
ploic, the mumps; see *pluic*.
plosg, palpitate, throb, Ir. *plosg* (O'R., Fol.), *blosgadh*, sounding, E. Ir. *blosc* ("ro clos blosc-béimnech a chride," the hitting sound of his heart). See *blosg*.
plub, a plump, sudden fall into water; from Eng. *plump*. Cf. *plab*. Hence **plubraich,** gurgling, plunging; etc.
plub, an unweildy mass or lump; from the Eng. *plump*.
plubair, a booby, one speaking indistinctly, blubberer; from Eng. *blubber*.
pluc, a lump, pimple, Manx *plucan*, pimple; seemingly a side form of *ploc*. M. Ir. has *plucc*, club or mace. Cf. Sc. *pluke*, a pimple.
pluc, pluck, Manx *pluck*; from the Eng.
plùc, beat, thump; from M. Eng. *pluck*, a stroke.
plucas, the flux; founded on Lat. *fluxus*?
plùch, squeeze, compress, Ir. *pluchaim*, Manx *ploogh*, suffocation:
pluic, cheek, blub cheek, Ir. *pluc*: "puffed cheek"; from *ploc*.
pluideach, club-footed; see *pliut*.
plùirean, a flower, Ir. *plúr*; from M. Eng. *flour* (now *flower*), O. Fr. *flour* (now *fleur*).
plum, plunge into water; see *plumb*.
plùm, one who sits stock still, dead calm:
pluma, plumba, a plummet, Ir. *plumba*; from Eng. *plumb*, Fr. *plomb*, from Lat. *plumbum*, lead.
plumb, noise of falling into water, plunge; from Eng *plump*.
plumbas, plumbais, a plum, Ir. *pluma*; from M. Eng. *ploume*, now *plum*.
plundrainn, plunder, booty; from Eng. *plundering*.
plùr, flour, Ir. *flúr*; from M. Eng. *flour*; same as Eng. *flower*, *flour* being for "flower of wheat."
plutadh, falling down, as of rain; from Sc. *plout*, Belg. *plotsen*, Ger. *plotzlich*, sudden, from **plotz*, "quickly falling blow."
pobull, people, Ir. *pobal*, O. Ir. *popul*, W., Br. *pobl*, Cor. *pobel*; from Lat. *populus*, whence Eng. *people*.
poca, a bag; from Sc. *pock*, Ag. S. *poca*, Norse *poki*, O. Fr. *poche*.

pòca, pòcaid, pocket, pouch. Ir. *póca, pócait* (F. M.), bag, pouch; from M. Eng. *póke,* A. S. *poca,* as above. Eng. *pocket,* M. Eng. *poket,* is a dimunitive. K. Meyer takes the Ir. from the Norse *poki.*

pòg, pàg, a kiss, Manx *paag,* Ir. *póg,* O. Ir. *póc, pócnat,* osculum, W. *póc,* Br. *pok*; from Lat. *pâcem,* "the kiss of peace," which was part of the ritual for the Mass; hence in Church Lat. *dare pacem,* means "to give the kiss." The old Celtic liturgies generally carry the rubric "Hic pax datur" immediately before the Communion.

pòireagan, rag, rags (M'D.):

poit, a pot, Ir. *pota,* W. *pot,* Br. *pod*; from Eng. and Fr. *pot,* from Lat. *potare* ultimately. See next.

pòit, drinking, tippling, Ir. *póit*: from Lat. *pôtus,* drunk (Eng. *potation, poison,* etc.). See *òl.*

poitean, a small truss of hay or straw; see *boitean.*

poll, a pool, a hole, mud, Ir., E. Ir. *poll,* W. *pwll,* Cor. *pol,* Br. *poull*; from Late Lat. *padulus,* pool, a metathesis of *palus, paludis,* marsh (Gaidoz), whence It. *padula,* Sp. *paúl.* Teutonic has Ag. S. *pól,* Eng. *pool,* Du. *poel,* O. H. G. *pfuol,* Ger. *pfuhl.* Skeat considers that *poll* is from Low Lat. *padulis,* and that the Ag. S. *pól* was possibly borrowed from the British Latin or Latin remains seen in place-names having *port, street, -chester,* etc. (*Principles*[1] 437).

poll, pollair, nostril, Ir. *polláire, poll-sróna*; from *poll.*

pollag, the fish pollock or lythe—gadus pollachius, of the cod and whiting genus, Ir. *pullóg*; from *poll*? Hence the Eng. name. The Irish Eng. *pollan,* Sc. *powan,* is a different fish—of the salmon genus.

pollairean, the dunlin (Heb.), polidna alpina. Mr Swainson (*Folklore of British Birds*) translates its Gaelic name as "bird of the mud pits (*poll*)," an exact description, he says.

ponach, boy, lad (Dial.), **poinneach** (W. Ross); cf. Manx *ponniar,* a boy, a small fish basket? In Arg. **boinnean** (Wh.), from *boinne.* Cf. use of **proitseach.** The word is for *bonach.*

pònaidh, a pony; from the Sc. *pownie,* from O. Fr. *poulenet* (*l* lost as usual), little colt, now *poulain,* a colt, from Med. Lat. *pullanus,* from Lat. *pullus,* foal, Eng. *foal, filly.*

pònair, bean or beans, Ir. *pónaire,* M. Ir. *ponaire*; from Norse *baun,* O. H. G. *pôna,* Ger. *bohne,* Eng. *bean,* Du. *boon* (Stokes' *Celt. Dec.*).

pong, a point, note, **pongail,** punctual; see *punc.*

pòr, seed, spore, Ir. *pór,* seed, clan, W. *par,* germ; from Gr. *σπόρος,* seed, Eng. spore.

port, harbour, port, Ir. *port*, harbour, fort, O. Ir. *port*, W., Corn. *porth*, Br. *pors*, *porz*; from Lat. *portus*, Eng. *port*.

port, a tune, Ir. *port*, M. Ir. *ceudport*, rhyme, prelude: "carry = catch"; from Lat. *porto*, carry. Sc. *port*, catch, tune, is from Gaelic. Cf. Eng. *sport*, from Lat. *dis-porto*.

pòs, marry, O. G. *pústa*, wedded (B. of Deer), M. Ir. *pósaim*; from Lat. *sponsus*, *sponsa*, betrothed, from *spondeo*, I promise (Eng. *spouse*, *respond*, etc.).

post, post, beam, pillar, Ir. *posda*, *posta*, W. *post*; from the Eng. *post*, from Lat. *postis*. Pl. *puist*, slugs for shooting (Wh.).

prab, discompose, ravel (**pràb,** H.S.D.), **prabach,** dishevelled, ragged, blear-eyed, Ir. *prábach* (O'R.): "suddenly arrayed," from *prap*?

pràbar, pràbal, a rabble; from *pràb*, *prab*, discompose. See above word.

prac, vicarage dues, small tithes, which were paid in kind (N. H. and Isles), **pracadair,** tithe collector; from Sc. *procutor*, Eng. *proctor*, *procurator*.

pracas, hotch-potch; cf. Sc., Eng. *fricassee*.

pràcais, idle talk; from Eng. *fracas*?

pràdhainn, press of business, flurry (M'A. for Islay), Ir. *praidhin*, O. Ir. *brothad*, a moment; see *priobadh*.

prainnseag, mince collops, haggis; from *prann*, pound (M'A.), a side form of *pronn*, q.v.

prais, brass, pot-metal (Arm.), pot (M'A.), **pràis,** brass (H.S.D., M'L., M'E.), Manx *prash*, Ir. *práis*, *prás*, W. *pres*; from M. Eng. *bras*, Ag. S. *bræs*. Hence **praiseach,** bold woman, concubine, meretrix.

praiseach, broth, pottage, etc., Ir. *praiseach*, pottage, kale, M. Ir. *braissech*, W. *bresych*, cabbages; from Lat. *brassica*, cabbage.

pràmh, a slumber, slight sleep:

pràmh, priam, heaviness; properly "blear-eyed-ness"; cf. Ir. *srám*, eye-rheum.

praonan, an earthnut; see *braonan*.

prap, quick, sudden, Ir. *prab*, M. Ir. *prap*; see under *priobadh*.

prasach, a manger, crib, **frasach,** (M'Rury):

prasgan, brasgan, a group, flock; cf. Ir. *prosnán*, a troop, company (O'R.):

prat, a trick (Wh.); **pratail,** tricky; see *protaig*.

preachan, a crow, kite, moor-bittern, Ir. *preachan*, crow, kite, osprey (according to the adj. applied), M. Ir. *prechan*, crow, raven:

preachan, a mean orator (M'A.), Ir. *preachoine,* crier, M. Ir. *prechoineadha,* præcones; from the Lat. *praeco(n),* crier, auctioneer.

preas, a bush, brier, W. *prys,* brushwood, covert: **qrst-,* root *qer* of *crann*? The G., which is borrowed, is doubtless of Pictish origin.

preas, a press, cupboard, Manx *prest*; from the Eng. *press.*

preas, a wrinkle, fold; from the Eng. *press.*

preathal, confusion of mind, dizziness; see *breitheal.*

prighig, fry; from the Eng. *frying.*

prine, a pin; from the Sc. *preen,* M. Eng. *prēon,* Ag. S. *préon,* Norse *prjónn,* Ger. *pfriem.*

priobadh, winking, twinkling (of the eye), Ir. *prap* in *le prap na súl,* in the twinkling of the eyes (Keating), from *prap,* sudden, *preaba* in *na bi preaba na sula muich* (B of Moyra), M. Ir. *prapud,* brief space (as twinkling of the eyes), *la brafad súla,* older *friha brathad sula,* where we get the series *prapud, brafad, brathad* (g. *brotto*), O. Ir. *brothad,* moment. Stokes compares the similar Gothic phrase—*in brahva augins,* where *brahv* might = a British **brap,* borrowed into Irish. The form *brafad* could easily develop into *brap*; the difficulty is the passing of *th* of *brothad* (which gives g. *brotto*) into *f* of *brafad* (but see *Rev. Celt.*[10] 57). The G. **priobadh** has its vowel influenced by **preabadh,** kicking, that is, *breabadh,* q.v. Zim. (Zeit.[32] 223) cites *brofte,* momentary, and says *brafad* is made from *bro,* eyebrow, falsely.

priobaid, a trifle, **priobair,** a worthless fellow; from Sc. *bribour,* low beggarly fellow, M. Eng. *bribour,* rascal, thief; from O. Fr. *bribeur,* beggar, vagabond, *briber,* to beg, *bribe,* morsel of bread, Eng. *bribe.* Hence **priobaid** is from an early Northern form of Eng. *bribe.* See *breaban* further.

priomh, prime, chief, Ir. *príomh,* a principal, *primh,* prime, O. Ir. *prím,* W. *prif*; from Lat. *primus,* first, Eng. *prime.*

prionnsa, a prince, so Ir., M. Ir. *prindsa*; from M. Eng. and Fr. *prince* (Stokes takes it from Fr. direct).

priosan, prison, Ir. *príosún,* M. Ir. *prísún*; from M. Eng. *prisoun,* from O. Fr. *prison* (Stokes takes it from O. Fr. *prisun*).

pris, price, W. *pris*; from M. Eng. *prīs,* from O. Fr. *prīs,* Lat. *pretium.*

probhaid, profit; from the Eng.

procach, a year-old stag (Rob Donn):

proghan, dregs, lees:

proinn, a dinner, O. G. *proinn* (B. of Deer), Ir. *proinn,* O. Ir. *proind, praind*; from Lat. *prandium.*

pròis, pride, haughtiness; from Sc. *prossie*, *prowsie*, nice and particular, Dut. *prootsch*, *preutsch*, proud, Eng. *proud*. The Arran Dial. has *pròtail* for *pròiseil*.

proitseach, a boy, stripling; cf. **brod balaich, brodan,** boy, from *brod*. The termination is *-seach*, really a fem. one. In Arg. **propanach,** a boy, from *prop*, also **geamht.**

pronn, food; see *proinn*.

pronn, bran, Manx *pronn*; see next word. Hence Sc. *pron*.

pronn, pound, bray, mash, Manx *pronney*, pounding; see, for root and form, *bronn*, distribute, from the root *bhrud*, break, which thus in G. means (1) distribute, (2) break or crush. Hence **pronnag,** a crumb, Sc. *pronacks*.

pronnasg, brimstone; formed on Sc. *brunstane*, Norse *brennisteinn*, Eng. *brimstone*. Dial. of Badenoch has the form **pronnasdail.**

pronndal, muttering, murmuring (Dial. **brundlais**):

prop, a prop, Ir. *propa*; from Eng. *prop*.

propanach, a boy (Wh.):

prosnaich, incite; see *brosnaich*.

protaig, a trick; from Sc. *prattick*, trick, stratagem, Ag. S. *prœtt*, craft, *prœtig*, tricky, Eng. *pretty*, Norse *prettr*, a trick.

prothaisd, a provost; from the Eng.

pubull, a tent, Ir. *pupal*, g. *puible*, O. Ir. *pupall*, W. *pabell*, *pebyll*; from Lat. *papilio*, butterfly, tent, Eng. *pavilion*. See *pàilliun*.

pùc, push, jostle; from the Sc. *powk*, thrust, dig, M. Eng. *pukken*, *pouken*, *póken*, to thrust, poke, Eng. *poke*, Ger. *pochen*, knock, Dial. **fùc.**

pucaid, a pimple; see *bucaid*.

pudhar, harm, injury, Ir. *púdhar* (O'B.), M. Ir. *pudar*, E. Ir. *púdar*, *pudar*; from Lat. *pudor*, shame. Usually taken as borrowed from Lat. *pûtor*, rottenness, Eng. *putrid*.

pùic, a bribe:

puicean, a veil, covering, Ir. *puicín*:

puidse, a pouch; from the Eng.

puinneag, sorrel:

puinneanach, beat, thump; from M. Eng. *pounen*, now *pound*, Ag. S. *punian*.

puinse, punch, toddy; from Eng. *punch*.

puinsean, puision, poison; from the Eng. Manx has *pyshoon*.

pùirleag, a crest, tuft, Ir. *puirleógach*, crested, tufted (O'B., Sh.), *puirleog* (O'R.)—an Irish word. See *pùrlag*.

pulag, round stone, ball, pedestal, also **bulag**; from M. Eng. *boule*, a ball or bowl, now *bowl*, Fr. *boule*.

pulaidh, turkey cock: Fr. *poulet*.

pùlas, pot-hook (Dial.) ; see *bùlas.*

punc, a point, note, Ir. *punc,* O. Ir. *ponc,* W. *pwnc* ; from Lat. *punctum,* Eng. *point.*

punnan, a sheaf, Manx *bunney,* Ir. *punnann,* E. Ir. *punann, pundand* (Corm.) ; from Norse *bundin,* a sheaf, bundle, Eng. *bundle, bind.*

punnd, a pound, Ir. *punta, punt,* M. Ir. *punt* ; from the Eng.

punnd, a place for securing stray cattle, a pound ; from the Eng. *pound.*

punntainn, funntainn, benumbment by cold or damp ; cf. Eng. *swoon,* M. Eng. *swoghne, *swog-.* Cf. Sc. *fundy.*

purgaid, a purge, Ir. *purgóid* ; from Lat. *purgatio,* Eng. *purgation, purge.*

purgadoir, purgatory, Ir. *purgadôir,* E. Ir. *purgatoir,* Br. *purgator* ; from Lat. *purgatorium,* Eng. *purgatory.*

pùrlag, a rag, tatter, fragment :

purp, purpais, sense, mental faculty ; from Eng. *purpose.*

purpaidh, purpur, purple, Ir. *purpuir,* M. Ir. *purpuir,* W. *porphor* : from Lat. *purpura,* Eng. *purple.* The old Gadelic form, borrowed through British, is *corcur.*

purr, thrust, push ; from Sc. *porr,* thrust, stab, Du. *porren,* poke, thrust, Low Ger. *purren,* poke about ; further Eng. *pore.*

pus, a cat, Ir. *pus* ; from the Eng.

put, the cheek (Stew., H.S.D.) ; from Eng. *pout.*

put, thrust, push ; from Sc. *put,* push, thrust, M. Eng. *puten,* push, now Eng. *put.* Also G. **but, butadh.**

pùt, young of moorfowl ; from Sc. *pout* (do.), Eng. *poult,* chicken, from Fr. *poulet,* from Lat. *pulla,* a hen, *pullus,* young fowl.

pùt, a large buoy, usually of inflated sheepskin ; seemingly of Scand. origin—Swedish Dial. *puta,* be inflated ; cf. Eng. *pudding,* W. *pwtyn,* a short round body, Cor. *pot,* bag, pudding.

putag, oarpin, also **butag** ; from Eng. *butt.* Cf. *Am Buta Leòdhasach,* the Butt of Lewis.

putag, a pudding, Ir. *putóg* ; from the Eng.

putag, a small rig of land (H.S.D.) :

putan, a button, W. *botwn* ; from Eng. *button.*

puth, puff, sound of a shot, syllable ; onomatopoetic. Cf. Eng. *puff,* etc.

puthar, power (M'A.) ; from the Eng. *power.*

R

ràbach, litigious, Ir. *rábach*, litigious, bullying :

rabhadh, a warning, so Ir., E. Ir. *robuth*, forewarning : *ro* + *buth*, latter from **buto-*, root *gu*, cry, Gr. *βοή*, shout, Skr. *gu*, be heard. W. *rhybudd* is from the root *qu* (Stokes, *Rev. Celt*[12]).

rabhairt, reothairt, springtide, Manx *royart*, Ir. *romhairt*, *rabharta*, M. Ir. *robarta*, O. Ir. *robarti*, malinas, (sing. **robarte*), W. *rhyferth* : *ro* + *bertio-*, "pro-fero," root *bher* of *beir*.

rabhan, rhapsody, repetition, Ir. *rabhán*, repetition : from *ro* and **ba*, say, root, *bhâ*, Lat. *fâri*, speak, Eng. *fame, fate.*

rabhart, upbraiding, senseless talk ; from *ro* and *ber* of *abair*, say, q.v.

rabhd, idle talk : **ro-bant*, root *ba*, speak, as in *rabhan*.

rac, the ring keeping the yard to the mast, the "traveller" ; from Norse *rakki* (do.).

ràc, a rake, Ir. *rάca*, W. *rhacan* ; from M. Eng. *rake*, Eng. *rake*.

ràc, a drake ; from the Eng., earlier Eng. *endrake*. The loss of *d* is due to the article.

racadh, tearing ; see *sracadh*.

racadal, horse-radish (Sh., H.S.D., Arm.), **ràcadal** (M'E.), Ir. *rάcadal* ; see *rotacal*.

racaid, noise ; cf. the Sc., Eng. *racket*. Skeat takes the Eng. from the Gaelic, referring the G. to *rac*, to make a noise like geese or ducks. See next word.

ràcail, noise of geese (H.S.D.) ; cf. Sc. *rackle*. See next word.

ràcain, noise, riot, mischief, **ràcaireachd**, croaking, Ir. *racan* ; cf. Br. *rakat*, *rakal*, croak, *raklat*, cry as a hen ; Lat. *raccare*, cry as a tiger, Lit. *rėkti*, cry, root *rak*. The words are greatly onomatopoetic.

racan, a bandy or crooked stick ; cf. *rac*.

racas, sail hoop ; see *rac*.

rach, go, Ir. *rachad*, I will go, E. Ir. *ragat*, ibo, O. Ir. *doreg*, veniam ; root *reg*, stretch. See *éirich* for the root connections.

rachd, vexation, moan, Ir. *rachd*, a fit as of crying or tears : cf. *racaid*.

rachd, strength (Carm.) :

rachdan, a tartan plaid worn mantle-wise :

racuis, rack, roasting apparatus, Ir. *raca* ; from the Eng. *rack*, M. Eng. *racke*.

radan, a rat ; from Sc. *ratton*, M. Eng. *raton*, now *rat*.

ràdh, saying, Ir. *rádh*, O. Ir. *rád*, *ráidiu*, I speak : I. E. *rôdh-éjô* ; Got. *rôdja*, I speak ; Skr. *râdhayati*, brings about ; root *rēdh*, *rē-dh*, *rē-*, of Lat. *reor*, think, *ratio*, reason.

radharc, sight, Ir. *radharc*, E. Ir. *radarc*, *rodarc*: *ro+darc*; for *darc* see *dearc*, behold.

rag, a wrinkle, Ir. *rag* (O'B., etc.); see *roc*.

rag, stiff, benumbed, unwilling, Manx, *rag*, stiff, Ir. *rag* (Fol.); **razgo-*, root *reg*, *rag*, Lat. *rigeo*, rigid, Eng. *rack*, N. *rakr*, straight, Lit. *rezgù*, knit. Hence **rogaim** (so Ir. in Lh., etc.), sneeze-wort (Cam.).

rag, a rag; from the Eng.

ragair, extortioner, villain; from Eng. *rack*, as in *rack-rent*. Dial. G. has **rògair**, for and from "rogue."

ragha, raghadh, choice; see *roghainn*.

raghan, churchyard (Sutherland); cf. Ir. *ráth*, barrow, the same as G. *ràth*.

raghar, radhar, an arable but untilled field (H.S.D., Dial.):

ràichd, impertinence, idle prating (M'F., etc.):

ràideil, inventive, sly, Ir. *raideamhuil*, cunning, sly:

raidhlich, rag, cast off clothes (Suth.); Lat. *reliquiae*.

ràidse, a prating fellow; founded on *ràdh*?

ràinig, came, Ir. *ránaig*, O. Ir. *ránic*, vênit; for *r-ánic*, *ro-ánic*; see *tháinig*.

raip, filth, foul mouth, **raipeas**, foul mouth, **rapach**, slovenly, foul-mouthed; M. Ir. *rap*, animals that draw food to them from earth, as the pig and its like (O'Cl.), E. Ir. *rap* (Corm., *rop* for cows, etc.): *rab-tho-*, root *rab*, *srab*, Lat. *sorbeo*? Stokes gives the stem as **rapno-*, root *rap* of Lat. *rapio*, I seize. The Ger. *raffen*, seize, snatch, has also been suggested.

raisean, goat's tail:

ràite, a saying, dictum; for *ràdhte*, a participial formation.

ràiteach, covenanting, affiancing (Suth.); see *ràth*, *ràthan*.

ràith, a quarter of a year, Ir. *ráithe*, M. Ir. *raithe*: **râtio-*, from *ṝt-*, Skr. *ṛtu*, season of the year, appointed time for worship, Zend (*ratu*) do.).

ràith, a threatening:

raith, prating largely (M'D.):

raithneach, raineach, fern, Ir. *raithneach*, *raith*, W. *rhedyn*, Cor. *reden*, O. B. *raten*, Br. *raden*, Gaul. *ratis*: **pratis*; Lit. *papartis*, Russ. *paporotĭ*; Eng. *fern*.

ramachdair, a coarse fellow:

ramair, a blockhead, a romp; cf. *ramalair*.

ramasg, sea tangle:

ràmh, an oar, Ir. *rámha*, O. Ir. *ráme*, W. *rhaw*, spade, Corn. *rêv*, oar, Br. *roenv*: **râmo-*; root *ere*, *rē*, *rō*; Lat. *rêmus*, (**resmo-*); Gr. *ἐρετμός*; Eng. *rudder*; Skr. *aritras*.

ramhlair, humorous, noisy fellow; from Eng. *rambler*. Also, Badenoch Dial., **ramalair**, rambler.

ràn, roar, cry ; Skr. *râ*, bark, *raṇ*, sound, *râyaṇa*, crying ; Ch. Sl. *rarŭ*, sonitus, Lettic *rát*, scold ; and cf. Lat. *râna*, frog.

rangoir, a wrangler ; founded on the Eng.

rann, a division, portion, Ir., O. Ir. *rann*, W. *rhan*, Cor. *ran*, later *radn*, O. Br. *rannou*, partimonia : **(p)rannâ*, **pratsnâ*, root *par*, *per* ; Lat. *pars*, *partis*, *portio* ; Gr. πορεῖν, supply, πέπρωται (perf. pass. of πορεῖν).

rann, a quatrain, stave, Ir. *rann*, E. Ir. *rann*, *rand* ; from *rann* above (*rann*, stave, is mas. in E. Ir., the other *rann* is fem.).

ranndair, a murmuring, complaining (H.S.D., Dial.) ; cf. *ràn*.

rannsaich, search, scrutinize, Ir. *rannsuighim* ; from Norse *rannsaka*, search a house, ransack, whence Eng. *ransack*.

ranntair, a range, extent of territory : "division," from *rann*.

raog, a rushing (H.S.D., Dial.) ; cf. *ruaig*.

raoic, **raoichd**, hoarse sound or cry, wild roaring, as of bull ; **raibheic** (M'A.), pronounced *raoi'c*, roar : **ro-beuc*.

raoine, a young barren cow that had calf ; cf. Sc. *rhind*, as in *rhind mart*, Ger. *rind*, cattle, beeves. In Suth. *reithneach*.

raoir, **an raoir**, last night, Ir. *a raoir*, *a réir*, O Ir. *aréir*, **prei-ri*, root as in *riamh* (Asc., St.). The Skr. *râtri*, night, has been compared, but the phonetics do not suit, and also Lat. *retro*. Cf. also *earar*, *uiridh*.

raoit, indecent mirth ; from Sc. *riot* (do.), Eng. *riot*.

raon, a field, plain, road, so Ir., E. Ir. *roen*, road, O. Ir. *roe*, *rói*, plain : **roves-no-*, **roves-jâ* ? Lat. *rus*, *rûris* ; Eng. *room*. Norse *rein*, a strip of land, suggests the possibility of a Gadelic **roino-*.

rapach, dirty-mouthed ; see *raip*.

ràpach, noisy, **ràpal**, noise, Ir. *rápal*, noise, bustle ; founded on Eng. *rabble*.

ras, a shrub (M'F., not M'A. or M'E.), Ir. *ras* (O'B., etc.) :

ràsan, harsh, grating noise, loquacity, **ràsanach**, discordant, Ir. *ráscach*, clamorous, talkative ; cf *ràn* for ultimate root.

ràsdail, a rake, harrow, E. Ir. *rastal* ; from Lat. *rastellus*, rake, hoe, *rastrum*, from *râdo*, scrape, Eng. *raze*, *rash*, etc.

ràsdail, sound of frying meat ; cf. *ròsd*.

rath, prosperity, so Ir., O. Ir. *rath*, gratia, W. *rhad*, grace, favour : **rato-n*, root *râ*, give ; Skr. *râti*, gift, *râs*, *rayis*, property, Zend *râta*, gift ; Lat. *rês*.

ràth, a raft, Ir. *rathannaibh*, (on) rafts (F. M.) ; Lat. *ratis*. The root is the same as that of *ràmh* (= *ret*, *rât* here).

ràth, **ràthan**, surety, vadimonium, Ir. *rath* (O'B., O'Cl.), O. Ir. *ráth* ; cf. O. Br. *rad*, stipulationes, which Stokes equates with Ir. *rath*, and says that it is from Lat. *rătum* (*ratum facere* =

"ratify"), a derivation to which Loth objects. Hibernian Lat. has *rata* for surety. The Lat. and G. are ultimately from the same root in any case (see *ràdh*).

† **ràth,** a fortress, residence, Ir. *ráth*, E. Ir. *ráth*, *ráith*, g. *rátha*, Gaul. *ratin*, *Argento-ratum*: **râti-s*, **râto-n*; cf. Lat. *prâtum*, a mead. W. *rhath*, cleared spot; borrowed from G.? (Rhys).

rathad, a road, Ir. *ráthad*, *ród*; from M. Eng. *roade*, road, Ag. S. *rád*; cf. M. Ir. *ramhad* (O'Cl.), E. Ir. *ramut* (Corm.).

ré, the moon, Ir., O. Ir. *ré*, luna: **revi*, Skr. *ravi*, sun.

ré, time, space, Ir. *ré*, O. Ir. *ré*, g. *ree*, space: **revesi-*, the *e* form of O. Ir. *rói*, **rovesjâ*, discussed under *raon*, q.v. Hence the prep. **ré,** during, which governs the genitive.

reabh, wile, trick, **reabhair,** subtle fellow, **reabhradh,** disporting, as boys (Badenoch), Ir. *reabh* (O'Cl.), *reabhach*, mountebank, the devil, *reabhradh*, E. Ir. *rebrad*, boys playing, sporting; root *reb*, play. Bez. compares M. H. G. *reben*, move, stir, Swiss *räbeln*, to brawl, be noisy, to which add Eng. *rabble*. Cf. Zim. *Stud.*[1] 83, 84.

reachd, law, statute, so Ir., O. Ir. *recht*, W. *rhaith*, Br. *reiz*, just: **rektu-*, from the root *reg*; Lat. *rectum*, right, *rego*, rule; Eng. *right*.

reachd, a loud sob, keen sorrow, Ir. *rachd* (also G. **rachd**), E. Ir. *recht*; cf. Eng. *reck*.

reamhar, fat, Ir. *reamhar*, *ramhar*, E. Ir. *remor* (*remro-*), W. *rhef*, thick; root *rem*, to be thick; Norse *ramr*, strong, stark. Stokes gives the alternatives of M. H. G. *fram*, *vrom*, sound, brave, O. Sax. *furm*, or Gr. *πρέμνον*, stem, thick end.

reang, a wrinkle in the face: "a rib;" see *reang*, boat-rib.

reang, a rank, series; from early Sc. *renk*, M. E. *reng*, now *rank*; Ir. *ranc*, W. *rheng*, Br. *renk*; O. Fr. *renc*.

reang, a boat-rib, **rangan** (Sutherland), *reang*, a bar, pole (Carm.); from Norse *röng*, g. *rangar*, a ship-rib. See *rong*

reang, kill, starve (M'F.), E. Ir. *ringim*, I tear, *reangadh*, to hang, *reng*, piercing or tearing. See *tarruing*.

reannach, spotted, striped: "starred;" see *reannag*.

reannag, a star, Ir. *reannán*, O. Ir. *rind*, constellation, signum, sidus: **rendi-*, root *red*, *r̥d*, order; Lit. *rinda*, row, order, Ch. Slav. *rędŭ*, ordo; Gr. *ἐρηρέδεται*, fixed; Lat. *ordo* (Fick, Prellwitz).

reasach, talkative, prattling (H.S.D., Dial.), Ir. *réascach*, *ráscach*; see *rásan*.

reasgach, stubborn, irascible, restive:

reic, sell, Ir. *reic*, a sale, O. Ir. *recc*, a sale, *reccaim* (vb.), also *renim*, I sell: root *per*, through, over ("sell over sea"); Gr.

περαω, sell, pass through, *πιπράσκω*, *πέρνημι*, I sell; Lit. *pirkti*, *perkù*, buy. The Gadelic and Lit. show a secondary root *perk*, *prek*, Gadelic **(p)rek-kâ*, while O. Ir. *renim* and Gr. *περνημι* give a stem *pernā-*, *prenă-* (Ir.).

réic, roar, howl (H.S.D.):

réidh, plain, smooth, Ir. *réidh*, O. Ir. *réid*, W. *rhwydd*, O. W. *ruid*, O. Br. *roed*, M. Br. *roez*, Br. *rouez*: **reidi-*; Eng. *ready*, Ger. *bereit*, Got. *garaids*, ordered. Also O. Ir. *riadaim*, I drive, Gaul. *rêda*, waggon, allied to Eng. *ride*, Ger. *reiten*, etc.

réilig, a burying ground, Manx *ruillick*, Ir. *reilig*, *roilig*, E. Ir. *relic(c)*, *relec(c)*, O. Ir. *reilic*, cemeterium; from Lat. *reliquiæ*, relics.

réim, dominion, power, Ir. *réim*:

réim, course, order, Ir. *réim*, O. Ir. *réimm*, inf. to *rethim*, I run: **reid-s-men-*, root *reid* of *réidh*, O. Ir. *riadaim*, I drive. Strachan suggests as alternates root *rengh*, spring, leap (cf. W. *rhamu*, soar), Gr. *ρίμφα*, quickly, Ger. *ge-ring*, light, Lit. *rengtis*, hurry; or root *ret*, run (see *ruith*), **retmen*, or, rather, **ret-s-men*, which would only give *rĕmm*.

réir, **a réir**, according to, Ir. *a réir*, *do réir*; dat. of *riar*, q.v.

réis, a race; from the Eng. (H.S.D.). Cf. *réise*, span, o. E. Ir.

réis, a span, Ir. *réise*: **prendsiâ*, from *sprend*, Lit. *sprésti*, to measure a span, root *sprend* (Strachan).

reisimeid, a regiment; from the Eng.

réit, **réite**, concord, conciliation, Ir. *réidhteach*; from *réidh*, with terminal *-tio-*.

reithe, **reath**, a ram, Ir. *reithe*, E. Ir. *rethe*: **retio-*; cf. Lat. *aries* (**eriét-*), Umbrian *erietu* (from *eri-*), Gr. *ἔριφος*, etc., as in *earb*.

reodh, **reotha**, frost, Ir. *reó*, *reodhadh*, E. Ir. *reo*, *reod*, O. Ir. *réud*, W. *rhew*, Corn. *reu*, gelu, Br. *reo*, *rev*. Stokes gives the stem as **regu-*, even suggesting that the Gadelic forms are borrowed from the Cymric; O. Ir. *réud* he refers to **presatu-*. I. E. *preus*, whence Lat. *pruina*, Eng. *freeze*, has been suggested, but the vowels do not immediately suit (*preus* would give *rua-*, *ró-* or *ro-*, in G.); yet **prevo-*, a longer form (with or without *s*) of *preu-s*, can account for the Celtic forms.

reub, **riab**, tear, wound, Ir. *reubaim*, *réabaim*, E. Ir. *rébaim*, *rép-gaeth*, rending wind: **reibbo-*, root *reib*, Eng. *reap*, *ripe*, and *rip* (?). Stokes gives the stem as **reip-nó-*, root *reip* of Gr. *ἐρείπω*, dash down, Lat. *rîpa*, Eng. *rive*, *rift*, Norse *rifna*, rumpi, *rífa*, break. G. **reubainn**, rapine, leans for its form and force on Lat. *rapina*. W. *rheibio*, seize, is from Lat. *rapio*.

reubal, a rebel; from the Eng.

reudan, a timber moth; cf. O. Ir. *rétan*, recula, small thing, from *rét*, now *rud*, q.v.

reul, pl., **reultan**, star, Ir *reult*, g. *réilte*, E. Ir. *retla*, g. *retland*, *retglu*, g. *retgland* ("*rét glé*, bright thing," Corm.); perhaps *rét*, thing, and **gland*, shining, Ger. *glanz* (see *gleus*).

reumail, constant (Arms.); from *réim*, course.

reusan, reason, Ir. *reusun*, M. Ir. *résún*, from M. Eng. *reisun*, now *reason*.

reusbaid, a beggar's brat (Arran), a rascal:

ri, to, against, Ir. *re*, O. Ir. *ri*, *fri*, in composition *frith-*, *fris-*, *fre-*, W. *gwrth*, *wrth*, versus, contra, re-, Cor. *orth*, Br. *ouz*; **vṛti*, root *vert*, turn; Lat. *versus*, against, to, *verto*, turn; Eng. *-wards*, etc.

riabhach, brindled, greyish, so Ir., M. Ir. *riab*, a stripe: **reibâko-*, Lit. *raíbas*, mottled grey, Lett. *raibs*, motley, O. Pruss. *roaban*, striped.

riabhag, a lark, Ir. *riabhóg*, "grey one," from *riabhach*.

riach, cut the surface, graze. Although there is I. E. *reiko-*, notch, break (Gr. ἐρείκω, tear, Lit. *raikýti*, draw a furrow, etc., Ger. *reihe*, row, Eng. *row*), yet it seems most probable that *riach* is a variant of *strìoch*, q.v.

riachaid, a distributing:

riachlaid, tattered garment (Suth.):

riadh, interest; from an older *ríad*, running, course (see *réidh* for root). Cf. for force M. Ir. *rith*, interest: "running."

riadh, a drill (as of potatoes, Badenoch): "course, running," as in the case of *riadh* above. See *riamh*.

riadh, a snare: **reigo-*, root *rig* in *cuibhreach*?

riaghailt, a rule, Ir. *riaghail*, O. Ir. *riagul*, *riagol*; from Lat. *rêgula*, Eng. *rule*. Hence also **riaghail**, rule thou.

riaghan, a swing, swinging; cf Ir. *riagh*, gallows, *riaghadh*, hanging, gibbeting, O. Ir. *riag*, gibbet. Cf. *riadh*, snare.

riamh, a drill (of potatoes, turnips, etc., M'A. for Skye); see *riadh*. H.S.D. gives the meaning of "series, number," Ir. *ríomh*, O. Ir. *rím*, number, W. *rhif*, as in *àireamh*, q.v.

riamh, ever, before, Ir. *riamh*, O. Ir. *riam*, antea: **reimo-*, *preimo-*, I. E. *pri*, *prî*, belonging as a case to *pro*, before, and *per*; Lat. *pri-* (in *pris cus*, *primus*, etc.), Lith. *pri*, Got. *fri-*, See *roimh*.

rian, order, mode, sobriety, Ir. *rian*, way or path, E. Ir. *rian*, way, manner: **reino-*, root *rei*; Lat. *rîtus*, Eng. *rite* (Strachan).

riar, will, pleasure, Ir. *riar*, O. Ir. *riar*, voluntas: **prîjarâ* (Stokes), root *prî*, love, please; Eng. *friend*, Got. *frijon*, to love ; Ch. Sl. *prijati*, be favourable ; Skr. *prîyate*, be gratified, *prîṇâti*, enjoy.

riasail, tear asunder, **riasladh**, mangling, tearing asunder: **reik-so-*, root *reik*, notch, break ; Gr. *ἐρείκω*, tear ? Cf *riastradh*, *riach* ; and *riaghan*, a swing.

riasg, dirk-grass, morass with sedge, land covered with sedge or dirk-grass, Manx *reeast*, wilderness, Ir. *riasg*, moor or fen, E. Ir. *riasc*, morass ; **reisko-* ; cf. Lat. *rûscum* (**roiscum* ?), butcher's broom, Eng. *rush*. Sc. *reesk*, coarse grass, marshy land, is from G.

riasglach, a mangled carcase (H.S.D., Dial.) ; from stem of *riasail*.

riaspach, **riasplach**, confused, disordered ; see next word.

riastradh, turbulance, confusion, wandering, E. Ir. *ríastrad*, distortion. For root, cf. *riasail*. W. *rhywstro*, obstruct (Hend.).

riatach, wanton, illegitimate ; cf. Eng. *riot*.

rib, hair, snare, Ir. *ribe*, *ruibe*, hair, whisker. See next words.

ribeag, rag, tassel, fringe, **ribean**, riband, Ir. *ribeóg*, rag, tassel, *ribleach*, a long line, anything tangled, *ribín*, riband ; from M. Eng. *riban*, O. Fr. *riban* (Br. *ruban*).

ribheid, a reed, bagpipe reed, musical note, Ir. *ribheid* ; from M. Eng. *rēod*, now *reed*.

rìbhinn, **rìoghann**, a nymph, young lady, quean, Ir. *ríoghan*, queen, E. Ir. *rígan*, a derivative of *rìgh*, king. Gaelic leans, by proper etymology, on *rìgh-bhean*.

rideal, a riddle ; from the Eng.

ridhe, field, bottom of a valley (H.S.D.) ; better **righe**. See *ruighe*.

ridir, a knight, Ir. *ridire*, E. Ir. *ritire*, W. *rheidyr* ; from Ag. S. *ridere*, horseman, *ridda(n)*, knight, Ger. *ritter*, knight, Norse *riddari*, rider, knight ; from the verb *ride* (see *réidh*).

rìgh, a king, Ir. *rígh*, O. Ir. *rí*, g. *ríg*, W. *rhi*, Gaul. *-rix*, pl. *-riges*: **rêks*, g. *rêgos* ; Lat. *rex*, *rêgis* ; Got. *reiks*, ruler, Eng. *rich*, *-ric* ; Skr. *râj*, King, our *rajah*.

righ, stretch (on a death bed), Ir. *righim*, stretch, reach, E. Ir. *rigim*, Lat. *rego*, etc., as under *righinn*.

righil, a reel, dance ; see *ruithil*.

righinn, tough, pliant, tenacious, Ir. *righin* : **reg-eni-* ; root *reg*, stretch, Gr. *ὀρέγω*, stretch, Lat. *porrigo*, *rego*, etc. See *éirich*.

rinn, a point, promontory, Ir. *rind*, O. Ir. *rinnd*, *rind*, W. *rhyn*, *penrhyn*, cape. It has been analysed as *ro-ind*, " fore-end," E. Ir. *ind*, end, Eng. *end*. Cf. *reannag*, however.

rinn, did, Ir. *rinn*, O. Ir. *rigni*, fecit ; from *ro* and *gni* of *nì*, will do, q.v. See also *gnìomh*.

riochd, appearance, form, Ir. *riochd*, O. Ir. *richt*, W. *rhith* : **riktu-*, **ṛktu-* (?) ; for root, see that of *dorch*.

riodag, kind of sea-gull (Lewis) ; N. *rytr*, sea-gull.

rioluinn, a cloud (Smith) :

riof, the reef of a sail ; from the Eng.

riofa, brimstone (Munro's Gr.) :

rìomhach, fine, costly, handsome, Ir. *rímheighe*, finery, delicateness : **rîmo-*, "measured" ; root *rîm* of *àireamh* ?

rionnach, **reannach**, a mackerel : "streaked, spotted," from *reann*, star, constellation. See *reannag*.

riopail, mangle, tear (H.S.D.) ; founded on Eng. *rip*.

riplis, weakness in the back (Suth.) ; Sc. *ripples*.

rìreadh, **a rìreadh**, really, in earnest, Ir. *ríreadh*, *da ríreadh* or *ríribh*, revera ; from **ro-fhìr*, very true ?

risteal, a surface plough, used in the Hebrides, drawn by one horse and having a sickle-like coulter, Sc. *ristle* ; from the Norse *ristill*, ploughshare, from *rísta*, cut.

rithisd, **rithis**, **ris**, **a rithisd**, etc., again, Ir. *arís*, O. Ir. *arithissi*, *afrithissi*, rursus. Ascoli suggests **frith-éisse*, from *éis*, vestigium (see *déis*). Others have derived it from **ar-fithis*, O. Ir. *fithíssi*, absidas, *fithis*, a circle, orbit. The *a* at the beginning is for *ar-* : **ar-frithissi*, that is, *air*, by, on, q.v. The root may well be *sta*, stand, reduplicated to **sistio-* : thus **frith(sh)issi-*, "resistere, backness."

ro, very, Ir. *ró*, O. Ir. *ro-*, W. *rhy-*, Br. *re*, O. Br. *ro-*, *ru-*, Gaul. *ro-* (*Ro-smerta*, *Ro-danos*, etc.) : **ro-*, **pro-*, which is both a verbal and an intensive particle ; Lat. *pro* ; Gr. *πρό*, before ; Eng. *fore*, *for* ; Skr. *pra*, before.

ròb, coarse hair ; founded on Eng. *rope*.

robair, a robber ; from the Eng. The Ir. has *robail* for "rob."

robhas, notification, information about anything lost ; cf. **robhadh** for root, the old form of *rabhadh*, q.v.

robhd, a runt ; Eng. *rout* ?

roc, a rock ; from the Eng. *roc*, a tempest covered rock (Heb.), so M'K., who derives from N. *rok*.

roc, a wrinkle, crease, Ir. *rocán*, *rug* ; from the Norse *hrukka*, wrinkle, fold, Eng. *ruck*, fold (Thurneysen). See *rug*.

ròc, a hoarse voice ; founded on the Norse *hrókr*, rook, croaker, G. *ròcas*, crow, Norse *hrókr*, rook. W. has *rhoch*, grunt, groan, Br. *roc'ha*, which Stokes refers to **rokka*, Gr. *ρέγκω*, snore.

rocail, tear, corrugate ; in the latter sense, it is from *roc*, wrinkle, and, probably, the first meaning is of the same origin. See, however, *racadh*.

ròcas, a crow; from Norse *hrókr*, rook, M. Eng. *rook*, Ag. S. *hróc*.

ròchd, a cough, retching (Dial.); see *ròc*.

ròd, a way, road, Ir. *ród*, E. Ir. *ród*; from Ag. S. *rád*, M. Eng. *rode*, now *road*.

ròd, a quantity of sea-weed cast on the shore; cf. Ir. *ród*, a cast, shot (O'R.), E. Ir. *rout*.

ròd, a rood (of land or mason-work); from the Eng.

rodach, sea-weed growth on timber under water; cf. *ròd*, sea weed.

rodaidh, ruddy, darkish, M. Ir. *rotaide*: **rud-do-*, root *rud*, *roud* of *ruadh*, q.v.

ròg, **rògair**, a rogue; from the Eng.

roghainn, a choice, Ir. *rogha*, g. *roghan*, E. Ir. *rogain*, n. pl., O. Ir. *rogu*: **ro-gu*, root *gu*, *gus* of *taghadh*, q.v. Stokes gives the stem as **rogôn* and the root as *rog*, which (*Bez. Beit.*[18]) he correlates with Lat. *rogo*, ask. Bez. suggests Lit. *rogáuti*, to cost.

ròib, fifth, squalid beard, filth about the mouth; cf. *ròpach* for root.

ròic, a sumptuous but unrefined feast; seemingly founded on the Sc. *rouch* as applied to a feast—"plentiful but rough and ready."

ròic, tear (H.S.D.; Sh. and Arm. have *roic*); see *rocail*.

roid, bog myrtle, Ir. *rideog* (O'R.), M. Ir. *raidleog*, darnel, *raideog*, bogmyrtle (St.): **raddi*. Cf. *ras*.

roid, a race before a leap, a bounce or spring: **raddi-*, **raz-di-*, root *ras*, as in Eng. *race*?

roilean, snout of a sow; really the "rolled" up part of the snout, and so possibly from Eng. *roll*.

roileasg, a confused joy, **roille**, a fawning or too cordial reception; cf. Ir. *róthoil*, exceeding pleasure, from *toil*, will. Also G. **roithleas**.

roimh, before, Ir. *roimh*, O. Ir. *rem-*: **(p)ṛmo-* (Stokes), root *per*, as in *ro* (=*pro*); in form, nearest allied to Eng. *from*, Got. *fruma*, Lit. *pirm*, before. In the pronominal compounds, where *s* begins the pronoun, the *m* and *s* develop an intermediate *p* coincident with the eclipse of the *s*: *rompa* = **rom-p-shu*, where *su* = *sôs* (see *sa*).

ròin, **ròineag** (also **ròinn**, **ròinneag**), Ir. *róine*, *róinne*, a hair, especially a horse hair, W. *rhawn*, coarse long hair, Cor. *ruen*, Br. *reun*, a hair, bristle, Skr. *roman*, hair, etc.: **râni-*; cf. Ir. *ruain*, hair of tail of cow or horse, *ruainne*, a hair.

roinn, division, share, Ir. *roinn*, M. Ir. *roinded*, divided: **ranni-*, an *i* stem from from *rann*, q.v.

ròisead, rosin ; from the Sc. *roset*, Eng. *rosin*.
roiseag, a small potato (M'D.) :
ròiseal, surge of a wave, the impetus of a boat, an assault, boasting ; from the Sc. *roust*, strong tide or current, Norse *röst*, a stream or current in the sea. In the sense of "boast," it is from Sc. *rouse*, *roose*, Norse *rausan*, boasting.
ròisgeul, a romance, rhodomontade ; from *ro*, very, and *sgeul*, a tale, q.v.
ròist, roast, Ir. *rósdaim*, W. *rhostio* ; from the Eng. *roast*, O. Fr. *rostir*, from O. H. G. *rôst*, craticula.
roithlean, a wheel, pulley, Ir. *roithleán* ; from *roth*, q.v.
rol, rola, a roll, volume, Ir. *rolla* ; from M. Eng. *rolle*, O. Fr. *rolle*, Lat. *rotula* ; now Eng. *roll*.
ròlaist, a romance, exaggeration ; cf. Sc., Eng. *rigmarole*.
ròmach, hairy, rough :
romag, meal and whisky (Sutherland) :
ròmhan, wild talk, raving, rigmarole (Dial.) ; from Eng. *row* ? from *Roman* ? Cf. W. *rhamant*, romance, Ir. *ramàs*, romance.
ròn, the seal, Ir. *rón*, O. Ir. *rón* (before 900), W. *moelron* : **râno-*; Lettic *rohns*, seal (W. Meyer, *Zeit.*[28] 119). Stokes holds *rón* as an old borrow from Ag. S *hron* or *hrón*, *hrán*, whale, while the Lit. *rùinis*, Lettic *rõnis*, seal, must be from Teutonic. Zimmer suggests Norse *hreinn*, reindeer, Ag. S. *hrán*. Cf. names *Rónán*, *Rónóc*, *Mac Ronchon*.
rong, a joining spar, rung, boat-rib, **rongas, rungas** (Dial.), Ir. *runga* ; from M. Eng. *ronge*, rung of a ladder, *runge*, Ag. S. *hrung* ; now Eng. *rung* ; N. *röng*, main rafter, pole. The words *reang* and *rang* or *rangan*, "boat-rib," are from the Norse.
rong, the vital spark, life :
rongair, a lounger ; cf. next word.
rongair, rong, a lean person ; from *rong*, rung : "like a ladder." The Sc. has *rung* in this sense : "an ugly, big-boned animal or person"
ronn, a slaver, a spittle, E. Ir. *ronna*, running of the nose : **runno-*; cf. Eng. *run*.
ròp, a rope, Ir. *rópa* ; from M. Eng. *rope*, *roop*, Ag. S. *ráp* ; now Eng. *rope*.
ròpach, slovenly, squalid, Ir. *rúpach*, a young slut : **roub-tho-* ; cf. Eng. *rub*.
ròram, dealing extensively with a family in provisions, etc. ; liberality (M'A.) :
ros, seed, **ros lìn,** flax seed (Armstrong's only use for it), Ir. *ros*, flax seed, M. Ir. *ros*, genealogy, E. Ir. *ross lín*, flax seed

(Corm.), *ros*, genealogy, to which Strachan compares Got. *frasts*, for *fra-sət-s*, from *pro-sto* (Stokes), a child. A usual word for seed is **fras**, which also means a "shower," but both are ultimately from **verso*, flow, whence Gr. ἕρση, ἔρση, dew, and ἄρσην, male. Dr. Cameron compared Gr. πράσον, leek (**pr̥so*), Eng. *furze*.

ros, a promontory, Ir. *ros*, promontory (North Ireland), wood (South Ireland ; its usual Ir. meaning), E. Ir. *ross*, promontory, wood ; in the former sense from **pro-sto-s*, "standing out before," root *sta*, stand, Lat. *sto*, Eng. *stand*, etc. ; especially Skr. *prastha*, plateau. In the sense of "wood," *ros* is generally regarded as the same word as *ros*, promontory, explained as "promontorium nemorosum," with which is compared W. *rhos*, a moor, waste, coarse highland, Br. *ros*, a knoll.

ròs, rose, Ir, *rósa*, M. Ir. *rós*, W. *rhosyn* ; from the M. Eng. *rose*, Ag. S. *róse*, from Lat. *rŏsa*. The word *ròs* has also the metaphoric meaning of "erysipelas."

ròs, knowledge (Carm.) :

rosad, mischance, evil spell : **pro-stanto-*, "standing before, obstruction," root *sta*. Cf. *faosaid*.

rosg, an eye, eyelid, Ir. *rosg*, O. Ir. *rosc*, oculus : **rog-sko-*, root *reg*, *rog*, see, Ir. *réil*, clear (**regli-*) ; Lit. *regiù*, I see (Bez. apud Stokes). See *dorch*.

rosg, incitement (to battle), war ode, Ir. *rosg*, E. Ir. *rosc* : **ro-sqo-*, root *seq*, say, as in *sgeul*, *cosg*, q.v.

rot, a belch, bursting as of waves (H.S.D., Dial.) ; from Fr. *rot*.

rotacal, horse radish ; from Sc. *rotcoll*.

rotach, a rush at starting, a running :

rotach, rough weather, *rótach* ? (Lewis) ; N. *róta*, storm.

rotach, a hand rattle to frighten cattle :

rotach, a circle of filth on one's clothes (M'A. for Islay), **rotair**, a sloven :

rotadh, cutting, dividing ; from Sc. *rot*, lines drawn on the ground to show the work to be done, to furrow, rut ; cf. Eng. *rut*.

rotal, a ship's wake ; cf. Eng. *rut*, *route*, Lat. *ruptâ*.

roth, a wheel, Ir., O. Ir. *roth*, W. *rhod* (f.), Br. *rod* : **roto-*, root *ret*, *rot* ; Lat. *rota*, wheel ; Ger. *rad* ; Lat. *rátas*, Lett. *rats* ; Skr. *ráthas*, waggon. Same root as *ruith*, q.v. Hence **rotha**, a roll (of tobacco), **rothaich**, roll thou, swathe.

rotha, a screw or vice :

ruadh, red, ruddy, Ir. *ruadh*, E. Ir. *rúad*, W. *rhudd*, Corn. *rud*, Br. *ruz* : **roudo-* ; Lat. *rûfus*, *rûber* ; Gr. ἐρυθρός ; Got. *rauþs*. Ag. S. *réad*, Eng. *red* (Sc. *reid*, *Reid*) ; Lit. *raudà*, red colour.

ruag, pursue, **ruaig**, flight, Ir. *ruaig* (n.), E. Ir. *ruaic*: **rounko-*, *rouk*, root *rou*, Lat. *ruo*, rush, fall.

ruaim, a flush of anger on the face, Ir. *ruaim*, *ruamnadh*, reddening: **roud-s-men*, from **roud* of *ruadh*.

ruaimhsheanta, hale and jolly though old (M'A. for Islay):

ruaimill, rumble (M'A.); from the Eng.

ruaimle, a dry pool, muddy water (Sh.), Ir. *ruaimle*. In G. the word means also the same as *ruaim* above, whence indeed *ruaimle* as "muddy pool" may also be. Cf. Sc. *drumblie*.

ruaimneach, strong, active, M. Ir. *ruamach*, E. Ir. *rúamna* (?): **rous-men-*; Lat. *ruo*, rush.

ruais, a rhapsody (M'A.):

ruamhair, dig, delve, Ir. *rómhairim*, *róghmhar*, digging, E. Ir. *ruamor*; root *rou*, *reu*, *rû*, dig; Lat *ruo*, dig, *rûta*, minerals; Lit. *ráuti*, dig up.

ruapais, rigmarole (M'A.):

ruathar, violent onset, skirmish, spell, so Ir., E. Ir., *rúathar*, W. *rhuthr*, impetus, insultus: **routro-*, root *rou*, to rush on; Lat. *ruo*, rush.

rub, rub; from the Eng.

rùbail, a tumult, rumbling (M'A.); formed on Eng. *rumble*.

ruc, **rucan** (H.S.D., M'A.), **rùc**, **rùcan** (M'E., etc.), a rick of hay; from Sc. *ruck*, Eng. *rick*, *ruck*, Norse *hraukr*, heap.

rucas, jostling kind of fondness:

rùchan, **rùcan**, the throat, wheezing; cf. Sc. *roulk* (= *rouk*), hoarse, Fr. *rauque*, hoarse, from Lat. *raucus*.

rùchd, a grunt, belch, rumbling noise; from Lat. *ructo*, belch, *erûgere*, spit out, Lit. *rúgiu*, belch. Cf. Sc. *ruck*, belch.

rud, a thing, Dial. **raod** (Arg., Arran), **rudach** (Arran **raodach**), hospitable, Ir. *rud* (g. *roda*), *raod*, O. Ir. *rét*, g. *réto*: **rentu-s*; Skr. *rátna*, property, goods; also root *rá* of *rath*, q.v.

rùdan, a knuckle, a tendon: **runto-*:

rudha, a promontory, Ir. *rubha*, E. Ir. *rube*: **pro-bio-*, "being before;" from root *bu* of the verb "to be; see *bi*.

rudha, a blush, E. Ir. *ruidiud*; from root *rud*, a short form of *roud* in *ruadh*, q.v.

rudhag, **rùdhag** (Suth.), a crab, partan:

rudhagail, thrift (M'A.):

rùdhan, a small stack of corn (H.S.D., M'E.); see *rùthan*, peat heap, with which and with *rùcan* this form and meaning are made up.

rùdhrach, searching, groping, Ir. *rúdhrach*, a darkening:

rug, wrinkle, Ir. *rug*; from Norse *hrukka*, a wrinkle, fold, Eng. *ruck*, a crease.

rug, caught, Ir. *rug*, E. Ir. *ruc*, *rucc*, tulit, O. Ir. *rouic* : **ro* + *ucc*-, where *ucc* = **ud-gos-a*, root *ges*, carry, Lat. *gero*, *gestum*. See *thug*.

ruga, rough cloth (M'A.); from Eng. *rug*, M. Eng. *ruggi*, hairy, Swed. *ruggig*.

rugadh, a greedy grasping of anything; from Sc. *rook*, deprive of, *rookit*, cleared out.

rugaid, a long neck (H.S.D.):

rugair, a drunkard (H.S.D. says Dial., M'A. says N.); from the Eng. For phonetics, cf. *ràc*, drake.

rugha, a blush; see rather *rudha*, but *rucce* (Corm.) shame, reddening (O'Cl.).

ruic, undesirable fondness (M'D.):

ruicean, a pimple: **rud-ki*-, from *rud*, *roud*, red, as in *ruadh*.

ruidhil, **ruidhle** (Arg.), a dance; see *ruithil*.

ruidhil, a yarn reel; from M. Eng. *reel*, *hréol*, Ag. S. *hréol*.

ruidhleadh, rolling; from *ruith*, *roth*.

ruidhtear, a glutton, riotous liver; from Eng. *rioter*.

ruididh, merry, frisky, Ir. *ruidéiseach*, from *ruidéis*, a sporting mood. Cf. *ruidhtear*.

ruig, half castrated ram; from Eng. *rig*, *ridgeling*.

ruig, reach, arrive at, O. Ir. *riccim*, *riccu*; from *ro* and *iccim*, for which see *thig*. Hence **gu ruig**, as far as, O. G. *gonice* (B. of Deer), E. Ir. *corrici*.

ruighe, an arm, forearm, Ir. *righ*, E. Ir. *rig*, forearm: **regit*-, root *reg*, stretch, Lat. *rego*, etc. See *ruigheachd*.

ruighe, the outstretched part or base of a mountain, shealing ground, E. Ir. *rige*, *rigid*, a reach, reaches; from the root *reg*, stretch, as in the case of the foregoing words.

ruigheachd, **ruighinn**, reaching, arriving, Ir. *righim*, I reach, inf. *riachdain*, *rochdain*, E. Ir. *rigim*, porrigo: **regô*; Lat. *rego*, *erigo*, *porrigo*, I stretch; Gr. ὀρέγω, stretch; further is Eng. *right*, etc. See *éirich*.

uighean, wool-roll ready to spin; from the same root as *ruighe*.

uinn, a point; see *rinn*.

uinnse, a long stick or stake, an animal's tail, rump:

uinnse, a rinsing, rinser; from Eng. *rinse*.

uis, a rash; formed from the Eng. Cf. Lit. *russus*, root *rud*.

uiteach, ruddy, E. Ir. *rutech*: **rud-tiko*-, from *rud*, *roud* of *ruadh*. (Stokes *Rev. Celt.*[8] 366) explained it as **rudidech*, but this would give G. *ruideach*.

uith, run, Ir. *riothaim*, O. Ir. *rethim*, perf. *ráith*, inf. *rith* (d. *riuth*), W. *rhedu*, to run, *rhed*, race, Br. *redek*, Gaul.

petor-ritum, four wheeler: **retô*; Lit., Lett. *ritù*, I roll; Lat. *rota*, wheel, *rotula*, Eng. *roll*, Lat. *rotundus*, Eng. *round*. See *roth*.

ruithil, a reel, dance, also **righil, ruidhil**: **retoli-*, root *ret*, run, wheel, as in *ruith*; Lat. *rotula*, little wheel, *rotulare*, revolve, Eng. *roll*. Hence Eng. *reel* (Skeat). The borrowing may be, however, the other way, and Eng. *reel*, dance, be the same as *reel*, a spindle or bobbin. **roteli*?

rùm, a room, Ir. *rúm*, M. Ir. *rúm*, floor (O'Cl.); from the Eng.

rumach, a marsh:

rumpull, the tail, rump; from the Sc. *rumple*, Eng. *rump*.

rùn, intention, love, secret, Ir., O. Ir. *rún*, W. *rhin*: **rûnes-*; Got., O. H. G., Norse *rúnar*, Eng. *runes*; Gr. ἐρευνάω, seek out; root *revo*, search.

rùsal, search, turn over things, scrape, **rùsladh, risleadh**, rustling, moving things about (Perth); from Eng. *rustle*; for ultimate root, see above word.

rùsg, a fleece, skin, husk, bark, Ir. *rusg*, O. Ir. *rúsc*, cortex, W. *rhisg*, cortex, Cor. *rusc*, cortex, Br. *rusgenn*, *rusk*, bark: **rûsko-*; whence Fr. *ruche*, beehive (of bark), O. Fr. *rusche*, *rusque*, Pied. *rusca*, bark. Stokes thinks the Celtic is probably an old borrow from the Teutonic—M. H. G. *rusche*, rush, Eng. *rush*, rushes; but unlikely. The Cor. and Br. vowel *u* does not tally with Gadelic *û*; this seems to imply borrowing among the Celts themselves.

rùta, a ram, ridgling; from Norse *hrútr*, ram.

rùtachd, rutting: from the Eng.

rutaidh, surly (Carm.): *rut*, ram (Carm.).

rùtan, the horn of a roebuck:

ruth, desire (Carm.):

rùthan (better **rùghan**), a peat heap (=*dais*); from the Norse *hrúgi*, heap.

rutharach, quarrelsome, fighting (H.S.D. marks it obsolete Arms.), Ir. *rútharach* (O'R.); from *ruathar*.

S

-sa, -se, -san, emphatic pronominal particle attached to personal pronouns and to nouns preceded by the possessive pronouns **mi-se**, I myself, **thu-sa, sibh-se, i-se** (she), **e-san, iad-san mo cheann-sa, a cheann-san**, his head. So also modern Ir. save that *esan* is *ésean*: O. Ir. *-sa*, *-se* (1st Pers.), *-su*, *-so*, pl. *-si* (2nd Pers.), *-som*, *-sem* (3rd Pers. *m.* and *n.*, sing., and pl. *-si* (3rd Pers. *f.*). All are cases of the pronominal root *so-*, *-se* Gr. ὁ, the (=σο); Ag. S. *se*, the (m.), Eng. *she*. See *so*, *sin*

sabaid, a brawl, fight; see *tabaid*:
Sàbaid, Sabbath, Ir. *Sabóid*, M. Ir. *sapoit*; from Lat. *sabbatum*, whence Eng. *sabbath*; from Hebrew *shabbáth*.
sabh, sorrel, Ir. *samh*; better *samh*, q.v.
sabh, ointment, salve; from Sc. *saw*, Eng. *salve*.
sàbh, a saw, Ir. *sábh*; from the Eng.
sàbhail, save, Manx *sauail*, Ir. *sabhailim* (*sábhálaim*, O'B.); from Lat. *salvare*, to save. Kuno Meyer says from Eng. *save*.
sabhal, a barn, so Ir., M. Ir. *saball*, Ir. Lat. *zabulum*; through Brittonic from Lat. *stabulum*, a stall, Eng. *stable*. Cf. M. Ir. *stéferus* = zephyr.
sabhd, a lie, fable (H.S.D., Dial.), straying, lounging; cf. *saobh*.
sabhs, sauce, Ir. *sabhsa*; from the Eng.
sabhsair, a sausage; founded on the English word.
sac, a sack, Ir. *sac*, E. Ir. *sacc*, W. *sach*; from Ag. S. *sacc*, Eng. *sack*, Got. *sakkus*, Lat. *saccus*.
sac, a load, burden, Ir. *sacadh*, pressing into a sack or bag, Low Lat. *saccare* (do.); from Fr. *sac*, pillage, the same as Eng. *sack*, plunder, all borrowed from *saccus*, a sack or bag.
sachasan, sand-eel:
sad, dust shaken from anything by beating, a smart blow, **sadadh,** dusting, beating.
sad, aught (M'D.: Cha 'n' eil sad agam, I have naught):
sagart, a priest, Ir. *sagart*, O. Ir. *sacart*, *sacardd*; from Lat. *sacerdos*, whence Eng. *sacerdotal*.
saidealta, soidealta, shy, bashful, Ir. *soidialta*, rude, ignorant; from *sodal*, q.v.
saidh, an upright beam, prow of a ship, a handle or the part of a blade in the handle:
saidh, bitch; see *saigh*:
saidh, saidhean, the saith fish (Arg.); from N. *seiðr*, the gadus virens, now *sei*.
saidhe, hay; formed from the Eng. *hay* by the influence of the article (*an t-hay* becoming a supposed de-eclipsed *say*).
saidse, sound of a falling body, a crash, noise (Badenoch Dial. **doidse,** a dint):
saigean, a corpulent little man:
saigh, a bitch, Ir. *saith* (Con., Lane, etc.), *sagh*, *saighín* (O'Br.), M. Ir. *sogh*, *sodh*, E. Ir. *sod*, bitch, she-wolf:
saighdear, soldier, archer, Ir. *sáighdiur* (do.), M. Ir. *saigdeoir*, sagittarius, W. *sawdwr*, soldier; from M. Eng. *soudiour*, *sougeour*, Sc. *sodger*, now *soldier*, confused in Gadelic with an early borrow from Lat. *sagittarius*, archer.
saighead, an arrow, so Ir., O. Ir. *saiget*, W. *saeth*, Cor. *seth*, Br. *saez*; from Lat. *sagitta*. For root see *ionnsuidh*.

sail, a beam, Ir. *sail* : **spali-*, allied to Ger. *spalten*, split, Eng. *spill*, *split*.

sàil, a heel, Ir., O. Ir. *sál*, W. *sawdl*, Br. *seuzl* : **sâtlâ*. Ascoli has lately revived the old derivation from **stâ-tlô-*, root *sta*, stand; but *st* initial does not in native words became *s* in Gadelic.

saill, fat or fatness, Ir. *saill*, fat, bacon, pickle : **saldi-*; Eng. *salt*, etc.; Lit. *saldùs*, sweet. See *salann* further.

saill, salt thou, Ir., O. Ir. *saillim*, condio, **saldio*, salt : **salni-*; see *salann*.

sailm, a decoction, oak-bark decoction to staunch blood, a consumption pectoral; founded on M. Eng. *salfe*, now *salve ?*

sàimhe, luxury, sensuality, Ir. *sáimhe*, peace, luxury, E. Ir. *sáim*, pleasant : **svadmi-*; Eng. *sweet*, Gr. ἡδύς, etc. But cf. *sàmhach*.

saimir, the trefoil clover (A. M'D.), Ir. *seamar*; see *seamrag*.

sainnseal, a handsel, New Year's gift; from Sc. *handsel*, M. Eng. *hansell*, *i.e.* *hand-sellan*, deliver.

saith, the back bone, joint of the neck or backbone, Ir. *saith*, joint of neck or backbone (Lh., O'B., etc.):

sàl, also **sàil, sáile**, sea, Ir. *sáile*, E. Ir. *sál*, *sáile* : **svâlos*, root *sval*, *svel*; Lat. *salum*, sea; Eng. *swell* (Stokes, who also refers Br. *c'hoalen*, salt). Shräder equates Gadelic with Gr. ἅλς, salt, the sea, and Lat. *salum*, root *sal*.

salach, dirty, Ir., so O. Ir., *salach*, W. *halawg*, *halog*, Cor. *halou*, stercora, O. Br. *haloc*, lugubri : **salâko-s* (adj.), root *sal*, to dirty; Eng. *sallom*, O. H. G. *salo*, dusky, dirty. *sal*, filth, is used.

salann, salt, Ir., O. Ir. *salann*, W. *halen*, Cor. *haloin*, Br. *halenn* (**salên-*) : **salanno-s*, salt; Lat. *sal*; Gr. ἅλς, salt, sea; Eng. *salt*, Ger. *salz*; Ch. Sl. *solĭ*.

salldair, a chalder; from Sc. *chalder*, Eng. *chalder*, *chaldron*, from O. Fr. *chaldron*, a caldron.

salm, a psalm, Ir., O. Ir. *salm*, W. and Br. *salm*; from Lat. *psalmus*, Eng. *psalm*.

saltair, trample, Ir. *saltairim*; from Lat. *saltare*, dance.

samh, the smell of the air in a close room, ill odour:

samh, sorrel, Ir. *samh* :

samh, a god, giant (Carm.):

samh, a clownish person; cf. Sc. *sow*, one who makes a dirty appearance, "a pig."

samhach, wooden haft, handle, Ir. *samhthach*, O. Ir. *samthach*; cf. O. Ir. *samaigim*, pono (which Ascoli refers to **stam*, root *sta*, stand). Cf. *sam*, together, of *samhuinn*.

sàmhach, quiet, Ir. *sámhach* (Coneys has *samhach*), still, pleasant, from *sámh*, (*samh*), pleasant, still, E. Ir. *sám*, *sáme*, rest, quiet, *sáim*, mild, quiet: **sâmo-*. Possibly allied to Eng. *soft*, O. H. G. *samfto*, softly, Got. *samjan*, please; and the root *sam* of *samhradh*. Stokes suggests connection with Zend *hâma*, like, Ch. Sl. *samŭ*, ipse, Norse, *sömr*, *samr*, Eng. *same*; or Gr. ἥμερος, tame. Cf. *sàimhe*.

samhail, samhuil, likeness, like, Ir. *samhail*, like, *samhuil*, likeness, simile, W. *hafal*, similis, O. W. *amal*, Corn *haval*, *avel*, Br. *haual*: **samali-*; Gr. ὁμαλός, like; Lat. *similis*; Eng. *same*.

samhan, savin-bush, Ir. *samhán*; from Eng. *savin*, M. Eng. *saveine*, Ag. S. *savine*, Lat. *sabina*.

samhnan, samhnachan, a large river trout (H.S.D., Dial.):

samhradh, summer, Ir. *samhradh*, *sámhradh*, E. Ir. *samrad*, *sam*, W., Corn. *haf*, M. Br. *haff*, Br. *hanv*: **samo-*; Skr. *sámâ*, year, Zend *hama*, summer, Arm. *am*, year; further Eng. *summer*, Gr. ἡμέρα, day. The termination *rad* = *rado-n* (n.).

samhuinn, Hallow-tide, Ir. *samhain*, E. Ir. *samuin*, *samain*, *samfhuin*: usually regarded as for **sam-fuin*, "summer-end," from *sam*, summer, and *fuin*, end, sunset, *fuinim*, I end, **vonesô*, root *nes*, as in *còmhnuidh*, q.v. (Stokes). For *fuin*, Kluge suggests **wen*, suffer (Got. *winnan*, suffer); Zimmer favours Skr. *van*, hurt (Eng. *wound*); and Ascoli analyses it into *fo-in-*. Dr Stokes, however, takes *samain* from the root *som*, same (Eng. *same*, Gr. ὁμός, like, Lat. *simul*, whence Eng. *assemble*; see *samhuil*), and makes **samani-* mean "assembly" —the gathering at Tara on 1st November, while *Cét-shamain*, our *Céitein*, was the "first feast," held on 1st May.

samplair, a copy, pattern, Ir. *samplair*, *sampla*; from Eng. *sampler*, *sample*.

-san, as in **esan,** ipse, **iadsan**; see *-sa*.

sanas, a whisper, secret, Manx *sannish*, whisper, Ir., E. Ir. *sanas*; **sanastu-*, root *sven*; Lat. *sonare*, Eng. *sound*; Skr. *svánati*, to sound.

sannt, desire, inclination, Ir., O. Ir. *sant*, W. *chwant*, Cor. *whans*, Br. *c'hoant*: **svandətâ*, desire, root *svand*, *svad*, desire, please: Gr. ἁνδάνω, please, ἡδύς, sweet; Skr. *svad*, relish; further Eng. *sweet*, etc.

saobh, erroneous, apt to err, dissimulation, Ir. *saobh* (adj.), O. Ir. *sáib*, *soib*, later *saeb*, falsus, pseudo-: **svoibo-s*, turning aside, wavering, W. *chwifio*, turn, whirl; Eng. *sweep*, *swoop*.

saobhaidh, den of a wild beast, fox's den:

saod, journey, intention, condition, good humour (Arg.), Ir. *saod*, *seud*, journey, O. Ir. *sét*, way, journey, W. *hynt*, Br. *hent*, O. Br. *hint*: **sento-s*; Got *sinþs*, journey, way, O. H. G. *sind*, Eng *send*. Hence **saodaich**, drive cattle to pasture: Cf. *soad*, drive animals slowly (Shet.), N. *saeta*, waylay, *sát*, ambush.

saoghal, the world, an age, life, Ir. *saoghal*, O. Ir. *saigul*, *saegul*; from Lat. *saeculum*, race, age, from **sai-tlom*, allied to W. *hoedl*, life.

saoi, saoidh, a good, generous man, a warrior, a scholar, Ir. *saoi*, a worthy man, a scholar, pl. *saoithe*, E. Ir. *sái*, *sui*, a sage, g *suad*: **su-vid-s*, root *vid* of *fios* (Thurneysen). Stokes (*Mart. Gorm.*) prefers *su-vet-*, root *vât*, say (see *fàith*). Rhys agrees.

saoibh, foolish, perverse, Ir. *saobh* (do.); see *saobh*.

saoibhir, rich, Ir. *saidhbhir*, E. Ir. *saidber*, opposed to *daidber*: **su-adber*, from **ad-berì-* (Lat. *adfero*), root *bher* of *beir*, bring, q.v.

saoibhneas, peevishness, dulness; from *saoibh*, *saobh*. Ir. has *saobhnós*, bad manners; but G. seems a pure derivative of *saobh*.

saoidhean, young saith (Lewis); cf. N. *seiðr*.

saoil, a mark, seal; see *seul*.

saoil, think, deem, Ir. *saoilim*, E. Ir. *sáilim*; cf. Got. *saiwala*, Eng. *soul*, which Kluge suggests may be allied to Lat. *saeculum*, root *sai*.

saoitear, oversman, tutor (Suth.); see *taoitear*.

saor, free, Ir. *saor*. E. Ir. *sáer*, O. Ir. *sóir*, *sóer*: **su-viro-s*, "good man," free; from *su* (= *so-*) and *viro-s*, *fear*, q.v.

saor, a carpenter, Ir. *saor*, W. *saer*, Cor. *sair*: **sairo-s*, from **sapiro-s*, root *sap*, skill, Lat. *sapio*, *sapientia*, wisdom, Ag. S. *sefa*, understanding, sense (Stokes, who thinks the Brittonic may be borrowed).

saothair, labour, toil, Ir. *saothar*, E. Ir. *sáethar*, O. Ir. *sáithar*, g. *sáithir*: **sai-tro-n*; also E. Ir. *sáeth*, *sóeth*: **sai-tu-*; root *sai*, trouble, pain; Got. *sair*, Ag. S. *sár*, Eng. *sore*, Ger. *sehr*, **sai-ra-*; Lat. *saevus*, wild; Lit. *síws*, sharp, rough.

sapair, sapheir, sapphire, Ir. *saphír*; from Lat. *sapphirus*, whence Eng. also.

sàr, oppression, **sàraich**, oppress, Ir. *sáruighim*, O. Ir. *sáraigim*, violo, contemno, *sár*, outrage, contempt, W. *sarhäed*, contumelia: **sâro-n*, **spâro-n*, root *sper*, kick, spurn; Lat. *sperno*; Eng. *spurn*; Lit. *spìrti*, kick; Skr. *sphur*, jerk (Stokes). The W. has the *a* pretonic short; is it borrowed from Ir. (Stokes)?

sàr, excellent, Ir., E. Ir., O. Ir. *sár-*, W. *hoer*, positive, stubborn, assertion, Ogmic *Netta-sagru*, *Sagarettos*, *Sagramni* : **sagro-s*, strong, root *seg* ; Gr. ὀχυρός, strong, fast, ἔχω, have ; Ger. *sieg*, victory ; Skr. *sáhas*, might.

sàrdail, a sprat ; from the Eng. *sardel* (Bailey), now *sardine*.

sàs, straits, restraint, hold, E. Ir. *sás*, a trap, fixing ; from *sàth*, transfix, q.v.

sàsaich, satisfy, Ir. *sásaighim*, O. Ir. *sásaim* ; from *sàth*, q.v.

sàth, plenty, satiety, Ir. *sáth*, *sáith*, E. Ir. *sáith* : **sâti-* ; Got. *sóþ*, satiety, Ger. *satt* (adj.) ; Lit. *sótis* ; Lat. *sat*, enough, *satur*, full, whence Eng. *satisfy*, etc.

sàth, thrust, transfix, Ir. *sáthadh*, a thrust, push, M. Ir. *sáthud*, driving, thrusting, E. Ir. *sádim* (L. U.), O. Ir. *im-sadaim*, jacio, W. *hodi*, shoot ; possibly from *sô*, *sê*, hurl, as in *sìol* :

sath, saith, bad (Dial. *maith na saith*, *math na sath*), M. Ir. *sath* (Lecan Glossary), *saith*, O. Ir. *saich* (*cid saich no maith*) : **saki-s*, root *svak*, *svag*, weak, Ger. *schwach*.

Sathairn, Di-sathairn, Saturday ; see under *di-*.

sè, sèa, sia, six, Ir. *sé*, O. Ir. *sé*, W. *chwech*, Cor. *wheh*, Br. *c'houec'h* : **sveks* ; Lat. *sex* ; Gr. ἕξ ; Got. *saíhs*, Eng. *six* ; Skr. *shash*.

seabh, stray (M'A.) : see *seabhaid*.

seabhach, trim, neat (H.S.D., Dial.) :

seabhag, a hawk, Ir. *seabhac*, E. Ir. *sebac*, O. Ir. *sebocc*, W. *hebog*, E. W. *hebauc* ; from Ag. S. *heafoc*, now *hawk*, Ger. *habicht*, Norse *haukr*, root *haf*, I. E. *qap*, Lat. *capus*, hawk, allied to *capio*.

seabhaid, an error, wandering, Ir. *seabhóid*, error, folly, wandering: **sibo-*, a short form of the root of *saobh* ?

seac, wither, Ir. *seacaim*, E. Ir. *seccaim*, *secc*, siccus, W. *sychu*, to dry, *sych*, dry, Corn. *seygh*, Br. *sec'h*, dry ; from Lat. *siccus*. See further under *seasg*.

seach, by, past, Ir. *seach*, O. Ir. *sech*, ultra, praeter, W. *heb*, without, Corn. *heb*, Br. *hep*, without : **seqos* ; Lat, *secus*, otherwise, by, *sequor*, I follow (Eng. *prosecute*, etc.) ; Gr. ἕπομαι, I follow, Skr. has *sácâ*, with, together, Zend *haca*, out, for. Hence G. and Ir. **seachad**, past, G. and Ir. **seachain**, avoid.

seachd, seven, Ir. *seachd*, O. Ir. *secht n-*, W. *saith*, Corn. *seyth*, Br. *seiz* : **septn̥* ; Lat. *septem* ; Gr. ἑπτά ; Got., O. H. G. *siban*, Eng. *seven* ; Lit. *septyni* ; Skr. *saptá*.

seachduin, a week, Ir. *seachdmhain*, O. Ir. *sechtman*, Corn. *seithum*, Br. *sizun* ; from Lat. *septimana*, from *septem*.

seachlach, a heifer barren though of age to bear a calf ; cf. O. Ir. *sechmall*, præteritio (= *sechm*, past, and *ell*, go, as in *tadhal*), Ir. *seachluighim*, lay aside. H. S. D. suggests ***seach-laogh***, **"past calf."** ***seach-la***, **surviving, still spared (Suth.).**

seachran, wandering, error, Ir. *seachrán*, E. Ir. *sechrán* : **sech-reth-an*, from *seach* and *ruith*, run ?

seadh, yes, it is, Ir. *'seadh*, for *is eadh*, it is ; see *is* and *eadh*, it.

seadh, sense ; usual spelling of *seagh*, q.v.

seagal, rye, so Ir., M. Ir. *secul* ; from Lat. *secale*, whence also Br. *segal*.

seagh, sense, esteem, Ir. *seagh*, regard, esteem, strength, *seaghdha*, learned (O'Cl.), M. Ir. *seg*, strength, Gaul. *sego-* : **sego-*, strength, pith ; Norse *sigr*, victory, Ger. *sieg* ; Skr. *sáhas*, might ; further Gr. ἔχω, have ; I. E. *segh*, hold.

seal, a while, space, Ir. *seal*, O. Ir. *sel*, W. *chwyl*, versio, turning, Br. *hoel*, "du moins, root *svel*, turn. Bez. (apud Stokes) compares Lettic *swalstit*, move hither and thither ; to which cf. Gr. σαλεύω, I toss.

sealbh, possession, cattle, luck, Ir. *sealbh*, E. Ir. *selb*, O. Ir. *selbad*, W. *helw*, possession, ownership : **selvâ*, possession, root *sel*, take, E. Ir. *selaim*, I take, Gr. ἑλεῖν, take ; Got. *saljan*, offer, Eng. *sell*. Windisch has compared Got. *silba*, Eng. *self* (pronominal root *sve*).

sealbhag, sorrel, Ir. *sealbhóg* ; usually regarded as for *searbhag*, "bitter herb" (cf. Eng. *sorrel* from *sour*). The change of *r* to *l* is a difficulty, but it may be due to the analogy of *mealbhag*.

sealbhan, the throat, throttle : **svel-vo-*, Eng. *swallow* (**svel-ko-*) ?

sealg, a hunt, Ir. *sealg*, O. Ir. *selg*, W. *hela*, *hel*, to hunt, O. W. *helghati*, venare, Cor. *helhia*, British *Selgovae*, now *Solway* : **selgâ*, a hunt, root *sel*, capture (see *sealbh*).

sealg, milt, spleen, Ir. *sealg*, M. Ir. *selg*, Br. *felc'h* : **selgâ*, **spelgâ* ; Gr. σπλάγχνα, the higher viscera, σπλήν, spleen (**splghēn*) ; Lat. *liēn* ; Skr. *plîhán*, spleen ; Ch. Sl. *slēzena*, Lit. *blużnis* ; also Eng. *lung*.

seall, look, E. Ir. *sellaim*, *sell*, eye, W. *syllu*, to gaze, view, Br. *sellet* ; cf. *solus*. Stokes gives the Celtic as **stilnaô*, I see, comparing the Gr. στιλπνός, shining.

sèam, seum, forbid, enjoin :

seaman (**sèaman**, H.S.D.), a nail, small riveted nail, a small stout person, Ir. *seaman*, small riveted nail, E. Ir. *semmen*, W., M. W. *hemin*, rivet : **seg-s-men*, root *seg*, *segh*, hold, as in *seagh*.

seamarlan, chamberlain, M. Ir. *seomuirlìn* ; from the Eng.

sèamh, mild, peaceful (**seamh**, Arms.), Ir, *séamh* ; see *séimh*, M'A. gives its meaning as an "enchantment to make one's friends prosper." See *seamhas*.

seamhas, good luck, also **seanns**, good chance, **seamhsail**, **seannsail**, lucky ; from Eng. *chance*.

seamlach, a cow that gives milk without her calf, an impudent or silly person ; Sc. *shamloch*, a cow that has not calved for two years (West Lothian) :

seamrag, shamrock, **seamair** (M'A.), Ir. *seamróg*, M. Ir. *semrach* (adj.), E. Ir. *semmor* (B.L.) :

seamsan, hesitation, quibbling, delay, sham ; from the Eng. *sham*, Northern Eng. *sham*, a shame, trick ?

sean, old, Ir. *sean*, O. Ir. *sen*, W., Corn., and O. Br. *hen*, Gaul. *Seno-* : **seno-s*, old ; Lat. *senex*, g. *senis*, old man ; Gr. ἕνος, old ; Got. *sinista*, oldest, Eng. *seneschal* ; Lit. *sénas* ; Skr. *sánas*.

seanachas, conversation, story, Ir. *seanachas*, *seanchus*, tale, history, genealogy, O. Ir. *senchas*, vetus historia, lex, O. W. *hencass*, monimenta. Stokes refers this to **seno-kastu-*, "old story," from **kastu-*, root *kans*, speak (see *cainnt* and Stokes' derivation of it). Regarded by others as a pure derivative of **seno-* or its longer stem **seneko-* (Lat. *senex*, Got. *sineigo*, old, Skr. *sanakás*, old), that is, **senekastu-*. Hence **seanachaidh,** a reciter of ancient lore, a historian, Ir. *seanchuidh*, a form which favours the second derivation.

seanadh, a senate, synod, Ir. *seanadh*, *seanaidh*, E. Ir. *senod*, W. *senedd*, Corn. *sened*, Br. *senez* ; from the Lat. *synodus*, now Eng. *synod*.

seanagar, old-fashioned, knowing ; cf. Ir. *senfha*, W. *henwr* :

seanair, a grandfather, Ir. *seanathair*, M. Ir. *senathair*, literally "old father."

seang, slender, lean, Ir. *seang*, E. Ir. *seng* : **svengo-s* ; Norse *svangr*, slender, thin, Sc. *swank*, *swack*, supple, Ger. *schwank*, supple, allied to Eng. *swing*.

seangan, an ant (S. Inverness and Perthshire **snioghan**), Manx *sniengan*, Ir. *seangán*, M. Ir. *sengán*, E. Ir. *segon* (Corm.) ; cf. Gr. σκνίψ (ι long), gen. σκνιφός or σκνιπός, κνίψ, root *skene*, *kene*, scratch (see *cnàmh*), Lit. *skanùs*, savoury (kittling), Stokes (*Bez* [18] 65) refers it to **stingagno-*, Eng. *sting*, Gr. στίζω, prick ; K. Meyer derives it from *seang*, slender.

seanns, luck ; see *seamhas*.

sèap, slink, sneak off, flinch, Ir. *seapaim* : "turn tail ;" see next word.

seap, a tail, an animal's tail hanging down (as a dog's when cowed :

sear, eastern ; see *ear*.

searadoir, a towel (Sh. *searbhadair*) ; from Sc. *serviter*, *servet*, napkin, from Fr. *servietta*, from *servir*, serve, Lat. *servio*.

searbh, bitter, Ir. *searbh*, O. Ir. *serb*, W. *chwerw*, Corn. *wherow*, Br. *c'houero* : **svervo-s* ; O. H. G. *sweran*, dolere, Ger. *sauer*, Eng. *sour* ; Lit. *swarùs*, salty.

searbhant, a servant maid : from the Eng. *servant.*

searg, wither, Ir. *seargaim,* O. Ir. *sercim, serg,* illness : **sergo-* ; Lit. *sergù,* I am ill ; O.H.G. *swërcan,* O. Sax. *swercan,* become gloomy.

searmon, a sermon, Ir. *searmóin,* M. Ir. *sermon* ; from Lat. *sermo, sermonis,* Eng. *sermon.*

seàrr, a sickle, saw, E. Ir. *serr,* O. W. *serr* ; from Lat. *serra.*

searrach, a foal, colt, so Ir., E. Ir. *serrach* : **serso-* ; Gr. ἕρσαι, young lambs ?

searrag, a bottle ; founded on the Eng. *jar ?*

sears, charge or load (as a gun) ; from Eng. *charge.*

searsanach, a sheriff officer, estate overseer, **seirseanach,** auxiliary (Arm., Sh., O'B.) ; Gaelic is from the Sc. *sergean, sergeand,* an inferior officer in a court of justice, Eng. *serjeant,* from Fr. *serjant,* Lat. *serviens,* etc. M. Ir. has *sersénach,* foot soldier. *sèarsaigeadh,* charging, citation (Suth.).

seas, stand, Ir. *seasaim,* E. Ir. *sessim,* O. Ir. *tair(sh)issim,* E. Ir. inf. *sessom,* G. **seasamh** : **sistami,* I stand, **sistamo-* (n.), root *sta* ; Lat. *sisto,* stop, *sto* ; Gr. ἵστημι, set ; Eng. *stand* ; Skr. *sthâ.* The W. *sefyll,* stare, Cor., Br. *sevell,* Br. *saff,* come from **stam* (Stokes).

seasg, barren, dry, Ir. *seasg,* E. Ir. *sesc,* W. *hysp,* Br. *hesk, hesp* : **sisqo-s,* from *sit-s-qo-,* root *sit,* dry ; Lat. *siccus* (= *sit-cus*), dry, *sitis,* thirst ; Zend *hisku,* dry.

seasgair, one in comfortable circumstances, comfortable, Ir. *seasgair,* cosy, dry and warm, quiet ; from *seasg.*

seasgan, a shock or truss of corn, gleaned land :

seasgann, a fenny country, marsh, Ir. *seisgeann,* E. Ir. *sescenn* ; from **sesc,* sedge, Ir. *seisg,* sedge, W. *hesg* (pl.), Cor. *hescen,* Br. *hesk,* whence Romance *sescha,* reed ; cf. Eng. *sedge,* I. E. root *seq,* cut. Zimmer refers *seasgann* to *seasg,* dry, though it denotes *wet* or marsh land.

seat, satiety of food (Dial.) : see *seid.*

seic, a skin or hide, peritoneum, brain pellicle ; see *seich.*

seic, meal-bag made of rushes (Lewis) ; N. *sekk,* sack.

seic, a rack, manger ; from Sc. *heck,* also *hack.* See next.

seiceal, a heckle (for flax) ; from Sc. and Eng. *heckle.* The W. is *heislan,* from Eng. *hatchel.*

seich, seiche, a hide, skin, Ir. *seithe,* E. Ir. *seche,* g. *seched* : **seket-* ; Norse *sigg,* callus, hard skin. The root is I. E. *seq,* cut, Lat. *seco,* etc. ; cf. for force Gr. δέρμα, skin, from δείρω, flay, Eng. *tear,* Lat. *scortum* and *corium,* from *sker,* Eng. *shear,* etc.

seid, a belly-full, flatulent swelling, **seideach,** swollen by tympany, corpulent :

seid, a truss of hay, a bed spread on the floor (especially **seideag** in the latter sense) : **seddi-* :

séid, blow, Ir. *séidim*, E. Ir. *sétim*, W. *chwyth*, a blast, M. Br. *huéz*, Br. *c'houeza*, blow, Cor. *whythe*, to blow : **sveiddo-*, **sviddo-*, from **sveizdho-*, **svizdho-* ; Ch. Slav. *svistati*, sibilare ; Lat. *sîbilus*, whistling (= *sîdhilus*), Eng. *sibilant*.

seidhir, a chair, from Eng. *chair*.

seilcheag, a snail, Ir. *seilide*, *seilchide*, *seilmide*, *slimide*, O. Ir. *selige*, testudo ; cf. Gr. σέσιλος (ι long), σέσηλος, σεσιλίτης, a snail. Stokes gives the root as *sel*, allied to Lit. *salė́ti*, creep, *slė̃kas*, earthworm, O. Pruss. *slayx* (do.). Stokes now, Lit. *seleti*, creep.

seile, placenta (Carm.) :

seileach, willow, Ir. *saileóg*, E. Ir. *sail*, g. *sailech*, W. *helyg*, willows, Corn. *heligen*, salix, Br. *halek* (pl.) : **saliks* ; Lat. *salix* ; Gr. ἑλίκη (Arcadian) ; Eng. *sallow*.

séileann, sheep-louse, tick :

seilear, a cellar, Ir. *seiléir*, M. W. *seler* ; from Eng. *cellar*.

seilisdeir, yellow iris or yellow water-flag, Ir. *soileastar*, *feleastar* (O'B.), *elestrom* (O'B.), M. Ir. *soilestar*, W. *elestr*, fleur de lys, iris, O. Br. *elestr*. Cf. L. Lat. *alestrare*, humectare (Ernault, Stokes in *R.C.*[4] 329).

seillean, a bee, **teillean** (Perth), **tilleag** (Suth.), W. *chwil*, beetle ; root *svel*, turn, as in *seal* ? W. *telyn*, harp ?

sèim, a squint :

sèimh, mild, placid, Ir. *séimh* (O'R., Fol.), *seimh* (Con.) :

seinn, sing, Ir. *seinnim*, M. Ir. *sendim*, O. Ir. *sennim*, play an instrument, psallo, perf. *sephainn* (**sesvanva*, Stokes) ; root *sven*, sound, as in Lat. *sonare*, *sonus*, Eng. *sound*, Skr. *svânati*, sound.

seipeal, a chapel, so Ir., M. Ir. *sépél* ; from M. Eng. and O. Fr *chapele*, now Eng. *chapel*.

seipein, a quart, choppin ; from the Eng. *choppin*, from Fr. *chopine*, *chope*, a beer glass, from Ger. *schoppen*.

seirbhis, service, Ir. *seirbhís* ; from the Eng.

seirc, love, Ir. *searc*, *seirc*, O. Ir. *serc*, W. *serch*, Br. *serc'h*, concubine, M. Br. *serch* : **serkâ*, **serko-* ; Got. *saúrga*, care, Ger. *sorge*, sorrow, Eng. *sorrow* ; Skr. *sûrkshati*, respect, reverence, take thought about something. The favourite derivation is to ally it to Gr. στέργω, I love, which would give a G. *teirg*.

seircean, burdoch (Carm.) :

seirean, a shank, leg, spindle-shanked person ; for connections see *speir*.

seirm, sound, musical noise, ring as a bell, O. Ir. *sibrase*, modulabor ; Celtic root *sver*, sing, I. E. *sver*, sound ; Skr. *svara*, sound, music; Eng, *swear*, *answer*, Got. *svaran*, swear; Lat. *sermo*, speech, Eng. *sermon*. The W. *chwyrnu*, hum, snort, is also allied.

seirsealach, robust (**séirsealach**, H.S.D.), Ir. *séirsean*, a strong person (O'R.); cf. *searsanach* for origin.

seis, one's match, a friend, sufficiency, Ir. *seas*, ship's seat, Lewis *seis*, bench, seat; cf. Norse *sessi*, bench-mate, oar-mate, from *sessa*, a ship's seat (I. E. root *sed*, sit).

seis, anything grateful to the senses, Ir. *seis*, pleasure, delight: **sved-ti-*, root *sveda*, *svâd*, sweet; Gr. ἑδανός, sweet, ἡδύς (do.); Lat. *suavis*, sweet; Eng. *sweet*.

seis, anus, the seat (Suth.):

seisd, a siege; formed from the Eng. *siege*.

seisean, session, assize, Ir. *seisiún*; from Lat. *sessio*, *sessiônis*, a sitting, session.

seisreach, a plough, six-horse plough, the six horses of a plough, Ir. *seisreach*, a plough of six horses, E. Ir. *sesrech*, plough team; from *seiseir*, six persons, a derivative of *sè*, six.

séist, the melody of a song, a ditty, M. Ir. *séis*, a musical strain: **sven-s-ti-*, root *sven*, *seinn*.

seòc, **seòcan**, a helmet plume, a helmet; cf. Eng. *shock*.

seochlan, a feeble person; from the Sc. *shochlin*, waddling, infirm, *shachlin*, verb *shachle*, shuffle in walking, allied to Eng. *shackle*, *shake*.

seòd, **siad**, a hero, a jewel, Ir. *seód*, a jewel; see *seud*, jewel.

seòg, swing to and fro, dandle; from Sc. *shog*, M. Eng. *shoggin*, M. Du. *shocken*.

seòl, method, way, Ir. *seól*, a method of doing a thing, *seólaim*, I direct, steer; E. Ir. *seól*, course; W. *hwyl*, course, condition. From *seól*, sail.

seòl, a sail, Ir. *seól*, O. Ir. *séol*, *seól*, *seol*, g. *siúil*, W. *hwyl*, O. W. *huil*: usually referred to **seghlo-* (root of *seagh*) or to Teutonic *seglo-*, sail (also from **seghlo-*), borrowed into Celtic. In either case we should expect Ir. **sél*, W. **hail*, but we have neither. Strachan suggests that *seól* is formed from gen. *siúil* on the analogy of *ceól*, etc.; while W. *hwyl* may have been effected by a borrow from Lat. *vêlum* (Cor. *guil*, Br. *goel*).

seòmar, a chamber, Ir. *seómra*, M. Ir. *seomra*; from M. Eng. and Fr. *chambre*, Lat. *camera*.

seòrsa, a sort, kind, Ir. *sórt*; from the Eng.

seot, a short tail or stump, the worst beast, a sprout; from Sc. *shot*, rejected sheep ("shot" from *shoot*), shoot, stern of a boat, from the root of Eng. *shoot*. Cf. Norse *skott*, fox's tail, *skotta*, dangle.

seotal, shuttle of trunk (M'D.) :
seth in **gu seth**, severally, neither (after negative) ; cf. Lat. *se-cum* ; "by one-self."
seuchd, a tunic or *léine* (Oss. Ballad of *Ionmhuin*) :
seud, a jewel, treasure, hero, Ir. *seud*, O. Ir. *sét*, pl. *séuti*, pretiosa, Med. Ir., Lat. *sentis*; from **sent-*, real, "being," I. E. *sents*, being, participle from root *es*, be ; Lat. *-sens*, praesens, etc. ; Gr. εἴς.
seul, seula, saoil, a seal, Ir. *seula*, M. Ir. *séla*, W. *sel*, O. Br. *siel* ; from Lat. *sigillum*, M. Eng. and Fr. *seel*, Ag. S. *sigle*.
seum, earnest entreaty ; see *sèam*.
seun, a charm, defend by charms, Ir. *seun*, good luck, E. Ir. *sén*, blessing, sign, luck, O. Ir. *sén*, benedic, W. *swyn*, a charm, magic preservative ; from Lat. *signum*, a sign, "sign of the cross."
seun, refuse, shun, Ir. *seunaim*, *séanaim*, M. Ir. *sénaim* ; probably from the above.
seunan, sianan in **breac-sheunain**, freckles :
seusar, acme or perfection (M'A. for Islay) ; from *seizure*, crisis ?
sgab, scab, **sgabach**, scabbed ; from the Eng.
sgabag, cow killed for winter provision (M'F.) :
sgabaiste, anything pounded or bashed (H.S.D.), Ir. *sgabaiste*, robbery :
sgaball, a hood, helmet, M. G. *sgaball*, a hood or cape (M'V.) ; Ir. *scabal*, a hood, shoulder guard, helmet, a scapular ; from Lat. *scapulae*, shoulder-blades, whence Eng. *scapular*.
sgabard, scabbard ; from the Eng.
sgabh, sawdust, Ir. *sgabh* (Lh.) ; Lat. *scobis*, sawdust, powder.
sgad, a loss, mischance ; from the Sc. *skaith*, Eng. *scathe*, *scath* (Shakespeare), Norse *skaði*, scathe, Ger. *schaden*, hurt.
sgadan, a herring, Ir. *sgadán*, E. Ir. *scatan* (Corm.), W. *ysgadan* (pl.) ; cf. Eng. *shad*, "king of herrings," Ag. S. *sceadda*, Prov. Ger. *schade*.
sgadartach, a set of ragamuffins (H.S.D.), anything scattered (M'A.) ; from Eng. *scatter*.
sgafair, a bold, hearty man (H.S.D., Arm., O'B.), a handsome man (H.S.D.), a scolding man (M'A.), Ir. *sgafaire*, a bold, hearty man, spruce fellow, a gaffer ; from the Eng. *gaffer* ?
sgag, split, crack, winnow, filter, Ir. *sgagaim*, filter, purge ; cf., for root, *gàg*.
sgaipean, a ninny, dwarf :
sgàil, a shade, shadow, Ir. *sgáile*, *scáil*, M. Ir. *scáil*, O. Br. *esceilenn*, cortina, curtain : **skâli-*, root *skâ* of *sgàth*, q.v.
sgailc, a smart blow, a slap, skelp, Ir. *sgailleóg* ; root *skal*, make a noise by hitting ; Norse *skella*, slap, clatter (*skjalla*), Ger.

schallen, resound; Lit. *skaliu*, give tongue (as a hunting dog). Cf. Sc. and M. Eng. *skelp*. Also **sgailleag**.

sgailc, a bald pate, baldness, **sgall**, baldness, Ir. *sgallta*, bald, bare, *scallach*, bald; from Norse *skalli*, a bald head, Swed. *skallig*, bald, *skala*, peel, *skal*, husk, Eng. *scale*. The G. *sgailc* is possibly from M. Eng. *scalc*, scalp; but **sgall** is clearly Norse.

sgàin, burst, rend, Ir. *sgáinim*: **skad-no-*, root *skhad*, *sked*, *skha*, split, rend, cut; Gr. *σκεδάννυμι*, scatter; Skr. *skhádate*, split,

sgainneal, a scandal, Ir. *scannail*, M. Ir. *scandal*; from the Lat. *scandalum*.

sgainnir, scatter, **sganradh** (n), Ir. *scanruighim*, scatter, scare; cf. Eng. *squander*, allied to *scatter*.

sgàinnteach, a corroding pain, pain of fatigue; from *sgàin*.

sgàird, flux, diarrhœa, Ir. *sgárdaim*, I squirt, pour out: **skardo-*; I. E. *skerdo-*; Lat. *sucerda*, swine-dung, *muscerda*, mouse-dung = *mus-scerda-*; Skr. *chard*, vomit; Ch. Sl. *skarędŭ*, nauseating; Eng. *sharn*. Another form is **skart*, W. *ysgarth*, excrement, Br. *skoarz*, *skarz*, void, cleanse, Gr. *σκῶρ*, g. *σκατός*, Skr. *çákṛt*, dung.

sgaireach, prodigal (Sh., etc.); from the root *skar* of *sgar*.

sgàireag, one year old gull, young scart; from Norse *skári*, a young sea-mew.

sgàirn, howling of dogs, loud murmur; see *sgairt*.

sgairneach, a continuous heap of loose stones on a hill side, the sound of such stones falling (**sgairm**, M'A.); cf. Sc. *scarnoch*, crowd, tumult, noise (Ayr). See *sgairn*. Badenoch Dial. **sgarmach**.

sgairt, a loud cry, Ir. *sgairt*: **s-gar-ti-*, root *gar*?

sgairt, activity, Ir. *sgairteamhuil*, active: root *skar*, skip, spring; Gr. *σκαίρω*, skip, *σκάρος*, a leap, run; Zend *çhar*, spring.

sgairt, midriff, intestine caul, Ir. *scairt*: "separater," from *skar* of *sgar*?

sgait, a skate; from the Eng. *skate*, Norse *skata*.

sgaiteach, sharp, edged, cutting, **sgait**, a prickle, a little chip of wood in one's flesh (Dial.); from *sgath*, lop.

sgal, howl, shriek, yell, Ir. *sgal*, M. Ir. *scal*, root *skal*, sound, cry; Norse *skjalla*, clash, clatter, *skvala*, squall, squeal, Ger. *schallen*; Lit. *skaliu*, give tongue (as a dog); Gr. *σκύλαξ*, whelp: I. E. root *sqel*, make a sound, allied to *sqel*, split, hit? Cf. W. *chwalu*, prate, babble, spread, root *sqvel*, *sqval*.

sgalag, a servant, Ir. *sgológ* (fem.), husbandman, rustic, M. Ir. *scolóc* (= *gille*), E. Ir. *scoloca*; from Norse *skálkr*, servant, slave, Got. *skalks*, servant, Ger. *schalk*, knave, Eng. mar*shal*, sene*schal*. It could hardly be from Lat. *scholasticus*, as Skene (*Celt. Scot.*[1] 448) thinks.

sgàlain, scales for weighing, Ir. *scála*, a balance, *scali* (B. of Dr.); from the early Eng. *scale*, Ag. S. *scále*, Norse *skál*, a balance.

sgàlan, hut, scaffold, Ir., M. Ir. *scálán*; from the Norse *skáli*, a hut, shed. Stokes (Bez. Beit.[18] 65) refers it to a stem **scânlo-*, cognate with Gr. *σκηνή* (Dor. *σκāνά*), a tent, roof, *skhâ*, cover, shade.

sgald, burn, scald, Ir. *sgall*, scald, singe; from the Eng. *scald*.

sgall, baldness, Ir. *sgallta*, bald, bare; see under *sgailc*.

sgalla, an old hat (M'A.):

sgàlla, a large wooden dish cut out of a tree (M'A.):

sgallais, insult, contempt; from the Norse *sköll*, mockery, loud laughter, *skjal*, empty talk, *skjall*, flattering (H.S.D. gives "flattery" as a meaning): allied to *sgal*, q.v.

sgamal, a scale, squama, Ir. *sgamal*; from Lat. *squâmula*, *squâma*. In G. and Ir. Bibles, *Acts*[8] 18, "Scales fell from his eyes"—*sgamail*.

sgamal, effluvia, phlegm, Ir. *sgamal*: same as above.

sgamh, dross, dust; see *sgabh*.

sgamhan, the lungs, liver, Ir. *sgamhán*, lungs, M. Ir. *scaman*, W. *ysgyfaint*, lights, Cor. *skefans*, Br. *skevent*; from Ir. *scaman*, levis, W. *ysgafn*, light, Cor. *scaff*, Br. *skanv*, light (cf. for force Eng. *lights*, Russ. *legkoe*, lungs, from *legkii*, light): **skamno-*; cf. Norse *skammr*, short, O. H. G. *scam*, short.

sgann, a multitude, drove:

sgann, a membrane, Ir. *sgann*; cf. Norse *skán*, a thin membrane, film, *skaeni*, film, membrane; **skad-no*?

sganradh, dispersing, terror; see *sgainnir*.

sgaog, a foolish, giddy girl; cf. Sc. *skeich*, *skeigh*, skittish, Eng. *shy*.

sgaoil, spread, scatter, let go, Ir. *sgaoilim*, M. Ir., E. Ir. *scáilim*; cf. W. *chwalu*, disperse, strew, root *sqval*, *sqvôl*, allied to root *sqel*, split (as in *sgoilt*, q.v.). Rhys says W. is borrowed.

sgaoim, a fright, a start from fear, skittishness: for *sgeum*? If so, for *sceng-men*, E. Ir. *scingim*, I start; Gr. *σκάζω*, I limp, *σκιμβάζω*, limp; Ger. *hinken* (do.); Skr. *khanj* (do.). See *sgeun*.

sgaoth, a swarm (as of bees), Ir. *scaoth*, *scaoith*: **skoiti-*, from *skheit*, separate; Ger. *scheiden*, Eng. *shed*; further Lat. *scindo* (from root *skheid*, split), split.

sgap, scatter, Ir. *scapaim*: **skad-bo-* (from *skhad*, divide, Gr. *σκεδάννυμι*, scatter), developing into *skabb*, which, as *skabb-th*, becomes *sgap*? But consider Eng. *scape*, *escape*.

sgar, sever, separate, Ir. *sgaraim*, O. Ir. *scaraim*, W. *ysgar*, separ_ ate, O. Br. *scarat*, dijudicari: **skaraô*, root *sker*, eparat sunder; Lit. *skiriù*, separate; O. H. G. *scëran*, Ger. *scheren*, shear, cut, Eng. *shear*; further Gr. *κείρω*, cut, etc.

sgarbh, cormorant; from the Norse *skarfr*, N. Sc. *scarf* (Shet., etc.).

sgarlaid, scarlet, Ir. *sgárlóid*, M. Ir. *scarloit*; from M. Eng. *scarlat*, *scarlet*, Med. Lat. *scarlatum*. Stokes and K. Meyer take it direct from Lat.

sgat, a skate (Dial.); see *sgait*.

sgath, lop off, Ir. *sgathaim*, E. Ir. *scothaim*; I.E., root *skath*, cut; Gr. *ἀσκηθής*, unscathed, *σχάζω*, cut; Eng. *scathe*, Ger. *schaden*, hurt; Skr. *chá*, lop. The root appears variously as *skhê*, *ska*, *skhêi*, *skhe* (Gr. *σκεδάννυμι*). It is possible to refer *sgath* to the root *seq*, cut, Lat. *seco*, Eng. *section*. See *sgian*.

sgàth, a shade, shadow, Ir. *sgáth*, *scáth*, O. Ir. *scáth*, W. *ysgod*, Cor. *scod*, umbra, Br. *skeud*: **skâto-s*; Gr. *σκότος*, darkness; Eng. *shade*, Got. *skadus*, shade, shadow, Ger. *schatten*; Skr. *cháya*, shadow.

sgath (Sh., Arm., **sgàth**, H.S.D.), a wattled door:

sgeach, **sgitheag**, hawthorn berry, Ir. *sgeach*, sweet-briar, haw, E. Ir. *scé*, g. *sciach*, also g. pl. *sciad*, W. *ysbyddad*, hawthorn, Cor. *spedhes*, Br. *spezad*, fruit, currant: **skvijat-*:

sgeadaich, dress, adorn, Ir. *sgeaduighim*, adorn, mark with a white spot, *sgead*, speck, white spot, *sgeadach*, speckled, sky-coloured; also **gead**, spot:

sgealb, a splinter, Ir. *sgealpóg*, splinter, fragment, *sgealpaim*, smash, split, make splinters of; see *sgolb*. Cf. Sc. *skelb*, *skelf*, a splinter, *skelve* (vb.).

sgeallag, wild mustard, Ir. *sgeallagach*, M. Ir. *scell*, a grain. kernel; root *sqel*, separate, Eng. *shell*, etc. Stokes equates Ir. *scellán*, kernel, with Lat. *scilla*, squill, sea-onion, Gr. *σκίλλα*.

sgealp, a slap; from Sc. *skelp*, M. Eng. *skelp*.

sgeamh, yelp, Ir. *sceamh*, E. Ir. *scem*, *scemdacht*; cf. next word. Also G. **sgiamh**, **sgiamhail**, to which Ernault compares M. Br. *hueual*, cry like a fox.

sgeamh, severe or cutting language, Ir. *sgeamhaim*, I scold, reproach: **skemo-*; Norse *skamma*, to shame, to scold, Eng. *shame*, *sham*? The word **sgeamh** also means "a disgust" in Gaelic; also, according to M'A., "a speck on the eye," "membrane." Also Ir. (and G.?) **sgeamh**, polypody.

sgean, cleanliness, polish; cf. for origin Norse *skína*, Eng. *shine*.

sgèan, sudden fright or start, a wild look of the face; see *sgeun*.

sgeanag, a kind of sea weed, so called from resembling a knife blade (Arg.).

sgeann, a stare, gazing upon a thing:

sgeap, a beehive; from the Sc. *skep*, M. Eng. *skeppe*, a skep, carrying basket, Norse *skeppa*, a measure.

sgeig, mockery, Ir. *sgige*, M. Ir. *scige*: **skeggio-*:

sgeigeach, having a prominent chin or a beard of strong, straight hair (Sutherland); from Norse *skegg*, a beard, from *skaga*, jut out, Eng. *shaggy*.

sgeilcearra, supple, active; cf. *sgiolcarra*.

sgéile, misery, pity, Ir. *sceile* (O'Cl., Lh. as obsolete, O'B.), *scéile* (O'R.):

sgeileid, a skillet, Ir. *sgiléad*; from the Eng.

sgeileas, a beak, thin face, talkativeness (H.S.D.); see *sgeilm*.

sgeilm, boasting, prattling (H.S.D., Arms.), a thin-lipped mouth, a prater's mouth (M'A.); also **sgiolam, sgeinm**. Root *skel*, as in *sgal*.

sgeilm, sgeinm, neatness, decency; cf. *sgean*.

sgeilmse, a surprise, sudden attack:

sgeilp, a shelf; from Sc. *skelf*, Ag. S. *scylfe*, now *shelf*.

sgèimh, beauty, Ir. *sgeimh*; see *sgiamh*.

sgeimhle, a skirmish, bickering, Ir. *sgeimhle*:

sgéinnidh, twine, flax or hemp thread; cf. Ir. *sgainne*, a skein or clue of thread. The Sc. *skiny*, pack thread (pronounced *skeenyie*) is apparently from G.; Eng. *skein* is from M. Eng. *skeine*, O. Fr. *escaigne*. Skeat derives the Eng. from Gaelic. The G. alone might be referred to **skein*, from *sghein*, *sghoin*, rope, string, Lit. *geinis*, string, Lat. *fûnis*, Gr. σχοῖνος.

sgeir, a rock in the sea, skerry; from Norse *sker*, a rock in the sea, whence Eng. *skerry*, *scaur*: "cut off," from root of Eng. *shear*, G. *sgar*.

sgeith, vomit, Ir. *sceithim*, E. Ir. *scéim*, *sceithim*, W. *chwydu*, Br. *c'houeda*: **sqveti-*; cf. Gr. σπατίγη, thin excrement as in diarrhœa (Bez.). *sgeith-féith*, varicose vein.

sgeò, g. **sgiach**, haze, dimness (Heb.): see *ceò*.

sgeòc, a long neck; cf. *geòc*.

sgeòp, a torrent of foolish words, also **sgeog**:

sgeul, sgial, a tale, Ir. *sgeul*, O. Ir. *scél*, W. *chwedl*, Cor. *whethl*, Br. *quehezl* (*que-hezl*, *que*=*ko-*): **sqetlo-n* (*sqedlo-n*, Rhys), root *seq*, say: Lat. *inseque*, dic, *inquam* (=*in-squam*?), say I; Gr. ἐννέπω, I tell, ἔνι-σπε, dixit; Ger. *sagen*, Eng, *say*; Lit. *sakýti*, say.

sgeun, dread, disgust, look of fear, Ir. *sgéan*, fright, wild look, M. Ir. *scén*, affright: **skeng-no-*, from *skeng*, start, spring, E. Ir. *scingim*, start, spring (for root see *sgaoim*). Strachan refers it to **skakno-*, root *skak*, spring, Lit. *szókti*, spring, Ch. Sl. *skakati*, Norse *skaga*, jut out.

sgiab, a snatch, sudden movement, Ir. *sgiob* ; see *sgiobag.*

sgiamh, beauty, Ir. *sgiamh,* O. Ir. *scíam* : **skeimâ* ; cf. Got. *skeima,* a light, Ag. S. *scíma,* Norse *skími,* a gleam of light, further Eng. *shine, shimmer.*

sgiamh, a squeal, yell, mew ; see *sgeamh.*

sgian, a knife, Ir. *sgian,* E. Ir. *scían,* W. *ysgíen,* slicer, scimitar, *ysgi,* cutting off, Br. *skeja,* cut : **skêenâ,* vb. *skêô,* cut ; Skr. *châ,* cut off, Gr. σχάζω, cut, σχάω ; I. E. root *skhê, skha,* split, cut. Lindsay refers Gadelic to **scênâ,* allied to Lat. *scêna,* a priest's knife, whose side-form is *sacena,* from *seco,* cut, Eng. *section, saw.* Others have compared Lat. *scio,* know, Gr. κείω, cut.

sgiath, a shield, Ir. *sgiath,* O. Ir. *sciath,* W. *ysgwyd,* O. W. *scuit,* O. Br. *scoit,* Br. *skoued* : **skeito-* ; Ch. Sl. *stitŭ,* shield ; O. Pruss. *scaytan,* Norse *skíð,* firewood, billet of wood, tablet (Schräder) ; to which Bez. queries if Lat. *scûtum* (**skoito-* ?) be allied.

sgiath, a wing, Ir. *sgiathán, sgiath,* E. Ir. *sciath* (*sciath n-ete,* shoulder of the wing), O. Ir. *scíath,* ala, pinna, W. *ysgwydd,* shoulder, Cor. *scuid,* scapula, Br. *skoaz* : **skeito-,* **skeidâ,* shoulder-blade ; I. E. root *sqid,* Lat. *scindo* ; Gr. σχίζω, split ; Skr. *chid,* cut ; further Ger. *scheiden,* divide (I. E. *shheit*), which agrees with the Gadelic form.

sgibeach, sgibidh, neat ; see *sgiobalta.*

sgid, a little excrement (M'A.) ; from the Eng.

sgideil, a plash of water ; see *sgiodar.*

sgil, skill ; from the Eng.

sgil, unhusk, shell, Ir. *sgiollaim, sgilc,* shellings of corn, *sgilice,* the operation of the mill in shelling corn : **skeli-,* I. E. *sqel,* separate ; Norse *skilja,* separate, Eng. *skill, shell,* etc. See *scoilt.* Cf. Sc. *shillin,* shelled or unhusked grain.

sgilbheag, a chip of slate (Arg.) ; from Sc. *skelve,* a thin slice, Eng. *shelf.*

sgilig, shelled grain (Dial.), from Norse, whence Sc. *shillin,* which see under *sgil.* Ir. *sgilige, sgileadh, sgiolladh,* shelling grain.

sgillinn, a penny, Ir. *sgillin,* shilling, M. Ir. *scilling, scillic,* from Ag. S. *scilling,* Norse *skillingr,* Ger. *schilling.*

sgilm, a mouth expressive of scolding aptitude (M'A.) ; see *sgiolam.*

sgimilear, a vagrant parasite, intruder ; from Sc. *skemmel.* Cf. *sgiomalair.*

sginn, squeeze out, gush out, Ir. *scinn,* gush, start, E. Ir. *scendim,* spring ; Skr. *skand,* leap ; Lat. *scando* ; Gr. σκάνδαλον, Eng. *scandal.* Arm. has **sginichd,** squeezing ; Badenoch Dial. has

sging, a squeeze, hardship. There is an E. Ir. *scingim*, I spring, from *skeng*, discussed under *sgaoim*.

sgioba, ship's crew; from the Norse *skip*, a ship.

sgiobag, a slap given in play, a hasty touch or snatch, **sgiob**, **sgiab**, snatch, Ir. *sgiobaim*, I snatch, W. *ysgip*, *ysgipiol*; cf. Manx *skibbag*, skip, hop, from Eng. *skip*.

sgiobair, a skipper; from the Sc. *skippare*, Eng. *skipper*, Norse *skipari*, a mariner.

sgiobal, **sgìobal** (Suth.), a barn, Ir. *sgiobál*:

sgioball, loose folds or skirts of a garment:

sgiobalta, clever, neat, Manx *skibbylt*, active, a skipping, Ir. *sgiobalta*, active, spruce; also G. **sgioblaich**, adjust the dress, etc., tidy up. Cf. Norse *skipulag*, order, arrangement, *skipa*, put in order, Eng. *ship shape*. The Gadelic is borrowed.

sgiodar, a plashing through bog and mire, diarrhœa; from Sc. *scutter*, *skitter*.

sgiogair, a jackanapes, Ir. *sgigire*, a buffoon, mocker; see *sgeig*.

sgiolam, forward talk, also **sgeilm**; also **giolam**. See *sgeilm*. *sgiol* (Lewis), empty talk; N. *skjal*.

sgiolc, slip in or out unperceived; cf. Eng. *skulk*.

sgiolbhagan, fibs (Wh.):

sgiomalair, an instrument to take the suet off a pot (M'A.); from Eng. *skim?*

sgìonabhagan, "smithereens" (Arg.); from *sgian?*

sgionnadh, starting, eyes starting with fear; see *sginn*.

sgionn-shuil, a squint eye; from Eng. *squint*, with a leaning on G. *sgionn*, *sginn*, start, protrude.

sgiord, squirt, purge, Ir. *sgíordadh* (n.), *sgiurdaim* (O'R.); either cognate with or borrowed from Eng. *squirt* (Stokes' *Lis.*).

sgiorr, slip, stumble, Ir. *sciorraim*:

sgiort, a skirt, edge of a garment, Ir. *sgiorta*; from Eng. *skirt*. O'Cl. has Ir. *sguird* for tunic or shirt.

sgiot, scatter; from Norse *skjóta*, shoot, *skyti*, shooter. M'A. says the word belongs to the North Highlands; Arm. does not have it. Ir. has *sgiot*, a dart, arrow: "something shot."

sgìre, a parish; from Ag. S. *scír*, county, now *shire*, O.H.G. *scîra*, charge.

sgirtean, a disease in cattle—black spauld or quarter-ill (H.S.D.): "stumbling disease," from *sgiorradh?*

sgìth, tired, Ir. *sgíth*, weariness, O. Ir. *scíth*, Corn. *sqwyth*, *skîth*, Br. *skouîz*, *skuîz*: **skîto-*, **skîtto-* (Brittonic **skvîtto-*, according to Stokes); root *skhei* beside *khsei*, decay, destroy, Gr. φθίω, decay, φθίσις, phthisis, Skr. *kshi*, destroy, *kshitás*, exhausted (Strachan, *Bez. Beit.*[17] 300).

sgithiol, a shealing hut (Carmichael); from Norse *skýli*, a shed, *skjól*, a shelter, Dan. and Swed. *skjul*, shed, Eng. *sheal.*

sgiùcan, sgiùchan, the cackling or plaint of a moorhen:

sgiùgan, a whimper; cf. the above word.

sgiùnach, a charm for getting all the fish about a boat or headland into one's own boat amidst the amazement of the neighbours (M'A.):

sgiùnach, a bold, shameless woman (H.S.D.):

sgiurdan, a squirt; from the Eng.

sgiùrs, scourge, Ir. *sgiúrsaim*, W. *ysgors*; from M. Eng. *scourge*, Lat. *excoriare.*

sgiùthadh, a lash, stroke with a whip (H.S.D. says Dial.; M'A. says North):

sglabhart, a blow on the side of the head; from Sc. *sclaffert* (do.), *sclaff*, a blow, Prov. Fr. *esclaffa*, to beat (Ducange), Med. Lat. *eclaffa.*

sglàib, ostentation (Hend.):

sglaim, questionably acquired wealth, **sglaimire**, usurper (M'A.); see *glam.*

sglamhadh, a seizing greedily upon anything, Ir. *sclamhaim*, I seize greedily, scold; also G. **sglamadh** (M'E.); see *glam.*

sglamhruinn, a scolding, abusive words; cf. Sc. *sclourie*, vilify, abuse, bedaub. Ir. *sglamhadh* means also "scold," and G. **sglamhadh**, scold of a sudden (M'A.). Sc. has *sklave*, to calumniate.

sglamhradh, clawing one's skin for itch (M'A.); see *clamhradh.*

sgleamhas, meanness, sordidness, **sgleamhraidh**, a stupid or mean fellow.

gleamaic, plaster (vb.), daub filthily (M'A.), **sgleamaid**, snotters (M'A.):

sglèap, ostentation, Ir. *sgléip*; M'A. gives the force of "to flatter, stare open-mouthed at one."

sgleò, dimness of the eyes, vapour:

sgleò, boasting, romancing, Ir. *scleo*, boasting, high language:

sgleò, misery, Ir. *scleo* (O'Cl.):

sgleòbach, sluttish:

sgleobht, a chunk (M'D.):

sgleog, a snot, phlegm, a knock:

sgleogair, a troublesome prattler, liar:

sgleòid, a silly person, slattern, Ir. *scleóid*; also **gleòid**:

sgliamach, slippery-faced (M'L.):

sgliat, slate, Ir. *scláta*; from M. Eng. *sclat*, now *slate.*

sglìmeach, troublesome, as an unwelcome guest:

sgliobhag, a slap (Dial.); cf. Sc. *sclaff, sclaffert.*

sgliùrach (**sgliurach**, H.S.D.), a slut, gossip, Ir. *sgliurach*. The G. also means "young of the sea-gull till one year old," when they become **sgàireag**.

sglongaid, a snot, spit; see *glong*.

sgob, snatch, bite, sting, Ir. *sgoballach*, a morsel, piece; also G. **sgobag**, a small wound, a small dram. Seemingly formed from **gob**, a bill, mouth (cf. O. Fr. *gobet*, morsel, *gober*, devour, Eng. *gobble*).

sgoch, gash, make an incision; for *scoth*; see *sgath*.

sgòd, the corner of a sheet, the sheet of a sail, a sheet-rope, M. Ir. *scóti*, sheets; from Norse *skaut*, the sheet or corner of square cloth, the sheet rope, a hood, Got. *skauts*, hem, Eng. *sheet*.

sgog, a fool, idler, **sgogach**, foolish, Ir. *sgogaire* (O'R.), W. *ysgogyn*, fop, flatterer:

sgòid, pride, conceit, Ir. *sgóid*; G. **sgoideas**, pageantry, ostentation:

sgoid, drift-wood (Lewis); N. *skiða*.

sgoil, school, Ir. *sgoil*, E. Ir. *scol*, W. *ysgol*, Br. *skol*; from Lat. *schola*, whence Eng. *school*.

sgoileam, loquacity; see *sgiolam*.

sgoilt, split, **sgoltadh**, splitting, Ir., M. Ir. *scoiltim*, inf. *scoltad*, O. Ir. *diuscoilt*, scinde (*St. Gal. Incant.*), Cor. *felja*, Br. *faouto*, split: **sqoltô*, split, root *sqvel*; Lit. *skêlto*, split, *skiliù*, split; Norse *skiljan*, separate, Ger. *schale*, shell, Eng. *shale*, *skill*; Gr. σκάλλω, hoe, σκύλλω, tear.

sgoim, wandering about, skittishness (Hend.); cf. *sgaoim*.

sgoinn, care, efficacy, neatness:

sgoirm, throat, lower parts of a hill (M'P. *Ossian*); for latter force, see under *sgairneach*.

sgoitich, a quack, mountebank:

sgol, rinse, wash; from Norse *skola*, wash, Swed. *skölja*, rinse, wash, Dan. *skylle*.

sgolb, a splinter, Ir. *sgolb*, M. Ir. *scolb*, a wattle, W. *ysgolp*, splinter, Br. *skolp*: **skolb-*, root *skel*, *skol*, split (see *sgoilt*), fuller root *skel-g*; Gr. κολοβός, stunted, σκόλοψ (σκόλοπος), stake; Swed. *skalks*, a piece, also Got. *halks*, halt, Eng. *shelf*, *spelk* (Persson *Zeit.*[33] 290 for Gr. and Teut.).

sgonn, a block of wood, blockhead; *sgonn-balaich*, lump of a boy: **skotsno-*, "section"; from the root of *sgath*.

sgonsair, an avaricious rascal (M'D.):

sgop, foam, froth (M'D.):

sgor, a mark, notch, Ir. *sgór*; from Eng. *score*, Norse *skor*, mark, notch, tally (G. is possibly direct from Norse).

sgòr, sgòrr, a sharp rock; from Sc. *scaur*, Eng. *scar*, cliff, of Scandinavian origin, Norse *sker*, skerry; O. H. G. *scorra*, rock; further Eng. *shore*, Ag. S. *score*. See *sgeir* further.

sgòrnan, a throat, Ir. *scornán*:

sgot, a spot, blemish, small farm; cf. Sc. *shot*, a spot or plot of ground.

sgoth, a boat, skiff, a Norway skiff; from Scandinavian—Dan. *skude*, Norse *skúta*, a cutter, small craft.

†**sgoth,** a flower, Ir. *sgoth*; Lat. *scateo*, gush (St. *Zeit.*[33]).

sgrabach, rough, ragged, Ir. *sgrábach*, *sgrabach* (Lh.); from Eng. *scrap*, *scrappy*, Norse *skrap*, scraps.

sgrabaire, the Greenland dove; hence Sc. *scraber*.

sgragall, gold-foil, spangle (Sh., Lh., etc.; not M'A. or M'E.), Ir. *sgragall*:

sgraideag, small morsel, diminutive woman, Ir. *sgraideóg*. M'A. gives **sgràid,** a hag, old cow or mare, and H.S.D. **sgraidht** (do.). Cf. Sc. *scradyn*, a puny, sickly child, *scrat*, a puny person, Norse *skratti*, wizard, goblin.

sgraig, hit one a blow:

sgràill (sgraill, H.S.D.), rail at, abuse:

sgraing, a scowling look, niggardliness; I. E. *sqrengo-*, shrink; Eng. *shrink*; Gr. κράμβος, blight.

sgràist, a sluggard, Ir. *scraiste* (Lh., etc.):

sgrait, a shred, rag:

sgràl, a host, a large number of minute things (Heb.); cf. *sgriothail*.

sgrath, outer skin or rind, turf (for roofing, etc.), Ir. *sgraith*, green sward, sod, *sgraithim*, I pare off the surface, W. *ysgraf*, what pares off, *ysgrawen*, hard crust; cf. Norse *skrá*, dry skin, scroll (**skrava*), Sc. *scra*, a divot (Dumfries).

sgrathail, destructive, Ir. *sgraiteamhuil* (O'R.):

sgreab, a scab, blotch, crust, Ir. *sgreabóg*, a crust; from Eng. *scrape?*

sgread, a screech, cry, Ir. *sgread*, M. Ir. *scret*: **skriddo-*, W. *ysgri*, root *skri*, *skrei*; O. H. G. *scrīan*, cry, Ger. *schrei*, Eng. *scream*, *screech*; Lat. *screô* (= *screjô*), a hawk.

sgreag, dry, parch; from the Scandinavian—Norwegian *skrekka*, shrink, parch, Swed. *skraka*, a great dry tree, Eng. *shrink*, *scraggy* (from Scandinavian).

sgreamh, abhorence, disgust, Ir. *screamh*: **skrimo-*, root *skri*, *skrei*; Norse *skræma*, scare away, Swed. *skräma*, Dan. *skræmme*.

sgreamh, thin scum or rind, ugly skin (M'A.); root *skr̥* of *sgar*.

sgreang, a wrinkle: **skrengo-*, I. E. *sqreng*, shrink; Eng. *shrink* (Dr Cameron). See *sgraing*.

sgreataidh, disgusting, horrible: **skritto-*, root *skri* of *sgreamh*, q.v. Cf. N. *skrati*, a monster, "Old Scratch."

sgreubh, dry up, crack by drought, **sgreath** (M'A., who has **sgreoth**, parch as cloth); cf. Eng. *shrivel*, from a Scandinavian source—base *skriv-*, O. Northumbrian *screpa*, pine, Norwegian *skrypa*, waste; or Sc. *scrae*, dry, withered person, old withered shoe, Norwegian *skrae*.

sgreuch, **sgriach**, a scream, screech, Ir. *sgréach*, E. Ir. *screch*: **skreikâ*, root *skrei*, as in *sgread*, q.v. Eng. *screech*, *shriek* are from the same root (not stem). W. *ysgrêch* seems borrowed from the Eng.

sgreunach, shivering (Arran), boisterous (of weather, Arg.): **sqreng-no-*; see *sgroing*.

sgriach, a score, scratch (Dial.); cf. *stríoch*.

sgribhinn, rocky side of a hill or shore (Arm., M'A.); for *sgridhinn*, from the Norse *skriða*, pl. *skriðna*, a landslip on a hill-side. See *sgrìodan*.

sgrid, breath, last breath of life: **skriddi-*, root *skri* of *sgread*.

sgrìob, a scratch, furrow, line, Ir. *scríob*, E. Ir. *scríb*, mark, *scrípad*, scratching; from Lat. *scribo*, write, draw lines, whence also Norse *skrifa*, scratch, write, W. *ysgrif*, a notch.

sgrìobh, write, Ir. *sgríobhaim*, O. Ir. *scríbaim*, W. *ysgrifo*, Br. *skriva*, *skrifa*; from Lat. *scribo*, write.

sgrìodan, a stony ravine on a mountain side, track of a mountain torrent, a continuous run of stones on a mountain side; from Norse *skriða*, pl. *skriðna*, a landslip on a hill-side, *skríða*, to glide, Ger. *schreiten*, stride; Prov. English *screes*, sliding stones, Sc. *scriddan* (from the Gaelic).

sgrios, destroy, Ir. *scriosaim*, M. Ir. *scrisaim*: **skrissi-* for **skṛ-sti-*, root *skar* of *sgar*, q.v.

sgriotachan, a squalling infant; from *scread*.

sgrioth, gravel (Islay), **sgriothail**, a lot of small items (Badenoch) (do.) as of children (Wh.): **skritu-*, root *sker*; cf. Eng. *short*, I. E. *skṛdh*, little, short.

sgròb, scratch, Ir. *scrobaim*: **skrobbo-*, from *skrob*, scratch; Lat. *scrobis*; a ditch, *scrōfa*, a pig ("scratcher up"); Eng. *scrape*; Lettic *skrabt*, scrape, Ch. Sl. *skreb*, scrape.

sgròban, a bird's crop, Ir. *scrobán*; cf. Eng. *crop*, Ger. *kropf*.

sgrobha, a screw, so Ir.; from the Eng.

sgrog, the head or side of the head (in ridicule), a hat or bonnet; vb. **sgrog**, put on the bonnet firmly, scrog; from the Sc. *scrog*, *scrug*, Eng. *shrug*. In the sense of "head" compare *sgruigean*.

sgrog, sgrogag, anything shrivelled, a shrivelled old woman, old cow or ewe, **sgrog,** shrivel; from the Sc. *scrog*, a stunted bush, *scroggy*, stunted, Eng. *scraggy*, Dan. *skrog*, Swed. *skrokk*, anything shrunken, Norse *skrokkr*.

sgroill, a peeling or paring, anything torn off; from Scandinavian —Dan. *skrael*, peelings or parings of apples, potatoes, Norse *skríll*, a mob.

sgrub, hesitate, **sgrubail,** a hesitating, Ir. *scrub*, hesitate, *sgrubalach*, scrupulous; from Eng. *scruple*.

sgrùd, examine, search, Ir. *scrúdaim*, O. Ir. *scrútaim*; from Lat. *scrûtor*, Eng. *scrutiny*.

sgruigean, neck of a bottle, the neck (in ridicule), Ir. *sgruigín*, neck of a bottle, short-necked person; cf. *sgrog*.

sgruit, an old shrivelled person, a thin person, Ir. *sgruta*, an old man, *sgrutach*, lean, *sgrut*, a contemptible person; cf. Norse *skrudda*, a shrivelled skin, old scroll.

sgrùthan (sgrù'an), a shock of corn (Assynt); from Norse *skrúf*, hay-cock.

sguab, a broom or besom, Ir. *sguab*, E. I. *scúap*, O. Ir. *scóptha*, scopata, W. *ysgub*, Br. *skuba*; from Lat. *scôpa*.

sguaigeis, coquetry; cf. *guag*.

sguainseach, hussy, hoyden (Arg.); possibly from Sc. *quean*: **s-quean-seach*; cf. *siùrsach*.

sguan, slur, scandal (Carm.):

sguch, sprain, strain a joint: "spring"; cf. E. Ir. *scuchim*, I depart, root *skak*, Lit. *szókti*, jump, spring (see *sgeun*).

sgud, lop, snatch; cf. W. *ysgûth*, scud, whisk, Eng. *scud*, Sc. *scoot*, *squirt*, etc. G. is borrowed.

sgùd, a cluster:

sgùd, a scout; from the Eng.

sgudal, fish-guts, offal; cf. *cut*.

sguga, coarse clumsy person, **sgugach,** a soft boorish fellow; see *guga*.

sguidilear, a scullion; from the Sc. *scudler*, *scudle*, cleanse.

sguids, thrash, dress flax, Ir. *sguitsim*; from Eng. *scutch*.

sgùillear, rakish person (Glenmoriston):

sguir, cease, stop, Ir. *sguirim*, O. Ir. *scorim*, desist, unyoke: **skoriô*, root *sker*, *skor*, separate; see *sgar*.

sgùird, sgùirt, the lap, a smock, apron, Ir. *sguird*; from Eng. *skirt*, Norse *skirta*, a shirt.

sguit, the footboard in a boat:

sguit, a wanderer (**scuite,** Shaw): Macpherson's *scuta*, whence he derives *Scotti*—an invention of his own?

sgùlan, a large wicker basket; from Scandinavian—Norse *skjóla*, a bucket, Sc. *skeil*, tub, *skull*, shallow basket of oval form. In Sutherland, **sgulag** means "a basket for holding the linen."

sgulanach, flippant, evil tongued (Carm.):

sgùm, scum, foam; from Norse *skúm*, foam, M. Eng. *scūm*, now *scum*, Ger. *schaum*, foam.

sgùman, a skirt, tawdry head-dress, corn rick; from *sgùm*, "skimmer"? *sguman* (Arran).

sgumrag, a fire-shovel, a Cinderella:

sgùr, scour, Ir. *sgúraim*; from the English.

sgùrr, sharp hill; Heb. for *sgorr*.

sì, she, Ir., O. Ir. *sí*; see *i*.

sia, six, Ir. *sé*; see *sè*.

siab, wipe, sweep along, puff away, Ir. *sìobadh*, blowing into drifts; **sveibbo-*, root *sveib*, Eng. *sweep*; Norse *sveipr*, sweep, Eng. *sweep*. Also **siabh**. Hence **siaban**, sand drift, sea-spray.

siabh, a dish of stewed periwinkles (Heb.):

siabhas, idle ceremony:

siabhrach, a fairy, **sìobhrag** (Arran), **siobhrag** (Shaw), **sìbhreach** (M'A.), Ir. *siabhra*, E. Ir. *siabrae*, *siabur*, fairy, ghost, W. *hwyfar* in *Gwenhwyfar*, *Guinevere* (?): **seibro-*:

siabunn, sìopunn, soap, Ir. *siabhainn* (Fol.), W. *sebon*; from Lat. *sapo(n)*, from Teut. *saipô*, whence Eng. *soap*, Ger. *seife*, Norse *sápa*.

siach, sprain, strain a joint:

siachair, a pithless wretch; another form of *sìochair*.

siad, a stink: **seiddo-*, blow; see *séid*. Cf. Eng. *shite*.

siad, sloth, Ir. *siadhail*, sloth:

sian, a scream, soft music (Carm.), Ir. *sian*, voice, shout, sound, E. Ir. *sian*: **svêno-*, which Stokes (*Zeit.*[28] 59) explains as **sesveno-*, root *sven*, sound (see *seinn*).

sian, a pile of grass, beard of barley, Ir., E. Ir. *sion*, foxglove, W. *ffion*, digitalis, *ffuon*, foxglove, O. W. *fionou*, roses, Br. *foeonnenn*, privet. Stokes gives the Celtic as **s(p)êâno-*. Gadelic might be allied to Lat. *spîna*, thorn.

sian, a charm; see *seun*.

sian, storm, rain, Ir. *síon*, weather, season, storm, O. Ir. *sín*, tempestas, W. *hin*, weather, M. Br. *hynon*, fair weather: **sênâ*; root *sê* (*sêi*) as in *sìn*, *sìor*; Norse *seinn*, slow, late, M. H. G. *seine*, slowly, Eng. *sith*, *since*.

sianan, breac-shianain, freckles; from *sian*, foxglove? See *seunan*.

siar, westward, aside, Ir. *siar*, O. Ir. *síar*; from *s-iar*, see *iar*, west, and *s-* under *suas*.

siaranachadh, languishing, **siarachd**, melancholy (Dial.); from *siar*, "going backwards"?

siasnadh, wasting, dwining (Suth.):

siatag, rheumatism; from Lat. *sciatica*.

sibh, you, ye, Ir. *sibh*, O. Ir. *sib*, *si*, W. *chwi*, O. W. *hui*, Cor. *why*, Br. *c'houi*: **sves*, for *s-ves* (Brug.; Stokes has **svês*); Gr. σφῶϊ, you two, Got. *izvis* (*iz-vis*); the *ves* is allied to Lat. *vos*. The form *sibh* is for **svi-svi*.

sic, the prominence of the belly (H.S.D.), peritoneum (M'A.):

sicear, particle, grain (Carm.):

sicir, wise, steady; from Sc. *sicker*, M. Eng. *siker*, from Lat. *securus*, now Eng. *sure*. W. *sicr* is from M. Eng.

sìd, weather, peaceful weather after storm, tide: **sizdi-*, "settling," root *sed*, sit? Ir. has *síde* in the sense of "blast," from *séid*. Also **tìd**, which suggests borrowing from N. *tíð*, tide, time, Eng. *tide*.

sil, drop, distil, Ir. *silim*, perf. *siblais*, stillavit, Br. *sila*, passez: **sviliô*. Stokes gives the root as *stil*, Lat. *stillo*, drop, Gr. στίλη (do.). Hence **silt**, a drop. Cf. Eng. *spill*; **spild*, destroy, spoil.

sile, spittle, saliva, Ir. *seile*, O. Ir. *saile*, W. *haliw*, Br. *hal*, *halo*: **salivâ* (Stokes); Lat. *saliva*. Stokes says that they appear to be borrowed from Lat., while Wharton thinks the Lat. is borrowed from Gaulish.

sìliche, a lean, pithless creature: "seedy," from *sìol*?

simid, a mallet, beetle, Ir. *siomaide*:

similear, a chimney, Ir. *seimileur*, *simnear*, *simne*; from Eng., Sc. *chimley*, Eng. *chimney*.

simleag, a silly woman; from the next word.

simplidh, simple, Ir. *simplidhe*, silly, simple; from Lat. *simplex*, whence Eng. *simple*, W. *syml*.

sin, that, Ir., O. Ir. *sin*, O. W. *hinn*, W. *hyn*, *hwn*, *hon*, Corn. *hen*, *hon* (fem.), Br. *hen*, Gaul. *sosin* (=*so-sin*); from root *so* (*sjo*), as in *-sa*, *so*, q.v.

sìn, stretch, Ir., O. Ir. *sínim*: **sêno-*, root *sê*, mittere, let go; Lat. *sino*, *situs*; Gr. ἵημι, send. Cf. *sìr* (from **sêro-*, long). Allied is root *sêi*, *sei*, *si*, mittere, Norse *síðr*, long, *seinn*, slow, Lit. *seinyti*, reach.

sine, a teat, Ir., E. Ir. *sine*, *triphne*, three-teated: **svenio-* for **spenio-*, root *spen* of Lit. *spénys*, udder teat, O. Pruss. *spenis*, teat, Norse *speni*, teat, Du. *speen*, udder, Sc *spain*, wean

sineubhar, gin, juniper tree (Suth.); Fr. *genièvre*.

sinn, we, us, Ir. *sinn*, E. Ir. *sinn*, *sinne*, O. Ir. *ni*, *sni*, *snisni*, *sninni*, W. *ni*, *nyni*, Cor. *ny*, *nyni*, Br. *ni*: **nes* (Brug.; Stokes gives *nês*), accusative form, allied to Lat. *nôs*, Skr. *nas*, Gr. *νώ*. The *s* of *sni* is due to analogy with the *s* of *sibh*, or else prothetic (cf. *is-sé*, he is).

sinnsear, ancestors, Ir. *sinnsear*, ancestors, an elder person, E. Ir. *sinser*, elder, ancestor: **senistero-*, a double comparative form (like Lat. *minister*, *magister*) from *sean*, old, q.v.

sinte, plough traces, from *sìn*.

sinteag, a skip, pace; from *sìn*.

siob, drift as snow (M'A.); see *siab*.

siobag, a blast of the mouth, puff, Ir. *siobóg*; cf. *siab*.

sioban, foam on crest of waves; see *siaban*.

siobail, fish, angle (M'A.), **sioblach**, fishing:

siobhag, a straw, candle wick:

sioblach, a long streamer, long person (M'A.); from *siab*?

siobhalta, civil, peaceful, Ir. *sibhealta*, from Ir. *síothamhuil*, peaceable, E. Ir. *sídamail*. Borrowing from Eng. *civil* has been suggested (*Celt. Mag.*[12] 169).

siochaint, peace, Ir. *síocháin*, peace, *síothchánta*, peaceful, *síodhchan*, atonement, M. Ir. *sídchanta*, peaceful; from *síth*.

siochair, a dwarf, fairy, M. Ir. *sidhcaire*, fairy host, *síthcuiraibh* (dat. pl.), E. Ir. *síthchaire*; from *síth*, fairy, and *cuire*, host (Ger. *heer*, army, Eng. *herald*).

sioda, silk, Ir. *síoda*, E. Ir. *síta*, W. *sidan*; from L. Lat. *sêta*, silk, from Lat. *sêta*, a bristle, hair; whence Ag. S. *síde*, silk, Eng. *satin*.

siogach, pale, ill-coloured, Ir. *síogach*, streaked, ill-coloured, *síog*, a streak, a shock of corn:

siogach, greasy (M'A.), lazy (M'F.):

siogaid, a starveling, lean person; from Lat. *siccus*?

siol, seed, Ir. *síol*, O. Ir. *síl*, semen, W. *hil*: **sêlo-n*, root *sê*, sow; Lat. *sêmen*; Eng. *seed*, Ger. *saat*; Lit. *pa-sėlýs*, a sowing.

siola, a gill; from the Eng.

siola, a wooden collar for a plough horse; from Scandinavian—Swed. *sela*, a wooden collar, Norse *seli*, harness, *sili*, a strap, Sc. *sele*, a wooden collar to tie cattle to the stalls.

siola, a syllable, Ir. *siolla*, E. Ir. *sillab*; from Lat. *syllaba*, whence Eng. *syllable*.

sioladh, straining, filtering, Ir. *síolthughadh*, E. Ir. *sithlad*, W. *hidlo*, *hidl*, a filter; also O. Ir. *síthal* = Lat. *situla*, a bucket; from Lat. *situla* (Stokes *Lismore*). G. **sioladh**, also means "subsiding," and leans for its meaning, if not its origin, upon *sìth*, peace.

sìolag, a sand-eel :

siolc, snatch, pilfer :

siolgach, lazy, dwarfish :

sioll, a turn, rotation (M'A.), W. *chwyl* ; see *seal*. Cf. Ir. *siolla,* whiff, glint, syllable ; root of *seal.*

siolp, slip away, skulk (Skye) :

sìolta, a teal, small wild duck ; from Eng. *teal* ?

sìoman, a rope of straw or hay ; from the Norse *síma*, g. pl. *símna,* a rope, cord, Sc. *simmonds*, heather ropes (Orkney), Teut. **sîmon-*, Ag. S. *síma*, fetter, Shet. *simmen* ; Gr. ἱμονία (ι long), well rope ; I. E. *sîmon-*, a bond, band, *seio-*, bind.

siomlach ; see *seamlach.*

sìon, something, anything ; also "weather," for *sian*, whence possibly this meaning of "anything" comes.

sionadh, lord (M'Pherson's *Fingal*[1], 341) : if genuine, the root may be *sen*, old ; cf. Lat. *senior*, now Eng. *sir.*

sionn, phosphorescent, solus **sionn,** phosphorus, also **teine-sionn-achain.** For root see next.

sionnach, valve of bellows, pipe-reed, **pìob-shionnaich,** Irish bag-pipe. From root *spend*, swing, play, Skr. *spand*, move quickly. Gr. σφεδόνη, sling, Lat. *pendeo*, hang, Eng. *pendulum.*

sionnach, a fox, so Ir., E. Ir. *sinnach*, *sindach*, O. Ir. *sinnchenae,* vulpecula :

sionnsar, bagpipe chanter, Ir. *siunsoir* ; from the Eng. *chanter.*

siop, despise ; *cuir an siop*, turn tail on (Hend.) ; see *sèap.*

sìopunn, soap ; see *siabunn.*

sìor, long, continual, Ir. *síor*, O. Ir. *sír*, comparative *sía*, W. *hir*, compar. *hwy*, Cor., Br. *hir* : **sêro-s* ; Lat. *sêrus*, late, Fr. *soir,* evening, Eng. *soiree* ; Skr. *sâyá*, evening. See *sian*, *sìn.*

siorra (M'A., M'E.), **siorraimh, siorram** (H.S.D.), a sheriff, **siorrachd, siorramachd,** county, Ir. *sirriamh*, M. Ir. *sirriam* ; from M. Eng. *shirreve*, now *sheriff*, "shire-reeve." The Sc. is *shirra* usually.

siorradh, a deviation, onset : **sith-rad*, from *sith* ?

sìorruidh, eternal, Ir. *síorruidhe* ; from **sír-rad*, eternity, *sìor.*

sìos, down, Ir. *síos*, O. Ir. *sís* : **s-ís*, from *s-* (see *suas*) and *ís*, or *ìos*, q.v.

siosar, a scissors, Ir. *siosur* ; from the Eng.

siota, a blackguard, a pet ; from Sc. *shit.*

sir, search, Ir. *sirim* (*sírim*, Con.), E. Ir. *sirim* : **s(p)eri-*, root *sper,* foot it ; Norse *spyrja*, ask, track, Sc. *spere*, ask after, Ger. *spüren*, trace, track, also further Eng. *spur* ; Lat. *sperno* (Eng. *spurn* allied), etc. The vowel of *sir* is short (otherwise

Stokes' *Dict.*, Rhys *Manx Pray.*[2] 71, who compares W. *chwilio*).

siris, sirist, a cherry, Ir. *siris*, W. *ceirios*; from M. Eng. **cheris*, from O. Fr. *cerise*, Lat. *cerasus*, Gr. κέρασος.

siteag, a dunghill; from the Eng. Cf. N. *saeti*.

sith, a stride, onset, a dart to, Ir. *sidhe*, gust, M. Ir. *sith*, onset; cf. Ir. *sith-*, intensive prefix (O'Don. *Gr.* 277), **setu-*, *seti-*, may be root *es*, ἐτυμός (Bez.[21] 123), E. Ir. *sith*, long, W. *hyd*, to, as far as, O. W. *hit*, longitudo, usque ad, Br. *hed*, length, during: **seti*, root *sē*, as in *sìor*, long (Stokes). Cf. N. *síðr*, long, Eng. *sith*; root *sit*.

sìth, peace, Ir. *síth*, *síoth*, E. Ir. *síth*, O. Ir. *síd*: **sêdos* (neut. *s* stem), root *sed* (*sêd*) of **suidhe,** q.v.; Lat. *sêdo*, settle; Lit. *sėdáti*, sit. W. *hedd*, peace, is from *sĕd*.

sìth, a fairy, **sìthich** (do.), Ir. *sídh*, a fairy hill, *sígh*, a fairy, *sígheóg* (do.), O. Ir. *síde*, dei terreni, whose dwelling is called *síd*; in fact, *síde*, the fairy powers, is the pl. (gen. s.?) of *síd*, fairy dwelling or mound, whild its gen. sing. appears in *mná síde*, *fir síde*: **sêdos*, g. *sêdesos*, as in the case of *sìth*, peace, which is its homonym (Stokes); root *sed*, *sêd*, Gr. ἕδος, a temple or statue, literally an "abode" or "seat;" Lat. *noven-sides*, *noven-siles*, the new gods imported to Rome. Thurneysen has compared Lat. *sîdus*, a constellation, "dwelling of the gods." Hence **sìthean,** a green knoll, fairy knoll.

sithionn, venison, Ir. *sídh* and *sídheann* (O'R.), M. Ir. *sieng*, *sideng*, deer, W. *hyddgig* (="stag's flesh"), from *hydd*, stag, red deer: **sedi-*, deer; to which is to be referred M. Ir. *segh* (=agh allaidh, O'Cl.), E. Ir. *ség* (=oss allaidh, Corm.).

sitig, the rafter of a kiln laid across, on which the corn is dried:

sitinn, roller for a boat:

sitir, sitrich, neighing, Ir. *sitreach*: cf. *séid*, blow (**svid-tri-*).

siubhal, walking, so Ir., M. Ir. *siubal*, for **siumal*, W. *chwyf*, motus, *chwyfu*, move, stir, M. Br. *fifual*, now *finval*, stir; root *svem*, move; O.H.G. Ag. S. *swimman*, Eng. *swim*. Cf. W. *syflyd*, move, stir.

siubhla; see *luighe-siubhla*.

siuc, a word by which horses are called:

siucar (**siùcar,** H.S.D.), sugar, Ir. *siúcra*, W. *sugr*; from M. Eng. *sugre*, Fr. *sucre*.

siùdadh, swinging; from Sc. *showd*, swing, waddle, O. Sax. *skuddian*, shake, O. Du. *schudden* (do.), Eng. *shudder*.

siug, call to drive away hens; cf. Eng. *shoo*!

siunas, lovage plant; see *sunais*.

siup, a tail, appendage; cf. *sèap*.

siùrsach, a whore; from the Eng., with the G. fem. termination *-seach* (see *òinnseach*).

siuthad, say away, begin, go on: **seo-tu*, " here you," from *so* and *tu*? Cf. *trobhad*, *thugad*.

slabhag, pith of a horn: Sc. *sluch*?

slabhagan, a kind of reddish sea-weed, sloke, Ir. *slabhacán*; from Eng. *sloke*, Sc. *sloke*, *slake*.

slabhcar, a slouching fellow (Suth.), a taunter; from Norse *slókr*, slouching fellow, whence Eng. *slouch*.

slabhraidh, a chain, Ir. *slabhra*, O. Ir. *slabrad*: **slab-rad*, from *slab*, root *lag* of Gr. λαμβάνω, I take, catch, Eng. *latch*.

slachd, thrash, beat, Ir. *slacairim*; root *slag*, *sleg*, or *sḷg*, E. Ir. *sligim*, beat, strike, *slacc*, sword: **slegô*, beside I. E., *slak*, as in Got. *slaha*, strike, Ger. *schlagen* (do.), Eng. *slay* (Stokes for *sligim*); further Lat. *lacerare*, lacerate, Gr. λακίζω, tear (Kluge). Hence **slachdan**, beetle, rod.

slad, theft, Ir. *slad*, M. Ir. *slat*: **sladdo-*. Stokes gives the Celtic as **stlatto-*, allied to Lat. *stlâta* (*stlatta*), pirate ship, and Eng. *steal*. The modern forms point to Gadelic **sladdo-*, for **stḷ-ddo-*, allied to Eng. *steal*?

sladhag, a sheaf of corn ready to be thrashed (H.S.D.):

sladhaigeadh, a kind of custard spread over bread (M'D.):

slag, a hollow (Lewis); N. *slakki*, slope, North Eng. *hollow*.

slàib, mire; see *làban*. Skeat refers Eng. *slab*, slime, but it is likely native (cf. *slop*, etc.).

slaid, a munificent gift:

slaightear, slaoightear, a rogue, Ir. *sloitire*, rogue, *sloitireachd*, roguery, M. Ir. *sleteoracht*, theft (O'Cl.); from *slad* (Ir. *sloit*), rob.

slaim, great booty, a heap: from the Sc. *slam*, a share or possession acquired not rightly, *slammach*, to seize anything not entirely by fair means, Swed. *slama*, heap together.

slais, lash; from the Eng.

slam, a lock of hair or wool, Ir. *slám*, E. Ir. *slamm*: **slags-men*, Gr. λάχνος, wool, λάχνη, down (otherwise Prellwitz, who refers Gr. to **vḷk-snâ*, root *vel* of *olann*, q.v.).

slaman, curdled milk, Ir. *slamanna*, clots, flakes (O'Cl.), E. Ir. *slaimred* (na fola). Cf. *lommen*, gulp.

slàn, healthy, whole, Ir., O. Ir. *slán*: **sḹ-no-* (Brug.), **səlâno-s* (Stokes); Lat. *salvus* (= *sḷ-vo-*, Brug.), safe, *solidus*, firm, Eng. *solid*; Gr. ὅλος, whole (= σόλϝος); Eng. *silly*, originally meaning "blessed," Ger. *selig*, blessed; Skr. *sárvas*, whole, all. W., Br. *holl* is referred here by Stokes, etc., more immediately allied to Lat. *sollus*, whole, all.

slaod, drag, trail, Ir. *slaodaim*, draw after, slide, *slaod*, a raft, float, E. Ir. *sláet*, a slide : **sloiddo-*, Celtic root *sleid*, *slid* ; W. *litthro*, Eng. *slide*, Ag. S. *slídan*, Ger. *schlitten*, slide, sledge (n.) ; Lit. *slidùs*, smooth, Gr. ὀλισθανω, **slid-d-*. Stokes explains the *d* of *slaod* as for *dd*, from *-dnó-* : **slaidh-nó-*.

slaop, parboil, **slaopach**, parboiled, slovenly, Ir. *slaopach*, lukewarm (O'R.) ; also *slaopair*, a sloven, for which see next.

slapach, slàpach, slovenly, Ir. *slapach*, slovenly, *slapar*, a trail or train ; from Scandinavian—Norse *slápr*, a good-for-nothing, *slaepa*, vestis promissa et laxa (Jamieson), *sloppr*, Eng. *slop*, Sc. *slaupie*, slovenly, Dutch *slap*, slack, remiss, Ger. *schlaff*.

slapraich, din, noise ; from Eng. *slap*.

slat, a rod, twig, Ir. *slat*, M. Ir. *slat*, *slatt*, W. *llath*, *yslath*, Br. *laz* : **slattâ* ; Eng. *lath* is from W. M. Eng. *latte*, Ag. S. *laetta*, O. H. G. *latta*, Ger. *latte* are also Celtic borrows, Fr. *latte* (Thurneysen), but Kluge regards them as cognate.

sleabhag, mattock for digging up carrots, etc. (Carm.) ; *sleidheag*, kind of ladle (Lewis) ; cf. N. *sleif*.

sleagh, a spear, so Ir., E. Ir. *sleg* : **sl̥gâ* ; Skr. *sr̥j*, hurl, sling.

sleamacair, sly person (Lewis) ; cf. N. *slaemr*, bad.

sleamhan, stye (Carm.) :

sleamhuinn, slippery, smooth, Ir. *sleamhuin*, O. Ir. *slemon*, W. *llyfn*, smooth, O. Br. *limn* (in compounds) : **slib-no-s*, root *slib*, *sleib* ; Norse *sleipr*, slippery, Eng. *slip*, slippery ; Gr. ὀλιβρός, λιβρός, slippery. See *sliabh* also.

sléigeil, dilatory, **sleugach**, drawling, slow, sly ; also **leug**, laziness ; from the Sc. *sleek* ?

sléisneadh, back-sliding (Heb.) : **sleið-s-*, root of *slaod* and Eng. *slide* ?

sleuchd, kneel, Ir. *sléachdain*, O. Ir. *sléchtaim* ; from Lat. *flecto*.

sliabh, a moor, mountain, Ir. *sliabh*, mountain, O. Ir. *slíab* : **sleibos*, root *sleib*, *slib*, glide, down, I. E. *sleigo-* ; Eng. *slope*, from *slip*, Norse *sleipr*, slippery ; see *sleamhuinn*. W. *llwyf*, platform, loft, seems allied to G. *sliabh*.

sliachdair, spread any soft substance by trampling, daub : **sleikto-*, *sleig*, Norse *slíkr*, smooth, Eng. *sleek*, Ger. *schlick*, grease, the original idea being "greasy," like soft mud. Cf. E. Ir. *sliachtad*, smoothing, preening.

sliasaid, **sliasad** (**sliaisd**, Dial.), thigh, Ir. *sliasad*, O. Ir. *sliassit*, poples : a diphthongal form of the root of *slis*, q.v.

slibist, a sloven ; cf. Ir. *sliobair*, drag along ; from Eng *slip*, *sloven*.

slige, a scale of a balance, a shell, Ir. *slige*, a grisset, shell, O. Ir. *slice*, lanx, ostrea : **sleggio-*, root *sleg*, for which cf. *slachd*.

slighe, a way, Ir. *slighe*, E. Ir. *slige*, g. *sliged* : **sleget-*, root *sleg* of Ir. *sligim*, I strike (*ro sligsetar*, *ro selgatar rotu*, they hewed out ways). See *slachd* further.

slinn, a weaver's sley or reed, Ir. *slinn*, a sley, M. Ir. *slind*, pecten, also *slige*, pecten, which suggests for *slinn* a stem : **sleg-s-ni-*, *sleg* being the same root as that of *slighe* and *slachd*. Cf. Eng. *sley* allied to *slay*, smite. Stokes refers both O. Ir. *slind*, tile and weaver's sley, to the root *splid*, *splind*, Eng. *split*, *splint*. See *slinnean* and *sliseag* further.

slinnean, shoulder blade, shoulder, Ir. *slinneán*, M. Ir. *slindén* : cf. O. Ir. *slind*, imbrex, tile, Ir. *slinn*, slate, tile, also E. Ir. *slind-gér*, smooth-sharp, slate-polished (?), *slind-glanait*, whetstone-cleaned : **slindi-*, root *slid*, *sleid*, smooth, glide, Eng. *slide*, Lit. *slidùs*, smooth. Stokes refers *slind*, imbrex, to the root *splid*, *splind*, split, Eng. *split*, *splint* ; see *sliseag*.

sliob, stroke, rub, lick, Ir. *sliobhaim*, polish, M. Ir. *slipthe*, whettened, *slibad*, whetting, W. *yslipan*, burnish ; from Norse or Ag. S.—Norse *slípa*, whet, make sleek, Ag. S. *slípan*, slip, glide, M. L. Ger. *slípen*, sharpen, M. Du. *slijpen*, polish, sharpen.

sliochd, posterity, tribe, Ir. *sliochd*, M. Ir. *slicht*, trace, track, O. Ir. *slict*, vestigium : **slektu-*, root *sleg* of *slighe* and *slachd*. For similar origin, cf. Ger. *geschlecht*, race, lineage.

sliogach, sly, Ir. *slíogach*, sleek, fawning, *slígtheach*, sly ; from Eng., Sc. *sleek*, Norse *slíkr*, smooth ; I. E. *sleig*, glide (see *sliabh*).

sliom, sleek, slippery, slim, the buttercup (Carm.), Ir. *slíomaim* flatter, smooth, gloss over ; from Eng. *slim*, sly, crafty, slender, now "slim," Sc. *slim*, naughty, *slim o'er*, gloss over, O. Du. *slim*, awry, crafty, Ger. *schlimm*, bad, cunning. Hence G. **sliomaire**, weakling, craven.

sliop, a lip, blubber lip ; from Eng. *lip*.

slios, the side of a man or beast, flank, Ir. *slios*, O. Ir. *sliss*, pl. *slessa*, W. *ystlis* : **stlisti-*, root *stel*, extend, Lat. *stlâtus*, *lâtus*, wide, Ch. Sl. *stelja*, spread.

slis, **sliseag**, a chip, Ir. *slis*, *sliseóg*, E. Ir. *sliss* : **slissi-*, from **splid-s-ti-*, root *splid*. Eng. *split*, *splice*, *splint*, Ger. *spleissen*, etc. Eng. *slice* has been compared, Eng. *slit*, root *slid*, which could also produce the Gadelic forms.

slisneach, a plant like the *slan-lus* (Carm.) :

sloc, a pit, slough, Ir. *sloc* : **slukko-*, for **slug-ko-*, root *slug*, swallow, as in *slug*, q.v. Skeat derives hence Ag. S. *slôh*, Eng. *slough*. Ger. *schlucht*, hollow, ravine, is referred by Kluge to the root *slup*, lubricus.

slod, a puddle, Ir. *slod*; see *lod*.

slòcan, sloke; from the Sc. or Eng. *sloke*.

sloinn, surname, Ir. *sloinnim*, I name, O. Ir. *slondim*, name, significo, *slond*, significatio, O. W. *istlinnit*, profatur, M. W. *cy-stlwn*, family and clan name, W. *ystlyned*, kindred, *ystlen*, sex: **stlondo-*, **stlondiô*, I speak, name.

sloisir, dash, beat against sea-like, daub; from Sc. *slaister*, bedaub, a wet liquid mass, to move clumsily through a miry road, also *slestir* (Badenoch Dial. **sleastair**, bedaub).

sluagh, people, Ir. *sluagh*, O. Ir. *sluag*, *slóg*, W. *llu*, Corn. *lu*, Gaul. *slôgi* in *Catu-slogi*: **slougo-s*; cf. Slav. *sluga*, a servant, Lit. *slauginti*.

sluaisreadh, act of mixing (lime, etc.) with a shovel; see next word. Cf. Eng. *slubber*.

sluasaid, a shovel, Ir. *sluasad*, a paddle, a shovel:

slug, swallow, **slugadh** (inf.), Ir. *slugaim*, E. Ir. *slucim*, *slocim*: **sluggô*, root *slug*, *lug*, swallow; Ger. *schlucken*, to swallow, M. H. G. *slucken*: Gr. λύζω, λυγγαίνω, have the hiccup. W. *llwnc*, gullet, a gulp, *llyncu*, to swallow, O. Br. *ro-luncas*, guturicavit, M. Br. *lloncaff* are allied to E. Ir. *longad*, now *longadh*, eating, which is a nasalised form of the root *slug*, *lug*.

smachd, authority, correction, Ir. *smachd*, O. Ir. *smacht*, M. Ir. *smachtaigim*, I enjoin, *smacht*, fine for breaking the law: **smaktu-*, from *s-mag*, root *mag*, I. E. *magh*, be strong; Eng. *may*, Got. *magan*, be able; Gr. μῆχος, means (see *mac*).

smad, a particle, jot: "spot, stain" (see *smod*). From Sc. *smad*, *smot*, a stain, Eng. *smut*. Ir. has *smadán*, soot, smut. Cf. also M. Ir. *smot*, a scrap, Ir. *smotán*, a block, W. *ysmot*, patch, spot.

smàd, threaten, intimidate, boast:

smàg, **smòg**, a paw; see *smòg*.

smal, dust, spot, blemish, Ir. *smál*, *smól*; root *smal*, *mal* (*smel*, *mel*), Lit. *smálkas*, dust, *smėlynas*, sand field, *smelalis*, sand, Lettic *smelis*, water sand, Got. *málma*, sand, Norse *melr*, sand hill, Eng. *mole*.

smàl, snuff a candle, Ir. *smál*, embers, snuff of candle; cf. the above word.

smalag, the young saith or cuddie:

smaoin, think; see *smuain*.

smarach, a lad, a growing youth (Badenoch); root *smar*, from *mar*, *mer*, Gr. μεῖραξ, boy, Skr. *maryakás*, a mannie, *máryas*, young man, Lit. *marti*, bride; also W. *morwyn*, girl, *merch*, daughter, Br. *merc'h.* Cf. Aran Ir. *marlach*, child of two to five years, either sex.

smarag, an emerald, Ir. *smaragaid* ; from Lat. *smaragdus*, whence through Fr. comes Eng. *emerald.*

smeachan, the chin, Ir. *smeach*, *smeachan*, E. Ir. *smech* : **smekâ* ; Lit. *smakrà*, Lettic *smakrs*, chin, palate ; Skr. *çmaçru*, moustache.

smeadairneach, a slumber, light sleep :

smeallach, smealach, remains, offals, dainties :

smèid, beckon, nod, Ir. *sméidim*, beckon, nod, hiss : **smeiddi-*, root *smeid*, smile, Gr. *μειδάω*, smile, Pruss. *smaida*, a smile, Eng. *smile.* W. *amneidio*, beckon, nod, O. W. *enmeituou*, nutus, O. Br. *enmetiam*, innuo, do not agree in vowel with Gadelic.

smeileach, pale, ghastly, **smeilean**, a pale, puny person ; cf. *meileach.*

smeòirn, the end of an arrow next the bowstring, **smeoirne**, back end of arrow head (Wh.), Ir. *smeirne*, a spit, broach (Sh., O'R.) :

smeórach, a thrush, Ir. *smólach*, *smól*, M. Ir. *smolach* ; W. *mwyalch*, blackbird, Corn. *moelh*, Br. *moualch* : **smugal-*, **smugl-*, from *mug* (see *mùch*)? Stokes derives W. *mwyalch*, blackbird, from **meisalko-*, Ger. *meise*, Eng. tit-*mouse.*

smeur, smiar, anoint, smear, Ir. *sméaraim*, grease, smear ; from the Eng. For root see *smior.*

smeur, smiar, a bramble berry, Ir. *smeur*, E. Ir. *smér*, W. *mwyaren*, Br. *mouar* (pl.) :

smeuraich, grope ; from *meur.*

smid, a syllable, opening of the mouth, a word, Ir. *smid* : **smiddi-*, root *smid*, *smeid*, smile, laugh, as in *smèid*?

smig, the chin, Ir. *smig*, M. Ir. *smeice* (O'C.) : **smeggi-*, for **smek-gi*, root *smek*, as in *smeachan*?

smigeadh, a smile, smiling, Ir. *smig*, *smigeadh* : **smĭggi*, root *smi*, smile, for which see *smèid.* Also *mìog*, q.v.

smiodan, spirit ; from Sc. *smeddum.*

smiolamus, refuse of a feast (M'A.) ; see *smolamas.*

smior, smear, marrow, Ir. *smior*, E. Ir. *smir*, g. *smera*, W. *mer* : **smeru-* ; O. H. G. *smero*, grease, Ag. S. *smeoru*, lard, Eng. *smear*, Norse *smjörr*, butter.

smiot, throw in the air with one hand and strike with the other ; formed on Eng. *smite.*

smiotach, crop-eared, short-chinned (R.D.), Ir. *smiot*, ear :

smiùr, smear ; from the Sc. *smear*, Eng. *smear.* See *smeur.*

smod, dirt, dust, also (according to M'A.) drizzling rain ; from Sc. *smot*, Eng. *smut.* See *smad.*

smodal, sweepings, crumbs, fragments, smattering, M. Ir. *smot*, a scrap; cf. above word.

smòg, smàg, a paw; cf. Norse *smjùga*, creep through a hole, Ag. S. *smúgan*, creep, Eng. *smuggle*. For **smàg**, see also *màg*.

smolamas, trash, fragments of victuals; cf. *strolamas*, *brolamas*.

smuain, a thought, Ir. *smuaineadh*, M. Ir. *smuained*: **smoudn-*, root *smoud*, *moud*; Got. *gamaudjan*, remind, cause to remember; Ch. Sl. *myslĭ-*, thought (Strachan). Cf. M. Ir. *muaidnig*, thought.

smuairean, grief, dejection: **smoudro-*, root *smoud* of above?

smuais, marrow, juice of the bones, Ir. *smuais*, marrow, E. Ir. *smuas*:

smuais, smash, Ir. *smuais*, in shivers, in pieces; from Eng. *smash*.

smùc, a snivel, a nasal sound (**smùch**, M'A.); for root, see *smug* (**s-mûc-c*).

smùcan, smoke, drizzle; from Eng. *smoke*.

smùdan, a particle of dust; see *smod*.

smùdan, a small block of wood, Ir. *smotan*, stock, block, log:

smùdan, smoke; see *smùid*.

smug, snot, spittle, **smugaid**, spittle, Ir. *smug*, *smugaid*: **smuggo-*, root *smug*, *mug*, mucus; Lat. *emungo*, wipe the nose. The root *mug* is a by-form of *muq*, mucus, seen in Lat. *mucus*, etc.; for which see *muc*.

smùid, smoke, Ir. *smúid*, E. Ir. *smúit*, *smútgur*, *smútcheo*: **smúddi-*, root *smud*. Cf. Eng. *smut*, Ger. *schmutz*, dirt; which Zim. thinks the Gadelic borrowed from, though the meaning makes this unlikely. There are three allied roots on European ground denoting "smoke"—*smûgh* (Gr. σμύχω, smoulder), *smúg* or *smaug* (Eng. *smoke*) and *smûd* (G. *smùid*).

smuig, a snout, the face (in ridicule): from the Eng. *mug*, ugly face.

smuilc, glumness, dejection; M. Ir. *smuilcín*, a small snout: "snoutyness."

smùrach, dross, peat dross, **smùir**, dust, a particle of dust, **smùirnean**, a mote; cf. Sc. *smurach*, peat dross, *smore*, *smurr*, a drizzling rain, M. Eng. *smóre*, dense smoke, Eng. *smother* (= *smorther*), O. Du. *smoor*. O'R. has *smur* from Sh., and K. Meyer translates M. Ir. *smur-chimilt* as "grind to dust."

smùsach, extracting the juice from (Suth.):

smut, a bill, snout, Ir. *smut*, a large flat nose, snout:

snag, a little audible knock, a wood pecker (**snagan-daraich**), Ir. *snag*, hiccup; cf. Eng. *snock*, a knock, and the next word. Ir. *snag*, *snagardarach*, *snaghairdara*, a wood pecker, seems from *snaidh*.

snagaireachd, cutting or hacking wood with a knife; from Dial. Eng. *snagger*, a tool for *snagging* or cutting off *snags*, that is branches, knots, etc., Sc. *snagger-snee*, a large knife, snicker-snee, *sneg*, *snag*, cut off branches.

snagarra, active; from the above roots; cf. *snasmhor*.

snaidh, hew, chip, shape, Ir. *snoighim*, *snaidhim* (O'D.) E. Ir. *snaidim*, *snaisi*, peeled, W. *naddu*, hew, chip, cut, O. Cor. *nedim*, ascia (W. *neddyf*, *neddai*, adze, Br. *eze*, *neze*), M. Br. *ezeff*: **snadô*; Ger. *schnat*, border, *schnate*, a young twig, Swiss *schnätzen* cut, Swab. *schnatte*, an incision in wood or flesh (Bez. apud Stokes). Strachan suggests the root *sknad*, Gr. κναδάλλω, scratch, κνωδών, tooth (see *cnàmh*). Hence **snas**, regularity.

snàig, creep; from Sc. *snaik*, sneak in walking, etc., *snaikin*, sneaking, Eng. *sneak*, *snake*. Cf. Ir. *snaighim*, I creep.

snaim, a knot, Ir. *snaidhm*, E. Ir. *snaidm*, d. *snaidmaimm*, *naidm*, bond, nexus: **nadesmen*, root *ned*, bind, I. E. *nedh*; Skr. *nah*, tie, *naddha-s*, tied; Ger. *nestel*, lace, O. H. G. *nestila*, a band; Lat. *nôdus*, for *noz-dos*, a knot. See *nasg*.

snàmh, swim, Ir. *snámhaim*, E. Ir. *snám* (inf.), *ro snó*, swam, W. *nawf*, natatio, *nofio* (vb.), M. Br. *neuff*, Br. *neunv*: **snâmu*, (n.), *snâô*, I swim; Lat. *no*, *nâre*; Gr. νάω, flow; Skr. *snâti*, bathe, float.

snaodh, head, chief; *ceann-snaodh*, head chief (Carm.):

snaois, a slice, piece; cf. E. Ir. *snaisse*, cut, caesus, from *snaidh*.

snaoisean, snuff, Ir. *snaoisín*, *snísín*; from Eng. *sneezing* in *sneesing pouder*, the old name for snuff, Sc. *sneeshin*, *sneezin*.

snaomanach, a strong, robust fellow, Ir. *snaománach*, stout, jolly fellow, hearty: "knotty," from **snadm-* of *snaim*?

snaoidh, a bier, Ir. *snaoi*:

snap, the trigger of a gun; from the English *snap*.

snas, regularity, elegance, Ir. *snas*: "good cut," from *snad* of *snaidh*; E. Ir. *snass*, a cut.

snàth, thread, Ir. *snáth*, O. Ir. *snáthe*, W. *ysnoden*, lace, fillet, *noden*, thread, Corn. *noden*, *snod*, vitta, Br. *neudenn*: **snâtio-*, **snâto-n*, root *snâ*, *snê*, wind, spin; Skr. *snâyu*, sinew, bow-string; Gr. εὔννητος, well-spun; Ger. *schnur*, lace, tie. See the allied **sniomh** and the next word below.

snàthad, a needle, Ir. *snáthad*, O. Ir. *snáthat*, W. *nodwydd*, O. Corn. *notuid*, Br. *nadoz*, *nadoez*: **snatantâ*, *snâteijâ*, from *snât* of *snàth* above; cf. Eng. *needle*, Goth. *nêþla*, O. H. G. *nâdala*, Ger. *nadel*.

sneachd, snow, so Ir., O. Ir. *snechta*, pl. *snechti*, nives, W. *nyf*: **sniqtaio-*, **snibi-* (Welsh), I. E. *snigh*, *sneigh*; Got. *snaiws*,

Eng. *snow*, Ger. *schnee*; Lat. *nix*, *nivis*; Gr. *νίφα* (acc.), *νείφει*, it snows; Lit. *sniñga* (vb.), *snẽgas*, snow; Zend. *çnizh*.

sneadh, a nit, Ir. *sneagh*, O. Ir. *sned*, W. *nedd*, nits, Corn., *nedhan*, Br. *nezenn*: **sknidâ*; Ag. S. *hnitu*, Eng. *nit*, Ger. *niss*; Gr. *κόνιδες*, nits.

snicean, a stitch of clothing (Arg.):

snigh, drop, fall in drops, ooze through in drops, Ir. *snidhim*, E. Ir. *snigim*, W. *di-nëu*, effundere, Br. *di-nou*, melt, thaw, I. E. *sneigho-*, wet; Skr. *snih*, *snéhati*, to be humid. Allied to *sneachd*.

snìomh, spin, wind, twist, Ir. *sníomhaim*, M. Ir. *snímaire*, a spindle. *sním*, spinning: **snêmu-*, root, *snê*, *nê*; Gr. *νῆμα*, yarn. See *snàth* further. W. has *nyddu*, nere, Corn. *nethe*, Br. *nezaff*. In the sense of "sadness," there is E. Ir. *sním*, distress, Br. *niff*, chagrin.

snòd, affix a fishing hook to the line, Manx *snooid*; from Sc. *snood*, the hair line to which the hook is attached, a fillet, Ag. S. *snód*, fillet, Eng. *snood*.

snodan, rapid motion of a boat:

snodha, snodha gàire, a smile; see *snuadh*.

snodhach, sap of a tree; root *snu*, flow, Ir. *snuadh*, a stream, Gr. *νέω*, swim, Eng. *snot*, Norse *snúa*, turn, Got. *sniwan*, go.

snoigeas, testiness; from Sc. *snog*, *snag*, snarl, flout.

snot, smell, snuff the wind, turn up the nose in smelling; founded on Eng. *snout*.

snuadh, hue, appearance, beauty, Ir. *snuadh*, M. Ir. *snúad*; root *snu*, flow, as in E. Ir. *snuad*, hair, head of hair, Ir. *snuadh*, stream (see *snodhach*).

so, here, this, Ir. *so*, E. Ir., O. Ir. *seo*, *so*: **sjo-* (beside **so*, as in *-sa*, *-se*), Skr. *syá*, *sá*, the, this, Ger. *sie*, she, they, O. H. G. *siu*, she (= Skr. *syā́*, G. **sì**).

so-, a prefix denoting good quality, Ir. *só-*, O. Ir. *so-*, *su-*, W. *hy*, Br. *he-*; Skr. *su-*, good, Zend. *hu-*.

sòbhaidh, sò'aidh, turn, prevent, O. Ir. *sóim*, inf. *sood*, root *sov*, discussed under *iompaidh*.

sobhrach, sòbhrach, (M'L.), primrose, Ir. *sobhróg* (Fol.), *somharcin* (O'B.), *sóbhrach* (O'R.), E. Ir. *sobrach*, g. *sobarche*:

soc, forepart of anything, ploughshare, snout, Ir. *soc*, E. Ir. *socc*, W. *swch* (f.), Cor. *soch*, Br. *soc'h*, *souc'h* (m.): **succo-*, snout, pig's snout, **sukku-*, a pig, W. *hwch*, Cor. *hoch*, Br. *hou'ch* (Ag. S. *sugu*, Eng. *sow*, Lat. *sûs*, etc.). So Thurneysen (*Rom.*, 112), who clinches his argument by E. Ir. *corr* being both "crane" and "beak." Fr. *soc*, ploughshare, Eng. *sock* are from Celtic. Stokes suggests the possibility of Celtic being from Med. Lat. *soccus*, vomer, or allied to O. H. G. *seh*, vomer, Lat. *secare*.

socair, ease, easy, Ir. *socair*, easy, secure, M. Ir. *soccair*; opposite is **deacair**, O. Ir. *deccair*: **di-acair*, **so-acair*, from **acar*, convenience, root *cor*, place, as in *cuir*. Hence *acarach*.

sochair, a benefit, emolument, Ir. *sochar*, emolument, wealth, ease, M. Ir. *sochor*, good contract (*Sench. Mór*); from *so-* and *cor*, q.v.

sochar, silliness, a yielding disposition, **socharach**, simple, compliant, Ir. *socharach*, obliging, easy, W. *hygar*, amiable, Br. *hegar*, benignus; from *so-* and *càr*, dear. The Ir. is also from *sochar*, ease.

sochd, silence, Ir. *sochd* (O'R., Sh.), M. Ir. *socht*: **sop-tu-*, root *svop* of *suain* (Dr Cameron).

sod, noise of boiling water, steam of water in which meat is boiled, boiled meat, Ir. *sod*, boiled meat (O'B.); from Norse *soð*, broth or water in which meat has been boiled, Eng. *sodden*, *seethe*, *sod*, Sc. *sotter*, boil slowly, *sottle*, noise of boiling porridge, etc.

sod, an awkward person, a stout person; from Sc. *sod*, a heavy person, *sodick*, *soudie*, a clumsy heavy woman.

sodag, a pillion, clout; from Sc. *sodds*, a saddle made of cloth.

sodal, pride, flattery, Ir. *sodal*, *sotal*, *sutal*, O. Ir. *sotla*, pride, insolence, *sotli*, animositates; this has been adduced as the source of Eng. *sot*, Fr. *sot*. According to Stokes **sput-tlo-*, W. *ffothyll*, pustula, Lat. *pustula*, Skr. *phutkar*, puff (Stokes).

sodan, caressing, joy, joyous reception:

sodar, trotting, a trotting horse (Sh., Lh., etc.), Ir. *sodar*, trotting:

sog, **sogan**, mirth, good humour, tipsiness; from **sugg*, a short form of the root of *sùgradh*.

sògh, luxury, riot, Ir. *sógh*, M. Ir. *sodh*, E. Ir. *suaig*, prosperous: **su-ag-*, root *ag* of *aghaidh*, *àgh*.

soidealta, bashful, ignorant; see *saidealta*.

soidean, a jolly-looking or stout person; see *sod*.

soighne, **soighneas**, pleasure, delight, Ir. *sóighneas*: *so-gne-*, root *gen*.

soileas, officiousness, flattery, Ir. *soilíos*; from Lat. *sollicitus*?

soilgheas, wind, a fair wind:

soilleir, clear, visible, Ir. *soilléir*: from *so-* and *léir*. The *ll* is due to the analogy of *soillse*.

soillse, brightness, so Ir., O. Ir. *soillse*, *soilse*: **svelnestio-*; see *solus* for connections.

soimeach, prosperous, easy, easy circumstanced, good-natured, seems to combine O. Ir. *somme*, dives, and O. Ir. *soinmech*, lucky, good, Ir. *soinmheach*, fortunate, happy. The former Stokes derives from *so-imbi-s*, for which see *iomadh*; the latter is *so-nem-ech*, root *nem*, under *nèamh*. M. Ir. *somenmnach*, good-spirited, is from *meanmna*.

soin, esteem (n.), **soineil**, handsome; cf. *sònraich* for the root.

soinionn, **soineann**, fair weather, Ir. *soinean*, M. Ir. *soinend*, E. Ir. *sonend*; the opposite of *soinionn* is *doinionn*, for *su-sîn-enn*, *du-sîn-enn*, from *sîn* now *sian*, weather, rain (Stokes).

soir, the east, Ir. *soir*, E. Ir. *sair*; from *s-* (see *suas*) and *air* (= **are*), on, q.v.

soir, sack, vessel, bottle; cf. *searrag*.

soirbh, easy, gentle, **soirbheas**, success, wind, flatulence (Arg.), Ir. *soirbh*, O. Ir. *soirb*, facilis, opposed to *doirb*, difficilis, root *reb* or *rib*, manare (Ascoli). But compare Gaelic *reabh*.

sois, snug, fond of ease (M'A.); from Sc. *sosh*, snug, *social*.

sòise, a ball of fire in the sky, a portent (M'A.):

soisgeul, gospel, Ir. *soisgéal*, *soisgeul*, O. Ir. *soscéle*; from *so-* and *sgeul*.

soisinn, taste, decency, rest, stillness; from Sc. *sonsy*?

soitheach, a vessel, Ir. *soitheach*, M. Ir. *soithech*, *saithech*: **satiko-*:

soitheamh, tame, docile, gentle: **so-seimh*, from *sèimh*? So Munro, who writes *soisheamh*.

sol, ere, before, Ir., E. Ir. *sul*; root *svel* of *seal*.

sòlach, highly delighted (M'A.; **sollach**, jolly, Arms.); founded on *sòlas*. Arm.'s word seems from Eng. *jolly*.

solar, a provision, purveying, preparing, Ir. *soláthar*; from *so-* and *làthair*.

sòlas, joy, comfort, solace, Ir. *sólas*; from Lat. *sôlatium*, Eng. *solace*.

sollain, a welcome, rejoicing, Ir. *sollamhuin*, a solemnity, feast, rejoicing, E. Ir. *sollamain*; from Lat. *sollemne*, Eng. *solemnity*.

solus, light, Ir., M. Ir. *solus*, E. Ir. *solus*, bright: **svl̥nestu-*, root *svel*; Ag. S. *svelan*, glow, Eng. *sultry*; Gr. σέλας, light, σελήνη, moon, ἑλάνη, torch; Skr. *svar*, sheen, sun.

somalta, bulky, large, placid; from M. Ir. *soma*, abundance, with adj. terminations *-ail* and *ta*. See *soimeach* further.

somh, convert, upset (Carm.); cf. Ir. *sóm*.

son, sake, cause, **air son**, on account of, Ir. *son*, *ar son*, M. Ir. *son*, *er son*; from E. Ir. *son*, word (root *sven* of *seinn*)?

sona, happy, Ir., E. Ir. *sona*, opposite of *dona*: **so-gná-vo-s*, "well-doing"; root *gna* of *gnìomh*.

sonn, a stout man, hero; from *sonn*, club, staff, M. Ir. *suinn catha*, captains, "staves of battle." Cf. N. *stafn-buar*, the *stem* men, or picked marines on the forecastle. Cf. *Tàillear dubh na tuaighe* was "ursainn chatha nan Camshronach." See *sonn*.

sonn, a staff, cudgel, beam, Ir., E. Ir. *sonn*, W. *ffon*, O. W. *fonn*: **spondo-*, Gr. *σφενδόνη*, a sling, *σφεδανός*, vehement; Skr. *spand*, draw, move; Lat. *pendo*, hang (Rhys). Stokes gives the stem **spundo*, allied to Norse *spjót*, a lance, O. H. G. *spioz*, spit, spear. Cf. M. Lat. *sponda*, trabecula, repagulum.

sònraich, appoint, ordain, Ir. *sonraighim*, *sonrach*. special, E. Ir. *sunnraid*, O. Ir. *sainriud*, especially, *sainred*, proprietas, *sain*, singularis, proprius, O. W. *han*, alium: **sani-*, especially; Got. *sundrô*, privately, Eng. *sunder*; Lat. *sine*, without; Skr. *sanutár*, without.

sop, a wisp, Ir. *sop*, E. Ir. *sopp*, W. *sob*, *sopen*; from Eng. *sop*, Norse *soppa*. Zimmer takes the Ir. from Norse *svöppr*, sponge, ball; Stokes derives it from Norse *sópr*, besom. The W. *sob*, *sopen* favours an Eng. source.

sòr, hesitate, grudge, shun:

soraidh, a farewell, blessing, Ir. *soraidh*, happy, successful, M. Ir. *soraid*, E. Ir. *soreid*; from *so-* and *réidh*.

† **sorcha**, light, bright, Ir., E. Ir. *sorcha*; opposite of *dorch*, q v.

sorchan, rest or support, foot-stool, light stand, peer-man; from *sorcha*.

sòrn, a flue, vent, Ir. *sórn*, E. Ir. *sornn*, W. *ffwrn*, Corn. *forn*; from Lat. *furnus*, oven, whence Eng. *furnace*.

sos, a coarse mess or mixture; from Sc. *soss*.

spad, kill, fell, Ir. *spaidim*, benumb, *spaid*, *spad*, a clod (cf. *spairt*), a sluggard, eunuch; cf. W. *ysbaddu*, exhaust, geld, from Lat. *spado*, eunuch. Hence **spadanta**, benumbed.

spad-, flat, Ir. *spad-*; from **spad* of *spaid*, spade?

spadag, a quarter or limb of an animal cut off; from L. Lat. *spatula*, a shoulder blade, *spatula porcina*, leg of pork, also *spadula*, a shoulder, *spadlaris*, a quarter of a beast. Cf. W. *yspaud*, shoulder.

spaḍair, fop, braggart; cf. Norse *spjátra*, behave as a fop. See *spaideil*.

spadal, a paddle, plough-staff, so Ir.; from M. Eng. *spaddle*, paddle, dim. of *spade*.

spadhadh, a strong and quick pull, the utmost extent of the outstretched arms, the grass cut by one scythe-stroke, *spadh*, a scythe's stroke (Bad.); from Lat. *spatium*. Meyer objects. If Stokes' theory were right *spadh* could be from root *spa*, pull, span. Cf. Eng. *swath*.

spàg, a claw or paw, limb of an animal, club-foot, **spàgach**, club-footed or awkward in the legs, Ir. *spág*, claw, club-foot, clumsy leg, W. *ysbach*, a claw; *spàga-da-ghlid*, a buffoon, tomfool (Wh.):

spagach, uttering words indistinctly, **spagadh**, obliquity of the mouth, **spaig**, a wry mouth :

spagluinn, ostentation, conceit :

spaid, a spade, Ir. *spád* ; from the Eng.

spaideil, foppish, well-dressed : "strutting," from Lat. *spatior*, as in *spaisdear* below? Cf., however, *spadair*.

spailp, pride, conceit, **spailpean**, fop, Ir. *spailp*, *spailpín*, rascal, mean fellow, "spalpeen" :

spàin, a spoon, Manx *spain* ; from Norse *spánn*, *spónn*, spoon, chip, M. Eng. *spōn*, Ag. S. *spón*, chip. Ir. *spúnóg*, spoon, is from the Eng.

spàirn, an effort, struggle, Ir. *spáirn*, *sbáirn*, wrestling, struggling ; from the Norse *sporna*, kick with the feet, struggle, *sperna*, kick, spurn, Eng. *spurn*. Hennessey derived it from Eng. *sparring* (*Athenæum*, 15/8/71).

spairiseach, foppish, **spairis**, having the hands in the trousers' pockets (M'A.) ; founded on Sc. *spare*, opening of the fore part of the breeches.

spairt, a turf, clod, a splash, Ir. *spairt* ; verb **spairt**, daub, plaster, splash, brain, Ir. *spairtim* : cf. N. *sparða*, pole-axe, whence M. Eng. *spert* or *spart*.

spaisdear, spaidsear, a saunterer, **spaisdeireachd**, sauntering, Ir. *spaisdeóireachd*, promenading, walking ; Norse *spázera*, walk, Dan. *spadsere*, Ger. *spazieren*, from Ital. (13th Cent.), *spaziare* : all from Lat. *spatior*, walk, promenade.

spàl, a shuttle, Ir. *spól* ; from Norse *spóla*, a weaver's shuttle, M. Eng. *spōle*, now *spool*, Ger. *spule*, bobbin, spool. Hence *spàlag*, pea pod.

spang, thin plate of metal, spangle ; from Norse *spöng*, g. *spangar*, a spangle, M. Eng. *spang*, now *spangle*, Ag. S. *spange*, a clasp, Ger. *spange*, buckle.

spann, sever, divide, wean (a child) ; from Sc. *spain*, *spane*, wean, prevent, confused with M. Eng. *spannen*, stretch, span.

spann, a hinge, hasp ; from the Eng. *spang*, a spangle, Ag. S. *spang*, a hasp ; or Ag. S. *spannan*, to clasp, Norse *spenna*, *spennir*, grasper, Sc. *spenn*, to button.

spaoill, speill, wrap, swathe : **svil*, **sveil*, as in *till*, etc.

spàrdan, a roost, from *spàrr*.

spàrr, a joist, beam, roost, Ir. *sparra*, wedge, spear, E. Ir. *sparr*, a beam, joist ; from Norse *sparri*, a spar, Swed., Dan. *sparre*, O. H. G. *sparro*, bar, balk, Ger. *sperren*, a spar, Eng. *spar*. Hence G. **spàrr**, drive as a nail or wedge, thrust, Ir. *sparraim* ; G. **sparrag**, a bridle bit, "little bar."

spathalt, a limb, a clumsy limb ; cf. *spoll*.

sparsan, the dew-lap of a beast, Ir. *sparsan* (Lh., O'B.); see *spursan.*

speach, a wasp, **connspeach,** for **conas-beach,** "wrangling or dog bee," from *beach,* bee? The Ir. for "wasp" is *eircbheach. connspeach* is referred by Stokes (Dict. 302) to **spekâ,* Gr. *σφήξ*; for phonetics cf. *padhadh, piuthar,* also *speir* and *speal.*

speach, a blow, thrust, stitch in the side, Ir. *speach,* a kick:

speach, door step (Carm.).

spead, a very small foot or leg (M'A.), **speadach,** sheepshanked (M'A.), kicking (Badenoch, where **spead** means a cow's or sheep's kick); cf. M. Ir. *spedudhud,* a musical instrument (?), Kuno Meyer's "King and Hermit." Root *sped-do-, spend-.*

speal, a scythe, Ir. *speal,* scythe, reaping hook, M. Ir. *spel*: **spelâ,* Gr. *ψαλίς,* shears, root *spal,* clip, pull, further Eng. *psalm* (so Stokes).

spealg, a splinter; from Sc. *spelk,* a splint attached to a fracture, M. E. *spelke,* a splinter, Norse *spjalk, spelkur,* splint, Du. *spalk.*

spealt, a splinter; from Teutonic—M. Eng. *spélde,* now a *spill,* M. H. G. *spelte,* a splinter, Ger. *spalten.*

spearrach, a cow-fetter, a fetter for wild goats; see *speireach.*

spéic, a spike, Ir. *spéice*; from Norse *spík,* a spike, Eng. *spike,* Ger. *speiche.* W. has *ysbig.*

speil, cattle, herd, Ir. *speil,* herd of cattle or swine; **speli-,* allied to Lat. *spolium* (Stokes).

spéil, slide, skate; from Sc. *speil,* play, *bonspel,* curling game, Ger. *spielen,* play.

speir, hoof or ham of cattle, claw, talon, ankle and thereabouts of the human leg, Ir. *speirr,* hough, ham: **s-peri-*; compare W. *ffer,* ankle, *ber,* leg, shank: Cor. *fer,* crus, E. Ir. *seir,* heel, *di pherid*: **speret-,* Gr. *σφυρόν,* ankle, heel; root *sper,* Eng. *spur, spurn,* Lat. *sperno,* etc.

speireach, spearrach, cow-fetter, foot fetter; from *speir* and **rich,* tie, for which last see *buarach.*

spéiread, strength, force, courage; founded on Lat. *spîritus.*

speireag, sparrow-hawk; from M. Eng. *sper-hauk,* Ag. S. *spear-hafoc,* Norse *sparrhaukr,* from *sparrow* and *hawk.*

spéis, esteem, liking, Ir. *spéis,* M. Ir. *sbéis*; seemingly from M. Ir. *sbesailte,* special, from Lat. *species,* look (cf. Eng. *re-spect*).

speuc, spiac, diverge, divaricate, tear asunder, branch; from Sc. *spaik,* a spoke (in a wheel), Eng. *spoke,* Ag. S. *spáca.*

speuclair, spectacles, Ir. *speucláir,* a glass, spectacles; from the Latin.

speur, the heaven, firmament, Ir. *speur*, *spéir*; from the L. Lat. *spera*, a hemisphere, circle (of each planet), celestial region, Lat. *sphaera*, a sphere (whence the Eng.), from Gr. *σφαῖρα*, globe. Cf. Sc. *spere*, sphere, circle, "the *speir* of the moon."

spìd, spite, Ir. *spíd*; from the Eng. Hence. **spìdeig** or **spideag**, a taunt.

spìd, speed, haste; from Eng. *speed*.

spideag, nightingale (**spìdeag**, M.F.), Ir. *spideóg*, robin:

spideag, a delicate or slender creature (Arms. **spìdeag**); from Sc. *spit*, a little, hot-tempered person, *spitten*, a puny, mischievous person, Eng. *spit*.

spideal, a spital, hospital, Ir. *spideul*, M. Ir. *spidél*; from M. Eng. *spitel*, from O. Fr. *ospital*, from Lat. *hospitale*.

spidean, pinnacle; "*spidean* an teampuill":

spiligean, a seedling, dwarfish person:

spioc, meanness, dastardliness, **spìocach**, mean:

spiocaid, a spigot, Ir. *spiocaid* (O'R.); from Eng. sources—M. Eng. *spigot*, Eng. *spike*.

spìochan, wheezing, Ir. *spiochan*; see *pìochan*.

spiol, nibble, peel, pluck, Ir. *spiolaim*, *spialaim*, snatch, pluck. See *piol*.

spiolg, unhusk, shell; from the Sc. *spilk*, *pilk*, shell pease, etc., *spilkins*, split pease. Cf. *spealg*.

spìon, pluck up, pull, tear, Ir. *spíonaim*, teaze, probe, pluck, examine; cf. M. Ir. *spín*, a thorn, from Lat. *spîna*, thorn.

spionnadh, strength, Ir. *spionnadh*, *spionnamhail*, strong (Keat.): **sphen* or **sven*; see *fuod*.

spiontag, a currant, a particle in the throat, a maggot, a drop of rain or flake of snow, Ir. *spionán*, a gooseberry, M. Ir. *spínan*; from Lat. *spîna*.

spiorad, a spirit, so Ir., O. Ir. *spiurt*, *spirut*; from Lat. *spiritus*, Eng. *spirit*. W. has *ysbryd*, Corn. *speris*, Br. *speret*.

spiosradh, spice, Ir. *spiosra*; from Eng. *spicery*, O. Fr. *espicerie*, spices, from Lat. *species*.

spiris, a hen-roost, hammock; from Norse *sperra*, a spar, rafter, with a leaning on G. **iris**, roost.

spisniche, pillar, support (Carm.):

spitheag, a chip, spelk, small bit of wood, bite, Ir. *spiothóg*, a finger stone for throwing at an object (Con., Sh.), *spitheóg*, a flake of snow; a borrowed word belonging to the Eng. group *spikè*, *spigot*, but likely taken from Norse *spík*, sprig, spike.

splang, a sparkle, flash, Ir. *splanc*:

splangaid, a snot, mucus, Ir. *spleangaid* (O'R.); a side-form of *sylongaid*?

spleadh, a splay foot; from Eng. *splay.*

spleadh, ostentation, romance, false flattery, Ir. *spleadh*; from M. Eng. *spleien,* display, from *displeien,* now *display.*

spleadhan, a sort of wooden paddle to dig up sand eels; see *pleadhag.*

spleuchd, spliachd, stare, squint, spread out by trampling:

spliùc, fluke of an anchor (M'A.); founded on Eng. *fluke.*

spliùchan, spliùcan, tobacco pouch, Ir. *spliuchán,* a pouch, bag, leather purse; hence Sc. *spleuchan.* Cf. W. *blwch,* a box.

spliug, a snot, icicle, anything hanging down: **s-cluig?* Cf. *cluigein.*

spliùgach, splay-footed:

spliùig, a discontented countenance:

spliut, a lame hand or foot, splay foot; see *pliut.*

spòc, a spoke; from the Eng.

spoch, address one quickly and angrily, intimidate, affront, attack, Ir. *spochaim,* provoke, affront, rob; cf. *spoth.*

spòg, spàg, a claw, paw, Manx *spaag,* Ir. *spág,* W. *ysbach*:

spoll, a quarter (as of a sheep, M'A.), **spòld,** a piece or joint of meat, Ir. *spódhla, spólla,* a piece of meat; from Sc. *spaul,* limb, *spald,* shoulder, from old Fr. *espaule, espalle,* L. Lat. *spatula,* shoulder, whence Eng. *epaulet.* Ir. *spolla* is also hence. Cf. *spadag, spathalt.*

spolladach, sottish:

spòlt, mangle, slaughter, hew down in battle, also (Dial. Badenoch) splutter; from the English. Cf. M. Eng. *splatten,* cut open, Sc. *sploit,* squirt, spout. *spoltadh,* drops flying out of a vessel when boiling or stirred carelessly.

spong, sponge, tinder, Ir. *sponc,* E. Ir. *sponge,* W. *ysbwng,* sponge, Corn. *spong,* Br. *spone, sponeñk*; from Lat. *spongia,* sponge, from Gr. *σπογγιά,* allied to Lat. *fungus.*

spor, a spur, claw, talon, Ir. *spor,* M. Ir. *sbor,* a spur for a horse; from Norse *spori,* a spur, *spor,* foot trace, Dan. *spore,* Swed. *sporre,* Eng. *spur,* Ag. S. *spora*; root *sper* of *speir,* etc. Hence **sporadh,** inciting, scraping the earth (as a hen), Sc. *spur.*

spor, tinder, flint, gun-flint; from Eng. *spar.*

sporan, a purse, Ir. *sparán, sporán, sbarrán,* M. Ir. *sboran,* W. *ysbur*: **s-burr-* from **burs,* from L. Lat. *bursa,* a purse, whence Eng. *purse,* bursary,; originally from Gr. *βύρση,* a hide.

sporracan, crumbs (M'F.):

spors, sport, Ir. *spórt* (Fol.); from the Eng.

spot, a spot; from the Eng.

spoth, geld, castrate, Ir. *spothaim*, M. Ir. *spochad* (n.), W. *dysbaddu*, Br. *spaza* ; from Lat. *spado*, eunuch, whence Eng. *spay*. The M. Ir. *spochad* is thought by Stokes to be from Br. *spac'hein* (inf.).

spracadh, strength, sprightliness, Ir. *spracadh* ; from Eng. *sprack*, lively, Norse *spraekr*, lively, Swed. *spräker* ; from Norse also comes Eng. *spark*—Norse *sparkr*.

spraic, a severe reprimand ; see *spreig*.

spraidh, a loud blast, report of a gun ; cf. Sc. *spraich*, a cry, Norse *spraki*, a report.

spreadh, burst, sound loudly while bursting, kill, Ir. *spréidhim*, spread, burst (*spreighim*, O'B.), E. Ir. *sprédaire*, brush for sprinkling the holy water; from M. Eng. *spraeden*, now *spread*.

spreangan, a cloven stick for closing the wound of bled cattle ; from Eng. *springe*, twig, rod, snare with flexible rod.

spréidh, cattle, Ir. *spré(idh)*, M. Ir. *spré*, *spreid*, W. *praidd*, flock, booty ; from Lat. *praeda*, booty. Hence Sc. *spreith*, booty.

spreig, blame, reprove, incite, Ir. *spreagaim* ; founded on M. Eng. *spraechen*, now *speak*, Ger. *sprechen*.

spreigh, scatter, burst ; see *spreadh*.

spreill, blubber lip : **s-breill*, from *breall ?*

spreisneach, the remains of a wreck :

spreòchan, weakness, weak person ; for **s-breòch-*, being the same in root as *breòclaid ?*

spreòd, **spreod** (H.S.D.), a projecting beam, **crann spreòid**, a bowsprit ; from M. Eng. *sprēot*, a sprit, now *sprit* ; Ag. S. *spréot*, M. Du. *spriet*. Hence **spreòd**, incite.

sprochd, dejection, sadness, Ir. *sprochd* : **s-broc*, M. Ir. *broc*, sorrow, anxiety (also *sbrog*). Cf. *murcach* for root ; or *bròn ?*

sprogan, **sprogaill**, dewlap, bird's crop, Ir. *sprogaille*, *sbrogaill*, also *sgroban*, *sgrogul*, neck : **s-broggo-*. See *bràghad*.

spronnan, a crumb ; from *pronn*.

sprot, single stick (Lewis) : N. *sproti*, stick.

spruan, brushwood, firewood, Ir. *sprudn* : **s-bruan*, from *bruan*. M'A. has **sprudhan**, fragments.

sprùdan, fingers, sprouts ; from the Eng. *sprout*.

spruileach, **spruidhleach**, crumbs, fragments, Ir. *spruille(ach)*, crumb, fragment, *sprudhaille* (Lh.), M. Ir. *sbruileach*. Cf. *spruan*. M. Ir. has also *spuirech*, fragmentum, W. *ysbwrial*, sweepings, *ysborion*, refuse of fodder.

spruiseil, spruce, neat, Ir. *sprúiseamhuil* ; from the Eng. *spruce*.

spruithean, claw (as of eagle) :

spuaic, crown of the head, a pinnacle, callosity, blister, Ir. *spuaic*, a welt, callus, pinnacle :

spùidsear, baling ladle (N.H.): cf. Eng. *spudge.*

spùill, spoil, plunder; from Sc. *spulye*, lay waste, plunder, Eng. *spoil*, Fr. *spolier*, Lat. *spoliare*. W. has *ysbail*, a spoil.

spùinn, spoil, plunder, Ir. *spúinim*; another form of *spùill*, borrowed directly from Lat. *spoliare?*

spuirse, spurge, milkweed, Ir. *spuirse*; from the Eng. *spurge*, M. Eng. *sporge*.

spùll, nail of a cat, a clutch, **spùllach,** nailed, greedy (M'A.):

spursan, a gizzard, Ir. *spursán*; cf. *sparsan*, dewlap.

spùt, a spout; from the Sc. *spoot*, Eng. *spout*.

sràbh, a straw; from the Eng.:

sràbh, falling water (Carm.):

srabhard, strife (Suth. R.D.):

srac, tear, rend, rob, Ir. *sracaim*; G. has also **racadh**: **srakko-*, for *rap-ko-*, root *rap* of Lat. *rapio?*

srad, a spark of fire, Ir. *srad*: **sraddâ*, from *strad* or *stṛ-d*, root *ster*, as in Eng. *star*, Gr. ἀστήρ. M. Ir. has *srab-tine*, lightning, from the same root.

sràid, a street, Ir. *sráid*, E. Ir. *sráit*; from Lat. *strâtā* (*via*), whence Eng. *street*. K. Meyer derives it from Norse *straeti*, which itself comes from Lat.

sraidean, the plant shepherd's purse, Ir. *sraidín* (*sráidín*, (O'B.); cf. *srad*.

sraigh, the cartilage of the nose, sneeze (M'A.); cf. root of *sròn*.

sramh, a jet of milk from the cow's udder, Ir. *sramh* (*srámh*, O'R.); root *ster*, *stṛ*, strew.

srann, a snore, buzz. Ir. *srann*, E. Ir. *srand*, O. Ir. *srennim*, sterto: **stre-s-no-*, root *ster*, *pster* of Lat. *sterto*, snore, *sternuo*, sneeze (see *sreothart* further). Stokes makes the Gadelic to be **strenvô*, like Lat. *sternuo*.

sraon, stumble, make a false step, rush forward violently; cf. Ir. *sraoinim*, defeat, overthrow, scatter, M. Ir. *sráined*, dragging down, defeat, E. Ir. *sroenim*, hurl, drag, defeat: **sroino-*, root *ster*, strew, scatter (Eng. *strew*, etc.).

sraonais, a huff, snuffiness; M'A. has **sròin,** a huff: from *sròn*, nose?

srath, a valley, strath, Ir., M. Ir. *srath*, meadow land or holm along banks of a river or loch, often swampy (Joyce), O. Ir. *israth*, in gramine, W. *ystrad*, strath, E. W. *strat*, *istrat*, planities: **stratu-*, root *ster*, spread, scatter; Lat. *strâtus*, from *sterno*, I strew; Gr. στρωτός, spread, στορέννυμι, scatter; Eng. *strew*, *strand* (?).

srathair, a pack-saddle, Ir., O. Ir. *srathar*, W. *ystrodyr*; from Med. Lat. *stratura*, from *stratum*, *sterno*, spread.

sream, rheum (M'A.), a wrinkle, **sreamach**, blear eyed, Ir. *srám*, eye rheum, *srámach*, blear-eyed, *sremach* (F. M.). Stokes derives this from Ag. S. *streám*, Eng. *stream*.

sreamadh, curbing or checking by the nose :

sreang, a string, Ir. *srang*, *sreang*, E. Ir. *sreng* : **srengo-*, *strengo-*, Gadelic root *streg* ; immediately allied either to Eng. *string*, Norse *strengr*, Ger. *strang* (I. E. *stregh*, Gr. *στρέφω*, turn), or to Lat. *stringo*, bind, draw, Ger. *strick*, string (I. E. *streg*). The I. E. roots *streg* and *stregh* are allied ultimately. *sraing*, lie, embroidery (Hend.).

sreath, a row, series, Ir. *sreath*, O. Ir. *sreth* : **srito-*, **sr̥-to-*, root *ser*, order, join ; Lat. *series*, row, *sors*, lot.

sreathan, filmy skin covering unborn calf (H.S.D., etc.). When dried, it was used for covering vessels :

sreothart, a sneeze, Ir. *sraoth*, *sraothfurtach*, earlier *sreod*, W. *trew*, *ystrew*, a sneeze, *ystrewi* (vb.), Br. *strefia*, *strevia* (vb.), root *streu*, *pstreu* (Stokes), further *ster*, *pster*, Lat. *sternuo*, sneeze, Gr. *πτάρνυμαι* (do.).

srian, a bridle, Ir. *srian*, E. Ir. *srían*, W. *ffrwyn* ; from Lat. *frênum* (through W.).

srideag, a drop, spark, **srideach**, white streaked with dark : **sriddi*, root *sr̥d* of *srad*.

sringlean, the strangles ; founded on the English.

sruit, a torrent of quick words ; founded on *sruth*.

srobadh, a push (Sh.), small quantity of liquor (A. M'D.) ; see *sruab*.

sroghall, a whip, so Ir., E. Ir. *sraigell*, O. Ir. *srogill* (gen.), W. *ffrowyll* ; from Lat. *flagellum*.

sról, a streamer, banner, silk, Ir. *sról*, satin, byssus ; from Lat. *stragulus*, coverlet, pall, whence Cor. *strail*, tapestry, W. *ystraill*, a mat. Stokes (*Lismore*) has suggested a form **fról*, **flór*, Fr. *velours*, velvet, Br. *flour*, velveted.

sròn, a nose, Ir., O. Ir. *srón*, W. *ffroen*, Br. *froan* : **srognâ* ; **sroknâ* (Stokes, Gr. *ῥέγχω*, snore, snort, *ῥέγκω*), **sprognâ* (Strachan), to which Lat. *spargo* has been compared. W. has also *trwyn* (**trugno-* or *trogni-*), Cor. *trein*.

sruab, drink up with noise of the lips, pull hastily out of the water : **sroubbo-*, root *sreub*? Cf. *srùb*, and Lit. *sriaubiu*, sup, lap up, Ch. Sl. *srŭbati*, swallow, Lat. *sorbeo*, Eng. *absorb*.

sruan, shortbread cake having five corners (M'A. for Islay) :

srùb, a spout ; from the Sc. *stroup*, spout, M. Eng. *strūpe*, throat, Norse *strjúpi*, the spouting trunk when the head is cut off, Swed. *strupe*, throat. Hence **srùban**, a cockle.

sruth, a stream, Ir., O. Ir. *sruth*, g. *srotha*, W. *ffrwd*, Cor. *frot*, alveus, Br. *froud* : **srutu-*, root *sreu*, flow ; Gr. *ῥύσις*, a flowing, *ῥεῦμα*, a stream, *ῥέω*, flow ; Eng. *stream*, Norse *straumr* ; Lit. *sravju*, flow. Some have referred the Celtic words to the root *spreut*, *spreu*, to well, Ger. *sprudel*, a well, *sprühen*, emit sparks, drizzle, further Eng. *spurt*, *spout*.

sruthladh, rinsing, half-washing, Ir. *sruthlaighim* ; from *sruth*.

stà, advantage, use ; from the Eng.—founded on *stay* ?

stàbhach, wide, asunder, straddling, Ir. *stabhaighim*, straddle :

stabhaic, a wry neck, a sullen attitude of the head (M'A.) ; see *stùichd*. Pronounced in Arg. **staoi'c, staghaic.**

stàbull, a stable, Ir. *stabla* ; from Lat. *stabulum*, through the English.

stac, a precipice, steep hill, M. Ir. *stacc*, a stack (F.M.), *stacc*, a pile, piece ; from Norse *stakkr*, a stack (of hay), *stakka*, a stump, Swed. *stack*, a stack, Sc. (Shetland, etc.) *stack*, a columnar isolated rock, Eng. *stack*.

stad, a stop, Ir. *stad*, E. Ir. *stad* (Cormac) ; founded on Lat. *status*, position, *stat*, stands (Hennessey, Stokes). Cf. Norse *staða*, a standing, a position. Ascoli compares O. Ir. *astaim*, sisto (= *ad-sad-to-*, root *sed* of *suidhe*).

stadh (better **stagh**), a stay, a certain rope in ship's rigging ; from Norse *stag* (do.), Eng. *stay*, Dan., Ger. *stag*.

stadhadh, a lurch, sudden bend :

staid, state, condition, Ir. *stáid*, M. Ir. *stait* ; from Lat. *statio* (K. Meyer). W. has *ystâd*, from Lat. *status*. Ir. *stáid* may be from the Eng. See next word.

stàideil, stately, Ir. *stáideamhuil* ; from Eng. *state*, *stately*.

staidhir, a stair, Ir. *staighre*, M. Ir. *staigre* ; from the Eng., and Ag. S. *stǽger*. The G. is possibly from Eng. *stair*, just as *paidhir* and *faidhir* are from *pair* and *fair* (Dr Cameron).

stail, a bandage, strap :

stailc, stubbornness, stop, stump, Ir. *stailc* ; cf. *tailce* ; cf. N. *stilkr*, stalk.

stàilinn, steel ; from Norse *stál*, steel, *stálin* weapons (pl.), Ger. *stahl*, Eng. *steel*.

staing, a peg, small pointed rock ; from Norse *stöng*, g. *stangar*, a pole, Sc. and Eng. *stang*.

staing, a well-built person or animal (M'A.), **staingean**, obstinate boorish person, Ir. *stainc*, incivility ; from the above.

staipeal, a stopple, Ir. *stapal* (O'R.) ; from the Sc. *stappil*, Eng. *stopple*.

staipeal, stapull, a staple, bar ; from Eng. *staple*.

stair, a path over a bog, stepping stones in a river. Dr Cameron has suggested connection with Du. *steiger,* waterside stairs, Eng. *stair.* For *s-tar,* from **tar,* cross (see *thar*)?

stairirich, a rattling, a rumbling noise; also **dairireach,** q.v. For *s-dairirich.*

stàirn, a particle, small quantity (Perth); from Sc. *starn,* particle, grain, star, from *star.*

stàirn, noise (as the tread of horses), a violent push: **s-tairn*; see *tàirneanach* for root. Cf. Ir. *stathruim,* clatter, din.

stàirneil, stairneanach (Suth.), conceited, ostentatious; from *stàirn,* noise: "creating a furore." Eng. *stern*?

stairsneach, stairseach, a threshold, Ir. *tairseach,* E. Ir. *tairsech*: "cross beam or stone"; for root see *tarsuinn,* transverse.

stairt, a considerable distance, trip (M'A.); from Eng. *start*?

stàit, a magistrate or great man, **stàitean,** great men; see *stàt.*

stalan, a stallion, Ir. *stail*; from the English.

stalc, stiffen, **stalcanta,** firm, strong; for *s-talc*; see *tailce.* M'A. gives **stalc** as meaning "dash one's foot against (Islay), thread a hook, thump, stare." In the meaning of "stalk," the word is from the Eng.

stalla, an overhanging rock, craggy steep, precipice, **stall,** a peat bank; from Norse *stallr,* any block or shelf on which another thing is placed, pedestal, step of a mast, stall, *stalli,* an altar, Eng. *stall,* Lit. *stalas,* table.

stallachdach, stupidly deaf, heedless (Wh.):

stalladh, dashing against, thumping (M'A.):

stamag, a stomach; from the Eng.

stamh, sea tangle, **staf** (Lewis), N. *stafr,* staff.

stamhnaich, reduce to order, subject, break in, drub (M'A.), **stannadh,** subject (Heb.); from N. *stafr,* a stick, *stafa fyir,* rule, *fyrir stafni,* aim at, *stafn,* stem?

stàmp, stamp, trample, Ir. *stampáil,* a stamping, prancing; from Eng. *stamp.*

† **stàn,** tin, Ir. *stán,* W. *ystaen,* Cor., Br. *stean*; from Lat. *stannum,* tin (for **stagnum*; cf. Ital. *stagno*). See *staoin.*

stàn, a stàn, below, down; Sutherland form of **a bhàn,** on analogy of *a' s t*-fhoghar, *a' s t*-samhradh, etc.:

stang, a ditch, pool; from Sc. *stank,* O. Fr. *estang,* now *étang,* from Lat. *stagnum.*

stang, sting, from Sc. *stang,* sting (as a bee), a sting, Norse *stanga,* prick, goad; further Eng. *sting.*

stangarra, the fish stickleback; from *stang,* sting.

stanna, a vat, tub, Ir. *stanna*, vat, barrel; from Eng. *tun, ton*, M. Eng. *tonne*. See *tunna*.

stannart, a standard, yard, limit; from the Eng. It also means "affected coyness."

staoig, a collop, steak, Ir. *staoig*, M. Ir. *stáic*; from Norse *steik*, Eng. *steak* (Stokes, K. Meyer).

staoin, pewter, tin; see *stàn*.

staoin, juniper, **caoran staoin**:

staoin, laziness:

staon, bent, awry, shallow (Hend.), Ir. *staon*:

staorum, bending of the body to a side; for *staon-um*.

stapag, a mixture of meal and cold water; from Sc. *stappack* (do.), *stap*, mix, hash, Norse *stappa*, bray in a mortar.

staplaich, loud noise, noise of the sea:

stapull, a bar, bolt, staple; see *staipeal*.

starach, cunning, deceitful (Suth.):

starachd, romping, blustering (M'A.):

starbhanach, a strong, robust fellow:

starcach, firm; from Norse *starkr*, strong, Eng., Ger. *stark*.

starr, shove, dash, **starradh**, pushing violently, dashing against, a failing or freak, **cnap-starradh**, a stumbling-block, obstruction, a ball on the end of a spear; cf. *starr-(shuileach)*.

starr-fhiacail, a tusk or gag-tooth, Ir. *stairfhiacail*; from *starr* and *fiacail*.

starr-shuileach, having the eyes distorted, **stard**, a moon-eye (M'A.); cf. Norse *starblindr*, blind with a cataract, O. H. G. *starablind*, Ger. *starr*, stiff, Eng. *stare*, "fixed" look, Sc. *stare*, stiff, *starr*, sedge, *star*, a speck on the eye.

stàt, pride, haughtiness, Ir. *státamhuil*, stately; from the Eng. *state*, M. Eng. *stát*, from Lat. *status*. Cf. *stàideil*, *stàta*.

stàta, the state or Government; from the Eng.

steach, a steach, (to) within, into, Ir. *steach, a steach*, M. Ir. *is tech*, E. Ir. *isa tech*: **in-san-tech*, "into the house;" from *teach*. Cf. *stigh*.

steadhainn, firm, pointed or punctual in speech (M'A.); cf. Eng. *steady*.

steafag, a little staff or stick, Ir. *steafóg*; from Eng. *staff*.

steàirn, a blazing fire (Perth), "a drop in the e'e":

steall, spout, cause to spout, pour out, Ir. *steallaim*, squirt, sprinkle, *steallaire*, a tap; from Lat. *stillo*, I drop, Eng. *distill*.

stear, a pole to kill birds with (Carm.):

steàrnal, a bittern, sea-bird, an inn-keeper's sign:

stéidh, foundation; from Norse *staeði*, *staeða*, establish, Ork. *steeth*, foundation, *steethe*, to found.

steill, a peg or pin for things hung; cf. Sc. *stell*, a prop.

stéilleach (steilleach, M'F.), lusty, stout, ruddy; cf. **stéidheil,** steady, solid, from *stéidh*.

steinle, the itch, mange, Ir. *steinle* (Lh., etc.); from *teine*, fire?

steòc, any person or thing standing (or sticking) upward, an attendant (**steòcair** also); from Sc. *stog, stug, stook*, stubble, stumpy horns, *stok*, Eng. *stick*.

steòrn, guide, direct, manage; from Norse *stjórna* (do.), *stjórn*, steering, rule, Eng. *stern, steer*. See *stiùir*.

steud, a horse, steed, Ir. *stead* (O'R.), M. Ir. *stéd*; from Ag. S. *stéda*, Ag. S. *stéda*, M. Eng. *stede*, now *steed*.

stiall, a strip, stripe, streak, Ir. *stíall*, E. Ir. *stíall*, girdle, strap, board; cf. W. *astell*, M. W. *ystyll*, shingle, plank, Corn. *stil*, rafter, O. Fr. *esteil*, pole, Lat. *astella*, splinter, or from O. H. G. *stihhil*, pole, post.

stic, a fault, blemish, pain; from Sc. *stick*, a bungle or botch, Eng. *stick, stitch* (older *sticke*).

stic, adhere, stick; from the Eng.

stìc, ghostly person, "imp" (Carm.); N. *stygr*, shy.

stìd, peep, Manx *steetagh*, to peep; see *dìd*.

stidean (stìdean, H.S.D.), a cat, the word by which a cat is called to one (also **stididh** and **tididh,** from Sc. *cheet, cheety*, puss, cat, Eng. *chit*, cub, youngster; from *cat*, like *kitten*).

stìg, a skulking or abject look or attitude; from Norse *stygr*, shy.

stigh, a stigh, inside, Ir. *'stigh, astigh*, E. Ir. *istig, istaig, isintig*; for **in-san-tig*, "in the house," from *tigh*, house.

stìnleag, the hinge of a box, hasp:

stìobull, a steeple; from the Eng.

stiocach, limping: "sticking"? From the Eng. anyway.

stìog, a stripe in cloth (M'A.); from Sc. *steik*, Eng. *stitch*.

stìom, stìm, a head-band, snood:

stiorap, a stirrup, Ir. *stioróip*; from M. Eng. *stirōp*, Ag. S. *stigráp*.

stiorc, stretch (at death, Arg.); from Eng. *stark?*

stiorlag, a thin, worn-out rag, an emaciated woman, **stiorlan,** a thin person; *stiorlach*, thin gruel (M'D.); *stirlean*, thin gruel or watery stuff (Bad.):

stiornach, sturgeon (M'A.), **stirean**; from Lat. *sturio(n)*, whence, through Fr., Eng. *sturgeon*.

stìpean, a stipend; from the Eng.

stiùbhard, a steward, Ir. *stíobhard*; from the Eng.

stiùir, steer, guide, Ir. *sdiuirim*, M. Ir. *stiurad* or *stiúrad*; from Ag. S. *steóran*, steer, now *steer*, Norse *stýra*, Got. *stiurjan*.

stiup, a long tail or train, a foolish person. In the latter sense, the G. is from Sc. *stupe*, from Lat. *stupidus*.

stiùireag, gruel; from the Sc. *stooram*, *stooradrink*, *stourreen*, *sturoch*, a warm drink, meal and water mixed, from *stoor*, to stir, agitate.

stob, thrust, stab, fix (as a stake), **stob**, a stake, stick, stob (Sc.), Ir. *stobaim*, stab, thrust; from Sc. *stob*, a side-form of Eng. *stab*. Cf. Norse *stobbi*, a stump, Eng. *stub*, M. Eng. *stob*.

stòbh, a stove; from the Eng.

stoc, a stock, pillar, stump, Ir. *stoc*; from Eng. *stock*.

stoc, a trumpet, so Ir., M. Ir. *stocc*, E. Ir. *stoc*; cf. Sc. *stock-horne*, *stock-and-horn*, a pipe formed of a sheep's thigh-bone inserted into the smaller end of a cut horn, with an oaten reed, from Eng. *stock*. Gadelic is borrowed.

stocain, a stocking, Ir. *stoca*; from the Eng.

stoim, a particle, whit, faintest glimpse of anything (Dial.); from Sc. *styme*.

stoirm, a storm, Ir. *stoirm*; from Eng., M. Eng. *storm*, Norse *stormr*, Ger. *sturm*.

stòite, prominent; cf. *stàt* for origin.

stòl, a stool, settle, Ir. *stól*, W. *ystôl*; from Ag. S. *stól*, now *stool*, Norse *stóll*, Ger. *stuhl*. Hence vb. **stòl**, settle.

stòp, a wooden vessel for liquor, a stoup, Ir. *stópa*, a "stoup" or wooden pail; from Sc. *stoup*, M. Eng. *stope*, now *stoup*, Du. *stoop*, a gallon, Norse *staup*, a stoup.

stop, stop, close up, Ir. *stopaim*; from the Eng.

stòr, a steep cliff, broken teeth; cf. *stùrr*, *starr*. Norse *stór*.

stòras, store, wealth, Ir. *stór*, *stórus*; from M. Eng. *stōr*.

stoth, lop off, cut corn high:

stoth, hot steam, vapour; see *toth*.

strabaid, a strumpet, Ir. *strabóid*; from an early form of Eng. *strumpet*, that is, **stropet*, from O. Fr. *strupe*, concubinage, *stupre*, from Lat. *stuprum*.

stràc, a stroke, ship or boat plank; from Sc. *strake*, Eng. *stroke*; from Sc. *straik*, strait-edge for measuring corn, comes G. **stràc** (do.). Similarly G. **stràc**, mower's whetstone, is from *strake*; all are from the root of Eng. *stroke*, strike.

stràcair, troublesome fellow, gossip, wanderer; from Norse *strákr*, a vagabond, etc.

straic, pride, swelling with anger, Ir. *stráic*:

straighlich, rattling, great noise, sparkles; root *sprag*, *sparg*, crackle, Eng. *spark*, *sparkle*, Lit. *sprageti*, crackle.

stràille, carpet; from Lat. *strâgulum*, coverlet.

strangair, a lazy, quarrelsome fellow, Ir. *strangaire*; cf. *dreangan*.

streafan, film, carpet (Carm.):

streap, climb, strive against obstacles, Ir. *dreapaim*; cf. *dreimire*.

streòdag, a little liquor (Skye):

streud, a row, line (Suth.); from Eng. *street.*
streup, strèapaid, strife, quarrel; from Lat. *strepitus.*
strì, strife, contention; from Norse *stríð*, Ag. S. *stríð*, Ger. *streit.*
strianach, a badger:
strìoch, a streak, line, Ir. *stríoc*; from Eng. *streak.*
strìochd, yield, Ir. *stríocaim, strìocail* (inf.), fall, be humbled, submit:
strìoghach, prodigal (Rob.):
strìopach, a prostitute, Ir. *stríopach*; from O. Fr. *strupe*, concubinage, from Lat. *stuprum*, dishonour, violation.
stròdh, prodigality, Ir. *stró, strógh*; seemingly (because of preserved *st* in all cases) borrowed from, rather than allied to, M. Eng. *strawen*, strew, Ag. S. *stréowian*, Got. *straujan*, I. E. *strou, stru.* Hence G. **struidheas,** prodigality, squandering.
stròic (stroic, Arm.), tear asunder, a long rag, strip torn off, Ir. *stroicim, stróicim, sroic*, a piece: **srakki-*, from *srac*, confused with *stródh*?
strolamas, mess (Glenmoriston):
stropach, wrinkled (H.S.D.):
struidheas, prodigality; see *stròdh.*
struill, a baton, cudgel, Ir. *sroghall*, whip, rod, O. Ir. *sraigell*; see *sroghall.*
strumpaid, a strumpet; from the Eng.
struth, ostrich, Ir. *struth*; from Lat. *struthio*, whence, through O. Fr. *ostruche* (= *avis struthio*), Eng. *ostrich.*
strùthan, cake made on St. Michael's eve and eaten on his day (Carm.):
stuadh, a wave, gable, pinnacle, scroll, Ir. *stuadh*, gable, pinnacle, scroll, *stuaidh-nimhe*, rainbow, M. Ir. *stuag-nime* (do.), *stuaid-léim*, leap of the waves, E. Ir. *stúag*, arch: **s-tuag*, from O. Ir. *tuag*, bow, belonging to the same root as *tuagh*, axe.
stuaic (M'A., Arm.), **stuaichd** (H.S.D.), a little hill, round promontory, Ir. *stuaic*: **s-tuag-c*, from *stuadh* above. M'A. has the meaning "wry-neck and sullen countenance, extreme boorishness," which is usually represented by *stùic.* Stokes gives the Celtic as **stoukki-*, Br. *stuchyaff*, to feather, Lit. *stúgti*, set on high, Eng. *steep.*
stuaim, modesty, Ir. *stuaim*, device, mien, modesty: **s-tuamm-*, **tous-men*, root *tus, teus* of *tosd*, silence.
stùc, stùchd, a little hill jutting out from a greater, a horn, Ir. *stucán*, a small conical hill, *stucach*, horned; from Teutonic —N. *stúka*, wing of a building; Sc., Eng. *stook*, M. Eng. *stouke*, a shock of corn (12 sheaves), *stooks*, small horns, Low Ger. *stūke* (properly a projection), a bundle, bunch. But cf. *stuaic.*

stùic, stùichd, a projecting crag, an angry or threatening aspect; from **stùc** above.

stuidearra, studious, steady, glum, Ir. *stuideurach, stuideur,* a study.

stuig, incite, spur on dogs; from Eng. *stick.*

stuird, huffiness, pride, Ir. *stuirteamhlachd* (Con.); from M. Eng. *sturte,* impetuosity, *sturten,* impetuous, quarrelsome, Sc. *sturt,* vexation, anger, a side form of *start.*

stùirt, vertigo, a disease in sheep caused by water in the head, drunkenness; from Sc. *sturdy,* from O. F. *estourdi,* dizzy-headed, now *êtourdi,* giddy-headed; from Lat. *extorpidire.* From Fr. comes Eng. *sturdy.*

stùr, dust; from Sc. *stour,* M. Eng. *stour,* tumult.

stùrr, the rugged point of a rock or hill, **sturrach,** rugged: **s-tùrr,* from *turr* = *tòrr,* q.v.? Cf. N. *staurr.*

stuth, stuff, metal; founded on the Eng. *stuff.*

stuthaig, dress with starch, starch (vb. and n.); from Sc. *stiffing,* starch, Eng. *stiff.* Perthshire has **stifinn.**

suabag, a sweeping blow (Suth. R.D.):

suacan, a pot (M'F.), earthen furnace (Arm.), a basket hung in the chimney containing wood to dry (Dial.), anything wrought together awkwardly, as clay (M'A.), Ir. *suachgan* (Lh.), an earthen pot; from *suath*?

suaicean, a bundle of straw or hay twisted together, a deformed person; see *sùgan.*

suaicheantas, ensign, escutcheon, Ir. *suaitheantas,* a streamer, standard, escutcheon, *su-aichintus,* ensigns, colours (K. Meyer), O. Ir. *suaichnid,* clear, demonstratio, for *su-aithne,* "easily known," from *aithne,* knowledge.

suail, small, inconsiderable (M'F.), Ir. *suaill,* E. Ir. *suail,* a trifle:

suaimhneach, genial, secure, Ir. *suaimhneach,* peaceful, gentle, peaceable: **su-menmnach*? See *meamna.*

suain, sleep, Ir. *suan,* E. Ir., O. Ir. *súan,* W. *hun,* Br. *hun*: **supno-s,* developing into **sofno-,* **sovno,* **souno-*; I. E. root *svop, svep,* sleep; Lat. *sopor,* sleep, *somnus*; Gr. *ὕπνος,* sleep; Ag. S. *swefn,* dream, *swefan,* sleep; Skr. *svápnas.*

suaineadh, twisting, rope-twisting anything, a line for twisting round anything, E. Ir., O. Ir. *súanem,* g. *suaneman,* funis: **sognemon-,* root *sug, soug,* Br. *sug,* trace, W. *syg,* chain, trace; Romance *soga,* rope, Ital. *soga,* rope, leather band, Sp. *soga,* a linear measure, Port. *soga,* rush rope, Churwälsch *saga.* Stokes finally refers *súanem* to a stem-root **sogno-* beside *segno-* (whence E. Ir. *sén,* a net for catching birds, gin, root *segh,* hold, Eng. *sail*), Lit. *segù,* fasten, *saga,* sledge.

This divorces *suaineadh* from G. *suaicean* and *sùgan*, q.v. Cf. W. *hwynyn*, *hoenyn*, a hair from a horse's tail, gin.

suaip, a faint resemblance ; from Sc. *swaup*, *swap*, cast or lineaments of the countenance, Norse *svipr*, likeness, look, a swoop or flash.

suaip, exchange, swop ; from the Sc. *swap*, Eng. *swop*.

suairc, civil, meek, so Ir., E. Ir. *suarc(c)*; opposed to *duairc*: **su-arci-* :

suaiteachan, wagging (tails) (Suth.) ; from *suath*?

suanach, a hide, skin, fleece, coarse garment, "plough rein" (Suth.) ; cf. Ir. *sunach*, a kind of plaid :

suarach, insignificant, careless, Ir. *suarach* : **svogro-*, root *sveg*, *sug*, Ger. *schwach*, weak, *siech*, sick, Eng. *sick*. Cf. Eng. *sour*, Ger. *sauer*, **sûra*.

suas, up, upwards, Ir. *suas*, O. Ir. *súas* : **s-uas*, from *uas*, as in *uasal*, and the prefix *s-*, allied to the final *s* of Lat. *abs*, *ex*, Gr. ἔξ, πρός, etc., and the initial *s* of Lat. *sub*, *super* ; possibly for **ens*, Gr. εἰς, from *en*, and meaning "into," "to" (Rhys' *M. Pray.*[2] 156).

suath, rub, mix, knead, Ir. *suathaim*, knead, mix, M. Ir. *súathaim* (do.), E. Ir. *suata*, polished down, root *sout*, *sut*, mix ; cf. Eng. *seethe*, Norse *sjóða*, cook, seethe, Got. *suaths*, a burnt offering.

sùbailte, supple ; from the Eng.

sùbh, **sùbhag** (**suibheag** or **sui'eag**, Dial.) a raspberry, **subh**, fruit generally (Arg.), Ir. *suibh*, a strawberry, *sughog*, raspberry (Fol.), O. Ir. *subi*, fragae, W. *syfi*, strawberry, Br. *sivi* ; a side form to root *sug* as in *sùgh*. Cf. Gr. ὕφεαρ, a kind of mistletoe.

subhach, merry, so Ir., E. Ir. *subach*, O. Ir. *sube*, joy ; opposite of *dubhach* : **so-bv-io-*, "well-being," from root *bu*, be (see *bu*, etc.).

subhailc, virtue, Ir. *subhailce* (*súbhailce*, Con.), O. Ir. *sualig*, virtus, *sualchi* (pl.) : **su-alich* (Asc., Zim.[1] 54), root *al* of *altram* (Dr Cameron).

suchd, sake, account (M'A.) :

sud (Dial. **sid**), yon, Ir. *súd*, E. Ir. *sút*, *siut*, illud, illic, W. *hwnt* (*h-wnt*), other, yonder, Br. *hont* ; from the root of *so* ; *sud* = *s-út* (Rhys). Also **ud**.

sùdh, a seam between the planks of a ship ; from Norse *súð*, a suture (only used for the clinching of a ship's boards), from *sýja*, sow, Eng. *sew*, *suture*.

sùg, **sùgradh**, mirth, Ir. *súgadh*, *súgradh*, E. Ir. *sucach* :

sùg, suck, imbibe ; from Sc. *souk*, *sook*, Eng. *suck*, Ag. S. *súcan*. See *sùgh*.

sugan, corra-shugain, the reflection of rays of light from any moving luminous body from the roof or wall of a house :

sùgan, a rope of twisted straw, Ir. *súgán*, *suagan*, straw or hay rope, *suag*, a rope (O'R.) : **souggo-*, root *soug* of *suaineadh*, q.v. Hence **suigean,** a circle of straw ropes in which grain is kept in a barn.

sùgh, juice, sap, also (as vb.) drain, suck up, Ir. *súgh*, *súghaim*, E. Ir. *súgim* : **sûgô*, suck, **sûgo-*, juice ; Lat. *sûgô*, suck ; Ag. S. *sûcan*, Eng. *suck*, *soak*. W. has *sug*, juice, *sugno*, suck. *súg*, *súch*, W. *sug*, from Lat. *sucus* (Stokes).

sùgh, a wave (A. M'D.), motion of the waves (H.S.D.) ; root *sup*, swing, Lit. *sùpti*, swing, Lat. *dissipo*, scatter ?

sùicean, a gag for a calf ; founded on *sùg*, Sc. *sook*.

suidh, sit, **suidhe,** a seat, sitting, Ir. *suidhim*, E. Ir. *suidim*, *sudim*, O. Ir. *suidigur*, *suide*, a seat : **sodeiô*, **sodio-n*, root *sed*, sod, W. *seddu*, *sedd*, Br. *azeza*, sit ; Lat. *sedeo* ; Gr. ἕζομαι, ἕδος, a seat ; Eng. *sit*, *seat* ; Lit. *sėdėti* ; Skr. *sádati*, *sā́dati*, sit, set.

sùil, eye, Ir., O. Ir. *súil* : **sûli-s*, allied to **sâvali-s*, sun, W. *haul*, *heul*, sun, Cor. *heuul*, Br. *heaul* ; Lat. *sôl*, sun ; Gr. ἥλιος, (=*sāvĕlios*), sun ; Got. *sauil*, sun ; Lit. *sáulė* (do.).

suilbh, cheer, hospitality, geniality : **su-lubi-*, root *lubh*, please, love, Lat. *libet*, Eng. *love*. It influences the meaning of **suilbhir,** originally "eloquent."

suilbhir, cheerful, so Ir., M. Ir. *suilbir*, O. Ir. *sulbir*, eloquence, E. W. *helabar*, now *hylafar*, eloquence : from *su-* or *so-* and *labhair*, speak : "easy-spoken."

suim, a sum, Ir. *suim*, W. *sum*, M. Eng. *summe* ; from Lat. *summa*, sum, chief.

suim, attention, respect, Ir. *suim* ; a metaphoric use of *suim*, sum (Dr Cameron).

suipeir, a supper, Ir. *suipéir* ; from the Eng.

suire, a maid, nymph, Ir. *súire* (O'Cl.), a siren (*suire*, O'B., Lh., etc., mermaids) ; from Lat. *siren*, with leaning on *suirghe*, courtship ? The word is doubtful Gaelic ; H.S.D. finds only an Ossian Ballad to quote.

suiridhe, a courting, **suiridheach** (better **suirtheach** or **suireach,** M'A.), a wooer, so Ir., also *surighim*, I woo, M. Ir. *suirge*, wooing, *suirgech*, procus : **su-reg-*, root *reg*, direct, etc. ?

sùist, a flail, Ir. *suist(e)*, M. Ir. *sust*, *suiste*, W. *ffust*, N. *thust*, *sust*, flail ; from Lat. *fustis*, club.

sùith, soot, Ir. *súithche*, M. Ir. *suithe*, O. Ir. *suidi*, fuligine, W. *huddygl* (cf. *hudd*, dark), Br. *huzel* (Fr. *suie*) : **sodio-*, root *sed*, sit, settle ; Eng. *soot*, Ag. S. *sôt*, Norse *sót*. Doubtful.

sùlair, the gannet; from Norse *súla*, *súlan*, the gannet, whence Eng. *solan*-goose.
sulchar, cheerful, affable; side-form of *suilbhir*?
sult, fat, fatness, joy, Ir. *sult*, E. Ir. *sult*: **sultu-*, root *svel*; Ag. S. *swellan*, Eng. *swell*; Lat. *salum*, sea; Gr. σάλος. tossing.
sumag, cloth below a pack-saddle; ultimately from L. Lat. *sauma*, pack-saddle, whence Fr. *sommier*, mattress, Eng. *sumpter*.
sumaich, give the due number (as of cattle for pasture); from Sc. *soum*.
sumaid, a billow, Ir. *sumaid* (O'R. and M'L., **sùmaid**); seemingly from Eng. *summit*. The G. also means "external senses" (H.S.D.).
sumain, summon, a summons; from the Eng.
sumainn, a surge, billow; see *sumaid*.
sumair, the drone of a bagpipe:
sùmhail, close-packed, tidy; opposite of *dòmhail*, q.v.
sunais, lovage—a plant, Ir. *sunais*; also **siunas**:
sunnd, sunnt, good humour, cheerfulness, Ir. *sonntach*, merry (O'Cl., O'B.), *sonnda*, bold, *súntaidh*, active, E. Ir. *suntich*, spirited: **sondeto-*, Eng. *sound*?
sunnag, an easy-chair of twisted straw:
supail, supple (M'A.); from the Eng.
sùrd, alacrity, cheerfulness; cf. W. *chwardd*, laughter, Corn. *wherzin*, ridere; root *sver*, sing, speak; Eng. *swear*, Lat. *susurrus*, whisper, etc. M. Ir. *sord*, bright (**surdo-*), is referred by Stokes to the same origin as Lat. *serenus*.
surrag, vent of a kiln; cf. *sòrn*.
surram-suain, a sound sleep; *surram*, snoring noise as of one asleep:
susbaint, substance, Ir. *substaint*; from Lat. *substantia*.
sùsdal, a bustling, pother, affected shyness:
suth, anything (Dial.), Ir., E. Ir. *suth*, weather; root *su*, produce, E. Ir. *suth*, milk; Gr. ὕει, it rains; as in *sùgh*, q.v. Further allied is root *su*, beget, O. Ir. *suth*, offspring, Eng. *sun*.
suthainn, eternal, Ir. *suthain*, O. Ir. *suthain*, *suthin*; from *su*, *so-* and *tan*, time, q.v.; *sú-tan-ìs* (Stokes *see*).

T

ta, tha, is, Ir. *tá*, E. Ir. *tá*, is, *táim*, I am, O. Ir. *táu*, *tó*, sum, *tá*, *táa*, est, especially *attáa* (at the beginning of a sentence), est (=*ad-tât*, Lat. *adsto*) and *itá*, *itáa*, "in which is": **tâjô*, **tâjet*, root *stâ*, stand; Lat. *stô*, *stat*, stand, Fr. *été*, having been; Ch. Sl. *stoją*, I stand; further Eng. *stand*, Gr. ἵστημι (for σί-στᾱμι), set, Lat. *sisto*. See *seas* further.

tabaid, fight, brawl; Br. has *tabut* of like force; see *sabaid*. Cf. Sc. *debate*.

tàbar, a tabor, Ir. *tabár*; from the Eng.

tabh, the sea, ocean; from Norse *haf*, Swed. *haf*, Dan. *hav*, the open sea, Ag. S. *haef*. From Norse also comes the Sc. (Shet.) *haaf*, open sea.

tàbh, a spoon-net; from Norse *háfr*, a pock-net.

tabhach, a sudden eruption, a forcing, a pull, Ir. *tabhach*, sudden eruption, compulsion, *tobhachaim*, I compel, E. Ir. *tobach*, levying, distraint, from *dobongaim*: for root see *buain*.

tàbhachd, substantiality, effectiveness, Ir. *tábhachd*, M. Ir. *tabhuchta* (Meyer):

tabhair, give, so Ir., E. Ir. *tabraim*, O. Ir. *tabur*, do, post-particle form of *dobiur*, now G. **bheir**, q.v.: inf. **tabhairt**, so Ir. See *thoir*.

tabhal, a sling, Ir. *tabhall*, E. Ir. *taball*, W. *tafl*, a cast, *taflu*, jacere, Cor. *toula*, Br. *taol*, a cast, blow: **taballo-*, root *tab*, to fire, sling; cf. Eng. *stab*.

tàbhairn, an inn, tavern, Ir. *tabhairne*; from Lat. *taberna*, Eng. *tavern*.

tàbharnach, noisy (Suth.):

tabhann, barking, Ir. *tathfan*: **to-sven-*, root *sven*, sound (see *seinn*).

tàbhastal, tedious nonsense:

tac, a lease, tack; from Sc. *tack*.

tacaid, a tack, tacket, Ir. *taca*; from the Eng.

tacan, a while, short time; from *tac*.

tacar (**tàcar**, H.S.D.), provision, plenty, support, Ir. *tacar*, a collection, gleaning, contrivance. Cf. N. *taka*, income.

tachair, meet, happen, Manx *taghyrt*, to happen, an accident, Ir. *tachair*, he arrived at; from *to-* and *car*, turn.

tàcharan, a ghost, yelling of a ghost, an orphan, Ir. *tacharán*:

tachas, itching, scratching, Ir. *tochas*:

tachd, choke, Ir. *tachdaim*, O. Ir. *tachtad*, angens. Stokes gives the root as *tak* and refers to it also W. *tagu* (and *ystagu*), choke, Cor., Br. *taga*. Brugmann and Ascoli analyse *tachd* into *to-acht*, root *angh*, Lat. *ango*, choke, Gr. ἄγχω, Eng. *anger*. Root *tak* as in Lat. *tacere* (Prellwitz).

tachras, winding yarn, Ir. *tocharais*, *tochardadh*, M. Ir. *tochartagh*: **to-cert-*, root *qert*, wind, as in *ceirtle*.

tacsa, tacas (Dial.), support, substance; cf. *taic*.

tàdh, a ledge, layer; cf. *spadh*.

tadhal, frequenting, visiting, Ir. *tadhall*, O. Ir. *tadal*, dat. *tadíll*, inf. of *taidlim*, *doaidlibem*, visitabimus, *adall*, diverticulum:

**to-ad-ell*, from **elnô* (Stokes), go, M. W. *elwyfi*, iero, Corn. *yllyf*, eam, root *ela*, Lat. *ambulare*, walk, Gr. ἐλαύνω, drive, proceed; likely also Fr. *aller*, go.

tadhal, goal, hail; from Eng. *hail*.

tagair, plead, Ir. *tagair* (imper.), *tagraim*, E. Ir. *tacraim*, O. Ir. *tacre*, argumentum: **to-ad-gar-*, root *gar*, as in *goir*, *agair*.

tagh, choose, Ir. *toghaim*, O. Ir. *togu*, eligo, electio: **to-gusô*, root *gus*, choose, taste; Lat. *gusto*, taste; Gr. γεύω, taste; Eng. *choose*.

taghairm, noise, echo, a mode of divination by listening to the noise of water cascades, Ir. *toghairm*, summons, petition, O. Ir. *togairm*, invocatio; from *to-* and *gairm*.

taghan, the marten:

tagradh, ghost (Suth. R.D.):

taibhs, taibhse, an apparition, ghost, Ir. *taibhse*, vision, ghost, M. Ir. *tadhbais*, phantasma, O. Ir. *taidbse*, demonstratio, *tádbat*, demonstrat, **tad-bat* or **to-ad-bat*, root *bat*, show, see, speak, I. E. *bhâ*, *bhan* as in *bàn*, q.v. Gr. φάντασμα, Eng. *phantasm* and *phantom* are closely allied to the G.

taibid, a taunt; see *teabaid*.

taibse, propriety of speech: "precision," E. Ir. *tepe*, cutting; see *teabaid*.

taic, support, proximity, Ir. *taca*, prop, surety, fastening, *toice*, prop, wealth, *tacamhuil*, firm, *aice*, support, food, near, M. Ir. *aicc*, a bond, E. Ir. *aicce*, relationship: **akki-*, **pakki-*, root *pak*, bind; Lat. *paciscor*, agree, *pax*, peace; Eng. *fang*, Got. *fahan*, seize: Zend *paç*, bind. The root is a triplet--*pak*, *pag*, *pagh* (Gr. πήγνυμι, make fast, Lat. *pango*, Eng. *page*, etc.). Zimmer refers E. Ir. *aicce* to the root of *agus*, *aig*.

taidhe, attention, heed, Ir. *uidh*, O. Ir. *oid*, *óid*, *con-ói*, servat: **audi-*, root *av*, watch, Lat. *aveo*, desire, *audeo*, dare, Skr. *av*, favour (see *àill* further). The *t* of G. is due to the phrase "Thoir taidhe (= *thoir do aidhe*)"—Take thy heed: a phrase to which the word is practically restricted, and which accounts for the short vowel of the G. and Ir., the sentence accent being on the verb.

taidheam, meaning, import; see *oidheam*.

taifeid, a bow-string:

taig, attachment, custom; cf. *aig*, at.

taigeis, haggis; from Sc. *haggis*, O. Fr. *hachis*, Eng. *hash*, from *hack*.

taighlich, chattels (Heb.); a side form of *teaghlach*.

tail, substance, wages, **taileas**, wages, Ir. *táille*, wages, M. Ir. *taile*, salarium, W. *tâl*, payment, Cor., O. Br. *tal*, solvit, root *tal*, *tel*, take, hold; Gr. τάλαντον, a talent, Eng. *talent*, τελος, toll; Lat. *tollo*, lift, Eng. *thole*, etc.

tailce, strength, Ir. *talcánta*, strong, E. Ir. *talce*, *tailce*: **t-alkiâ*, root *alk*, strong, Gr. ἀλκή, strength, ἀλέξω, defend.

tailceas, contempt; cf. *tarcuis*.

tàileasg, backgammon, chess, Ir. *táibhleis*, backgammon table, back-gammon, M. Ir. *taiflis*, draught-board, tables, W. *tawl-fwrdd*, draught-board; from M. Eng. *tables*, backgammon, from *table*, Norse *tafl*, game, chess.

tailebart, halberd; from the Eng. The Ir., M. Ir. is *halabard*, which Stokes regards as derived from the Fr. *hallebard*.

taileas, wages; see *tail*.

tailgneachd, prophecy; for *tairgneachd*, q.v.

tàille, apprentice fee, premium (M'A., who has **tàilleabh**); see *tail*.

tàille, **tàilleabh** (M'A.), consequence, **air tàille**, on account of; cf. M. Ir. *a haithle*, after, *as a haithle sin*, thereafter, O. G. *as á áthle*, thereafter (B. of Deer), *aithle*, remnant.

tàillear, a tailor, Ir. *tailiur*, W. *teiliwr*; from the Eng., M. Eng. *tailor*, *taylor*, from Fr. *tailleur*.

tailm, a tool, sling, noose, Ir. *tailmh*, a sling, E. Ir. *tailm* (do.), W. *telm*, laqueus, Br. *talm*, sling: **talksmi-* (Stokes); Ch. Sl. *tlŭką*, strike.

tailmrich, bustle, noise; for **tairmrith*, E. Ir. *tairmrith*, transcursus, from *tairm-*, cross, trans (see *thar*), and *ruith*, run.

tailp, a bundle, bunch (Sh., O'R.):

tàimh, death, mortality, Ir. *táimh*, E. Ir. *tám*, plague: **tâmo-*, death; cf. Skr. *támyati*, choke, Ch. Sl. *tomiti*, vexare. Cf., however, *tàmh*, rest.

taimhlisg, traduce (Carm.):

tàin, cattle, drove, Ir. *táin*, cattle, spoil, E. Ir. *táin*: **to-ag-ni*, root *ag*, drive, Lat. *ago*, etc.

taing, thanks; from the Eng. *thank*.

tainneamh, thaw (Arran), Manx *tennue*, Ir. *tionadh*, O. Ir. *tinaid*, evanescit, root *ten* as in *tana*. See *aiteamh*.

taip, a mass, Ir. *taip*; see *tap*.

tàir, contempt, Ir. *táir*, E. Ir. *tár*; for **to-shár*; see *sàr*.

tàir, get, obtain, come, Ir. *tair*, come thou, E. Ir. *tair* (do.), *tair*, venies; from *tairicim*, I arrive at, come, catch, for **to-air-ic*, root *ic* of *thig*, q.v.

tairbeart, an isthmus, peninsula: **tar-bertâ*, from *tar* (see *thar*, cross) and *ber* of *beir*: "cross-bringing, portage."

tairbhe, profit, so Ir., O. Ir. *torbe*: **to-for-be*, where *-be* comes from **bv-iâ*, root *bu*, be (see *bu*).

tairbheartach, profitable, so Ir., E. Ir. *tairbert*, yielding, giving up : **to-air-ber-*, from the verb *beir*, bring.

tairbhein, surfeit, bloody flux (Carm.) :

tairg, offer, **tairgse,** an offer, Ir. *tairgim*, *tairgsin*, E. Ir. *tairgim*, *tharscin* (dat.) : **to-air-ges-*, root *ges*, carry (Lat. *gero*), as in *agus*? Ascoli compares O. Ir. *taircim*, affero, *tairciud*, oblatio, tribuere, from *to-ad-ro-ic*, root *ic* of *thig*.

tairgneachd, tailgneachd, tairgire, prophecy, Ir. *tairrgire*, *tairgire*, prophecy, promise, O. Ir. *tairngire*, promissio : **to-air-ind-gar-iâ*, root *gar* as in *goir*.

tairiosg, a saw ; see *tuireasg*.

tairis, the dairymaid's cry to calm a cow : cf. O. Ir. *tairissim*, sto, **to-air-sess*, from *sess* as in *seas*, q.v.

tairis, kind, loving, Ir. *tairis*, loyal, E. Ir. *tairisse*, true, loyal : "stable," from *to-air-sess*, from *sess*, stop, stand, as in *seas*, q.v.

tairisgein, peat-spade ; see *toirsgian*.

tairleas, turlas, cupboard or aumrie (Perth) : Sc. *tirless*, lattice, wicket, Fr. *trellis*.

tairm, necromancy (Sh., O.R.) ; see *taghairm*.

tàirneanach, thunder, Ir. *tóirneach*, *tóirn* ; see *torrunn* for root, etc.

tàirng, tarrang, a nail, Ir., E. Ir. *tairnge* ; from *tarruing*?

tais, soft, Ir. *tais*, E. Ir. *taise*, *tasse*, weakness : **taxi-*, soft (Gaul. *Taxi-magulus*?), root *tak*, weak, melting, Gr. τακερός (do.), τήκω, melt ; further Lat. *tabes*, Eng. *thaw*. Bezzenberger suggests Gr. τάγηνον, a melting pot, saucepan.

taisbean, reveal, Ir. *taisbeanaim*, E. Ir. *taispenim*, *taissfenim*, O. Ir. *asfenimm*, testificor, *doairfenus*, exploravi ; the old Gaelic root is *fen*, *ben*, which may be cognate to Gr. φαίνω (see *taibhse*). Zeuss regarded the *s* as put before the *b* by metathesis, the word being of the same origin as *taibhse*.

taisdeal, a journey, *taisdil* (Cars.), journey (v. imp.) Ir. *taisdiol*, : **to-asdel*, **ad-sod-*, root *sod-*, as in *astar*.

tàisealan, taisealan (M'E.), saints' relics, E. Ir. *taisse* :

taisg, deposit, store away, **tasgaidh,** depository, Ir. *taisgim*, E. Ir. *taiscim*, *doroisecht-sa*, id deposui : **to-ad-sec-*, root *seq*, follow, beside, as in *seach*, past ; the idea of the verb being "put past." (Ernault Zeit. Celt.[2] 384. *segh*).

taisgeal, finding of anything, **taisgealach,** a spy, Ir. *taiscealladh*, spying, betraying, M. Ir. *taiscelad*, O. Ir. *taiscelaid*, explorator, pl. *taisceltai*, *do-scéulaim*, experior ; from *to-scél-*, from *sgeul*, story (Windisch). Hence **taisgealadh,** news.

taitheasg, a repartee, Ir. *taitheasg*, *aitheasg* (O'Br., etc.), O. Ir. *taithesc*, answer, *aithesc*, admonitio, W. *ateb*, a reply : **ati-seq*, root *seq*, say, as in *sgeul*.

taitinn, pleasing, Ir. *taithneamhach*, M. Ir *taitnemach*, bright, shining, E. Ir. *taitnim*, I shine, *taitnemach*, shining, O. Ir. *taitnem*, lucina, light : **taith-tennim*, *to-aith-tenn*, root *ten* of *teine*, fire (Windisch). Stokes (*Bez. Beit.*[18], 112), divides *taitnem* into *tait-* and *nem*, Pictish *namet*, albus.

tàl, adze, Ir., O. Ir. *tál* : **to-aglo-* (rather *t-aglo-*?), Got. *aqisi*, axe, Eng. *axe* (Strachan). Stokes gives a pre-Gaelic **tâkslo*, root *tek*, Ch. Sl. *tesla*, axe, Lat. *telum* (=*tex-lum*), weapon, Gr. τέκτων, carpenter ; but *tek* does not appear to have a side form *tâk*, and *tâkslo-* would produce *táll* (*tôkslo*, Foy). But cf. Lat. *pâla*, spade, for root, and for phonetics G. *torc* and Lat. *porcus*.

talach, complaining, Ir. *talach*, dispraise, reproach :

tàladh, enticing, hushing, caressing ; from Norse *tál*, allurement, bait, trap, Ag. S. *tál*, calumny, root *dâl*, *del*, Lat. *dolus*, guile, δηλέομαι, hurt (Dor. δᾱλέομαι).

talainte, a partition or dividing wall ; from Sc. *halland*, *hallon*. Dial. G. has also **tallaid**.

talamh, earth, so Ir., O. Ir. *talam*, g. *talman*: **talmon-*, for *tḷ-mon*, root *tel* ; Lat. *tellus*, earth (for *tēl-ōs*), **têl*, flat ; Gr. τηλία, a board ; Ag. S. *thelu*, board (root *tēl*) ; Skr. *talas*, level ground ; Ch. Sl. *tĭlo*, pavement (root *tḷ*). Stokes joins here Celtic *talo-s*, brow, Gaul. *Dubno-talos*, *Argio-talos* (Pictish *Talorgan*), W. *tâl*, brow, Cor. *tâl*, Br. *tal*.

tàlan, feats of arms, chivalry, Ir. *talan* (O'B., Sh., etc.) ; see *tàlann* for origin.

tàlann, a talent, Ir. *tallann*, O. Ir. *talland* ; from Lat. *talentum*, Eng. *talent*.

tàlfuinn, a hoe ; from *tàl* and *fonn*.

talla, a hall, Ir. *alla*, M. Ir. *all* ; from Norse *hall*, *höll*, Eng. *hall*, allied to G. *ceall*, q.v.

talmaich, honour (Carm.) :

tàmailt, an insult, offence, Ir. *támailt*, Br. *tamall*, reproach, root *stemb*, abuse, I. E. *stengo*, stamp, Gr. στέμβω, shake, misuse, abuse, στόβεω, scold, Eng. *stamp* (Stokes, Jubainville *Rev. Celt.*[16], 365).

tàmh, rest, Ir. *támh*, E. Ir. *tám* : **tâmo-*, root *stâm*, *stâ*, *sta*, stand, Eng. *stand*, *station*, *stamina* ; see *seas*. Usually *tàmh*, rest, and *tàimh*, death, are referred to the same root.

tamhasg, blockhead, brownie ; see *amhas*. For termination, cf. *ùruisg*, *tannasg*.

tamhladh, a gulping movement (M'D.) :

tamull, a while, space of time, Ir. *tamall* : **to-ad-melno-*, from *melno-*, linger, Gr. μέλλω, linger (Stokes). See *mall*.

tan, time, **an tan**, when, Ir. *tan*, *an tan*, O. Ir. *tan*, *intain*, *intan*, quum, quando: **tanâ*, time; Skr. *tan*, duration, *tanâ*, continually. Root *tan*, *ten*, extend, as in *tana*, q.v.

tana, thin, Ir., O. Ir. *tana*, Cor. *tanow*, Br. *tanaw*, but W. *teneu*: **tanavo-*, thin; Lat. *tenuis*, thin, *tendo*, stretch; Gr. ταναός, ταvυ-, long, stretched, τείνω, stretch; Eng. *thin*, Ger. *dünn*; Ch. Sl. *tĭnŭkŭ*; Skr. *tanú*.

tànaiste, next heir, tanist, anything second, Ir. *tánaiste*, lieutenant, second in command, heir apparent, O. Ir. *tánaise*, secundus, *imthanu*, alternation, *innimthána*, talionem: **to-atn-*, root *at* of *ath*, "re," Skr. *at*, also **at-s-men*, of *àm*, time, q.v. (Strachan). Rhys (*Celt. Br.*[2], 308) suggests connection with W. *tan*, till, Lat. *tenus*, root *ten* (no root *tân*?).

tancard, a tankard, Ir. *tancárd*; from Eng.

tannas, tannasg, an apparition, ghost; from the root of *tana*?

taobh, a side, Ir. *taobh*, E. Ir. *tóeb*, *táib*, O. Ir. *tóib*, W., Cor., Br. *tu*: **toibos*, root *steibh*, *sti*, stiff, standing; Lat. *tîbia*, shin-bone (pl.); Lit. *staibis*, post, shin-bone (pl.), *staibus*, strong; Gr. στιφός, strong; further Eng. *stiff*, Lat. *stipes*, log.

taod, a halter, cable, hair-rope, Ir. *téad*, a rope; see *teud*.

taodhair, an apostate, Ir. *taodhaire* (Lh., O'B.):

taodhal, frequenting; see *tadhal*.

taoghas, the grave:

taoig, a fit of passion (Sh., O'R.):

taois, dough, Ir. *taos*, E. Ir. *toes*, O. Ir. *táis*, massam, W. *toes*, Br. *toas*: **taisto-*, **stajesto-*, root *staj*, concrescere; Gr. σταίς (g. σταιτός), dough, στέαρ (g. στέᾱτος for **stājatos*, **stājn̥tos*); Lat. *stîria*, a drop.

taoitear, oversman, tutor (Sutherland, etc.); from Lat. *tutor*, Eng. *tutor*. See *saoitear*.

taom, pour out, empty (vb.), a jet, torrent (n.), **taoim**, bilge-water, Ir. *taomaim* (*taodhmaim*), *taodhm* (n.), E. Ir. *tóem*, a jet, *taeim*, sentina, O. Ir. *tuismiud*, delivery, **to-fo-ess-sem*: **to-ad-sm-men*, root *sem*, let go, from *sê*, Lit. *semiù*, draw (as water), Lat. *simpulum*, ladle (Stokes). Cf. O. Ir. *teissmim*, I pour out (= *to-ess-sem-im*). Borrowing from Norse *tómr*, empty, Eng. *toom*, is not to be thought of.

taom, a fit of rage, Ir. *taom* (O'B., etc.), M. Ir. *taem*:

taosg, a pour, rush, exact full of a liquid measure, Ir. *taosgaim*, I drain, pour out, E. Ir. *tóesca*, spilling, *taescaire*, a baler, pumper: **to-ad-sem-sko-*, root *sem* as in *taom*?

taosnadh, horseplay (R. D.):

tap, tow or wool on the distaff, forelock, "busk a hook," (Arg.), Ir. *tap*, *tapán*; from M. Eng. *top*, tuft of hair or flax, top, Sc. *tap*.

tapaidh, clever, active, so Ir., E. Ir. *tapad*, suddenness, alertness, *top*, sudden; from the same root as *obann* (Stokes).

tap-dubh, tattoo (R. D.).

taplach, a wallet, repository, Ir. *taplaigh*; for *tap-lach*, from *tap*, tow, etc.

tarachair, augur, so Ir.; for *tarathar*. See *tora*.

taraid, truncheon or staff of authority (Hend.):

taran, the ghost of an unbaptised infant (Sh., O'R.); for *tacharan?*

tarbh, a bull, Ir. *tarbh*, E. Ir. *tarbh*, W. *tarw*, Corn. *tarow*, Br. *taro*, *tarv*, Gaul. *tarvos*: **tarvos*; Lat. *taurus*; Gr. ταῦρος (= τάρϝος); Pruss. *tauris*, buffalo, Ch. Sl. *turŭ*, auroch. Prellwitz thinks the Celtic not allied to Gr. ταῦρος, etc., which he refers to the root *tau*, *tu* (*stû* gives Eng. *steer*).

tarcuis, also **talcuis**, contempt. Ir., M. Ir. *tarcuisne*, E. Ir. *tarcusul*:

targadh, ruling, governing, assembly (Lh., etc.), Ir. *targadh*:

targaid, a target, Ir. *targáid*; from Eng.

targair, foretell, Ir. *tairrghirim*; see *tairgneachd*.

tàrladh, it happened; see *thàrladh*.

tàrlaid, a slave, thrall; from Eng. *varlet?*

tàrmachadh, producing, originating, source, dwelling, Ir. *tórmach*, an increasing, a growing ripe for bearing, magnifying, O. Ir. *tórmach*, an increase: **to-for-mach*, root *mag*, power (Eng. *may*, *might*, etc.).

tàrmachan, a ptarmigan, Ir. *tarmochan*; Eng. *ptarmigan* is hence (Skeat). Also **tarman**, from *tarm*, murmur (Carm.):

tarmachan-dé, white butterfly (Carm.):

tàrmus, dislike of food: **to-air-meas*; see *meas*.

tàrnach, thunder-clap; see *tàirneanach*.

tàrnadair, inn-keeper; from L. Lat. *tabernator*, tavern-keeper, Lat. *taberna*, Eng. *tavern*.

tarp, a clod, lump (Sh., O'B., etc.), Ir. *tarp*, *tarpán*; from Norse *torf*, a turf, sod, Eng. *turf*.

tàrr, lower part of the belly, tail, breast, Ir. *tárr*, belly, lower part of the belly, E. Ir. *tarr*, W. *tor*, Br. *tor*, O. Br. *tar*: **tarsâ*, *tarmsâ*; Sc. *thairm*, belly, gut, Eng. *tharm*, Ger. *darm*, bowels; Gr. τράμις, tail, entrail, hip joint. Stokes gives the Celtic **targsâ*, allied to Lat. *tergus*, back.

tarrag, a nail; see *tàirng*.

tarruing, pull, draw, so Ir., E. Ir. *tairrngim*: **to-air-rengim*, from E. Ir. *ringim*, hang, tear, from *reng*, a nasalised form of *reg*, stretch (see *ruighe*).

tarraid, also **tèarraid**, sheriff officer, tipstaff (Dial.); see *earraid*.

tarsuinn, transverse, across, Ir. *tarsna*, *tarsa*, *trasna*, M. Ir., E. Ir. *tarsnu*, across; from *tar*, across (see *thar*), and *sainn* of *ursainn*, q.v.

tart, thirst, Ir., O. Ir. *tart*: **tar(s)to-*; Eng. *thurst*, Ger. *durst*, Gr. *τέρσομαι*, become dry; Lat. *torreo*, burn, *tostum* (**torstum*), Eng. *toast*; Skr. *tarsh*, thirst, Zd. *taresh*; I. E. *ters*, dry.

tartan, tartan; from Eng., Sc. *tartan*, from Fr. *tiretaine*, linsie-wolsie.

tartar, noise; reduplication of root *tar*, *tor* in *tòirneanach*.

tàsan, tedious discourse or scolding, Ir. *tasanach*, tedious, slow (Lh. marks it obsolete and queries meaning):

tasdan, a shilling; from Sc. *testan*, *testoon*, a silver coin of the 16th century with Mary's head (*teste*) on it, the "inglis testane" being worth 8 shillings Scots, Eng. *tester*, worth 6d; originally so called from the coins of Louis XII. (1500) with his head (*teste*, Fr. *tête*, head) on them.

tasgaidh, depository, a treasure: "A thasgaidh"—Thou treasure; see *taisg*.

tataidh, attract, attach one to oneself, **tadadh** (inf.), **taiteadh** (Perth), tame: **tad-dam*, root *dam* of *aidich*.

tàth, cement, join (M'F., Lh.), Ir. *táthaim*, *táth*, solder or glue, W. *todi*, construct, join: **táto-*, **stâto-*, constitute, root *sta*, stand?

tathaich, visit, frequent, tendency to vomit (Hend.), Ir. *tathuighim*, M. Ir. *aithigim*; formed from the prep. *aith*, back, rather than a compound of *tiagaim* as in *imthich*, our *imich* (that is, **ati-tig-*, go back again). Stokes prefers root *at*, go, formerly discussed under *tànaiste*.

tathunn, barking; see *tabhunn*.

té, a woman, female, she, Ir. *an tí*, she who, *an té*, he who (O'Donovan says either means "he or she who" or "person who"), O. Ir. *intí*, is(qui), *indí* ea(quae), *aní* id(quod): the article and the enclitic particle *-í*, for which see *nì*, and cf. *tì*, he who.

tè, tèa, insipid, slightly fermented; from root of *teas*; cf. *tepid*.

teabaid, a taunt, repartee (Dial.), **teab**, a flippant person's mouth (M'A.), **teibidh**, smart: "cutting," E. Ir. *tepe* (*to-aith-be*, Stokes), a cutting, O. Ir. *taipe*, concisio, brevitas: **tad-be* (=*to-ad-be*), reduced root *be*, cut, *imdibe*, circumcisio, etc., root *bi*, *bin*, as in *bean*, touch, q.v.

teach, a house, Ir. *teach*, O. Ir. *tech*, *teg*, g. *tige*, W. *ty*, Cor. *ti*, O. Br. *teg*, *tig*, *ti*, now *ti*: **tegos*, g. *teges-os*; Gr. *τέγος*, roof, *στέγω*, cover; Lat. *tego*, cover, *tectum*, house; Eng. *thatch*,

Ger. *dach* ; Lit. *stẽgiu*, cover ; Skr. *sthagati*, cover. See *tigh* for usual nom. case.

teachd, coming, arrival, Ir. *teachd*, O. Ir. *techt*, aditus, itio, W. *taith*, iter, Br. *tiz*, diligence, haste : **tiktâ*, root *stig*, *steig*, as in *tighinn*, q.v. Some derive it from *thig* or *tig*, q.v. Hence **teachdaire**, messenger.

teachd, legal, lawful, M. Ir. *techta*, *téchta*, O. Ir. *téchte*, fitting, legalis, lex : **tenctio-*, root *tenq*, become, chance, produce, Eng. *thing*, Lit. *tenkù*, chance, befall, Lat. *tempus*. Dial. form **deic, cha deic**, q.v.

tèachd, teuchd, silly boasting (Arg.).

teadalach, slow, dilatory :

teadhair, a tether ; from Sc., Eng. *tether*, *tedder*, Norse *tjóðr*, *tjor*, Swed. *tjuder*.

teagair, collect, provide, shelter, Ir. *teagar*, provision, shelter, *teagarach*, warm, snug, *teagairim*, store, provide ; cf. *eagar*.

teagamh, doubt, suspense ; see *theagamh*.

teagasg, teaching, so Ir., E. Ir. *tecosc* : **to-aith-cosc-*, for which see *caisg*.

teaghlach, family, household, so Ir., O. Ir. *teglach*, W. *teulu*, O. W. *telu*, Corn. *teilu*, familia : **tego-slougo-*, from the stems of *tigh* and *sluagh*. The termination *-lach* from **slougo-s* makes abstract collective nouns, which are used for single objects or persons ; as *òglach*, young man, really "youth," or "young-people," just as "youth" is also used in Eng. as a concrete noun—"a youth."

teallach, hearth, forge, Ir. *teallach*, E. Ir. *tenlach*, *tellach* : **tene-lach*, from *teine*, fire, and terminal *-lach* (see *teaghlach*).

teallaid, a lusty or bunchy woman (M'F.) :

teamhaidh, pleasant, Ir. *teamhair*, pleasant, Tara, E. Ir. *temair*, delightful, omnis locus conspicuus : **stem-ri-* ?

teamhair, time (Suth.) : Lat. ?

teamhall, slight swoon or stun, Ir. *teimheal*, darkness, O. Ir. *temel* (do.), Skr. *támas*, Lit. *tamsa*, Lat. *tenebrae*, *temere*, rashly.

teampull, temple, church, Ir. *teampoll*, O. Ir. *tempul*, W. *teml*, Corn. *tempel* ; from Lat. *templum*.

teanacadh, deliverance, succour, **teanacas**, healing : **tind-ioc*, from *ìoc*, heal.

teanchair, pincers, smith's tongs, Ir. *teanchoir*, tongs, pincers, O. Ir. *tenchor*, forceps : **ten-cor*, "fire-putter," from the stem of *teine*, fire, and *cor*, seen in *cuir*, put.

teanga, teangadh, a tongue, Ir. *teanga*, O. Ir. *tenge*, gen. *tengad* : **tengot-*, from *stengh*, sting (Eng. *sting*, Ger. *stengel*, stalk), which is from *zdn̥gh*, from *dn̥gh*, whence Lat. *dingua*, Eng. *tongue?* Stokes (*Academy*, Oct. '91) has compared Lat. *tango* (so Windisch, *Scot. Celt. Rev.*, 34). Rhys has considered the probabilities of alliance with W. *tafod*, Corn. *tavot*, Br. *teod*, older *teaut* (**tebâto-*) in *Manx Pray.*², 136-7.

teann, tight, tense, near to, Ir. *teann*, O. Ir. *tend*, W. *tyn*, tight, stretched : **tendo-* ; Lat. *tendo*, I stretch, *tentus*, stretched (Stokes, *Rev. Celt.*[13], 124) ; in any case from root *ten* of *tana*. Foy gives *sten* ; N. *stinnr*, rough, hard. Cf. Gr. *στενός*.

tearb, separate, Ir. *tearbadh* (O'Cl.), severance, M. Ir. *terpúd*, E. Ir. *terbaim*, *terbud* : **ter-be-*, Gadelic reduced root *be*, cut, for which see *teabaid?*

tearc, scarce, rare, Ir. *tearc*, E. Ir. *terc* : **ter(s)qo-s*, rare, root *ters*, dry (as in *tart*) ; Lat. *tesqua* (= *tersquo-s*), deserts.

tearmann, a sanctuary, protection, so Ir., M. Ir. *termain*, *termonn*, W. *terfyn* ; from Lat. *termo(n)*, *terminus*, end, "end of race for life by reaching church lands" or *Termon landes* (Ducange).

tearr, tar, Ir *tearr* ; from M. Eng. *terve*, Norse *tjara*.

tèaruinn, save, escape, **tèarnadh** (inf.), Ir. *tearnaim*, E. Ir. *térnaim*, *ternam*, an escape, *érnaim*, I escape : **es-rn-*, root *r̥n*, Eng. *run?*

teas, heat, Ir. *teas*, O. Ir. *tess*, g. *tesa*, W., Corn. *tes*, Br. *tez* : **testu-*, for **tepstu-*, root *tep*, burn, heat ; Lat. *tepeo*, be warm, Eng. *tepid* ; Ch. Sl. *teplo*, hotly ; Skr. *tap*, be hot, Zd. *tap*, burn. See, also from *tep*, **teine**, **teth**. Hence **teasach**, fever.

teasairg, save, deliver, Ir. *teasargaim*, O. Ir. *tessurc*, servo, *dumesurcsa*, defendo me : **to-ess-arc*, root *ark*, defend : Lat. *arceo*, ward off ; Gr. *ἀρκέω* (do.). See *adharc*.

teasd, die, Ir. *teasdaighim*, die, fail, M. Ir., O. Ir. *testa*, deest, fails ; **to-ess-tá*, from *tá*, I am. Cf., for force, Lat. *desum*.

teasdam, I preserve, help (Carm.) :

teasg, cut, cut off, Ir. *teasgaim*, E. Ir. *tescaim* : **to-ess-sc*, root *sec*, cut, Lat. *seco*, Eng. *saw*.

teibideach, irresolute : "halting, failing ;" cf. Ir. *tebim*, disappoint, fail, for which see *theab*.

teich, flee, Ir. *teithim*, E. Ir. *techim*, O. Ir. *teichthech*, vitabundus, W. *techu*, skulk, M. Br. *techet*, flee : **tekô*, **tekkô*, flee, I. E. root *teq-*, flow, run ; Ch. Sl. *teku*, a run, Lit. *tekù*, flow ; Skr. *takti*, runs, Zd. *taka-*, course.

teididh, wild, fierce (H.S.D.), wild fire (M'A.) :

teilg, a fishing line : "a cast," from *tilg*, cast, Ir. *teilgean*, casting?

teilinn, musical instrument, **teilig**, a chord (Carm.), W. *telu* or *telyn*, harp. Cf. *seillean*.

teilleach, a blub-cheeked fellow (Dial.) ; cf. *meilleach*.

teine, fire, Ir. *teine*, O. Ir. *tene*, g. *tened*, pl. *tenti*, W. *tân*, Cor., Br. *tan* (in proper names also *tanet*) : **tenet-*, **tenos*, Celtic root *te*, from *tep*, hot, as in *teas*, q.v. Not for **te(p)ne-*, as usually said, which would give *téine* now, nor **tepsne-*, which would produce *tenne* now ; *teine-sionnachain*, phosphorescence, *teine-fionn*, will o' the wisp (Suth.).

teinn, calamity, strait ; an abstract noun from *teann*.

teirig, fail, be spent, die, **teireachduinn** (inf.), Ir. *teiricim* (O'B.), E. Ir. *tarnic*, it ended, from **tar-ic*, transire (*tar*, across, and *ic* or *nic* of *thig*, *thainig*). Atkinson joins it with *tairicim*, arrive (= *to-air-ic-*), as in *tàir*, but the meanings scarcely suit.

teiric, hake, herring hake (Carm.) :

teirinn, tèarn, descend, Ir. *tearnaim*, *túrnaim*, E. Ir. *tairnim*, O. Ir. *tairirnud*, dejectio (= *to-air-innud*), from **endô*, go, root *end*, *ed*, I. E. *ped*, go (Eng. *foot*, Lat. *pes*, etc., G. *uidhe*, q.v).

teirisi ! the dairymaid's cry to calm a cow ; see *tairis*.

teirm, a term, Ir. *tearma*, earlier, *térma* (F.M.) ; from M. Eng. *terme*, from Lat. *terminus* through Fr.

tearmasg, tiormasg, a mistake, mischance ; cf. *eirmis*. Here *te* may be for *de*, on the analogy of *to*, *do*.

téis, a musical air ; see *séist* for derivation.

teismeid, last will and testament ; from Lat. *testamentum*.

teis-meadhon, the exact or very middle ; *teis* = *to-ess*, as in *teasairg*.

teist, testimony, Ir. *teisd*, *teist*, O. Ir. *teist*, W. *tyst*, Br. *test* ; from Lat. *testis*, Eng. *test*, etc.

teó, teódh, make warm ; from *teò-*, q.v. The Ir. verb is *teighim*, inf. *téaghadh*.

teò-, warm, **teò-chridheach**, warm-hearted ; **tepu-*, Skr. *tapus*, hot, root *tep* as in *teth*. Cf. Keating's (*Three Shafts*, 282), *teó-ghrádhuigheas*, qui ardentius amat, where Atkinson considers *teó* a comparative.

teòm, a dole (Carm.) :

teòma, skilful, expert, **teòm**, cunning (Carm.) :

teth, hot, Ir. *teith*, comp. **teotha** (G. and Ir.), M. Ir. *te*, comp. *teou* : **teps* (?), root *tep*, hot, as in *teas*. The O. Ir. is *tee*, *té*, fervidus, pl. *téit*, from **tepents*, g. **tepentos*, Lat. *tepens*.

teuchd, congeal, be parched, Ir. *teuchdaim*, curdle, coagulate, M. Ir. *téchtaige*, frozen, O, Ir. *coiteichtea*, concretionis : **tenkto-*, from I. E. *tenq*, firm, fast ; Eng. *tight*, Ger. *dicht*, close.

teud, a string, Ir. *teud*, *téad*, O. Ir. *tét*, fidis, W. *tant* : *tn̥tâ*, chord ; Skr. *tântu*, *tánti*, cord : root *ten*, stretch, thin, as in *tana*.

teugmhail, battle, contest, disease, Ir. *teagmháil*, a meeting, retribution : **to-ex-com-dháil*, see *comhdhail*. In the sense of "disease," see *eugail*.

teum, a bite, sudden snatch, wound, E. Ir. *temm*, W. *tam*, a bite Corn. *tam*, pl. *tymmyn*, Br. *tamm*: **tendmen*, root *tend*, cut; Lat. *tondeo*, shear, *tineo*, a worm; Gr. *τένδω*, gnaw; Ch. Sl. *tęti*, caedere.

thà, is; see *tà*. The aspiration is due to the use of *tà* in relative sentences, where the *t* is intervocalic.

thàinig, came, Ir. *thánaic*, *tháinig*, vēnit, O. Ir. *tánic*, *ránic*, vēnit, *tânac*, vēni: **ananka*, I have come—a reduplicated perfect; Skr. *ânamca*, has reached; Gr. *ἤνεγκε*, brought: root *enk*, *nak* (*nank*), attain, bring, for which see *thig*. The aspiration is due to the analogy of other perfects which follow *do*.

thairis, over, across, Ir. *tairis*, E. Ir. *tairis*, over it, him; from *tar* (*thar*) and *sé* or *é*, he, it. The aspiration is, due to a sup pressed, or supposed suppressed, *do* or *a*.

thall, over, beyond, Ir. *thall*, O. Ir. *thall*, *tall*: **t-all*, O. Ir. *ol*, quam, *indoll*, *altarach*, ultra, *al*, ultra; root *ol*, *el*, *ol*, Lat. *ille* (= *olle*), *alius*. Also **eile**, other, which see. The form **thallad** stands for *thall-ud*.

thalla, come, come along, "age," **thallaibh** (pl.), E. Ir. *tallaim*, take away, **talnô*, root *tel*, bear (see *tlàth*, *tail*, etc.). Also interjection: **thalla! thalla!** well! well!

thar, across, Ir. *tar*, O. Ir. *tar*, *dar*, W. *tra-*, over, *trach*, beyond, root *ter*, through, past, Lat. *trans*, *terminus*; Skr. *tar-*, pass; I. E. *ter*, pass through, bore. See *tora*, *troimh*.

thàrladh, accidit, Ir. *tarla*, E. Ir. *dorala*, *dorla*, O. Ir. *tarla*: **to-ro-la*, the *la* being the remains of root *plu*, as in *dol* (Ascoli).

theab, nearly did (with inf.), Ir. *do theib sé*, he failed (O'B.): "grazed" it, from **tebb*, graze, cut, as in *teabaid*?

theagamh, mayhap, perhaps, O. Ir. *tecmaing*, accidit, *tecmang*, eventus, *do-é-cm-aingim*, accido, for **to-ex-com-ang*, root *ang*, near, as in *cumhang*, q.v. Meyer takes O. Ir. *ecmaing* from *ad-com-bangim*, *bang* root of *buain*. It has also been referred to root *mang*, *mag*, Eng. *may*, etc.

théid, will go, Ir. *téid*, goes, O. Ir. *téit*, venit, it: **to-éit*, **entô*, **pentô*, go, reach, root *pet*, *pent*, go, fly, fall; Lat. *pet*, seek, "fall on"; Gr. *πίπτω*, fall; Got. *finþan*, Eng. *find*.

their, will say; see *deir*.

thig, will come, Ir. *tigim*, come, E. Ir. *tic*, *ticc*, venit, O. Ir. *ticfa*, veniet: **tó-icc*, from *icc*, **enkô*, come, reach, root *enk*, *nak*, *nank*, attain, bring; Gr. *ἤνεγκα*, brought (= G. **thàinig**), a reduplicated perf. from *εγκ*; Skr. *ānamça*, attained; further *nank* of *adhlac* and Lat. *nanciscor*.

thoir, give, G., Ir. **tabhair**, give thou, q v. The G. is for *toir*, a crushed form of *tabhair*, and this is aspirated on the analogy of *bheir*, *gheibh*, and especially of *thug*, its past tense.

thud, an interjection of dislike or impatience : Sc. *hoot*, *hoot-toot*, Swed. *hut*, whence Eng. *hoot*. The G. is borrowed.

thug, gave, brought, Ir. *thug*, *thugas* (1st pers.), E. Ir. *tuc*, *tucas*, *do-fuc*, from *uc*, *ucc*, **ud-ge*, from *s-* aorist **e-ges-s-t*, **e-ges-s-m*, root *ges*, carry, Lat. *gero*, *gessi* (Zimmer, *Zeit.*[30] 156-7); whence also W. *dug*, he bore, Cor. *duk*, Br. *dougas*.

thugad, thugaibh, thuige, etc., to thee, to you, to him; for *chugad*, etc., q.v. Similarly **thun** is for **chun, gun, gu**, q.v. **thun** with gen. is for *chum*.

tì, any one, person, Ir. *tí*, person, *an tí*, *an té*; see *té*, *nì*.

tì, intention, Ir., E. Ir. *tí*; *ar ti* = intends (Glenmassan MS.) :

tiachair, perverse, ill-disposed, sick, a dwarf, Ir. *tiachair*, perverse (O'Cl., Lh., O'B.), M. Ir. *tiachair*, troublesome, E. Ir. *tiachaire*, affliction, peevishness :

tiadhan, a little hill, small stone, Ir. *tíadhan*, a stone, testicle :

tiamhaidh, gloomy, lonesome, Ir. *tiamdha*, dark (O'Cl.), E. Ir. *tiamda*, dark, afraid :

tiarmail, prudent; cf. *tìorail*.

tibirt, fountains (Uist; Hend.); see *tiobart*.

tìde, time; from Icel. *tíð*, Sc., Eng. *tide*. Ag. S. *tíd*, Ger. *zeit*.

tigh (for **taigh**), a house, Ir. *tigh*, O. Ir. *teg*, *tech*; see *teach*.

tighearn, tighearna, lord, master, Ir. *tighearna*, O. Ir. *tigerne*, W. *teyrn*, O. W. *-tigern*, Cor. *teern*, O. British *tigernus* : **tegerno-s*, *tegernio-s*, root *teg* of *tigh*, q.v.

tighil, call when passing (M'A.); the *t* being as in *tigh*, the word seems a variant of *tadhal*.

tighinn, coming, Ir. *tighim*, I come, E. Ir. *tiagaim*, O. Ir. *tiagu*, *tíchtu* (*tíchtin*), adventus : **tigô*, **teigô*, from root *steigh*, *stigh*, go; Gr. *στείχω*, walk; Got. *steigan*, ascend, Ger. *steigen*, Eng. *stair* : Skr. *stighnute*, stride.

tilg, cast, cast out, vomit, Ir. *teilgim*, O. Ir. *teilcim* : *to-es-leic*, "let out," from the original of G. **leig**, let, q.v.

till, pill, return, Ir. *tillim* (Keating), *fillim*, *pillim* (O'B.) (Ulster has *till*) : **svelni-*, turn round, W. *chwylo*, turn, revolve, *chwyl*, a turn, course, while (for which see G. **seal**). Cf. *fill*.

tìm, time; from the Eng.

timchioll, around, a circuit, so Ir., O. Ir. *timchell* : **to-imm-cell*, from I. E. *qel*, move, go; Lat. *colo*, tend, *celer*, swift; Gr. *πελομαι*, go, be, *ἀμφίπολος*, attendant; Skr. *cárâmi*, move, go. See *buachaill*.

tinn, sick, Ir. *tinn*, E. Ir. *tind*: **tenni-*, root *ten* of *tana*, *teann*, *teinn*. Cf. O. Ir. *tinaim*, evanesco, Lat. *attenuo*, Eng. *attenuate*.

tinne, a chain, link, piece of a column, M. Ir. *tinne*, flitch, E. Ir. *tinde*, ring, link, bar, O. Ir. *tinne*, chalybs; from the root *ten* of *tana*. Cf. Norse *þind*, diaphragm.

tioba, a heap (Arg.); from Eng. *heap* or G. *iob*?

† **tiobart,** a well, O. G. *tiprat* (gen., Bk. of Deer), Ir. *tiobar*, *tiobrad*, E. Ir. *tipra*, d. *tipraít*, **to-aith-brevant-*, Celtic verb **bervô*, seethe, boil; Gr. *φρέαρ*, *φρέατος*, a well; Ger. *brunnen*, Eng. *burn*. See *tobar*.

tiodhlac, a gift, Ir. *tiodhlacadh*, E. Ir. *tidnacul*, O. Ir. *tindnacul*, traditio, *do-ind-naich*, distribuit: *to-ind-naŋk-*, root *nank*, bring, get, Lat. *nanciscor*, obtain; also root *enk* as in *thig*, q.v. Hence also **tiodhlaic,** bury, and **adhlac,** q.v.

tiolam, a short space, a snatch:

tiolp, snatch, grasp eagerly, Ir. *tiolpaim*:

tiom, soft, timid, G. *tioma*, tenderness, Ir. *time*, fear, E. Ir. *tim*, soft, timid, *timme*, fear: **temmi-*, root *tem*, faint, Lat. *timeo*, fear, Eng. *timid*; Skr. *tam*, to faint, Zd. *tam*, perish.

tiomnadh, a will or testament, Ir. *tiomna*, O. Ir. *timne*: **to-imm-ne*, the *n* of *ne* being the remains of *-ân-*, mandare, mittere (Ascoli); cf. O. Ir. *adroni*, deposuit, *immerâni*, delegavit, G. **àithne,** command, q.v.

tiompan, a musical instrument—a cymbal, Ir. *tiompán*, tabor, cymbal, drum, E. Ir. *tiompan*, a small stringed instrument; from Lat. *tympanum*, a timbrel, drum (Windisch). The difference of meaning between E. Ir and Lat. has caused some to doubt the connection; and Stokes gives the Celtic root as *temppu-*, a chord or string, Lit. *tempiù*, stretch, Ch. Sl. *tętiva*, chorda.

tiomsach, collecting, bringing together, Ir. *tiomsughadh*, E. Ir. *timmsugud*: **to-imm-sag-*, root *sag* as in *ionnsuidh*, q.v.

tionail, gather, Ir. *tionólaim*, O. Ir. *tinólaim*, *tinolaim*, *do-in-ola*, applicat: **to-in-ōla-im*, where *ōla* is referred by Stokes to **oklo-*, **poklo-*, joining, uniting, Ger. *fügen*, to fit, *füge*, joint; Lat. *paciscor*, bargain, bind; Skr. *pā́ças*, a knot, Zd. *paç*, bind. Ascoli regards it as **to-in-od-lu*, root *lu*, *plu* of *dol*, but **od-lu-* would rather mean "go out," "go off." W. *cynnull*, gathering, Corn. *cuntell*, O. Br. *contullet*, are, according to Ernault, borrowed from Lat. *contuli*.

tionnail, likeness of any person or thing: **t-ionnail*, from *ionnan*, like.

tionndadh, turning, Ir. *tiontodh*, O. Ir. *tintuith*, g. *tintuda tintathigh*, interpretes: **to-ind-sout-*, root *su* of *iompaidh*, q.v.

tionnsgainn, a beginning, devising, **tionnsgal**, ingenuity, Ir. *tionnscnadh*, a beginning, device, plotting, *tionsgiodal*, managing, industry, O. Ir. *tinscnaim* (= *to-ind-scannaim*), I begin, *tindscetal*, a beginning, root *sqend*, start, spring, Lat. *scando*, ascend, Skr. *skandati*, hurry, spring. The W. has *cy-chwyn*, ortus (**sqenô*). The form *-scetal* is for *sqen-t-* (?).

tiop, pilfer (M'A.); cf. *tiolp*.

tìor, dry (as corn), kiln-dry, Ir. *tiortha*, kiln-dried (Con.), M. Ir. *tírad*, kiln-drying, E. Ir. *tír*, to dry; from the root of *tioram* (O. Ir. *tírim*).

tìorail, warm, cosy, sheltered, Ir. *tíoramhuil*, cosy; W. *tirion*, pleasant, a familiar object; cf. Ir. *tíoramhuil*, *tíorthamhuil*, homely, national, from *tír*. Dr Cameron regarded it as taken from the root of *tioram*, which is ultimately the same as that of *tìr*. Borrowing from Eng. *cheerful* is unlikely.

tioram, dry, Ir. *tirim*, M. Ir. *tirimm*, O. Ir. *tírim*, *tír* (vb.): **tersmi-*, root *ters*, dry, as in **tart**, q.v. See also *tìr* for phonetics.

tiorc, save, deliver from peril: **t-erc-*, **to-arki-*, root *ark* of *teasairg*, q.v.

tiort, an accident:

tiosan, water-gruel; from Eng. *ptisan*, Lat. *ptisana*, barley water, from Gr. πτισάνη.

tiot, tiota, tiotan, a moment, while; cf. Ir. *giota*, something small, jot, appendage, from Lat. *iota*, whence Eng. *jot*. Gaelic is *t-iot*.

tìr, land, earth, Ir., O. Ir. *tír*, W., Corn., Br. *tir*, tellus, la terre: **têrsos* (**têrses-*); Lat. *terra* (**tersâ*), Oscan *teerum*, territorium. The further root is *ters*, be dry, as in *tart*; the idea of *tír*, *terrâ* is "dry land" opposed to sea.

tit, an interjection expressive of wet being perceived suddenly (H.S.D.): Eng. *chut ?*

tiugainn, come, let us go; from deaspirated *thugainn*, "to us," for *chugainn*, q.v.

tiugh, thick, Ir. *tiugh*, E. Ir. *tiug*, W. *tew*, O. W. *teu*, obtuso, Corn. *tew*, Br. *teu*: **tegu-*, thick; Eng. *thick*, Norse *þykkr*, Ger. *dick*; Gr. στεγνός, fast, tight.

tiurr, a beach out of reach of the sea; for *an t-iurr*, from Norse *eyrr*, a gravelly bank by a river or a promontory, Swed. *ör*, Dan. *örr*. **tiur**, mark of sea on shore, tear, stamp (Carm.).

tlachd, pleasure, so Ir., M. Ir. *tlacht*: *tḷ-ko-*, "willing," from *toil*, will, q.v. O. Ir. *todlugud*, petitio, *tothlaigim*, I desire, is from **tloq-*, of *altach*.

tlàm, teaze (wool), handful of wool. Strachan and Stokes give the stem as **tlagm* (read *tlâg-s-m-*) allied to Ger. *flocke*, flock of wool, Eng. *flock*.

tlàth, mild, smooth, Ir. *tlaith* (*tláith*, O'B.), *tlath*, E. Ir. *tlaith*, W. *tlawd*: **tlâti-*, "long-suffering," from *tel*, bear, endure; Gr. τλητός, τλάω, endure; Lat. *tollo*, raise, *tuli*, *lâtus* (for **tlâtus*), borne; Eng., Sc. *thole*.

tligheachd, liquid, spume: *t-lighe*?

tlus, pity, tenderness, M. Ir. *tlusach*, wealthy, W. *tlws*, jewel (Stokes), E. Ir. *tlus* (S. n. R.); from root *tl̥*, *tel* of *tlàth*, q.v.

tnùth, envy, Ir., E. Ir. *tnúth*; from the root *ten*, stretch: "grasping?"

to-, do-, verbal prefix = to, ad, Ir., O. Ir. *to-*, *do-*. Stokes compares Gothic *du-* to, from *þu* (?). W. has *du-*, *dy-*, *y*, Cor. *dhi*, Br. *do*, *da*.

tòbairt, flux, diarrhœa spasms: *to-fo-od-ber-t*, root *ber* of *beir*.

toban, wreath of wool or flax on a distaff; from Sc. *tappin*.

tobar, a well, Ir. *tobar*, O. Ir. *topur*, fons: **to-od-bur*, root *bhur*, *bhru*, to well, boil; Gr. φύρω, mix; Lat. *ferveo*, well, Eng. *fervid*; Skr. *bhur*, move quickly: further see root *bhru* in **bruith** and *bhrev* in **tiobar.** Some have referred **tobar** to the root *ber* of *inbhir*, *abar* (*obair*).

tobha, a rope, from Sc. *tow*, rope, Eng. *tow*, pull, Norse *tog*, rope, Lat. *duco*.

tobhta, tota, turf, roofless walls, knoll; from Norse *toft*, *topt*, a clearing, a space enclosed by roofless walls, Eng. *toft*, *tuft*, and *top*.

tobhta, tota, a rower's bend; from Norse *þopta*.

toch, hough or thigh of an animal: **t-hoch*, from the Sc. *hough*.

tochail, dig, Ir. *tochuilim*, *tochlaim*: **to-cladh*; see *cladh*.

tochar, tochradh, dowry, Ir. *tochar*, M. Ir. *tocra*, (acc.); cf. O. Ir. *tochur*, placing, from *cuir*, put. The idea is "something assigned to one." Hence Sc. *tocher*.

tòchd, tòch, an unpleasant smell, **tòchar** or **tàchar,** dense volume of smoke (Arg.); root *stou*, as in *toth*.

tòchd, a disease of the eye in cattle; cf. Sc. *hock* (H.S.D).

† **tochmharc,** a wooing, so Ir., O. Ir. *tochmarc*: **to-com-arc*; see for root *iomchorc*.

tocsaid, a hogshead; from the Eng.

todan, small tuft of wool (Lewis); N. *toddi*, a tod of wool. So Badenoch.

todhar, manure, a bleaching, seaweed for manure, Ir. *tuar*, a bleach-green, *tuarachan*, a bleacher:

todhlair, mastiff, better *tobhlair*:

tog, raise, **togail**, lifting, Ir. *tógaim*, *tógbhail*, E. Ir. *tócbaim* : **to-od-gab-im-*, from *gab*, **gabh**, take, q.v.
togair, desire, Ir. *togairim*, please, choose, G. inf. **togradh**, Ir. *togra* : **to-od-gar*, root *gar* of *goir*.
toghaidh, attention, care (H.S.D.) ; a variant of *taidhe*.
toghlainn, exhalation (M'A.) ; cf. *tòch*.
toithbheum, reproach, blasphemy, Ir. *toibhéim*, blemish, reproach, E. Ir. *toibeim* : **to-béim*, from *béim*, that is, *beum*, q.v.
toic, wealth, riches, Ir. *toice* ; cf. *taic*.
tòic, a swelling, a puffed up state of the face :
tòiceil, purse-proud ; from *tòic*.
toichiosdal, arrogance (Sh., O'B.) ; see *tostal*.
toigh, agreeable, cordi (mihi est), **docha**, preferable, **is docha leam**, I prefer, O. Ir. *toich*, acceptus, *tochu*, acceptior : **to-gus-*, root *gus*, choose, as in *tagh*. It has also been analysed as **do-sech*, or **do-fech*, roots *seq*, *veq*? Stokes derives this from **togi-s*, root *tag*, take, Lat. *tango*, etc.
toil, will, Ir. *toil*, O. Ir. *tol* : **tolâ*, root *tel*, take, lift, endure ; Lat. *tollo*, *tolero* ; Eng. *thole*, *tolerate*, etc. See *tlachd*, *tlàth*.
toill, deserve, Ir. *tuillim*, O. Ir. *tuillim*, *atroilli*, *asroille*, meruit, later *do-sli*, meruit, from *sli* (Thur., Strachan).
toimhseachan, a riddle, Ir. *toimseachán*, a riddle, measure ; from *tomhas*, q.v.
toimhsean, good sense, **toimhseil**, sensible (Suth.) ; from *tomhas*.
toinisg, understanding :
toinn, twist ; from Norse *tvinna*, twine, twist thread, Eng. *twine*.
toinneamh, the miller's share of meal for grinding (S. Argyle) :
tòir, **tòrachd**, pursuit, Ir., E. Ir. *tóir*, Ir. *tóruigheachd*, *tóireacht* : **to-fo-racht*, root *reg* of *éirich*. Rhys agrees. Cf. O. Ir. *toracht*, successus, processus (=*to-racht*), *tíarmóracht*, pursuit (**to-iarm-fo-racht*). From Ir. *tóruighe*, pursuer, comes Eng. *Tory*.
toirbheart, efficiency, bounty, Ir. *toirbheart*, gift, munificence ; see *tairbheartach* for the roots.
tòirleum, a mighty leap ; cf. E. Ir. *tairlingim*, jump out of, jump off, alight, *turlaim* (inf.) : **to-air-ling-*, for which see *leum*. Hence **tòirlinn**, alight (M'A.).
toirm, a noise, Ir. *toirm*, *tormán*, E. Ir. *toirm*, *tairm* : **tor-s-men*, root *tor* of *torrunn*. Cf. W. *twrf*, *tyrfan*, tumult, Lit. *tarmė*, declaration. Cf. *seirm*, *foirm*.
toirmisg, forbid, so Ir., M. Ir. *tairmiscim*, prohibit, hinder : **tarmi-sc*, from *tarmi*, the composition form of *tar*, across, and *sc* or *sec*, say, as in *caisg*.
toirn, **toirne**, a great noise, sound, Ir. *tóirn* ; root *tor* of **torrunn**.

toirnichte, foetid, "high" (Wh.):
toirp, a sod (M'A.); from Norse *torf*, Eng. *turf*.
toirrcheas, conception (Bible):
toirsgian, a peat-cutting spade, **toirpsgian** (M'A.); a hybrid from Norse *torf*, turf, peat, and G. *sgian*. Cf. Norse *torf-skeri*, peat-cutter.
toirt, respect, value, taste, Ir. *toirt*, quantity, value:
toirt, giving; for *tabhairt*. See *tabhair, thoir*.
toiseach, the beginning, front, Ir. *tosach*, O. Ir. *tossach*, initium. See the next word.
tòiseach, a beginning, a chief, Ir. *toiseach*, a captain, O. Ir. *tóisech*, praestans, leader, W. *tywysog*, dux, princeps, Welsh Ogmic *tofisac* and *tovisaci* (Lat.): **to-vessiko-s*, root *ved*, lead, bring; Lit. *wedù*, lead, Ch. Sl. *vedą*, duco; Zd. *vádhayeiti*, bring, lead. O. Ir. has also *do-fedim*, I lead.
toisg, an occasion, opportunity, Ir. *toisg*, circumstances, state, journey, business, M. Ir. *toisc*, business, O. Ir. *toisc*, necessity: **to-sech*, root, *seq*, follow, as in *seach*.
toisgeal, the left, unlucky:
toisgeal, reward for finding a lost thing; see *taisgeal*.
toit, smoke, fume, Ir. *tóit*, M. Ir. *tutt*, smoke: **tutto-*, root *tu*, *stu*, Eng. *steam*? See *toth*.
toitean, a little heap; from Eng. *tuft*. In the sense of "piece of flesh," Ir. *tóiteán*, this is from **tóit**, roast, smoke (see *toit*), scarcely to be derived from Fr. *tôt*, hastily roasted, from Lat. *tostus*.
tolg, tulg, a hollow in metal, dent, Ir. *tolc*, hole, crevice, E. Ir. *tolc*, W. *tolc*. Rhys says W. is borrowed.
toll, a hole, Ir., E. Ir. *toll*, W. *twll*, Br. *toull*: **tukslo-*, root *tuk*, pierce, punch; Gr. *τύκος*, hammer; Ch. Slav. root *tuk*, pierce, *is-tŭknati*, effodere, *tŭkalo*, cuspis.
toll-dhubh, tollbooth, a gaol; from the Eng.
tolm, a hilloch of round form; from Norse *hólmr*, a holm, islet, "inch," Sc. *holm*, Eng. *holm*, Ag. S. *holm*, mound, billow, Ger. *holm*, hill.
tom, a hillock, Ir. *tom*, M. Ir. *tomm*, W. *tom*, Br. *das-tum*, to heap: **tumbo-*, hillock; Gr. *τύμβος*, cairn, mound, Eng. *tomb*; Skr. *tunga*, high, height; further Lat. *tumulus*. W. *tom* has been regarded as from the Eng. *tomb*. But *stom*, Skr. *stamba*, "busch."
tomad, tomult, bulk; see *somalta*.
tomh, offer, threaten, M. Ir. *tomaithim*, O. Ir. *tomad*, g. *tomtho*, minationes: **to-mat-*, root *mat*, throw, Lit. *metù*, throw.

tomhas, measure, so Ir., O. Ir. *tomus*: **to-mus*, where *mus* (**messu-*) comes from root *met*, *mê*, measure; Lat. *mêtior*, *mensus*, Eng. *measure*; Gr. *μέτρον*, a measure. Allied is G. *meas*, q.v.

tomult, bulk; also **tomad.** Cf. **somalta,** large, bulky:

tòn, anus, Ir., E. Ir. *tón*, W. *tin*: **tuknâ*, *tûkno-* (Welsh), root *teuk*, Ag. S. *þeóh*, Eng. *thigh*, Teut. **theuha-* (Strachan, Stokes); from root *tu*, swell.

tonn, a wave, Ir., E. Ir. *tond*, O. Ir. *tonn*, W., Corn. *ton*, Br. *tonn*: **tunnâ*, root *tu*, swell; Lit. *tvanas*, a flood, *tvinti*, swell; further Lat. *tumeo*, swell, Eng. *thumb*. Stokes gives the Celtic as **tundâ*, Ag. S. *þeótan*, howl, Norse *þjóta*, whistle (as the wind, etc.). Some have correlated it with Lat. *tundo*, beat, root *tund*, *tud*, Skr. *tud-*, push.

† **tonn,** † **toinnte,** skin, Ir. *tonn*, hide, skin, E. Ir. *tonn*, skin, surface, W. *tonn*, cutis, Br. *tonnenn*, rind, surface, hair of the head: *tunnâ*, skin, hide, whence possibly Low Lat. (9th cent.) *tunna*, a cask, "wine-skin," now Eng. *ton*.

tonnag, a woman's shawl or plaid; from Lat. *tunica*. Cf. M. Ir. *tonach*, tunic.

tora, augur, Ir. *tarachair*, E. Ir. *tarathar*, O. Cor. *tarater*, W. *taradr*, Br. *tarazr*, *tarar*: **taratro-*; Gr. *τέρετρον*; Lat. *terebra*: root *ter*, through, as in *thar*.

toradh, produce, fruit, so Ir., O. Ir. *torad*: **to-rad*, from **rato-*, root *rat*, *ra*, give, as in *rath*, q.v.

toranach, grub-worm, Ir. *torain*, corn maggots (O'B.), *torán* (Con., etc.); from *tor*, bore, as in *tora*?

torc, a boar, Ir., O. Ir. *torc*, W. *twrch*, Cor. *torch*, Br. *tourc'h*, O. Br. *turch*: **t-orko-s*, from **orko-*, in **uircean,** q.v.: I. E., *porko-s*, swine, Lat. *porcus*, Lit. *parsza-s*, Eng. *farrow*. Stokes gives Celtic as **torko-s*, Jubainville as **turco-s*.

torc, a cleft, notch (Carm.):

torcan, species of bere, biforked carrot, Ir. *turcan*? (Carm.):

torchar, a fall, killing, **torchuir** (vb.), Ir. *torchair*, fell, O. Ir. *torchar*, I fell, *doro-chair*, cecidit, *ara-chrinim*, difficiscor, root *ker*, Skr. *çar*, break to pieces, *çṛnâmi*, break; see *crìon*.

torghan, a purling sound; from *tor* of *torrunn*.

tòrr, a hill of conic form, heap, castle, Ir. *tor*, tower, castle, crest, E. Ir. *tor*, *tuir*, d. *turid*, a tower, W. *twr*, Cor. *tur*, Br. *tour*: **turi-*, **turet-*, I. E. root *tver*, hold, enclose, Lat. *turris*, Gr. *τύρσις*, tower. Some hold that the Celtic is borrowed from Lat. G. **tòrr,** with *rr*, is possibly for *torth* (cf. **turet-*). It also means "crowd" in G. and E. Ir., and "heap" also in W.

torrach, pregnant, Ir. *torrach*, pregnant, fruitful, E. Ir. *torrach* : **torth-aco-*, from **torato-*, **toradh**, fruit, q.v. W. *torwy* big-bellied, has been compared, from *tor*, belly, G. *tàrr*.

tòrradh (**torradh**, H.S.D.), burial, funeral solemnities, Ir. *tórradh*, watching or waking of the dead, E. Ir. *torroma*, attending, watching :

torrunn, thunder, Ir. *toran*, a great noise, E. Ir. *torand*, thunder, W. *tarann*, Cor. *taran*, tonitruum : **toranno-s* ; Gr. *τόρος*, sound ; Lit. *tàrti*, say. Gaul. *Taranis*, the Gaulish Jove or Thor, and G. *tàirneanach* show an *a* grade of the root.

tosd, silence, so Ir., O. Ir. *tost* : **tusto-*, root *tus*, *teus*, whence E. Ir. *tó*, *tua*, silent ; O. Pruss. *tussîse*, silet, Ch. Slav. *tichu*, silent ; Skr. *tush*, silere, *tushnîm*, silently. **tòs**, calm = clos (Hend.).

tosg, a tusk ; from the Eng.

tosg, a hack, gash, dent (Wh.) :

tosg, a peat-cutter (Dial.) ; from Sc. *tusk* in *tusk-spawd* (Banff), *tuskar* (Ork. and Sh.), *tusk*, cut peats. Cf. Shet. *tushker*, from N. *torfskeri*, turf-cutter.

tosgair, an ambassador or post, Ir. *toisg*, a journey, business. See *toisg*.

tostal, arrogance, Ir. *tósdal*, *toichiosdal* (O'B.), O. Ir. *tochossol*, violation : **to-con-sal*, from *sal*, leap (see *tuisleadh*)? Also **toichiosdal**.

tota, rower's bench, turf ; see *tobhta*.

toth, a foul blast of vapour, also **stoth**, q.v. ; see *toit* for root.

trabhach (**tràbhach**, M'F.), rubbish cast ashore, the grass fiorin ; from *tràigh*? Cf., however, *drabhas*. *tràibheanach*, bedraggled fellow (R.D.). Cf. Sc. *drab*.

trabhailt, mill-hopper (M'A.) ; possibly from Lat. *trabula*.

trachdadh, negotiating, proposal, so Ir. ; from Lat. *tracto*, treat.

trachladh, fatigue ; from Sc. *trachle*, draggle, fatiguing exertion.

tradh, a lance, fishing spear, Ir. *tradh*, lance, *treagh*, spear ; from the root *tar*, *tra* (see *thar*), through, Lat. *trâgula*, a dart.

tràigh, the shore, Ir. *tráigh*, E. Ir. *tráig* : **trâgi-* ; see *traogh*.

tràill, a slave, Ir. *traill* (O'B.), M. Ir. *tráill* (not well known to glossographers) ; from Norse *þraell*, Eng. *thrall*.

traille, the fish tusk :

trait, **tròidht**, a poultice, cataplasm, rag, Ir. *treata* (*tréata*, Con.), plaster :

tramailt, a whim (M'A.) :

trang, busy ; from Sc. *thrang*, Eng. *throng*.

traod, one wasting away with sickness (Hend.) ; cf. Ir. (Keat. *traothaim*, wear out, am weary.

traogh, ebb, Ir. *tráighim*, *traoghaim*, E. Ir. *trágim*, W. *treio*, ebb, *trai*, ebb-tide, *traeth*, shore: **trâgô*, from *trâg*, I. E. *tragh*, draw, Lat. *traho*, etc.; see *troidh* for root.

traona, the corncrake, Ir. *traona*; see *trèan-ri-trèan*.

trapan, a cluster, Ir. *trapán*:

trasd, across, **trasdan,** cross beam, crozier, O. Ir. *trost*, trabs, from *tar*, *tra* of *thar*. Cf. W. *trawst*, rafter, which Stokes and Loth think to be borrowed from Lat. *transtrum*, as also O. Ir. *trost* mentioned above. Sc. has *trast* or *trest*, beam, from early Fr. *traste*, Lat. *transtrum*.

trasg, a fast, Ir. *trosgadh*, O. Ir. *troscud*: **truskô*, **trud-skô*, root *trud*, distress, burden, Lat. *trûdo*, push, Eng. *threaten*. See *trod*, *trom*.

tràth, time, season, Ir., E. Ir. *tráth*: **trâtu-*, root *tra*, *tar*, through (see *thar*). Cf. W. *tro*, turn, time, Br. *tro*, occasion, round; Eng. *turn*.

tre, through, Ir. *tré*, *tre*, E. Ir. *tré*, *tria*, *tri*, O. Ir. *tri*, *trí*, *tre*, O. W. *troi*, now *trwy*, Cor., Br. *dre*, O. Br. *tre*, *dre*: **trei*, **tri*, root *ter*, pass over, through; Lat. *trans*, across; Skr. *tirás*, through, over, Zd. *tarô* (do.). See the root in *thar*, *tora*, *troimh*; also in Eng. *through*.

treabh, plough, till, Ir. *treabhaim*, E. Ir. *trebaim*, inhabit, cultivate, *treb*, a dwelling, W. *tref*, homestead, O. W., O. Br. *treb*: **trebo-*, a house; Lat. *tribus*, *trebus*, a tribe, Eng. *tribe*; Eng. *thorp*; Lit. *trobà*, dwelling, building. Hence **treabhair,** houses, **treibhireach,** prudent.

treabha, a thrave; from Norse *þrefi*, Eng. *thrave*.

treachail, dig, **treachladh** (1) digging (2) fatiguing: **tre-clad*; for (1) see *cladh* and cf. *tochail*; for (2) cf. Sc. *trachle*.

treaghaid, a darting pain, stitch, Ir. *treagh(d)aim*, I pierce through, M. Ir. *treghat*, pangs, smart, *treaglad*, transpiercing; Ir. *treagh*, a spear: "piercing." See *tradh*.

trealaich, lumber, trash, Ir. *trealamh*, lumber, apparel, instruments, E. Ir. *trelam*, weapons, furniture, apparel: **tre-lam*; for *lam*, see *ullamh*.

trealais, the spleen (M'F.):

trèalamh, indisposition (M'F.):

trealbhaidh, adult, grown-up (M'A. for Islay):

treall, treallan, a short space or time, Ir. *treall*, M. Ir. *trell*, root *ter*, through, Eng. *thrill*, pierce.

trèan-ri-trèan, corn-crake, Ir. *traona*:

treann, cut (Carm.):

treas, third, Ir. *treas*, O. Ir. *tress*: **tristo-*, from *tris*, thrice, Gr. τρίς, Skr. *tris*, root *tri* of *tri*, three. W. *trydydd*, third, is for **tritijo-s*.

† **treas,** battle, skirmish, Ir. *treas*, E. Ir. *tress*. For root, cf. the next word. W. has *trîn*, battle, bustle, *treis*, violence.

treasa, stronger, Ir. *treas*, strong, *treise*, stronger, O. Ir. *tressa*, W. *trech*, fortior, Br. *trec'h*: **treksjôs*, fortior, root *treg*, *streg*, *sterg*, strong, Eng. *stark*, Lit. *strégti*, stiffen, Pers. *suturg* (**stṛg*), strong. Stokes refers it to the root *treg*, *trag*, draw, leap, as in *troigh*, *traogh*. See *treun* further; *treasa* is its comparative really.

treasdach, thorough-paced (of a horse); cf. Ir. *trosdán*, a pace, jump; root *treg*, draw, walk, as in *troigh*.

treasg, refuse of brewed malt, groats, Ir. *treasúmha*, dross, copper dross, *treascach*, draffy, M. Ir. *tresc*, refuse, offal: **tre-sco ?*

treibhireach (treibhdhireach, Dictionaries), prudent, upright, O. Ir. *trebar*, prudent, M. Ir. *trebaire*, prudence; from *treb* of *treabh*, q.v.

tréig, forsake, Ir. *tréigim*, E. Ir. *trécim*, W. *trancu*, perish: **trankjô*, abandon, root *trak*, push, press, as in **dùrachd** (Stokes).

treis, a while, space, also **greis,** Ir. *treibhse*, *dreibhse* (O'B.), *treimhse* (Con.); see *greis*.

treisg, treisginn, weaver's paste, trash (M'A., Arg.), Ir. *treisgin* (Con., etc.), *dreislinn* (Monaghan); cf. Sc. *dressing*.

treodhair, a smith's nail mould, Ir. *treóir*, *treoir*; from *tre*, *trem*, through ?

treòir, strength, Ir. *treóir*, conduct, strength, M. Ir. *treorach*, strong, E. Ir. *treóir*, vigour: **treg-ri-*, root *treg* of *treasa*.

treòraich, guide, Ir. *treóruighim*, M. Ir. *treoraigim*: **trag-ri-*, root *trag* of *troigh* ?

treubh, a tribe; from Lat. *trĭbus*, a tribe. See *treabh*.

treubhach, valorous, strenuous, **treubhantas,** bravery; for **treuntas*, from which *treubhach* is deduced. M'Kinnon (*Gael. Soc. Tr.*[13], 341) refers it to *treubh*, tribe.

treud, flock, heard, Ir. *tréad*, *treud*, E. Ir. *trét*: **trento-*, root *trem*, Lat. *turma*, troop, Ag. S. *þruma*, heap, company (Strachan, Stokes). Windisch has compared Gr. *στρατός* (**strṇtos*) to *treud*.

treun, brave, Ir. *treun*, O. Ir. *trén*, fortis, W. *tren*, strenuous, force: **tregno-*, root *treg* of *treasa*, q.v. Stokes gives the Celtic as **treksno-*, which would produce **tresno-*, modern *treann*.

tri, three, Ir., O. Ir. *trí*, W. *tri*, Cor. *try*, Br. *tri*: **treis*; Lat. *três* (**trei-es*); Gr. *τρεῖς*; Got. *þreis*, Eng. *three*; Lit. *trýs*; Skr. *tráyas*.

triall, going, journey, Ir. *tríall*, E. Ir. *triall*: **tri-all*, "go-through," root *ell* of *tadhal* ?

trian, third part, a third, Ir., E. Ir. *trían*, W. *traian* : **treisano-* ; see *treas*, *tri*.

triath, lord, chief, E. Ir. *tríath* : **treito-s*. Stokes compares Lat. *trîtavus*, *strîtavus*, ancestor in the 6th degree.

tric, frequent, often, Ir. *tric*, E. Ir. *trice* : **trekki-*, root *treg* of *troigh* (Stokes, Strachan).

trid, **trìd**, through, by, Ir. *tríd*, E. Ir. *trít*, per eum, id : **trei-t*, from root *trei* of *tre*, through ; the final *-t* is the demonstrative pron. *to* (Eng. *that*, Gr. *το*) ; a pron. **em-ti*, **en-ti* (Stokes).

trìd, rag, clout, stitch ; "Cha'n 'eil trìd air" :

trileanta, thrilling, quavering ; cf. E. Ir. *trílech*, song, O. Ir. *trírech*, song of birds. Cf. Eng. *trill*, Ital. *trillare*, Sp. *trinar* : an initiative word, Eng. *thrill* is from the root *tre*, *ter* (see *tora*), "piercing," which may also be the ultimate origin of the G. words.

† **trilis**, locks of hair, Ir. *trilis* (obs.), E. Ir. *triliss* ; cf. Eng. *tress*, from Lat. *tricia*, *trica*, plait, Gr. *τρίχα*, in three parts, root *tri*, three.

trill, sand plover (Heb., Miss Freer) :

trilleachan, **trìleachan** (**drilleachan**, M'A.), the pied oyster-catcher, sea-piet :

trillsean (**drillsean**, M'A.), lantern, rush-light, a glimmer, Ir. *triliseán*, torch, lantern, earlier *trilsen*, facula, *trillsech*, sparkling : "piercing," from *tre*, *ter*, as in *trileanta* ?

trinnseir, a plate, trencher, Ir. *trinsiur* ; from Eng. *trencher*.

trioblaid, trouble, tribulation, Ir. *trioblóid*, E. Ir. *tréblait* ; from Lat. *tribulatio*, Eng. *tribulation*.

triobuail, vibrate, quiver ; from Eng. *tremble* ?

trionaid, a trinity, Ir. *tríonóid*, *tríonoid*, E. Ir. *trínóit*, O. Ir. *trindóit* ; from Lat. *trinitât-*, *trinitas*, a trinity, from *tres*, three. The Gadelic is developed from **trin(i)tâti-*.

triubhas, trews, trousers, Ir. *triús*, M. Ir. *tribus*, O. Ir. *trebus*, breeches, L. Lat. *tubrucus* (Isidore), *tribuces* (Du Cange), "thigh breeches" (D' Arbois) ; from Sc. *trews*, Eng. *trooze*, *trouses*, now *trousers*, trunkhose.

triùcair, a rascal ; from Sc. *truker*, *trukier*, a deceitful person, from O. Fr. *tricher*, to trick, allied to Eng. *trick*.

triuchan, a stripe of distinguishing colours in tartan :

triuthach, **triuth** (M'F.), hooping cough, **triogh** (M'A.), a fit of laughing or coughing, Ir. *triuch*, *trioch* : root *pster* of *sreothart* ?

trobhad, come thou hither to me ; opposite of **thugad** : **to-ro'-ad*, **to-romh-t*, "to before you ?"

tròcair, mercy, Ir., O. Ir. *trócaire*, W. *trugaredd*, Cor. *tregereth*, M. Br. *trugarez*, O. W. *trucarauc*, merciful: **trougo-karja*, "loving of the wretched," from the roots of *truagh* and *car*, love.

trod, a quarrel, scolding, Ir. *troid*, M. Ir. *trot*, quarrel, combat, *trottach*, quarrelsome: **truddo-*, root *trud*, distress, bother; Eng. *threat*, Norse *þrjóta*, fail, lack; Lat. *trûdo*, push, Eng. *obtrude*; Ch. Sl. *trudŭ*, difficulty.

trog, raise, **trogail**, raising, Manx *troggal*, earlier *trogell*: *to-ro-od-gab*, that is to say, **tog** with the prep. *ro* inserted. See *tog*. Rhys (*Manx Pray.*[2], 138) compares E. Ir. *turcbál*, a rising (as of the sun): **to-for-gab-*.

trog, trash (Dial.), busy dealing, **tròg**, busy dealing, from Sc. *troke*, to bargain, barter, *trog*, old clothes, *troggin*, pedlar's wares, Eng. *truck*, from Fr. *troquer*, barter, truck.

trogbhoil, grumbling (M'A.), **trògbhail**, quarrel (Nich., *trogbhail*, Arm., Sh., O'R.):

troich, a dwarf; see *droich*.

tròidht, cataplasm, rags, shapeless worn shoe (Skye); see *trait*.

troigh, misspelt **troidh**, a foot, Ir. *troigh*, O. Ir. *traig*, g. *traiged*, W. *traed*, O. Cor. *truit*, pes, M. Br. *troat*: **traget-* (**troget-* ?), foot, root *trag*, leap, draw, Gaul. *vertragos*, greyhound; I. E. *tragh*; Got. *þragjan*, run, Ag. S. *þrah*, course; Lat. *traho*, draw.

troileis, any trifling thing; founded on Eng. *trifles* ?

troimh, through, O. Ir. *tremi-*, trans-, super-: **trimo-*, from *tri* of *tre*. For the *mi* or *mh*, cf. *roimh*, *comh-*.

trom, heavy, Ir. *trom*, O. Ir. *tromm*, W. *trwm*, Cor. *trom*, Br. *troum*, : *trud-s-mo-s*, "oppressive," from *trud*, oppress, distress; Got. *us-þriutan*, oppress, Eng. *threat*; Lat. *trûdo*, push. See *trod* further. For other views, see Rhys' *Lect.*[2], 114, Zimmer *Zeit.*[24], 208.

troman, dwarf, elder, Ir. *tromán*, O. Ir. *tromm*, g. *truimm*; also G. **droman** (M'A.):

tromb, the Jew's harp; from Sc. *trump* (do.), Eng. *trump*, from Fr. *trompe*.

trombaid, a trumpet, Ir. *trompa*, L. M. Ir. *trompadh*; from the Eng.

troraid, a spire, steeple (M'F.); founded on Eng. *turret*.

trosdail, dull, seriously inclined, Ir. *trosdamhuil*, serious, confident:

trosdan, a crutch, support, Ir. *trostán*, crutch, pilgrim's staff, W. *trostan*, long slender pole. See *trasd* for root.

trosg, a codfish, Ir. *trosg*; from Norse *þorskr*, Dan. *torsk*, Ger. *dorsch*.

trot, trot, **trotan**, trotting; from the Eng.

truacantas, compassion, Ir. *truacánta* (O'B.) : **troug-can-*, "expressing pity," from *truagh* and *can*, say.

truagh, wretched, pitiful, so Ir., E. Ir. *trúag*, O. Ir. *tróg*, W. *tru*, Corn. *troc*, miser, Br. *tru*, Gaul. *Trôgos* : **trougo-*, miser, root *streug*, rub, wear; Gr. *στρεύγομαι*, am worn out, distressed; Ch. Sl. *strugati*, scratch, distress, Lit. *strugas*, carving instrument; Norse *strjúka*, to stroke, Ger. *straucheln*, stumble (Windisch, Prellwitz). Stokes refers it to the root of Norse *þrúga*, press, *þrúgan*, compulsion, O. H. G. *drûh*, compes. From Celtic comes Eng. *truant*.

truaill, a sheath, so Ir., E. Ir. *trúaill* : **troud-s-li-*, root *treud*, *trud*, push; Eng. *thrust*, Lat. *trûdo*. See further *trod*, *trom*.

truaill, pollute, violate, Ir. *trúaillim*, E. Ir. *trúalnim*, O. Ir. *druáilnithe*, corruptus, *œllned*, inquinatio, illuvies, *élnithid*, violator, from *éln-*, O. Ir. *as-lenaimm*, polluo, G. root *len* (*lēn*, Ascoli), fœdare (Lat. *lino*, smear, as in *lean*?). Ascoli analyses *truaill* into *der-uad-lēn* (*der-* intensive), while Thurneysen refers the *tru-*, *dru-*, to the root of Lat. *trux*, *trucis*. *dru-es-lén* (Stokes). E. Ir. *trú*, wretched, Eng. *throe* (Stokes).

trudair, a stammerer, a dirty or obscene person, Ir. *trudaire*, a stammerer (Lh., O'B., Con.). In the first sense, the word is Ir.; in the second sense, it is G. only, and likely of the same origin as *trusdar*. Norse *þrjótr*, knave, bad debtor, has been adduced as its origin.

truilleach, a dirty or base person, filthy food : **trus-lic-*, root *trus* as in *trusdar*? Or from Sc. *trolie*, a person of slovenly habits, *trollop*?

truis, tear, snatch, truss; from Sc. *truss*, to eat in a slovenly, scattering fashion (Ork.), Icel. *tros*, Eng. *trash*. In the sense of "truss," the G. is from Eng. *truss*. Hence the cry to dogs to get out—**truis**!

trùp, a troop; from the Eng.

trus, truss or bundle, collect, Ir. *trusdalaim*, truss up, girdle, W. *trwsa*, a truss; from Eng. *truss*, O. Fr. *trusser*, from L. Lat. *tortiare*, *tortus*, twisted. See also *triubhas*.

trusdar, a filthy fellow, filth; cf. Ir., E. Ir. *trist*, curse, profligacy, L. Lat. *tristus*, improbus.

trusgan, clothes, apparel, Ir. *truscán*, *trosgán*, clothes, furniture; founded on **trus**. Cf. Eng. *trousseau* from the same origin.

truthair, a traitor, villain; from Sc. *trucker*, deceiver, trickster? Or from Eng. *traitor*? Cf. *trudair*.

tu, thu, thou, Ir., O. Ir. *tú*, W. *ti*, Corn. *ty*, *te*, Br. *te* : **tû* ; Lat. *tū* ; Gr. *σύ* ; Eng. *thou* ; Pruss. *tou* ; Zd. *tū*.

tuagh, axe, so Ir., M. Ir. *tuag*, E. Ir. *túagach*, hitting : **tougâ* root *teugh*, *tuq*, hit, strike ; Gr. *τεύχω*, fashion, *τύκος*, hammer, *τυκάνη*, flail ; Ch. Sl. *tŭkalo*, cuspis. Stokes prefers comparison with Skr. *tuj*, hit (**tug*).

tuaicheal, dizziness, **tuachioll** (Sh.), winding, eddying, moving against the sun, left-about : **to-fo-cell* (for *cell*, see *timchioll*), Ir. *tuachail*, going, confused with **tuath-cell*, "left (north) going"? Cf. *tuaineal*.

tuaileas, reproach, scandal, so Ir. (Lh., O'B., etc.) : **to-fo-less* ; from **lisso-*, blame, discussed under *leas-* ?

tuailt, tubhailt, a towel ; Ir. *tudhoille* ; from the Eng.

tuainig, unloose (Dial.) ; see *tualaig*.

tuaineal, dizziness, stupor, Ir. *toinéall*, swoon, trance (Dineen) : **to-fo-in-el*, root *ell* of *tadhal* ? Or **to-fo-neul* ?

tuaiream, a guess, aim, vicinity, Ir. *tuairim* ; also **tuairmse** : **to-for-med-*, root *med* of *meas*.

tuaireap, turbulence :

tuairgneadh, confusion, sedition, Ir. *tuargán*, noise, discontent :

tuairisgeul, description, report, Ir. *tuarasgbháil*, M. Ir. *túarascbal*, description, O. Ir. *túarascbaim*, for *to-for-as-gab-*, root *gab* of *gabh*.

tuairmeis, hit on, discover : **do-fo-air-mess* ; see *eirmis*.

tuairneag, anything round, a boss, tidy female, **tuairnean,** a mallet, beetle, Ir. *tuairnín*, mallet ; cf. next word.

tuairnear, a turner, Ir. *túrnóir* ; from the Eng.

tuaisd, a dolt, sloven, **tuaisdeach,** unseemly :

tuaitheal, wrong, left-wise, Ir. *tuaithbhil*, E. Ir. *tuathbil* ; from *tuath* and *seal* : see *deiseil* for latter root and form. Ir. has *tuathal*, the left hand, awkward.

tualaig, loose (Arm.), have flux, **tuanlaig** (*n.* elided, Perth), **tuainig, tuanag,** loosening (Dial.) : from *leig*, **to-fo-leig*.

tuam, tuama, a tomb, Ir. *tuama* ; from Lat. *tumba*, Eng. *tomb*.

tuar, food, O. Ir. *tuare* : **taurio-*, root *staur*, place, store, Eng. *store*, Skr. *sthávara*, fixed : root *sta*.

tuar, hue, appearance ; cf. Ir., M. Ir. *tuar*, an omen, presage : **to-vor-*, root *ver*, *vor*, of *fhuair* ?

tuarasdal, wages, so Ir., M. Ir. *tuarustul*, *tuarastal* : **to-fo-ar-as-tal*, root *tal*, *tel*, take, lift, M. Ir. *taile*, salarium, W. *tâl*, payment, Cor., Br. *tal*, solvit ; I. E. *tel* ; Gr. *τέλος*, tax, *τάλαντον*, talent ; Lat. *tollo* ; Eng. *thole*. See *tail*, *tlàth*.

tuasaid, a quarrel, fight, Ir. *fuasaoid*, animosity, spite, E. Ir. *fúasait*, "entwickelung," development : *to-fo-ad-sedd-*, G.

root *sedd* from *sizd*, *si-sed*, set, "set-to" being the idea? Root *sed* of *suidhe*. But cf. *faosaid*.

tuasgail, loose, untie, Ir. *tuaslagadh*, releasing, E. Ir. *tuaslaicim*: **to-fo-as-léc-im*, from *lēc* of *leig*, let, q.v.

tuath, people, tenantry, so Ir., O. Ir. *túath*, populus, W. *tud*, country, nation, Cor. *tus*, Br. *tud*, Gaul. *Tout-*, *Teuto-*: **toutâ*, people; Lat. Umbr. *toto*, state, Oscan *túvtú*, populus, Lat. *tôtus*, all; Got. *þiuda*, people, *Teutonic*, *Deutsch*, German, *Dutch*; Lettic *táuta*, people, O. Pruss. *tauto*, land.

tuath, north, Ir. *tuath*, *tuaith*, O. Ir. *túath*, left, north: **toutâ*, **touto-s* (adj.), left hand, left, "good," Got. *þiuþ*, good; cf. Gr. εὐώνυμος, left hand, "good-omened." Rhys (*Manx Pray.*[2], 62) suggests that the root is *su*, turn (see *iompaidh*): **do-hūth* (**to-su-*), "turning to"; W. *aswy* or *aseu*, left hand, being also hence—**ad-sou-i-*.

tuba, a tub; from the Eng.

tubaist, mischance, M. G. *tubbiste* (D. of L.), Arran G. *tiompaiste*, Ir. *tubaiste*:

tuban, tuft of wool on the distaff; see *toban*.

tùch, smother, become hoarse, **tùchan**, hoarseness: **t-úch*; cf. W. *ig*, sob, hiccup.

tudan, a small heap or stack (**dud**, M'A.):

tug, brought; see *thug*.

tugaidean, witticisms (Dial., H.S.D.):

tugha, thatch, covering, **tugh** (vb.), Ir. *tuighe* (n.), *tuighim* (vb.), E. Ir. *tuga*, *tugim*, W. *to*, a cover, thatch, *toi*, tegere, Cor. *to*, *tectum*, Br. *to*, *toenn*: **togio-*, **togo-*, root *tog*, *steg*, as in *tigh*, *teach*.

tughag, a patch:

tuig, understand, Ir. *tuigim*, O. Ir. *tuiccim*, *tuccim*: **to-od-ges-*, root *ges* of *tug*. Some have given the stem as **to-od-cesi*, root *qes* of *chì*; but this would give G. *tuic*. O. Ir. *tuicse*, electus: **to-od-gus-*, root *gus*, taste, Eng. *gusto*.

tuil, a flood, Ir., O. Ir. *tuile*: **tuliâ*, root *tu*, swell; Gr. τύλος, knob, weal; Skr. *tûla*, tuft; Eng. *thumb*, *tumid*, etc. (See *tulach*). So Stokes *Zeit.*[31], 235. The O. Ir. root *ōl*, to flood, abound, gives *tólam*, a flood, *imról*, *foróil*, abundance, etc. The root *pol*, *pel* has also been suggested, as in *iol-*.

tuilis, overloading stomach (Carm.):

tuille, tuilleadh, more (n.), Ir. *tuille*, *tuilleadh*, addition, *tuilleamh*, wages, addition, E. Ir. *tuilled*, *tuillem*, addition, inf. to *tuillim*, enhance, deserve, as in G. **toill**. Two words are mixed: **to-eln-*, deserve, and *to-oln*, much, more, E. Ir. *oll*, great, *huilliu*, plus, **olniôs*, root *pol*, *pel*, many, Gr. πολύς, Lat. *plus* etc. (see *iol*). Stokes equates the O. Ir. *uilliu*, *oll*, with Lat. *pollere*, which is from **pol-no-*, root *pol* as above (Wharton). The G. syntax of *tuille* shows its comparative force in *tuille na* (more than) as well as *tuille agus*, Ir. *tuilleadh agus* (addition and).

tuimhseadh, beating, thumping, **tuinnse,** a blow (*Gael. Soc. Tr.*[15], 260), M. Ir. *tuinsim*, calco, *tuinsem*, bruising, **to-ud-nessim* (Str.); founded on Lat. *tundo*, beat. Stokes queries if cognate.

tuineadh, an abode, possession, Ir. *tuinidhe*, possession (O'Cl.), E. Ir. *tunide*; also **tuinneadh** (Ir. and G.): **to-nes-*, root *nes* as in *comhnuidh*, q.v.

tuinneasach, deathful, Ir. *tuinneamh*, *tuineamh*, death:

tuinnidh, firm, hard, Ir. *tuinidhe* (O'B., Sh.), immovable, *clocha tuinidhe*; from *tuineadh*, the idea being "settled, fixed."

tuir, relate, **tuireadh,** relating, Ir. *tuirtheachda*, relation, rehearsal, E. Ir. *turthiud*, pl. *tuirtheta*, tale, from *ret*, run (as in *ruith*). Cf. *aithris*. E. I. *tuirem*, reciting, is from **to-rím*, root *rīm*, number (as in *àireamh*).

tuireadh, a dirge, lamentation, Ir. *tuireamh*, dirge, elegy; for root see *tuirse*.

tuireann, a spark of fire from an anvil, Ir. *tuireann* (O'B., etc.), E. Ir. *turend* (?): **to-rind*? For *rind*, see *reannag*.

tuireasg, a saw, Ir. *tuiriosg*, E. Ir. *turesc*: **tar-thesc*, from *teasg*, cut. q.v.

tuirl, tuirling, descend, Ir. *tuirlingim*, E. Ir. *tairlingim*, O. Ir. *doarblaing*, desilit **to-air-ling-*; for *ling*, jump, see *leum*.

tuirse, sadness, Ir. *tuirse*, M. Ir. *tor*, sad, E. Ir. *toirsi*, *torsi*, O. Ir. *toris*, *toirsech*, tristis; root *tor*, *ter*, *tre*, Lat. *tristis*, sad.

tùis, incense, Ir., M. Ir., E. Ir. *túis*; from Lat. *tūs*, Gr. *θύος*.

tuisleadh, a stumbling, fall, so Ir., O. Ir. *tuisled*, prolapsio, *tuisel*, casus, *dofuislim*, labo: **to-fo-ess-sal-im*, root *sal*, spring; Lat. *salio*, leap, dance, Eng. *insult*; Gr. *ἅλλομαι*, leap; cf. Lit. *selé'ti*, glide, creep. Ascoli analyses it into **to-fo-isl-*, where *isl* is what remains of *ísel* or *ìosal*, low.

tuit, fall, Ir. *tuitim*, O. Ir. *tuitim*, inf. *tutimm*, acc. pl. *totman*, also *tothimm*, **tod-tim*, Gadelic root *-tim-*, W. *codwm*, a fall (cf. Ir. *cudaim*), *codymu*, cadere, Cor. *codha*; cf. Eng. *tumble*, Fr. *tomber*, fall. Usually explained as **to-fo-thét-*, from *théid*, which would naturally be *tuid* in G., even granting that the crasis of *-ofothé-* simply landed in *-ui-*, not to mention the inf. in preserved *m* (**tuiteam**). Root *tud* (Thur.); *to-tud* = *think*.

tul, entirely, Ir. *tul* (*i.e. tuile*, O'Cl.), increase, flood: an adverbial use of the root form of *tuil*, flood? Cf. Ir. *tola*, superfluity.

tul, fire, hearth, heap (Carm.):

tulach, a hillock, Ir., E. Ir. *tulach*; root *tu*, swell; Gr. τύλος, knob, τὺλη (υ long), swelling, weal; Lat. *tumor*, *tūber*, a swelling; Eng. *thumb*.
tulag, the fish whiting, Ir. *tullóg*, the pollock; cf. *pollag*.
tulchann, tulchainn, a gable, posterior, Ir. *tulchán*, hillock; from *tulach*?
tulchuiseach, plucky (Hend.):
tum, dip, **tumadh**, dipping, so Ir., E. Ir. *tummim*: **tumbô*; Lat. *tinguo*, *tingo*, wet, Eng. *tinge*, *tincture*; O. G. H. *duncôn*, dip, Ger. *tunken*, dip, steep.
tunna, a tun, ton, Ir., E. Ir. *tunna*; Ag. S. *tunne*, M. Eng. *tonne*, Norse *tunna*, Ger. *tonne*; all from Lat. *tunna*, a cask. Stokes (*Bez. Beit.*[18]) suggests borrowing from the Norse; Kluge regards the words as of Celtic origin. On this see †**tonn.**
tunnachadh, beating, dashing; see *tuimhseadh*.
tunnag, a duck, Ir. *tonnóg*?
tunnsgadh, upheaval (R. D.):
tur, gu tur, entirely, Ir. *tura*, plenty (*tura namhad*, plenty of enemies), E. Ir. *tor*, a crowd (dat. *tur*); see *tòrr*.
tùr, a tower, Ir. *túr*; from M. Eng. *tour*, *tūr*, from O. Fr. *tur*, Lat. *turris*.
tùr, understanding; cf. M. Ir. *túr*, research, examination, O. Ir. *túirim*, *rotuirset*, scrutati sunt, for *to-fo-shirim*, from *sir*, search.
turadh, dry weather, **tur**, dry (without condiment), so Ir., E. Ir. *turud*, *terad*, adj. *tur*, dry, *tair*: root *tor*, *ter* of *tioram*?
turag, a trifling illness (as of a child)—Arg:
turaman, rocking, nodding; see *turraban*.
turcais, tweezers (M'A.), pincers; see *durcaisd*.
turguin, destruction (H.S.D. from MSS.), M. Ir. *tuarcain*, smiting, E. Ir. *tuarcaim* (dat.), hitting: **to-fo-argim*, root *org*, O. Ir. *orgun*, *orcun*, occisio, O. Br. *orgiat*, Cæsar's Gaul. *Orgeto-rix*: **urg-*, root *vṛg*, *verg*, press, Lat. *urgeo*. Stokes suggests connection with Gr. ἐρέχθω, tear; Bezzenberger gives Zend *areza*, battle, fight; Brugmann compares Skr. *ṛghāyati*, raves, rages, O. H. G. *arg*, what is vile or bad.
turlach, a large fire: **t-ur-lach*, from Ir. *ur*, *úr*, fire, Gr. πῦρ, Eng. *fire*.
turlach, a bulky, squat person; see *tòrr*, *turadh*. Cf. W. *twrllach*, a round lump.
turlas, small cupboard (Perth); see *tairleas*.
turloch, a lake that dries in summer, Ir. *turloch*; from *tur* and *loch*.
tùrn, a turn, job; from the Eng.

turraban, turraman, rocking of the body, nodding, grief (**turadan,** Sh.). Hence **turra-chadal,** a slumbering drowsiness, "nodding sleep":

turrag, an accident:

turradh, a surprise, taking unawares (Skye):

turraig, air do thurraig, at stool (M'A.):

turram, a soft sound, murmur; onomatopoetic. But cf. *toirm*, *torrunn*.

turtur, a turtle, so Ir., W. *turtur*; from Lat. *turtur*.

turus, a journey, Ir., E. Ir. *turus*, O. Ir. *tururas*, incursus, *aururas*, properatio: **to-reth-s-tu*, root, *ret*, run (see *ruith*).

tùs, the beginning, Ir. *tús*, O. Ir. *túus*, *tús*, W. *tywys*, leading; see *tòiseach*.

tut, interjection of cold or impatience; from Eng. *tut*. See *thud*.

tùt, a quiet breaking of wind, stench, Ir. *tút*, M. Ir. *tútt*, stench: allied to *toit*, q.v. Cf. Keating's *tútmhar*, smoky.

tuthan, a slut (Arm., M'L.), Ir. *túthán*; from the root of the above word.

U

ua, o, from, Ir. *ua*, *ó*, O. Ir. *ua*, *hua*, *ó*: **ava*, ab; Skr. *áva*, ab, off; Lat. *au-* (*au-fero*), away; Ch. Sl. *u-*, ab, away. See *o*.

uabairt, expulsion: **od-bert-*, prefixed by *ua*? from the root *ber* (in *beir*).

uabhar, pride, so Ir., O. Ir. *úabar*, vainglory, W. *ofer*, waste, vain (Ascoli): **oubro-*, root *eug*, rise, Gr. *ὕβρις*, insolence (see *uasal*). It has also been analysed into **ua-ber* like *uabairt* = "e-latio," elation.

uachdar, surface, summit, so Ir., O. Ir. *uachtar*, *ochtar*: **ouktero-*, root *eug*, *veg*, rise, be vigorous, as in *uasal*, q.v. Cf. W. *uthr*, admirandus.

uadh- in **uadh-bheist,** monster, **uadh-chrith,** terror; see *uath* below.

uaigh, a grave, Ir. *uaigh*, M. Ir. *uag*, E. Ir. *uag*, **augâ*, allied to Got. *augo*, eye, Eng. *eye*. See for force *dearc*. So Stokes, and rightly.

uaigneach, secret, lonesome, so Ir., M. Ir. *uagnech*: **uath-gen-*, "lonesome-kind," from *uath*, lonesome, single; Norse *auðr*, empty, Got. *auþs*, waste, desert; Lat. *ôtium*, rest.

uaill, pride, Ir. *uaill*, E. Ir. *úaill*, O. Ir. *uall*: **ouksl̂â*, root *eug*, *veg* of *uasal*.

uaimh, a cave, den, Ir. *uaimh*, g. *uamha*, M. Ir. *uaim*, g. *uama*, O. Ir. *huam*, specus (also *huád*, specu): **oumâ*. Bezzenberger suggests **poumâ*, allied to Gr. *πῶμα*, a lid (**πωυμα*); Strachan compares Gr. εὐνή, bed (Ger. *wohnen*, dwell). W. *ogof*, cave, den, is correlated by Ascoli.

uaine, green, Ir. *uaine*, *uaithne*, E. Ir. *úane*. Strachan suggests the possibility of a Gadelic **ugnio-*, root *veg*, be wet, Gr. ὑγρός, wet (see *feur*).

uainneart, bustle, wallowing, Ir. *únfuirt*, wallowing, tumbling; also G. **aonairt, aonagail**:

uair, an hour, Ir. *uair*, O. Ir. *huar*, *uar*, g. *hóre*, W. *awr*, Cor. *our*, O. Br. *aor*, Br. *eur*, *heur*; from Lat. *hora*, Eng. *hour*. Hence **uaireadair**, a watch, time-piece, Ir. *uaireadóir* (**horatorium?*).

uaisle, pride, nobility, so Ir.; from *uasal*, q.v.

uallach, a burden, Ir. *ualach*: **podl-*; O.H.G. *fazza*, a bundle, Ger. *fassen*, hold (Strachan). Also G. **eallach**, q.v.

uallach, gay, proud, so Ir.; from *uaill*.

uamhag, sheep-louse:

uamharr, dreadful, Ir. *uathmhar*, E. Ir. *úathmar*; from *uath*, fear, q.v. Used adverbially, like Eng. *awfully*, to denote excess. Dial. **uarraidh.**

uamhas, dread, horror, **uathbhas**, Ir. *uathbhás*, E. Ir. *úathbhás*: **uath-bás*, "dread death"; see *uath* and *bàs*.

uamhunn, horror, Ir. *uamhan*, awe, horror, E. Ir. *uamun*, *hóman*, O. Ir. *omun*, *homon*, rarely *ómun*, fear, W. *ofn*, fear, awe, Cor. *own*, Br. *aoun*, Gaul. *-obnos*, *Ex-obnus*, Fearless: **obno-s*, fear. Bez. cfs. Got. *bi-abrjan*, be astounded (but *abrs* means "powerful"), and Gr. ἄφνω, suddenly.

uan, a lamb, Ir., M. Ir. *uan*, W. *oen*, pl. *wyn*, Cor. *oin*, Br. *oan*: **ogno-s*; Lat. *agnus*; Gr. ἁμνός (for ἀβνός); Ch. Sl. *jagne*; also Ag. S. *éanian*, to yean or lamb (**aunōn*).

uar, waterfall, heavy shower, confluence (Sutherland Dial.), Ir., E. Ir. *úarán*, fresh spring; see *fuaran*. Arm. has **uaran**, fresh water.

uarach, hourly, temporary (H.S.D), homely (M'L.); from *uair*.

uasal, noble, proud, Ir., O. Ir. *uasal*, W. *uchel*, Br. *uhel*, *huel*, Gaul. *uxello-*: **ouksel‌o-*, high, root *eug*, *veg*, rise, increase; Gr. ὑψηλός, high, αὔξω, increase; Lat. *augeo*, increase, *vigeo*, be strong; Eng. *up*, Ger. *auf*; Lit. *áuksztas*, high.

† **uath**, dread, Ir. *uath*, O. Ir. *úath*, Cor. *uth*, Br. *eus*, *heuz*, horror; **pouto-*, root *pu*, foul; Lat. *putris*, Eng. *putrid*, *foul?*

ub! ubub! interjection of contempt or aversion, O. Ir. *upp*.

ubag, ubaidh, a charm, Ir. *uptha*, *upadh*, sorcerer, O. Ir. *upta*, fascinatio, *uptha*, Manx *obbee*, sorcery: **od-ba-t-*, from *ba*, speak (see *ob*, refuse). Zimmer refers it to root *ben* of *bean*, hurt, touch.

ubairt, rummaging among heavy articles, bustle (Dial.); see *ùbraid*.

ubh! ubh! interjection of disgust or amazement; cf. Eng. *phew*.

ubh, an egg, Ir. *ubh*, *ugh*, O. Ir. *og*, *ub* (?), W. *wy*, pl. *wyan*, Cor. *uy*, *oy*, Br. *u*, *vi*: **ogos*; Gr. *ὤβεον*, egg, further *ᾠόν*, Lat. *ovum*, Eng. *egg*. The phonetics as between Celtic and the other languages is somewhat difficult; but the connection is indisputable.

ubhal, apple, Ir. *ubhall*, E. Ir. *uball*, *ubull*, O. Ir. *aball*, W. *afal*, Cor. *auallen*, Br. *avallen*: **aballo-*, **aballôn-*; Eng *apple*, Ger. *apfel*; Lit. *obůlys*. Stokes now queries Ger. *obst*, fruit, O. H. G. *obaz*, Ag. S. *ofet*, fruit.

ùbhla, a fine, penalty:

ùbraid, confusion, dispute, also **ùprait**: **ud-bert-*, from *ber* of *beir*.

ucas, ugsa, coal-fish, stenlock:

uchd, the breast, so Ir., O. Ir. *ucht*: **poktu-*; Lat. *pectus?* Stokes and Bezzenberger give **puptu-*, Lettic *pups*, woman's breast, Lit. *pápas*, breast (Eng. *pap* from Lat. *pappa*). St. now gives *poktus*, allied to *pectus*. See *iochd*.

ud, yon, yonder, Ir. *úd*, E. Ir. *út*; for *sud* (*sút*), q.v. For loss of *s*, cf. the article.

udabac, outhouse, porch, back-house (**ùdabac,** Uist); from Norse *úti-bak*, "out-back"?

udail, cause to shake, waver, remove, Ir. *udmhall*, quick, stirring (O'Cl.), O. Ir. *utmall*, unsteady, *utmaille*, instability: *út* of *sud* + *tamall* (Rhys).

ùdail, inhospitable, churlish, **ùdlaidh,** gloomy; cf. Norse *útlagi*, an outlaw, *útlagð*, outlawry.

udalan, a swivel, Ir. *udalán* (Fol., O'R.); from *udail*. Cf. *ludnan*.

udhar, a boil, ulcer; also **othar,** q.v.

ùdlaiche, a stag, old hart (Arm.):

ùdrathad, ùtraid, free egress and regress to common pasture; from the Norse—cf. *útreið*, an expedition, "out-road."

ugan, the upper part of the breast, Ir. *ugán*, craw of a fowl, *ugann*, fish gill (Heb.):

ùghdair, author, Ir. *úghdar*, E. Ir. *ugtar*, O. Ir. *augtor*; from Lat. *auctor*.

ugsa, coal-fish; see *ucas*.

uibe, a mass, lump (as of dough), **iob**; cf. *faob*: **ud-bio-*, "out-being." But cf. Lat. *offa*, ball.

uibhir, a number, quantity, Ir. *uibhir*, *uimhir*, E. Ir. *numir*, number; from Lat. *numerus*, Eng. *number*.

ùidh (uidh), care, heed, Ir. *uidh* (obs.), O. Ir. *oid*; see *taidhe*.

ùidh, a ford, that part of a stream leaving a lake before breaking into a current; also an isthmus (M'Kinnon, *uidh*, *aoi*); from

Norse *eið*, an isthmus, neck of land. Hence *Eye* or *Ui* near Stornoway, older *Ey*, *Huy*, *Eie*.

uidh, uidhe, a journey, distance, Ir. *uidhe*, E. Ir. *ude*, O. Ir. *huide*, profectio: **odio-n*, root *pod*, *ped*, go; Lat. *pes*, *pedis*, foot; Gr. πούς, ποδός, foot; Eng. *foot*; Skr. *padyâ*, footstep.

uidheam, accoutrements, apparatus, Ir. *ughaim*, harness, trappings, O. Ir. *aidmi*, armamenta, W. *iau*, jugum, O. Cor. *iou*, Br. *geo*, *ieo*, **yougo-*, yoke; Eng. *yoke*, Ger. *joch*; Gr. ζυγόν; Lat. *jugum*; Lit. *jungas*. The Gadelic requires a form **ad-jung-mi-*. Cf. O. Ir. *adim*, instrumentum, pl. n. *admi*.

ùig, a nook, cove; from Norse *vík*, bay, creek, Eng. *wick*, *-wich*. Hence the place-name *Uig* (Skye, Lewis). Hence **ùigean,** a fugitive, wanderer.

uigheil, pleasant, careful; from *aoigh* in the first meaning and from *ùidh* in the second.

uile, all, the whole, Ir. *uile*, O. Ir. *uile*, *huile*: **polio-s*, root *pol*, *pel*, full, many, Gr. πολλός (=πολιος), much, many; see *iol-*. Stokes and most philologists refer it to **oljo-s*, Eng. *all*, Ger. *all*, Got. *alls* (**olnó-s*, Mayhew). Some have derived it from **soli-*, Lat. *sollus*, whole, Gr. ὅλος, whence Stokes deduces the Brittonic words—W. *oll*, all, Corn. *hol*, Br. *holl*, *oll* (see *slàn*).

uileann, elbow, Ir. *uille*, g. *uilleann*, M. Ir. *uille*, pl. acc. *uillinn*, O. Ir. *uilin* (acc.), W., Cor. *elin*, Br. *ilin*, *elin*: **olên-*; Gr. ὠλήν, ὠλένη; Lat. *ulna*; Ag. S. *eln*, Eng. *ell*, *elbow*.

uilear, enough, etc.; see *fuilear*.

uill (**ùill,** H.S.D.), oil thou, **uilleadh,** oil (n.); see *ola*.

uilleann, honeysuckle, so Ir. (O'B.), M. Ir. *feithlend*, woodbine; see under *feith*.

uilm, coffer (Carm.):

uim-, circum, Ir. *uim-*, O. Ir. *imm-*; a composition form of *mu*, q.v. Hence **uime,** about him, it, Ir. *uime*, O. Ir. *uimbi*; **uimpe,** about her (=*imb-sì* or *imb-shi*).

ùin, ùine, time, Ir. *uain*, time, opportunity, E. Ir. *úine*, O. Ir. *úain*, leisure, time: **ut-nio-*, root *ut*, *vet* of *feith*, wait. Strachan gives **ucn-* as a reduced form, from *euq*, Skr. *ókas*, comfort, εὔκηλος, free from care, at ease.

ùinich, bustle, tumultus; see *uainneart*.

uinicionn, lambskin (Carm.); for *uainicionn*.

uinneag, a window, M. G. *fuinneóg*, M. Ir. *fuindeog*, *fuindeoc*; from Norse *windauga*, Sc. *winnock*, Eng. *window* (=*wind-eye*). From Ag. S. *windaége* (Stokes, *Lis.*).

uinnean, an onion, Ir. *uinniun*, M. Ir. *uinneamain*, *uindiun*, W. *wynwynyn*; from Lat. *union-em*, O. Fr. *oignon*, Eng. *onion*, from *unus*, one.

uinnean, ankle :

uinnseann, ash, Ir. *uinseann*, M. Ir. *fuindseog*, ash-tree, O. Ir. *ind-huinnius*, W. *on*, *onen*, earlier *onn*, *onnen*, Br. *ounnenn*, Cor. *onnen* : **osnâ*, **osnestu-* ; Lat. *ornus* (**osinos*) ; Lit. *ũsis*, ash, Russ. *jasenĭ*. Cf. Eng. *ash*.

uipear, unhandy craftsman, bungler :

uipinn, a treasure, hoard ; cf. *uibe*.

ùir, mould, dust, earth, Ir., M. Ir. *úir*, E. Ir. *úr*, g. *úire* : **ûrâ* ; Norse *aurr*, loam, wet clay, mud, Ag. S. *eár*, humus. Stokes hesitates between **ûrâ* and **ugrâ*, Gr. ὑγρός, wet.

uircean, a young pig, Ir. *uircín*, M. Ir. *orcán*, porcellus, *oircnín* (do.), *orc*, porcus ; **porko-s* ; Lat. *porcus* ; Eng. *farrow*, *pork* ; Lit. *pàrszas*, boar.

uiread, as much, amount, Ir. *oiread*, O. Ir. *erat*, *airet*, length of time, distance, *cia eret*, quamdiu : **are-vet-to-*, root *vet* of *feith*.

uireas, below, down ; see *ioras*.

uireasbhuidh, need, poverty, so Ir., M. Ir. *auresbadh* ; from *air* and *easbhuidh*, q.v.

uirghioll, faculty of speech, speech, Ir. *uirghíol*, a command (O'B.), *uraghall*, *uradhall*, speech (Keat.), E. Ir. *uirgill*, for *ur-fhuigell*, M. Ir. *urfhoighill* :

uiridh, an uiridh, last year, Ir. *annuraidh*, E. Ir. *inn uraid*, O. Ir. *urid* : **peruti* ; Skr. *parut*, last year ; Gr. πέρυσι, Dor. πέρυτι ; root *vet* of *feith*.

uirigh, a couch, bed : **air-sed-*, root *sed* of *suidhe* ?

uiriollach, a precipice (H.S.D. from MSS.) : **air-ailech*, from *ail*, rock, q.v.

uirisg, offspring of fairy and mortal (M'F.) ; see *ùruisg*.

ùirlios, a walled garden, Ir. *uirlios* (O'B., etc.) ; from *air* and *lios*.

ùirneis, a furnace, Ir. *uirnéis*, *fúirnéis* (O'B.), M. Ir. *forneis* ; from Eng. and O. Fr. *fornaise*, Lat. *fornacem*, *fornax*, oven.

ùirneis, tools, implements, Ir. *úirnéis* (Fol., O'R.), *úirlis* (Con.) ; see *airneis*.

uirsgeil, a spreading (as of dung or hay to dry) ; from *air* and *sgaoil*.

uirsgeul, a fable, romance, so Ir. ; from *air* and *sgeul*.

ùis, use, utility ; from the Eng. *use*, Lat. *ûsus*.

uiseag, a lark, Ir. *uiseóg*, *fuiseóg*, W. *uchedydd*, Br. *ec'houedez*, also W. *ucheda*, to soar ; from **ux*, up, as in *uas*, *uasal* ?

uisg, uisge, water, Ir. *uisge*, O. Ir. *uisce*, *usce* : **ud-s-kio*, root *ud*, *ved* ; Gr. ὕδωρ, ὕδος ; Eng. *water*, etc. ; Skr. *udán* ; further Lat. *unda*, wave. Stokes suggests the possibility of ***uisge*** being for **uskio-*, and allied to Eng. *wash*.

uisliginn, disturbance, fury :

uislinn, sport, diversion, Ir. *uslainn* (Lh., etc.) :

uist, hist ! whist ! Lat. *st !* Eng. *hist !*

ula, ulachan (pl.), beard, Ir., E. Ir. *ulcha*, g. *ulchain* : **ulukon-* ; **pulu-*, beard ; Skr. *pula*, *pulaka*, horripilation ; Gr. *πύλιγγες*, hair of chairs (Hes.). Hence *Ulaid*, Ulster. It may be root *ul*, *vel*, cover (see *olann*).

ulag, block, pulley, "snowball" (Wh.) ; from Eng. *pulley*, L. Lat. *polanus ?*

ulag, oatmeal and water mixed :

ulaidh, a treasure, Ir. *uladh*, charnel-house, E. Ir. *ulad*, stone tomb ; root *ul*, *vel*, cover ? A Gadelic **alveto-*, allied to Lat. *alvus*, a belly, *alveus*, channel, has been suggested.

uloh, you brute ! (Sutherland) ; from Norse *úlfr*, wolf.

ulbhach (ul'ach), ashes, W. *ulw*, pl. *ulwyn* : **polviko-*, **pôlven-* ; Lat. *pulvis*, dust, *pollen*, pollen.

ulartaich, ulfhartaich, howling ; from **ul*, bark (Gr. *ὑλάω*, bark, Lat. *ulula*, owl, etc.), and *art* of *comhart*, q.v.

ullachadh, preparation, preparing, Ir. *ullmhuighim*, I prepare ; from *ullamh*, ready.

ullag, a mouthful of meal (Sh.) ; cf. *ulag*.

ullamh, ready, Ir. *ullamh*, for *urlamh*, E. Ir. *erlam*, paratus ; from *air* and *lam*, the latter being from *làmh*, hand : "to hand, handy." Usually referred to root *las*, desire, Lat. *lascivus*, Eng. *lascivious*.

ultach, a lapful, armful, Ir. *ullthach* (O'B.), M. Ir. *utlach*, lapful, *urtlach*, lap : **ar-tḷ-ac-* ; root *tol*, *tel*, lift (see *toil*, *tlàth*). G. *ulathach*, burden in one's arms = *ultach* (Wh.).

ùmaidh, dolt, blockhead ; see *umpaidh*.

umha, copper, brass, Ir. *umha*, O. Ir. *humæ*, *ume*, copper, brass, *umaide*, *humide*, aeneus, W. *efydd*, O. W. *emid*, aere ; **umâjo-* (Stokes), **omja* (Ascoli), **um-ajo-*, *-ajo-* = *aes* (Bez.).

umhail, heed, attention, Ir. *umhail*, *úmhail* (O'B., Con.) ; cf. next word.

ùmhal, obedient (**umhailt,** Dial.), Ir. *umhal*, E. Ir., O. Ir. *umal*, W. *ufyll*, Corn. *huvel*, Br. *vuel* ; from Lat. *humilis*, Eng. *humble*.

ùmlagh, a fine, **unlagh** (Arg.) ; from Sc. *unlaw*, *unlach*, a fine, transgression, *un-law*.

umpaidh, a boor, clown, idiot (Sh., O'R.) ; see *ùmaidh*.

ung, anoint, Ir. *ungaim*, O. Ir. *ongim* ; from Lat. *unguo*. W. has *enenio* from **o*[i]*nj-*.

unnsa, an ounce, Ir. *únsa*, W. *wns* ; from Eng. The O. Ir. is *unga*, from Lat. *uncia*.

unradh, adversity (Campbell's Tales, II. Mac-a-rusgaich); a form of *an-rath ?*

ùp, push, **ùpag**, a push; cf. W. *hwp*, a push, effort. Cf. *pùc*. Onomatopoetic.

ùr, fresh, new, Ir., E. Ir. *úr*, O. Ir. *húrde*, vividarium, W. *ir*, fresh, green: **ûro-s*, **pûro-s*; Lat. *pûrus*, Eng. *pure*. Usually referred to **ugro-s*, Gr. ὑγρός, wet, Lat. *uvidus*, moist, root *veg*.

urcag, thole pin (N. Lochaber). Cf. *àrcan*, a cork.

urchair, a shot, cast, Ir. *urchur*, E. Ir. *urchur*, *aurchor*, *erchor*, W. *ergyr*, O. B. *ercor*, ictum: **are-koru-*, a cast; from *cuir*, send, q.v.

urchall, fetters, shackles, so Ir. (Lh., etc.): **are-col-*, root, *col*, *cel* of *timchioll ?*

urchasg, physic, antidote, Ir. *urchosg*, preservative, antidote: **air-chosg*, from *cosg*, *casg*, stop, q.v.

urchoid, hurt, mischief, Ir. *urchóid*, O. Ir. *erchoit*: **are-konti-*, Gr. κεντέω, stick, prick, καίνω, kill. Stokes prefers **skonti-* as stem, allied to Eng. *scathe*.

urla, face, hair, breast, Ir. *urla*, lock of hair, long hair of the head, E. Ir., *urla*, *irla*: **air-la-*, where *la* is for *vla*, root *vel* of *falt ?*

ùrlabhairt, eloquence, Ir. *urlabhair*, elocution, E. Ir. *erlabra*: * *air-labhair*; see *labhair*.

ùrlach, stag (R.D.):

ùrlaich, turn from in disgust (Arg.):

ùrlaim, readiness (M'F.), Ir. *úrlamh*, ready; see **ullamh**. Hence also **ùrlaimh**, expert, O. Ir. *erlam*, *irlam*.

ùrlamhas, possession, Ir. *úrlámhus*, *forlamhus*; from *for*, super, and *làmh*, hand: "upper-handed-ness."

ùrlann, a staff, Ir. *úrlann*, a staff, spear staff, M. Ir. *urlann*, staff of a spear: * *air-lann*, from *lann*: also E. Ir. *irlond*, hinder end of a spear or ship.

ùrlar, a floor, lowest part, Ir. *urlár*: * *air-lár*, from *làr*, floor, q.v.

ùrnuigh, a prayer, Ir. *urnuighe*, O. G. *ernacde* (B. of Deer), O. Ir. *irnigde*, *irnichte*: * *are-nakô*, I strive for, root *nak*, *enk*, as in *thig ?* Zimmer gives the root *igh*, desire, Gr. ἰχανᾶν, desire, Lit. *igiju*, strive after, Skr. *îh*, long for, dividing it into **air-con-ig* (* *air-in-ig ?*). O. ? Ir. *arnigim*: *ig* = Gr. ἶχαρ; *arn* = **paran*, Gr. παρά (St. Zeit. 36).

urra, a person, infant; cf. next word.

urradh, **urrainn**, authority, guarantee, author, Ir. *urra(dh)*, surety, author, defendant, *urrain*, stay, prop, M. Ir. *errudus*, responsibility; from *ràth*, *ràthan*, surety. *Urradha* were a chief's "gentlemen," paying rent or service (Sil. Gad.).

urrainn, power, **is urrainn**, can ; Ir. *urra*, power, *urrain*, stay. See above word.
urrail, forward, bold, **urranta**, Ir. *urránta*, bold, confident in one's might ; from *urradh*.
urram, honour, respect, Ir. *urram*, *urraim*, honour, deference, submission, M. Ir. *urraim*, homage : **air-réim ?*
urras, surety, guarantee, Ir. *urrúdhas*, *urrûs* ; from *urradh*.
ursainn, a door-post, Ir. *ursa*, g. *ursann*, E. Ir. *ursa*, *aursa*, *irsa*, d. *ursaind*, W. *gorsin* : **are-stan-*, root *sta*, stand.
ùruisg, a Brownie ; from *uisge*, *air + uisg*.
us, impudence (M'A.) :
usa, easier, Ir. *usa*, O. Ir. *assu*, facilius, *asse*, facilis ; cf. W. *haws*, from *hawdd*, easy ; further Fr. *aisé*, Eng. *easy*, Got. *azets*, easy.
usaid, querulousness (M'A. and Wh.) :
usgar, a jewel, bell on liquor :
usga(r), holy, sacred (Carm.) :
uspag, a push, pang, Ir. *uspóg* ; cf. *ospag*.
uspair, an ugly or lumpish fellow, Ir. *uspán*, a shapeless lump, chaos, clumsy fellow. See *uspan*.
uspairn, strife, Ir. *uspairneachd* : **ud-spairn*, from *spàirn*.
uspan, a shapeless mass, Ir. *uspán* : also **usp** (**ùsp**) ; cf. *uibe*, **uibs- ?*
ut ! ut ! interjection of disapprobation, Eng. *tut*, *hoot*, W. *hwt*, etc.
utag, **ùtag** (Arg.), strife, confusion ; also "push, jostle," **ut**, push. Cf. *put*, *putag*.
ùtan, a knuckle (Sh., O'R.), better *utan* :
ùth, an udder, E. Ir. *uth*. Stokes gives the stem as *(*p*)*utu-*, Lit. *suputimas*, a swelling, *putlùs*, swollen. Lat. *ûber*, Gr. οὖθαρ, Eng. *udder* have been compared, but the Gadelic lacks the terminal *-er*, and the consonant is *t* rather than *d* or *dh*. Cf. Lat. *uter*, skin-bag.
uthard, above, on high, Ir. *ós*, *árd*. Gaelic is for **for-ard*, "on high ;" see *air* and *àrd*.
utraid, district road (Carm.) ; see *udrathad*.
ùtrais, a confused mass of anything, a fidgeting.

SUPPLEMENTARY WORDS NOT GIVEN IN THE BODY OF THE DICTIONARY.

I. From the Sutherland Dialect

(Per Rev. Adam Gunn).

bòrc, thatch, afterwards manure.
ceàldair, slow-moving fellow; from the "r"-like instrument used for making hanks of yarn.
cionlas, "confound you," = string for tying fingers of dead.
dàm, mud, gutter.
dusd, dead body.
failmisg, bold, stormy day; "teamhair fhailmisg," "stormy weather."
faoirisgeadh, sprinkling.
fìr-iasg; *muinntir an fhìr éisg,* salmon fishers. See *fìreun* (Ed.).
garra-gartan, corncrake.
giorrasach, hare.
goireag, cole.
lampan, curdled milk. See *lamban* (Ed.).
leumachan, frog.
meanmainn, itch on point of nose prognosticating news.
meireachadh, starving with cold. See *meilich* (Ed.).
milis, white button; cf. Sc. *smylies.*
mùrd-mhàrd, mumbling.
rangan, putting off time unnecessarily.
smàgach, toad. See *màgan* (Ed.).
snéip, turnip. See *nèip* (Ed.).
stiùcan; "is fhiach e stiùcan dheth," twelve times better.
t'ig, why?
tighinn-toghainn, vacillating.

II. From the Perthshire Dialect

(Per Rev. C. M. Robertson).

aoghaist, fishing tackle (line and hook). *ad-gaoisd?*
bata: gu bata, to abundance. Cf. M'A. *buta,* surplus.
beò, air: "tha am beò fàs fuar," "the air is getting colder"; "beo-ghaoithe," "breath of wind."
bleithteach, kind of gruel.
brabhd, anything bulky (especially a person).
braodag, a tantrum, huff.
buidean(-reòtaidh), icicle. *bod?*
bulbhag (chloiche), a boulder.
bùta, young bird. See *put* (Ed.).
ceabhgach = ciagach, q.v.
ciad, opinion, impression; cf. *ceudfath.*
clòimhneag, flake of snow; *cloimh + boinne?*
clionach, partition.
cnèadag, fir cone.
cramhuinn, a large (hearth) fire.

curraidh, sitting on hunkers. Sc. v. *curr*, "On his coorie-hunkers," said of sliding on ice in a crouching position (Ed.).
deanaich, at work.
diaghaltach, fond of.
dràichd, stallion (Arms.), drudge.
drug, illness : unnamed illness ; cf. *dreag*.
dubh - reabha (-reabhgan), a mole ; cf. Arm.'s *dubh-reotha*, Shaw's *ùir-reothadh = dubh-threabhadh*.
faghairt, ask = farraid.
frioghlaisg, shred of skin rising at nails.
fucadh, pushing heavily.
fùrlaich, revolt against. "Dh' fhurlaich mi ris" = abhor.
futhair, the dog days. See *futhar* (Ed.).
geabhag, a twist.
giolc = *sgiolc*.
iomaltas, hesitation.
lad, loud talk.
leatach, remote.
leiceid, a slap.
liab, a rag, tatter. See *leòb* (Ed.).
lomh, a diet = *longadh*.
lùig, desire, long.
luis, outrush of water.
luthasaích, allow. See *ludhaig* (Ed.).
maoidheanach, friendly.
moislich, stir (out of sleep).
mùganach, thick and damp.
murthail, grumbling; *murlaich*.
niannradh (clach), grinding (stone) ; (*nn* elided).
niarraidh, middling (as to health, when asked).
prio-taoil (accent on last syll.), clatter, heavy noise of falling things.
pròis, beseech, pray, urge.
ràidh (*air*), scolding, threatening.
raigealtach, rascal, rollicking fellow.
ràmh, pl. **ramhchan,** a root (of tree).
reamalair = *ramhlair*.
riasgach, blustering (of weather).
riodach, kind.
ruaig, shower of rain.
saich, sick (Arms. *soithich*, s. "ill"), *saoich*. Cf. *maith no saith*.
samht, a thud.
seanagair, a sagacious one. See *seanagar* (Ed.).
sgeilceil, crackling (of wood).
sgiorlaich, crush (anything soft and juicy).
sgiut = *sgiot*.
sglogaid = *sglongaid*.
siach, avoid.
siochadh, peace.
sic (*air*), attempt upon.
sladaig (*air*), working hard at.
smaiteard, youth, "young spark."
snaoic, chunk (of food).
spacadh, wrestling.
suigeartach, merry.
toman - eallaidh, spider. See *damhan-allaidh* (Ed.).

NATIONAL NAMES.

ALBION, Great Britain in the Greek writers, Gr. Ἄλβιον, Ἀλβίων, Ptolemy's Ἀλουίων, Lat. *Albion* (Pliny), G. **Alba**, g. **Albainn**, Scotland, Ir., E. Ir. *Alba*, *Alban*, W. *Alban* : **Albion-* (Stokes), "white-land"; Lat. *albus*, white; Gr. ἀλφός, white leprosy, white (Hes.); O. H. G. *albiz*, swan.

ARMORIC, belonging to Brittany, Lat. (Cæsar) *Armoricus*, *Aremoricus* (Orosius), **are-mori*, "by the sea" (see *air* and *muir* in Dict.), M. Br. *Armory*, Brittany, *armor*, land by the sea, Br. *arvor*, maritime.

BRITAIN, G. **Breatann**, Ir. *Breatain*, E. Ir. *Bretan*, n. pl. *Bretain*, the Britons, W. *Brython*, Briton, Corn. *Brethon*, Br. *Breiz*, Brittany, Lat. *Brittania* (Cæsar), *Brittani*, Britons, Βρεττανοί (Strabo). The best Gr. forms are Πρεττανοί, Πρεττανική, W. *Prydain*, Britain, E. Ir. *Cruithne*, a Pict, O. Ir. (Lat.) *Cruithnii* (Adamnan, *Cruthini* Populi): **Q̣ṛtaniâ*, root *q̣ṛt*, to which Stokes refers G. **cruithneachd**, wheat, though the usual reference is to G. **cruth**, picture, form, still retaining the notion of "pictured" men as in the old explanations of *Pict*. Stokes, Rhys, etc., regard the Lat. *Brittania* as a word of different origin from the Gr. Πρεττανία, and G. *Cruithne*: though, as a matter of fact, the Lat. seems to have been a bad rendering of the Greek. The Cruithne or Picts thus gave their name to Britain, as being, about 300 B.C., its then Celtic inhabitants.

BRITTANY; the BRETON language; from *Britain* above. Britons poured into France in the fifth and sixth centuries.

CALEDONIA, northern Scotland (Tacitus), Gr. Καληδόνιοι (Ptol., etc.), Lat. *Calēdonii* (Lucan, Martial, etc.), O. G. Dun-*Callden*, Duni-*Callen*, Dun-*Keld*, fort of the Caledonians, G. Dùn-**Chaillinn**; explained by Windisch as from **cald*, the root of G. *coille*, the force being "wood-landers." Stokes and others object because of the η (Lat. *ē*) in Καληδ-; but if the Eng. and Gaelic modern forms are the descendants of the word Caledonia as locally spoken, the objection cannot hold.

CELTS, Lat. *Celtæ* (Cæsar), Gr. Κελτοί, Κελταί, Κελτικός, appearing in the fifth and fourth cent. B.C. in Herodotus, Xenophon, etc.: **Kelto-s*, "the lofty," root *qel*, raise, go, Lat. *celsus*, high, Eng. *excel*, Lit. *kėltas*, raised. Rhys refers the name to the root *qel*, slay, Ag. S. *hild*, war, Norse, *hildr*, Lat. *percello*, hit, Lit. *kalti*, strike : the Celtæ being "smiters."

CORNWALL : CORNISH, Ag. S. *Cornwalas*, the *Walas* or Welsh of the Corn or Horn, E. Ir. *i tírib Bretann Cornn* (Corm.), in the lands of the Britons of the Corn. For *Walas* see *Wales*.

CRUITHNE, a Pict ; see under *Britain*.

CYMRY, the Welsh (pl.), *Cymraeg*, the Welsh name for the Welsh language ; the singular of *Cymry* is *Cymro*, older *Cym-mro* : **Com-mrox*, pl. *Com-mroges* or *Combroges* (cf. Cæsar's Allobroges, "Other-landers"), country-men, "co-landers," from *brog*, *mrog* of *brugh* in Dict., q.v. The E. Ir. Gaelic for Wales is found in the phrase *isinchomreic* = im Kymrischen (Zim. Zeit. [32] 162).

ERIN ; see *Ireland*.

GAELIC, GAEL, the name of the language and people of the Scottish Highlands, G. **Gàidhlig, Gàidheal**, Ir. *Gaoidhilig*, *Gaedhilig*, the Irish language, *Gaoidheal*, Irishman, E. Ir. *Góedel* (1100 A.D.), *Gaideli* (Giraldus), W. *Gwyddel*, Irishman : **Gâdelo-s* (for Sc. Gaelic) or **Gâidelo-s* (for Irish), root *ghâdh*, Eng. *good*, Ger. *gut*, etc.? The Scotch form seems the best, as its use has been continuous, the race being only a fourth item in Scotland. Stokes gives a proto-Gaelic **Goidelos* or **Geidelos*, which Bez. compares to the Gaul. *Geidumni*, and which Stokes compares with Lat. *hoedus*, goat ("Goat-men," cf. Oscan *Hirpini*) or Lit. *gaidys*, cock.

GALLI, GAUL, now France, Lat. *Gallus*, *Galli* (fourth to first cent. B.C.), Gr. Γαλάτης, Γαλάται (third and second cent. B.C.) ; from the root *gal*, bravery, which see in Dict., with discussion of Galli and G. **Gall**, Lowlander, stranger.

IRELAND, IRISH ; G. **'Eireann**, Ir. *'Eire*, g. *'Eireann*, E. Ir. *'Eriu*, *'Erenn*, W. *Ywerddon*, *Iwerddon*, M. W. *Ewyrdonic*, Irish Ptol. Ἰουερνία Ἰέρνη (Strabo), Lat. *Hibernia*, *Iverna* (Mela), *Ierne* (Claudian, fourth cent. A.D.), *Evernili*, Irish (Adamnan) **Iverjôn-*, **Everjôn-*, usually referred to *Piverjo-*, Skr. *pîvarî* fat, Gr. Πιερία, the Grecian seat of the Muses, πίων, fat (Windisch, Stokes) : "rich-soiled, swelling." Others refer it to G. *iar*, west, or Skr. *ávara* (from *ava*, G. *bho*), western lower. No derivation can be satisfactory which does not at the same time account for the similarly named Highland rivers called **'Eire, 'Eireann**, Eng. *Earn*, *Findhorn*.

MAN, MANX ; Manx *Manninagh*, Manx (adj.), *Gailck*, *Gaelk*, the Manx Gaelic, E. Ir. *inis Manann*, Isle of Man, a genitive from **Mana* (= Lat. *Mona*), early W. *Manau*, Lat. *Mona* (Cæsar)

Ptol. Μονάοιδα, *Monapia* (or *Mona ?*) The E. Ir. god-name *Manannán Mac Lir* (son of the Sea) is connected with the Island; Skr. *Manu*, the Law-giver; Teutonic *Mannus* (Tacitus), Eng. *man*.

PICTS; G. **Cruithnich,** for which name see under *Britain*. The name *Picti* can scarcely be separated from the Gaul. *Pictavi*, now *Poitiers;* and, if this be the case, the usual derivation from Lat. *pictus*, painted, must be abandoned. Windisch adduces E. Ir. *cicht*, engraver, carver, for which a Brittonic *piht*, *pict* may be claimed as a parallel (**qict*); this again leaves the idea of tattooing intact, and so agrees with the historical facts.

SCOTLAND, SCOTS; E. Ir. *Scott*, pl. n. *Scuit*, d. *Scottaib*, Irishmen; Adamnan—*Scotia*, Ireland, *Scoti*, the Irish, *Scoti Britanniae*, Scots of Dalriada, etc., *Scoticus*, Irish, *Scotice*, in the Gaelic language, Lat. (fourth cent.) *Scotti*, *Scôti*, **Skotto-s*. Stokes translates the name as "masters, owners," allied to Got. *skatts*, money, Ger. *schatz*, treasure, stock, Ch. Sl. *skotŭ*, property, cattle. The root *skat*, hurt, scathe, cut, of Eng. *scathe*, has been suggested, either as "cutters" or "tattooed ones" (so Isidore of Saville). Rhys has suggested connection with W. *ysgwthr*, a cutting, carving—"tattooed or painted men."

WALES, WELSH; Ag. S. *Wealas*, *Walas*, the Welsh—the name of the people in pl. being used for the country, *Wylisc*, *Welsh*, *Wylisce men*, the Welsh; sing. of *Wealas* is *Wealh*, a foreigner, Welshman, O. H. G. *walh*, foreigner, Celt, Ger. *wal-* in *walnuss*, Eng. *wal-nut*: from the Gaul. nation of the *Volcae*, bordering on the Germans, * *Volko-s*, * *Volkâ*, "the bathers," from *volc*, bathe (see *failc* in Dict.). Stokes connects the name with Lit. *wìlkti*, pull, referring to the restless wanderings of the Gauls.

PERSONAL NAMES AND SURNAMES.

ADAM, G. **Adhamh**, *Ahū* (Fer. MS.), *Awzoe* (D. of L.), E. Ir. *Adam*, O. Ir. *Adim* (g); from Hebrew *Adam*, red. Hence *Mac-adam*, *M'Caw*, and from Dial. G. **'Adaidh** (a diminutive from Sc.) *M'Cadie*, **M''Adaidh.**

ADAMNAN, G. **Adhmhnan** (pronounced *Yownan* or *Yōnan*), earlier *Adhamhnan* (*Oghamhnan*, M'V.), E. Ir. *Adamnán*, Lat. *Adamnanus* (seventh cent.), St Adamnan (died 704 A.D.), "little Adam," a Gaelic diminutive from *Adam*. Hence the personal name *Gilleownan* (1495), *Giolla-Adhamhnáin*, father of Somerled (twelfth cent.), *Gilla-agamnan* (1467 MS.), whence Skene deduces the *Mac-lennans*, q.v.

ALEXANDER, G. **Alasdair**, *Allex*[r] (D. of L.), *Alaxandair*, (1467 MS.), M. Ir. *Alaxandair*; from Lat. *Alexander*, from *Gr.* Ἀλέξανδρος, "defending men." Hence G. **M'Alasdair**, *Mac-alister*; further *Mac-andie* (from *Sandy*).

ALLAN, G. **Ailean**, E. Ir. *Ailéne*, Adamnan's *Ailenus*, from *al*, rock? The Norman *Alan*, whence Scotch *Allan* mostly, is O. Br. *Alan*, *Alamnus*, Nennius *Alanus*, from *Alemannus*, the German tribe name—"All Men." Cf. Norman, Frank, Dugall, Fingall. Hence *Mac-allan*.

ALPIN, G. **Ailpein**, E. Ir. *Alpin* (Dalriadic king 693); from Pictish or Welsh sources—M. W. *Elphin*, *Elfin*, which Stokes suggests to be from Lat. *Albînus*, from *albus*, white (or allied rather?). Hence G. **M'Ailpein**, *Mac-alpine*.

ANDREW, G. **Aindrea** (**Anndra**, Dial.), **Gilleanndrais**, Eng. *Gil-landers*, St. Andrew's *gille*, M. G. *Andro* (D. of L.), *Ainnrias*, *Gille-ainnrias* (1467 MS.), E. Ir. *Andrias*; from Lat. *Andreas*, g. *Andreæ*, from Gr. Ἀνδρέας, a reduced double-stemmed name now showing only ἀνδρ-, man (see *neart*). Hence *Mac-andrew*, *Gillanders*, *Anderson*.

ANGUS, G. **Aonghas**, Ir. *Aonghus*, g. *Aonghusa*, E. Ir. *'Oengus*, O. Ir. *'Oingus*, W., Cor. *Ungust*: *Oino-gustu-s*, "unique choice," from *aon* and *gus*, choice (Eng. *choose*, Lat. *gustus*, taste, as in G. *tagh*). Hence **M'Aonghuis**, *Mac-innes*; further *M'Ainsh*.

ARCHIBALD, G. **Gilleasbuig**, Bishop's *gille* (see *easbuig* in Dict.), M. G. *Gillespik* (D. of L.), *Gilla-espic* (1467 MS.). Hence *Gillespie*. The name *Archibald*, Ag. S. *Arcebald*, *Arcenbald* or *Ercenbald*, which vaguely means "right-bold" (O. H. G. *erchen*, right, real), has no apparent connection with *Gillespic* in meaning or origin (cf. similarly Ludovic and *Maol-domhnuich*).

ARTHUR, G. **Artair,** M. G. *Artuir*, E. Ir. *Artuir*, *Artur*, Ir. Lat. *Arturius*, son of *Ædan* (Adamnan), W. *Arthur*, to which the Lat. *Artorius* (Juvenal) has been compared and suggested as its source (it being maintained that the Gens Artoria of Yorkshire lasted from Roman to Domesday-Book times, where *Artor* appears in the days of Edward the Confessor). If native to Brittonic (which is probable), it is from **arto-s*, a bear, W. *arth*, O. Ir. *art*, whence the names *Art*, *Artgal*, *Artbran*. Rhys prefers to render the **arto-* as "cultor," from *ar*, plough (*Arth. Leg.*, 40-48), allying Arthur to the idea of a "Culture God." Hence G. **M'Artair,** *Mac-arthur*.

BAIN, from G. *bàn*, white. The Bains of Tulloch appear in the sixteenth century variously as *Bayne* or *Bane*, with a contemporary near them called John Makferquhair *M'Gillebane* (1555). This last name is now **M'Ille-bhàin,** "Fair-*gille*," rendered into Eng. by *Whyte*; whence also *M'Gilvane*.

BARTHOLOMEW, G. **Parlan,** Ir. *Parthalon*, E. Ir. *Partholón*, Lat. *Partholomæus* or *Bartholomæus* (Nennius, ninth cent.), the name of a personage who is represented as the first invader of Ireland after the Flood (278 years after!). The *p* proves the name to be non-Gadelic; and as the historians take *Partholon* from Spain, the Spanish *Bar Tolemon* of legend has been suggested as the original. Prof. Rhys thought it came from the Ivernians or Pre-Celtic race in Ireland. Hence the Clan *Mac-farlane*, G. **M'Pharlain.**

BROWN, G. **M'A'-Bhriuthainn,** M. G. *M'abhriuin* (1408 Gaelic Charter), from *britheamhain*, the former (Sc. Gaelic) genitive of **britheamh,** judge, q.v. Hence *Mac-brayne*.

CAMERON, G. **Camshron, Camaran,** M. G. *Cámsroin*, g. (M'V.), *Camronaich* (D. of L.), *Gillacamsroin* (1467 MS.), Charter Eng. *Camroun* (1472); explained as from *càm-sròn*, "wry-nose," which is the most probable explanation (cf. *caimbeul*, E. Ir. *cerrbél*, wry mouth). Connection with *camerarius* or *chamberlain* (of Scotland) unlikely, or with the fourteenth century *De Cambruns* or *Cameron* parish in Fife.

CAMPBELL, G. **Caimbeul,** M. G. *Cambel* (1467 MS.), *Cambell* (1266, etc.), from *cambél*, wry-mouthed (*càm* and *beul*; see *Cameron*). There is no *De Cambel* in the numerous early references, but *De Campo-bello* appears in 1320 as a Latin form and an etymology; this, however, should naturally be *De Bello-campo* as Norman-French idiom and Latin demand—a form we have in *Beau-champ* and *Beecham*. *De Campello* or *De Campellis* (little plain) has been suggested; but unfortunately for these derivations the earliest forms show no *de*: *Cambell* was an epithet, not a place-name.

CARMICHAEL, G. **M'Gillemhicheil,** Son of the *gille* of St Michael, M. G. *Gillamichol* (1467 MS.), O.G. *Gillemicel* (B. of Deer). The name Carmichael is really Lowland—from the Parish name of Carmichael in Lanark (Michael's *caer* or *cathair*, q.v.).

CATTANACH, CHATTAN, G. **Catanach,** M. G. plural *Cattanich* (D. of L.), "belonging to Clan Chattan," *Clann Gillacatan* (1467), which claims descent from *Gillacatain* (1467 MS.), servant of St Catan, whose name denotes "little cat" (see *cat*).

CHARLES, G. **Tearlach,** M. Ir. *Toirrdhealbhach* (Maclean Genealogy), Englished as *Tirlagh* and *Turlough*, E. Ir. *Toirdelbach*, Latinised and explained as *Turri-formis*, "Tower-shaped," but the *toir* in Gaelic took the phonetics of the prefix *tair*, super, and hence the modern G. form. Hence *M'Kerlie*.

CHISHOLM, G. **Siosal, Siosalach,** *De Chesholme* (thirteenth century documents), *De Cheseholme* (1254), a Border name, the place-name Chisholm being in Roxburgh: *Ches-holm* (a holm, but *Ches ?*).

CLARK, G. **Cléireach**; see *cléireach* in Dict. Also **M' A'-Chléirich,** whence Galwegian *M'Chlery*.

COLL, G. **Colla,** M. G. *Colla* (M'V., 1467 MS.), E. Ir. *Colla*: **Colnavo-s*, from *col*, *cel*, high, as in *Celtæ* (see above).

COLIN, G. **Cailean,** M. G. *Callane* (D. of L.), *Cailin* (1467 MS.), *Colinus* (Lat. of 1292). This is a personal name, once more or less peculiar to the Campbells, the Chief being always in Gaelic **M'Cailein.** Its relation to Eng. and Continental *Colin* is doubtful. Cf. *Coileán*, "whelp," and personal name; the G. is a dialectic form of old *coileán* (see Fol.), *cuilean*, whelp.

CRERAR, G. **Criathrar,** the name of a Lochtay-side clan who regard themselves as Mackintoshes, explaining the name as "riddler," from *criathar* (which see in Dict.): the derivation is right, but for the meaning compare the Eng. noun and name *Sieve(w)right*. See *Celt. Mag.* [6], 38.

CUMMING, G. **Cuimein, Cuimeanach,** earliest Eng. form *Comyn*, a Norman family dating from the Conquest, belonging to the Norman house of De Comines, a territorial designation.

DAVID, G. **Daibhidh** (Classical), **Dàidh** (C.S.); hence **Clann Dàidh** or the *Davidsons*, a branch of the Clan Chattan. In C.S., *Davidson* appears as **Déibhiosdan.**

DERMID, G. **Diarmad,** M. G. *Dermit* (D. of L.), *Diarmada*, gen. (1467 MS.), E. Ir. *Diarmait*, O. Ir. *Diarmuit*, *Diarmit*, Ir. Lat. *Diormitius* (Adamnan). Zimmer explains the name as *Día-ermit*, "God-reverencing," from *dia* and *ermit*: **are-ment-*, "on-minding," root *ment*, as in *dearmad*, q.v.

DEWAR, G. **Deòir, Deòireach,** documents *Doïre* (1487), *Jore* (1428); from *deòradh*, a pilgrim, q.v. Hence *Macindeor*.

DONALD, G. **Domhnall,** M. G. *Domnall* (1467 MS.), gen. *Donil* (D. of L.), O. G. *Domnall* (B. of Deer), E. Ir. *Domnall*, Ir. Lat. *Domnallus* (Adamnan), *Domnail* (do., ablative), Early W. *Dumngual*, later *Dyfnwal*: **Dumnovalo-s*, from *dubno-* of *domhan*, and *valo-* (see *flath*), meaning "world-wielder, world-ruler," much the same in meaning as *Dumnorix*, world-king, Cæsar's opponent among the Aedui. See *domhan*, *flath*. Hence **M'Dhòmhnuill,** *Mac-donald*.

DUFF, M. Ir. *Dubh* (*Clann Dubh*, Clan Duff, of which was Macbeth, etc.), earlier *Dub*, King Duff in tenth century; from Gadelic *dub*, now *dubh*, black, q.v. As a personal name, it is a curtailment of some longer or double-stemmed name (cf. *Fionn*, *Flann*, red). Hence *Macduff* (*Clen m*[c] *Duffe*, 1384). The family name *Duff* is merely the adjective *dubh* used epithetically.

DUFFY, Ir. *Dubhthaigh*; see *Mac-phee*.

DUGALD, G. **Dùghall,** M. G. *Dowgall*, g. *Dowle* (D. of L.), *Dubgaill*, gen. (1467 MS.), thirteenth century documents give *Dugald* (1289), *Dufgal* (1261), M. Ir. *Dubgall* (first recorded Dubgall is at 912 A.D.), from Early Ir. *Dubgall*, a Dane, "Black stranger," as opposed to *Finngall*, a Norwegian, "Fair foreigner." See, for derivation, *fionn* and *Gall*. Hence **M'Dhùghaill,** *Mac-dougall*, *Mac-dowel*, etc.

DUNCAN, G. **Donnchadh** (Dial. **Donnach**), M. G. *Duncha* (D. of L.), *Donnchaid*, gen. (1467 MS.), O. G. *Donchad* (B. of Deer), E. Ir. *Donnchad*: **Donno-catu-s*, **Dunno-catu-s*, "Brown warrior," from *donn* and *cath*, q.v. The Gaulish *Donno-* of personal names has been referred by De Jubainville to the same meaning and origin as M. Ir. *donn*, king, judge, noble—a word occurring in O'Davoren's glossary.

EDWARD, G. **'Eideard** (**'Eudard,** Dial.), **Imhear, Iomhar**; the first is the Eng. *Edward* borrowed, the second is the Norse *Ivarr* borrowed (see *Mac-iver*). Hence **M''Eideard,** *M'Edward*.

Ewen, G. **Eòghann** (Dial. **Eòghainn**), M. G. *Eogan*, *Eoghan*, E. Ir., O. Ir. *Eogan* : **Avi-gono-s* (**Avigenos*, Stokes), "well born, good," from **avi*, friendly, good, Skr. *ávi* (do.), Got. *avi-liud*, thanks, Lat. *aveo*, desire, possibly Gr. εὐ-, good (cf. here Εὐγένης, *Eugenius*), W. has *Eu-tigirn*, *Eu-tut*, O. Br. *Eu-cant*, *Eu-hocar*, Gaul. *Avi-cantus*. Rhys (*Hib. Lect.* 63) refers Ir. *Eoghan* and W. *Owen* to **Esu-gen-*, Gaul. *Esugenus*, sprung from the god *Esus*. Zimmer regards *Owen* as borrowed from Lat. *Eugenius*. Cf., however, the *evo-* of Ogmic *Eva-cattos*, now *Eochaidh*. Hence *Mac-ewen*.

Farquhar, G. **Fearchar,** M. G. *Fearchar*, *Fearchair*, Ir. *Fearchair* (F. M., year 848 A.D.) : **Ver-caro-s*, "super-dear one"; for *fear*, see *Fergus*, and for *car* see Dict. above. Hence **M'Fhearchair,** *Mac-erchar*, *Farquharson*, *M'Farquhar*.

Fergus, G. **Fearghas,** M. G. *Fearghus*, *Fergus*, E. Ir., O. Ir. *Fergus*, g. *Fergusso*, W. *Gurgust*, O. Br. *Uuorgost*, *Uurgost* : **Ver-gustu-s*, "super-choice"; for *ver-* or *fear-*, see in Dict. *far*, *air* (allied to Lat. *super*), and for *gustus*, see under *Aonghus* above. Some regard *Fer* here as G. *fear*, man, **viro-* or **vir*.

Fingal, G. **Fionn,** Macpherson's Gaelic **Fionnghal,** which really should mean "Norseman," or Fair-foreigner, M. G. *Fionnghall*, a Norseman (M'V.), *ri Fionn-gal*, king of Man and the Isles (M'V.), *Fingal* (*Manx Chron.*), king of Man and the Isles from 1070 to 1077 : from *fionn* and *Gall*, q.v. *Fingal* as the name of the Gaelic mythic hero is an invention of Macpherson's, as likewise is his Gaelic **Fionnghal.** As a matter of fact the name is a Gaelic form of the female name *Flora!* See *Fionnaghal* in the addendum to this list.

Finlay, G. **Fionnla, Fionnlagh** (misspelt **Fionnladh**), M. G. *Finlay* (D. of L.), *Finlaeic*, gen. (1467 MS.), *Fionnlaoich*, gen. (*Duan Albanach*), E. Ir. *Findlæch* (Lib. Leinster), *Finnloech* and *Finlaeg*, gen. (Marianus Scotus). Those early forms and the Norse *Finnleikr* prove that the name means "Fair hero" (*fionn* and *laoch*). It is a popular (10th and 11th century) rendering of *Finnlug*, "Fair attractive one," the older name. It has been explained as "Fair calf," which would suit the phonetics also. Hence *Finlayson*, *Mackinlay* (**M'Fhionnlaigh**).

Forbes, G. **Foirbeis, Foirbeiseach,** early document form *De Forbes* (thirteenth cent.), so named from the place-name *Forbes* in Aberdeenshire.

Fraser, G. **Friseal, Frisealach,** circ. 1298 the patriot's name is variously Simon *Fraser*, *Frasel*, *Fresel*, *Frisel*, in Domesday B. *Fresle*, Battle Abbey Rolls (?) *Frisell* or *Fresell*; usually referred to O. Fr. *freze*, a strawberry, **frezele*, from Lat. *fragula*, *fragum*, Fr. *fraisier*, strawberry plant. For sense, cf. the name *Plantagenet* (broom). Strawberry leaves form part of the Fraser armorial bearings. The word may also mean "curled" (Eng. *frizzle*, *frieze*).

GALBRAITH, G. **M' A'-Bhreatnaich**, son of the Briton (of Strathclyde). The name appears in the thirteenth century in Lennox, etc., as *Galbrait* (from *Gall* and *Breat-* of Breatann above).

GEORGE, G. **Seòras, Seòrsa, Deòrsa**, ultimately from Gr. γεωργός, a farmer, "worker of the earth" (γῆ, earth, ὀργός, Eng. *work*). Hence the Border *M'George*.

GILBERT, G. **Gilleabart, Gillebrìde**. *Gilbert* is from Ag. S. *Gislebert*, "Bright hostage" (see *giall* in Dict.); **Gillebrìde** is St Bridget's slave, an exceedingly common name once, but now little used.

GILCHRIST, G. **Gillecrìosd**, M. G. *Gillacrist*, Ir. *Gillacrist* (several in eleventh century): "servant of Christ." Hence *M'Gilchrist*. It translates also *Christopher*.

GILLESPIE, G. **Gilleasbuig**; see *Archibald*.

GILLIES, G. **Gillìosa**: "servant of Jesus." From **M'A-Lìos** comes the "English" form *Lees*, *M'Leish*.

GLASS, G. **Glas**, an epithet, being *glas*, grey. See *M'Glashan*.

GODFREY, G. **Goraidh**, M. G. *Gofraig* (1467 MS.), *Godfrey* (do.), Ir. *Gofraidh* (F.M.), M. Ir. *Gothfrith*, *Gofraig*, also *Gofraig* (Tigernach, 989), E. Ir. *Gothfraid* (Lib. Lein.), E. W. *Gothrit* (*Ann. Camb.*). The Norse name, for it is Norse-men that are referred to, is *Goðröðr* or *Gudrod* (also *Góröðr*), but the earlier Gaelic shows rather a name allied to the Ag. S. *Godefrid*, Ger. *Gottfried*, "God's peace." Modern Gaelic is more like the Norse. The Dictionaries give G. **Guaidhre** as the equivalent of *Godfrey*; for which, however, see *M'Quarrie*.

GORDON, G. **Gòrdan, Gòrdon, Gòrdonach**; from the parish name of *Gordon* in Berwickshire. The De Gordons are well in evidence in the thirteenth century. Chalmers explains the place-name as *Gor-dyn*, "super-dûnum" (see *far* and *dùn*).

GOW, G. **Gobha**, a smith, now usually **gobhainn**, q.v. Hence *Mac-cowan*, *Mac-gowan*, *Cowan*.

GRANT, G. **Grannd**, *Grant* (1258), an English family which settled about Inverness in the thirteenth century, Eng. *Grant*, *Grand*, from Fr., Eng. *grand*.

GREGOR, G. **Griogair, Griogarach**, M. G. *M'Gregar* (D. of L.), M. Ir. *Grigoir*, E. Ir. (Lat.) *Grigorius* (Gregory the Great, died 604), from Lat. *Gregorius*, Gr. Γρηγόριος, a favourite ecclesiastical name from the third century onward (cf. Gr. γρηγορέω, be watchful, Eng. *care*). Hence **M'Griogair**, *Macgregor*, *Gregory*.

GUNN, G. **Guinne, Gunnach,** early documents *Gun* (1601), *Clangwn* (1525), in Kildonan of Sutherland, originally from Caithness; from the Norse *Gunni* (twelfth century), the name then of a son of Olaf, a Caithness chief (*Ork. Saga*). This *Gunni* is a short or "pet" form of some longer name of two stems, with *gunn-r*, war, as the first and chief one (cf. *Gann-arr*, which is an old Orkney name, *Gunn-björn*, *Gunnlaugr*, *Gunn-ólfr*, war-wolf, *Gunn-stein*, *Gunn-valdr*).

HAROLD, G. **Harailt,** M. Ir. *Aralt*, from Norse *Haraldr* (same in roots and origin as Eng. *herald*). Hence *Mac-raild*.

HECTOR, G. **Eachunn** (Dial. **Eachainn**), M. G. *Eachuinn*, g. (M'V.), *Eachdhuin*, g. (M'V.), *Eachdhonn*, g. *Eachduinn* (1467 MS.), Ir. *Eachdonn* (year 1042): **Eqo-donno-s*, "horse lord," like *Each-thighearna* of *Mac-echern*. Of course "Brown-horse" is possible; cf. Gr. Ξάνθιππος. The phonetics are against **Each-duine*, "horse-man," as an explanation.

HENRY, G. **Eanruig**; from O. Eng. *Henric*, now Henry, from Germanic *Heim-rik*, "home-ruler" (Eng. *home* and *ric* in *bishop-ric*, *rich*). Hence *Mackendrick*, *Henderson*.

HUGH, G. **'Uisdean (Hùisdean),** in Argyle **Eòghan,** M. G. *Huisduinn*, which comes from Norse *Eysteinn*, "*Ey*(?)-stone." The Dictionaries also give the G. **Aodh** (see *Mackay*) as equivalent to Hugh, which is itself from Germanic sources, Teutonic root *hug*, thought.

JAMES, G. **Seumas,** M. G. *Sémus* (M'V.); from the Eng. *James*, a modification of Hebrew *Jacob*.

JOHN, G. **Iain,** older **Eòin,** in compounds **Seathain,** as *Mac-Gille-Sheathainn*, now **M'Illeathainn.**

KATHEL, G. **Cathal,** M. G. *Cathal* (M'V.), Ir. *Cathal* (common from seventh century onwards), O. W. *Catgual*: **Katu-valo-s*; see *cath*, war, and *val* under *Donald*. Hence *M'All*, *Mackail*.

KENNEDY, G. **Ceanaideach, Ceanadaidh,** *Kennedy* (*Kenedy*, John *M'Kennedy*, fourteenth century) is the family name of the old Earls of Carrick, now represented by the Marquis of Ailsa; it is a famous Irish name borne by the father of Brian Boru in the tenth century—Ir. *Ceinneidigh*, E. Ir. *Cennétich*, gen.; from *ceann*, head, and *éitigh*, ugly: "ugly head." Called also **M'Ualraig** from Walrick Kennedy (sixteenth century), who first settled in Lochaber: *Walrick* may be G. **Ualgharg** confused with Teutonic *Ulrick*, older *Uodalrich*, "rich patrimonially."

KENNETH, G. **Coinneach,** M. G. *Coinndech, Coinnidh,* g. *Coinndigh,* g. (M'V.), O. G. *Cainnech,* g. *Caennig* (B. of Deer), E. Ir. *Cainnig,* gen., Ir. Lat. *Cainnechus* (Adamnan): **Cannico-s,* "fair one," from the same stem as *cannach* (root *qas*), q.v. The Eng. *Kenneth* is a different word: it is the old Scotch king name *Cinæd* (E. Ir. form), O. G. *Cinathá* (B. of Deer), Ir. *Cinaedh,* "fire-sprung," from *cin* of *cinn* and *aed* of *Mackay.*

LACHLAN, G. **Lachlann** (Dial. **Lachlainn**), **Lachunn,** M. G. *Lochlinn,* g. (M'V.), *Lochloinn,* n. and g., *Lachlan,* g. (1467 MS.), Ir. *Lochlainn Mac Lochlainn* (F.M., year 1060); probably from *Lochlann,* Scandinavia, possibly commencing as *Mac-Lochlainne,* a Scandinavian ("son of L."). *Lochlann* evidently means "Fjord-land."

LAMOND, G. **M'Laomuinn, Làman,** M. G. *Ladmann,* early documents *Lawemundus* (Lat. of 1292), *Laumun* (circ. 1230), M. Ir. *Laghmand, Lagmand*; from Norse *lagamaðr, lögmaðr,* lawman, pl. *lögmenn,* "law-men," by meaning and derivation. Hence *M'Clymont,* D. of L. *V'Clymont, Clyne lymyn.*

LAURENCE, G. **Labhruinn,** M. G. *Labhran* (1467), Ir. *Laurint* (*Saint*), from Lat. *Laurentius,* St Laurence, the ultimate stem being that of Lat. *laurus,* a laurel. Hence **M'Labhruinn,** or *Mac-laren.*

LEWIS, G. **Luthais**; from Fr. *Louis,* from *Chlovis,* the Frankish king (fifth century), degraded from old German *Chlodwig,* now *Ludwig* (**Kluto-vigo-s,* famed warrior, roots in *cliù* and Eng. *victory*). Hence Eng. *Ludovic,* which is rendered in G. by **Maoldònuich,** shaveling of the Church.

LIVINGSTONE, G. **M'An-léigh**; see *Mac-leay.*

LUKE, G. **Lùcais.** Hence *Mac-lucas.*

MAGNUS, G. **Manus, Mànus,** M. G. *Magnus, Manuis,* g. (1467 MS.), Ir. *Maghnus,* Norse *Magnúss,* from Lat. *magnus,* in the name of Charle*magne*—Carolus *Magnus.*

MALCOLM, G. **Calum,** earlier **Gillecalum,** M. G. *Mylcollum* (D. of L.), *Maelcolaim,* O. G. *Malcoloum, Malcolum, Gilliecolaim,* Ir. *Maelcoluim*: from *maol,* bald, and *calum,* a dove (Lat. *columba*), the particular *Calum* meant here being St Columba. Hence *Maccallum.*

MALISE, G. **Maoliosa,** E. Ir. *Maelísu,* servant of Jesus. Hence also *Mellis.*

MATHESON, G. **M'Mhathan, Mathanach,** M. G. *Mac-Matgamna* (1467 MS.), *Macmaghan* (*Exchequer Rolls* for 1264), the Ir. *Mac-mahon,* "son of the bear," for which see *mathghamhuin.* Matheson in Perthshire and Kintyre is, as elsewhere outside the Highlands, for *Mathew-son,* G. **M'Mhatha.**

MENZIES, G. **Mèinnear, Mèinn** and **Mèinnearach** locally, early documents *de Mengues* (1487), *de Meyners* (1249); *De Meyneria* would mean much the same as *De Camera*, that is, "of the household," from *mesn-*, *masn-*, giving Fr. *mén-* (our *ménage*, *menagerie*, *menial*), from Lat. *mans-* (our *mansion*), from *maneo*, remain. The root anyway is *man* of *mansion* and *manor*, and the name is allied to *Manners* and *Mainwaring*.

MORGAN, M. G. *Clann Mhorguinn* (M'V.), O. G. *Morgunn*, g. *Morcunt*, W. *Morgan*, Cor. and O. Br. *Morcant*: *Mori-canto-s*, "sea-white," from the stem of *muir* and root *kṇd*, burn, as in *connadh* (Lat. *candeo*, shine, Eng. *candle*). See *Mackay*.

MORRISON, G. **Moireasdan,** earlier **M'Gille-mhoire,** Mary's servant, M. G. *Gillamure*, whence *Gilmour*. The name *Morris* is for *Maurice*, from the Latin saint's name *Mauricius*, "Moorish."

MUNRO, G. **Rothach, Mac-an-Rothaich** (Dial. **Munro**). In the fourteenth century the name is "of Monro," which shows it is a territorial name, explained as *Bun-roe*, the mouth of the Roe, a river in County Derry, Ireland, whence the family are represented as having come in the eleventh century.

MURDOCH, G. **Muireach, Murchadh**; the first is M. G. *Muiredhaigh*, gen. (M'V.), *Murreich* (D. of L.), *Muireadhaigh*, g. (1467 MS.), Ir. *Muireadhach*, E. Ir. *Muiredach*, O. Ir. (Lat.) *Muirethachus*, Adamnan's *Muiredachus*, "lord," allied to *muirenn* and *muriucán*; Ag. S. *masre*, clarus; Br. *conomorios* (?) (Stokes R. C. 1876.) The form **Murchadh** is in Ir. the same, E. Ir. *Murchad*: **Mori-catu-s*, sea warrior. Hence (from the first) **M'Mhuirich** (in Arran, etc., becoming *Currie*), and from the second, *Murchison*, *Murchie*, and Ir. *Murphy*. See *murrach* above.

MURRAY, G. **Moirreach**; from the county name Moray or Murray, early Gadelic forms being *Moreb*, *Muref*, and Norse *Morhæfi* (influenced by Norse *haf*, sea): **Mor-apia*, from *mor* of *muir*, sea, and **apia*, the termination of several Celtic place-names. Andrew *Morrich*, Kiltearn, 1672.

MYLES, G. **Maolmoire,** servant of Mary, an old and common name. *Myles* is from the Med. Lat. *Milo*, with a leaning on *miles*, soldier—a common name in the Middle Ages.

MAC-ALISTER; see *Alexander*.

MAC-ANDREW; see *Andrew*.

MAC-ARTHUR; see *Arthur*.

MAC-ASKILL, G. **M'Asgaill**; from Norse *'Askell*, for **'As-ketill*, the kettle (sacrificial vessel) of the Anses or gods: "a vessel of holiness."

MAC-AULAY, G. **M'Amhlaidh**, Ir. *Mac Amhlaoibh*, M. Ir. *Amlaibh*, E. Ir. *Amláib*, *'Alaib*; from Norse *'Oláfr*, *Anlaf* (on coins), "the Anses' relic" (Eng. *left*).

MAC-BEAN, G. **M'Bheathain**, from **Beathan**, Englished as *Bean* (1490, *Beane*, 1481) or *Benjamin*: **Bitâtagno-s*, life's son, from *beatha*, life, with the termination *-agno-s*, meaning "descendant of," Eng. *-ing*, now used like the Eng. to form diminutives. Also *Mac-bain*, *Mac-vean*.

MAC-BETH, G. **M'Bheatha** (Dial. **M'Bheathain** and **M'Bheathaig**), M. G. *Macbethad*, O. G. *Mac-bead* (B. of Deer), M. Ir. *Macbethad*, Macbeth 1058, 1041 A.D.): "son of life," from *beatha*, life. It is a *personal* name originally, not patronymic. From *Macbeth* come *M'Bey*, *M'Vey*, *M'Veagh*.

MAC-CAIG, G. **M'Caog**, Ir. *Mac Taidhg*, son of Teague, E. Ir. *Tadg*, possibly allied to Gaul. *Tasgius*, etc. *Tadg* explained by O. Cl. and Dav. as "poet."

MAC-CALLUM, G. **M'Caluim**; see under *Malcolm*.

MAC-CODRUM, G. **M'Codrum**; from Norse *Guttormr*, *Goðormr*, Ag. S. *Guthrum*: "good or god serpent" (*orm*).

MAC-COLL, G. **M'Colla**; see *Coll*.

MAC-COMBIE, G. **M'Comaidh**, M. G. *M'Comie* (D. of L.): "son of Tommie," or Thomas.

MAC-CONACHIE, G. **M'Dhonnchaidh**, son of Duncan, which see. The Clan Donnachie are the Robertsons of Athole, so-named from Duncan de Atholia in Bruce's time: the English form of the name is from Robert, Duncan's great-grandson, who helped in bringing the murderers of James I. to execution.

MAC-CORMIC, G. **M'Cormaig**, from **Cormac** (**Cormag**), E. Ir. *Cormac*, Adamnan's *Cormacus*: **Corb-mac*, charioteer, from *corb*, chariot, Lat. *corbis*, basket. See *carbad*. From *corb* also comes **Cairbre**, O. Ir. *Coirbre*.

MAC-CORQUODALE, **M'Corcadail**, M. G. *Corgitill*, g. (D. of L.), early documents *Makcorquydill* (1434); from Norse *Thorketill*, Thor's kettle or holy vessel (see *Mac-askill*).

MAC-CRIMMON, G. **M'Cruimein**; from *Rumun* (on a Manx Rune inscription), from Norse *Hrômundr* (for *Hróð-mundr*, famed protector)? Ceannfaelad Mac *Rumain*, Bishop, d. 820; *Ruman*, the poet, d. 742; *Ruman*, the bishop, d. 919. Erig a n-agaid *Rumuind*, MS. Bodl. Lib. Laud. 610, fol. 10, a, a (O. Don's Gram.).

MAC-CULLOCH, G. **M'Cullach**, early documents *M'Culloch* (1458), *M'Cullo*, *M'Cullach* (1431)—in Easter Ross: "son of the Boar" (*cullach*)? *M'Lulach*, son of *Lulach* (little calf?), has been suggested, and this appears as *M'Lulich*.

MAC-DERMID; see *Dermid.*

MAC-DONALD; see *Donald.*

MACDUFF; see *Duff.*

MAC-ECHERN, G. **M'Eachairn,** M. G. *M'Caychirn* (D. of L.), early documents *Mackauchern* (1499), Ir. *Echthighern* (Annals 846 A.D.): "Horse-lord," from *each* and *tighearna.* Also Englished as *M'Kechnie* (**Mac-Echthigerna*).

MAC-FADYEN, G. **M'Phaidein,** early documents *M'Fadzeane* (1540); from *Paidean,* Pat, a pet form of *Patrick.*

MAC-FARLANE; see *Bartholomew.*

MAC-GILL; from a G. **M'Gille,** used as a curtailment, especially of Mac-millan or **M'Gille-mhaoil.**

MAC-GILLIVRAY, G. **M'Gillebhràth,** son of the Servant of Judgment, from *bràth,* judgment, q.v.

MAC-GLASHAN, G. **M'Glaisein,** a side-form of **M'Ghilleghlais,** the Grey lad, M. G. *M'Illezlass* (D. of L.), documents *M'Gilleglasch* (1508). For the formation of this name, cf. **Gille-naomh** (Mac-niven), **Gille-maol** (Mac-millan), *M'Gillebane* (1555), *M'Gille-uidhir* (M'Clure, dun lad), *Gilroy,* red lad.

MAC-GOWAN; see under *Gow.*

MAC-GREGOR; see *Gregor.*

MAC-HARDY, G. **M'Cardaidh:**

MAC-INDEOR; see *Dewar.*

MAC-INNES; see *Angus.*

MAC-INTYRE, G. **Mac-an-t-saoir,** son of the carpenter; see *saor.*

MAC-IVER, G. **M'Iamhair,** M. G. *M'Imhair* (1467 MS.), Ir. *Imhar,* E. Ir. *Imair,* g.; from Norse *'Ivarr.*

MACKAY, G. **M'Aoidh,** from **Aoidh,** O. G. *Aed,* O. Ir. *Aed,* Adamnan's *Aidus,* g. *Aido*: **Aidu-s,* fire, E. Ir. *aed,* fire, Gr. *αἶθος,* fire, brand, Lat. *aedes,* house (= hearth), *aestus,* heat, O. H. G. *eit,* fire, pyre. Hence the Gaul. *Aedui.*

MAC-KELLAR, G. **M'Ealair, M'Eallair,** old documents *Makkellar* (1518), *Makalere* (1476), *M'Callar* (1470), all "of Ardare" in Glassary, Argyle. *Ellar M'Kellar,* 1595, proves the name to be **Ealair.** M. Ir. *Elair,* the Gaelic form of Lat. *Hilarius* borrowed.

MAC-KENZIE, G. **M'Coinnich**; from *Coinneach,* which see under *Kenneth.*

MACKERCHAR, G. **M'Fhearchair**; see *Farquhar.*

MACKESSACK, for G. **M'Isaac,** son of *Isaac.* Also MACKIESON, *M'Kesek,* 1475; *Kessokissone, Kessoksone,* 1488; *Makesone,* 1507; *Makysonn,* 1400 (mostly in Menteith and S. Perth), from *Kessoc, Kessan,* personal names circ. 1500, also St. *Kessog* or *Kessock.*

MACKILLOP, G. **M'Philib**, for **Philip** (= *Filip*), where *f* (= *ph*) is aspirated and disappears; from Lat. *Phillipus*, from Gr. Φίλιππος, lover of horses (see *gaol* and *each*).

MACKINLAY, G. **M'Fhionnla(idh)**; from *Finlay*.

MACKINNON, G. **M'Fhionghuin**, M. G. *Fionghuine*, g. (M'V.), in *Macfingon* (1400), O. G. *Finguni*, gen. (B. of Deer), Ir. *Finghin*, M. Ir. *Finghin*, *Finnguine*, E. Ir. *Finguine*: **Vindogonio-s*, "fair-born" (*fionn* and *gin*); cf. for force and partial root Gr. Καλλιγένης, and -γονος in proper names.

MACKINTOSH, G. **Mac-an-tòisich**, the Thane's son (see *tòiseach*), M. G. *Clanna-an-tóisaigh*, Clans Mackintosh (M'V.), *Toissich* (D. of L.), Mackintoshes, *Clann-an-toisigh* (1467 MS.), early documents *M'Toschy* (1382).

MACKIRDY, G. **M'Urardaigh**, *M'Urarthie*, 1632; *M'Quiritei*, 1626; *Makmurrarty*, 1547; *Makwerarty*, 1517; common in Bute and Arran of old, from *Muircheartach*, "sea-director" (*muir* and *ceart*); whence also *M'Murtrie*, *M'Mutrie*.

MAC-LACHLAN, G. **M'Lachlainn**; see *Lachlan*.

MACLAGAN, G. **M'Lagain** (**Lathagain** in its native district of Strathtay), documentary *Maklaagan* (1525): **M'Gillaagan*, sed quid?

MAC-LAREN, G. **M'Labhruinn**; see *Lawrence*.

MAC-LARTY, G. **M'Labhartaigh** and **Lathartaich**, from *Flaithbheartach*, Eng. *Flaherty*: "dominion-bearing" or "princely-bearing" (see *flath* and *beartach*).

MAC-LEAN, G. **M'Illeathain**, for **Gill' Sheathain**, John or *Seathan's* servant, M. G. *Giolla-eóin* (M'V.), *Gilleeoin* (1467 MS.), documents *Makgilleon* (1390); from *gille* and *Seathain* (*Iain*) or *Eòin*, John, the latter being the classic G. for the name. John means in Hebrew "the Lord graciously gave."

MAC-LEARNAN, so G.; from *Gill' Ernan*, St Ernan's *gille*. The Latin name of this saint is *Ferreolus*, "Iron-one"; from *iarunn*.

MAC-LEAY, G. **M'An-léigh**, or earlier **M'An-léibh**, documents *M'Conleif* (1498 in Easter Ross), *Dunslephe*, gen. (1306-9, Kintyre), *Dunslaf* Makcorry (1505), M. G. *Duinsleibe*, gen., Ir. *Donnsléibhe*, E. Ir. *Duindslébe*, gen.: "Brown of the Hill," from *donn* and *sliabh* (not "Lord of the Hill," as other similar names exist in *dubh*, *e.g.* *Dubhsléibhe*; see *Mac-phee*). Capt. Thomas regarded the M'Leays of the north-west as descended from *Ferchar Leche*, F. the physician, who gets lands in Assynt in 1386, being thus *M'An-léigh*, physician's son, Manx *Cleg*, *Legge*. The Appin M'Lea clan Englished their name as Livingstone, of whom was the celebrated traveller.

Mac-lellan, G. **M'Gillfhaolain,** M. G. *M'Gillelan* (D. of L.), *Gilla-faelan* (1467 MS.), St Fillan's slave, E. Ir. *Faelán,* O. Ir. *Fáilan,* from *fáil,* now *faol,* wolf, q.v. Hence *Gilfillan.*

Mac-lennan, G. **M'Illinnein,** Servant of *St Finnan,* Ir. *Mac-Gilla-finnen* (common in fourteenth and fifteenth century), M. Ir. *Finden,* E. Ir. *Finnian,* Adamnan's *Vinnianus* = *Finnio, Finnionis* = *Findbarrus*; from *finn, fionn,* white: the full name, of which Finnan is a pet form, was *Findbarr* or "Fair-head," Eng. Fairfax. Skene deduced *Mac-lennan* from M. G. *M'Gilla-agamnan,* Adamnan's *gille,* documents *Gilleganan* Macneill (1545), *Gilleownan* (1427).

Mac-leod, G. **M'Leòid,** M. G. *M'Cloyd* (D. of L.), *M'Leod* (MS. 1540), documents *Macloyde* (fourteenth century), O. G. *Léot* (B. of Deer), Norse Sagas *Ljótr,* earl of Orkney in tenth century, and otherwise a common Norse name; the word is an adj. meaning "ugly" (!), Got. *liuta,* dissembler, Eng. *little.*

Mac-mahon, G. **M'Mhathain**; see *Matheson.*

Mac-martin, G. **M'Mhairtinn,** no doubt for earlier *Gillamartain,* gen. (1467 MS., an ancestor of the Cameron chiefs): Eng. *Martin,* from Lat. *Martinus,* the name of the famous fourth century Gaulish saint; it means "martial."

Mac-master, G. **M'Mhaighistir,** son of the Master.

Mac-michael, G. **M'Mhìcheil,** doubtless for earlier *Gillamichol*; see *Carmichael.*

Mac-millan, G. **M'Mhaolain, M'Ghille-mhaoil,** son of the Bald *gille* (cf. *M'Glashan*). To *Maolan* must be compared the Ogmic *Mailagni.*

Mac-nab, G. **M' An-aba,** M. G. *m' ynnab* (D. of L.), *M' An Aba* (1467 MS.): "son of the Abbot"; see *aba.*

Mac-nair, G. **M'An-uidhir**; for *Mac Iain uidhir,* son of dun (odhar) John (cf. *Makaneroy,* 1556, now *Mac-inroy,* and *Makaneduy,* 1526, now *Mac-indoe*). Such is the source of the Gairloch branch of the name. The Perthshire sept appears in documents as *M'Inayr* (1468), *Macnayr* (1390), which is explained as *M' An-oighre,* son of the heir. *M'Nuirs* in Cowal (1685), John *Maknewar* (1546, in Dunoon); Tho. *M'Nuyer* (1681, Inverness). Prof. Mackinnon suggested *M'An-fhuibhir,* son of the smith or *faber*; nor should *M'An-fhuidhir,* the stranger's son, be overlooked as a possible etymology.

Mac-naughton, G. **M'Neachdainn,** M. G. *M'Neachtain* (1467), O. G. *Nectan,* Pictish *Naiton* (Bede), from *necht,* pure, root *nig* of *nigh,* wash.

MAC-NEE, G. **M'Righ**; D. of L. *M'onee*, *M'Nie*, 1613; *M'Knie*, 1594; *M'Kne*, 1480 (Menteith and Breadalbane). From *mac-nia*, champion?

MAC-NEILL, G. **M'Neill,** documents *Makneill* (1427). See *Neil.*

MAC-NICOL, G. **M'Neacail,** M. G. *M'Nicail*, from Lat. *Nicolas*, Gr. Νικόλας, "conquering people." Hence *Nicholson.*

MAC-NISH, G. **M'Neis**; from **M'Naois,** the *Naois* being a dialectic form of **Aonghus** or Angus.

MAC-NIVEN, G. **M'Ghille-naoimh,** the saintly *gille* (cf. for form in Eng. *Mac-glashan*). Documentary form *Gilnew* M'Ilwedy (1506). The M. G. and Ir. *Gilla Nanaemh*, servant of the saints (1467 MS.), is a different name. The Ir. *M'Nevin* is for *M'Cnaimhin. Mac Nimhein* (*Oranaiche* 520).

MAC-PHAIL, G. **M'Phàil**; son of Paul. See *Paul.*

MAC-PHEE, G. **M'a-Phì,** M. G. *M'a ffeith* (D. of L.), *M'Duibsithi* (1467), documents *Macduffie* (1463), for *Dub-shíthe*, Black of peace (*dubh* and *sìth*).

MAC-PHERSON, G. **M'Phearsain,** son of the Parson, M. G. *M'a pharsone* (D. of L.), documents *M'Inphersonis* (1594 Acts of Parl.). Bean *Makimpersone* (1490, Cawdor Papers), *Makfarson* (1481, Kilravock Papers), Archibald M'Walter vic Doncho vic *Persoun* (who in 1589 has lands in Glassary of Argyle); Tormot *M'Farsane* (vicar of Snizort, 1526). The Badenoch M'Phersons are known as *Clann Mhuirich*; the Skye sept are called *Cananaich* (from Lat. *canonicus*, canon).

MAC-QUARRIE, G. **M'Guaire,** M. G. *Guaire*, *M'Guaire* (1467 MS.), *Macquharry* (1481), *M'Goire* of Ulva (1463, *Makquhory* in 1473); from Gadelic *Guaire*, **Gaurio-s*, E. Ir. *guaire*, noble; Gr. γαῦρος, proud, exulting; further Lat. *gaudeo*, rejoice, Eng. *joy.*

MAC-QUEEN, G. **M'Cuinn,** documents *Sween M'Queen* (1609, Clan Chattan Bond), *M'Queyn* (1543, *Swyne* then also as a personal name, in Huntly's Bond), *Makquean* (1502, personal name *Soyne* also appears), M. G. *Suibne*, gen. (1467 MS., Mackintosh genealogy), *M'Soenith* (D. of L.), documents *Syffyn* (1269, the Kintyre Sweens), Ir. *Suibhne* (Sweeney), E. Ir. *Subne*, Adamnan's *Suibneus*: **Subnio-s*, root *ben*, go: "Good going?" The opposite *Duibne* (O'Duinn, etc.) appears in Ogam as *Dovvinias* (gen.). Cf. *dubhach*, *subhach*. Usually Mac-queen is referred to Norse Eng. *Sweyn*, Norse *Sveinn*, which gives G. *M'Suain*, now *Mac-Swan*, a Skye name. Pronounced in Arg. Mac *Cui'ne* or *Cuibhne*, for **M'Shuibhne,** which is the best spelling for Argyle.

MAC-RAE, G. **M'Rath,** M. G. gen. *Mecraíth*, documents *M'Crath* (1383 in Rothiemurchus), Ir. *Macraith* (years 448, onwards):

"Son of Grace or Luck," from *rath*, q.v. A *personal* name like Macbeth.

MAC-RAILD; see under *Harold*.

MAC-RANALD, G. **M'Raonuill**; see *Ranald*.

MAC-RORY, MAC-RURY; see *Rory*. Documents give *Makreury* in 1427.

MAC-TAGGART, G. **M'An-t-Sagairt,** son of the priest.

MAC-TAVISH, G. **M'Thàimhs,** for **M'Thàmhais,** son of Thomas or Tammas, M. G. Clyne *Tawssi* (D. of L.), documents *M'Cawis* and *M'Cause* (1494, 1488, in Killin of Lochtay).

MAC-VICAR, G. **M'Bhiocair,** documents *Makvicar* (1561, when lands are given near Inveraray to him): "Son of the Vicar."

MAC-VURICH, G. **M'Mhuirich,** M. G. *Mhuireadhaigh* (M'V.): the Bardic family of M'Vurich claimed descent from the poet Muireach Albanach (circ. 1200 A.D.). They now call themselves Macphersons by confusion with the Badenoch Clann Mhuirich.

NEIL, G. **Niall,** so Ir., E. Ir. *Níall*, Adamnan's *Nellis*, gen.: **Neillo-s*, **Neid-s-lo-*; see *niata* for root, the meaning being "champion." Hence *Mac-neill*. The word was borrowed into Norse as *Njáll*, *Njal*, and thence borrowed into Eng., where it appears in Domesday Bk. as *Nigel*, a learned spelling of *Neil*, whence *Nelson*, etc.

NICHOLSON, G. **M'Neacail**; see *Mac-nicol*.

NORMAN, G. **Tormoid, Tòrmod** (Dial. **Tormailt,** for earlier *Tormond*), documents *Tormode* (David II.'s reign); from Norse *Thórmóðr*, the wrath of Thor, Eng. *mood*. The form *Tormund* alternates with *Tormod* (1584, 1560): "Thor's protection;" whence the Dial. **Tormailt** (cf. *iarmailt* for phonetics). Cf. *Gearmailt*, Germany.

PATRICK, G. **Pàdruig, Pàruig** (with pet form **Para**), for *Gillephadruig*, M. G. *Gillapadruig*, Ir. *Pádraig*, *Giollaphátraicc*, O. Ir. *Patricc*; from Lat. *Patricius*, patrician. Hence *Macphatrick*, *Paterson*.

PAUL, G. **Pòl** (Classic), **Pàl** (C.S.); from Lat, *Paulus*, from *paulus*, little, Eng. *few*.

PETER, G. **Peadair**; from Lat. *Petrus*, from Gr. Πέτρος, rock, stone.

PHILIP, so G.; see *Mackillop*.

RANALD, G. **Raonull,** M. G. *Raghnall* (M'V.), *Ragnall*, *Raghnall* (1467 MS.), Ir. *Ragnall* (common); from Norse *Rögnvaldr*, ruler of (from) the gods, or ruler of counsel, from *rögn*, *regin*, the gods, Got. *ragin*, opinion, rule; whence *Reginald*, *Reynold*, etc. Hence **M'Raonuill**, *Mac-ranald*, *Clanranald*.

ROBERT, **Raibert, Robart, Rob,** M. G. *Robert* (D. of L.), *Roibert* (1467 MS.); from Eng. *Robert*, Ag. S. *Robert*, from *hrô*, *hrôð*, fame, praise, and *berht*, bright, now *bright*, "bright fame." Hence *Robertsons* (= **Clann Donnchaidh**), *Mac-robbie*.

Roderick, Rory, G. **Ruairidh,** M. G. *Ruaidri* (1467 MS.), O. G. *Rúadri*, Ir. *Ruaidhri*, gen. *Ruadrach* (Annals at 779, 814), O. Ir. *Ruadri*, E. W. *Rotri*, *Rodri*; from *ruadh*, red, and the root of *rìgh*, king? The Teutonic *Roderick* means "Famed-ruler" (from *hrôð* and *rik*, the same root as G. *rìgh*). The terminal *-ri*, *-rech* (old gen.) is a reduced form of *rígh*, king (Zimmer, who, however, regards *Ruadri* as from N. *Hrôrehr*, but this in Galloway actually gives *Rerik*, *M'Rerik*, *M'Crerik*, 1490, 1579, thus disproving Zimmer's view). *M'Cririck* still exists.

Ross, G. **Rosach, Ros**; from the County name *Ross*, so named from *ros*, promontory.

Roy, G. **Ruadh,** red. Hence *Mac-inroy*, earlier *Makaneroy* (1555), for **M'Iain Ruaidh,** Red John's son.

Samuel, G. **Samuel, Somhairle.** The latter really is *Somerled*, M. G. *Somuirle* (M'V.), *Somairli* (1467 MS.); from Norse *Sumarliði*, which means a mariner, viking, "summer sailor," from *sumar* and *liði*, a follower, sailor.

Shaw, G. **Seaghdh,** Englished as *Seth*; evidently formerly *Si'ach* or *Se'ach*, *Schiach M'Keich*, Weem in 1637 (= Shaw M'Shaw), *Jo. Scheach*, Inverness in 1451, *Jo.* and *Tho. Scheoch*, king's "cursors" 1455-1462, *Sythach* Macmallon in Badenoch in 1224-33, Ferchar filius *Seth* there in 1234, *M'Sithig* in B. of Deer: **Sithech*, M. Ir. *sidhach*, wolf. The female name **Sitheag** was common in the Highlands in the 17th century (*Shiak*, *Shihag*). The Southern Shaws—of Ayrshire and Greenock—are from *De Schaw* (1296), from Sc. and Eng. *shaw*, *shaws*; the southern name influenced the northern in spelling and pronunciation. In Argyle, the Shaws are called Clann Mhic-ghille-*Sheathanaich*.

Simon, G. **Sim.** This is the Lovat personal name; hence **M'Shimidh,** Simmie's son, the name by which the Lovat family is patronymically known. Hence in Eng. *Sime*, *Mac-kimmie*, *M'Kim*, *Simpson*, etc.

Somerled; see *Samuel*.

Sutherland, G. **Suthurlanach**; from the county name.

Taggart; see *Mac-taggart*.

Thomas, G. **Tòmas, Tàmhus** (M'F.), M. G. *Tamas* (1467 MS.). Hence *Mac-tavish*, *Mac-combie*.

Torquil, G. **Torcull (Torcall)**; from Norse *Thorkell*, a shorter form of *Thorketill*, which see under *Mac-corquodale*.

Whyte, G. **M'Illebhàin**; son of the fair *gille*. See *Bain* above.

WILLIAM, G. **Uilleam,** M. G. *William* (1467 MS.); the G. is borrowed from the Eng., O. Eng. *Willelm*, Ger. *Wilhelm*, "helmet of resolution" (from *will* and *helm*). Hence *Mac-william.*

SOME NATIVE FEMALE NAMES.

Beathag, SOPHIA, M. G. *Bethog* (M'V.), *Bethoc* (*Chronicles of Picts and Scots*: name of King Duncan's mother), for **Bethóc*, the fem. form of *Beathan*, discussed under *Mac-bean.*

Brìde, BRIDGET, E. Ir., O. Ir. *Brigit*, g. *Brigte* or *Brigtae*: **Bṛgṇtî* (Stokes), an old Gaelic goddess of poetry, etc. (Corm.); usually referred to the root *bṛg*, high, Celtic *Brigantes*, high or noble people; Skr. *bṛhatî*, high (fem.); further Ger. *berg*, hill, Eng. *burgh*. The Norse god of poetry was *Bragi*, whose name may be allied to that of *Brigit*. The name of the Gr. goddess Ἀφροδίτη (*Bhṛg-îtâ*) and the Teutonic name *Berhta* (from the same stem as Eng. *bright*), have been compared to that of *Bridget* (Hoffman, *Bez. Beit.* [18], 290); but this derivation of *Aphrodite* ("foam-sprung"?) is unusual.

Diorbhàil, Diorbhorguil, DOROTHY, M. G. *Derbhfáil* (M'V.), Ir. *Dearbhail*, *Dearbhforghaill*, respectively translated by O'Donovan "true request" (see *àill*) and "true oath" (E. Ir. *forgall*, O. Ir. *forcell*, testimony, from *geall*). Hence the historic name *Devorgilla.*

Fionnaghal, FLORA, M. G. *Fionnghuala* (1469 MS.), documents *Finvola* (1463), *Fynvola* (1409), Ir. *Finnghuala*: "Fair-shouldered"; from *fionn* and *guala.*

Mòr, Mòrag, SARAH, M. G. *Mór* (M'V.), Ir. *Mór* (year 916); from *mór*, great, while Hebrew *Sarah* means "queen."

Muireall, MARION, MURIEL, Ir. *Muirgheal* (year 852): *Mori-gelâ*, "sea-white"; from *muir* and *geal.*

Oighrig, Eighrig, EUPHEMIA, M. G. *Effric* (D. of L.), med. documents *Africa*, Ir. *Aithbhric*, older *Affraic* (two abbesses of Kildare so called in 738 and 833); from *Africa?*

Raonaild, Raonaid, RACHEL; from Norse *Ragnhildis*, "God's fight." Cf. *Ronald.*

Sorcha, CLARA, Ir. *Sorcha*; from the adj. *sorcha*, bright, the opposite of *dorcha*, q.v.

Una, WINIFRED, WINNY, Ir. *Una*; usually explained as from *úna* (*núna*, M. Ir. = *gorta*), hunger, famine, whence the Ir. proverb: "Ní bhíon an teach a mbíon Una lá ná leath gan núna"—The house where Una is is never a day or half one without hunger." W. *newyn*, Cor. *naun*, Br. *naon*, M. Br. *naffin*, **novengo-*, Eng. *need*. Cf. E. Ir. *uinchi*, scarcity, Eng. *want*, *wane*. Una, daughter of the King of Lochlan, is represented by Keating as Conn Cédcathach's mother (second century).

Also of Interest from Hippocrene...

SCOTTISH PROVERBS

Through opinions of love, drinking, work, money, law and politics, the sharp wit and critical eye of the Scottish spirit is charmingly conveyed in this one-of-a-kind collection. The proverbs are listed in the colloquial Scots-English language of the turn-of-the-century with modern translations below. Included are twenty-five witty and playful illustrations. There is something for everyone in this collection.

130 pages • 6x 9 • 25 • illustrations • 0-7818-0648-8 • $14.95 • W • (719) • May 1998

Love Poetry from the Gaelic Tradition...

SCOTTISH LOVE POEMS
A Personal Anthology

edited by Lady Antonia Fraser, re-issued edition

Lady Antonia Fraser has selected her favorite poets from Robert Burns to Aileen Campbell Nye and placed them together in a tender anthology of romance. Famous for her own literary talents, her critical writer's eye has allowed her to collect the best loves and passions of her fellow Scots into a book that will find a way to touch everyone's heart.

220 pages • 5 1/2 x 8 1/4 • 0-7818-0406-x • $14.95pb

IRISH LOVE POEMS

edited by Paula Redes

A beautifully illustrated anthology that offers an intriguing glimpse into the world of Irish passion, often fraught simultaneously with both love and violence. For some contemporary poets this will be their first appearance in a U.S. anthology. Included are poets Thomas Moore, Padraic Pearse, W.B. Yates, John Montague, and Nuala Ni Dhomnaill.

Gabriel Rosenstock, famous poet and translator, forwards the book, wittily introducing the reader to both the collection and the rich Irish Poetic tradition.

176 pages • 6 x 9 • illustrated • 0-7818-0396-9 • $14.95

Language Guides...

SCOTTISH GAELIC-ENGLISH/ ENGLISH-SCOTTISH GAELIC

R.W. Renton & J.A. MacDonald

Scottish Gaelic is the language of a hearty, traditional people, over 75,000 strong. This dictionary provides the learner or traveler with a basic, modern vocabulary and the means to communicate in a quick fashion. This dictionary includes 8,500 modern, up-to-date entries, a list of abbreviation and appendix of irregular verbs, a grammar guide, written especially for students and travelers.

416 • pages • 5 1/2 x 8 1/2 • 0-7818-0316-0 • NA • $8.95pb

BEGINNER'S WELSH

Heini Gruffudd

The Welsh language, with its rich culture and heritage, has successfully survived to this day. More than half a million people speak the language throughout the country in Wales, while thousands in England, the U.S. and elsewhere have continued to keep the language alive. Beginner's Welsh is an easy to follow guide to grammar, pronunciation and rules of the language. A clear and concise introduction to Welsh politics, the economy, literature, and geography preface the language guide.

Heini Gruffudd is a native of Wales and has published Welsh learning guides on Wales.

IRISH-ENGLISH/ENGLISH/IRISH DICTIONARY AND PHRASEBOOK

160 pages • 3 3/4 x 7 • 1,400 entries/phrases • 0-87052-110-1 • NA • $7.95pb • (385)

British

BRITISH-AMERICAN/ AMERICAN-BRITISH DICTIONARY AND PHRASEBOOK

160 pages • 3 3/4 x 7 • 1,400 entries
0-7818-0450-7 • W • $11.95pb • (247)

Travel Guides..

LANGUAGE AND TRAVEL GUIDE TO BRITAIN

266 pages • 5 1/2 x 8 1/2 • 2 maps, photos throughout, index • 0-7818-0290-3 • W • $14.95pb • (119)

Cookbooks...

New!

ENGLISH ROYAL COOKBOOK: FAVORITE COURT RECIPIES

Elizabeth Craig

Dine like a King or Queen with this unique collection of over 350 favorite recipes of the English royals, spanning 500 years of feasts! Start off with delicate Duke of York Consommé as a first course, then savor King George the Fifth's Mutton Cutlets, and for a main course, feast on Quails a la Princess Louise in Regent's Plum Sauce, with Baked Potatoes Au Parmesan and Mary Queen of Scots Salad. For dessert, try a slice of Crown Jewel Cake, and wash it all down with a Princess Mary Cocktail. These are real recipes, the majority of them left in their original wording. Although this book is primarily a cookery book, it can also be read as a revealing footnote to Court history. Charmingly illustrated throughout.

187 pages • 5 1/2 x 8 1/2 • 0-7818-0583-X • W • $11.95pb • (723) • May

CELTIC COOKBOOK: Traditional Recipes from the Six Celtic Lands Brittany, Cornwall, Ireland, Isle of Man, Scotland and Wales

Helen Smith-Twiddy

This collection of over 160 recipes from the Celtic world includes traditional, yet still popular dishes like Rabbit Hoggan and Gwydd y Dolig (Stuffed Goose in Red Wine).

200 pages • 5 1/2 x 8 1/2 • 0-7818-0579-1 • NA • $22.50hc • (679)

TRADITIONAL RECIPES FROM OLD ENGLAND

Arranged by country, this charming classic features the favorite dishes and mealtime customs from across England, Scotland, Wales and Ireland.

28 pages • 5 x 8 1/2 • 0-7818-0489-2 •W $9.95pb • (157)

Ireland

THE ART OF IRISH COOKING

Monica Sheridan

Nearly 200 recipes for traditional Irish fare.

166 pages • 5 1/2 x 8 1/2 • 0-7818-0454-X • W • $12.95pb • (335)

Scotland

TRADITIONAL FOOD FROM SCOTLAND: THE EDINBURGH BOOK OF PLAIN COOKERY RECIPES

A delightful assortment of Scottish recipes and helpful hints for the home—this classic volume offers a window into another era.

336 pages • 5 1/2 x 8 • 0-7818-0514-7 • W • $11.95pb • (620)

Wales

TRADITIONAL FOOD FROM WALES

A Hippocrene Original Cookbook

Bobby Freeman

Welsh food and customs through the centuries. This book combines over 260 authentic, proven recipes with cultural and social history

332 pages • 5 1/2 x 8 1/2 • 0-7818-0527-9 • NA • $24.95 • (638)